Royal Commission on Civil Liability and Compensation for Personal Injury

Chairman: Lord Pearson

REPORT
Volume One

Presented to Parliament by Command of Her Majesty
March 1978

LONDON
HER MAJESTY'S STATIONERY OFFICE
£7·60 net

Cmnd 7054–I

The Report of the Royal Commission on Civil Liability and Compensation for Personal Injury

VOLUME ONE   REPORT

VOLUME TWO   STATISTICS AND COSTINGS

VOLUME THREE   OVERSEAS SYSTEMS OF COMPENSATION

The estimated total expenditure of the Royal Commission is £1,337,446. Of this sum £50,546 represents the estimated cost of printing and publishing.

THE ROYAL WARRANTS

ELIZABETH R.

ELIZABETH THE SECOND, by the Grace of God of the United Kingdom of Great Britain and Northern Ireland and of Our other Realms and Territories QUEEN, Head of the Commonwealth, Defender of the Faith, to

Our Right Trusty and Well-beloved Counsellor Colin Hargreaves, Baron Pearson, Commander of Our Most Excellent Order of the British Empire;

Our Trusty and Well-beloved:

Sir Philip Allen, Knight Grand Cross of Our Most Honourable Order of the Bath;

John Cameron (commonly called Lord Cameron), one of the Senators of Our College of Justice in Scotland, upon whom has been conferred the Decoration of the Distinguished Service Cross;

Walter Charles Anderson, Esquire, Commander of Our Most Excellent Order of the British Empire;

Ronald John Kerr-Muir, Esquire, Officer of Our Most Excellent Order of the British Empire;

Margaret Anne Brooke;

Robert Buchan Duthie, Esquire;

Robert Alexander MacCrindle, Esquire, one of Our Counsel learned in the law;

Norman Stayner Marsh, Esquire, one of Our Counsel learned in the law;

Denis Alfred Marshall, Esquire;

Alan Richmond Prest, Esquire;

Arthur Edward Sansom, Esquire;

Richard Selwyn Francis Schilling, Esquire;

Ronald Sidney Skerman, Esquire;

Olive Stevenson;

James Stewart, Esquire.

Greeting!

Royal Commission on
Civil Liability and Compensation
for Personal Injury

iii

WHEREAS We have deemed it expedient that a Commission should forthwith issue to consider to what extent, in what circumstances and by what means compensation should be payable in respect of death or personal injury (including ante-natal injury) suffered by any person—

a. in the course of employment;

b. through the use of a motor-vehicle or other means of transport;

c. through the manufacture, supply or use of goods or services;

d. on premises belonging to or occupied by another or

e. otherwise through the act or omission of another where compensation under the present law is recoverable only on proof of fault or under the rules of strict liability,

having regard to the cost and other implications of the arrangements for the recovery of compensation, whether by way of compulsory insurance or otherwise:

NOW KNOW YE That We, reposing great trust and confidence in your knowledge and ability, have authorised and appointed, and do by these Presents authorise and appoint you the said Colin Hargreaves, Baron Pearson (Chairman); Sir Philip Allen; John Cameron; Walter Charles Anderson; Ronald John Kerr-Muir; Margaret Anne Brooke; Robert Buchan Duthie; Ronald Alexander MacCrindle; Norman Stayner Marsh; Denis Alfred Marshall; Alan Richmond Prest; Arthur Edward Sansom; Richard Selwyn Francis Schilling; Ronald Sidney Skerman; Olive Stevenson and James Stewart, to be Our Commissioners for the purpose of the said inquiry:

AND for the better effecting the purposes of this Our Commission We do by these Presents give and grant unto you, or any five or more of you, full power to call before you such persons as you shall judge likely to afford you any information upon the subject of this Our Commission; to call for information in writing; and also to call for, have access to and examine all such books, documents, registers and records as may afford you the fullest information on the subject and to inquire of and concerning the premises by all other lawful ways and means whatsoever:

AND We do by these Presents authorise and empower you, or any of you, to visit and personally inspect such places as you may deem it expedient so to inspect for the more effectual carrying out of the purposes aforesaid:

AND We do by these Presents will and ordain that this Our Commission shall continue in full force and virtue, and that you, Our Said Commissioners, or any five or more of you may from time to time proceed in the execution thereof, and of every matter and thing therein contained, although the same be not continued from time to time by adjournment:

AND We do further ordain that you, or any five or more of you, have liberty to report your proceedings under this Our Commission from time to time if you shall judge it expedient so to do:

AND Our further will and pleasure is that you do, with as little delay as possible, report to Us your opinion upon the matters herein submitted for your consideration.

GIVEN at Our Court at Saint James's the nineteenth day of March, 1973; In the Twenty-second Year of Our Reign

By Her Majesty's Command

ROBERT CARR

NOTES

Mr Kerr-Muir died on 29 January 1974. Sir Philip Allen was created a life peer in June 1976 with the title of Lord Allen of Abbeydale. Mr Skerman, Professor Schilling and Mr Marsh were each awarded the CBE in January 1974, June 1975 and January 1977 respectively. Mrs Brooke was awarded the OBE in June 1976.

v

ELIZABETH R.

ELIZABETH THE SECOND, by the Grace of God of the United Kingdom of Great Britain and Northern Ireland and of Our other Realms and Territories QUEEN, Head of the Commonwealth, Defender of the Faith, to Our Trusty and Well-beloved Alan Willis Ure, Esquire, upon whom has been conferred the Royal Naval Reserve Officers' Decoration,

Greeting!

WHEREAS by Warrant under Our Royal Sign Manual bearing date the Nineteenth day of March, One thousand nine hundred and seventy-three, We appointed a Commission, to be called the Royal Commission on Civil Liability and Compensation for Personal Injury:

NOW KNOW YE that We reposing great trust and confidence in your knowledge and ability do by these Presents appoint you the said Alan Willis Ure, to be a Member of the said Commission, in the room of Our Trusty and Well-beloved Ronald John Kerr-Muir, Esquire, deceased.

GIVEN at Our Court at Saint James's the twenty-fourth day of June, 1974; In the Twenty-third Year of Our Reign

By Her Majesty's Command

ROY JENKINS

WARRANT appointing Alan Willis Ure, Esquire,
to be a Member of the Royal Commission on
Civil Liability and Compensation for
Personal Injury.

Contents

Contents

Contents

Contents

Contents

Tables

ROYAL COMMISSION ON CIVIL LIABILITY AND COMPENSATION FOR PERSONAL INJURY

Report

To the Queen's Most Excellent Majesty

MAY IT PLEASE YOUR MAJESTY

We, the undersigned Commissioners, having been appointed by Royal Warrant

'To consider to what extent, in what circumstances and by what means compensation should be payable in respect of death or personal injury (including ante-natal injury) suffered by any person—

a. in the course of employment;

b. through the use of a motor-vehicle or other means of transport;

c. through the manufacture, supply or use of goods or services;

d. on premises belonging to or occupied by another or

e. otherwise through the act or omission of another where compensation under the present law is recoverable only on proof of fault or under the rules of strict liability,

having regard to the cost and other implications of the arrangements for the recovery of compensation, whether by way of compulsory insurance or otherwise.'

HUMBLY SUBMIT TO YOUR MAJESTY THE FOLLOWING REPORT

PART I

Introductory

CHAPTER 1

Introduction

Appointment and terms of reference

1 We were appointed on 19th March 1973:

'to consider to what extent, in what circumstances and by what means compensation should be payable in respect of death or personal injury (including ante-natal injury) suffered by any person—

a. in the course of employment;

b. through the use of a motor vehicle or other means of transport;

c. through the manufacture, supply or use of goods or services;

d. on premises belonging to or occupied by another or

e. otherwise through the act or omission of another where compensation under the present law is recoverable only on proof of fault or under the rules of strict liability,

having regard to the cost and other implications of the arrangements for the recovery of compensation, whether by way of compulsory insurance or otherwise'.

2 When the then Prime Minister (Mr Heath) announced the decision to establish the Royal Commission on 19 December 1972 he said:

'The Government have been considering proposals made from time to time in the past, which are now particularly relevant in the light of the Report of the Robens Committee on Safety and Health at Work and in connection with the recent concern over the thalidomide cases, that there should be an inquiry into the basis of civil liability in the United Kingdom for causing death or personal injury. It is the Government's view that a wide-ranging inquiry is required into the basis on which compensation should be recoverable'.

Extracts from Hansard for the House of Commons and the House of Lords are in Annex 1.

3 The interpretation of our terms of reference was not free from difficulties; and some of the special problems which arise will be dealt with in later chapters. But the main points are clear. The terms of reference do not cover property damage or any loss not resulting from death or personal injury. They cover injury but, subject to special points, not illness except when it results from injury. Moreover, not all injuries are covered, but only those within the five categories which are specified, with the result that many injuries, including many suffered

3

in the home, are outside our remit. The terms of reference clearly do not envisage as immediately practicable a comprehensive scheme dealing with all injuries, still less a 'universal' scheme dealing with all incapacity whether caused by injury, disease or congenital defect.

4   Nevertheless, we have had to deal with a wide range of subjects. Our membership was drawn from several fields—including the law, medicine, economics, social and public administration, insurance and industry – reflecting the extensive scope of knowledge and experience required to consider the variety of issues remitted to us.

5   Owing to the sad death of Mr R J Kerr-Muir, who had given valuable help in the early stages of our work, Mr A W Ure was appointed on 24 June 1974. Mr A Sansom, who contributed so much to our work in the first four years, was prevented by illness from participating to the end.

Our work

6   We held our first meeting in March 1973. In the following month we issued our first circular. It asked for evidence about the two main categories covered by our terms of reference – injuries in the course of employment, and injuries through the use of motor vehicles or other road transport. In February 1974 we issued a second circular, relating to the remaining categories, and a third circular on general issues. The terms of the three circulars are reproduced in Annex 2.

7   The subjects we were commissioned to study are not peculiar to the United Kingdom. They are of worldwide concern, and we soon learned that reforming action had been taken or was under discussion in many countries. Indeed, in the announcement about setting up the Commission, the then Prime Minister mentioned the adoption of no-fault motor insurance in some parts of the USA; and the then Lord Chancellor, after making his announcement in the House of Lords, referred specifically to the schemes operating in Massachusetts and New Zealand, adding that obviously these and other possible models would require examination. We were also conscious of a need to understand the likely interrelation of the United Kingdom's international obligations with anything we might decide to recommend. We found that the available literature, although considerable, was inadequate for our purpose, and although we were able to see in London some witnesses from overseas (and derived much help from them) it became clear that only by going to selected countries and talking to people on the spot could we properly inform ourselves.

8   In considering how these overseas enquiries could be carried out in the most economical way, we thought that those countries with a similar social and political background to our own would be the most likely to yield useful information. Small groups of us visited Canada and the USA in 1974. Early in 1975 similar groups visited Switzerland, France, the Federal Republic of Germany, the Netherlands and Sweden. Some of our members went to Geneva, Brussels and Strasbourg to meet representatives of the International Labour

Organisation, the Commission of the European Communities and the Council of Europe. One of us, while visiting Singapore, looked at a new scheme of workmen's compensation then about to be introduced there.

9 Late in 1975 we went to New Zealand and Australia. We had arranged for this visit to be the last so that we could study the New Zealand scheme – the only comprehensive one of its kind actually in operation – after it had been running for over a year. We were also able to consult with those in Australia who were then working on a possible new scheme of 'universal' no-fault compensation (applying to all incapacity however caused).

10 On most of our overseas visits we split up so as to enable an extensive programme of discussions and interviews to be carried out in the shortest possible time. Altogether, we held 252 such meetings – 125 in North America, 86 in New Zealand and Australia and 41 in Europe.

11 In the United Kingdom, we held 225 meetings, either of the full Commission or of committees. Most were in London, but we also met in Edinburgh and Belfast. The meetings ranged from quite short ones to working weekends.

Evidence

12 We received 865 written submissions from 766 organisations and individuals. Oral evidence was taken, in the United Kingdom, from 113. Some of these witnesses appeared before us more than once; almost all of them had first sent written evidence. A list of those who gave evidence is in Annex 3.

13 We have given much thought to the question of publishing the evidence. We realise that it may seem anomalous to publish in some detail the results of our enquiries abroad, but not to publish the evidence we received in the United Kingdom. This evidence was so voluminous however that, on grounds of cost, we were forced to the conclusion that we should not be justified in publishing it all; and it would be invidious to publish only some, even if we could devise criteria for distinguishing between the various documents and statements put to us. Some of those concerned have published their evidence themselves. For our part, we discuss the relevant evidence in the course of our report and give quotations where we feel that this would best illustrate a point or bring out the views of a particular organisation or individual. For the rest, we felt that the appropriate course was to put copies of the memoranda we had received, together with notes of oral evidence, in the Public Record Offices in London and Belfast, the Scottish Record Office, and the National Library of Wales in Aberystwyth, together with the United Kingdom copyright libraries and the libraries of the House of Commons and the House of Lords – providing the witness has raised no objection. The material so deposited will be available for inspection.

The form of our report

14 We are publishing our report in three volumes. Volume One constitutes the main part and includes all our recommendations. Volume Two contains information on statistics and costings and includes the results of a household

survey commissioned by us. Volume Three contains a summary of the information we gathered in connection with our overseas visits, supplemented by relevant information obtained about other countries which we did not visit. We are not aware of any comparable collection of published information.

15 Volume One is arranged as follows. After this introductory Part, Part II describes the present systems of compensation in the United Kingdom and touches on some popular misconceptions. Part III considers how the systems might be changed, looking first at some points of special interest in overseas systems, and then developing our main strategic conclusions. Part IV deals with detailed issues relating to the assessment of tort damages. Part V deals with the various classes of injury within our remit, applying to each in turn the broad principles we have adopted. Part VI assesses the cost of our proposals and contains some concluding reflections. Part VII is a summary of conclusions and a list of recommendations. There is a glossary near the end of the Volume.

16 We are unanimous in our main recommendations, but we differ among ourselves on a number of particular issues. Where possible, differences of opinion are dealt with by explaining both points of view before giving the majority recommendation. Elsewhere, those disagreeing with particular recommendations have written dissenting notes. Where these notes are short they are normally incorporated in the text. Where they are longer they are put at the end of the relevant chapter.

17 Our remit covered the United Kingdom. Where appropriate, we point to differences between the law and the legal systems of England and Wales, Scotland and Northern Ireland.

Statistics

18 Many of the statistics in our report are estimates. Some combine information from surveys carried out for us with information from existing sources. The estimates vary in accuracy. Where it is appropriate, uncertain estimates of magnitudes of significance are given, rather than none at all. Indications of the degree of accuracy of the most important sets of figures are in Volume Two. All figures relate to the United Kingdom except where otherwise stated.

19 Information derived from the surveys we commissioned at the outset of our work relates to 1972, 1973 or 1974. Other figures are for the most recent year or years available. Where appropriate, figures for two or three years are averaged.

20 Throughout our report values and benefit rates are at January 1977 levels unless otherwise stated. The same date has been used for currency conversions.

21 Some classes of injury or accidental death, in particular those relating to work and transport, are by definition within our terms of reference. But for other classes, and for injuries and deaths in total, it was not possible to make a clear distinction in the statistics between those within and those outside our terms of reference. Some of the figures given therefore relate to all injuries or accidental deaths, or to all those of a particular kind.

22   The definition of injury adopted is that leading to four or more days off work, or an equivalent degree of severity for those not at work. This definition corresponds to the period after which national insurance sickness or injury benefit ordinarily becomes payable.

23   Where figures have been rounded to the last significant digit, the sum of constituent items may not be exactly equal to the total shown.

Acknowledgments

24   It is difficult to acknowledge adequately all the help we have received. We express our gratitude to all those who helped us with evidence, written or oral. Special thanks are due to the British Insurance Association and Lloyd's, who undertook a statistical survey for us, and with whom we had several discussions; to a number of Government departments; to Sir Roy Allen, our statistical consultant; to Dr J H Renwick of the London School of Hygiene and Tropical Medicine for a report on ante-natal injury; to Professor J P M Tizard of the University of Oxford for a report on birth injury; to Mr M Freeman of the University of London for a survey of the literature on the pros and cons of tort; to Professor A M Linden of York University, Ontario for a survey of Canadian schemes; and to Professor R Henderson of the University of Nebraska for an analysis of no-fault schemes in the USA. We wish to thank those who arranged our overseas visits and also those who generously gave their time to discussing the common problems and the differing factors involved in the various countries.

25   We wish to express gratitude to our Secretary, Mrs Elizabeth Parsons, for her dedicated service to this Commission, her skill in organising its activities both in the United Kingdom and overseas, and the help which she has given to us all. We are also grateful to her and to the present and past members of the Secretariat for their work in connection with the consideration of written evidence and information, the compilation of statistics and costings and the production of the report. We also thank those who carried out the typing, copying and circulation of the numerous papers required by our wide-ranging enquiry.

CHAPTER 2
The meaning of compensation

26   When we started our work we came across two initial problems: the use of words, and the interpretation of our terms of reference. Central to both problems is the word 'compensation'.

27   Our terms of reference, at any rate in part, seemed to envisage 'compensation' as being largely confined to an award by the courts, or a settlement out of court, arising out of the liability of one person to pay damages in respect of the death or personal injury of another. We were in no doubt that the word must be given a wider meaning.

28   We define compensation for personal injury as the provision of something to the injured person (or to his dependants if he has been killed) in consequence of the injury and for the purpose of removing or alleviating its ill effects. What is provided may be money, services, goods or real property. We are directly concerned only with monetary or cash compensation, but in considering how much money is required we must take account of compensation provided in other ways.

29   Services include the medical and other services provided free of charge or at low cost by the National Health Service and by local authority social service departments. Services may also include help towards rehabilitation, domestic help and travel facilities. Goods may include such things as wheelchairs, walking aids, special clothing or special equipment. Real property may include a suitable dwelling or adaptation of an existing dwelling. All these diminish the need for cash compensation. If they had to be paid for, more money would be required. The wide provision of medical and social services in the United Kingdom is an important factor too in any comparison with overseas systems of compensation.

30   Cash compensation involves a payment to the injured or bereaved person from a source other than his own resources. Within our definition, there are several important, and quite different, sources of payment.

31   To take first the source most obviously covered by our terms of reference, compensation may be paid by the person who has caused or is responsible for the injury, either directly or indirectly. Payment may be made from that person's own resources or, more usually, by his insurer. This is the province of civil liability in tort or (in Scotland) delict. Usually, but not invariably, the law of tort requires payment only where the person who caused the injury was at 'fault'. We describe the essential features of the tort system, including the meaning and scope of 'fault', in chapter 4.

8

32   The biggest single source of compensation, however, is the social security
system. Social security payments are normally made irrespective of the cause
of the injury or death. Even where the cause is relevant, as in the industrial
injuries scheme, payments do not depend on whether the injury was due to
someone else's fault. Payment is made instead to meet a particular need or
other circumstance, which for the injured is most commonly that of incapacity
for work. We describe in chapter 5 those features of the social security system,
including the main benefits, which are of particular relevance to us. We also
briefly describe in that chapter the criminal injuries compensation schemes,
which are the only other major source of cash compensation provided by the
state for death or personal injury.

33   In addition to the tort system and the state, there are two other important
sources of compensation. First, there is the employer, who may compensate
an employee through sick pay, through some form of private insurance policy
taken out for the employee or through an occupational disability pension.
Again, compensation of these kinds is normally paid irrespective of the cause
of the injury and irrespective of fault. Secondly, there is private insurance,
whereby the injured person has taken out and paid for his own policy, and
payment is in effect made from a fund into which others running a risk of
injury have also contributed. The terms of the policy will have determined
whether or not compensation is payable in the circumstances concerned. We
describe in chapter 6 the types of provision made by employers and by private
insurance. We refer also in that chapter to certain other forms of compensation
which are provided outside the tort and state systems.

34   Finally, we must explain our use of the term 'no-fault'. We use it to refer
to compensation which is obtainable without proving fault and is provided
outside the tort system. No-fault compensation is a system of obtaining payment from a fund instead of proceeding against the person responsible for the
injury. In practice, 'no-fault' includes nearly all the forms of compensation
described in chapters 5 and 6. The relationship between tort compensation
and no-fault compensation is a central theme of our report.

CHAPTER 3
Facts and figures

35 Every year in the United Kingdom some three million people are injured, and about 21,000 die as a result of injury. Since our concern is with the compensation available to those of the injured and bereaved who fall within our terms of reference, one of our first tasks was to find out more about these injuries, their circumstances, their seriousness, and the kinds of people most affected by them. We found it necessary to supplement the available information by commissioning our own survey of people who had sustained injuries.

36 The purpose of this chapter is to set out basic facts and figures by way of background to the examination of compensation systems which follows. The figures are derived from various sources. A fuller study of the available statistics, including the results of our own personal injury survey, is in Volume Two.

Injuries

37 Of the three million or so injuries, about a million occur at work or on the roads, and so come within the first two categories of our terms of reference. As to the remaining two million, precise allocation is not feasible, but from the available information we estimate that rather less than a million come in the last three categories – mainly the residual category e – and that rather more than a million, including many injuries occurring in private homes, are outside our terms of reference. A more detailed breakdown of these figures is given in table 1.

38 All these numbers relate to injuries which are sufficiently serious to lead to four or more days off work, or to an equivalent degree of incapacity for those not in work. They may differ from statistics prepared on other bases, for example in respect of motor vehicle injuries. (The bases of the various statistics are described in Volume Two.)

39 We estimate that no more than 3 per cent of men and 8 per cent of women will escape injury, as we have defined it, during an average lifetime. Injuries happen in the course of every kind of human activity – at work or at school, when driving, when playing games, in the street or at home. In infancy and in old age, accidents at home predominate; in the school years, accidents at school; and in the middle years, accidents at work. Until around retirement age, and even in infancy, males are more susceptible to injury than females. Manual workers and their families are more subject to injury than non-manual workers.

10

Table 1   Numbers of injuries each year

United Kingdom, 1973–1975   Thousands

	All	Males 15 and over	Females 15 and over	Children under 15 and students
Injuries at work	720	630	90	—
Motor vehicle injuries[1]	290	160	80	50
Other injuries	2,040	660	620	760
Of which possibly due to the act or omission of another	880	260	160	460
All injuries	3,050	1,450	790	810

1 Other than while at work.

Figures estimated by the Commission.

40   Most injuries have no long lasting consequences. Reliable figures are available only in respect of the working population, among whom incapacity for work due to injury usually lasts for less than three weeks, and rarely for more than six months, as shown in table 2. There may be some residual disability, however, even when incapacity for work is fairly short.

Table 2   Duration of incapacity for work due to injury

Working population

Great Britain, 1973–1975   Percentage of annual spells of incapacity

	Percentage of spells terminating in period	Cumulative percentage of spells terminating by end of period
Duration:		
Over 3 days–1 week	18·5	18·5
Over 1 week–2 weeks	27·4	45·9
Over 2 weeks–4 weeks	27·5	73·5
Over 4 weeks–8 weeks	16·0	89·5
Over 8 weeks–3 months	5·5	94·9
Over 3 months–6 months	3·4	98·3
Over 6 months	1·6	

Source: Based on Department of Health and Social Security records of 1·7 million spells of incapacity due to injury qualifying for sickness or industrial injury benefit.

Deaths

41   About 21,000 people die each year in the United Kingdom as a result of accidental injury or purposely inflicted violence. This number represents some

3 per cent of the 670,000 total deaths. We have no way of estimating what proportion of the 21,000 come within our terms of reference, although we know that between 8,000 and 9,000 are the result of accidents on the roads or at work. Further details are given in table 3; it is noteworthy that, whereas there are more than twice as many non-fatal injuries at work as there are on the roads, there are more than five times as many deaths following injury on the roads as deaths following injury at work.

Table 3   Numbers of deaths following injury each year

United Kingdom, 1972–1975   Numbers

	All	Males over 15	Females over 15	Children 15 and under
At work	1,300	1,270	30	—
Motor vehicle[1]	7,220	4,330	2,080	810
Other	12,900	5,100	6,540	1,260
All deaths	21,420	10,700	8,650	2,070

1 Excluding deaths while at work.

Source: Registrars General, except that estimates of deaths at work, including those involving motor vehicles, were made by the Commission.

42   Accidental injury and purposely inflicted violence together represent the commonest cause of death up to the age of 35. They account for 24 per cent of all deaths in this age range. This proportion has increased as fatal diseases which used to be common have become rarer.

Trends

43   Measures aimed at promoting safety have had some success. For example, the number of casualties on the roads fell by 10 per cent in the period immediately following the introduction of breath tests in 1967, although it has since risen again. More generally, there has been a substantial decline in the number of casualties per vehicle mile, counterbalanced by the continuing growth of traffic. A reduction in recent years in the number of accidents at work was partly due to a shift in the pattern of employment away from some of the more dangerous occupations, but partly also to better accident prevention. There is, however, no indication of a downward trend in the number of accidents of all kinds.

Compensation

44   In the next Part of our report, we discuss the various ways in which compensation is provided at present. We estimate that the total amount of compensation for personal injury and death resulting from injury is over

£800 million a year, but we have no adequate basis for estimating what proportion of this figure relates to injuries within our terms of reference. About a half comes from social security and a quarter from the tort system. Table 4 gives a broad indication of the relative importance of the different sources of compensation available at present.

Table 4   Scale of present sources of compensation for injury

United Kingdom, based on data for 1971–1976

	Aggregate value of compensation payments	Approximate number of new beneficiaries
	£ million a year[1]	Number a year
Social security	421	1,550,000
Tort/delict	202	215,000
Other	204	
Occupational sick pay	125	1,000,000
Occupational pensions	5	4,000
Private insurance[2]	51	200,000
Criminal injuries compensation	17	18,000
Other forms of compensation[3]	6	150,000
All forms of compensation	827	1,700,000[4]

1 At 1 January 1977 prices.

2 Excluding life insurance, for which we can make no reliable estimate.

3 Rent and rate rebates, trade unions, friendly societies and charities.

4 After double counting has been excluded.

Figures estimated by the Commission.

PART II

The present system

CHAPTER 4
Tort

45 Civil liability in tort and in delict is the oldest method of obtaining compensation for personal injury. For a long time it was the most important. Tort (in England, Wales and Northern Ireland) and delict (in Scotland), in their legal senses, cover wrongful acts and omissions, other than breaches of contract, in respect of which damages can be claimed by the victim from the wrongdoer in respect of a loss or injury. In its original sense 'tort' (derived from the Latin *tortus*, meaning 'twisted') meant any wrong. The overall scope of both tort and delict is much wider than their application to cases of personal injury and death, but all tortious and delictual acts in such cases are within our terms of reference. When we refer to 'tort' in the remainder of our report we intend to include 'delict' unless we indicate otherwise.

46 We come later in the report (chapter 10) to consider the criticisms which are levelled at tort. The purpose of this chapter is to describe its essential features.

Origins and development

Historical background

47 The historical roots of civil liability in tort lie in the earliest traditions, common to many societies, of paying a forfeit for harm done. Under the customary European systems, including those of England and Scotland, there was no clear distinction between crime and tort, and, where personal injury or death occurred, a single proceeding served for buying off the vengeance of the injured person or his family and placating the king or lord for the disturbance of the peace. The amount of the payment reflected the affront to dignity or the rank of the person injured, rather than the actual loss occasioned by the injury. Little consideration appears to have been given to fault or blameworthiness; a man acted at his peril.

48 In England and Wales, with the growth of central power in the centuries following the Norman Conquest, actions which today would be serious crimes came increasingly to be punishable by the state, rather than by private vengeance and the exaction of compensation by the injured party or his relatives. But there remained the less serious cases, and probably too a continuing demand for payment of compensation, and the principle of reparation began to be acknowledged by the common law. The presence or absence of fault remained largely immaterial until the nineteenth century, when the idea that the

17

defendant's liability might be modified began to emerge in cases arising from road traffic accidents involving horses or carriages. The trend of judicial thinking in such cases can be illustrated by a passage from the judgment in *Holmes* v. *Mather* (1875) L.R. 10 Ex. 261, 'For the convenience of mankind in carrying on the affairs of life, people as they go along roads must expect, or put up with, such mischief as reasonable care on the part of others cannot avoid'.

49   A failure to use reasonable care when doing or omitting to do something is an essential element in the modern test of negligence, with which much of our report will be concerned. It gradually came to be applied more widely than just in traffic cases. An early example had been the Fires Prevention (Metropolis) Act 1774, which had substituted liability for fault for the previous strict liability in respect of the escape of fire. By the end of the nineteenth century, liability for fault had largely superseded the stricter liability of the past.

50   Northern Ireland law is based to a large extent on the principles of English common law.

51   In Scotland, the modern test of negligence emerged by a different path. In or around the fourteenth century, when any personal injury or death resulting from the act of another was treated as a crime, the quasi-criminal action of assythment became established. Originally, assythment was available as a remedy for the victim himself, if he survived, or for his relatives, if he died, in respect of all bodily injuries; but later it became limited to cases of death. Assythment constituted the compensation payable by the person causing the injury or death for the mutilation or slaughter, and for 'the pacifying of the rancour' of the injured person or his next of kin. The modern claim for *solatium* was developed out of the claim for assythment, as a head of damages in purely civil actions.

52   In the meantime, by the beginning of the eighteenth century, accidental or negligent acts had become characterised as civil rather than criminal, and the action of assythment was falling into disuse. At the end of the century, the principle of reparation for fault emerged to fill the gap. Several of the early successful actions related to injuries incurred by falling into unfenced pits and drains during the construction of the Edinburgh new town. To the extent that they encompassed negligence by omission (an omission to fence off pits and drains) these and other cases also extended the scope of potential reparation even beyond the range of medieval criminal law. In England, the emergence of the test of negligence represented in some respects a contraction of liability. In Scotland, it represented an expansion.

Donoghue v. *Stevenson*

53   The classic statement of the principles behind the test of negligence, applicable throughout the United Kingdom, is in the speech of Lord Atkin in the Scottish case of *Donoghue* v. *Stevenson* [1932] A.C. 562, 1932 S.C.(H.L.) 31.

That was the case in which legal history was made by an alleged snail in a ginger beer bottle. The pursuer (plaintiff) alleged that a bottle of ginger beer had been bought for her, and that when she drank it she found in it a decomposed snail and in consequence became ill. The question before the court was whether, if all the pursuer's allegations were proved, the pursuer's relationship to the defender (defendant) – the manufacturer of the drink – was such as to enable her to succeed in her action against him on the grounds of his negligence towards her, there being no contract between them. It was held in the House of Lords, by a majority of three to two, that if the pursuer proved her allegations she would be entitled to succeed. Thus the principle was established. The case was subsequently settled extra-judicially for a small sum.

54   Lord Atkin, one of the majority, said:

'The liability for negligence, whether you style it such or treat it as in other systems as a species of 'culpa', is no doubt based upon a general public sentiment of moral wrongdoing for which the offender must pay. But acts or omissions which any moral code would censure cannot in a practical world be treated so as to give a right to every person injured by them to demand relief. In this way rules of law arise which limit the range of complainants and the extent of their remedy. The rule that you are to love your neighbour becomes in law, you must not injure your neighbour; and the lawyer's question, Who is my neighbour? receives a restricted reply. You must take reasonable care to avoid acts or omissions which you can reasonably foresee would be likely to injure your neighbour. Who, then, in law is my neighbour? The answer seems to be – persons who are so closely and directly affected by my act that I ought reasonably to have them in contemplation as being so affected when I am directing my mind to the acts or omissions which are called in question.'

55   That passage shows the basis of the action for negligence. The duty to take care in order to avoid injury to others is an aspect of the duty to one's neighbour. A possible analysis, not accepted by all of us, is that, if a person by rash or careless conduct causes injury to another, the wrongdoer has or ought to have a feeling of guilt which needs to be expiated and the victim has a feeling of indignation which needs to be appeased, and that the expiation and appeasement are achieved by a payment of compensation. This could be regarded as the simple idea of liability for negligence, although extensions of the liability will be referred to later in this chapter.

56   In an action for negligence, therefore, the plaintiff has to show that the defendant owed to him a duty of care, that the defendant in breach of that duty behaved negligently and that the defendant's negligent behaviour caused the plaintiff's injuries. The first question is whether the plaintiff was within the category of those to whom the defendant owed a duty of care. Often, an affirmative answer can readily be given. It is well settled and taken for granted that, for instance, a duty of care is owed by a road user to any other road user near enough to be affected, by an employer to his employees, by a carrier to his passengers and by an occupier of premises to any person whom he has invited or permitted to enter his premises.

57   The questions that are more frequently disputed are whether the defendant was negligent; if so, whether his negligence caused the plaintiff's injuries; and, then, what are the extent and effect of the plaintiff's injuries. Nearly always the questions in dispute are questions of fact, which the judge, or in Scotland or Northern Ireland the judge or jury, must decide on the evidence to the best of his or their ability. The burden of proof is lighter in a civil action than in a criminal prosecution, in that the plaintiff has only to establish a balance of probabilities in his favour, whereas the prosecutor has to prove his case beyond reasonable doubt.

58   The defendant can defeat the plaintiff's claim or secure a reduction of the damages, by showing that the accident was wholly caused or contributed to by the negligence of the plaintiff. Until 1945, contributory negligence on the part of the plaintiff was a complete defence to any tort claim. The Law Reform (Contributory Negligence) Act of that year altered the position. It provided that negligence by the plaintiff which was merely contributory would no longer bar his claim entirely, but would reduce the damages awarded to the extent to which he was to blame for the accident. In determining whether there is negligence, the standard of care is the same for the plaintiff as for the defendant.

Liability insurance

59   The development of liability for negligence has been accompanied by a growth of what is described as liability insurance or, more commonly, as third party insurance. The insured person is the first party, the insurer is the second party, and the potential plaintiff is the third party. The availability of liability insurance modifies the concept of individual responsibility implied by the test of negligence, since it allows potential defendants to pool their risks. It is also in the interests of the plaintiff. Without insurance, a defendant may be unable to meet a claim for damages if he has few resources himself, and the more so if the claim is in respect of the death or serious injury of a breadwinner.

60   Third party insurance has been made compulsory by statute for motorists in relation to other road users (including passengers) and for employers in relation to their employees. In each case, this is a recognition of its importance in ensuring that compensation is available to the victims of negligence. It has also developed substantially in other fields, where compulsion does not exist. For example, virtually all businesses are now insured against their liabilities to the public. With the growth of negligence claims, nearly all specialist areas in the realm of professional liabilities are covered, sometimes by mutual associations.

61   Insurance enables the defendant to pay the damages if he loses the action. In practice, the insurer nearly always takes over the conduct of the action and makes a direct payment to the injured party if he succeeds. Usually, there is a settlement by agreement between the defendant's insurer and the plaintiff or his representative.

Extensions of negligence

62 There are at least five extensions or elaborations of the simple idea of negligence.

Vicarious liability

63 First, there is the rule of vicarious liability. A defendant employer is vicariously liable for the negligence of his employees acting within the scope of their employment, even if the employer himself was wholly free from blame. An employer may be held liable in respect of an injury suffered by one of his employees through the negligence of another of them.

64 This rule of vicarious liability is an application of the principle of agency, that he who acts through another is taken to be acting himself. It has the practical advantage that the need for insurance is placed on the employer, who can insure more economically than could individual employees; and it may be considered reasonable to expect the employer to insure because, by instructing his employees to engage in activities on his behalf, he creates the risk that they may negligently injure other persons. At any rate the rule is clear and well established.

Breach of statutory duty

65 Secondly, there is the action for damages for personal injury caused by the defendant's breach of statutory duty. Breach of statutory duty is sometimes referred to as 'statutory negligence', but more naturally regarded as a separate species of fault distinct from negligence. There can be a breach of statutory duty without any failure to take reasonable care. For practical purposes, liability for breach of statutory duty operates as an extension of liability for negligence, because the plaintiff may allege both in the same action and, if he fails to prove negligence, may still succeed by proving a breach of statutory duty.

66 The theory of it is that, when an Act imposes a duty, or provides for regulations to impose a duty, for the protection of a class of persons, it may be inferred that Parliament must have intended a person of that class injured by a breach of that duty to have a civil cause of action for damages against the wrongdoer. That can be held to be the intention of Parliament even in an Act which provides a criminal penalty for the breach of duty and makes no mention of a civil remedy. The original decision to that effect was given by the courts in 1898 (*Groves* v. *Wimborne* [1898] 2 Q.B. 402). It has been affirmed and applied in many subsequent cases, especially cases concerned with duties under the Factories Acts, for example failure to fence dangerous machinery. The practical effect is that a factory worker injured by his employer's breach of some duty imposed by the Acts or regulations is entitled to succeed in his action without proving that the employer was negligent.

The standard of care

67 Thirdly, the standard of care that is to be exercised, at least where the defendant is an adult, is the standard of the reasonable man. The defendant cannot free himself from liability by showing he is by nature forgetful,

inattentive, absent-minded, impulsive or unskilful and so could not help behaving as he did. If his behaviour falls short of the standard of the reasonable man, that is negligence. There can be negligence without moral fault, when the person concerned is doing his best but is doing badly when judged by the objective standard.

The burden of proof

68   Fourthly, although the burden of proof is on the plaintiff to prove that there was negligence on the part of the defendant causing the plaintiff's injury, there are in the practice of the courts certain principles which assist the plaintiff to discharge this burden. There is the rule of *res ipsa loquitur* (the facts speak for themselves). The plaintiff may be able to prove facts which, without directly proving such negligence, raise a *prima facie* inference that there must have been such negligence somehow. Then the plaintiff will win the case unless the defendant can rebut the inference by contrary evidence. Examples of *res ipsa loquitur* are an air crash and a train collision. In such cases the inference may be virtually conclusive, so that the only serious dispute, if any, will be as to the amount of the damages. In motor accident cases, the facts are usually not so clear, but if the car mounts the pavement and strikes a pedestrian there will be a *prima facie* inference of negligence which he may or may not be able to rebut.

Dangerous things

69   Fifthly, there is another principle which may assist the plaintiff. A person who has in his charge a dangerous thing, which will do great damage if a mishap occurs, is required to exercise a high degree of care to prevent any mishap occurring. An example is the use of blow lamps or oxy-acetylene cutting equipment involving a serious risk of fire. Another example is a motor vehicle carrying a load of some explosive or flammable chemical. Even without such a load, the driver of a motor vehicle is required to exercise a high degree of care in view of its capacity for causing injury.

70   In all cases, the law pays regard both to the degree of the risk and to the nature and extent of the damage or injury which might arise if the risk were to materialise. Both considerations are relevant to the question whether a duty of care arises, and to the extent of that duty. For example, a high degree of care may be required of those in charge of a large department store, an hotel, a stand at a football ground, a concert hall, theatre, circus or assembly hall, or a tall block of flats, even if there is little probability that an accident will occur, because if it does occur it could well be a catastrophe.

Strict liability

71   There are in the United Kingdom a few cases of strict liability imposed by law. Strict liability may be defined as liability irrespective of the negligence of the defendant, based solely on proof that he caused the loss or injury in respect of which the claim is made. Under statute law, strict liability applies to nuclear installations, the underground storage of gas, surface damage caused by aircraft and, in England, Wales and Northern Ireland, certain animals. At English common law, there is a measure of strict liability imposed

on a person who has kept on his land a thing which will cause serious damage if it escapes, and who fails to prevent its escape; but actions based on this principle are rare.

The Unfair Contract Terms Act 1977
72   Under the Unfair Contract Terms Act 1977, and except as permitted by any international convention to which the United Kingdom is a party, it will no longer be possible to exclude or restrict, by contract or by notice, liability for negligence arising in a business context and resulting in death or personal injury. With certain exceptions, the Act covers not only the supply of goods and services but also contracts of employment and the liability of occupiers of the premises or land used for business purposes to persons entering on or using those premises or land.

Damages
Damages for personal injury
73   In the assessment of damages, different principles apply to the damages for pecuniary loss and to those for non-pecuniary loss.

74   Damages for pecuniary loss relate to additional expenses and loss of income up to the date of the award and for the future; and the broad principle is that the court should award the injured party such a sum of money as will put him in the same position as he would have been in if he had not sustained the injuries. Only lump sum damages can be awarded; there is no power to award periodic payments. To replace lost future income, the established method is to award such a sum as, when suitably invested, will over the relevant period, by receipt of interest and dividends and drawings from capital, provide annually the amount of the lost income. Grave problems at present arise in seeking to apply this method realistically in face of the uncertainties as to future rates of inflation, of taxation on investment income and of interest and dividends; and we discuss these problems in later chapters.

75   Damages for non-pecuniary loss relate to pain and suffering, and loss of amenity, and usually one sum is awarded for the whole. Non-pecuniary loss is understood as covering physical pain and suffering, nervous shock, mental distress, loss of faculty, disfigurement, inconveniences, and discomfort, loss of enjoyment of life and also loss of expectation of life (in so far as damages are awarded for this element). No sum of money could be exact compensation for non-pecuniary loss, because no sum of money could restore or be a true equivalent for the lost sight, hearing, limb, power of movement or capacity to enjoy life. The trial judge (or jury when there is one) can award only such sum of money as appears fair and reasonable and in line with comparable previous awards.

Damages following death
76   In the case of a fatal injury, damages in England, Wales and Northern Ireland may be sought on one or both of two bases. First, the representatives of the deceased's estate may claim on behalf of the estate under any of the heads that would have been available to the deceased had he not died; the

principle of trying to restore the injured party to the position he would have been in is applied posthumously to the benefit of his estate. Secondly, the dependants of the deceased have a statutory right of action for damages for loss of their dependency. This right of action is confined to pecuniary loss. Where the dependants and the beneficiaries of the estate are one and the same, no duplication of damages is permitted.

77 In Scotland, the respective claims of the executors and relatives are now defined in the Damages (Scotland) Act 1976. An executor is entitled to sue for patrimonial (pecuniary) loss up to the date of death, but is barred from claiming for any non-pecuniary loss to which the deceased himself would have been entitled. The relatives may claim for their subsequent pecuniary loss, that is to say their loss of support; and, in addition, members of the deceased's immediate family are entitled to an award for loss of society when this can be justified as compensation to them for losing the benefit of his society and counsel.

Tort in practice

Claims and settlements

78 About a quarter of a million tort claims in respect of personal injury are made in the United Kingdom each year; between 85 and 90 per cent of them are successful, in whole or in part. Nevertheless, taking all injuries, including those outside our terms of reference, the proportion attracting tort compensation is low – about 6·5 per cent. There are some wide variations, depending on the type of injury, the type of person who is injured, and the duration of incapacity, as shown by the following table:

Table 5 Proportion of injuries for which tort compensation is obtained
Great Britain, 1973

(i) By type of injury	Percentage obtaining tort compensation
Injuries at work	$10\frac{1}{2}$
Motor vehicle injuries[1]	25
Other injuries	$1\frac{1}{2}$
All injuries	$6\frac{1}{2}$

(ii) By population group	Percentage obtaining tort compensation
Working men	10
Working women	8
Other men	5
Other women	4
Children under 15	1
All injuries	$6\frac{1}{2}$

24

(iii) By duration of incapacity for work[2]	Percentage obtaining tort compensation
4 days–1 month	6
Over 1 month–2 months	12
Over 2 months–3 months	13
Over 3 months–6 months	20
Over 6 months	31

1 Including injuries while at work.
2 Injuries to people in employment.

Figures estimated by the Commission.

79   Of all tort claims, 47 per cent relate to work injuries or illnesses, 41 per cent to motor vehicle injuries and 12 per cent to other injuries. Eighty six per cent are disposed of without the issue of a writ or service of a summons. Not quite half the claims are settled within a year of the injury. Only 1 per cent of claims reach the courts. Even so, personal injury cases in England and Wales make up over three quarters of the cases set down for hearing in the Queen's Bench Division of the High Court.

80   Most tort settlements are small. About 60 per cent of them amount to £500 or less. About 1 per cent exceed £10,000. A breakdown is given in Table 6.

Table 6   Distribution of tort payments by size[1]

Great Britain, based on data for 1973

Size of payment	Percentage of total number of payments	Percentage of total amount paid
£		
1– 100	17	1
101– 200	15	3
201– 500	28	10
501– 1,000	19	14
1,001– 2,000	11	16
2,001– 5,000	7	22
5,001–10,000	2	13
Over 10,000	1	21
All payments	100	100

1 At January 1977 prices.

Figures estimated by the Commission from BIA data.

81   More than a half of the total amount paid out under the present tort system is for non-pecuniary loss. In the biggest claims, compensation for future loss of earnings plays a larger part and the proportion of non-pecuniary loss is lower.

82   Amounts awarded have been increasing over the last few years and in some cases have exceeded £100,000. Until recently, the highest award made was £142,000, in February 1977. In December 1977, the High Court awarded damages of £243,000, although only £132,000 of this was payable immediately pending an appeal.

Administration costs

83   We estimate that the operating costs of the tort system amount to about 85 per cent of the value of tort compensation payments, or about 45 per cent of the combined total of compensation and operating costs. Of these operating costs, about 40 per cent is accounted for by the costs of insurers in handling claims and on general administration. The remaining elements are the commissions paid by insurers to brokers and agents, claimants' legal fees, and profit. Each represents about a fifth. On small claims, the expenses can be greater than the damages paid.

Statistics

84   We have illustrated this chapter with some of the more important figures indicating the way in which the law of tort works in practice. Further information is given in Volume Two, which includes a statistical picture of the operation of the law of tort built up in the course of our enquiries.

CHAPTER 5

State provision

85 The development of the modern social security system can be traced back to the poor laws of the seventeenth century in England, Wales and Scotland and the nineteenth century in Northern Ireland. From these beginnings there grew a parish based system of almshouses, hospitals and payments in cash and kind for those in want as a result of incapacity or loss of a bread-winner. The late seventeenth century saw the start of systematic arrangements for compensating disabled soldiers and sailors, first by accommodation in the Royal Hospitals at Chelsea and Greenwich and then by pensions for those for whom there was not room in the hospitals.

The extent of state provision

86 There has been a dramatic growth of state provision over the last 70 years. Measures aiming at no more than the bare relief of extreme poverty have given place to a system in which cash benefits are provided as of right, together with comprehensive medical services and supporting social services to meet a wide variety of contingencies.

87 In 1977–78 the cost of this provision is expected to be about £18,000 million, about a third of all public expenditure. As table 7 shows, only a small part of this expenditure, less than 6 per cent, is for the victims of personal injuries. The estimated expenditure in respect of civilian injury relates to all injuries, or deaths resulting from injury, whether or not these are within our terms of reference, since provision for injuries and deaths within our terms of reference could not be distinguished.

88 In this chapter, we summarise those developments of the social security system which are relevant to our enquiry. We begin with workmen's compensation.

Workmen's compensation

89 Apart from provision for war pensions, tort damages were for centuries all that stood between an injured or bereaved person and destitution or dependence on charity. The break away from dependence on tort came in the field of industrial accidents in 1897. The Workmen's Compensation Act of

Table 7 State provision

United Kingdom 1977/78 £ million a year

	Total expenditure[1]	Estimated expenditure in respect of civilian injury[2]
Benefits for civilian injury, sickness or death[3]	1,986	407
War pensions	274	—
Retirement and old persons' pensions	5,705	—
Other cash benefits[4]	3,389	14
Social security administration and miscellaneous services	531	47
Total social security	11,885	468
Hospitals and community health services	3,869	390
Family practitioner and other health services	1,196	120
Personal social services	941	50
Other services	147	15
Total services	6,153	575
Total, cash benefits and services	18,038	1,043

1 Estimates for 1977/78 at 1976 public expenditure survey prices.

2 Broad estimates made by the Commission at January 1977 prices.

3 Excluding £17 million criminal injuries compensation.

4 Total expenditure includes £300 million estimating margin. No deduction has been made for the reduction in child tax allowances accompanying increased child benefits.

Sources: Public expenditure estimates (Cmnd 6721-II, Feb 1977), and estimates made by the Commission.

that year introduced into employment law the concept of liability without fault and the provision of cash benefits as of right and without a test of means. Section 1(1) of the Act stated:

'If in any employment to which this Act applies personal injury by accident arising out of and in the course of employment is caused to a workman, his employer shall, subject as herein-after mentioned, be liable to pay compensation . . .'

90 The Act applied only to certain hazardous industries, namely employment on or in railways, factories, mines, quarries, engineering works or buildings over 30 feet high. Under the Act, the negligence of the employee himself,

unless it amounted to his 'serious and wilful misconduct', was no defence. In fatal cases compensation was in the form of a lump sum equal to three years' earnings, subject to a minimum of £150 and a maximum of £300, payable to the dependants. For total incapacity for work, compensation was a weekly payment not exceeding 50 per cent of the average pre-accident earnings, subject to a maximum of £1. For partial incapacity, the payment was based on the difference between earnings before and after the accident. The employee retained the right, as an alternative, to sue for damages under the tort system.

91   In 1906, a further Workmen's Compensation Act extended the scheme to most people working under a contract of service or apprenticeship. The number of people who were covered rose from an estimated $7\frac{1}{4}$ million to some 15 million. The most important exception was non-manual workers earning more than £250 a year. Compensation for incapacity or death due to certain industrial diseases was also provided. Although the 1906 Act was frequently amended, the structure of the workmen's compensation system which it established lasted until 1948.

National insurance

92   The National Insurance Act 1911, which made provision for sickness and unemployment benefits, was the start of our national insurance system. It was later extended by the Widows', Orphans' and Old Age Contributory Pensions Act 1925. Sickness benefit was paid by friendly societies, trade unions, insurers and other bodies under arrangements approved under the provisions of the National Insurance Act. Unemployment benefit was paid by the Ministry of Labour. Pensions were paid by the Health Departments. Workmen's compensation continued as a separate system, under the aegis of the Home Office and the Ministry of Labour for Northern Ireland, with benefits considerably higher than those paid under the insurance schemes.

The Beveridge Report

93   The publication in 1942 of the Beveridge Report on Social Insurance and Allied Services (Cmd 6404) was a landmark in the history of social security. Its philosophy was a world away from that of the nineteenth century poor law, which treated poverty as a sign of moral fault in the pauper, to be eliminated by rigorous measures. Beveridge held that people would not voluntarily be paupers if they were given the chance of maintaining themselves and that it was the business of the state to see that the chance was available.

94   Beveridge's proposals for a new structure of social security and supporting services were implemented, with some changes, soon after the war. The insurance schemes were unified and extended by the National Insurance Act 1946; the workmen's compensation system was replaced by the National Insurance (Industrial Injuries) Act 1946; and the public assistance system was replaced by the National Assistance Act 1948. Other welfare provisions were family allowances, under the Family Allowances Act 1945, and comprehensive medical services, under the National Health Service Acts 1946 and 1947.

95 The legislation departed in some respects from the Beveridge proposals. Among the modifications were, first, the introduction of full rate retirement pensions from the outset, instead of starting at a modest rate and gradually increasing over a period of 20 years. Secondly, family allowances were set at a lower level than Beveridge had proposed. Thirdly, national assistance, with the inclusion of an allowance for rent, was set at a higher level than insurance benefits. Householders with no income other than insurance benefit were entitled from the outset to national assistance to supplement their benefit.

96 Beveridge acknowledged in his report that the workmen's compensation system had conferred great benefits, but he noted two major disadvantages. First, employer's liability insurance was not compulsory (except in the mining industries), so that there was no complete security for the payment of compensation. Secondly, the system rested, in the last resort, on litigation. The original intention that disputes should usually be resolved by friendly and informal arbitration had not been realised; instead, the parties almost invariably resorted to court proceedings. Beveridge concluded that:

'The pioneer system of social security in Britain was based on a wrong principle and has been dominated by a wrong outlook. It allows claims to be settled by bargaining between unequal parties, permits payment of socially wasteful lump sums instead of pensions in cases of serious incapacity . . . and over part of the field, large in the numbers covered, though not in the proportion of the total compensation paid, it relies on expensive private insurance. There should be no hesitation in making provision for the results of industrial accident and disease in future, not by a continuance of the present system of individual employer's liability, but as one branch of a unified Plan for Social Security.'

The survival of the industrial preference

97 Beveridge considered whether the consequences of industrial accidents and diseases should be treated in exactly the same way as other accidents and diseases. He concluded, not without reluctance, that an element of industrial preference should remain, where the individual died or where he was incapacitated for more than 13 weeks. Three reasons were advanced. The first was that many industries vital to the community were especially dangerous. It was essential that men should enter them and it was more likely that they would do so if they were assured of special provision against their risks. The second was that a man disabled during the course of his employment had been disabled while working under orders. The third was that it would be possible to limit the employer's liability at common law only if provision were made for the results of industrial accidents and disease irrespective of negligence.

98 Beveridge proposed that, for the first three months, those disabled through work should receive the same benefit as those disabled from any other cause, and that thereafter preference would come into operation. A pension of two thirds of the workman's earnings in full employment should be paid, and

30

should continue as long as inability to work lasted. Partial disablement benefit should be payable for a partial loss of earning capacity. There should be a lump sum for dependants of those killed while of working age.

99 The Government accepted that workmen's compensation should be replaced by a scheme integrated with the social security system, but did not implement all of Beveridge's proposals. One of the most important changes was its decision that long term industrial pensions should be based not on loss of earnings, but on loss of faculty. This decision marked a departure not only from the basis of workmen's compensation but also from the principle still followed today in industrial injuries compensation schemes in nearly all other countries. The concept of compensation for loss of faculty offered the prospect of escaping from one of the most contentious aspects of workmen's compensation – the assessment of earnings before and after the accident. It also met the criticism that the scheme discouraged an injured workman from returning to work or increasing his earnings.

100 The method adopted for assessing the degree of disablement followed that which had been used in the war pensions scheme since 1917. The principle was that the degree of disablement should be assessed by comparison with that of a healthy person of the same age. Degrees of disablement were on a scale from 20 to 100 per cent, in steps of 10 per cent. Compensation for disablement of less than 20 per cent was not payable for the first few years of the industrial scheme, but was then paid as a gratuity or temporary allowance.

101 In addition to the basic disablement benefit, certain allowances were payable, in particular when constant attendance or hospital treatment were needed. During the passage of the legislation through Parliament, provision was added for a limited loss of earnings supplement, known as special hardship allowance. The allowance was originally intended to overcome the criticism that the scheme provided inadequate compensation for the man who might suffer a comparatively minor disablement which nevertheless might prevent him from following his regular occupation. But the allowance has come to be paid to many more people than was first envisaged. One reason has been the removal of the restriction on payment of disablement benefit (and its allowances) in cases where the assessment was less than 20 per cent.

102 For short term cases, the industrial injuries scheme provided industrial injury benefit at a rate of 73 per cent higher than sickness benefit. It was payable from the start of incapacity, up to a maximum of six months.

103 The Government did not accept the Beveridge proposals that a lump sum related to the husband's earnings should be payable to a widow. Instead, provision was made for a pension. Widows of men killed in industrial accidents had three advantages over other widows – their pensions were at a higher rate; they were not subject to an earnings rule; and they were entitled to a small pension even of they were likely to be able to earn their own living.

104 One reason for keeping a preference in cases of industrial injury or disease may well have been that it was thought unlikely that any new provisions would be acceptable if they provided less benefit than workmen's compensation already provided; and it was even more unlikely that benefit could be provided at workmen's compensation rates for all. At the time of the Beveridge report, workmen's compensation was double the rate of sickness benefit, with allowances for dependants payable in addition.

Developments in social security since 1948

Increase in benefit rates
105 Since 1948, benefit levels have been regularly increased in real terms, so that beneficiaries have shared in rising living standards. For example, sickness benefit increased some tenfold between 1948 and 1977. It kept in step with the increase in average earnings, and ahead of prices which, over the same period, increased by a factor of $6\frac{1}{2}$.

106 Section 125 of the Social Security Act 1975 now provides for benefits to be reviewed once in each tax year. Short term benefits are increased by reference to increase in prices, and long term benefits by reference to increase in prices or earnings, whichever is the more favourable. Except where otherwise stated, the rates of social security benefits quoted in this report are those in force in January 1977.

Erosion of the industrial preference
107 In the process of uprating benefits, the lead which the recipients of industrial injury benefit have over their national insurance counterparts has been eroded. It has remained at £2·75 a week since 1965. In relative terms it has dropped from an increase over sickness benefit of 73 per cent in 1948 to 21 per cent in 1977. The lead for widows in receipt of industrial death benefit has similarly been eroded. It has remained at 55p a week since 1967.

108 The provision of disablement benefit for those injured at work, and payable whether earnings are affected or not, remains as the most important feature of the industrial preference.

New contributory benefits
109 New benefits have been introduced within the contributory national insurance scheme. After six months' incapacity for work, sickness benefit is now succeeded by invalidity pension of £15·30 (and, as such, £2·40 higher than sickness benefit). An invalidity allowance is added to the invalidity pension. This allowance is related to the age at which the incapacity began. If under age 35 it is £3·20 a week, between 35 and 45 it is £2, and between 45 and 60 (55 for women) it is £1. Over 60 (55) no addition is made.

110 The relationship between the original benefits has also altered. The principle of uniform rates for unemployment, sickness and retirement has been abandoned. Increasing emphasis has been put on providing higher benefits for the long term sick and disabled.

Earnings relation

111   The original concept of flat rate national insurance contributions and benefits has been modified. Contributions graduated according to earnings were first added to the flat rate contributions in 1961. Since April 1975, the national insurance contributions paid by employees and their employers have been wholly earnings related (although there is an upper limit). They are now collected through the income tax PAYE system.

112   Small graduated additions to the flat rate pensions began to be earned from 1961. Earnings related supplements to short term benefits followed in 1966. They were intended to act as a cushion to cover a temporary loss of earnings. The supplement was paid for 26 weeks starting with the third week of incapacity or unemployment. The amount payable was related to earnings in the most recent tax year for which records were available.

The new pensions scheme

113   The trend towards earnings relation has continued with the Social Security Pensions Act 1975, which introduces a new pensions scheme starting in April 1978 in which the state scheme will work in partnership with occupational pension schemes. Over a period of 20 years, there will be a change from a basically flat rate pension system to a combination of flat rate and earnings related addition. The new pensions will be payable as retirement and widows' pensions and, as invalidity pension, to those who have to retire early because of sickness or injury.

114   The Act provides that, for retirement and widows' pensions, occupational schemes may be contracted out of the earnings related element in the new state scheme, if certain basic requirements are met. State invalidity benefits on early retirement will be payable in full, irrespective of whether the scheme is contracted out.

New non-contributory benefits

115   A significant change, made in 1970, was the introduction of special benefits to help severely disabled people and their families; such benefits were neither contributory nor subject to a test of means. They include attendance allowance for those unable to care for themselves; mobility allowance for those unable, or virtually unable, to walk; invalid care allowance for people looking after an invalid entitled to attendance allowance; and a non-contributory invalidity pension for those who are not entitled to a full invalidity pension but are too severely disabled to be able to work.

116   This departure from the contributory principle marks a growing recognition of the needs of the disabled. Many of those disabled from birth or early in life may not be able to satisfy contribution conditions; and the severely disabled may have special requirements beyond those which can be met by the benefits of the contributory scheme.

Child benefit
117 Taxable family allowances have been replaced by non-taxable child benefit as a result of the Child Benefit Act 1975. The scheme has not yet been fully implemented but the intention is to provide a new system of family support payable to the mother for all children, including the first. This will replace both family allowances and child tax allowances.

Industrial injuries scheme
118 A striking feature of the last 30 years is the way in which the structure of the industrial injuries scheme has survived, in contrast to the variety of changes made elsewhere. There have been an erosion of the industrial preference and a change in the financing arrangements, but the basic scheme has been virtually unaltered.

119 The change in financing arrangements introduced in the Social Security Act 1975 meant that the distinction between the national insurance scheme and the industrial injuries scheme became technically unnecessary. Throughout our report, however, we refer to the two schemes separately, so as to distinguish between the benefits available to the two categories of beneficiary.

Contributions
120 The basis of the national insurance contribution has changed over the years. Originally intended to fund future pensions, these contributions are now calculated so as to provide sufficient income to pay the current benefits, on a 'pay as you go' basis.

Administration
121 The social security system is administered by the Department of Health and Social Security (DHSS) in Great Britain and by the Department of Health and Social Services in Northern Ireland. Procedures for claiming benefit are comparatively simple. Payment of short term benefit is normally made within a few days of claiming. Appeals are to administrative tribunals, and do not ordinarily involve the appellant in significant expense. The cost of administering sickness benefit is about $8\frac{1}{2}$ per cent of the total paid in benefits. For industrial injury and disablement benefit, where more medical investigation is required, the proportion is about 12 per cent. The combined cost of administering social security benefits for injured people is about 11 per cent of the value of the compensation payments, or 10 per cent of the cost of payments and administration. These costs include collecting contributions, investigating claims and paying benefit. They do not include any administrative costs incurred by employers or others in handling contributions or providing information on the circumstances of injuries.

An illustration of the effect of the changes
122 In 1948, an employed man who was injured in an accident not at work, and was never able to work again, could receive flat rate sickness benefit with increases for dependants. As long as he was incapable of work, sickness benefit

would be paid and would cover the whole period of his sickness from the first day until he was 65. He could then draw a retirement pension at the same rate as his sickness benefit for the rest of his life.

123 A man in a similar position in 1977 would receive no payment for the first three days, then a flat rate benefit for two weeks (increased if he had a dependent wife or children). After two weeks, he could qualify for an earnings related supplement. After 28 weeks, his benefit would change to an invalidity pension (at a different rate) which could also be increased for any dependants. Invalidity allowances could be paid at various rates according to his age when his incapacity began. Benefits will be further changed by the new pension scheme.

Other state provision

Criminal injuries
124 The non-statutory Criminal Injuries Compensation Scheme in Great Britain authorises the payment of *ex gratia* sums to victims of crimes of violence and to those hurt trying to arrest offenders or to prevent offences. A separate statutory scheme is in operation in Northern Ireland. Both schemes are financed by grant-in-aid from public funds.

125 Compensation under the scheme for Great Britain is assessed on the basis of common law damages, but the rate of loss of earnings to be taken into account cannot exceed twice the average of industrial earnings from which a notional income tax deduction is made. In Northern Ireland no deduction is made, and terrorist injuries are exempt from the upper limit. In Great Britain 14,000 payments were authorised between 1 April 1976 and 31 March 1977, averaging £700. Total compensation paid out during the 12 months was £9·7 million. In Northern Ireland, the most recent figures show 3,600 awards in 1976–77. The aggregate value was £6·3 million, and the average amount awarded was about £1,700.

Tax relief, rent and rate rebates
126 Other provisions which may not always be regarded as methods of compensation give substantial assistance to the victims of personal injury. Tax relief is one. Sickness benefit, injury benefit, invalidity benefit and disablement benefit (including its allowances) are tax free. A registered blind person can receive an additional income tax allowance of £180 a year, but this may be reduced if other benefits are paid.

127 The disabled are often entitled to special travel rates and can benefit from rent and rate rebates. Rating relief is given on a garage for the disabled, and there are postal concessions for the blind.

The National Health Service
128 All medical advice and treatment, including rehabilitation, are provided free under the National Health Service. So is accommodation in hospitals and

other health service institutions. Aids such as wheelchairs are provided where necessary. There are charges for dentures and spectacles, and also for medicine and appliances prescribed by general practitioners or in certain cases by hospital out-patient departments. The charges can, however, be remitted on grounds of low income and in some other circumstances. In road accident cases, a charge of £1·25 can be levied on the owner of the vehicle which caused the injury. Where damages have been paid, hospitals can recover the cost of treatment (subject to a maximum of £200 for an in-patient and £20 for an out-patient) from the insurer. Only a small proportion of the total cost of treating road casualties is, however, recovered under these provisions.

Personal social services

129   Benefits and services are provided for the disabled under the National Assistance Act 1948 and the Chronically Sick and Disabled Persons Act 1970. In Scotland and Northern Ireland, similar powers and duties are contained in the Social Work (Scotland) Act 1968, the Chronically Sick and Disabled Persons (Scotland) Act 1972 and the Health and Personal Social Services (Northern Ireland) Order 1972. There is statutory provision for local authorities to ascertain the numbers and needs of chronically sick and disabled persons in their areas, and where necessary to provide benefits and services, generally subject to a means test. These include adaptations to homes, installation of telephones, domestic assistance, holidays and sheltered accommodation. Despite these wide ranging powers and duties, recent economic difficulties, in particular restraints and cuts in public expenditure, have prevented local authorities from developing the comprehensive support for disabled people in the community which was the intention of the Acts.

Industrial rehabilitation

130   The Employment Services Agency provides employment rehabilitation courses for those who need to re-adjust themselves mentally and physically to normal working conditions after illness or accident. About 14,000 pass through the employment rehabilitation centres each year. In addition, the Training Services Agency provides vocational training courses for disabled people who require training to take up employment suited to their age, experience and qualifications. Over 500 different courses are available for this purpose.

Sheltered employment

131   Remploy Ltd operates as a non-profit making concern engaged in ordinary production and trading activities, but with the object of providing employment under conditions suited to severely disabled people. Any loss on its operations is met from public funds. Local authorities are empowered to set up workshops for severely disabled workers and have a statutory duty to provide sheltered employment for blind people. The Government provides financial assistance in the form of grants towards trading losses, capital expenditure and training. About 115 approved undertakings are now receiving assistance. Some voluntary organisations which provide sheltered employment for particular classes of workers also receive assistance from the Government.

Social security now

132 The social security system has now moved a long way from the Beveridge concept – the provision of fixed benefits to cover basic need. At any one time, almost 20 million social security benefits, pensions and allowances are being paid in the United Kingdom. About 9 million of these are retirement pensions. In the course of a year, about 11 million people receive sickness and injury benefit.

133 Increasing provision is now being made for those who are severely disabled, irrespective of the cause of their disability and independently of their status as contributors to the national insurance scheme. National assistance has been replaced by a system of means-tested supplementary pensions and allowances.

134 The result of the changes made over the last 30 years is not only to increase the range of persons covered and the level of benefits, but also to increase the complications. For instance, 122 leaflets are issued to explain different aspects of the social security scheme. The complications are further increased by the somewhat haphazard incidence of taxation of social security benefits.

135 Annex 4, which was provided for us by DHSS, is a résumé of the social security benefits now available and includes a reference to the new state pensions scheme. Annex 5 lists the principal rates of social security benefits and allowances.

CHAPTER 6

Other provision

136 State cash benefits and tort damages together account for three quarters
of all compensation for personal injury in the United Kingdom (see table 4,
paragraph 44). The rest is provided in a variety of ways, which are briefly
described in this chapter. As in the previous chapter, the amounts of compensation quoted relate to all injuries, or deaths resulting from injury, since it is
not possible to distinguish provision for injuries and deaths which are within
our terms of reference from those which are not.

Occupational sick pay

137 About two thirds of those in employment are entitled to continued
payments from their employer in replacement of loss of earnings, at least in part,
for a limited period of absence from work through sickness or injury. It has
been held by the courts that there is an implied term in a contract of employment that the employee is entitled to wages when away sick unless the contract
clearly specifies otherwise; and that wages during sickness are payable only as
long as the contract subsists (*Orman* v. *Saville Sportswear* [1960] 1 W.L.R. 1055).

138 Nearly all professional and managerial employees are now covered by
sick pay schemes. Among manual workers, the proportion is lower. Women
are less likely to be entitled to sick pay than men. This is because a higher
proportion of them work part time, and part time workers receive less favourable
sick pay treatment than full time workers. Sick pay provision also varies between
industries.

139 Sick pay is usually short term, lasting only for a few weeks. Some people
exhaust their entitlement before they are fit to return to work. From data
supplied by DHSS, we estimate that, even among those who have been absent
as the result of injury for less than six months, only about a half will be receiving
sick pay. The proportion drops to less than 10 per cent for those absent for
more than six months. After a year, it becomes negligible.

140 Most sick pay schemes are non-contributory. Many provide full pay for
an initial period, although this provision may not include bonuses, commission
or overtime. Some grant half pay or a flat rate, or provide for payment at the
employer's discretion. Social security benefits to which the employee may be
entitled are usually, but not always, deducted. The period of entitlement may
be discretionary, or it may depend on length of service.

141 We estimate that the amount of compensation for personal injury provided by occupational sick pay schemes totals some £125 million a year.

Accident and health insurance by employers

142 Some employers supplement their sick pay schemes by taking out insurance policies which provide benefits similar to those provided by private, first party insurance. Both 'personal accident' and 'permanent health' insurance – described in more detail a little later in this chapter – may be taken out by employers in the form of group policies. Permanent health insurance of this kind is usually designed to make some continuing provision for an employee when his entitlement to sick pay ends after, say, six months. We have made no estimate of the relatively small amount of compensation provided by employers in this way.

Occupational health services

143 The existence of health services provided by employers for employees may also be noted, although they do not constitute compensation payments as such. Most large firms provide some medical or nursing services, and group industrial health services provide facilities for some smaller firms. The Robens report, 'Safety and Health at Work' (Cmnd 5034), refers to an estimate made by the group services that about a third of their time is devoted to employees who are injured. We estimate that the contribution of employers' medical services towards the cost of dealing with work injuries is of the order of £50 million a year.

144 Employers may also pay on behalf of their employees contributions to insurance schemes designed to meet the cost of private medical treatment. Such payments amount to some £2 or £3 million a year. They cover sickness as well as injury.

Occupational pensions

145 In 1975, 8·7 million male and 2·8 million female employees were members of occupational pension schemes. The scope and level of the benefits provided by such schemes are varied, but most members are entitled to some element of compensation, over and above their social security entitlement, if they are forced to retire early as a result of personal injury. This compensation can take one of three forms. The member may receive from the date of his premature retirement such pension as has accrued to him, but with a reduction to allow for its being paid earlier than normal pension age. Or he may receive an accrued pension without such a deduction. Or he may receive the accrued pension with some enhancement; for example, the scheme may credit to him some or all of the years he might have continued to work but for early retirement. According to the Government Actuary, in 1971, 33 per cent of all scheme members qualified for the first of these forms of compensation, 20 per cent for the second, and 41 per cent for the third. Of the remaining 6 per cent, some no doubt receive some other form of payment. In addition, some public

sector employers provide for special benefits to be payable where the injury is suffered at work. We note that improvements in pension scheme provisions for early retirement due to ill health have recently been recommended by the Occupational Pensions Board in their report 'Occupational Pension Scheme Cover for Disabled People' (Cmnd 6849).

146 Most occupational pension schemes provide benefits for the widow where her husband has died while in service. As shown in table 8, the benefit is usually either wholly or partly in the form of a lump sum.

Table 8   Occupational pension schemes – benefits on death in service[1]

United Kingdom: 1971

	Male members
	%
-Widow's pension and lump sum	42
Widow's pension, no lump sum	14
Lump sum, no widow's pension	39
Neither	5
Total	100

1 Other than return of members' contributions.

Source: Fourth Survey by the Government Actuary.

147 We estimate the amount of current payments from employers under occupational pension schemes – in respect both of early retirement and death – at not more than £5 million a year.

148 We have already referred to the developments in social security benefits which will follow from the Social Security Pensions Act 1975, and in particular to the provision that occupational pension schemes may be contracted out of the earnings related element in the new state scheme provided that certain basic requirements are met.

First party insurance

149 In many cases, the person killed or injured will himself have taken out an insurance policy providing for benefits in the event of his death or personal injury. First party insurance, which is personal and normally voluntary, is to be distinguished from third party insurance, which provides benefits to those injured by the insured person if they can establish his liability.

150 The three main types of policy are life assurance, permanent health insurance and personal accident insurance. Of these, life assurance is by far the most common.

151 Precise information about the number of people covered by life assurance is not available. Most policies provide an agreed sum on the death of the person insured, sometimes limited to death occurring within a certain period ('term' policies). Some provide periodic payments rather than a lump sum. It has not been possible to estimate the value of payments under life policies generally.

152 The number of people covered by personal accident insurance is not known. Personal accident policies provide cover for short periods only, normally a year. They cover death, loss or disablement resulting from accidental injury, and may be extended to cover sickness or hospital treatment (including private treatment). Benefits usually consist of periodic payments for a fixed period (normally limited to two thirds or three quarters of previous earnings for 104 weeks), together with lump sums which vary according to the type of injury. We estimate at £50 million a year the amount of benefits from such policies paid out in respect of personal injuries.

153 The number of people covered by permanent health insurance has been growing, and is probably now approaching a million. Permanent health policies are intended to replace income. They provide periodic payments if the insured person becomes unable to follow his normal occupation because of sickness or accident. The cover available is often limited to two thirds or three quarters of previous earnings, less state insurance benefits. Many policies also provide for part payment if the insured person has to change his job and suffers a partial loss of income. Benefit is normally payable after six months' incapacity, although policies offering earlier payment in return for higher premiums are also available. Contracts normally run for at least five years, or until retiring age. Permanent health insurance cover can be of particular value to the self employed. We estimate at £1 million a year the amount of permanent health insurance benefits paid out in respect of personal injuries.

154 Our personal injury survey found that about 10 per cent of those injured in 1973 had relevant private insurance cover – presumably either permanent health or personal accident insurance – and 7 per cent had made successful claims. The average amount received was only £70 at January 1977 prices.

Trade unions, friendly societies and charities

155 Our personal injury survey suggests that about 10 per cent of employees receive some payment from trade unions or friendly societies during absence from work due to sickness or accident. The practice of individual trade unions varies. Most unions provide benefits for both sickness and injury, but some for injury only. Payments for injury are usually restricted to work injuries, sometimes including accidents while travelling to and from work (which are

not covered by the industrial injuries scheme). The duration of payment also varies. Several unions, including the National Union of Mineworkers, make special grants for fatal accidents.

156   It is difficult to assess the contribution made by charities to compensation for personal injury. Many of the larger charities provide substantial amounts of compensation within their own field of concern, and the activities of charities concerned with disabled and handicapped people within our remit are particularly significant.

157   On the basis of our personal injury survey we estimate that, taken together, trade unions, friendly societies and charities provide some £5 million a year to the injured.

Disaster funds

158   Where the scale or the circumstances of injury are particularly horrifying, a disaster fund may be set up to help the victims and their dependants. The overall impact of this form of compensation is small, but the amount received by individual victims can be substantial. The Aberfan Appeal Fund raised £1·6 million following the death of 116 schoolchildren and 28 adults when a coal tip engulfed a village school in South Wales in 1966.

CHAPTER 7

Interrelationships

159 We have now described separately each of the main sources of compensation currently available. The purpose of this chapter is to consider the scope of the various types of provision looked at together, including the scope for obtaining compensation from more than one source.

The limited cover of compensation provisions

160 Most cash compensation is designed to replace lost income, and therefore goes to earners or their dependants. Of the 3 million injuries resulting in death or in four or more days' incapacity each year, close on 1·8 million (nearly 60 per cent) are suffered by the working population. Of these, some 1·6 million (about 90 per cent) attract some compensation. Social security is by far the most important source of compensation. The 10 per cent of the working population who receive no compensation includes those, many of them married women, who are not entitled to contributory national insurance benefits, and others who for one reason or another fail to claim benefit.

161 About 1·3 million injuries (over 40 per cent of all injuries) are suffered each year by those who are not part of the work force. Of this 1·3 million, no more than 100,000 (well under 10 per cent) attract some compensation – from three main sources. According to our personal injury survey, the most important source is tort, followed by first party insurance and then social security.

162 The relative importance of the various sources of compensation is changing, and in the future social security will probably achieve even greater importance. Married women will not be able to opt out of contributing, and so eventually nearly all those at work should qualify for some benefit. For those outside the work force, the introduction of non-contributory social security benefits means that the most severely handicapped can obtain payment although they have not contributed.

163 In broad terms, injuries with less than serious or long lasting consequences are likely to go uncompensated by any cash payments unless the injured person was at work; or he had taken out some relevant first party insurance cover; or the injury occurred in circumstances which would justify a tort award. We estimate that nearly 1·4 million (about 45 per cent) of the 3 million or so injuries and deaths each year are not compensated. The proportion is no doubt less than 45 per cent in respect of the 1·9 million injuries within our terms of reference, because a higher than average proportion of those 1·9 million will have been suffered by earners.

Overlapping and offsetting

164   Just as there are gaps in the availability of compensation, so compensation may be available from two or more sources in respect of the same injury. Our personal injury survey suggests that more than a half of those compensated receive payments from more than one source. It also suggests that some 2 per cent receive money from four or more sources, and that the commonest such combination is occupational sick pay, social security benefits, private insurance and a tort award.

165   Within the social security system itself there are provisions for ensuring that no more than one benefit is paid to meet the same need. Indeed, this is an important part of the social security structure as a whole. But social security benefits – other than supplementary benefit – are paid without regard to the claimant's resources, and other compensation payments are disregarded. Occupational disability pensions are also normally payable irrespective of the availability of other compensation, although the level of pensions payable may take them into account.

166   It is the usual practice of employers to reduce sick pay by the amount of any social security benefits payable. Because sickness benefit is not taxable, however, employees in this position may benefit from a reduction in their liability for tax. Some employers also take account of any tort award, perhaps by requiring repayment of sick pay from any tort damages subsequently recovered. Benefits under first party sickness insurance and permanent health insurance are often limited to a proportion of income less social security benefits.

167   The question whether to offset any other compensation is of particular importance in the context of tort. A tort award will not usually be made until after other compensation payments have been settled. Beveridge recognised the problem of overlap between social security benefits and tort damages, and suggested that, as a general principle, an injured person should not have the same need met twice. He acknowledged that this principle raised questions of some complexity and recommended that the problem should be examined by an expert committee. Following this recommendation, the Departmental Committee on Alternative Remedies (the Monckton Committee) was appointed.

168   The Committee reported in 1946 (Cmd 6860). A majority accepted the principle suggested by Beveridge, and recommended that, 'The injured person or his dependants should not be permitted to recover by way of damages and benefits more than the maximum which he could recover from either source alone'. A minority took the view that social security benefits should be disregarded in the assessment of damages.

169   In the result, a compromise was adopted. Section 2(1) of the Law Reform (Personal Injuries) Act 1948 and section 3(1) of the Law Reform (Miscellaneous Provisions) Act (Northern Ireland) 1948 provide that, in assessing damages for loss of income due to personal injury, the court shall take into account one half of the value of certain social security benefits for five years. (There are

difficulties in implementing this provision, particularly in times of inflation.) In assessing damages following death, legislation provides for social security benefits to be left out of account.

170   The partial offsetting of social security benefits constitutes an exception to what is in effect a rule that benefits accruing to the plaintiff as a result of the accident are not to be deducted from his award of damages. By decisions of the courts in cases of personal injury, and in accordance with legislation in respect of fatal cases, payments under first party insurance policies, payments out of a distress fund and other charitable or gratuitous payments are disregarded. Occupational pensions are also disregarded (except that, where damages are awarded in respect of prospective lost income after retirement, any disability pension which is expected to continue in payment is offset against the lost retirement pension). Sick pay, however, is taken into account; earnings have obviously not been lost to the extent that they continue in payment despite absence from work.

171   The assessment of compensation under the criminal injuries schemes is in general based on the assessment of damages in tort, but the schemes provide that social security payments and tort awards should be offset in full. In practice, this provision, not surprisingly, presents considerable difficulties.

172   The overall scope for the duplication of compensation is substantial. It is possible even for those not at work to benefit, because, with the exception of non-contributory invalidity pension, non-contributory social security benefits are not even partially taken into account in the assessment of a tort award. For those who are at work the possibility of duplication is much greater.

CHAPTER 8

Popular misconceptions

173　In this chapter we comment briefly on half a dozen popular misconceptions which have coloured many of the submissions made to us.

'Only tort provides real compensation'

174　The first is the belief, which is widely held, that only tort provides real compensation, and that failure to succeed in a tort claim means failure to obtain compensation. This sentiment emerges from the evidence of many witnesses who sent us accounts of individual cases. Social security benefits received were either disregarded or considered to be quite insufficient.

175　In part, this attitude springs from the belief that social security payments are payments as of right, to which the injured person knows himself to be entitled anyway because of his contributions. The victim feels that, if he is injured because of someone else's fault, he should get something over and above what he would have got if the accident had been due to his own fault or nobody's, or if he had been sick. This attitude completely overlooks the fact that only a small part of the cost of social security benefits is in any event met by the individual's contributions; that full benefit rights can now be obtained by the payment of a few months' contributions; and that, as regards industrial injury benefits, the full benefit rights can be obtained as soon as employment has begun even if no contribution has yet been paid.

No-fault as a novelty

176　Secondly, we have found a widespread ignorance of the fact that in this country we already have a considerable element of no-fault provisions. Many witnesses urged the introduction of no-fault schemes, either for particular categories of injury or for all injuries, as though this would be a complete novelty. It is true that what was generally envisaged was a scheme which would replace, or at least substantially modify, tort, but the advocates of no-fault schemes did not appear to recognise that we have had no-fault provision on quite a considerable scale since the 1897 Workmen's Compensation Act. Now, as well as the contributory benefits of the social security scheme, we have non-contributory no-fault benefits available to disabled people, the medical benefits of the National Health Service, and local authority social services provision of various kinds.

177   In some respects, this no-fault provision for the whole population already exceeds that provided by the no-fault schemes of limited scope which have been introduced in other countries. For example, medical and hospital cover under the National Health Service is open ended, whereas most United States no-fault schemes for road accidents provide only limited medical and hospital cover. Additional no-fault schemes for those injured in accidents in the United Kingdom would for most of them be a matter of building on to the no-fault provision which already exists.

Lump sums

178   Thirdly, there is a tendency to take it for granted that only a lump sum constitutes acceptable compensation. We shall have more to say about lump sum tort awards, but this particular assumption ought to be dismissed as a misconception at the outset. As we shall show, there is considerable room for discussion as between lump sums and periodic payments, but compensation can be in either of these forms.

Going to court

179   Fourthly, it is widely thought that many, if not most, plaintiffs have to go to court in order to get tort compensation. Witnesses describing individual cases have attributed their failure to obtain compensation to a refusal by their union to take their claim to court (although the union might have had good reason for dropping the claim), or to their own inability to afford the cost of litigation. Other witnesses have called for a system which would make it possible to obtain adequate compensation without going to court, and incurring the expense and strain of court proceedings.

180   But in fact only a small proportion of tort claims ever reach the courts. A survey by the British Insurance Association (BIA) showed that 86 per cent of claims were settled without the issue of a writ, 11 per cent after the issue of a writ but before the case was set down for hearing, and 2 per cent after setting down but before trial. Only 1 per cent were concluded in court, and this total included cases settled at the door of the court.

'Delay is never justified'

181   Fifthly, while the law's delay is a reality, there are cases in which delay is justified. It may be in the plaintiff's own interests that the case should not be settled before his medical condition has sufficiently stabilised to allow of a proper prognosis; and a quick settlement may well result in less compensation being paid. Delay does not always indicate a fault in the system.

The value of social security benefits

182   Sixthly, we have found that even well informed witnesses consistently underestimate the present and prospective value of social security benefits. It is possible for a person with family responsibilities to receive £40 or £50 a

week, or more, tax free, by way of sickness or invalidity benefits. If industrial disablement benefit is payable, the weekly payment may exceed £70, again tax free. Additional amounts may be paid if the disablement is severe. A man totally incapacitated early in life through an accident at work could, by the time he is 65, receive in all a total of £150,000 in benefits at current prices. The payments are 'inflation proofed', and most of them free of tax. Except where particularly high earnings have been lost, the overall value of social security benefits, particularly for industrial injuries, compares favourably with lump sum damages which make no allowance for future inflation.

183   The tendency to disregard social security benefits is no doubt reinforced by the fact that, where a tort claim is successful, the compensation can be received in addition to such benefits, subject only to a limited degree of offset.

PART III

Changing the system

CHAPTER 9

A look overseas

184   The subjects we studied are of worldwide interest. In developing our strategy we took into account information about overseas systems, and we describe these systems in Volume Three, something that has not been done before in such detail. In this chapter we confine ourselves to points of special interest which are of particular relevance to our recommendations. These are the spread of no-fault compensation and its effect on tort; the interaction of different compensation payments; the effect of inflation; and comprehensive approaches to compensation. We illustrate these points by reference to particular schemes.

The spread of no-fault compensation and the effect on tort

185   For centuries, tort was the only means of obtaining compensation for personal injury. In most countries, compensation is now provided from a variety of no-fault sources, in addition to tort or in partial or total replacement of it.

186   In overseas tort systems, fault based liability is found in all the common law countries and those with civil codes. In some countries, compensation is made easier to obtain by a reversal of the burden of proof. Strict liability, which is based on causation rather than fault, has become increasingly prominent in the laws of continental European countries. Under the French Civil Code, a person is liable for damage caused by things of which he is in charge. 'Things' include motor vehicles. Strict liability is imposed by road traffic laws in the Federal Republic of Germany, the Netherlands and Switzerland.

No-fault: work injuries

187   The break away from tort started in Germany in the nineteenth century with Bismarck's scheme of industrial accident insurance. No-fault provision for work accidents has since spread all over the world. In many countries, including Canada, Australia and the USA, workmen's compensation has virtually replaced tort as a source of compensation for work injuries.

No-fault: road injuries

188   The twentieth century has seen the introduction of no-fault compensation for road injuries. By the middle of the century, as motor cars multiplied and

51

became more powerful and to some extent more lethal, thoughts turned to special provision for victims of road accidents. This time the movement started in North America.

189   The first Canadian scheme was in the province of Saskatchewan in 1946. Schemes are now operating in all the provinces of Canada.

190   The first state of the USA to adopt a scheme was Massachusetts in 1971. There are now no-fault schemes in 24 – nearly half the states of the USA.

191   We have spent some time in considering no-fault schemes for road injuries, paying particular attention to those in North America and Australia. These we now describe in more detail.

192   The two-tier systems operating in North America include no-fault first party insurance and third party liability insurance. The policy in respect of a motor vehicle provides first party insurance for the owner of the vehicle, any authorised driver of it, any passenger in it and any person struck by it (unless he is the driver or a passenger in another vehicle and so covered by insurance in respect of that vehicle). If any person for whom such first party insurance is provided suffers an injury while travelling in or embarking in or disembarking from the vehicle or is struck by the vehicle, he has a direct claim under the policy against the insurer for pecuniary loss. If his claim is disputed, he has a right of action in his own name against the insurer. The same policy also provides third party insurance for the owner and any authorised driver of the vehicle against any liability which he may incur for injury caused by his negligence in the driving or control of the vehicle.

193   So far the tort action for motor vehicle accidents has not been abolished in any province of Canada or any state of the USA. But the two-tier system could well prove to be a step on the way. Such abolition was indeed proposed for Quebec in the Gauvin Report and for Ontario in a report of the Ontario Law Commission.

194   The addition of the no-fault element in the motorist's insurance policy may have the effect of increasing the premium, but the motorist gains the advantage of first party accident insurance for himself, his family and other passengers, and there should be some diminution of the third party liability element.

195   In Canada some no-fault schemes for road injuries are run by public corporations. In the USA they are run by insurance companies.

196   A considerable variety of provision exists in the USA. Some states have adopted what are known as 'add-on plans', giving no-fault cover for road injuries without any restriction of tort liability other than an offset of no-fault compensation paid or payable. The majority have adopted 'modified plans', permitting tort for pecuniary loss subject to offset of no-fault compensation

paid, but restricting tort for pain and suffering to claims for injuries which are particularly severe or result in losses exceeding a certain figure. Limits of benefits payable for medical expenses, wage loss and cost of substitute services range from $1,000 in South Carolina to $50,000 in New York. In New Jersey, Michigan and Pennsylvania medical benefits are unlimited.

197   We think it may be of interest to give some details of the schemes of three of the states we visited – Massachusetts, New York and Michigan.

198   The *Massachusetts* scheme, originally introduced in January 1971, provides no-fault benefits for medical and funeral expenses, 75 per cent of wage loss and the cost of substitute services, within an overall limit of $2,000 a person injured or killed. Tort is available for pecuniary loss above this figure. For non-pecuniary loss tort is available only if medical expenses exceed $500, or in case of death or serious injury.

199   There was an initial mandatory cut of 15 per cent in insurance premiums for bodily injury. In the light of a dramatic fall in the number and cost of claims made and savings resulting from the $500 medical expenses threshold, this was soon followed by refund of 25 per cent of premiums paid. It has since become clear that before the no-fault scheme was introduced there had been many fraudulent claims.

200   A fairly recent study by Widiss and others[1] suggested that, on the whole, the no-fault scheme was not being abused. Many did not bother to claim because of ignorance or because their losses were covered in other ways. Over 90 per cent of claims had been for amounts below the $2,000 ceiling, but inflation was changing this. The use of lawyers in claiming had dwindled and the number of tort trials had been greatly reduced.

201   The *New York* scheme, originally introduced in February 1974, provides no-fault benefits for medical expenses, wage loss and substitute services of up to $50,000 in the aggregate. The wage loss benefit is limited to 80 per cent of actual loss up to $1,000 a month for three years. Tort is available for pecuniary loss above this threshold; but it is not now available for pain and suffering unless there is serious injury or disfigurement or inability to function normally for 90 of the 180 days following the accident. (Between 1974 and 1977, tort for pain and suffering was conditional upon medical expenses exceeding $500, or there being defined serious injuries, or death.)

202   The scheme began with a statutory requirement to reduce premiums by 15 per cent. In the event, a reduction of 19 per cent was achieved. The official view in 1976 was that no-fault was a cost saver but that inflation and the low medical expenses threshold of $500 were pushing up premium levels – hence the abolition of the money threshold.

203   The *Michigan* scheme, which was introduced in October 1973, provides for unlimited medical expenses, limited funeral expenses, wage loss of up to $1,285 a month for three years (adjusted annually for changes in the cost of living), and limited costs of substitute services. Tort is available for pecuniary

loss above these limits but is available for pain and suffering only if the injuries result in death or in serious impairment or disfigurement.

204   The official view in 1976 was that the scheme was fulfilling its objective of guaranteeing prompt, sure and more adequate recovery of injury costs; that there had been a significant decline in the number of minor tort claims; that there was less overlap with other health and accident benefits through the exercise of options to take up policy exclusions; and that the cost of insurance premiums appeared to be less in real terms.

205   In *Australia*, two states, Victoria and Tasmania, operate no-fault schemes under which insurance is compulsory. Benefit, for pecuniary loss only, is given for a limited period. Both schemes are administered by statutory boards. In Victoria, the board meets its outgoings from premiums fixed by a state government committee and collected by the state Government Insurance Office, any losses being covered by state guarantee. In Tasmania, the board recoups itself from premiums fixed by the state Government on the advice of a statutory board and collected on an agency basis by the state Government Insurance Office and participating private insurers. Any losses are met from state funds.

206   The right to tort action remains, but a tort claim can relate only to loss not covered by the no-fault claim. The no-fault schemes have served to reduce substantially the number of small tort claims.

207   *Sweden* is the only European country operating a no-fault scheme for road accident injuries. Insurance is compulsory and provided by private insurers. Tort is not excluded but since the amount of no-fault compensation is assessed on the same principles as tort damages (which are laid down by statute) tort action is unlikely to be taken in practice.

No-fault: medical accidents in Sweden
208   Sweden has a patient insurance scheme, negotiated between the county councils and the main insurance companies, which provides no-fault compensation to patients injured by medical accidents. The patient has to prove only that the physical injury suffered has resulted accidentally from health care. Health care, for this purpose, includes ordinary medical and dental treatment, and also services such as blood donation, therapy and ambulance transport. Injury which is a foreseeable result of a medically justified act is not covered; nor is injury resulting from risks which are justified to avoid a threat to life or the possibility of permanent disability. Other injuries not covered are those resulting from the side effects of drugs; those resulting from infection, unless they are the result of failure to sterilise equipment; and those not involving incapacity for work for at least 14 days.

209   Following a recent examination of the Swedish law on medicines, proposals have been made for setting up an insurance fund, to which producers and importers of medicines would be required to contribute, covering serious and unexpected injuries caused by medicines. Compensation would be payable,

within certain global limits, provided that the injured person could show 'a predominant probability' that the injury was due to the medicine or combination of medicines.

Interaction of different compensation payments

210 In most countries, payments made under one system of compensation take account of payments made under another system.

211 In the Federal Republic of Germany, for example, an invalidity pension or a retirement pension payable to an injured person is reduced or suspended to ensure that the total payment does not exceed 85 per cent of reckonable earnings under the accident insurance provision. In Switzerland, where there is entitlement to invalidity benefit under the general social security scheme and also benefit under the workers' accident scheme, both can be received subject to a limit of 100 per cent of earnings. Where that limit would otherwise be exceeded the accident scheme benefit is reduced.

212 Under most no-fault schemes for work injuries overlapping with tort damages is prevented by removing the right to tort damages if a claim is made to workmen's compensation. This is so in Canada and the USA. In European countries the right to tort damages is restricted so that there is no double compensation. In France and the Federal Republic of Germany, awards under the work accident schemes replace the right to bring an action in tort against the employer unless the employer intentionally caused the injury.

213 In Sweden, no-fault schemes provide benefits not only for road injuries and medical injuries but also for work injuries at levels approaching or matching the damages payable under the tort system. For work injuries, benefits for the first 90 days (amounting to 90 per cent of earnings) are made under the general sickness benefit arrangements. Payments are then continued under a separate industrial accidents scheme. Under yet another scheme additional payments bringing the benefit up to 100 per cent and providing non-pecuniary compensation equivalent to that available in tort are made on the understanding that the employer is not sued. All the systems of compensation are integrated so as to avoid double compensation.

214 Sometimes there is subrogation whereby an authority paying compensation under a statutory social security or no-fault scheme is entitled to take over the injured party's right of action against the wrongdoer to the extent of its own expenditure. In Switzerland the Accident Insurance Agency, responsible for administering the work accident scheme, has subrogation rights in respect of the cost of benefits which it has provided. Payments under the social security scheme do not affect damages and the social security authorities have no subrogation rights. In the Netherlands, the industrial insurance boards and health insurance funds have the right to seek reimbursement of their costs from third persons liable for damage because of injury for which benefits have been provided. The reimbursement right is regarded as an independent claim, but the amount is nevertheless determined by the extent of the third party's liability.

Effect of inflation

215 The effect of inflation on the real value of awards of tort compensation has been a widespread problem. In France, as far back as 1951, legislation provided for the reassessment of accident compensation periodic payments under civil law. The system was financed by a state fund to which insurers contributed 5 per cent. The increases were low by comparison with corresponding increases in social security payments. Between 1962 and 1973, increases of 23 per cent were made in civil awards, whereas increases of 193 per cent were made for work accidents and invalidity pensions under social security schemes. Attempts were made by the lower courts in the late 1960s to link periodic compensation payments to an index, for example to railway fares in rail accident cases or to variations in the cost of living. These attempts were frustrated by the *Cour de Cassation*, which refused to recognise awards of this sort on the ground that a sum in reparation should be determined on the basis of the actual loss occasioned by the wrongful act as at the date of the decision.

216 Legislation now provides for index linked periodic payments of compensation in road accident cases where there is permanent disability of at least 75 per cent. The costs are met from a central fund financed by a levy of $1\frac{1}{2}$ per cent on all compulsory motor insurance premiums. The scheme started at the beginning of 1975. It has not been in operation long enough for conclusions to be drawn about its success.

217 In Sweden private insurers have been required by law since January 1974 to add a maximum of 5 per cent a year to tort damages paid in the form of pensions in order to provide some protection against inflation. The rate of inflation was between 10 and 15 per cent during 1974 and 1975.

218 Indexed annuities have long been an accepted method of compensation in Finland. There are indications that the idea may be spreading to other European countries.

Comprehensive approaches

New Zealand

219 In 1974, New Zealand introduced the first comprehensive no-fault compensation scheme in the world for personal injury by accident. Injury by accident is defined as the physical and mental consequences of any injury or accident. It includes medical, surgical, dental or first aid misadventure; and actual bodily harm arising from a criminal act.

220 This unique accident compensation scheme mainly followed the recommendations made in 1967 by the Royal Commission of Inquiry on Compensation for Personal Injury in New Zealand ('The Woodhouse Commission'). It comprises three separate schemes: one for earners, another for persons injured by motor vehicles, and a supplementary scheme for non-earners. Tort action has been abolished in respect of all injuries covered by the schemes but the no-fault benefits are not at a level which fully replaces tort in every case.

221   The earners scheme covers all employed or self employed persons (or their dependants, in fatal cases) who suffer injury by accident. It is financed by levies on employers (a percentage of wages) and on the earned income of the self employed (a percentage of business income), within a ceiling. Employers must themselves pay the employee his wages for the first week of incapacity if he was injured at work or on the way directly to or from work. Thereafter the Accident Compensation Commission, which administers the scheme, pays for pecuniary loss at the rate of 80 per cent of the person's average weekly earnings before tax (90 per cent for the low paid) within a ceiling of 15,600 dollars (about £9,000) a year. Potential earning capacity can be taken into account to a limited extent, mainly for younger workers. The self employed receive nothing for the first week and thereafter 80 per cent of their average weekly earnings within the ceiling during the last financial year.

222   The motor vehicle accident scheme covers persons injured by accident caused by, through or in connection with the use of a vehicle in New Zealand. The scheme is financed by annual levies on motor vehicles, including motor cycles. Compensation for pecuniary loss is on the same basis as for the earners scheme.

223   The supplementary scheme covers anyone injured or killed by accident who is not covered by the other two schemes. Non-earners such as pensioners, housewives and visitors to New Zealand (while in New Zealand), and their dependants, can receive benefits for non-pecuniary loss and for loss of potential earning capacity. The scheme is financed from national revenue.

224   For non-pecuniary loss, a lump sum of up to 7,000 dollars (about £3,900) is payable under each of the schemes for permanent loss or impairment of some bodily function or loss of any part of the body. Common impairments attract fixed percentages. A lump sum of up to a further 10,000 dollars (about £5,600) is payable for loss of amenities or capacity to enjoy life and for pain and suffering.

225   Compensation may also include reasonable medical expenses and other out-of-pocket expenses. In fatal cases reasonable funeral expenses are payable.

226   Before the scheme was introduced, financial provision for compensation, apart from the negligence action, was through worker's compensation or means tested social security. Compensation through the negligence action was provided in less than 1 per cent of industrial accidents. In the words of the Woodhouse Commission, describing the situation as they found it, 'The Worker's Compensation Act provides meagre compensation for workers, but only if their injury occurred at their work. The Social Security Act will assist with the pressing needs of those who remain, provided they can meet the means test. All others are left to fend for themselves'.

227   The earners scheme compares most favourably with the former arrangements. The new scheme not only gives earners compensation cover against

injury by accident throughout the 24 hours, but also provides compensation at much higher rates. Whereas previously an injured worker would receive worker's compensation of 42 dollars a week for six years at the most, under the new scheme he can receive 80 per cent loss of earnings up to a maximum of 240 dollars a week (about £135), payable for life if necessary, and lump sums for non-pecuniary loss of up to £9,500. For the earner, therefore, the new scheme was indeed a major step forward.

228   But in the following important respect the scheme has not followed the recommendations of the Woodhouse Commission. One of the guiding principles of the Commission was 'community responsibility', involving protection by the community of 'all citizens . . . and the housewives who sustain them from the burden of sudden individual losses when their ability to contribute to the general welfare by their work has been interrupted by physical incapacity'. On this basis, the Woodhouse Commission recommended a weekly payment to housewives and others without direct loss of earnings of (at December 1967 values) about £5·50 a week for temporary total incapacity and £9·30 a week for permanent total incapacity. The scheme as implemented makes no such provision. Indeed, with the removal of the right to tort action and the more limited provision for non-pecuniary loss the non-earner may get nothing at all.

229   It is still too early to judge the schemes' financial soundness, particularly in an inflationary situation. At present, there are surpluses of income over outgo in the earners and motor vehicle accident schemes, but awards for permanent disability have so far not been made on any significant scale and the Government Actuary in New Zealand has not yet made his first statutory report. Other possible areas of concern to the schemes' administrators are the effect of the no-fault schemes on accident prevention, the possible weakening of incentive on the part of manufacturers to guard against the production of defective goods, and the increased incidence of short term claims under the earners scheme. In 1975, an investigation started into the possibility of extending the accident compensation scheme to cover incapacity as a result of sickness or congenital defect.

Australia
230   In Australia, in 1974, a national committee of inquiry, also chaired by Mr Justice Woodhouse, proposed a national scheme of compensation for all incapacity, whether caused by sickness, injury, disease or congenital defect. This compensation would replace tort. With the change of government in November 1975 the drafting of implementing legislation ceased. A halfway house has been suggested under which states would be responsible for compensation for personal injury to earners and road accident victims for the first year of incapacity and the federal government would be responsible thereafter. Tort would be retained for non-pecuniary loss. No decision has been taken on this proposal.

No blueprint for the UK

231   While we need to take overseas experience into account, it is important to remember some of the relevant differences between our country and other countries.

232   In the USA (where, as explained, 24 out of the 50 states now have some form of no-fault road scheme) there are more motor vehicles and greater use and dependence on them than in this country. There is a less well developed social security system and there is no National Health Service. Medical bills can be enormous, and the cover provided by the voluntary medical schemes known as Blue Cross and Blue Shield may be limited depending on the premiums paid.

233   Litigation in the USA costs more than in this country and the general level of damages is much higher. The system of trial by jury makes trials longer and more expensive. Costs as such are not awarded by juries, but the lawyer will have met all legal costs; and if the action succeeds, these will be covered under the contingent fee system which may well absorb as much as 40 or 50 per cent of the damages awarded. Although many feel that abolition of the jury trial in accident cases might be advantageous this could not be done without an amendment of the Constitution.

234   Apart from the demand for provision for wider compensation, it was agreed in the late 1960s that some reform was necessary in order to clear the congestion in the courts in many states. The trial of an action could be considerably delayed. In Massachusetts, for example, in spite of an increase in the number of judges it was sometimes five years before a case could be heard.

235   The pattern of reform was influenced by the fact that there is a good deal of property damage insurance against collision. This is first party insurance, and it eases the transition to no-fault insurance for personal injuries. Also the long established system of workmen's compensation in the USA excludes any action of tort by employees against their employer in respect of injuries at work, so that the notion of excluding tort in full or in part was a familiar one.

236   In considering the relevance of the New Zealand schemes to our own country, it needs to be remembered that New Zealand has a much smaller population and is predominantly agricultural. But, more importantly, its former provision of worker's compensation, its current flat rate means tested social security and its state provided medical care are less complete than our industrial injuries scheme, our earnings related social security without a means test and our National Health Service respectively.

237   One thing emerged clearly from our investigations. There are too many differences between our country and the others we examined, for example in health and social security provision and in social attitudes, to allow any one of the schemes to be used as a blueprint for this country.

CHAPTER 10

The scope for change

238 We have described the main features of the present systems of compensation in the United Kingdom, and some features of particular interest in overseas systems. We now look at the constraints within which we worked, and then summarise and assess some of the main criticisms of the present systems of compensation in the United Kingdom.

Constraints and relevant developments

Our terms of reference

239 In considering what changes could be made, we were subject to a number of constraints. The most important was our terms of reference. As we interpreted these, they excluded not only most sickness, but also about 35 to 40 per cent of all injuries, notably the bulk of injuries suffered through accidents in the home. We were therefore not free to consider recommending a comprehensive compensation scheme covering all injuries, still less a universal scheme covering sickness as well.

Cost

240 Our terms of reference enjoined us to have regard to cost. This has two aspects. First, there is the total expenditure on compensation in the country. This, in turn, consists partly of a transfer of purchasing power from non-injured to injured, and partly of the usage of real resources in the operation and administration of any such transfer. Secondly, there is the division of the total expenditure between that which is disbursed through the public sector and that which is not. Current restrictions on levels of public expenditure and on the use of public manpower pose severe limits on our recommendations for the short run. At the same time, in any consideration of additional Exchequer expenditure on compensation, it is necessary, in appraising the overall position, to take account of any reductions in such expenditure in the private sector.

Public opinion

241 Some aspects of our remit have been the subject of extensive publicity. When we were set up, the then Prime Minister referred particularly to the thalidomide tragedy and to the Robens report on 'Safety and Health at Work' (Cmnd 5034), which had expressed concern about the relationship between tort and work accidents. More recently, there has been a demand for compensation for vaccine damaged children. By and large, however, we have not had

evidence of a strong public demand either for or against major change over the whole area of our remit. The problems involved have not been the subject of widespread debate in this country, perhaps because people tend not to be aware of these problems until they are themselves injured, and perhaps because the problems are so complicated. Bur we have had no lack of evidence from those who have been injured to satisfy us beyond all doubt that real difficulties exist; and it is certainly our function to identify them and suggest solutions.

International developments
242 A number of recent international developments have helped to set the framework. Within the EEC, for example, a draft directive on products liability is under consideration, and there is a Recommendation, dating from 1966, on occupational diseases. In recent years, the Council of Europe has prepared conventions on both products liability and road injuries. In the field of international transport, both existing and potential international commitments have been central to our deliberations.

Developments in the United Kingdom
243 We have borne in mind recent developments within the United Kingdom. Two of the most important were, first, the gradual extension of non-contributory social security benefits for the severely disabled; and, secondly, the Social Security Pensions Act 1975, which has set a new framework for long term social security benefits. There has been some other relevant legislation. For example, the Damages (Scotland) Act 1976 has codified a number of aspects of the Scottish law of damages on death. The Congenital Disabilities (Civil Liability) Act 1976 has established in English law the right of a child to sue for damages in respect of ante-natal injury. The Unfair Contract Terms Act 1977 will limit the scope for excluding liability for death or personal injury.

244 Our attitude to a number of issues, and especially to the assessment of damages in tort, has been affected by the difficulty of arriving at a fair lump sum in the light of inflation and high levels of taxation. We have also been conscious of a growing concern to protect the consumer, as evidenced, for example, by the Government's 1976 consultative document on consumer safety.

Criticisms of the present systems
245 As well as bearing in mind a number of constraints and recent developments, we considered some of the main criticisms which are levelled at the present systems of compensation. In selecting these criticisms, we have drawn on published work, on our own experience, and on the evidence we have received.

Criticisms of tort
246 The case against the tort system as it operates in the field of personal injury has been expounded with authority by many writers both in this country and abroad. The volume of criticism has increased notably over the past 10 or 15 years. Prominent among critics in this country have been judges – the

late Lord Parker of Waddington[2] and Lord Kilbrandon[3]; academics – Professor
T G Ison[4], Professor Harry Street[5] and Professor P S Atiyah[6]; and an industri-
alist, Lord Robens. A number of these and other critics of tort further developed
their views in evidence to us. Many of their criticisms were supported by other
witnesses, and by those interviewed in our survey who attempted to claim tort
compensation. We group the various criticisms of tort under seven heads.

247   First, there is criticism of the fault principle itself, the fact that the
plaintiff's entitlement to tort compensation normally depends on proof that
the defendant was negligent. One strand to the argument is that the outcome
of a tort claim is unpredictable, so that an injured person does not know
whether or not his losses will be recompensed and cannot plan his personal
finances accordingly. There is clearly much force in this argument. For example,
the injured person may be unable to discharge his burden of proof, the defendant
may not be sufficiently affluent or well insured to pay the damages, or it may
not be possible to trace the wrongdoer at all. The unpredictability of the
system is perhaps greater in some circumstances than in others, and we shall
be arguing that it is especially capricious in respect of road accidents.

248   The other main strand to the argument is that, in any event, compensation
should not depend on whether or not an injury had a particular cause.
Compensation, it is argued, should be designed to compensate for loss actually
suffered, irrespective of what caused it, whereas tort is limited by its concern
to meet losses incurred only in certain circumstances. This argument, too,
has force; and it retains much of its validity even where the test of negligence
has been extended or dispensed with.

249   Having said all this, it is important not to consider tort in isolation.
Most earners, and the most severely injured non-earners, are by no means
wholly dependent on tort for their compensation. For them, the criteria
stipulated by the law of tort, whether negligence or otherwise, determine only
the availability of compensation over and above social security benefits. To
define the problem in this way does not invalidate criticism of the fault
principle, but helps to put the criticism in perspective.

250   Secondly, and closely related to criticisms of the fault principle, there
are criticisms to the effect that the tort system is difficult for the injured person
to understand and operate. We tried to form an assessment of this kind of
criticism through our personal injury survey. Details of the relevant findings
are in chapter 18 of Volume Two. We found that, of those who thought that
their injury had been caused by something another person had done or failed
to do, some two thirds took no steps towards making a claim for tort compensation. Of these, about a fifth either did not know that they could claim or did not
know how to go about it. Others, too, had been inhibited by practical difficulties,
feeling for example that it was just too much trouble, or that they would be
unable to prove their case.

251   Even when a claim was pursued, practical difficulties remained. Many
felt themselves to be in an unequal bargaining position. Some who had dropped
their claim said that they had become discouraged, for example by difficulty

in finding witnesses, or were uncertain what to do next; some who had settled had been afraid that, had they not done so, they might have ended up with nothing; others in both categories had been deterred by the cost from pressing the matter any further. Indeed, the cost of pursuing a tort action was a common source of criticism in the evidence we received. Even those who consulted a solicitor often continued to find the law frightening or difficult to understand. The complexity of the system can also cause difficulty for the defendant.

252   Thirdly, there is criticism of the delays which can occur before a claim is settled. Our personal injury survey showed delay to be the most important reason for dissatisfaction with the legal system. This again was reflected in the evidence we received. As we suggest in chapter 8, delay is sometimes justifiable; but it can often aggravate pressure on the plaintiff to settle prematurely, and can be a source of worry and distress. Nor is it necessarily in the interests of the defendant. The problem of delay is also linked with the medical condition sometimes known as 'compensation neurosis'. The causes variously ascribed to this condition range from genuine anxiety to an attempt by the plaintiff to magnify and prolong his loss until a settlement is reached; but, whatever the cause, we accept that it is a commonly recognised phenomenon in personal injury cases.

253   We made a statistical assessment of the problem of delay through the survey of insurance claims undertaken for us by the BIA. The details are in chapter 22 of Volume Two. The survey showed that the median period from the date of a claim to the date of its disposal was $9\frac{1}{2}$ months. The range was wide, going up to five years or more in isolated cases. Unsuccessful claims tended to take considerably longer than claims in which compensation was secured. Where payment was made, the more serious cases, measured in terms of the size of the payment, tended to take considerably longer than the rest. Well over half the payments in excess of £5,000 were made more than two years after the date of the claim, as against one tenth of all payments.

254   The survey of insurance claims also threw some light on the reasons for delay in respect of the 90 per cent of claims which took more than three months to dispose of. Nearly half these delays were attributed to disputes over liability or quantum or both, nearly a fifth to establishing and agreeing a medical prognosis, and nearly a third to delay by the claimant or to other reasons. This suggests that much of the delay is inherent in a system which is adversarial in nature and often reliant on an agreed medical prognosis.

255   Fourthly, there is the criticism from the defendant's viewpoint that it is unreasonable for a tortfeasor to have to pay damages where he is not to blame in the ordinary sense of the word. It is certainly true that the tortfeasor may have been doing his best, as an inexperienced driver, for example, but may still have fallen short of the standard of the 'reasonable man'. Moreover, the scale of the damages he is liable to pay may be quite out of proportion to the degree of his fault, related as they are to the circumstances of the plaintiff.

256   We believe there is limited, if real, importance in the suggestion that the system is unfair to the tortfeasor. Most tortfeasors are insured; a motorist may

find his premium increased but he is unlikely to suffer serious financial hardship. Other tortfeasors may be either 'self insurers', such as Government departments, or substantial companies well able to meet the cost. Nor is the criticism really apt where liability is not based on the test of negligence and therefore carries no implication of 'fault'. In broad terms, however, there remains an important potential impact on the tortfeasor's reputation as, say, a professional or business man. This is the more significant in that the cases attracting most publicity will tend to be those in which the tortfeasor contests his liability, and in which liability is therefore the least clear cut.

257   Fifthly, there are criticisms of the levels of damages paid. We have already discussed the possibility that a plaintiff may settle prematurely for an unduly low sum. Leaving this aside, the two quite different charges levelled at the tort system are that it compensates minor injuries too fully, and that it compensates serious injuries, or death, not enough.

258   Although there is no clear statistical evidence for either charge, we believe them both to be justified. Indeed, they have an important bearing on some of our conclusions, and we discuss them more fully in the next Part of our report. On the first charge – that minor injuries are compensated too fully – it is often maintained that insurers may tend to make excessive payments in settlement of minor cases, especially under the head of non-pecuniary loss, rather than incur the costs of defending actions. We find this contention plausible, and such statistics as we have did not contradict it.

259   We are in still less doubt about the justification for the second charge, that the tort system under compensates the most serious injuries. The problem concerns the assessment of damages for future pecuniary loss; whereas there is usually no need for damages under this head in the least serious cases, future pecuniary loss accounted for 45 per cent of all payments of over £25,000 in 1973. It is clear to us that the present method of assessing damages for future loss of income results in awards which are insufficient to provide for its full replacement, particularly in times of inflation. Moreover, a lump sum cannot in any event restore the injured person to the position he was in before his injury. He then had an income, not a capital sum.

260   Sixthly, there are criticisms relating to the adversarial nature of tort, both as it affects the parties themselves and as it affects accident prevention. We accept that there is some force in these criticisms. A tort action may be damaging to family relations or to friendships. It may also have an adverse impact on industrial relations when the action is between employee and management. Also in the context of work injuries, the two parties may be more interested in proving or avoiding blame than in helping to find, or being prepared to admit to, the real cause of an accident.

261   Finally, there is the criticism that the tort system is expensive to administer. The best estimate we can make, albeit an uncertain one, is the one we have given in chapter 4, that the total costs of operating the tort system represent about 85 per cent of the value of tort compensation payments, or about 45 per cent of the combined total of compensation and operating costs. These are high

figures by any standards, and the more so in comparison with the figures of about 11 and 10 per cent, respectively, which apply to social security compensation for the injured (see chapter 5). The reasons for the administrative expense of tort are broadly the same as the reasons for complexity and delay. In particular, the system is concerned not only with the exact circumstances of each individual accident but also with the exact losses of each individual plaintiff. On the other hand, as we shall suggest, the capacity of tort to deal with individual losses is perhaps its greatest strength.

262   As against these various criticisms, it is to be remembered that there are various arguments in favour of retaining tort liability. The deterrent effect of tort is in many cases blunted by insurance, but may be partly preserved by the insurers' premium rating systems – for example, no claims bonuses. Moreover, not all injuries caused by negligence or other fault are covered by insurance, and where there is no insurance, or inadequate insurance, the risk of incurring civil liability can still deter. There is elementary justice in the principle of the tort action that he who has by his fault injured his neighbour should make reparation. The concept of individual responsibility still has value. In addition, a tort action may draw attention to dangerous practices, especially in the industrial sphere.

263   The question whether tort should be retained as a source of compensation for personal injury is not just a matter of weighing criticisms, but also of assessing the function of tort in the context of other forms of compensation. We explain our conclusions in the next chapter. In the meantime, our assessment of criticisms serves to underline the importance of directing attention to cases of prolonged incapacity and substantial loss. It is here that the difficulties of operating the system matter most, and that delay and under compensation are most likely to occur. Concern with the more serious cases became an important theme in our deliberations.

Criticisms of state provision
264   Our discussion of the main criticisms of state provision must necessarily be briefer and more tentative than our discussion of the criticisms of tort. Whereas tort compensation for personal injury is entirely within our terms of reference, the social security system and other state provision extend well beyond them. There is a significant body of opinion which maintains that the social security system should not differentiate according to the nature of the injury, but that all disabled people should be treated alike. It is urged that there should be a comprehensive income scheme for disabled people of all ages, regardless of the type and origin of the disability. Alternatively, it is suggested that the benefits under the industrial injuries scheme should be extended to all disabled people. The possibility of comprehensive provision on these lines, however, takes us well outside our terms of reference.

265   Similarly, we can offer no comment on the general level of social security benefits. For example, some people contend that benefits should seek more fully to replace lost earnings, others that the social security system makes

provision which is too generous. Suffice it to say that, in considering the benefits with which we are directly concerned, we found that the present rates afforded an adequate foundation on which to build.

266   There is one criticism of the present system which goes beyond our terms of reference, but on which we do wish to comment. We have been repeatedly struck by the complexities of the system, and we have considerable sympathy with the view that state provision has become too complicated and too difficult to understand. There are also inconsistencies in the taxation of social security benefits. The practice adopted in part is that long term benefits are taxable, but short term benefits are not. But we find it difficult to understand why widow's allowance, which is a short term benefit, is taxable, whereas invalidity benefit, paid in respect of prolonged incapacity, is not. We are also puzzled by the fact that mobility allowance is taxable, whereas attendance allowance is not.

267   We are not suggesting that such anomalies and complexities are without justification, nor do we underestimate the difficulties of rectifying the position. But we should like to add our voice to those which are urging the Government to simplify the social security system, and to rationalise the arrangements for taxing benefits.

268   The main criticisms of state provision which fall squarely within our terms of reference concern the industrial injuries scheme. In particular, it is often maintained that the self employed should be included, that benefit should be paid for accidents that occur on the way to and from work, and that provision for partial loss of earnings should be extended. These are important issues, and we consider them in chapter 17.

269   Despite the various criticisms which are levelled at the social security system, the principle of social security provision is widely accepted, and the system itself works quickly and cheaply.

Criticisms of the systems in combination
270   Criticisms of the way in which social security and tort interact, unlike criticisms of social security as such, are basic to our remit. Many people maintain that social security benefits should be more fully offset against tort damages. More generally, it is suggested that there is a need for a more effective co-ordination of compensation systems. Whereas on the one hand there is overlapping and over compensation, many instances have been cited in which, for one reason or another, no compensation was received. It is contended that the present situation results in anomalies, injustice, confusion and waste of resources.

271   It is clear to us that the two systems have for too long been permitted to develop in isolation from each other, without regard to the fact that, between them, they meet many needs twice over and others not at all. In practice, each system hardly recognises the existence of the other. We are determined that they should do so in future, and many of our recommendations will be directed to this end.

CHAPTER 11
Our strategy

272 In this chapter, against the background set out in the previous chapter, we explain our main conclusions. Most of these conclusions are developed in more detail in subsequent chapters, where we also make our specific recommendations.

A mixed system

273 The fundamental problem with which we were faced was the balance between no-fault and tort. The extreme options might be thought of as exclusive reliance on one or the other. A total dependence on the tort system, however, would be unrealistic – there could be no question of sweeping away the growing structure of social security provision. On the other hand, the possibility of relying exclusively on no-fault required more careful consideration, particularly as this was a model which had gained wide support following the Woodhouse report in New Zealand, and the subsequent implementation of a comprehensive accident compensation scheme in that country. Our consideration of such a possibility involved asking two main questions – how far no-fault should be extended; and whether tort should be abolished.

274 As we have already explained, and leaving aside the merits of the issue and the matter of cost, our terms of reference precluded us from considering whether to recommend a no-fault scheme covering all injuries. To recommend a scheme for all injuries within our terms of reference would have been impracticable. In a no-fault scheme, such as the social security system, it would not be feasible to adjudicate on the dividing line between injuries inside and outside our remit; this would involve determining such issues as whether or not a given injury was suffered through the act or omission of another. We therefore came of necessity to ask ourselves whether there were persuasive reasons for extending no-fault provision for particular categories of injury, and whether any new no-fault schemes could be satisfactorily financed.

275 Our decision to approach the extension of no-fault in this manner had an obvious bearing on the question whether tort should be abolished. It was clear to us that social security should be regarded as the primary method of providing compensation – it is quick, certain and inexpensive to administer, and it already covers a majority of the injured. But, in the absence of a no-fault scheme covering all injuries, the abolition of tort for personal injury would deprive many injured people of a potential source of compensation, without

67

putting anything in its place. We concluded that tort must be retained; and most of us saw good reason for keeping tort even where all injuries in a given category are covered by a no-fault scheme.

276   The retention of a mixed system, including both social security and tort, still leaves a wide variety of mixed systems to choose from. We now summarise our main strategic conclusions.

Overlapping compensation

277   Under a mixed system, compensation must be considered as a whole. The current provision that social security benefits should be offset against tort awards to the extent of 50 per cent for up to five years was a compromise between two principles – first, that the injured person should not be compensated twice in respect of the same loss; and, secondly, that social security benefits, at least in so far as they had been paid for by the individual himself, represented the fruits of his own thrift and should be disregarded. We do not accept that the social security system can any longer be regarded in this way as a form of first party insurance.

278   We also noted a further argument against a full offsetting of social security benefits, namely that the tortfeasor should pay in full. This argument received little support from our witnesses. Tort does not have a criminal or punitive function; it is meant to compensate the injured plaintiff for actual loss or damage. It is usually the tortfeasor's insurance company who pays, and this would be inappropriate if tort were punitive.

279   Consequently, one of our earliest strategic conclusions was that the duplication of compensation should be ended, and in particular that relevant social security benefits should be fully offset against tort awards. For those entitled to social security benefits, including most earners, the function of tort would become that of supplementing the no-fault compensation already provided by the state.

280   At first sight it might appear that abolishing the duplication of compensation would penalise married persons and those with dependants in favour of single persons and the childless. This outcome is more apparent than real. There is no such discrimination if compensation from tort and from social security are regarded as a whole. The social security system does not aim to provide a full replacement of earnings. Social security benefits contain a flat rate as well as an earnings related element, the earnings related element is subject to a ceiling, and there are flat rate allowances for dependants. The result is that a greater degree of income replacement is provided for low earners and those with dependants than for high earners and single people. Tort on the other hand has the aim, in theory, of restoring the injured person to the position he was in before his accident. If therefore no one is to receive as total compensation for his lost income more than 100 per cent of his loss, it must follow that, of two injured persons, if one receives a higher percentage of his loss in benefits he must receive a lower percentage in damages. The low earner and the married man with children would receive a higher percentage of their loss in benefits, and so must receive a lower percentage in damages.

No-fault

281 We reached three main conclusions on the extension and improvement of no-fault provision. These were that the structure of the industrial injuries scheme should remain basically unchanged, albeit with some improvements; that a new scheme should be introduced for road injuries; and that a new social security benefit should be introduced for severely handicapped children.

282 We considered the introduction of new no-fault schemes for other categories covered by our terms of reference, but, in broad terms, we thought that the case for such schemes was less compelling; that our proposals as they stood would be enough, for the present at any rate, for the administrative system to absorb; and that the miscellaneous circumstances of accidents would make it difficult, and sometimes impracticable, to construct and finance schemes other than those covered by our main conclusions.

Work injuries

283 There was a remarkable unanimity among our witnesses that the structure of the industrial injuries scheme had stood the test of time. We could see no better alternative in overseas models, nor any way of devising one ourselves. We concluded that the scheme should remain essentially as it is, but extended and improved in some respects.

284 The present degree of overlap between social security and tort is especially marked in this field. Nearly all those who obtain tort compensation in respect of work injuries will also have been entitled to industrial injury benefit. A decision to recommend an end to the duplication of compensation, without anything to balance it, would have implied a drop in entitlement for those injured through the fault of their employer.

285 We were particularly concerned about those suffering from long term incapacity. We sought a solution which would improve long term industrial injury benefits in such a way as to harmonise them with long term earnings related benefits under the Social Security Pensions Act 1975. Our conclusion was that maximum benefits under the Act should become payable immediately. Among other things, we shall also be recommending cover for the self employed; an extension of the range of occupational diseases qualifying for compensation; and, by a majority of one, an extension of cover to accidents on the way to and from work. Along with full offsetting against tort awards, the outcome of these and other changes would in our view be to combine suitable no-fault provision with a more rational deployment of work injury compensation.

Road injuries

286 Our decision to recommend a special no-fault scheme for road injuries sprang largely from our review of the operation of the tort system in this field. We were impressed by evidence that some of the criticisms levelled against tort applied with especial force to road accident compensation. In particular, we were convinced that the fault principle operates with particular capriciousness, as we shall explain further in chapter 18.

287 There were other considerations, too. Road accidents are numerous, particularly likely to be the cause of serious injury, and an unavoidable hazard for most of the population. It was noticeable that those witnesses who pressed for more no-fault compensation tended to consider road injuries an exceptionally strong case. Similar considerations have led other countries to the same conclusion.

288 In seeking a model, the industrial injuries scheme was the obvious choice, in that it would provide inflation proofing and adequate benefits for long term incapacity. In using it, we thought it essential to make one important modification. There is necessarily no place in that scheme for benefits for non-earners, but we felt that there should be some provision for non-earners injured in road accidents. In chapter 18, we make recommendations accordingly.

Industrial preference
289 Our conclusion that the structure of the industrial injuries scheme should be preserved, and that it should be used as a model for a new road scheme, raised a further important issue. This concerns the so-called 'industrial preference'. At present, injury benefit under the industrial injuries scheme is somewhat higher than national insurance sickness benefit, and industrial death benefit higher than national insurance widow's pension, although by amounts which have been eroded in real value over the years. More importantly, the provision for loss of faculty, in the form of disablement benefit and its related allowances, is unique to the industrially and war disabled. Our proposals for work injuries would preserve this level of benefits. Indeed, our recommendations on long term benefits would improve the preference until maximum benefits become payable generally under the Social Security Pensions Act 1975.

290 But this does not mean that we endorse such a preference in principle. Although Beveridge concluded that an element of industrial preference should remain it seemed to us that his arguments carry a good deal less weight now, especially as the scheme has been applied to all industries, whether dangerous or not.

291 We considered whether the preference should be extended in full to road injuries, and concluded that, with minor exceptions, it should. To move the boundary of the preference seemed simpler and less anomalous than any alternative solution.

Children
292 In proposing a new social security benefit for severely handicapped children, we have, exceptionally, gone beyond our terms of reference. We found this unavoidable. Our remit explicitly includes ante-natal injury, and it is often impossible to distinguish the results of such injury from other congenital defects. Congenital defects, in turn, account for 90 per cent of all severe disability among children.

293 Because it is seldom possible to identify the causes of ante-natal injuries and therefore to provide compensation for them separately, we looked at the position of disabled children as a whole. We found no strong grounds for

providing compensation for all injuries to children. Those with severe disability, however, need all possible assistance if they are to achieve their maximum potential in later life; and the whole family may suffer if support is not available. In this context, we concluded that the no-fault provision at present available was not adequate, and that an addition to child benefit should be paid to parents or guardians of all severely handicapped children. Our detailed recommendations are in chapter 27.

Vaccine damage

294 We found special problems when we came to consider disabilities resulting from vaccination. It is not always possible to establish whether vaccination is the cause of a disability. But the argument was strongly urged upon us that, where this can be established, those affected – who are mainly children – have a special claim to compensation from the public purse when they have been placed at risk in the interests of the health of the public generally. We concluded that the Government should be held strictly liable in tort for vaccine damage, whether to children or to adults, where the vaccination was recommended by the Government or a health authority in the interests of the community. For those children who are sufficiently seriously disabled to be eligible for the allowance we are recommending, or for any other social security benefits, the tort award could provide a supplement. Our detailed proposals are in chapter 25.

Administration and finance

295 We gave much thought to the financing of our proposed no-fault schemes for road injuries and children, and of the industrial injuries scheme and our proposed improvements to it. For none of these could we see any alternative to the state assuming responsibility for administering the payment of benefits. But we were anxious to minimise the burden on the Exchequer by ensuring so far as possible that the cost of the benefits should be borne by those creating the risks. We also considered whether, say, the industries or road users who tended to create the greatest risks should pay more towards the schemes.

296 We considered first the possibility of subrogation. By 'subrogation' we mean that the state would pay the benefits to the injured person in each case; but that, where the injury had been caused by the fault of another, the paying authority would be enabled to bring an action against the wrongdoer in order to recover the cost. This would parallel an existing principle by which an insurer, or anyone who had contracted to indemnify against loss, may have a right to bring an action in the name of the victim against the wrongdoer. State benefit paying authorities currently have no such right.

297 In the event, we found that there were formidable objections to the idea. Perhaps the most important was that it would reintroduce an element of fault into schemes which were intended to dispense with it. This would involve practical difficulties, and, once the cost of litigation and other costs had been taken into account, the result might well be a rather unprofitable extension to the administrative machinery.

298   We took the view that the additional costs of our proposals on work injuries, and the whole cost of our proposed new road scheme, should be met by some form of special revenue rather than out of general taxation; and that the cost should be borne by employers and motorists respectively. Deciding on the precise form of special revenue gave us considerable difficulty. We explain the options and our conclusions in chapters 17 and 18. For severely handicapped children, there seemed to be no feasible source of risk related funding. We concluded that the new benefit for them would have to be financed directly by the Exchequer (see chapter 27).

Tort

Possible exceptions to the retention of tort
299   In the light of our conclusions on the extension of no-fault, we considered the possibility of abolishing tort for certain categories of injury. In doing so, we kept in mind two considerations which could apply to any such category, although not all of us would place the same emphasis on each.

300   First, we were not convinced that the social security system could provide machinery suitable for determining the appropriate award under certain heads of damage which most of us felt should be compensated, in particular, pain and suffering and promotion prospects, in such a way as to take account of individual circumstances.

301   Secondly, the earnings relation of social security benefits is subject to limits, for the present at least. Whilst this is so, most of us thought it not unreasonable that high income earners should be free to pursue full reparation in tort.

302   If tort were to be abolished for any particular categories of injury, the most obvious possibility would be where all injuries would be within a no-fault scheme, that is to say, under our proposals, for work and road injuries. In either case, however, there would be the difficulty that other categories of injury would remain covered by the tort system. This means that someone injured by the fault of another at work or on the roads might receive less compensation than if he had suffered an identical injury, also through the fault of another, in different circumstances.

303   We felt unable to defend such an anomaly for road injuries. For work injuries, however, there is a strong case for abolishing tort on accident prevention grounds, as we have already briefly suggested. The Robens report, 'Safety and Health at Work' (Cmnd 5034), referred to a number of ways in which the tort system was said to work to the detriment of accident prevention. The main argument was that the task of framing and enforcing statutory provisions for prevention of accidents, and the task of investigating individual accidents, were made more difficult than they should be. Employers and trade unions were inevitably concerned with safeguarding or strengthening their respective positions in the event of a tort action. If employers were no longer to be held liable in tort, it was argued, everyone could concentrate on the task of preventing accidents, and perhaps devote to it some of the money previously spent on

litigation. It was also suggested that the tort system had a detrimental impact on industrial relations.

304 Our evidence showed that not everyone accepted these arguments in the Robens report. We for our part acknowledge the force of the arguments, but most of us concluded that they were not sufficiently powerful to justify depriving the work injured alone of the right to claim tort compensation. We recommend in chapter 17 that tort should be retained for work injuries as a means of supplementing industrial injury benefits.

305 We considered the possibility of abolishing tort for two other categories of injury, medical and ante-natal. In relation to medical injuries, it was put to us that it was particularly difficult to prove negligence and, still more important, that it was often impossible to ascertain whether or not the injury was indeed a 'medical injury'. It might not be clear whether a given deterioration in the patient's condition would have occurred but for the act or omission complained of. It was also put to us that there were widespread fears that the risk of litigation was proving an obstacle to good and economical medical practice, and that, if litigation became more common, insurance premiums might rise to prohibitive levels. But we did not find these arguments strong enough to justify making medical injuries a special case where tort liability would not apply, especially as we received much evidence from medical and other witnesses which favoured the retention of tort. These topics are discussed in detail in chapter 24.

306 In relation to ante-natal injuries, the main problem is one we have already mentioned in another context, namely that it is only rarely that a physical cause of a congenital deformity can be identified. There is also the risk that acts or omissions of the child's parents may be called into question, with serious consequences for relationships within the family. Again, however, we did not find these arguments strong enough to justify removing the right to a tort action, save in certain exceptional cases. These conclusions are discussed in more detail in chapter 26.

Assessment of damages

307 We are not proposing the retention of tort without recommending a number of important changes. Some of these concern the assessment of tort compensation.

308 In chapter 13, many of our detailed recommendations arise from our conclusions that social security benefits should be fully offset against tort awards, and that the offsetting of other forms of compensation should be considered. The effect of implementing these recommendations would be a significant reduction in the level of many tort awards. Although other recommendations might lead to higher awards, we expect a net reduction overall. We hope that, as a consequence, the forces of competition would operate to set insurance premiums at lower levels than they would otherwise have reached.

309 Our main concern with the assessment of damages for pecuniary loss was that the tort system did not appear to be achieving what it in theory aimed

to achieve, namely to put the injured person in the same position as he would have been in if he had not sustained the injury. The major doubt related to the assessment of damages in respect of any expected loss of earnings after the date of the settlement or court award. Consider the simple and common example of a man with a regular income whose injury prevents him from working. At present, his tort compensation for loss of future income, like the remainder of his damages, would take the form of a lump sum. Yet what he has lost is a flow of income. Most of us concluded that there should be a scheme of periodic payments for the most serious cases. Most of us also became convinced that the present method of calculating the lump sum is not the best that could be designed if that sum, when invested, is to give the closest possible approximation to the actual loss of purchasing power. There is no way of achieving perfection in these matters, but we concluded that there should be a revised method of calculating lump sums – although there were two differing views on how this should be done. Periodic payments and the calculation of lump sums are discussed in detail in chapters 14 and 15.

310 Quite different problems were posed by the assessment of damages for what is for convenience called 'non-pecuniary loss', that is to say pain and suffering and loss of amenity. There is, by definition, no measurable financial loss, whether incurred or prospective. Although there are obvious practical and conceptual difficulties involved in compensating non-pecuniary loss, and especially in compensating pain and suffering, most of us concluded that the main heads of damage should be retained. Moreover, most of us also concluded that the 'loss of society' award currently payable in fatal cases under Scots law should be extended to the remainder of the United Kingdom, although with an upper limit. Nevertheless, we found that a good deal is spent on damages for pain and suffering and loss of amenity in the settlement of small claims. Most of us took the view that this is wasteful and that the payment of non-pecuniary damages is not justifiable where the injury is a minor one; and reached the conclusion that damages should not be payable for non-pecuniary loss suffered in the first three months after the injury. These conclusions are discussed in more detail in chapter 12.

311 We hope that these changes would have two particularly desirable consequences. First, by offsetting social security benefits in full, and by cutting down on awards for non-pecuniary loss in minor cases, a major role of the tort system would be seen more clearly as that of supplementing the no-fault compensation provided by the state. Secondly, in fulfilling this role, the system would tend to concentrate more on compensating serious and lasting damage.

Liability

312 To describe the future role of tort as essentially one of supplementing no-fault compensation is not to say that that role would be insubstantial. For example, not all long term social security benefits are earnings related and it will be some time before they are. Even then, the upper limit on the earnings related element would continue to leave high earners with a substantial gap to try to fill. There would continue to be cases where substantial losses or expenses were incurred over and above lost earnings. There would remain considerable

scope for compensating non-earners who were injured otherwise than in a road accident and were not entitled to non-contributory social security benefits.

313   We considered whether it should be made easier for an injured or bereaved person to recover tort compensation. For most categories of injury, the basis of liability remains the proof of negligence. We reviewed each category separately and considered two main options – either a statutory reversal of the burden of proof or strict liability.

314   In the event, we decided not to recommend a reversal of the burden of proof for any category of injury, and we decided against strict liability for work or road injuries. But there remained a wide range of other circumstances for which we found we had to consider strict liability.

315   By definition, strict liability is not concerned with fault (except in so far as fault on the part of the injured person may be permitted to reduce or eliminate his entitlement to damages). Subject to any defences which might be allowed, its effect is to impose the cost of compensation on the person who causes an accident or is responsible for something which causes it.

316   A relevant question is the insurability of the risk. Can those who may cause an injury take out insurance more conveniently and cheaply than those who may be injured? This is a practical issue. For example, depending on market conditions, the owner of a business might be able to spread the financial burden over those who ultimately pay for his goods or services. Another question is whether the victim is likely to experience particular difficulty in proving fault.

317   Our answers to these questions have led us to conclude, as we explain in chapter 22, that strict liability should be imposed on producers for injuries caused by defective products.

318   We also felt that where particular things or activities involved exceptional risks of injury, the cost of compensating such injury ought to be charged to those responsible for the things or activities concerned. This principle already lies behind the imposition of strict liability on the 'keepers' of dangerous animals in England, Wales and Northern Ireland. We concluded that the principle should be extended and applied systematically to things or activities which either have a high risk potential (such as highly flammable gases or liquids), or where a malfunction might cause multiple casualties (such as dams). In chapter 31, we recommend a scheme whereby strict liability would be imposed on the controllers of such things or activities.

319   In most other areas of our remit, strict liability was less clearly appropriate, for reasons which we shall explain in each of the chapters concerned. In broad terms, we concluded that liability should continue to be for negligence except where there were exceptional risks or where, as with defective products, there were other reasons for introducing a scheme of strict liability.

Compulsory insurance
320   Our terms of reference mentioned specifically the possibility of recovering compensation through compulsory insurance. At present, third party insurance

cover is compulsory for employers and motorists, and also in respect of nuclear installations, dangerous wild animals, riding establishments, and oil pollution from merchant ships. The central argument in its favour is that it ensures, so far as is possible, that those entitled to tort compensation actually receive it.

321 We saw a number of practical difficulties in the way of widening the scope of compulsory insurance. A requirement to insure would have to be effectively enforced. All the present requirements are linked to a system of licensing or certification; but for many other risks the cost of effective enforcement – in money and manpower – might prove disproportionate.

322 Furthermore, the cost of the cover required would have to be economic; it might not be reasonable to compel the insurance of small risks. The cover required would also have to be available; it would not be sensible to require unlimited cover which insurers would consider unrealistic to provide.

323 We also considered whether the basis of liability was relevant. It can be argued that insurance is essential to the effectiveness of tort as a provider of compensation; and that, if legislation were to impose strict liability with the object of improving a victim's chances of being entitled to compensation, it would be logical also to insist that such liabilities should be insured. On the other hand, it may be thought no less unfortunate for people not to receive damages when they have gone to the trouble and expense of proving negligence.

324 We concluded that the imposition of compulsory insurance was essentially a matter of weighing up the practical possibilities. We shall be recommending that consideration be given to imposing a new requirement in only two areas, namely in respect of exceptional risks for which strict liability would be imposed (chapter 31), and in respect of private aircraft (chapter 19). We shall not be recommending the removal of the requirement in any instance where it exists at present, although we doubt whether we should ourselves have proposed introducing one or two of the provisions in minor areas had we been starting afresh.

The application of our strategy

325 We now go on to consider how the strategic decisions outlined in this chapter should work out in detail. Our strategic survey has concealed the fact that there are a good many points of importance and difficulty to be considered before these decisions could be implemented.

PART IV

The assessment of tort damages

CHAPTER 12

The heads of claim

326 Before turning to the various categories of injury within our remit, we consider the assessment of tort damages – a subject which is common to all categories. This demands lengthy, and at times rather technical, treatment. Nevertheless, this Part of our report contains some of our key recommendations. In this chapter we discuss the heads of claim. In subsequent chapters we consider the offset of social security and other benefits from tort damages; the form of damages; the calculation of damages; and adjudication.

327 We have been greatly assisted in this part of our task by the work of other bodies. Following their Working Paper No 41, the Law Commission published, in July 1973, a Report on Personal Injury Litigation – Assessment of Damages (Law Com No 56, HC 373). Simultaneously, the Scottish Law Commission published a Report on the Law Relating to Damages for Injuries Causing Death (Scot Law Com No 31, HC 393). This report led to the enactment of the Damages (Scotland) Act 1976. Towards the end of 1975, the Scottish Law Commission also published a consultative memorandum on Damages for Personal Injuries: Deductions and Heads of Claim (Memorandum No 21). They expect their report to be ready for submission to the Lord Advocate early in 1978.

328 The Law Commissions made recommendations on many topics of direct relevance to our own enquiry. We have had the advantage of studying their reasoning, and in most cases we have reached similar conclusions. But on some points we have formed different views, if only because – as both the Law Commissions recognised – our terms of reference were much wider than theirs.

329 This chapter is in four sections, dealing with pecuniary loss due to personal injury, non-pecuniary loss due to personal injury, damages following death, and the actions for loss of services and society.

PECUNIARY LOSS DUE TO PERSONAL INJURY

330 We consider, first, the heads of claim for pecuniary loss incurred by a living plaintiff. We see no reason to depart from the principle which underlies the present heads of claim that, in an action for damages for personal injury, pecuniary loss should be compensated in full. But in the following paragraphs we comment on certain types of pecuniary loss.

Future loss of income: the rule in Oliver v. Ashman

331   In England, Wales and Northern Ireland, as a result of the decision of
the Court of Appeal in *Oliver* v. *Ashman* [1962] 2 Q.B. 210, damages for future
loss of income are awarded only for the period for which the plaintiff is expected
to remain alive. The plaintiff in *Oliver* v. *Ashman* was a young boy, whose life
expectation had been reduced by about 30 years as a result of a serious brain
injury. It was held that damages for loss of income during the 'lost years',
when the plaintiff would probably have remained alive if he had not been injured,
were to be regarded as part of the damages for loss of expectation of life. These
had in effect been set at a small conventional figure by the House of Lords in
Benham v. *Gambling* [1941] A.C. 157.

332   The rule in *Oliver* v. *Ashman* has been criticised – by the Law Commission,
and more recently by the Court of Appeal in *Pickett* v. *British Rail Engineering
Ltd* (*The Times*, 19 November 1977) – on the grounds that it can operate unfairly
when applied to adult plaintiffs with dependants. If, for example, the life
expectancy of a young married man is reduced by an injury from 40 years to
5 years, he can recover damages for loss of income for 5 years, and the small
conventional sum for loss of expectation of life. After his death, his dependants
can recover nothing further, since they cannot bring a second action for the
same injuries. If, however, the young man had been killed instantaneously
(or if he had died before winning his case) his dependants could have claimed
damages for lost dependency in respect of the full 40 years.

333   We consider this result to be unsatisfactory, as did almost all those who
expressed a view on the rule in *Oliver* v. *Ashman* in evidence to us. If someone
is prevented from fulfilling his obligations towards his dependants by an injury
for which somebody else is liable, the person liable for the injury should in our
view make good the loss.

334   The Law Commission concluded that the best substitute for the rule in
Oliver v. *Ashman* would be the formula adopted by the High Court of Australia
in *Skelton* v. *Collins* [1966] A.L.R. 449. This was to award the plaintiff damages
for his full pecuniary loss in the lost years, less the amount which he would
have spent on his own living expenses. The Scottish Law Commission, who
considered the matter in the context of clarifying rather than altering Scots
law, reached the same conclusion in their report on damages for injuries causing
death. Their recommendation was incorporated in section 9 of the Damages
(Scotland) Act 1976, which came into force in May 1976.

335   We agree with the Law Commissions that the solution propounded in
Skelton v. *Collins* is the right one. **We recommend** that, in England, Wales and
Northern Ireland, as under the present law in Scotland, damages for loss of
income by a living plaintiff should be recoverable on the basis of his pre-
accident life expectancy, subject to a deduction for the amount which he would
have spent on his own living expenses.

336   One probable consequence of our recommendation, although by no
means the most important, would be an increase in the level of pecuniary
damages awarded to a child who suffered an injury which was sufficiently

serious to reduce his life expectancy. But we would not expect any such increase to be dramatic, since there would be many uncertainties in assessing a child's lifetime loss of income and lifetime expenditure. A similar task faces the courts now in cases where a child's injuries do not reduce his life expectancy; and in practice only moderate amounts are as a rule awarded.

Loss of earning capacity

337 Loss of earning capacity may be regarded by the courts as a separate item of damages from loss of income. Recent cases, including, for example, *Moeliker* v. *A Reyrolle & Co Ltd* [1977] 1 All E.R. 9, seem to have established that damages for loss of earning capacity should be awarded if there is a significant risk that the plaintiff, because of his injury, will at some time in the future lose his job – even if he is not suffering any loss of earnings at the time of the trial.

338 The Law Commission have suggested that there is no real distinction between damages for loss of earning capacity and damages for future loss of earnings. We agree. If the plaintiff's earning capacity is diminished because of his injury, the loss may sooner or later be experienced by him as a loss of income. In our view, it should be so regarded for the purpose of assessing damages. The chance of the loss materialising would then fall to be taken into account by the court in the same way as many other contingencies. **We recommend** that loss of earning capacity should be regarded as a factor to be taken into account when assessing damages for future loss of earnings.

Expenses

339 Damages are at present recoverable for all expenses reasonably incurred or likely to be incurred by the plaintiff as a result of his injury. These may, for example, include the cost of domestic help, nursing care or similar attendance, extra wear and tear on clothes, and the purchase of special appliances needed to cope with physical disability.

340 Medical expenses may also be compensated. Section 2(4) of the Law Reform (Personal Injuries) Act 1948, which applies to Great Britain, and section 3(4) of the Law Reform (Miscellaneous Provisions) Act (Northern Ireland) 1948, require the courts to disregard, in determining the reasonableness of medical expenses, the possibility of avoiding all or part of them by taking advantage of National Health Service facilities.

341 We do not think that the requirement to disregard the availability of the National Health Service reflects present day realities. It gives rise to the possibility of double compensation where a plaintiff recovers damages on the basis that he will incur private medical expenses, and then in the event seeks treatment under the National Health Service. The Scottish Law Commission assumed in their Memorandum No 21 that the matter would be one which we would consider, and suggested that a test of reasonableness – such as applies, under the existing law, to expenses generally – would arguably lead to more satisfactory results. We consider that the criterion of reasonableness in relation to private

medical expenses should be a medical one. If a plaintiff decides to seek private treatment for his injuries when the same treatment would have been equally available under the National Health Service, we do not think that the defendant can reasonably be expected to meet the cost.

342   **We recommend** that section 2(4) of the Law Reform (Personal Injuries) Act 1948 and section 3(4) of the Law Reform (Miscellaneous Provisions) Act (Northern Ireland) 1948 should be repealed; and that in their place it should be provided that private medical expenses should be recoverable in damages if and only if it was reasonable on medical grounds that the plaintiff should incur them.

Services rendered and expenses incurred by others for the plaintiff's benefit

343   Services may be rendered by others to help the plaintiff to cope with his injury. Probably the most common example is that of a wife who looks after her injured husband at home. A relative or friend of the plaintiff may incur expenses for his benefit, such as travelling expenses when visiting him in hospital.

344   The problem of compensating for losses of this kind was considered by the Court of Appeal in *Donnelly* v. *Joyce* [1974] Q.B. 454. Lord Justice Megaw, delivering the decision of the court, said:

> 'We do not agree with the proposition ... that the plaintiff's claim, in circumstances such as the present, is properly to be regarded as being ... "in relation to someone else's loss" merely because someone else has provided to, or for the benefit of, the plaintiff – the injured person – the money ... to provide for needs of the plaintiff directly caused by the defendant's wrongdoing. The loss *is* the plaintiff's loss. The question from what source the plaintiff's needs have been met, the question who has paid the money or given the services, the question whether or not the plaintiff is or is not under a legal or moral liability to repay, are, so far as the defendant and his liability are concerned, all irrelevant. The plaintiff's loss, to take this present case, is not the expenditure of money to buy the special boots or to pay for the nursing attention. His loss is the existence of the need for those special boots or for those nursing services, the value of which for purposes of damages – for the purpose of the ascertainment of the amount of his loss – is the proper and reasonable cost of supplying those needs. That, in our judgment, is the key to the problem. So far as the defendant is concerned, the loss is not someone else's loss. It is the plaintiff's loss'.

345   We were attracted by this reasoning. If the plaintiff needs to have services rendered or expenses incurred for his benefit, and if this need arises from an injury for which a defendant is liable, then we think he should be able to recover damages. The way in which the need is met is indeed irrelevant. If, for example, the plaintiff's need for attendance is met gratuitously by his wife rather than by a suitable paid person, he should not recover less damages. This point of equity assumes considerable practical importance where the gratuitous rendering of a service brings about a fall in family income, for example, if a member of the plaintiff's family gives up work to care for him. In such cases, it is in our view just to consider the value of the services rendered, and the impact of the defendant's action on the family as a whole.

346   Our view accords with that of the Law Commission in their 1973 report, and with the subsequent decision of the Court of Appeal in *Donnelly* v. *Joyce*. In Scotland there has been no authoritative decision on the point and variant views have been expressed at first instance. But the Scottish Law Commission's proposed recommendation is that where any member of the family group renders necessary services to an injured person in consequence of those injuries, and where the injured person is successful in his claim for damages, it should be presumed that the services have been rendered, not gratuitously, but on such terms as to repayment or remuneration as may seem reasonable to the court. We would not ourselves wish to exclude the recovery of damages in respect of services rendered gratuitously by someone outside the victim's family group. On the approach in *Donnelly* v. *Joyce* the damages are awarded for the plaintiff's need to have services rendered to him. It seems to us that this need is not different in character if it is met by a friend rather than a member of the family.

A duty to account?
347   The English courts, until the decision in *Donnelly* v. *Joyce*, sometimes insisted that the plaintiff should give an undertaking to repay the damages to the person who actually rendered the services or incurred the expense (see, for example, *Schneider* v. *Eisovitch* [1960] 2 Q.B. 430). We understand that the Scottish Law Commission are to propose that the plaintiff should be under a legal duty to account for such damages as are recovered in respect of the services. In *Cunningham* v. *Harrison* [1973] Q.B. 942, Lord Denning, Master of the Rolls, said, referring to services rendered by a wife, that the husband should recover compensation for the value of the services and hold it in trust for his wife.

348   We think it follows from Lord Justice Megaw's reasoning in the later case of *Donnelly* v. *Joyce* that such arrangements are unnecessary. The damages are awarded for the plaintiff's loss, and it is for him to dispose of them as he thinks fit. In practice, the damages will often compensate for a loss suffered by a family income pool.

349   There are also, in our view, practical objections. In particular, it is difficult to see how an undertaking to repay could be enforced as part of a settlement; or what form it might take where the services were expected to be rendered at some time in the future. A requirement to set up a trust fund could present practical difficulties if several people were involved. The court would have to ascertain the amounts expended and the value of the services rendered by each, so that the plaintiff could hold the right sum in trust for each of them.

Assessment
350   There remains the question of how damages for services rendered by others should be assessed. One possible approach would be to award the approximate market value of the services; but this would bear hardly on those who gave up a highly paid job to help an injured relative. On the other hand, to award damages based on the loss actually sustained by the person rendering the services might encourage him or her to leave work unnecessarily. We came to

the conclusion that there could be no hard and fast rule which would be fair in every case; and that compensation should continue to be assessed by the court on the basis of what is reasonable.

351 **We recommend** that damages should continue to be recoverable for an injured person's need to have services rendered and expenses incurred by others for his benefit; that such damages should be recoverable by the injured person in his own right; that the injured person should not have a legal obligation to account to, or hold the damages in trust for, those rendering the services or incurring the expenses; and that such damages should continue to be assessed on the basis of what is reasonable.

Services rendered by the plaintiff

352 Another result of an injury may be that the plaintiff loses his capacity to render services to others. The most important example is the loss suffered by an injured housewife, who is deprived of her capacity to look after her family. Damages for the loss of gratuitously rendered services are not usually recoverable where the victim survives.

353 It seems to us that a person who loses the capacity to render services to others suffers a real loss. The housewife who can no longer care for her family has not lost money, but she has lost money's worth. If her services are partly replaced by hired help, the family as a whole may suffer substantial pecuniary loss. But we do not think her claim should be determined by the way in which her services are replaced. Even if they are replaced free of charge by a friend or relative, we consider that damages should be recoverable. We note that Resolution (75)7 of the Council of Europe, on Compensation for Physical Injury or Death, adopted in March 1975, envisages compensation in recognition of the victim's inability to carry out household tasks.

354 Again, we think it is right to regard the loss of the capacity to render services gratuitously as primarily the plaintiff's loss, rather than the loss of those who used to benefit from the services. We consider therefore that damages should be recoverable by the plaintiff in his own right.

355 It would in our view be necessary to place some limit on the types of service for which damages should be recoverable under this head. The Law Commission recommended that the action should be confined to services rendered by the victim to anyone within the class of dependants having a remedy under the Fatal Accidents Acts (see paragraph 401 below). We understand, too, that the Scottish Law Commission are to recommend that the law should be changed so that an injured person who has been prevented as a result of his injuries from performing his ordinary duties within the family group would be able to recover the reasonable value of the personal services he rendered. They define 'the family' for this purpose as the class of relatives who would have been entitled to claim damages for loss of support under section 1 of the Damages (Scotland) Act 1976, if the injured person had died of his injuries.

356   We agree with this approach. The loss of the plaintiff's capacity to render services to those dependent on him could bring about substantial pecuniary loss for the family in replacing them; but the loss suffered by those not dependent on the plaintiff seems to us to be altogether more remote. There are advantages in consistency with the right to recover damages for lost services in fatal cases.

357   Compensation for loss of the capacity to render services should in our view continue to be assessed by the court on the basis of what is reasonable. Any expenses incurred in providing replacement services would be a useful guide, but would be more relevant for some types of services than for others. In *Regan* v. *Williamson* [1976] 1 W.L.R. 305, for example – a case under the Fatal Accidents Acts – the court held that the services of a wife and mother should not be regarded as limited to the services of a housekeeper; account should also be taken of the fact that a wife does not work set hours, and that she is able to give instruction to her children. The extent to which less tangible services of this nature should be taken into account, and the value to be put on them, must in our view remain matters for the court to decide according to the facts of the case.

358   We propose below that the class of relatives entitled to claim damages for lost dependency under fatal accidents legislation in England, Wales and Northern Ireland should be brought into line with the class of relatives entitled to claim damages for loss of support in Scotland (listed in paragraph 402 below). **We recommend** that damages should be recoverable by an injured person for the loss of his capacity gratuitously to render services to others, where those to whom the services were rendered are within the class of relatives entitled to bring an action for loss of support under the Damages (Scotland) Act 1976; and that such damages should be assessed on the basis of what is reasonable.

NON-PECUNIARY LOSS DUE TO PERSONAL INJURY

The function of damages for non-pecuniary loss

359   By definition, money cannot make good a non-pecuniary loss. Yet damages for non-pecuniary loss are recoverable in both English law and, as *solatium*, in Scots law. Indeed, they are recoverable in some form in almost all tort systems.

360   What, then, is the purpose of an award for non-pecuniary loss? Clearly it cannot provide full compensation – no amount of money can drive away pain and suffering, or restore a lost limb. But at least three functions may be suggested. First, a conventional award may serve as a palliative. Pain and suffering and loss of amenity are real enough, at least for the seriously injured plaintiff; and he may well feel entitled to some reparation where these misfortunes befall him because of an injury for which someone else is liable. Secondly, an award for non-pecuniary loss may enable the plaintiff to purchase alternative sources of satisfaction to replace those he has lost. Thirdly, it may help to meet hidden expenses caused by his injury. Although in theory all expenses resulting from injury are recoverable as pecuniary loss, in practice some of them may well be unquantifiable or unforeseen.

361 There was no significant pressure in the evidence we received for the abolition of damages for non-pecuniary loss, and neither the Law Commission nor the Scottish Law Commission have so recommended. Compensation for non-pecuniary loss, in the form of disablement benefit for loss of faculty, is an important part of the existing industrial injuries scheme, although it is not intended to compensate for pain and suffering. We note also that the Council of Europe resolution on compensation for physical injury or death provides for compensation for 'aesthetic damage, physical pain and mental suffering'.

362 We consider that there is a place for damages for non-pecuniary loss. But we feel that the main aim of any compensation system should be to make good pecuniary loss. Our recommendations on the assessment of damages for non-pecuniary loss are made with this in mind.

Loss of expectation of life

363 Where a plaintiff's life expectancy is reduced by an injury for which a defendant is liable, the fact may be reflected in his damages in three ways. First, his pecuniary damages under the present law in England, Wales and Northern Ireland will be assessed on the basis of his life expectancy following the accident. In paragraph 335, we recommended that this rule should be changed so that pecuniary damages would be recoverable on the basis of the plaintiff's life expectancy before the accident. Secondly, throughout the United Kingdom, any mental suffering caused by knowledge of his shortened life expectancy will be taken into account in assessing damages for pain and suffering and loss of amenity. We do not propose any change. Thirdly, he will be awarded non-pecuniary damages for the fact of loss of expectation of life itself. It is to this third element (commonly referred to as damages for loss of expectation of life) that we now turn.

364 The recovery of damages for loss of expectation of life in England, Wales and Northern Ireland stems from decisions of Mr Justice Acton and the Court of Appeal in *Flint* v. *Lovell* [1935] 1 K.B. 354, and of the House of Lords in *Rose* v. *Ford* [1937] A.C. 826. The question of how such awards were to be assessed was considered by the House of Lords in *Benham* v. *Gambling*, a case which concerned a two year old child killed in a road accident. The House of Lords decided that damages should be awarded not for 'the prospect of length of days, but the prospect of a predominantly happy life'. Observing that any estimate of prospective happiness was bound to be uncertain, Viscount Simon (with whom the other Lords agreed) concluded that, 'in assessing damages under this head, whether in the case of a child or an adult, very moderate figures should be chosen'. Damages of £200 were awarded.

365 The effect of this decision was to set a conventional figure of £200 as damages for loss of expectation of life. The amount was raised to £500 in *Yorkshire Electricity Board* v. *Naylor* [1968] A.C. 529, to take account of the fall in the value of money. Subsequent awards have varied between £500 and £750.

366   In Scotland, although there may be no conventional figure, awards for loss of expectation of life are in practice made at much the same level as in the rest of the United Kingdom, as part of damages for *solatium*.

367   For living plaintiffs, damages for loss of expectation of life are usually of little practical importance. Where the injuries are serious enough to reduce life expectancy, such damages seldom form a significant proportion of the total award.

368   In England, Wales and Northern Ireland, a deceased person's right to damages for loss of expectation of life survives for the benefit of his estate. Again, such damages are often of little practical importance, since they are deducted from damages for lost dependency. Where, for example, a widow sues both as a dependant and as administrator of her husband's estate, damages for loss of expectation of life will be awarded to the estate but deducted from damages for lost dependency. If, however, there is no claim for lost dependency, damages for the deceased's loss of expectation of life may constitute a small sum paid to the beneficiaries of his estate. The main example is the death of a child, where the parents may recover the conventional sum on behalf of his estate. Usually they will have no other basis for a claim in English law.

369   In Scotland, claims for the deceased's loss of expectation of life do not survive for the benefit of the deceased's estate. But members of the deceased's immediate family may recover non-pecuniary damages in their own action, in the form of an award for loss of society.

Proposals for change
370   We received evidence from several parents who had lost children in accidents. A number of them felt strongly that damages for loss of expectation of life, paid to them under English law as beneficiaries of their child's estate, provided an inadequate – even derisory – acknowledgment of their loss. While we have some sympathy with this view, we do not think it would solve the problem to raise the present level of damages for loss of expectation of life. We propose below that their present function in providing an indirect acknow-ledgment of the loss suffered by close relatives of the deceased should be met by the introduction of an award for loss of society on Scottish lines.

371   In our view, damages for loss of expectation of life have an air of unreality. It is not possible to assess how happy the victim might have been if he had lived out his days. Still less is it possible to evaluate such a loss. These difficulties have led the courts to fix damages for loss of expectation of life at a level which means that they are usually of no practical significance. In some overseas legal systems, such as Ontario and British Columbia, loss of expectation of life has been abolished as a separate head of damages. In others, notably the USA, it has never been recognised as such. The Law Commission have recommended the abolition of damages for loss of expectation of life in England and Wales.

372   **We recommend** that damages for loss of expectation of life as a separate head of damage should be abolished.

Pain and suffering and loss of amenity

373 The present practice of the courts in compensating for non-pecuniary loss is to award a single sum of damages for pain and suffering and loss of amenity. Both the pain caused by the injury and any pain caused by subsequent operations or treatment are taken into account. So is the plaintiff's suffering because of his awareness of his injuries and their consequences. The court considers his awareness of physical disability or shortened life expectancy, his fear of future incapacity, his embarrassment or humiliation at disfigurement, and so on.

374 Loss of amenity is broadly interpreted as covering physical impairment and its non-pecuniary results, apart from pain and suffering. The court considers the loss of amenity of the individual plaintiff. He may expect, for example, to receive more damages for the loss of a leg if he used to play football rather than chess.

375 The translation of the court's assessment of the gravity of pain and suffering and loss of amenity into a sum of damages is necessarily an arbitrary process. The approach of the English courts to this problem was described as follows by Lord Morris of Borth-y-Gest, in *West* v. *Shephard* [1964] A.C. 326:

'All that judges and courts can do is to award sums which must be regarded as giving reasonable compensation. In the process there must be the endeavour to secure some uniformity in the general method of approach. By common assent awards must be reasonable and must be assessed with moderation. Furthermore, it is eminently desirable that so far as possible comparable injuries should be compensated by comparable awards. When all this is said it still must be that the amounts which are awarded are to a considerable extent conventional'.

376 The present method of assessment of non-pecuniary damages relies heavily on the judge's view, having regard to precedent, of what is a reasonable sum. Under the present procedure in Scotland and Northern Ireland, the same question may be decided there by a jury; their decision is subject to the power of the court on appeal to direct a re-trial, on the grounds that an award is grossly excessive, or grossly inadequate.

A legislative tariff?

377 The Law Commission considered, but in the end rejected, the possibility of substituting for the judge's assessment some form of legislative tariff relating damages to specified injuries or to the loss of specified faculties. We ourselves considered whether it would be possible, for example, to base a scale of damages on the present method of assessment for disablement benefit under the industrial injuries scheme.

378 The treatment of loss of faculty as a separate head of non-pecuniary loss would mean that the more subjective, and therefore more intangible, elements of present awards – pain and suffering and the loss of amenity caused by loss of faculty in a particular case – could be isolated. Awards might then be subject to some form of limit; or non-pecuniary damages other than for loss of faculty

might simply be abolished. The New Zealand Accident Compensation Act 1972, as amended, provides lump sum compensation for non-pecuniary loss under two heads:

i   permanent loss or impairment of bodily function;

ii a   the loss suffered by the person of amenities or capacity for enjoying life, including loss from disfigurement; and

    b   pain and mental suffering, including nervous shock and neurosis.

Compensation under the second head is not payable except where recovery from the injury is prolonged. Awards under both heads are subject to monetary limits. In Sweden, tables drawn up by insurance companies are used in assessing compensation for pain and suffering which is paid during the acute period.

379   While we saw some attractions in the idea of a tariff, we concluded that damages for pain and suffering and loss of amenity should continue to be assessed on broadly the present basis. There is clearly some overlap between, say, pain and loss of faculty. Loss of a limb may cause continuing pain, and the consciousness of its loss may cause mental distress. The judge should, in our view, be able to take an overall view of these interrelated losses. The introduction of a scale of damages for loss of faculty would not eliminate the arbitrariness of pecuniary awards for non-pecuniary loss; nor would it avoid the problem that similar awards for similar losses of faculty represent greater compensation for a poor man than for a rich man.

380   **We recommend** that damages should continue to be recoverable for loss of amenity; that such damages should continue to be awarded as a single sum; and that a scale of damages should not be introduced.

381   By a majority, **we also recommend** that damages should continue to be recoverable for pain and suffering; and that such damages should continue to be awarded, together with damages for loss of amenity, as a single sum. Professor Schilling and Professor Stevenson dissent and recommend that pain and suffering should be eliminated as a basis for compensation and that loss of amenity should be the main head of damages under non-pecuniary loss. Professor Stevenson's views are recorded in a note of reservation at the end of this chapter.

A threshold for non-pecuniary damages
382   We were struck by the high cost of compensation for non-pecuniary loss. It accounts for more than half of all tort compensation for personal injury, and for a particularly high proportion of small payments.

383   We think it likely that payments for minor non-pecuniary loss represent, in part, the price of a settlement. It may well be in the interests of the defendant's insurance company to offer more than a court would award as compensation for the plaintiff's pain and suffering and loss of amenity, in order to avoid the expense of continuing argument and possible litigation. We think this is wasteful.

384   Most of us find it hard to justify payments for minor or transient non-pecuniary losses, such as may equally be incurred through sickness or some

everyday mishap. We find it impossible to justify their use as bargaining counters. The emphasis in compensation for non-pecuniary loss should in our view be on serious and continuing losses, especially loss of faculty.

385   We considered that some limit should be applied so as to eliminate minor claims for non-pecuniary loss, and that it would best be expressed in terms of the duration of the loss. Damages would then be awarded only for lasting pain and suffering and loss of amenity. Another possibility would have been to set a financial threshold, so that only claims for which the court could be expected to award substantial damages would be admissible. But a monetary threshold would have a number of disadvantages. It would relate less closely than would a time threshold to the severity of the loss, since the monetary valuation of non-pecuniary loss is largely a matter of convention; it would need adjustment in line with changes in the value of money; it could encourage people to exaggerate the seriousness of their claims; and it would add to the uncertainties of litigation, since the plaintiff would have to attempt to evaluate his claim for non-pecuniary loss before deciding whether to bring an action.

386   The choice of a period to act as a threshold is necessarily arbitrary. We think it should be long enough to eliminate the bulk of small claims, but short enough not to exclude prolonged suffering. On balance, a period of three months seems to us to be fair. We recognise that, at the margin, there may be a tendency to adduce evidence of prolonged pain and suffering in order to surmount the threshold; but most injuries could not be represented as causing non-pecuniary loss for this length of time.

387   A three month threshold might operate in two ways. Non-pecuniary loss in the first three months after an injury might be totally disregarded; or damages in respect of the first three months might become payable if, and only if, the loss continued thereafter. Our view is that it would be fairer not to compensate anyone for pain and suffering and loss of amenity incurred within three months of the date of injury.

388   By a majority, **we recommend** that no damages should be recoverable for non-pecuniary loss suffered during the first three months after the date of injury. Lord Cameron and Mr Anderson dissent from this recommendation. They consider that damages should continue to be recoverable for non-pecuniary loss suffered during the first three months after an injury.

389   Although our proposal would not entirely eliminate small claims for non-pecuniary loss, the saving in the cost of tort compensation would be substantial. We estimate that the reduction would be £44 million a year, at January 1977 prices – about one fifth of all tort compensation for personal injury.

A ceiling for non-pecuniary damages

390   The possibility of imposing a ceiling on awards for non-pecuniary loss raises similar, though not identical, issues. It could be argued that large awards represent an excessive allocation of money to the compensation of intangible losses; and that they, too, could be used as bargaining counters in the settlement

process. It would be particularly unfortunate if, in the absence of a limit, this led to the large scale switching of payments between the heads of pecuniary and non-pecuniary loss.

391   We are equally divided on this issue. Half of us consider that there should be an upper limit as well as a lower limit to damages for non-pecuniary loss. Those who take this view recognise that there might be a tendency for the maximum to act as a target for awards, but think that this would be a danger only in a small number of serious cases. They believe that a maximum could, indeed, act as a useful point of reference for the courts in awarding damages, and that awards for lesser injuries could then be assessed roughly in proportion. They consider that the maximum should be set at five times average annual industrial earnings (about £20,000 in 1977).

392   Half of us, however, are against an upper limit. There was no strong demand for one in the evidence we received, and those who take this view think that in practice the Court of Appeal, and the Court of Session in Scotland, can – and do – secure a reduction of awards which are excessive. They believe that the introduction of a statutory maximum would be an unnecessary complication.

The unconscious plaintiff

393   The assessment of non-pecuniary damages raises particular difficulties where the plaintiff has been rendered permanently unconscious by his injuries. Such cases are comparatively rare, but they have given rise to two distinct judicial approaches.

394   The view which has prevailed in both the English and Scottish courts is that substantial damages should be awarded to a permanently unconscious plaintiff, in recognition of the gravity of his injuries, even though he is neither aware of his condition nor able to enjoy the use of his damages. Majority decisions based on this approach were given by the Court of Appeal in *Wise* v. *Kaye* [1962] 1 Q.B. 638, and by the House of Lords in *West* v. *Shephard*. In the latter case, Lord Morris of Borth-y-Gest said:

'An unconscious person will be spared pain and suffering and will not experience the mental anguish which may result from knowledge of what has in life been lost or from knowledge that life has been shortened. The fact of unconsciousness is therefore relevant in respect of and will eliminate those heads or elements of damage which can only exist by being felt or thought or experienced. The fact of unconsciousness does not, however, eliminate the actuality of the deprivations of the ordinary experiences and amenities of life which may be the inevitable result of some physical injury'.

A similar approach was adopted by the Scottish Court of Session in *Dalgleish* v. *Glasgow Corporation* 1976 S.L.T. 157.

395   The alternative approach, adopted by the minority in both *Wise* v. *Kaye* and *West* v. *Shephard* and by the High Court of Australia in *Skelton* v. *Collins*,

was that only a small award or none at all should be made. In *Skelton* v. *Collins*, Mr Justice Windeyer put the argument as follows:

'I am unable myself to understand how monetary compensation for the deprivation of the ability to live out life with faculties of mind and body unimpaired can be based upon an evaluation of a thing lost. It must surely be based upon solace for a condition created not upon payment for something taken away'.

396   We do not think it is possible to regard either of these approaches as necessarily right and the other as necessarily wrong. The 'majority' approach reflects a natural human feeling that substantial injuries call for substantial damages. The 'minority' approach, on the other hand, treats permanent unconsciousness as a form of living death which it seeks to compensate on approximately the same basis as for a fatal accident.

397   On balance, we favour the view that no non-pecuniary damages should be awarded. We think the approach should be to award non-pecuniary damages only where they can serve some useful purpose, for example, by providing the plaintiff with an alternative source of satisfaction to replace one that he has lost. Non-pecuniary damages cannot do this for a permanently unconscious plaintiff. As Justice argued in their evidence to us, 'When we compensate someone for non-economic loss, we are essentially seeking to relieve his suffering, and suffering is by its nature an experience subjective to the victim'.

398   **We recommend** that non-pecuniary damages should no longer be recoverable for permanent unconsciousness.

DAMAGES FOLLOWING DEATH

399   Claims for damages following death may be made under the present law on behalf of the relatives of the deceased and on behalf of his estate.

The relatives' claim for pecuniary loss

400   An action may be brought on behalf of certain dependent relatives of the deceased for pecuniary loss (lost dependency) under the Fatal Accidents Acts in England, Wales and Northern Ireland. In Scotland, the equivalent action is for loss of support and funeral expenses under the Damages (Scotland) Act 1976.

The entitlement to claim

401   Claims under the Fatal Accidents Acts may be made on behalf of the deceased's spouse, parent, grandparent, child, grandchild, brother, sister, uncle, aunt, and – in the case of the last four relatives – their issue. Relationships by marriage are treated as blood relationships; a legally adopted child is treated as a natural child; and an illegitimate child is treated as the legitimate child of his mother and reputed father. 'Half' and 'step' relationships are treated as full relationships.

402   In Scotland, those entitled to claim damages for loss of support also include all ascendants and descendants; any person accepted by the deceased as a child of his family (whether or not legally adopted); and a divorced spouse. The full list, contained in Schedule 1 to the Damages (Scotland) Act 1976, is as follows:

a   any person who immediately before the deceased's death was the spouse of the deceased;

b   any person who was a parent or child of the deceased;

c   any person not falling within paragraph b above who was accepted by the deceased as a child of his family;

d   any person who was an ascendant or descendant (other than a parent or child) of the deceased;

e   any person who was, or was the issue of, a brother, sister, uncle or aunt of the deceased; and

f   any person who, having been a spouse of the deceased, had ceased to be so by virtue of a divorce.

403   We think that there is a good case for extending the present entitlement in England, Wales and Northern Ireland to conform with Scots law. We agree with the Law Commission that a child accepted by the deceased and maintained by him as a 'child of the family', even though not legally adopted, has at least as good a claim to damages for lost dependency as, say, a stepchild; and that where a divorced spouse can demonstrate dependency on the deceased (if, for example, he or she has been awarded maintenance payments) he or she should also be able to claim damages. The inclusion under Scots law of all ascendants and descendants further means that claims by a dependent great-grandparent or great-grandchild can be considered. Although the likelihood of such claims is in practice remote, we see no reason why they should in principle be excluded.

404   **We recommend** that the relatives entitled to claim damages for lost dependency in England, Wales and Northern Ireland should be the same as those entitled to claim damages for loss of support under the Damages (Scotland) Act 1976.

405   Some of our witnesses felt that the entitlement to claim damages for lost dependency should be further extended, so as to include a common law husband or wife. Although some of us sympathised with this view and would have liked to find a formula to include such claims, we recognised that there were likely to be practical difficulties. We were aware, in particular, that national insurance widows' benefits are paid only to a person who was a legal wife at the time of the death. We were reluctant to propose a change in tort which would conflict with the social security position, since it was fundamental to our approach that the two systems should be co-ordinated; and we felt that the complex issues involved in paying benefits such as widows' benefit to common law spouses were largely outside the scope of our remit. We decided therefore to make no recommendation for or against allowing claims for lost dependency by a common law spouse. We note that the Law Commission suggested, in their report on the assessment of damages, that there might be a case for examining the legal position of a common law wife in all its aspects.

Changes in dependant's earnings
406 In assessing damages for lost dependency, difficulties arise with changes in the dependant's own earnings after the death. If a change takes place before the trial as a direct result of the death, we think the court should – as at present – take it into account in assessing the lost dependency. Such a case might arise where the deceased had been in need of constant attendance before the accident. After his death, the person who had looked after him could go out to work. But if the change in the dependant's earnings would probably have taken place even if the deceased had lived, we think it should be left out of account.

407 We consider that possible changes in the dependant's earnings after the trial should normally be left out of account. It would be difficult enough for the court to form a view on what changes were likely, but it seems to us that it would sometimes be almost impossible for the court to decide whether the change in question (for example, a widow going out to work) would or would not have taken place if the deceased had lived. We think it would be wrong to base what could be quite substantial adjustments to damages for lost dependency on such speculative foundations.

408 **We recommend** that, in assessing damages for lost dependency, changes in a dependant's earnings which have taken place before the trial as a direct result of the death should be taken into account; but that the possibility of changes in a dependant's earnings after the trial should normally be left out of account.

Remarriage
409 Section 4 of the Law Reform (Miscellaneous Provisions) Act 1971 provides that in assessing damages for lost dependency no account should be taken of a widow's remarriage or prospects of remarriage. This provision, in its application to England and Wales, is now in section 3(2) of the Fatal Accidents Act 1976. It was extended to Northern Ireland by the Fatal Accidents (Northern Ireland) Order 1977.

410 This legislation was intended to take account of criticism that the assessment of a widow's marriage prospects was distressing for her and distasteful for the judge. It was recognised that ignoring such prospects could sometimes result in considerable over compensation, since the widow would be supported both by the defendant and by her new husband.

411 The rationale for also ignoring a remarriage which had actually taken place before damages were assessed was, no doubt, that otherwise the widow would have an incentive to delay her marriage. In our view, this argument does not justify the manifest absurdity of awarding damages for a loss which is known to have ceased. This was the view of the Scottish Law Commission in their report on damages for injuries causing death; and it seems to us consistent with our approach to changes in a dependant's earnings before trial.

412 **We recommend** that, in assessing damages for lost dependency, the court should be able to take into account the remarriage of a widow before trial; and that the court should continue to be able to take into account the remarriage of a widower before trial.

413   The question of possible remarriage after the trial raises rather different issues, which would take on a new aspect if our majority proposals for periodic payments (set out in chapter 14) were adopted.

414   We were unable to devise any very satisfactory solution to this problem; and we are almost equally divided on what should be done. We are, however, all agreed that, whatever changes are made, the same approach should be adopted for widows and widowers. Some of us think that periodic payments should cease automatically on remarriage, without further reference to the courts, and that a dowry should become payable, perhaps in the form of a lump sum equivalent to five years' compensation.

415   Others of us consider that the disadvantages of terminating compensation are such that it would be better to allow continued over compensation in some cases. Those who take this view believe that, if compensation were terminated, the need to preserve equivalence between periodic payments and lump sums could present serious difficulties. In order not to discourage widows and widowers from accepting periodic payments, it would be necessary to take account of marriage prospects in assessing the lump sum; and this would involve the courts in precisely the kind of speculation which the present law was designed to avoid. The termination of periodic payments could act as a disincentive to remarriage; and it would be necessary to devise a review procedure capable of monitoring changes in marital status. This might be thought objectionable, and it would certainly add to the administrative complexity of periodic payments. Moreover, if provision were made for periodic payments to terminate on remarriage, it would, under our proposals, be open to a widow contemplating remarriage to apply for commutation of her future periodic payments, in the hope of obtaining more favourable compensation in the form of a lump sum.

416   Mr Marsh and Professor Schilling are unable to align themselves with either of the two points of view. They think that Parliament in the Law Reform (Miscellaneous Provisions) Act 1971 was concerned with the unseemliness of estimating a particular widow's chances of remarriage for the purpose of assessing a lump sum payment. Whether a periodic payment should be made when a spouse has in fact remarried is in their view an entirely different question. If, as their colleagues think, a lump sum in respect of future loss of support should not be awarded to a widow who has remarried before trial, they consider that similarly it is hard to justify a periodic payment at a time when the widow is known to have remarried. The other view put forward – that periodic payments should cease on the spouse's remarriage but that a kind of 'dowry' equivalent to five years' periodic payments should be awardable – appears to them to be arbitrary. They admit that it is desirable, if no account of a particular individual's marriage prospects is to be taken when assessing a lump sum for a spouse's future loss of support, that the choice of a periodic payment, which would cease on remarriage, should not by comparison be unattractive. They do not think there is any easy solution to the problem, but to either of the views put forward by their colleagues they would prefer a *formal test* of remarriage prospects based on the age of the spouse at the time of the other spouse's fatal accident; the correct ages for this purpose would depend on the national statistics of

remarriage of widows and widowers; the maximum percentage deduction would be for the youngest category of spouses and there would be no deduction if the bereaved spouse was over a certain age. This would be a rough and ready test but it would not involve embarrassing assessments of personal remarriage prospects and it would make a periodic payment continuing until actual remarriage more attractive.

Divorce
417   We do not think that any account should be taken of the possibility of divorce between the plaintiff and the deceased if he had lived, if this would be to the detriment of the plaintiff. Such a change could theoretically have affected the dependency, but the chances of its taking place cannot be ascertained with any degree of certainty; and the attempt to make a forecast could lead to undesirable inquiries into the nature of the relationship. **We recommend** that, in assessing damages for lost dependency, the possibility of divorce between a widow or widower and the deceased if he or she had lived should be disregarded, if taking the possibility into account would be to the detriment of the plaintiff.

The relatives' claim for non-pecuniary loss
418   In Scotland, a spouse, parent or child of the deceased may claim damages 'for the loss of such non-patrimonial (non-pecuniary) benefit as the relative might have been expected to derive from the deceased's society and guidance' (section 1(4) of the Damages (Scotland) Act 1976). Damages under this head constitute a 'loss of society' award.

419   In the rest of the United Kingdom, relatives of the deceased have no direct claim to compensation for any non-pecuniary loss they may suffer. But as we have already pointed out, the conventional damages awarded to the deceased's estate for his loss of expectation of life may sometimes serve as an indirect acknowledgment of their loss. The main example we gave was the damages recovered by parents on behalf of the estate of a child. In the light of our recommendation that damages for loss of expectation of life should be abolished, we considered whether provision should be made for some form of loss of society award in England, Wales and Northern Ireland. We were also mindful of the fact that the 1975 resolution of the Council of Europe on compensation for physical injury or death provides that compensation should cover the mental suffering of a spouse, child, parent or fiancée who has maintained 'close bonds of affection' with the victim up to the time of his death.

420   This difficult topic was considered by the Law Commission, who concluded that an award for bereavement caused by the death of a close relative could be justified in two, and only two, circumstances. These were an award to a parent for the death of a child; and to a husband or wife for the death of the other. They based their recommendation on the belief that, in these two circumstances, a small conventional award of damages could have some slight consoling effect.

421   The evidence we received lends some support to this view. One witness suggested that the absence of a claim for personal bereavement under English

law caused indignation among widows. Of those parents who had lost children in accidents, there were several who felt not only that they should receive compensation, but that the conventional damages for loss of expectation of life were far too small. Among them were parents of children killed in the fire at Summerland, Isle of Man in August 1973, and in the Moorgate tube disaster in February 1975. We should be surprised if the abolition of damages for loss of expectation of life, without replacement, were not widely resented.

422   In our view, awards for non-pecuniary loss suffered by the close relatives of the deceased should be directed at loss of society, rather than at sorrow or suffering. In this we concur with the view of the Scottish Law Commission, which was given effect by the Damages (Scotland) Act 1976:

'... over and above the quantifiable loss of income which they sustain when a man is killed, we think that a wife and children suffer damage through the loss of his help as a member of the household and of his counsel and guidance as a husband and father. A similar situation arises when a wife is killed leaving a husband and young family: even if she was not herself earning, her husband and family suffer considerable loss on her death, which is only partially quantifiable in financial terms. These are facts which ought to be acknowledged by the law.'

423   Most of us also agree with the Scottish Law Commission that the entitlement to a loss of society award should extend to a child of the deceased, as well as to a spouse or parent, but not – as provided in the Council of Europe resolution – to a fiancée. In this respect we differ from the Law Commission's view that awards in England and Wales to a child for the loss of a parent's society would not be justified. We think that if it is right to acknowledge the loss of society suffered by a bereaved husband or wife, it would be inconsistent not to do the same for a child who has lost one or both parents. Furthermore, we recognise the need to avoid, if possible, discrepancies between English and Scots law in this respect. We agree, however, with the Law Commission that a parent should be entitled to recover these damages only in respect of the death of an unmarried minor child; and we consider that, similarly, only an unmarried minor child should be entitled to recover damages for loss of society in respect of the death of a parent.

424   By a majority, **we recommend** that damages for loss of society should be recoverable by a husband or wife for the death of the other, by a parent for the death of an unmarried minor child, and by an unmarried minor child for the death of a parent. We agree with the Law Commission that, in England, Wales and Northern Ireland, such damages should be recoverable under the Fatal Accidents Acts.

425   Professor Schilling and Professor Stevenson dissent from this recommendation. Where no pecuniary loss is involved, they can see no justification for a payment fixed at an arbitrary figure, which is low, as a gesture of consolation. They are not convinced by arguments about public opinion. In their view, there will always be bereaved persons who regard such a payment as derisory, and, in a sense, they will be right.

97

426   Mr Marsh also dissents from this recommendation. He considers that, in view of the controversial nature of loss of society awards, they should be available only where there is evidence of a real demand and need for them. In his view, there is no such demand or need in the case of children who have lost one or both parents. He therefore remains of the opinion, to which he subscribed as a Law Commissioner in the Law Commission's report on the assessment of damages, that damages for non-pecuniary loss suffered by close relatives of the deceased should be recoverable only by the parents of an unmarried minor child and by a surviving spouse.

427   There is a further point, on which the Law Commissions did not agree. In Scotland, awards for loss of society are unlimited; but the Law Commission proposed (in their 1973 report) that in England and Wales awards should be fixed at £1,000. We see considerable force in the Law Commission's view that a small fixed award would be consistent with the conventional nature of damages for loss of society, and would avoid the need to enquire into the nature of family relationships. We consider, however, that a figure related to the level of average annual industrial earnings would be preferable to a fixed amount of money, since it would automatically be revised to take account of inflation. **We therefore recommend** that damages for loss of society in England, Wales and Northern Ireland should be set at half average annual industrial earnings (about £2,000 in 1977).

428   We agree with the Law Commission that where both parents succeed in a claim for the death of a child, each should be awarded half the fixed amount. Where more than one child, or one parent and one or more children, claim in respect of the death of a parent, those of us who think that damages for loss of society should be recoverable consider that the award should be divided equally between them.

429   We are, however, reluctant to set a fixed level for loss of society awards in Scotland. Non-pecuniary damages have long been recoverable there by relatives of the deceased (until recently as an award of *solatium*). This tradition provides a background against which loss of society awards can be assessed, whereas in the rest of the United Kingdom, loss of society would be a novel head of damage. **We recommend** that damages for loss of society in Scotland should continue to be unlimited.

Possible overlap with pecuniary damages for lost services
430   Our proposals for a loss of society award could sometimes be regarded as giving rise to the possibility of overlap with pecuniary damages for lost services which are recoverable under the Fatal Accidents Acts as an element in damages for lost dependency. The sort of difficulty we have in mind is well illustrated by the judgment in *Regan* v. *Williamson* [1976] 1 W.L.R. 305. After pointing out that the present law allows compensation only for the value of lost services, Mr Justice Watkins said:

> 'I am . . . of the view that the word "services" has been too narrowly construed. It should, at least, include an acknowledgement that a wife and mother does not work to set hours and, still less, to rule. She is in constant

attendance, save for those hours when she is, if that is the fact, at work. During some of those hours she may well give the children instruction on essential matters to do with their upbringing and, possibly, with such things as their homework. This sort of attention seems to be as much of a service, and probably more valuable to them, than the other kinds of service conventionally so regarded.'

431   Some of the elements of loss cited in this judgment are similar in character to the loss of help and counsel which the Scottish Law Commission think should be compensated by a loss of society award. We would have thought it right to include in the pecuniary damages all those services which can theoretically be replaced in return for money, or can at least be valued in terms of money; and to regard the loss of society award as something quite separate, intended to acknowledge the loss of those intangible services which defy attempts at valuation.

The estate's claim

432   The recovery of damages by the estate of a deceased person is governed in England and Wales by the Law Reform (Miscellaneous Provisions) Act 1934; in Scotland, by the Damages (Scotland) Act 1976; and in Northern Ireland, by the Law Reform (Miscellaneous Provisions) Act (Northern Ireland) 1937.

Pecuniary loss

433   The rule is that causes of action vested in the deceased at the time of his death survive for the benefit of his estate. Any pecuniary loss incurred by the plaintiff because of his injury and before his death is recoverable by his estate. We think it should remain so.

434   In England, Wales and Northern Ireland, by virtue of the rule in *Oliver* v. *Ashman*, the deceased has no right to damages for lost income in the years following his death. Consequently they cannot be recovered by his estate. We agree with the Law Commission that, if – as we propose – the rule in *Oliver* v. *Ashman* is reversed, a right to damages for pecuniary loss in the lost years should not survive for the benefit of the deceased's estate.

435   If such claims were to survive, the defendant might well find himself paying damages twice over – once to the deceased's dependants, and once to his estate. This would be unfair. In our view, the loss of the victim's income in the lost years is in practice felt by those dependent on him. We think it is in their hands that the right to recover damages should lie.

436   This result is already achieved by the law in Scotland, where damages for pecuniary loss in the lost years may be recovered by a living plaintiff, but not by his estate, by virtue of section 2(3) of the Damages (Scotland) Act 1976.

437   **We recommend** that in England, Wales and Northern Ireland, as under the present law in Scotland, a claim for damages for pecuniary loss in the 'lost years' should not survive for the benefit of the claimant's estate.

Non-pecuniary loss

438   The Scottish Act also provides that no claim should survive for *solatium* or for loss of society. By contrast, under present English law, the estate may recover damages for any pain and suffering and loss of amenity suffered by the deceased before his death, as well as the conventional damages for loss of expectation of life.

439   Like the Law Commission, we have recommended that damages for loss of expectation of life should be abolished and that an award for loss of society, on Scottish lines, should be introduced in England, Wales and Northern Ireland.

440   The Scottish Law Commission, whose recommendation was incorporated in the Damages (Scotland) Act 1976, took the view that claims for non-pecuniary loss should not survive, since they were personal to the victim and it would be artificial for others to benefit from them. For much the same reason, the Law Commission recommended that in England and Wales claims under their proposals for damages for bereavement should not survive for the benefit of the claimant's estate. We take the same view in relation to our proposals for awards for loss of society.

441   **We recommend** that, in England, Wales and Northern Ireland, as under the present law in Scotland, a claim for loss of society should not survive for the benefit of the claimant's estate.

442   The Law Commission considered, however, that in England and Wales claims for pain and suffering and loss of amenity should continue to survive. In their Working Paper No 41, which they quoted in their report, they put the argument as follows:

> 'The deceased may have suffered severe pain over a considerable period before death and may even, during that time, have spent some of the damages he was advised he would recover; and, during this period, relatives may have so acted in looking after him as to be not undeserving of the reward he may have intended to bestow upon them. We can see no reason why, in justice, a victim's death, perhaps wholly unconnected with the injury, should lead to this compensation being taken away.'

443   We have considerable sympathy with this line of argument; and we consider that, in England, Wales and Northern Ireland, claims for pain and suffering and loss of amenity should continue to survive for the benefit of a deceased person's estate, even though this means retaining an inconsistency between English and Scots law.

444   **We recommend** that, in England, Wales and Northern Ireland, claims for pain and suffering and loss of amenity should continue to survive for the benefit of the claimant's estate; and that in Scotland such claims should continue not to survive.

THE ACTIONS FOR LOSS OF SERVICES AND LOSS OF CONSORTIUM

445   Finally, we deal with the common law actions for loss of services and loss of consortium (*per quod servitium amisit* and *per quod consortium amisit*).

These actions, which are available in England, Wales and Northern Ireland, provide a limited remedy for a husband who is deprived of his wife's society; for a parent who is deprived of a child's services, provided that the law regards the parent as entitled to the services; and for an employer who is deprived of the services of a menial servant. The actions are not available if the victim is killed rather than injured.

446   The Law Commission took the view that the actions for loss of services and loss of consortium now have little importance or relevance, and recommended their abolition. We agree. Our proposals on the heads of claim would make redundant the limited remedies which these actions in theory provide. Where, by an injury for which a defendant is liable, a woman is deprived of her capacity to render services to her family, we have recommended that she should be able to recover damages in her own right. Where a husband is deprived of his wife's society by an injury for which a defendant is liable, we have recommended that he should be entitled to an award for loss of society. Lastly, as we point out in chapter 13, an employer who continues to pay wages to an injured employee can in effect recover the cost from the person responsible for the injury if the employee is obliged by his contract of service to refund such payments from damages.

447   **We recommend** that the actions for loss of services and loss of consortium (*per quod servitium amisit* and *per quod consortium amisit*) should be abolished.

NOTE OF RESERVATION ON NON-PECUNIARY LOSS

by Professor Stevenson

448   I am one of those members of the Commission who would wish to see the tort system 'wither away'. In the long run, I would prefer to see our social security provision developed so that all citizens, regardless of the cause of their injury or sickness, are compensated to ensure, first, that they do not suffer serious and lasting pecuniary loss, and secondly, that they have the resources to enable them to live as full a life as possible. The acquisition of such resources is not, of course, solely dependent upon the money which the citizen has in his pocket. The provision of services to those suffering from major disability turns on the availability of the requisite resources. This in turn depends on national and local policies for the improvement of both practical and professional services, for example, in more sophisticated aids for daily living and a sufficiency of occupational therapists.

449   In my view, therefore, the long term goal should be to abolish discrimination between citizens which arises solely from the causation of the injury. The only 'head of damages' in tort which has no clear parallel in our social security system is that of 'pain and suffering'. Therefore, I do not wish to see this play a significant part in compensation for 'non-pecuniary loss' as it does at

present in the tort system. It widens the gap between the two systems and, for reasons discussed below, I do not consider the gap should be narrowed by a movement of the social security system towards the use of such a concept.

450   Albeit with reluctance, I have agreed with my colleagues that, for a variety of reasons, the tort system of compensation should be retained for the time being. Two reasons have weighed heavily with me. The first is that our system of social security and services is not at present adequate, either in terms of replacement of lost earnings or in the provision of services. It is therefore, simply, 'dog in the manger' to say that because adequate compensation is not available to all, it should not be given to some who at present can obtain under the tort system a more generous sum for their needs. Secondly, although too much can, in my view, be made of the merits of 'judicial discretion', the tort system does permit a degree of individualised justice which social security schemes find very difficult to operate. This tension between so-called 'creative' and 'proportional' justice is a recurrent theme in the debate about a 'just' society and it is incorrect to suggest that tort is only concerned with the former and social security only with the latter. The phrase is used to distinguish between the individual's need, on the one hand, for special treatment and, on the other, to be treated the same as others. Nonetheless, it remains broadly true that the balance between the two systems differs and the privileged few of the injured and the sick who achieve a financial settlement through a tort claim can at present be better catered for as individuals.

451   I do not differ from my colleagues that, if the tort system is retained, there must be an attempt to compensate as justly as possible for monetary loss, both in relation to loss of earnings and in relation to the payment of expenses incurred as a result of the injury. In the serious and prolonged cases with which we, as Commissioners, have been much concerned, these expenses are likely to be substantial, and I would wish them to be generously assessed, taking fully into account such matters as the care which has to be provided for children as well as the injured spouse, even if that care is provided by relatives or friends. (See paragraphs 343 to 351.)

452   That leaves the question of non-pecuniary loss, elements of which are described in Fleming[7] under two main heads:

a actual pain and suffering, 'an entirely subjective sensation of conscious distress';

b an element 'variously referred to as loss of faculty, of capacity, or of amenities, the inability to enjoy the normal activities and functions'.

It is a pity that the phrase 'pain and suffering' is commonly used by lawyers to embrace both these aspects of non-pecuniary loss, for this obscures the very real differences between the criteria for awards made under the head of 'non-pecuniary' loss.

453   On pain and suffering, as a basis for compensation, I am not persuaded by anything I have read or heard in evidence that this is satisfactory. No one disagrees that it is *de facto* unquantifiable. Atiyah[6] puts it well.

454   He points out that the phrase 'pain and suffering' is a blanket term used to cover mental distress generally, and which can include 'humiliation, indignity, and embarrassment'. He argues:

'Something which cannot be measured in money is "lost" and the award of damages requires some monetary value to be placed upon it. There appears to be simply no way of working out any relationships between the value of money – what it will buy – and damages awarded for pain and suffering and disabilities. All such damage awards could be multiplied or divided by two overnight and they would be just as defensible or indefensible . . . .'

455   Economists, Atiyah suggests, have struggled with this in vain. 'There is no "market" for pain or lost limbs.' A further difficulty is that 'the value of money differs according to the wealth of the recipient', so that one is trapped between the manifest absurdity of awarding a rich man more for his pain and suffering or offering a sum which might seem derisory to one and riches to another.

456   It may be argued that the law is well accustomed to quantifying the unquantifiable, as for example in damages for libel. But that, in my view, does not constitute a sufficient justification for retaining this concept as an essential component of non-pecuniary loss, given the long term objectives for this area of compensation, which I have discussed earlier.

457   I therefore consider that pain and suffering *per se* should be eliminated as a basis for compensation. I accept that it is deeply embedded in our own and other legal systems. But I think it unlikely that the public would be much outraged, especially if, as I have suggested, expenses are generously calculated and an alternative basis for the calculation of other aspects of non-pecuniary loss is included in the scheme. I believe that to cling to a system which is generally acknowledged to be fairly 'rough justice' may actually hinder a more precise assessment of other losses which are non-pecuniary.

458   In this connection, the study of O'Connell and Simon[8] is relevant. Their research was conducted in a different social and legal setting. It is nonetheless of considerable interest. Their study focused upon the victims' understanding of, experience with, and attitudes towards 'pain and suffering', and out of a randomly drawn sample of 700, they contacted 73 per cent of such people, who had been awarded compensation in 1966. They found 'large scale confusion' on the question of awards for pain and suffering. Seventy per cent had no knowledge or expectation of such payment at the time of the accident. Eighty nine per cent in fact received payment above their economic loss. The great majority of people interviewed believed that the more serious the accident and the larger the awards, the more likely they were to include awards for pain and suffering. The opposite was in fact the case. '. . . Respondents with smaller losses were more likely to be paid at a higher rate for pain and suffering . . .' (Our recommendation to allow compensation only after three months reflects our concern on this last point.)

459   Fleming's second element under b in paragraph 452 in fact describes two different kinds of loss. One, loss of 'faculty and capacity', refers to damage

to the person; 'amenity' refers to what he has lost as a result of the injury. There are thus two logically distinct categories which have different implications for awards. The industrial injuries scheme gives benefits for loss of faculty, on a percentage basis. The situation in the social security scheme in respect of 'loss of amenity' is somewhat ambiguous. For example, mobility and attendance allowances are in theory compensation for expenses incurred in the extra cost of caring at home for the disabled. In fact, no check is made as to how this money is spent and it is implicitly accepted that some recipients may choose to use it to make life easier in other ways which comes close to compensation for 'loss of amenity'.

460   I am inclined to the view that, for serious and lasting cases, *loss of amenity* should be the main head of damages under non-pecuniary loss. This enables the judge to exercise discretion, having regard to the alternative satisfactions which the injured plaintiff may have to seek in his daily life, which will be all the more important when he is unable to work.

461   However, there are cases in which a seriously injured plaintiff has suffered little or no loss of amenity but some loss of faculty. An example might be of a man who lost some fingers of one hand but whose career and daily life were in no way affected. It would be reasonable, I believe, for some very modest award to be made in such cases. Unlike the 'loss of amenity' which is clearly a matter for discretionary decisions, it would seem more just, and feasible to have some kind of 'tariff', as has the industrial injuries scheme. But I consider this as relatively unimportant, compared with provision for loss of amenity.

462   It will, of course, be regarded by some as harsh that I propose taking no account of the pain and suffering consequent upon injuries. My arguments for doing so, as set out above, reflect in part my wish not to perpetuate a concept which separates the tort claimant from his counterpart on social security. But a second and most important point is that we may better serve the injured person who claims under tort by *a very careful assessment of the financial consequences of social disability* than by the present fairly arbitrary calculations of 'pain and suffering'. This in turn may in the longer run benefit the social security claimant when it can be seen, by analogy, how such damages can be calculated with some precision.

463   To clarify the argument, I take one example:

Mrs X, a young married woman with children, is seriously disabled as a consequence of an accident for which another can be held responsible. She was not working outside the home before the accident and there is therefore no loss of earnings. However, under the arrangements proposed by the Commission (paragraphs 343 to 351), she and the family would receive generous compensation for the *expenses* incurred in her care at home and for the care which has to be bought for her young children as a result of her incapacity. Such expenses would take into account not only services but, for example, adaptations to the home necessitated by her injuries. (The provisions of the Chronically Sick and Disabled Persons Act 1970 and the Chronically Sick and Disabled Persons (Scotland) Act 1970 should, in theory, meet these but the practice falls far short of the intention and affords a good example of the need at present to give to some even if all can not receive equally.)

That leaves a head 'loss of amenity'. What might be the criterion for such an award if it concerned an assessment of social disability? The fundamental criterion would be concerned with alternative sources of satisfaction. If the injured woman is not now able to enjoy the same activities as heretofore, it is obviously psychologically important for her, and for her family, that alternatives should be sought. Supposing she had been a good amateur musician, now unable to play the instrument in which she had previously been skilled. Is there another one that she could play? What would the cost of it be and of the lessons necessary to learn it? If attendance at concerts is now impossible or difficult, would it be a source of pleasure for her to increase her collection of discs beyond that she could previously have afforded, or are cassettes (much more expensive at present than discs) much easier for her to manipulate when she is on her own? The variations on the theme are many and various. Clearly, lawyers will try to make out the best case for their clients and there will be an element of exaggeration in some claims under this head. But judges are well accustomed to considering such evidence and there is at least some factual basis upon which to assess both the validity of the claim and its financial implications.

464   This example, I hope, serves to illustrate that a combination of compensation for expenses incurred and for loss of amenity might add up to a considerable sum. One is, inevitably, left with 'the hard cases', for example, the woman with no evident disability, who complains of headaches since the accident and who could under this present system claim for pain and suffering. If it could be demonstrated that any condition – visible or invisible – had seriously altered the plaintiff's way of life, it is likely that a claim under 'loss of amenity' could be sustained. If that case cannot be made out, then I consider there should not be compensation which serves to emphasise so sharply the distinction between this tort plaintiff 'in pain' and the vast majority who do not receive, or indeed expect, to be given money for pain *per se*.

CHAPTER 13

Offsets

465 Having decided that compensation should be considered as a whole, we came to the conclusion that there should be no overlap between tort compensation and social security benefits. In this chapter, we discuss the considerations which led us to this conclusion, and the way in which we think it might be translated into practice.

466 We deal first with social security benefits and then go on to consider other payments.

Tort and social security

467 We explained in chapter 7 the provisions made in section 2(1) of the Law Reform (Personal Injuries) Act 1948 and section 3(1) of the Law Reform (Miscellaneous Provisions) Act (Northern Ireland) 1948. In assessing damages for loss of income due to personal injury, the court is obliged to take into account one half of the value of certain social security benefits for five years, if these are payable as a result of the injury for which damages are awarded. The benefits, including those added by subsequent legislation, are sickness benefit, invalidity benefit, non-contributory invalidity pension, injury benefit, and disablement benefit. The court may take other benefits into account, but is not required to do so. Unemployment benefit, for example, has been deducted in some cases, but not in others.

468 In assessing damages for lost dependency, social security benefits are left out of account. The relevant provisions are now contained in the Fatal Accidents Act 1976, the Damages (Scotland) Act 1976, and the Fatal Accidents (Northern Ireland) Order 1977.

469 The Law Commission recommended, in their report on the assessment of damages (Law Com No 56, HC 373) that social security benefits not specified in the 1948 Acts, as amended, should be left out of account. We are told that the Scottish Law Commission, in their forthcoming report on deductions and heads of claim, are expressing the view (without making any formal recommendation) that the benefits covered by the 1948 Acts should be deducted in full.

470 The weight of opinion in the evidence we received was in favour of a fundamental change in the compromise represented by the 1948 Acts. Although there was by no means unanimity as to the form such a change should take, there was widespread agreement that greater account should be taken of social

security benefits in the assessment of damages. The TUC said that they were not opposed to such changes, provided that some improvements were made in the no-fault benefits of the industrial injuries scheme.

471   Two main arguments were advanced in favour of the present law. First, it was said that, as social security benefits were paid for by the victim's own contributions, they should be treated in the same way as payments from first party insurance (which, under the present law, are not deducted from damages). This argument seems to have carried some weight with the Law Commissions. Our own view is that it is not realistic to regard social security benefits as the fruits of individual thrift. A number of important benefits, including non-contributory invalidity pension as well as mobility allowance and attendance allowance, are non-contributory. Others are only partly financed by the contributions of potential recipients; and the tendency in recent years has been for the relative importance of individual contributions as a source of finance for benefits to decrease, and for contribution conditions to be relaxed. Furthermore, the fact that national insurance contributions are compulsory seems to us to distinguish them from premiums paid voluntarily in respect of private insurance.

472   Secondly, it was argued that the defendant should not be relieved of part of his liability by the state; the tortfeasor should pay in full. This view seems to us to be based on a wrong conception of the tort system, which is directed at the compensation of loss rather than the punishment of wrongdoing. The aim should be for the damages to be equal to the actual net loss suffered. We think the argument is also undermined by the fact that tort compensation is usually paid, not by the defendant, but by his insurers.

473   We therefore agree with a majority of our witnesses that the present law should be changed. The 1948 compromise no doubt seemed reasonable at a time when the social security system as we now know it was in its infancy; but it has no justification in principle. Nor is it in practice fully implemented by the courts. The usual procedure is to ascertain the annual value of relevant benefits paid to the plaintiff at the time of the trial, and to multiply this figure by five and divide it by two in order to arrive at the deduction. This calculation takes no account of probable increases in benefits over the five year period, even though all the benefits listed in the 1948 Acts must now be reviewed annually.

474   Some of our witnesses suggested other possible compromises, which would take fuller but not complete account of social security benefits. The BIA suggested that benefits might be set off in full, but for only five years – largely on the practical grounds that long term flows of benefit were difficult to capitalise in order to deduct them from a tort award. The Faculty of Advocates proposed that there should be no time limit, but that two thirds of the benefits should be deducted. They argued that this would reflect the increasing proportion of benefits paid for nowadays by employers' rather than employees' contributions.

475   We decided not to accept these suggestions. We think the time has come for full co-ordination of the compensation provided by tort and social security. An injured person, or his dependants, should not have the same need met twice,

not only because it is inequitable, but because it is wasteful. This principle has been adopted in most countries where compensation may be provided through both tort and social insurance.

476 Our conclusion is that there should be no overlap between the compensation provided by tort and that provided by social security.

Method of avoiding overlap

477 We referred in chapter 7 to the report of the Monckton Committee in 1946. The majority recommended that there should be no overlap; and the Committee considered three ways in which this recommendation might be put into effect.

478 First, they examined the possibility of requiring the injured person to elect between compensation through damages and compensation through benefit. This would have been analogous to the situation under the Workmen's Compensation Acts, whereby a workman had to elect between claiming under the Acts and claiming at common law. We explored a refinement of this possibility, whereby an injured person who succeeded in recovering damages would have them reduced by the amount of benefits received, and would be eligible for no further benefits. If he lost his case, or decided not to bring an action, his right to benefit would be unaffected. We thought this arrangement might provide an element of freedom of choice, but concluded that it would have overriding disadvantages and should not be recommended. We thought that it would be wrong to allow an injured person in effect to opt out of the social security system, which is uniquely well suited to the provision of long term income support. Such an option would not in our view be in the best interest of injured people and their dependants, and it would be foreign to the nature of social security. It would also put an onerous responsibility on those who have to advise injured people whether to pursue tort claims.

479 Secondly, the Committee considered the possibility that, where a person recovered or was entitled to recover damages for his injury, no benefit would be payable, unless the damages were less than the benefit. In that event, only the difference would be payable. The benefit paying authority, however, would have a discretionary power to advance benefit, pending the settlement of a tort claim. We ourselves rejected any such scheme. We thought that an injured person's entitlement to social security benefits should not depend on whether or not he succeeded, or was likely to succeed, in a tort action. Still less, did we think that entitlement should depend on the benefit paying authority's view of whether or not he was likely to succeed.

480 Thirdly, the Committee considered the possibility of requiring the court to deduct social security benefits when assessing damages. The majority of the Committee thought that this should be the approach, rather than the other two courses they considered, and we agree with them. This course would involve an adaptation, rather than a complete change, of the present practice (under the 1948 Acts). We think that the deduction should be made both from damages

for an injured plaintiff and from damages for dependants in the case of a fatal accident. The arguments for avoiding overlap between tort and social security seem to us to apply with equal force in both cases.

Benefits to be offset

481   We agree with the principle in the 1948 Acts that the benefits deducted should be limited to those payable to the plaintiff as a result of the injury for which damages are awarded. In practice, this means that such benefits as state retirement pensions, child benefit, and maternity benefit should be disregarded.

482   **We recommend** that the full value of social security benefits payable to an injured person or his dependants as a result of an injury for which damages are awarded should be deducted in the assessment of the damages.

483   We would include as part of the benefit to be deducted any increase in respect of dependants. These increases result in a greater degree of income replacement for an injured married person with children than for an injured single person. They are part of social security compensation for loss of income, and should in our view be taken into account in assessing the injured person's need for further compensation. Tort damages should compensate for the actual net loss after taking the benefits into account. In chapter 15 we discuss the effect on the level of tort damages of taking dependency increases into account as part of the benefits.

Method of deduction

484   The deduction might be made in one of several ways. One possibility would be to deduct lump sum benefits from lump sum damages, and benefits in the form of periodic payments from damages in the same form. We decided not to recommend this course, however, in the light of our conclusion that periodic tort payments should be restricted to future pecuniary loss resulting from serious and lasting injuries or from death.

485   Another possibility would be to deduct the total value of the benefits from the total tort award. But this approach would run counter to our view – which we share with the Law Commission – that the functions of compensation for pecuniary and non-pecuniary loss are distinct, and that they should be separately assessed. In particular, we think it would be wrong if a plaintiff receiving loss of earnings benefits was to find that all or most of his award for pain and suffering and loss of amenity disappeared.

486   This led us to consider the possibility of classifying social security benefits as either pecuniary or non-pecuniary, and deducting those in each category from the corresponding portion of the tort award. Most of us thought that this approach, too, could give rise to difficulties. Certain important social security benefits, including mobility allowance and attendance allowance, are directed at meeting specific expenses of disability. These benefits might sometimes exceed the value of tort damages for expenses, so that, if the benefits were classified as pecuniary, they might sometimes be partially set off against damages for loss

of income. We felt this would be unfair, since the benefits are not intended to provide income support. Equally, most of us thought it would be unfair to classify the benefits as non-pecuniary and deduct them from damages for pain and suffering and loss of amenity. It seemed to us that these damages served a different purpose. Most of us concluded that both tort damages and social security benefits could involve three distinct types of compensation – for loss of income, for expenses, and for non-pecuniary loss – and that anomalies were inevitable unless this fact was recognised in arranging offsets.

487 **We recommend** that, for the purpose of offsetting, social security benefits should be divided into categories; that the benefits in each category should be deducted in assessing the corresponding portion of the tort award; and that there should be no carry over between categories.

488 By a majority, **we also recommend** that, for the purpose of offsetting, there should be three categories of social security benefits – those compensating for loss of earnings, for expenses, and for non-pecuniary loss. Our Chairman, Lord Cameron, Mrs Brooke and Mr Marshall think that there should be only two categories; their views are set out in a minority opinion at the end of this chapter.

489 If social security benefits were divided into three categories and deducted without any carry over between categories, the total deduction might not be as great as if they were divided into only two categories. A consequence would be that the total amount of compensation, including both social security benefits and tort damages, would be slightly higher on the majority approach than on the minority approach.

Categorisation of benefits
490 The main social security benefits payable in respect of personal injury may be divided into three categories as follows:

Compensation for loss of income	*Compensation for expenses*	*Compensation for non-pecuniary loss*
Sickness benefit	Attendance allowance	Disablement benefit
Invalidity benefit	Constant attendance allowance	Hospital treatment allowance
Non-contributory invalidity pension	Exceptionally severe disablement allowance	
Injury benefit	Mobility allowance	
Special hardship allowance	Death grant	
Unemployability supplement		
Industrial death benefit		
Widows' benefit		

We have suggested in this list that disablement benefit should be set off against compensation for non-pecuniary loss, and that the allowances payable as additions to disablement benefit should be divided between the categories according to their function. Under the present law, constant attendance allowance is disregarded; all the other allowances are treated as part of disablement benefit, and taken into account in assessing damages for loss of earnings. We think that hospital treatment allowance, which brings a disablement pension up to the 100 per cent level when the recipient is in hospital, should be deducted from damages for non-pecuniary loss, and all the other allowances allocated to loss of income or expenses.

491   All the benefits listed in the previous paragraph should in our view be fully taken into account. But special considerations apply to unemployment benefit, invalid care allowance, supplementary benefit, and family income supplement.

492   When as a result of the injury the plaintiff is unemployed and receives unemployment benefit the benefit diminishes the plaintiff's loss of income and so should be set off against it. But as unemployment benefit is payable only if the claimant is fit for work, we doubt whether the question of offset would often arise. One possible example might be where a man was not able to do his job as well as before because of an injury, and was made redundant although he was still fit for work.

493   Invalid care allowance is a taxable non-contributory benefit which is payable to men or single women who are unable to go out to work because they have to look after a severely disabled relative receiving attendance allowance or constant attendance allowance. It is in a different category from the other benefits because it is not payable to the plaintiff but to the person who is looking after him. In chapter 12, we considered how damages for services rendered by others should be assessed; we concluded that there could be no fixed rule which would be fair in every case; and that compensation should be assessed by the court on the basis of what was reasonable. We cannot therefore make specific provision for offsetting invalid care allowance; but we think that the payment of this allowance is one factor which should be taken into account by the court when assessing damages for the plaintiff's need for services.

494   Supplementary benefit received up to the date of the award diminishes the plaintiff's loss and should be deducted in the assessment of damages for past loss of income. But, after the award, the plaintiff will have his damages and these will be taken into account in deciding whether he is eligible for supplementary benefit. We think it follows that, in assessing the damages for future loss of income, supplementary benefit should not be taken into account. The same considerations apply to family income supplement.

495   Finally, we propose in chapter 27 the introduction of an allowance for all severely handicapped children, payable as an addition to child benefit. The majority of us think that it would be right to regard the new allowance as a benefit intended to compensate for expenses. By a majority, **we recommend** that the proposed allowance for severely handicapped children should be set off against damages for expenses, where a child succeeds in a tort claim for the injury which caused his handicap.

Contributory negligence

496   The majority of the Monckton Committee considered two ways in which social security benefits might be deducted in cases where tort compensation was reduced because of the plaintiff's contributory negligence. Either the full value of the benefits received might be deducted from the reduced damages, or the equivalent proportion might be so deducted. In a case where the total damages were £1,000, the benefits were £200, and there was 50 per cent contributory negligence, the alternative final tort awards would be:

either i $\frac{1}{2}$ (£1,000 – £200)=£400
or   ii $\frac{1}{2}$ (£1,000) – £200=£300

In either case the plaintiff would receive the benefits of £200 as well.

497   Most of us agree with the majority of the Committee that the first method of deduction would produce the fairer result. If the plaintiff had not been negligent, he would have received £800 in tort damages and £200 in social security benefits. It seems to us that considerations of fault are relevant only to the tort element of this compensation; and that the plaintiff who is 50 per cent contributorily negligent should receive half the tort element (£400), and the full social security element (£200).

498   With one dissentient, **we recommend** that, where damages are reduced on account of contributory negligence, only the equivalent proportion of the relevant social security benefits should be deducted.

Payments by an employer

499   Payments made by an employer to an injured employee, whether or not the employer is liable for the injury, may take several forms.

Ex gratia payments

500   There are *ex gratia* payments, by which we mean payments which the employer has no contractual obligation to make and are not a condition of the employee's service. Such payments are in our view in the nature of a gift. We think they should be left out of account in assessing damages. We certainly would not wish to discourage employers from making *ex gratia* payments, as might sometimes happen if they were deducted from damages so that the employee derived no benefit from them.

501   **We recommend** that *ex gratia* payments made to the plaintiff by his employer should continue to be left out of account in the assessment of damages, unless the employer is the defendant (see paragraph 536 below).

Occupational sick pay

502   Then, there are payments made by the employer to an injured employee under a contract of employment, or as a condition of service. Such payments may vary in amount and duration. We refer to them collectively as occupational sick pay.

503 Occupational sick pay diminishes the plaintiff's loss, and to avoid over compensation we think that it should normally be taken into account in the assessment of damages. There are, however, two circumstances which in our view justify making an exception to this rule. First, the employee may by his contract of service be under a contractual obligation to refund sick pay to his employer if he succeeds in recovering damages. Secondly, the employer may provide sick pay as a loan, on the express understanding that it is to be repaid if damages are recovered. The present law permits the plaintiff to recover the cost of sick pay from the defendant in these circumstances.

504 Arrangements of this sort seem to us to provide a legitimate means whereby an employer can, indirectly, recover the cost of sick pay from the person responsible for the injury to his employee (or probably from that person's insurers), without either putting the employee at a disadvantage or compensating him twice over. (They have no practical effect where the employer is also the defendant. Technically, the plaintiff recovers the cost of the sick pay from the employer as defendant, and repays it immediately to the employer as employer.)

505 **We recommend** that occupational sick pay should continue to be taken into account in the assessment of damages, unless either the plaintiff is by his contract of service under a contractual obligation to refund it from damages, or it was advanced by his employer as a loan on the express understanding that it would be repaid if damages were recovered.

506 In that our proposals amount to a clarification rather than an alteration of the present law, we are in agreement with the Law Commission (who recommended no change). Our recommendation also accords with the proposed recommendation of the Scottish Law Commission.

Repayment by 'custom and practice'

507 In some fields of employment, repayment of sick pay may be customary, even though it is not the subject of a contractual obligation or a loan agreement. In our view, this sort of uncertainty is unsatisfactory, particularly for the employee. We hope that, as a result of our proposals, those employers who now rely on repayment 'by custom and practice' will take steps to obtain the agreement of their employees to the insertion of an appropriate term in contracts of employment, or to a stipulation that sick pay is advanced as a loan to be repaid if damages are recovered.

Expenses saved

508 It was held by the Court of Appeal in *Shearman* v. *Folland* [1950] 2 K.B. 43 that expenses saved by the plaintiff as a result of his injury could be set off against damages, provided that the expenses concerned were equivalent in nature to the expenses being compensated. The plaintiff was an elderly woman who, until her injury, was accustomed to living in hotels. After her injury, she moved to a nursing home. The court held that, if evidence had been adduced to show what proportion of the nursing home fees was attributable

to board and lodging, a deduction of that amount from the damages could have been made. Beyond the common element of board and lodging, however, hotel expenses and nursing home fees were not equivalent in nature.

509 Like the Law Commission, who observed in their report that deductions from expenses saved were seldom a significant feature of a final assessment of damages, we see no reason to recommend a change in the rule in *Shearman* v. *Folland*. Apart from expenses which are equivalent in nature, and apart from the point in the following paragraph, we do not think there should be any deduction of expenses saved. If, for example, the plaintiff is no longer able to follow some expensive hobby because of his injury, that is part of his loss; and we do not think the saving should be taken into account in assessing damages. We think that the same principle should apply in Scotland, where there is no judicial authority on the deduction of expenses saved.

510 There is, however, one aspect of the present rule for deducting expenses saved which we think calls for change. In *Daish* v. *Wauton* [1972] 1 Q.B. 262, the Court of Appeal held that no deduction should be made in respect of maintenance provided by a public authority. The decision was based on an analogy with the majority view of the House of Lords in *Parry* v. *Cleaver* (see paragraph 517 below). We cannot help feeling that the analogy is misconceived. In chapter 12, we recommended that private medical expenses should be recoverable only where the plaintiff could show that for medical reasons it was reasonable for him to incur them. In the light of this decision, and of our conclusion that tort and state compensation should be co-ordinated, we think that the rule in *Daish* v. *Wauton* should be reversed.

511 Most social security benefits are reduced when the beneficiary is receiving long term treatment in hospital under the National Health Service. Unless the present rule was reversed, the effect of our proposals for the full offset of benefits would be that the defendant would have to make up the reduction. This would lead to over compensation.

512 **We recommend** that the value of maintenance provided by a public authority should be taken into account in the assessment of damages.

First party insurance

513 It is well established under the present law that benefits received under a contract of insurance should not be deducted from damages for personal injury. As regards damages following death, the Fatal Accidents Act 1976, the Damages (Scotland) Act 1976, and the Fatal Accidents (Northern Ireland) Order 1977 specifically provide that insurance money shall not be taken into account.

514 The leading English case is *Bradburn* v. *Great Western Railway Co* (1874) L.R. 10 Ex. 1, in which Baron Piggott said, '. . . there is no reason or justice in setting off what the plaintiff has entitled himself to under a contract with third persons . . .' The Scottish Law Commission said in their Memorandum

No 21 that, although there was no direct authority on the point in relation to claims for personal injury, it was not the practice of the Scottish courts to deduct accident insurance benefits.

515 Payments under a private insurance contract are left out of account in assessing damages in most foreign legal systems, although in the Netherlands they are taken into account in fatal accident claims. We do not think that any change in the present law in the United Kingdom is necessary. Payments under a private insurance contract are in our view to be regarded as paid for by the beneficiary himself; and we do not think it would be right to deprive him of the benefit of them. This was also the view of both the Law Commissions.

516 **We recommend** that payments received under a first party contract of insurance should continue to be left out of account in the assessment of damages. We deal separately, at paragraph 529 below, with permanent health insurance taken out by an employer for an employee or for his employees collectively.

Occupational pensions

Occupational disability pensions
517 It was held by a majority of the House of Lords in *Parry* v. *Cleaver* [1970] A.C. 1 that a disability pension, whether or not discretionary and whether or not contributory, should be left out of account in assessing a plaintiff's lost earnings. The decision was influenced by the fact that, in the case of damages following death, it is provided by statute that all pensions should be disregarded.

518 The majority and minority opinions in *Parry* v. *Cleaver* reflected two distinct views of the nature of occupational disability pensions. The majority argued that a disability pension should be regarded as a form of first party insurance, which was in large measure paid for – either directly in the form of contributions, or indirectly in lieu of higher wages – by the beneficiary himself. (A benefit paid for exclusively by the employee would not fall within the statutory definition of an occupational pension.) The minority view was that an occupational pension should be regarded as a benefit provided by the employer, analogous to sick pay; and that it should be deducted from damages because it diminished the plaintiff's actual loss.

519 We do not think either of these views exactly reflects the realities of occupational pensions provision. Although the relative proportions may vary, most disability pensions are financed partly by the employer and partly by the employee. As was pointed out in *Parry* v. *Cleaver*, this is true even of non-contributory schemes, since pensions are in practice part of the remuneration taken into account by employees in choosing jobs, and – increasingly – in pay negotiations.

520 On balance, we think that it would be nearer the truth to regard occupational disability pensions as benefits provided by the employee rather than by the employer. **We recommend** that occupational disability pensions should

continue to be left out of account in the assessment of damages for loss of earnings. In this respect, we are in agreement with the Law Commission and the Scottish Law Commission.

521   Our conclusion that disability pensions should be left out of account relates only to pensions provided under occupational pension schemes. These pensions are entirely separate from the state invalidity benefits, which as we have already indicated, should in our view be deducted from damages. Our conclusion also relates only to the assessment of damages for lost earnings. We now turn to the assessment of damages for lost pension.

Occupational retirement pensions
522   It was conceded in *Parry* v. *Cleaver* that occupational disability pensions should be taken into account in assessing damages for loss of a retirement pension – for example, where the plaintiff, after completing his service, would have received a full retirement pension rather than a lower disability pension. Lord Reid said:

'. . . with regard to the period after retirement we are comparing like with like. Both the ill-health pension and the full retirement pension are the products of the same insurance scheme; his loss in the later period is caused by his having been deprived of the opportunity to continue in insurance so as to swell the ultimate product of that insurance from an ill-health to a retirement pension.'

523   We agree with this reasoning. **We recommend** that occupational disability pensions should continue to be taken into account in the assessment of damages for loss of retirement pension.

Occupational widows' pensions
524   The effect of the new state pension scheme is that a widow of a member of an occupational scheme which is not contracted out of the state scheme can look to receive such benefits as the scheme provides in addition to any state widow's benefit to which she may be entitled. Benefits – if any – provided for widows by these occupational schemes may take the form either of a pension or of a lump sum.

525   In the light of our decision that occupational disability pensions should be left out of account in assessing damages, we think that any benefits provided for widows by participating occupational schemes should also be disregarded. (We have proposed earlier in this chapter that state widows' benefits should be fully taken into account.)

526   The position regarding widows of members of contracted out occupational pension schemes is, however, more complicated. A contracted out scheme will have to provide a widow with a pension equal to at least half of the guaranteed minimum pension accruing to her husband at the date of his death. The state widows' benefit will make up the difference between this minimum level of occupational widows' pension and the full state benefit which would have been payable to the widow if her husband had not been a member of a contracted out scheme.

116

527 We think the right course would be simply to deduct from damages the full equivalent state benefit – that is, half the guaranteed minimum pension accruing to the husband at the time of his death, plus the amount paid to the widow by the state. This solution would in our view take into account both the need to avoid double compensation, and the need to preserve benefits paid for by the widow's husband.

528 **We recommend** that widows' benefits provided by occupational pension schemes which are not contracted out of the state scheme should be left out of account in the assessment of damages; and that, in the case of contracted out schemes, only the full equivalent state benefit should be deducted.

Permanent health insurance

529 We referred to permanent health insurance in chapter 6, and explained that policies covering employees as a rule provide long term benefits which take over after occupational sick pay ceases – often after six months. Although we recognise that these benefits are not paid for directly by the employee, we think that it would be fair to leave them out of account in assessing damages. As we have argued in the case of non-contributory pension schemes, long term cover of this sort is in practice part of the employee's remuneration, so that he may be said to pay for it indirectly. **We recommend** that benefits provided under a policy of permanent health insurance taken out by an employer for his employees should be left out of account in the assessment of damages.

530 If permanent health insurance is taken out by the insured person himself, for example, by a self employed person, we think that as with other forms of first party insurance the proceeds should be left out of account in assessing damages.

Private benevolence

531 Like both the Law Commissions, we are in no doubt that charitable gifts and other donations to the victim of a personal injury, or to his dependants, should be left out of account in assessing damages. This is the present law throughout the United Kingdom. The justification may be found in the words of Lord Reid in *Parry* v. *Cleaver:*

> 'It would be revolting to the ordinary man's sense of justice, and therefore contrary to public policy, that the sufferer should have his damages reduced so that he would gain nothing from the benevolence of his friends or relations or of the public at large, and that the only gainer would be the wrongdoer.'

In this category of benefits we would include not only charitable gifts and private donations, but also payments made by trade unions and friendly societies.

532 Subject to the recommendation in paragraph 536, **we recommend** that charitable gifts and other donations to the plaintiff should continue to be left out of account in the assessment of damages.

Payments by the defendant

533   The Scottish Law Commission suggested in their Memorandum No 21 that the argument for discounting gifts to the injured party might be less strong where the defendant was himself the giver. They cited as an example the case of *Dougan* v. *Rangers Football Club Limited* 1974 S.L.T. (Sh. Ct.) 34. The action was brought by the children of a person killed in an accident at a football ground. It was held that the payments received by the children from a disaster fund set up after the accident should not be taken into account, even though the defendants had themselves contributed to the fund.

534   The Scottish Law Commission reached the provisional conclusion, in line with this decision, that no exception should be made to the general rule that private benevolence should be disregarded. We understand, however, that having reconsidered the matter they now take the view that payments by the defendant should be taken into account in assessing damages, in the absence of an express contractual provision to the contrary. They feel in particular that, if such payments were always to be disregarded, potential defendants might become more reluctant to make them.

535   In general, we agree with the Scottish Law Commission's final view. We think that it probably reflects the existing law in the rest of the United Kingdom that – in the absence of an express contractual provision to the contrary – payments made by the defendant should be taken into account in the assessment of damages. But this should not apply if, as was the case in *Dougan* v. *Rangers Football Club*, the payment is in the form of a contribution to a general fund, to be dispersed among a number of victims. We think that in these circumstances the plaintiff's share of the payment should be ignored.

536   **We recommend** that payments made by the defendant should be taken into account in the assessment of damages unless

either i   the payments were made subject to an express contractual provision that they would be repaid from any damages recovered;

or   ii   the payments were in the form of contributions to a general fund from which people other than the plaintiff also benefited.

Benefits derived from the deceased's estate

537   Under the present law in England, Wales and Northern Ireland, pecuniary benefits derived by a dependant of a deceased person from his estate are taken into account in assessing damages under the Fatal Accidents Acts. Usually, any deduction is unimportant because, if the sum would have been paid to the plaintiff in any event in the future (for example, under a will), it is not deducted in full. Instead, an allowance may be made for accelerated payment and certainty of receipt. Nor does the rule apply to payments under a life insurance policy, or to the use of a home or property. A full deduction is, however, made where the dependant receives a sum awarded to the estate of the deceased for non-pecuniary loss.

538   The Law Commission pointed out that the present rule could give rise to unfairness, for example by penalising the widow of a man who saved by

buying shares as opposed to one who saved by taking out life insurance. A circuit judge told us that he had always considered it a serious injustice that the widow of a careful and thrifty man should receive less under the Fatal Accidents Acts than the widow of a spendthrift whose net income was the same but who managed to save none of it. We agree with the Law Commission that benefits derived from the deceased's estate should be disregarded in assessing damages for lost dependency. This is already the law in Scotland, under section 1(5) of the Damages (Scotland) Act 1976.

539 **We recommend** that, in England, Wales and Northern Ireland, as under the present law in Scotland, benefits derived from the deceased's estate should be disregarded in the assessment of damages for lost dependency.

The effect of our proposals

540 The main change proposed in this chapter is that relevant social security benefits should be fully taken into account in the assessment of tort damages. Most other payments would be treated as at present.

541 The elimination of overlap between tort and social security would bring about a substantial saving in costs. The effect of fully offsetting benefits presently available would be to reduce the cost of tort compensation by about £38 million a year, out of a total of £202 million a year. A further reduction of about £19 million a year would result from full offsetting of the new benefits we propose (primarily those for work and motor vehicle injuries).

542 The full offset of social security benefits is only one of a number of the changes in tort compensation we propose which would affect the levels of individual awards.

MINORITY OPINION ON CATEGORISATION OF SOCIAL SECURITY BENEFITS

by our Chairman, Lord Cameron, Mrs Brooke and Mr Marshall

543 We are not fully in agreement with the majority views expressed in paragraphs 486 to 490 and 495. For the purpose of offsetting social security benefits in the assessment of tort damages, we think that there should be only two classes of benefits, corresponding to the familiar two classes of damages – pecuniary and non-pecuniary. Most of the benefits fall readily into the one class or the other.

544 There are, however, certain benefits which cannot be readily placed in such a classification, because in some cases they compensate for pecuniary loss and in others for non-pecuniary loss: it depends on what is done with the money in each particular case. For instance, attendance allowance is available for paying the cost of hiring attendance, but the injured person does not have to use the money in that way. There may be no hiring, the attendance being provided free of charge by a kind relative or friend, in which case there is no expense but the injured person suffers the worry and humiliation of imposing

a burden on the relative or friend and incurring a moral indebtedness. The attendance allowance compensates, in one way or the other, for the plaintiff's need for attendance. If his claim for pecuniary loss includes an item for past or expected future expenses of hiring or otherwise paying for attendance, the attendance allowance should be offset against that item. Subject to that, the attendance allowance should be taken into account in the assessment of the non-pecuniary loss. The judge in assessing the damages for non-pecuniary loss would take into account the plaintiff's need for attendance, and as against that he would also take into account the fact that the plaintiff is receiving and will receive the attendance allowance, which will be available for meeting attendance expenses, if any are incurred, and otherwise as compensation for the hardship of needing attendance and being a burden on the family.

545 The same considerations apply to constant attendance allowance and to exceptionally severe disablement allowance.

546 Similarly, mobility allowance cannot be readily placed in the classification, because it is available for paying the cost of transport but does not have to be spent in that way. The injured plaintiff can spend the allowance in other ways and do without transport or have transport provided for him by kind relatives or friends, who would often refuse an offer of payment. But in one way or another the mobility allowance compensates for the plaintiff's lack of mobility. If his claim for pecuniary loss includes an item for past or expected future cost of transport, the mobility allowance should be offset against that item. Subject to that, the mobility allowance should be taken into account in the assessment of the non-pecuniary loss. The judge in assessing the non-pecuniary loss would take into account the plaintiff's lack of mobility, and as against that he would take into account the fact that the plaintiff is receiving and will receive the mobility allowance, which will be available for meeting transport expenses, if any are incurred, and otherwise as compensation for the hardship of having to have transport provided for him or else be immobile.

547 The proposed new weekly allowance for a severely handicapped child would be available primarily as compensation for the extra expense caused by his condition, but, if it was more than the expense, the excess would be some slight compensation for the hardship. The allowance should not be left out of account but it would not make much if any difference, because it would be wholly or mainly used up in meeting the expenses.

548 We explain elsewhere (chapter 15, paragraph 726) our view that in the assessment of the damages for non-pecuniary loss, which essentially depends on an impression of what is reasonable and not on any precise calculation, the relevant social security benefits should be offset not by capitalisation and deduction but by being taken into account in forming the impression as to what is reasonable in all the circumstances.

CHAPTER 14
The form of damages

549 At present, damages invariably take the form of a lump sum. In this chapter, we consider whether it would be desirable to introduce a system of periodic payments for certain types of loss. The chapter is in three sections, dealing with damages for past pecuniary loss, future pecuniary loss and non-pecuniary loss.

PAST PECUNIARY LOSS

550 As regards damages for past pecuniary loss (special damages), we see no reason to depart from the present practice. Losses which are a thing of the past by the time a claim comes to be tried or settled should be compensated once and for all. The sums involved are usually a matter of record; and even in cases which go for trial they are commonly agreed between the partie's solicitors.

551 **We recommend** that damages for past pecuniary loss should continue to be awarded as a lump sum.

552 In principle, all pecuniary losses up to the date of the award should be regarded as past losses; but in practice the loss agreed or fixed usually covers only losses incurred before the commencement of the trial. This difference is seldom significant, since most personal injury trials are completed in a single day. But if judgment is reserved for more than a few days, some addition would naturally be made for pecuniary losses incurred between the date of trial and the date of judgment.

FUTURE PECUNIARY LOSS

553 Only about 8 per cent of tort payments include compensation for pecuniary loss extending beyond the date of trial or settlement. But the injuries which give rise to such claims are often serious or fatal; and individual awards tend to be substantial. Nearly 20 per cent of all tort compensation is for future pecuniary loss.

554 It is in considering the form of compensation for future pecuniary loss that major and difficult issues arise; and we are not agreed on whether provision should be made for periodic payments. The views of the majority, who are in favour of provision being made in cases of death or serious and lasting injury,

121

are set out below. Lord Cameron and Mr Marshall consider that no such provision should be made. Their views are set out in a minority opinion at the end of this chapter.

Periodic payments – the majority view

555 The main component of a claim for future pecuniary loss is, almost invariably, loss of income or, in fatal cases, lost dependency. The plaintiff's loss is therefore in periodic form, whether it is made up of weekly wages, a monthly salary, or regular contributions to a family budget. Any expenses included in a claim for future pecuniary loss also tend to be regular outgoings.

556 It seems to most of us that the lump sum is not the most natural form of compensation for losses of this sort, given the objective of tort of restoring the plaintiff as closely as possible to his position before the injury. Yet it is at present the only form of tort compensation. In assessing damages, the court must translate a periodic future loss into a capital sum.

557 This process is inevitably inexact. The court must compare the plaintiff's expected income with the income which he might have enjoyed if he had not been injured. Allowance must be made for the likely duration of incapacity, and for the chances of promotion or increase in earnings; and, on the other hand, for the chances of loss of earnings, unemployment, unconnected illness or death. The court must also make assumptions about future economic conditions. In particular, it must make some assumptions about future rates of inflation, tax, and return on invested capital.

558 None of these factors is certain. The plaintiff may live for a longer or shorter period than was assumed; his medical condition may improve or deteriorate unexpectedly; he may lose his job or fail to find another; or he may be unable to derive the hoped-for return on his investment. As a result, he may be extensively over compensated or under compensated.

559 In one sort of case, which the Law Commission have termed a 'chance' case, a degree of error is inevitable. Suppose, for example, that the court is satisfied that there is a 50 per cent chance that the plaintiff will develop epilepsy as a result of his injury at some time in the future. All the court can do is to assess the damages appropriate if he is to develop epilepsy and the damages appropriate if he is not, and take a half way figure. If, in the event, the plaintiff does develop epilepsy, he will have been under compensated. If he does not, he will have been over compensated.

560 The lump sum is said, however, to have a number of advantages. Among those urged upon us was finality in litigation. A lump sum completely disposes of a tort claim. This is said to be in the interest both of the parties and of the community, in that there is an end of legal dispute and an end of expense. The defendant can discharge his liability fully and then forget the matter. In practice, this means that his insurer can close his file without incurring the expense (which would ultimately be reflected in higher premiums) of continued administration. The plaintiff, if he is not too badly injured, can concentrate his

efforts on recovery and put his injury and his grievance behind him. Because people like to finish with their claims a final lump sum award is said to promote settlements, and thus to help to contain the cost of the tort system.

561   The lump sum is also said to give freedom of choice. Although the compensation is awarded for future pecuniary loss, the plaintiff may, if he wishes, spend all or a large part of it immediately. He may, for example, use it to buy a house or to pay off his existing mortgage; or to buy a business; or simply to purchase some luxury which he could not otherwise afford but which may give him pleasure that to some extent makes up for his loss.

562   Some information about the use people make of lump sum awards was provided by our personal injury survey. The sample was of recipients of tort compensation generally, not just of those who recovered compensation for future pecuniary loss. Most of the sums involved were small. The money was most commonly spent on current living expenses or on a holiday or other luxuries. More than one third of those who responded used part or all of the money in each of these ways. Thirteen per cent banked at least some of their award. Only 5 per cent invested any of it.

563   We noted the results of research into the use made of lump sums won on the football pools, recorded in 'The Pools Winners' by Stephen Smith and Peter Razzell.[9] The average amount covered by the sample was much larger than that in the tort claims covered by the personal injury survey. Over three quarters of the sample of 89 winners invested half or more of their winnings, although most of them also purchased a house and gave some part of the money to relatives. New cars, holidays, consumer goods and luxuries also featured largely in the spending. Nearly half of the winners in the sample were advised what to do with their money by the pools companies.

564   In the less serious cases, we think, the arguments in favour of lump sums should normally prevail. There is no doubt that any system of periodic payments would require more elaborate and expensive administration than the present system of lump sum awards; and although, as we point out in paragraph 580, we would not rule out periodic payments otherwise than for serious and long term pecuniary losses, we would not expect such cases to be very common. It is in the interests of the community that most of the smaller tort claims, even for future pecuniary loss, should be finally, and so far as possible quickly, disposed of.

565   Most of us feel, however, that in cases of death or serious and lasting injury the arguments in favour of lump sums are not convincing. The finality of the lump sum may operate to the plaintiff's disadvantage if the forecast on which it is based proves erroneous – for example by overstating his chances of physical recovery or underestimating the effect of inflation on income from his invested damages. Its relative immediacy may not be preferable to the provision of assured long term financial support, either from the point of view of the plaintiff or from the point of view of the community who have to support him if his damages prove inadequate. Indeed, the payment of supplementary benefit to a person whose damages were exhausted would be a form of double

compensation paid for by taxpayers. Finally, the freedom of choice offered by the lump sum is something which the plaintiff would not have enjoyed if he had not been injured.

566 By contrast, periodic payments seem to us to offer important advantages in serious cases, although we recognise that it would not be practicable to eliminate all the uncertainties of awards of damages for future pecuniary loss.

567 Periodic payments would, first of all, restore the plaintiff more closely to his original position than would a lump sum.

568 Secondly, periodic payments would enable account to be taken of some of the actual, rather than forecast, changes after the trial. If a partially incapacitated plaintiff suffered a deterioration in his medical condition so that he became completely unable to work, it would be possible, if suitable review procedures could be established, to adjust his compensation accordingly. Similarly, if his condition improved so that he could take a better paid job than was first thought, his compensation might be reduced. In this respect, periodic payments would produce fairer results both for the plaintiff and for the defendant. Certain changes in economic conditions after the trial might also be taken into account. For example, provided that the necessary financial arrangements could be devised, the payments might be inflation proofed.

569 Thirdly, if periodic payments were taxed as earned income, they would avoid the high rates of tax which, by reason of the investment income surcharge, may be payable on the income derived from the investment of large lump sum awards. This difficulty could become more acute in the future if tort awards in the form of a lump sum were to become subject to a wealth tax.

570 Fourthly, other compensation received by the plaintiff could be more accurately offset from damages if the damages were awarded in the form of periodic payments. Most of the benefits which we think should be offset are themselves periodic; and they are likely to vary in amount from time to time. Broad adjustment of the periodic payments in line with changes in the level of benefits would be more accurate than any method of allowing for such changes in advance in the assessment of the lump sum. We consider this question in more detail in the next chapter.

571 Finally, we note the view expressed by the Royal College of Physicians and Surgeons of Glasgow, in their evidence, that the dangers of periodic payments prolonging incapacity were outweighed by their advantages in relieving financial anxiety.

572 We note the conclusion reached by the Law Commission after consultations on their Working Paper No 41 that, 'the introduction of a system of periodic payments would meet with vehement opposition from almost every person or organisation actually concerned with personal injury litigation'. But the Law Commission were working within, and consulting on the basis of, narrower terms of reference than our own. The evidence we received reflected a somewhat different balance of opinion. In terms of numbers, just over half of those who commented on the lump sums and periodic payments issue were in favour of

some form of periodic payments for future pecuniary loss. The BIA told us
that, although they were not in favour of periodic payments and stressed the
difficulties of inflation proofing, the commercial insurance market could if
necessary service a system of periodic payments.

573   By a majority, **we recommend** that provision should be made, in accordance
with the following proposals, for damages in the form of periodic payments
for future pecuniary loss caused by death or serious and lasting injury. We are
under no illusions as to the practical difficulties which would be posed by our
recommendation; and it is to these that we now turn.

Periodic payments – the majority proposals

Scope of the scheme
574   We have indicated that in our view, subject to our recommendation
in paragraph 580, a scheme of periodic payments should be confined to cases
of death or serious and lasting injury. The injury should in our view be one which,
subject to our proposals for declaratory judgments (paragraphs 584 and 585),
affects earning capacity or otherwise causes substantial pecuniary loss. Losses
of an annual value of less than 5 per cent of average annual earnings, and those
likely to last for less than four or five years from the date of the award, should
not normally attract periodic payments.

Compulsory or optional?
575   In considering whether such payments should be compulsory or optional,
we were mindful of the fact that some successful plaintiffs would probably prefer
lump sums, even when presented with an alternative. The fund administering
indexed annuities in France (the *Caisse Centrale de Réassurance*) reported that
only 44 annuities were granted in 1975, and 57 in 1976. But we did not think this
was the end of the argument. Opinions as to the merits of lump sums in serious
cases might well change if the results of our scheme were favourable, and if
inflation continued to erode the value of income from invested capital. We have
already pointed out, too, that the state has an interest in the form of compensation for pecuniary loss. In the field of occupational pensions, where somewhat
similar considerations applied, Parliament decided to insist on the preservation
of accrued benefits on leaving employment, and to prevent the return of contributions as a lump sum. We consider that the benefits of periodic payments for
pecuniary loss caused by serious and fatal injuries are such that the courts
should be bound to award them, unless the plaintiff can show that in the circumstances of his particular case a lump sum award would be more appropriate.
He might seek to satisfy the court, for example, that he was in a good position
to use a lump sum to set up a business, which would itself provide him with a
source of income at least as favourable as periodic payments.

576   **We recommend** that the court should be obliged to award damages for
future pecuniary loss caused by death or serious and lasting injury in the form
of periodic payments, unless it is satisfied, on the application of the plaintiff,
that a lump sum award would be more appropriate.

Settlements

577   We do not think it would be practicable or justifiable to prevent a plaintiff from settling his claim before trial for a lump sum. But we think it should be the duty of the plaintiff's professional adviser to point out the advantages of periodic payments as a form of compensation for pecuniary loss caused by death or serious and lasting injury (especially when the payments were inflation proofed according to our proposals in paragraphs 598 to 608); and to make it clear that the courts would normally award periodic payments in such cases. We would certainly hope that settlements would increasingly take the form of periodic payments as their advantages became more widely appreciated. But we recognise that in a residue of cases, and particularly in the early days of a scheme of periodic payments, settlements would be likely to continue to take the form of a lump sum.

578   **We recommend** that the parties in a claim for future pecuniary loss caused by death or serious and lasting injury should remain free to negotiate a settlement for damages in the form either of a lump sum or of periodic payments; but that the plaintiff's professional adviser should be under a duty to point out the advantages of periodic payments and the normal court practice in such cases.

579   Our proposals do not envisage any change in the present requirement of English law that settlements reached on behalf of children should be approved by the courts. As a rule, we think periodic payments for future pecuniary loss would be to the advantage of a seriously injured child; and we would expect the courts to take this consideration into account when considering settlements. But the court would not be precluded from approving a lump sum settlement, even for a serious and lasting injury to a child; and if the court awarded periodic payments, there would be nothing to prevent an application for commutation being made. In Scotland, there is unfortunately no equivalent machinery for approving settlements reached on behalf of children. We hope that this will be one of the matters considered by the Procedure Committee of the Court of Session, under the chairmanship of Lord Kincraig, in its review of procedure in personal injuries litigation.

Discretionary awards

580   Although we believe that the need for periodic payments is greatest in cases of death or serious and lasting injury, we would not wish to exclude them in other circumstances, notwithstanding our comments in paragraph 564 above. Accordingly, **we recommend** that the court should have a discretion to award damages in the form of periodic payments for future pecuniary loss caused by injuries which are not serious and lasting. As regards settlements, we recognise that the parties would be unlikely to agree on periodic payments for a loss caused by injuries which were not serious and lasting, unless in the circumstances of the particular case the court would probably exercise this discretion.

Commutation

581   We have recommended that the plaintiff in a claim following death or serious and lasting injury should be entitled to ask the court for an award of a lump sum rather than periodic payments. We think that the recipient of an

award of periodic payments should also be entitled to apply for commutation for a lump sum at a later stage. We consider that the court should have a discretionary power to grant or refuse such an application, and that in exercising its discretion it should adopt the same criteria as for applications for lump sums at the time of the award. It should be open to the defendant to support or oppose the application. The commuted amount should be the value of the plaintiff's expectation of periodic payments in the future, based on his circumstances (for example, his medical condition) at the time of the commutation. It should be calculated by a multiplier method along the lines discussed in the next chapter.

582   **We recommend** that the recipient of an award of damages in the form of periodic payments should be entitled to apply to the court for its commutation at any stage during the currency of the award, based on his total future expectation of periodic payments in the light of his circumstances when the application is considered; that the court should have a discretionary power to grant or refuse the application; and that, in exercising this discretion, the court should apply the same criteria as for applications for lump sums at the time of the award.

583   In the case of a settlement, we think the consent of both parties should be essential before the agreed form of compensation was altered from periodic payments to a lump sum. It would naturally be open to the parties to make a new agreement at any stage. But the court would not normally have any jurisdiction except for settlements reached on behalf of children in England and Wales.

Declaratory judgments
584   We think provision should be made for declaratory judgments, where the plaintiff is suffering from a serious and lasting injury which is not, at the time of the trial, causing him pecuniary loss. The declaration should define the relevant injury, and the proportion, if any, of contributory negligence. If the injury later caused the plaintiff pecuniary loss, it would be open to him, under the procedure which we describe below, to apply for review of his award. **We recommend** that, where the plaintiff is suffering from a serious and lasting injury which is not, at the time of the trial, causing him pecuniary loss, the court should, subject to the recommendation in paragraph 585, be able to give a declaratory judgment.

585   Our proposals for declaratory judgments would meet the same need as the Law Commission's proposals for provisional awards. The Law Commission suggested that these should be made only where the defendant was a public authority, or was insured in respect of the plaintiff's claim, or was secured against third party risks by means of a deposit under section 144 of the Road Traffic Act 1972 (see chapter 18, paragraph 971). We think that declaratory judgments should be restricted in a similar way. **We recommend** that declaratory judgments should be given only if the defendant is a public authority, or is insured in respect of the plaintiff's claim. (We recommend in chapter 18 that the deposit provision contained in section 144 of the Road Traffic Act 1972, and equivalent legislation in Northern Ireland, should be abolished.) Only a small number of tort claims would in practice be excluded by this recommendation from the scope of declaratory judgments, since few claims are made against uninsured individuals.

Review

586 To make it possible to realise the advantage that periodic payments can take account of actual changes following trial, we think that a review procedure would be essential. Many successful plaintiffs also receive social security benefits in respect of the same injury. These are subject to review. It would be desirable from the plaintiff's point of view if both periodic tort damages and benefits were subject to the same – or at least consistent – review. We therefore considered whether this should be undertaken by the existing social security tribunals.

587 We concluded, however, that we should not recommend this course. The review of periodic tort payments would necessarily involve three parties (the plaintiff, the defendant or his insurers, and DHSS); and we did not think that this tripartite adversarial structure would be appropriate for the social security tribunals. The fact that insurers would almost always be legally represented at a hearing would mean that the plaintiff would often be at a disadvantage unless legal aid was made available. This would be a departure from present policy regarding representation at administrative tribunals which we do not feel it is for us to recommend in the narrow context of periodic tort payments. But anyway, we think it unlikely that Parliament would accept the use of social security tribunals for the resolution of private disputes.

588 It seems to us that the courts are better fitted to handle adversarial disputes of this sort; and we do not think that the number of reviews would impose an intolerable burden. In England and Wales, most awards of periodic payments would be made by the High Court, since county courts cannot handle claims worth more than £2,000 in all. In Northern Ireland, the existing limit to the jurisdiction of the county court, of £1,000, would have a corresponding effect. We think the review of a High Court order should be carried out by a Master if in London, and by the District Registrar if on circuit. Any county court orders should be reviewed by a judge in the same county court. In Scotland, where there is no equivalent of a Master, we consider that review should in all cases be carried out by a judge of the court which made the order. For practical reasons, we think it preferable that only the Court of Session should have power to award and review periodic payments.

589 **We recommend** that awards in the form of periodic payments should be subject to review by the courts.

590 In principle, if periodic payments were to keep pace with the actual extent of the victim's pecuniary loss, it would be desirable to provide a broadly based review which could consider such factors as changes in other compensation for the injury (such as social security benefits), and in the victim's tax liability, as well as changes in his medical condition. But we consider that a comprehensive review along these lines would be too complicated, at least initially. It would be necessary, for example, to take into account any increase in the plaintiff's income if he returned to work. This would lead to the further problem of whether his compensation should then be reduced by the full amount of his increase in earnings, or by some lesser amount, or whether some form of earnings rule should be introduced.

591   **We recommend** that the review of an award in the form of periodic payments should be confined to changes in the plaintiff's pecuniary loss brought about by changes in his medical condition, and to cases which are the subject of a declaratory judgment. (We discuss below arrangements for the automatic revision of awards to take account of changes in the value of money and in the general level of earnings.)

Registration of settlements

592   We think that where a settlement has been reached the parties should be able to use the review procedure. **We recommend** that, if both the parties to a settlement for damages in the form of periodic payments wish its terms to be subject to the review procedure, they should be able either to register the settlement with the court or to ask the court to make an order by consent. As regards changes falling outside the scope of review (for example, commutation), we think the consent of both parties should be essential.

Premature death

593   We have recommended in chapter 12 that compensation for future pecuniary loss suffered by a living plaintiff should be based on his pre-accident expectation of life. Our recommendation is designed to ensure that, where a person dies prematurely as a result of his injury, his dependants should not be left without compensation during the 'lost years' when he would, but for his injury, have still been alive. Special arrangements would be necessary to achieve this result where an injured person recovered damages in his lifetime in the form of periodic payments, and then died prematurely (whereupon the payments would cease). We think that the best course would be to allow his dependants to claim damages in their own action for the years which would have remained to the deceased but for his injury, even though we recognise that this would be a departure from the usual rule that more than one action should not be brought for the same injury. The dependants would need to establish only that the deceased died prematurely as a result of his injury. Under our proposals, the damages would normally be awarded in the form of periodic payments, although the dependants would have the right to apply to the court for a lump sum at the time of the trial, or for subsequent commutation.

594   **We recommend** that, where the recipient of an award in the form of periodic payments dies prematurely as a result of his injury, his dependants should be able to bring an action for lost dependency in respect of the years when but for his injury he would still have been alive.

Administration

595   The method of administration of the payments raises similar issues to those raised by the method of review. On the one hand it would be easier to arrange for the offset of social security benefits if DHSS (and the Department of Health and Social Services in Northern Ireland), administered the tort payments as well. But on the other hand this would impose new burdens on the public sector in respect of a private remedy.

596   We think that DHSS should not be asked to administer periodic tort payments, and that the administration of payments should be the responsibility of the defendant, or in practice usually his insurers. (We consider the position of the uninsured defendant below.) We have no reason to doubt that the insurers could provide the necessary machinery. Indeed, many companies already make a substantial number of regular monthly payments to occupational pensioners.

597   **We recommend** that periodic payments provided by insurance should be administered by insurers; and that payments should be made no less often than monthly.

Finance

598   If periodic payments are to provide the continuing income replacement which the seriously injured victim needs, we think it would be essential to protect their value against inflation. It is from this need, rather than from the periodic nature of the payments, that the problems of finance primarily stem.

599   The payments might be revalued in line with either average earnings or retail prices. Since damages for future pecuniary loss are largely intended to replace lost income, the movement of average earnings seems to us the fairer choice. The recipients of periodic damages would not enjoy a special advantage at a time when prices rose faster than earnings, but would share in the general increase in prosperity when, as we hope can be expected in the long term, earnings rose faster than prices. In other words, they would be protected from inflation to the same extent as the average earner.

600   **We recommend** that periodic payments should be revalued annually in line with the movement of average earnings.

601   We held a series of discussions with the BIA and Lloyd's about the difficulties posed by inflation proofed periodic payments. It became clear to us that conventional insurance could not be provided to cover the uncertain future liabilities associated with inflation proofed payments, and we examined other ways in which the risks might be covered.

602   We looked overseas. In France, the cost of inflation proofing compensation for the victims of motor vehicle injuries is met from a central fund, financed by a levy on insurance premiums which can be varied from time to time. There is no state guarantee. In Finland, periodic payments are also inflation proofed; but insurance companies are obliged to make them only until the limit of cover is reached.

603   We formed the view that there would be difficulties in assuring the solvency of a scheme if in times of high inflation its only recourse was to levy current premiums to meet excess liabilities. The market for the class of insurance might contract because of the size of the levy, leading to spiralling increases in premiums; or large insurance companies might decide to withdraw from the relevant class of business. We concluded that a viable scheme of inflation proofed compensation would require some form of government involvement.

We nevertheless rejected a suggestion made to us by the BIA that the Government should make available index linked bonds, in which insurers could invest in order to cover their inflation proofed liabilities; we did not feel able to recommend such a substantial innovation for the limited purpose of financing periodic tort payments.

604   We attempted to devise financial arrangements which either made government intervention unlikely, or gave the taxpayer at least an equal chance of making a profit or a loss. One possibility was to establish an independent, self-financing agency which, in return for a lump sum, would take over an insurer's commitment to make periodic payments. If the assumptions on which the lump sums were calculated proved seriously incorrect, so that the agency could not meet its liabilities, it could surcharge new business. In the last resort, it could call on government support. A second possibility was for insurers to be financially responsible for inflation proofed payments in the first instance, but able also to re-insure with an independent re-insurance agency against the risk of inflation exceeding a planned level. This agency could then surcharge new business if it found itself unable to meet its liabilities from its own funds, with recourse to a government guarantee if necessary.

605   The third possibility had a precedent in the contracting out provisions of the new state pensions scheme. Insurers would undertake to provide periodic payments escalating at one of two fixed rates (at present 5 per cent and $8\frac{1}{2}$ per cent). If the lower rate was chosen, the insurer would also pay a 'limited revaluation' premium to the Government. In return, the Government would supplement the payments in order to provide full inflation proofing in years when the inflation rate exceeded the fixed escalation. If the higher rate was chosen, the Government would again supplement the payments if necessary, but, in years when the inflation rate was lower than the fixed escalation, the Government would have the benefit of the difference. In either case, there would be an agreed minimum period of notice before the escalation rate could be changed.

606   We decided to reject both the schemes which would require a separate agency in favour of the fixed escalation scheme. Apart from its relative simplicity this scheme would have the advantage of following an established precedent. It is also the only one of the three options which could provide an equal chance of the Government making a profit or a loss. At the same time, the funds required to pay tort compensation would remain substantially in private hands, in keeping with the role of tort as a private remedy. There would be no need for insurers to make provision for meeting inflation proofed liabilities of uncertain extent.

607   We think the fixed escalation scheme could reasonably be regarded as a fair deal between insurers and the Government, although the Government has given no assurance that it would be prepared to participate. We would not ourselves wish to express a preference between the two types of partnership we have described. Both have been incorporated in the new pensions scheme, and we think that any choice between them in the field of periodic tort payments should be a matter for negotiation between insurers and the Government.

608   **We recommend** that periodic payments provided by insurance should be financed by a fixed escalation scheme based on the contracting out provisions of the Social Security Pensions Act 1975.

The uninsured defendant

609   In much of the foregoing, we have assumed that the defendant will be insured. Occasionally he will not be. If he is also impecunious, the plaintiff may be unable to recover the damages which he has been awarded. Our proposals for periodic payments would not overcome this problem. But it is one which already applies to damages generally.

610   The defendant might be uninsured but at the same time be able to command substantial resources. To safeguard an award of periodic payments in these circumstances, we think that the court should have a discretionary power to require the defendant to deposit with an insurance company a lump sum of an amount determined by the company. The income derived from this lump sum would then be inflation proofed, according to the arrangements we have described. The lump sum should be calculated by a multiplier method along the lines proposed in the next chapter. Where the defendant is a public authority carrying its own risks, we do not envisage that the courts would find it necessary to exercise their discretionary power.

611   **We recommend** that the court should have power to require an uninsured defendant to deposit a lump sum with an insurance company, in order to provide an income to meet an award for periodic payments; and that the income derived from this lump sum should be inflation proofed by the fixed escalation scheme (see paragraphs 605 to 608).

NON-PECUNIARY LOSS

612   We do not think that the arguments in favour of periodic payments apply with equal force to damages for non-pecuniary loss. Such damages are an arbitrary acknowledgment of an essentially unquantifiable loss. They are not intended to provide financial support; and we do not think there is the same need to take account of post-trial changes. Indeed, there is no rational basis for saying whether a particular award represents over compensation or under compensation, except by comparison with other awards.

613   We nevertheless considered whether there was a case for awarding damages for loss of faculty in the form of periodic payments. We had in mind a possible analogy with the industrial injuries scheme, under which disablement benefit is usually payable weekly to those whose disability is assessed at 20 per cent or more. But, in the light of our decision not to regard loss of faculty as a separate head of non-pecuniary damage, we rejected this possibility. Periodic payments are inevitably more complex, and more expensive to administer, than lump sums. We do not think it would be right to introduce them as a form of compensation for losses which are unrelated to financial loss. Many of our witnesses, including the TUC, the Medical Protection Society and the Industrial Law Society, took the same view.

614 **We recommend** that damages for non-pecuniary loss should continue to be awarded as a lump sum.

MINORITY OPINION ON PERIODIC PAYMENTS
by Lord Cameron and Mr Marshall

615 In order to explain our reasons for expressing in some detail the grounds of the minority's dissent we feel it is first necessary to set out what we understand to be the recommendations of the majority in summary form. They are as follows:

  i that in cases of serious and lasting injury or death, plaintiffs should receive from the court an award in the form of a lump sum, except for compensation for future pecuniary loss which shall be by award of periodic payments unless the plaintiff has satisfied the court a lump sum award would be more appropriate;

  ii that the parties in such cases should remain free to compromise the claim for a lump sum for all heads of damage prior to the action coming to trial;

  iii that the court should have a discretion to award periodic payments for future pecuniary loss for injuries which are not lasting and serious;

  iv that the plaintiff (but not the defendant) should have power to apply to commute a periodic payment award for a lump sum on showing good grounds to the court;

  v that either party should have the right to apply to the court for a review of a periodic payments award limited to those cases where there has been a change in the plaintiff's pecuniary loss brought about by changes in his medical condition;

  vi that the death of a plaintiff holding an award for periodic payments would give his dependants a fresh right of action against the defendant for lost dependency in respect of the years when, but for his injury, he would still have been alive;

  vii that payment of the award by the defendant or his insurers should be made at intervals no less than monthly, and the award itself should be indexed against inflation as set out in paragraphs 598 to 608;

  viii that an uninsured defendant might be required to deposit a lump sum with an insurance company to provide income for the periodic payments.

616 These proposals are both far reaching and complicated in operation. Their professed purpose is to remedy two shortcomings in the present system of assessment of damages for future loss of income or future expense. These are said to be:

  i that the lump sum, payments being based on uncertainties as to future physical condition and income position, will almost never succeed in producing compensation exactly matching the lost income or future expense;

  ii that in conditions of inflation, the plaintiff almost certainly will be the loser in that the lump sum award will not in the event replace the lost income unless it is increased by an amount sufficient to cover future inflation, and over-assessment of future inflation might leave the plaintiff over compensated.

617   When the Law Commission considered and reported on the proposed introduction of awards for periodic payments, the tentative conclusion was that the objections outweighed the possible advantages, but that consideration should be given to introducing provisional awards in the limited 'chance' or 'forecast' case – that is, where there is a risk of the onset at some uncertain future date of disability due to, say, epilepsy or osteo-arthritis or, on the other hand, to the uncertainty of recovery from an existing condition. We have no disagreement with the majority as to the possible use of declaratory judgments of potential liability in such cases. Our objection to the introduction of a periodic payments system is in the main in line with the view expressed by the Law Commission but on somewhat different specific grounds.

618   In support of the majority view it is asserted that:

 i At the date when judgment is given the uncertainties as to the future make it virtually certain that a lump sum assessed and awarded for future pecuniary loss will be wrong.

 ii Continuing inflation operates to prevent a lump sum award restoring the plaintiff financially to his pre-accident condition.

 iii The application of the income tax investment surcharge payable on the income from investment of the lump sum award will, unless the lump sum is invested with considerable skill, leave the plaintiff still further under compensated than results from inflation. Periodic payments can be regarded as earned income and this problem is avoided.

 iv Plaintiffs will in some cases fritter away their lump sum damages, and ultimately become a charge on the social security system.

 v Offsetting social security payments receivable in the future will be facilitated and capable of being exactly calculated as an offset against the damages award.

619   While we acknowledge that these arguments have force, they are not in our considered opinion of such weight as to warrant so radical a change in our system of assessment and payment of awards of damages for personal injuries. It is our view, based upon evidence given to us, that plaintiffs prefer lump sums to periodic payments, as is demonstrated in those few countries which have instituted such a system. The investigations made into other systems of compensation operated throughout the world appear to us to support the conclusion that lump sum awards are made and regarded as acceptable almost universally through the rest of the world. In such circumstances there is likely to be popular reaction against proposals restricting a plaintiff's long established and understood right to receive full compensation in a lump sum.

620   We have noted that there is opinion evidence, which should not be readily disregarded, that periodic payments tend to destroy initiative and produce lack of incentive towards rehabilitation.

621   The introduction of a periodic payments system must of necessity be accompanied by a review procedure to consider changed conditions and if necessary to alter the amount of the award. This in our opinion must lead to

an undesirable continuation of the adversarial process and relationship which is not in the plaintiff's best interests; as well as to a continuing uncertainty as to the ultimate limit of a defendant's liability. To convert a plaintiff into a pensioner of the defendant throughout the period of disability is an innovation which cannot be desirable even if practicable.

622 Further it is indisputable that all but a very small percentage of personal injury actions are at present settled by compromise agreement prior to the case coming to trial. It is our opinion that in the interests of all parties this should be so and that every incentive and encouragement should be given to the early and just settlement of claims. Introduction of a system of periodic payments would be likely in our view to have the reverse effect.

623 As we foresee it, more actions than before would proceed to trial and judgment, with consequent increase in costs and delay in settlement and receipt of compensation by the victim.

624 Plaintiffs will be faced with an undesirable enforced decision prior to trial whether to settle their whole claim on a lump sum basis on such terms as are offered by the defendant or his insurers, or of continuing to trial when, except for special circumstances, they will be required to receive at least part of their award in the form of periodic payments.

625 In addition, the legal advisers of a plaintiff will be faced with an undue burden in offering advice to their client as to whether to settle a claim or to proceed to seek an award of compensation measured in terms of period payments – so settlements out of court on a long term basis will tend to diminish rather than increase.

626 A periodic payments system will increase the cost of administering claims being dealt with in this way, so far as defendants or their insurers are concerned, and there will be further substantial costs incurred by one party or the other in obtaining continuing fresh medical evidence periodically in order to monitor changes in physical condition, and the legal costs involved in review hearings in court to argue and determine alterations in the amount of such awards. It seems to us unlikely as a practical issue that periodic payments will be involved to any substantial extent in out of court settlements.

627 Although lump sum awards may not at present or in the future produce exact payment of full compensation for future pecuniary loss, the view of the minority is that a closer approximation to achievement of full compensation on a lump sum basis than at present would be achieved by adopting one of the different multiplier methods discussed elsewhere in this report. It is our view that the adoption of such a procedure would go far to solving the problem of inflation and its influence upon awards and is preferable to the introduction of a system of periodic payments for future pecuniary loss. While it may be conceded that a lump sum award for future loss based on uncertainties at the date of trial as to future physical condition and future earnings prospect of the plaintiff does not produce exact compensation, this does not appear to have been a cause of serious complaint, until the comparatively recent onset of

inflation, the failure of the law to recognise and make allowances for its effect, and the very high incidence of liability to tax on the income from invested damages.

628   Further and in any event we do not believe that it is right to take away from a plaintiff his entitlement to receipt of the whole of his damages from a defendant in the form of a lump sum awarded by the court on trial and to compel him – against his will – to accept a series of periodic payments in its place. The action in tort or delict is designed to produce justice between the parties and we doubt the fairness of imposing on a defendant who may be uninsured a continuing liability for periodic payments of damages over many years, particularly when such damages are likely progressively to increase for the reasons mentioned above. Further, it is not to be assumed that every defendant will be insured and thus able to pass his liability for payment of periodic payments on to his insurers.

629   Finally, in the event of death of a claimant entitled to periodic payments, we doubt the fairness to a defendant of according to the dependants of a deceased plaintiff a fresh cause of action, quite apart from any consideration of the practical difficulties in the operation of such a procedure. We appreciate the argument that the defendant will not have paid his full liability by way of periodic payments to the deceased plaintiff, but to submit a defendant to a second and entirely fresh claim and possibly a second action seems to be undesirable.

630   For all these reasons, we are unable to accept the views of the majority and are not convinced that there are sufficient reasons for making such radical changes, for depriving plaintiffs of existing and long standing rights and for imposing a system of compensation which will in our view be cumbrous in operation, extravagant in administration, and inimical to the rapid and just settlement of claims. We therefore consider that damages for tort or delict should continue to be calculated by way of a lump sum under all heads of claim, but should be assessed with reference to the appropriate recommendations contained elsewhere in this report.

CHAPTER 15

The calculation of damages

631   This chapter is in four sections, dealing with the calculation of damages for past and future pecuniary loss, the assessment of damages for non-pecuniary loss taking account of social security offsets, and our proposals in practice.

PAST PECUNIARY LOSS

632   We are not proposing any change in the method of calculating damages for past pecuniary loss, although the amounts involved could be substantially affected by our recommendations on the heads of claim and on offsets. The plaintiff's loss of income in the period between the date of injury and the date of the award is calculated by taking the hypothetical income (net of tax and social security contributions) which he would have received, and deducting the net income which he has actually received (including any earnings, sick pay, and relevant social security benefits). Any damages for expenses are added. The resultant total is the amount of the damages for past pecuniary loss.

633   The calculation can be made from the facts, simply proved by evidence from the injured plaintiff, his employer, and DHSS. In practice, we see no reason why the amount of damages for past pecuniary loss should not in most cases continue to be agreed between the parties' solicitors.

634   **We recommend** that there should be no change in the present method of calculating damages for past pecuniary loss, except that relevant social security benefits should be deducted in full.

FUTURE PECUNIARY LOSS

635   The calculation of damages for future pecuniary loss is more complex. Later in this chapter we set out in detail the procedures which most of us think should be adopted. But first we describe the main features of the calculation.

The net annual loss

636   The starting point, common both to the present method and to our own proposals, is the plaintiff's net annual loss. In broad terms, the net annual loss suffered by a living plaintiff is equal to the annual value of his lost 'take home' earnings (that is, his lost earnings net of tax and social security contributions), plus the annual cost of any additional expenses resulting from the injury, less the annual value of relevant social security benefits. In fatal cases, the net annual

137

loss is – broadly – the amount which the deceased would have spent or applied for the benefit of his dependants, less the annual value of relevant social security benefits. The necessary figures for determining the net annual loss are usually obtained when the damages for past pecuniary loss are calculated.

637   Under the present law, adjustments to the net annual loss may be made for proved prospects of changes in the plaintiff's position. These may include both hypothetical changes which might have occurred if he had not been injured (for example, as a result of promotion), and changes which probably will occur in the period following injury (for example, as a result of retraining).

638   Under our proposals, some of these changes would be allowed for in other ways. In the case of an award in the form of periodic payments, possible changes in earnings resulting from a change in the plaintiff's medical condition would be covered by the review procedure. Other changes could be allowed for by specifying percentage changes in the payments at specified future dates. In the case of awards in the form of a lump sum, the method of calculation which we propose below could allow for prospective changes in take home earnings, at a constant annual percentage rate, without requiring any adjustment of the net annual loss.

639   There would remain, however, a variety of possible changes which could be taken into account only by an approximate adjustment of the net annual loss. We have in mind, for example, the partial loss of an occupational retirement pension suffered by a plaintiff who is unable to pay contributions after losing his job as a result of injury. The appropriate adjustment for a change of this sort would depend on the facts of the particular case, and in our view no rule could usefully be laid down.

640   Certain refinements of the calculation of the net annual loss would be necessary in order to take proper account of the effect of taxation. In particular, tax free social security benefits should be deducted from a figure which is net of tax, whereas taxable social security benefits should be deducted from a gross figure. We explore the effect of taxation later, in describing the procedure which most of us think should be adopted for determining the net annual loss.

641   **We recommend** that the starting point for the assessment of damages for future pecuniary loss should be the plaintiff's net annual loss, that is his net pecuniary loss at the date of the award adjusted as necessary and expressed as an annual figure.

642   By a majority, **we also recommend** that the net annual loss should be calculated according to the procedure set out in paragraphs 662 to 674. Our Chairman, Lord Cameron, Mrs Brooke and Mr Marshall do not agree; their views are set out in a minority opinion at the end of this chapter.

Periodic payments

643   Once the net annual loss had been obtained, the calculation of the initial amount of an award of periodic payments would be straightforward. On the assumption that periodic payments for future pecuniary loss would be taxed

as earned income in the hands of the recipient, the only step required would be to 'gross up' the net annual loss. In practice, we envisage that the amount needed before tax at the earned income rate to provide the plaintiff with a given amount of after tax income could readily be supplied to the court as a figure agreed between the parties' professional advisers.

644 **We recommend** that the initial annual amount of damages for future pecuniary loss in the form of periodic payments should be the gross equivalent of the net annual loss; and that the payments should be taxed as earned income in the hands of the recipient.

645 We recommended in the previous chapter that periodic payments for · future pecuniary loss should be revalued annually in line with the movement of average earnings. We think that, for practical reasons, this revaluation should apply to the gross amount of the payments. The net value of the payments would also be maintained, assuming that tax allowances as well as social security benefits would in the long term increase approximately in line with average earnings. It seems to us that this would be a reasonable assumption. Long term social security benefits must by statute be revised annually in line with either earnings or prices, whichever is more favourable to the recipient. In the long term, the revaluation could be expected to keep pace with earnings.

Lump sums

646 Whatever method of calculation is adopted, the calculation of lump sum damages for future loss of income is subject to considerable uncertainty. But where the scope for error is greatest – that is, in cases of substantial pecuniary loss caused by death or by serious and lasting injury – our majority proposals for periodic payments would apply. The effect should be to remove many substantial awards of damages from the sphere of lump sum compensation.

647 The traditional method of calculating lump sum damages for future pecuniary loss has been to multiply the plaintiff's net annual loss by an appropriate factor representing a number of 'years' purchase'. This factor, known as the 'multiplier', has always been less than the number of years for which compensation is to be provided, since it is scaled down to take account of the fact that the plaintiff receives his compensation in advance as a lump sum. A reduction is also made for future contingencies, such as the chance that the plaintiff would have died for a reason unconnected with the injury. The method in theory provides a lump sum sufficient, when invested for this purpose, to produce an income equal to the lost income over the relevant period, when the interest is supplemented by withdrawals of capital.

648 The present range of multipliers used by the courts – which has an effective maximum of 18 – approximately corresponds to the assumption that a person who invests a sum of money in the United Kingdom will enjoy a rate of return on his investment of $4\frac{1}{2}$ per cent a year, after the effects of tax and inflation have been taken into account. This assumption is not now realistic. The net real rates of return (that is, the net rates after tax, less the rate of inflation) derived from investments in this country have over a number of years been considerably lower than $4\frac{1}{2}$ per cent. Furthermore, they vary

substantially according to the individual investor's tax liability, and for those who are subject to tax at the highest rate have been negative. Recent trends in inflation, and their effect on real rates of return, are discussed in chapter 28 of Volume Two.

649   Because insufficient account is taken of the effects of tax and inflation, lump sums calculated on the present basis are unlikely to provide full year by year replacement of the plaintiff's lost income.

650   The multiplier method is simple and well understood, and it can readily be operated by practitioners. **We recommend** that damages for future pecuniary loss in the form of a lump sum should continue to be calculated by multiplying the net annual loss by the appropriate multiplier.

651   We are all agreed, however, that because of the effects of tax and inflation a new procedure for determining the appropriate multiplier is needed. There is a difference of opinion among us as to what the new procedure should be. The views of our Chairman, Lord Cameron, Mrs Brooke, and Mr Marshall, are set out in their minority opinion, at the end of this chapter. The views of the rest of us are set out in the following paragraphs (652 to 687).

652   The view of the majority is based on the starting assumptions that the calculation of lump sum damages for future pecuniary loss should continue to aim at year by year replacement of the plaintiff's loss; and that, in order to achieve this aim, fuller account ought to be taken, in determining the multiplier, of the effects of tax and inflation. The majority have reached this conclusion for two main reasons.

653   First, it seems to follow from the principle of full compensation, on which the tort system is based. A lump sum award for future loss of income can hardly be said to provide full compensation unless it is capable of approximately replacing that income, even though the recipient may choose to use it in other ways; and it seems too that replacement of income entails a provision in each year of compensation which is equal in money terms to the plaintiff's loss in that year.

654   Secondly, there should be as little difference as possible between the cost to the defendant (or rather his insurers) of paying compensation in the form of a lump sum rather than in the form of periodic payments. For if lump sums were substantially cheaper from the defendant's point of view, undesirable pressure might be put on those suffering from serious and lasting injury, and on the dependants of those killed in fatal accidents, to forgo their right to periodic payments under the proposals set out in chapter 14.

655   The majority recognise that no method of lump sum calculation can achieve mathematical perfection. But they consider that use should be made of such practical assistance as mathematics can provide.

656   Details of the procedure which they propose are in paragraphs 675 to 687. There would be not one range of multipliers, but several. The appropriate range in an individual case would depend on the plaintiff's average tax rate, which would be the rate used to 'gross up' his net annual loss. The appropriate multiplier within that range would depend on the period of years for which damages were awarded. In fixing the period, the court would – as now – make an allowance for contingencies ('the chances and changes of life'). But no further reduction would be needed for the fact that the award would take the form of a lump sum, since this would automatically be taken into account in the calculation of the multiplier. In other words, any further reduction would be a form of double counting.

657   A table relating ranges of multipliers to various average tax rates could readily be constructed for the use of the courts. In constructing the table, it would be necessary to assume values for the rate of interest and the rate of inflation of earnings, and it is envisaged that the Government Actuary might from time to time suggest suitable values for these variables, as he does when preparing reports on the state pensions scheme.

658   By a majority, we recommend that the appropriate multiplier for calculating lump sum damages for future pecuniary loss should be determined by the modified multiplier method described below (paragraphs 675 to 687).

Procedure for determining the net annual loss – the majority view
659   Different procedures for determining the net annual loss are appropriate in claims for personal injury and for lost dependency, since in the one case most benefits are tax free, whereas in the other most benefits are taxable. Before describing these procedures, we (the majority) explain the average tax rate – a term which is common to both.

Average tax rate
660   A person's average tax rate is the total amount of income tax which he pays, expressed as a proportion of his income. Suppose, for example, that the basic rate of income tax is 33⅓ per cent and that the single person's allowance is £1,000 a year. A single man with no other allowances, earning £4,000 a year, will have a taxable income of £3,000. He will therefore pay a total of 33⅓ per cent of £3,000, that is £1,000 in tax. His average tax rate will then be £1,000 expressed as a proportion of his gross income of £4,000, that is 25 per cent.

661   If tax allowances other than personal allowances are ignored, and once the child tax allowances have been largely phased out to make way for child benefit, the relationship between gross income, average tax rate and net income after tax in the United Kingdom can be summarised approximately in two tables – one for a married person and one for a single person. Table 9 gives the relationships for the tax year 1976/77.

Table 9   Tax payable on earned income in the 1976/77 tax year

Single person with no dependants			Married person with no children		
Gross income	Approximate average tax rate	Net income	Gross income	Approximate average tax rate	Net income
£	Percentage	£	£	Percentage	£
800	3	777	800	—	800
900	6	842	900	—	900
1,000	9	907	1,000	—	1,000
1,250	14	1,070	1,250	5	1,192
1,500	18	1,232	1,500	10	1,355
1,750	20	1,395	1,750	13	1,517
2,000	22	1,557	2,000	16	1,680
2,500	25	1,882	2,500	20	2,005
3,000	26	2,207	3,000	22	2,330
3,500	28	2,532	3,500	24	2,655
4,000	29	2,857	4,000	26	2,980
4,500	29	3,182	4,500	27	3,305
5,000	30	3,507	5,000	27	3,630
6,000	31	4,144	6,000	29	4,280
7,000	33	4,706	7,000	31	4,863
8,000	35	5,217	8,000	33	5,392
9,000	37	5,679	9,000	35	5,872
10,000	39	6,091	10,000	37	6,301
15,000	48	7,764	15,000	47	8,009
20,000	55	9,051	20,000	53	9,314

Claims by a living plaintiff

662   The first stage in the determination of the annual loss of income suffered by a living plaintiff would be to ascertain what his total income, including both earned and unearned income, would have been at the date of the award if he had not been injured. We shall refer to the total income as A. If the pre-injury average tax rate (taking account of all tax allowances) would have been t, then his total after tax income B would have been equal to A $(1 - t)$. All amounts would be expressed as annual amounts.

663   The second stage would be to take account of additions to and deductions from net of tax income. Social security contributions C which the plaintiff would no longer have to pay would be deducted. So would any tax free social security benefits for loss of income D which were being received by the plaintiff at the date of the award. Any expenses E, less social security benefits for expenses F, would be added (unless the relevant benefits exceeded the value of the expenses, in which case no tort compensation would be payable and both E and F would be left out of the calculation). The second stage would result in a net figure G equal to $[B - C - D + (E - F)]$.

664   The third stage would be to take account of deductions from gross income. The average post-injury tax rate T corresponding to a net amount G could be found from the appropriate tax table, and thus the gross amount H

corresponding to the net amount G could be ascertained. From H would be deducted any relevant taxable social security benefits I and any other income J which the plaintiff had not lost as a result of his injury (for example investment income, or reduced earnings where he had suffered only a partial loss of earnings). This would give the plaintiff's gross annual loss K equal to $H-I-J$.

665   The gross annual loss would be the initial annual amount of an award in the form of periodic payments.

666   The net annual loss L, which would be the basis for calculating lump sum damages by a multiplier method, would be given by $K(1-T)$.

667   The procedure for claims by a living plaintiff which we have described above may also be expressed diagrammatically.

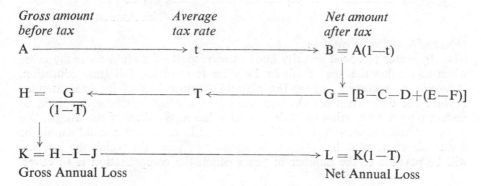

Gross amount   *Average*   *Net amount*
before tax   *tax rate*   *after tax*

$A \longrightarrow t \longrightarrow B = A(1-t)$

$H = \dfrac{G}{(1-T)} \longleftarrow T \longleftarrow G = [B-C-D+(E-F)]$

$K = H-I-J \longrightarrow L = K(1-T)$
Gross Annual Loss   Net Annual Loss

Claims by dependants

668   The procedure for determining the annual loss (of dependency) suffered by dependants would be simpler, since all the relevant social security benefits are taxable, and there would be no continuing expenses.

669   The first stage would be to determine the dependency. This would be the amount M of take home pay (that is, of earned income net of tax and social security contributions) which the deceased would have devoted to the support of his dependants and to the upkeep of the family home, plus any damages for the value of the deceased's lost services.

670   The second stage would be to take account of deductions from gross income. The gross equivalent N of the dependency figure M would be found from the appropriate tax table (in the case of a widow or widower, from the table for a single person), and any social security benefits P payable to the dependants would be deducted. This would give the gross annual loss $K=N-P$.

671   The gross annual loss would be the initial annual amount of an award in the form of periodic payments.

672   To determine the net annual loss for the purpose of lump sum calculations, it would be necessary to add to K any other income Q of the claimant, including earned income and any investment income. The tax rate T corresponding to a gross income of $K+Q$ could be found from the tax table. The net annual loss L would be given by $K(1-T)$.

673   This procedure may also be expressed diagrammatically.

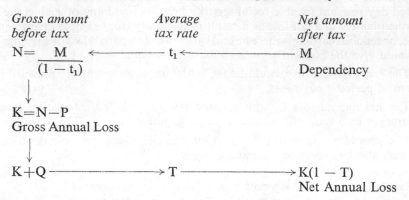

Gross amount before tax   *Average tax rate*   *Net amount after tax*

$$N = \frac{M}{(1 - t_1)} \longleftarrow t_1 \longleftarrow M$$

Dependency

$$K = N - P$$
Gross Annual Loss

$$K + Q \longrightarrow T \longrightarrow K(1 - T)$$
Net Annual Loss

Offset of benefits for children

674   Increases to social security benefits in respect of a child normally cease when he reaches the age of 16, or 19 if he is receiving full time education. It would be necessary, where the plaintiff's future loss of income extended beyond the time when his children ceased to qualify for these increases, to deduct only a proportion of their annual value at the date of the award. We suggest that a proportion p of an increase paid in respect of a child should be deducted, where p is the ratio of the number of years for which the increase will be payable to the number of years which the compensation is to cover.

The modified multiplier – the majority view

675   If the simplifying assumption is made that the plaintiff pays tax at a constant rate on the income from his invested damages throughout the period of the award, the calculation of a lump sum award becomes a straightforward example of a discounted cash flow calculation. This is a standard type of calculation for converting a series of future payments into a capital sum, at a given discount rate.

676   As we (the majority) have already mentioned, the present range of multipliers is implicitly equivalent to the use of a discount rate of $4\frac{1}{2}$ per cent, even though in practice explicit calculations are not made, awards being based on experience and precedent.

677   A more realistic calculation in present day circumstances would use a lower discount rate, and one which made explicit allowance for inflation and for tax. The discount rate would be the real rate of return after tax, that is, approximately the net rate of return after tax less the rate of inflation. If compensation for loss of income were to keep pace with average earnings, as we have proposed in the context of periodic payments, the relevant rate of inflation would be the rate of inflation of earnings. Any increments in the plaintiff's earnings which were likely to take place, apart from those associated with inflation, could be allowed for at a constant annual percentage rate by adjustment of the discount rate.

678   We considered whether it would be sufficient to use multipliers based on the same real rate of return after tax for all plaintiffs. A rate of zero, for example, would result in the simple rule that the plaintiff's net annual loss should be multiplied by the number of years for which damages were to be awarded in order to give the appropriate lump sum. But we thought that such a proposal would create too great inequities between those taxed at high rates and those taxed at low rates or not subject to tax.

679   The appropriate discount rate for an individual with a nil average tax rate would be the difference between the rate of interest which he could obtain on his investments and the rate of inflation of earnings. We understand that the Government Actuary has used, in the context of the new pensions scheme, long term average values of 9 per cent a year for the rate of interest, 8 per cent a year for the rate of inflation of earnings, and 6 per cent a year for the rate of inflation of prices. On these assumptions, the appropriate discount rate for a non-tax payer would be 1 per cent. For a man who paid tax at a high rate, the real rate of return after tax, used as the discount rate, would be likely to be negative. A rate of −2 per cent would be of the right order, for a single man earning £250 a week, if account were taken of compensation provided by tax-free social security benefits; or −3 per cent if his take home pay was expected to increase by 1 per cent a year more than the rate of increase of average earnings.

680   The following table of multipliers shows the extent of the inequity that would result from the use of a fixed discount rate for all plaintiffs. For example it shows that a plaintiff for whom a discount rate of −2 per cent would be appropriate would need 50 per cent more compensation than a man for whom a discount rate of 1 per cent would be appropriate in order to replace the same annual loss for 25 years.

Table 10   Multipliers based on various discount rates

Period of years	Present basis[1]	Discount rate (%)					
		2	1	0	−1	−2	−3
5	5	5	5	5	5	5	5
10	8	9	10	10	11	11	12
15	11	13	14	15	16	18	19
20	13	17	18	20	22	25	28
25	15	20	22	25	28	33	37
30	16	23	26	30	35	41	49
35	17	25	30	35	42	51	63
40	18	28	33	40	49	62	78

1 Corresponds approximately, but not exactly, to a discount rate of 4½% a year.

681   The use of the same range of multipliers for all plaintiffs regardless of their individual tax position would also give rise in an acute form to the problem of equivalence between the cost to the defendant of awards in the form of lump sums and periodic payments. Assuming a 9 per cent rate of interest and an 8 per cent rate of inflation of earnings, the cost to the defendant's insurer of providing a gross inflation proofed periodic payment would be equivalent to applying

to the plaintiff's net annual loss a multiplier based on a 1 per cent discount rate, divided by $(1 - T)$ where T is the individual plaintiff's average tax rate. For a single man earning £80 a week, for whom the appropriate tax rate after taking account of social security benefits would be 0·12 in 1976/77, the relevant multiplier for an insurer making periodic payments for 25 years would be the 1 per cent multiplier (22) divided by 0·88 – that is, 25. For a single man earning £250 a week, for whom the appropriate tax rate after taking account of social security benefits would be 0·33 in 1976/77, the relevant multiplier for an insurer making periodic payments would be 22 divided by 0·67 – that is 33. It would cost the insurer 32 per cent more to make periodic payments in respect of the same annual loss to the second man than to the first. Unless the lump sum calculation also took account of the individual's tax position, this differential in costs would not be reflected; and it would be much cheaper for an insurer to settle a claim by a relatively high earner for a lump sum rather than by periodic payments.

682 We concluded that the individual plaintiff's tax position ought to be taken into account in selecting the discount rate to be used for the determination of the multiplier. The relationship between the discount rate R and the plaintiff's average tax rate T is given approximately by the following formula:

$$R = r (1-T) - i - e$$

where r is the rate of interest (the nominal rate of return), i is the rate of inflation of earnings and e is the plaintiff's expected average annual increase in take home pay (other than due to changes in the level of average earnings). T is the post-injury average tax rate, defined in paragraph 664 for a living plaintiff and in paragraph 672 for a dependant.

683 This formula gives the theoretical basis on which we think the multipliers used for calculating damages for future loss of income should be determined. It does not exactly reproduce the cost to an insurer of providing inflation proofed periodic payments gross of tax, but it provides a broad equivalence which we think would in practice be sufficient to prevent serious injustice, in a way which no multiplier based on a single discount rate could do.

684 The net annual loss is calculated on the basis of rates of tax and social security benefits applicable at the date of the trial. To capitalise this loss in the way proposed by the majority implicitly assumes that, in the calculation of the net annual loss in future years, these rates will maintain a constant relationship with average earnings; and to calculate multipliers in the way proposed by the majority implies consistent assumptions. The method also assumes that United Kingdom rates of tax and social security benefits would apply. Adjustments to the calculation may be needed in a case involving overseas tax or benefit rates.

685 As an example of the calculation of the multiplier, suppose that the plaintiff's net annual loss is £2,000 and that his average tax rate is 22 per cent (that is 0·22). Suppose also that the judge considers that loss of income will continue for a period of 20 years, and that the plaintiff has shown that if he

had not been injured his take home pay would have increased by an average of 1 per cent a year (0·01). Again assuming a 9 per cent rate of interest and an 8 per cent rate of inflation of earnings, the appropriate discount rate R is given by:

$$R = r(1-T)-i-e$$
$$= 0·09\,(1-0·22)-0·08-0·01$$
$$= -0·0198 \text{ or approximately } -2\%$$

The appropriate multiplier corresponding to a discount rate of −2 per cent and a period of 20 years may then be looked up in the table of multipliers (table 10). It is 25. The damages for future loss of income would be obtained by applying this multiplier to the plaintiff's net annual loss. The award in this example would be 25 × £2,000, that is £50,000.

686   Table 11 illustrates modified multipliers for various categories of plaintiff, based on 1976–77 tax rates, a rate of interest of 9 per cent a year, and a rate of inflation of earnings of 8 per cent a year. Multipliers under the present system (taken as corresponding to a discount rate of 4½ per cent) are included for the sake of comparison. The examples are of a single man earning up to £66 a week, £80 a week, and £240 a week; and of a married man earning up to £111 a week, and £240 a week. The lowest figure in each case is the maximum amount which could be earned before the net amount after deduction of social security benefits exceeded the tax threshold.

Table 11   Modified multipliers

	Modified multipliers					
	Single man earning			Married man earning		Present system
	Up to £66 a week	£80 a week	£240 a week	Up to £111 a week	£240 a week	
Tax rate	0	12	33	0	29	0
Discount rate	+1	0	−2	+1	−1½	+4½[1]
Period of years						
5	5	5	5	5	5	5
10	10	10	11	10	11	8
15	14	15	18	14	17	11
20	18	20	25	18	23	13
25	22	25	33	22	30	15
30	26	30	41	26	38	16
35	30	35	51	30	46	17
40	33	40	62	33	55	18

1 Approximately.

687   The multipliers given in table 11 do not in themselves indicate the overall financial effect of our proposals relating to the calculation of damages for future pecuniary loss. The combined effect of these proposals is discussed in paragraphs 701 to 708 below.

NON-PECUNIARY LOSS

688 We have recommended that, in assessing non-pecuniary damages, full account should be taken of social security benefits, designed to compensate for non-pecuniary loss. The main relevant benefit is disablement benefit, which is paid as a weekly pension where disability is assessed as 20 per cent or more. The damages would, as at present, take the form of a lump sum.

689 The amount awarded as damages for non-pecuniary loss depends on the judge's impression of what is reasonable, and not on calculation. No account is taken of the rate of tax paid by the recipients. We do not think that it would be appropriate to lay down hard and fast rules for calculating the offset. But we think that the court should take full account of the compensation provided by the social security benefits in forming an impression of what would be a reasonable amount of damages.

690 An approximate capitalisation may be helpful to the courts as a guide to the weight to be put on the benefits. Tax considerations are not relevant, since both the damages and the benefits are free of tax. Accordingly, multipliers based on the same discount rate for all plaintiffs may be used. On the basis of the assumptions as to rates of inflation and interest which we have used elsewhere, we think that multipliers based on a discount rate of 2 per cent would give a reasonable guide. Table 12 shows the capitalised value on this basis of a disablement pension of £25 a week (£1,305 a year) for varying periods.

Table 12 Capitalised value of disablement pension of £25 a week

Period of years	Multiplier[1]	Capitalised value of benefit
		£
5	5	6,500
10	9	11,700
15	13	16,900
20	17	22,100
25	20	26,000
30	23	29,900
35	25	32,500
40	28	36,400

1 Based on 2% discount rate.

691 **We recommend** that there should be no fixed rule for calculating the offset of social security benefits from damages for non-pecuniary loss; but that multipliers based on a 2 per cent discount rate for all plaintiffs may be helpful as a guide to the value of the benefits.

THE MAJORITY PROPOSALS IN PRACTICE

Example of the calculation of damages for future pecuniary loss
692 The majority's proposals for calculating damages for future pecuniary loss can be illustrated by the following numerical example of the full calculation of an individual award.

693   Suppose that the plaintiff is a single man, permanently incapacitated at the age of 35, and that his gross earnings at the time of the award would have been £80 a week (£4,174 a year, on the basis of 52·18 weeks in a year) if he had not been injured. Suppose for the sake of simplicity that he has no other income; that there are no tax allowances apart from the personal allowance; and that there are no expenses. Suppose also that he would have paid income tax of £1,204 a year, and social security contributions of £240 a year, out of his gross earnings; and that at the date of the award he is receiving £33·55 a week (£1,752 a year) in social security benefits for loss of income. (These figures are based on 1976/77 tax and benefit rates for a single man, on the assumption that the improved earnings related benefits which we have proposed for work and road injuries would be payable.)

694   The procedure in paragraphs 662 to 667 may be used to determine the initial amount of an award of periodic payments (the gross annual loss). The net figure G, as there are no expenses, is given by:

$$G=B-C-D$$
$$=2,970 - 240 - 1,752$$
$$=978$$

The average tax rate T corresponding to G may be found by interpolation from table 9. It is 12 per cent.

695   Since both I (taxable social security benefits) and J (other income) are zero, the plaintiff's gross annual loss K is given by:

$$K=H= \frac{G}{(1-T)}$$
$$= \frac{978}{0·88}$$
$$= 1,111$$

He would therefore qualify for an award of periodic payments of £1,111 a year subject to inflation proofing.

696   The starting point for calculating the corresponding award in the form of a lump sum is the net annual loss L (equal to K (1 – T)), which in this case is equal to G (£978).

697   The discount rate R for the multiplier may be found from the formula in paragraph 682. Assuming as before that r=0·09 and i=0·08:

$$R=r (1-T)-i-e$$
$$=r (1-0·12)-0·08-0$$
$$=(0·09 \times 0·88)-0·08$$
$$=0 \text{ approximately}$$

698   The period of years for which the plaintiff's loss of income would continue is the number of years until he reaches retirement age, reduced for 'the chances and changes of life'. Assuming a period of 25 years, the multiplier based on a discount rate of 0 would be 25 (from table 10).

699   The lump sum award would be the product of the multiplier and the net annual loss, that is 25 × £978, or £24,450.

Table 13   Examples of tort damages supplementing social security benefits for loss of earnings.

Lump sums on present and proposed basis after full offset of improved benefits

i Single person, permanently incapacitated at age 35

A *Earnings and benefits*[1]					
Gross earnings	£ per week	60	80	105	240
	£ per year	3,131	4,174	5,479	12,523
Income tax[2]	£ per year	839	1,204	1,660	5,512
Social security contributions[3]	£ per year	180	240	315	315
Net earnings[4]	£ per year	2,112	2,730	3,504	6,696
	£ per week	40·5	52·3	67·2	128·3
Social security benefits:					
Flat rate[5]	£ per week	17·3	17·3	17·3	17·3
Earnings related[6]	£ per week	11·25	16·25	22·5	22·5
Total	£ per week	28·55	33·55	39·8	39·8
Adjusted total[7]	£ per week				
Annual loss[8]	£ per week	11·95	18·75	27·4	88·5
	£ per year	624	978	1,430	4,618
B *Present basis*					
Multiplier		15	15	15	15
Lump sum, gross[9]	£	31,680	40,950	52,560	100,040
Benefit offset[10]	£	2,970	3,490	4,140	4,140
Lump sum, net	£	28,710	37,460	48,420	95,900
C *Present multiplier with full offset of benefits*					
Multiplier		15	15	15	15
Lump sum[11]	£	9,360	14,670	21,450	69,270
D *Proposed basis* (Full offset of benefits and modified multiplier)					
Tax rate[2]	%	Nil	12	21	33
Real rate of return after tax[12]	%	1	0	−1	−2
Period[13]	Years	25	25	25	25
Multiplier		22	25	28	33
Lump sum[14]	£	13,730	24,450	40,000	152,000

1 At January 1977 rates, but with improved social security benefits in force.

2 At 1976/77 rates, assuming no other income, and no tax allowances apart from personal allowances (in particular no tax allowance for children).

3 At rates in force from April 1977, i.e. 5·75% of earnings up to £105 a week.

4 Gross earnings less tax and social security contributions.

5 Benefits for loss of earnings, consisting of invalidity pension £15·30, invalidity allowance £2·00, allowance for wife £9·20, allowance for each child £4·95 (£7·45 less an assumed child benefit equivalent to £2·50).

6 25 per cent of earnings between £15 and £105 a week, assuming the benefit is based on the current level of earnings, not on a previous period.

700 Table 13 sets out this example and other examples of the calculation of lump sums using modified multipliers, allowing for full offset of the improved benefits proposed for work and motor vehicle injuries. It also includes, for purposes of comparison, lump sums based on the present range of multipliers, with offsets on the present basis of one-half of the benefits for five years, and with full offsets.

ii Married man with two children, permanently incapacitated at age 35

				A *Earnings and benefits*[1]	
60	80	105	240	Gross earnings	£ per week
3,131	4,174	5,479	12,523		£ per year
716	1,081	1,538	5,286	Income tax[2]	£ per year
180	240	315	315	Social security contributions[3]	£ per year
2,235	2,853	3,626	6,922	Net earnings[4]	£ per year
42·8	54·7	69·5	132·7		£ per week
				Social security benefits:	
36·4	36·4	36·4	36·4	Flat rate[5]	£ per week
11·25	16·25	22·5	22·5	Earnings related[6]	£ per week
47·65	52·65	58·9	58·9	Total	£ per week
41·05	46·05	52·3	52·3	Adjusted total[7]	£ per week
1·75	8·65	17·2	80·4	Annual loss[8]	£ per week
91	451	897	4,195		£ per year
				B *Present basis*	
15	15	15	15	Multiplier	
33,525	42,795	54,390	103,830	Lump sum, gross[9]	£
4,955	5,475	6,130	6,130	Benefit offset[10]	£
28,570	37,320	48,260	97,700	Lump sum, net	£
				C *Present multiplier with full offset of benefits*	
15	15	15	15	Multiplier	
1,365	6,765	13,455	62,925	Lump sum[11]	£
				D *Proposed basis* (Full offset of benefits and modified multiplier)	
Nil	Nil	Nil	29	Tax rate[2]	%
1	1	1	$-1\frac{1}{2}$	Real rate of return after tax[12]	%
25	25	25	25	Period[13]	Years
22	22	22	30	Multiplier	
2,000	9,900	19,700	126,000	Lump sum[14]	£

7 Allowing one third of benefits for the two children over the whole period (£3·30 per week instead of £9·90 per week).
8 Net earnings less benefits or adjusted benefits.
9 Product of net earnings and the multiplier.
10 Half unadjusted benefits for 208 weeks, assuming that of the 5 years for which deduction is made, one had elapsed by the time of settlement or judgment, and no deduction of disablement benefit.
11 Product of the annual loss and the multiplier.
12 Assuming a 9 per cent money rate of return and an 8 per cent rate of earnings inflation.
13 Period to retirement age, reduced to allow for the chances and changes of life.
14 Product of the annual loss and the multiplier.

151

The financial effect

701   Our proposals relating to the calculation of damages for future pecuniary loss are designed to do two things – to take account of social security benefits in assessing the plaintiff's net annual loss; and to take account of tax and inflation in determining the appropriate multiplier. Taken together, these proposals would have a substantial effect on the level and distribution of damages for future pecuniary loss.

702   Our proposals for the full offset of relevant social security benefits are designed to eliminate a great deal of double compensation. They would lead to an aggregate saving in the cost of tort compensation for future pecuniary loss of the order of £20 million a year at January 1977 prices. This saving would be effected by a reduction at all income levels in the net annual loss taken into account when assessing damages. The effect of full offset of improved social security benefits on the net annual loss is illustrated by part A of table 13; part B shows awards on the present basis; and part C shows the effect of full offset on lump sum awards using the present multipliers. If present multipliers were retained, full offset would lead to a reduction of tort awards for future pecuniary loss at all income levels.

703   Our proposals for modified multipliers would lead to an increase in multipliers for all incomes and for all periods. The effect on multipliers for short periods would be small; but there would be substantial increases in multipliers relating to long periods and to high incomes which bear a relatively high average rate of tax. We estimate that the aggregate increase in the cost of compensation for future pecuniary loss under our proposals, separate from the effect of offsets, would be of the order of £25 million a year.

704   Taken together, our proposals would lead to a small increase of some £5 million a year in the aggregate cost of tort compensation for future loss of income.

705   At the level of individual awards, our proposals would have two effects which, we recognise, may at first sight appear socially unattractive. First, tort awards to high earners would be higher than at present, whereas tort awards to low and medium earners would be lower. In the extreme case of a man with a five figure after tax income and good prospects of promotion, who was seriously injured in his twenties, an award of £$\frac{1}{2}$ million would be possible. But such a case would be exceedingly rare; and, if it happened at all, would be covered by our proposal that awards for future pecuniary loss caused by death or serious and lasting injury should normally take the form of periodic payments. Secondly, a married man with children would receive a lower tort award than a single person who suffered the same loss. These effects are illustrated by part D of table 13. We think it important that they should not be misunderstood.

706   The social security system at present provides a greater degree of income replacement for a low earner who is injured than for a high earner who is injured, and for an injured person with dependants than for an injured single person; and we have reflected this differentiation in favour of low earners and people with families in our proposals relating to no-fault compensation. But

the tort system does not differentiate in this way. Indeed it would be incompatible with the objective of tort, which is to restore an injured person as closely as possible to the position which he was in before he was injured.

707   We do not think that it would be right for tort to provide full replacement of income for some but not for others. Our proposals are designed to ensure that, so far as possible, the distribution of compensation which includes tort damages reproduces the distribution of disposable income among uninjured people. Hence the supplementary tort damages in isolation appear to differentiate in the opposite way to social security, that is to favour single people and higher earners.

708   Finally, in the light of the observations made by our colleagues in their minority opinion, we wish to make two further points. First, the high income earner who is injured would not be better off in real terms when compensated under our proposals than he would have been if he had not been injured. It is not over compensation to provide a plaintiff with a lump sum award which gives him immediately a greater nominal purchasing power than the total purchasing power which he will require over the period of the award if, because of the effects of tax and inflation, he cannot preserve the purchasing power which he is awarded until it is needed. Secondly, any calculation of lump sum damages based on a multiplier method, including the standard fraction method proposed by our colleagues, implies some assumptions about future rates of interest, inflation, tax and social security benefits.

MINORITY OPINION ON THE CALCULATION OF LUMP SUM DAMAGES FOR FUTURE PECUNIARY LOSS

by our Chairman, Lord Cameron, Mrs Brooke and Mr Marshall

709   We are in general agreement with the majority as to the assessment of the special damages (paragraph 634) and as to the ascertainment and adjustment of the net annual loss (paragraph 641) which is the starting point of the assessment of damages for future loss of income, to which net expenses can be added. But owing to the inevitable uncertainty of prophetic forecasts as to the future (see paragraph 723) we do not think that elaborate calculations are appropriate for these purposes. We have at the end of chapter 13 stated our views as to the proper allocation of social security benefits for the purposes of offsetting, and we are not dealing with that subject here, except incidentally in paragraph 726. Nor are we dealing here with the calculation of periodic payments, two of us being opposed to the introduction of periodic payments. We are here dealing only with the calculation of lump sums of damages for future pecuniary loss, except that we shall add a paragraph (paragraph 726) on the assessment of damages for non-pecuniary loss.

710   In assessing a lump sum of damages for future pecuniary loss the sum to be multiplied is the net annual loss as at the date of the award, adjusted as may be necessary. But what is the appropriate multiplier? That is the question on which there is substantial disagreement.

711   What are the criteria? One has to take into account the interests of the
plaintiffs or claimants (the injured persons or the dependants of the deceased),
those of the defendants or their insurers and those of the community. First,
justice is the paramount consideration. An award of damages should, so far as is
reasonably possible, provide full compensation for the effects of the wrongdoing, but not more than full compensation. The award should be fair to the
plaintiff and fair to the defendant. Secondly, it is in the interests of all concerned
that there should be finality in litigation; that so far as possible claims should be
settled by agreement without being taken to court; and that claims, whether
settled by agreement or decided by a court, should be disposed of as quickly
and cheaply as possible without detriment to justice. Thirdly, there should be
fairness as between different plaintiffs. Fourthly, we should think in terms of
real value rather than nominal values in a depreciating currency. Fifthly, a lump
sum is different in kind from a lost income: it brings different and wider opportunities: it can be a reasonable equivalent of a lost income, but it is a substitute
compensation, not a replacement.

712   In the old days the rates of inflation and taxation were much lower than
they are now. In those days it was possible to assess a reasonable (not extravagant or fantastic) lump sum which, if suitably invested for this purpose, could be
expected, as things then stood, to produce an income equal to the lost income
over the relevant period. The theory of it was that in each year the required
income could be provided partly by the interest and dividends from the investments and partly from capital by a sale of part of the investments, with the result
that the interest and dividends would dwindle and more of the capital would have
to be used as time went on and the whole fund would be exhausted at the end of
the relevant period. The lump sum was arrived at by the multiplier method, and
there was a range of multipliers up to a maximum of about 16 'years purchase'
or 18 as an outside figure. We understand that this range of multipliers would be
consistent with a real net return of about $4\frac{1}{2}$ per cent on the investments. It is
inherently probable, and the evidence tends to show, that most successful
plaintiffs have not used their lump sums of damages in this way, preferring to
take advantage of the wider opportunities afforded by a lump sum available
immediately. Nevertheless, the method was rational, providing a useful measure
of, or check upon, the suitability of the sum awarded or proposed to be awarded.

713   But the old days have gone, and the position now is very different. The
interest and dividends no longer provide their fair share of the lost income which
has to be made good. A striking example of the effect of high taxation, taken by
itself without any help from inflation, arises in the case of very high lost earnings;
the top slice of investment income is taxed at 98 per cent; therefore an additional
£10,000 of gross income is required in order to yield £200 of net income. But
even with more moderate lost earnings the combination of high inflation and
high rates of taxation reduces the real net return on investments to zero or a
minus figure. Thus the income from the damages fund makes a nil or negative
contribution to the replacement of the lost income, and the replacement has to
be effected by payments out of the capital of the fund, and the capital of the
fund has to be large enough for that purpose, if replacement of the lost income,
pound for pound, without considering inflation, is still to be the objective.

ROYAL COMMISSION ON CIVIL LIABILITY AND COMPENSATION FOR PERSONAL INJURY

REPORT

Volume One

Cmnd 7054–I

CORRECTIONS

Page 237, Table 16 II:
for '£11,700' read '£10,700'.

Page 299, Paragraph 1418 (line 5):
the first word should be 'offer'.

March 1978

LONDON: HER MAJESTY'S STATIONERY OFFICE

714   If full theoretical allowance were to be made for inflation, very large sums indeed would be required. If inflation continues, earnings may be expected to rise at least as fast as prices. As a matter of convenience, let us assume for the moment that they will increase at the same rate. If the plaintiff had not been injured, he would over the years have received more and more pounds but each pound would have been worth less and less. If one assumes inflation continuing at a constant rate of 8 per cent a year, and a compound interest table is used, one finds that earnings of £1,000 a year would become £8,000 a year after about 27 years, that is in 2004. The real value which £1,000 now has in 1977 is equal to the real value which £8,000 will have in 2004.

715   Now we should apply the principle of working with real values in preference to nominal values. If we took simply nominal values, the defendant or his insurers would have to provide £8,000 in 1977 in the pounds of 1977 to compensate the plaintiff's future loss of £8,000 in 2004 in the greatly depreciated pounds of 2004. The plaintiff would receive a real value eight times as large as the real value which he will be losing in 2004. That cannot be right: in extreme cases the multipliers would be very high and the resulting lump sums also very high. On the other hand, if we work with real values, the principle is clear. The plaintiff should receive in 1977 a sum of 1977 pounds having a real value equal to the total of the real values which he will be losing (would have been receiving but for the injury) over the relevant period.

716   Then how does one find the appropriate multiplier? One can start with the number of years in the oustanding period from the date of the award to the age of retirement (normally 65 for a man and 60 for a woman). That must be scaled down for the 'chances and changes of life': the injured plaintiff or the deceased, if this injury had not occurred, might have died or been incapacitated by illness or some other injury or might have become unemployed. Secondly in our opinion there should be a further scaling down for the advantages of a lump sum as compared with the prospect of a long series of future and therefore uncertain periodic payments. The lump sum has advantages of immediacy, certainty and flexibility, and the evidence tends to show that people prefer it, and if so they should not be accused of imprudence. The importance of certainty becomes evident if one bears in mind the number and variety of misfortunes which can befall nations as well as individuals.

717   Adjustment might be needed if, contrary to the assumption made hitherto, earnings were expected to rise faster than prices: that is, if real earnings were expected to increase. Such an increase is indeed expected during the next few years. However, we are concerned with periods of up to 45 years, about which there can be no such confidence, having regard to increasing competition for the available world supplies of food and raw materials, and the growing desire for leisure rather than for further material possessions. How fast real earnings will increase in the longer term, or even whether they will increase at all, must be a matter of speculation. If an upward trend were to be re-established and were expected to continue, allowance for it could be made, on the method we propose, by increasing the standard fraction.

155

718   We are reluctant to be very precise as to the range or level of multipliers, because it needs discussion, but we would say that the existing level is too low, because it was settled at a time when the lump sum could provide pound for pound replacement of the lost income and that is no longer practicable. A very convenient method would be to use a standard fraction (variable in exceptional cases) of the outstanding period from date of award to retirement age. The standard fraction might be three-fifths or two-thirds or seven-tenths. If two-thirds were the standard fraction, the normal multiplier for an outstanding period of 30 years would be 20, and for a 36-year period it would be 24, and for a 42-year period it would be 28. That seems a reasonable result, and the method is easy and eminently workable. It might not be appropriate to apply the standard fraction to a short outstanding period (say less than 15 years), where the degree of uncertainty would be small and the appropriate multiplier would be not much less than the period of years. For the short outstanding periods there could be a graduated scale on these lines:

Outstanding period	Multiplier	Outstanding period	Multiplier
1 year	1		
		8 years	$8 \times \dfrac{82}{100} = 6 \cdot 56$
2 years	2		
3 years	$3 \times \dfrac{97}{100} = 2 \cdot 91$	9 years	$9 \times \dfrac{79}{100} = 7 \cdot 11$
4 years	$4 \times \dfrac{94}{100} = 3 \cdot 76$	10 years	$10 \times \dfrac{76}{100} = 7 \cdot 60$
5 years	$5 \times \dfrac{91}{100} = 4 \cdot 55$	11 years	$11 \times \dfrac{73}{100} = 8 \cdot 03$
6 years	$6 \times \dfrac{88}{100} = 5 \cdot 28$	12 years	$12 \times \dfrac{70}{100} = 8 \cdot 40$
7 years	$7 \times \dfrac{85}{100} = 5 \cdot 95$	13 years	$13 \times \dfrac{67}{100} = 8 \cdot 71$

719   How would the suggested method – which may be called the 'standard fraction method' – be applied to claims for lost dependency resulting from a fatal accident? 'Lost dependency' means the financial loss suffered by those who were financially dependent or partially dependent on the deceased. The standard fraction method could solve some of the difficult problems dealt with in chapter 12, paragraphs 406 to 417. As proposed in paragraph 716 of the present chapter the number of years in the outstanding period is scaled down to allow for the chances and changes of life and for the advantages of an immediate lump sum as compared with a long series of future periodic payments. In the case of a widow's claim the chances and changes of life include the hypothetical possibility that if the fatal accident had not happened the marriage might have

been dissolved at some later time and also the actual possibility that the widow might marry again. These are relevant factors and do not have to be artificially disregarded, but evidence on them could be excluded because they are taken into account as general possibilities in determining the standard fraction for such cases. It can be argued that, as there are more chances and changes of life in the case of a widow's claim than in the case of an injured plaintiff's claim, the standard fraction for the widow should be smaller than that for the injured plaintiff. But that would be harsh treatment for the widow, who suffers the dislocation of her life resulting from the loss of her husband. We think the standard fraction should be the same for the widow as for the injured plaintiff. If there was an actual remarriage by the time of the award, that would, in the absence of special circumstances (for example, if the second husband was an invalid), terminate the period of lost dependency because a new dependency would take its place.

720   We understand that as a result of the use of our standard fraction method the amount of compensation payable, separate from the effect of offsets, might be increased by some £5 to £10 million a year. This compares with an increase of £25 million as a result of the use of the modified multiplier method.

721   Though we are reluctant to join issue directly with our colleagues, we feel that we ought to state our main reasons for being unable to join with them in recommending the 'modified multiplier method' which they propose.

722   First, we think the method is wrong in principle, because it gives to the very high earner a lump sum of damages having a real value several or many times greater than the total of the future real values which he will be losing over the relevant period (see paragraphs 714 and 715). Consequently a very high earner would receive an extravagant award. There might exceptionally be an award of as much as £$\frac{1}{2}$ million (at present values). We feel that such an award would be excessive and unreasonable. Also there would be an excessive disproportion between the lump sum awards to low earners and the lump sum awards to high earners. Some disproportion is inevitable when social security payments are taken into account as compensation, and leave uncompensated a greater part of a high income than of a low income. But the method greatly enhances the disproportion.

723   Secondly, owing to the inevitable uncertainty as to future developments, any mathematical calculation based on prophetic forecasts can only be of limited value. In the modified multiplier method the calculation is based on a number of assumptions, which are prophetic forecasts covering periods from, say, 2 to 45 years. It has to be predicted and assumed that there will be a specific constant rate for 45 years, or the same average rate for any period up to 45 years, for

 a inflation (though it has varied between 5 per cent and 25 per cent in the last few years),

 b interest (though Minimum Lending Rate has been changed some 19 times in 12 months),

 c tax (though it may be changed in every annual Finance Act),

 d social security benefits.

157

We do not think a defendant or his insurer could reasonably be required to pay out £½ million in pursuance of a calculation having these unstable foundations. Moreover there is an element of artificiality in the calculation itself, because it makes the simplifying assumption (referred to in paragraph 675) that the plaintiff pays tax at a constant rate on the income from his invested damages throughout the period of the award.

724 Thirdly, we have doubts whether the Government would wish to prescribe, or give a lead as to, the rates of inflation and other rates to be assumed. If the Government did so, they would be taking a responsibility and a risk. If it became clear in a few years that the assumptions were not being borne out by the course of events, one party or the other in each case would have a grievance against the Government. It might be said that the Government had misled the courts. On the other hand, without decisive Government intervention, the rates would have to be estimated by any court on the basis of expert evidence given in the particular case, and the resulting uncertainty would impede settlements and increase the number and length of trials and appeals.

725 Fourthly, we think that the calculations required for the method proposed by the majority would in themselves tend to impede settlements and increase the number and length of trials and appeals.

Non-pecuniary damages

726 The amount of the damages to be awarded for non-pecuniary loss (pain and suffering and loss of amenity) depends upon the judge's impression of what is reasonable and not upon calculation. In deciding the amount the judge should, according to this Commission's recommendations, take fully into account the social security benefits designed to compensate for non-pecuniary loss. We think he should do this in the course of forming his impression as to what is reasonable and not by way of capitalisation and deduction. For instance he should in forming his impression take into account both the loss of faculty and the disablement allowance, both the need for attendance and the attendance allowance, and both the loss of mobility and the mobility allowance. No amount of money can restore the lost faculty or the lost independence or the lost mobility. But a plaintiff who is receiving, for example, disablement benefit and attendance allowance and mobility allowance is already receiving a large amount of financial compensation for his non-pecuniary loss. The damages to be awarded to him should be much less than the damages to be awarded to someone not receiving those benefits. That is as far as we would go. We do not think any precise rule or formulation would assist. A capitalisation might sometimes be helpful as a guide to, or check upon, the weight to be given to a particular factor or set of factors, but we do not think it should be used as a basis of assessment in this field of intangibles and imponderables. Thus to a large extent we are in agreement with the majority as to the method for assessing damages for non-pecuniary loss. But in our view, as explained in chapter 13, paragraphs 543 to 548, the functions of the attendance allowance, the mobility allowance, and similar social security benefits in providing some compensation for the need of attendance, the lack of mobility and similar hardships should not be disregarded.

158

CHAPTER 16

Adjudication

727 In this final chapter on the assessment of damages, we deal with aspects of adjudication in personal injuries litigation.

728 Our task has been considerably lightened by the work of several other bodies. As regard England and Wales, we have taken into account the Report of the Committee on Personal Injuries Litigation, Cmnd 3691 (the Winn Committee), and the preliminary views of the Working Party on Procedure in Personal Injuries Litigation under the chairmanship of Mr Justice Cantley. We have also studied those aspects of the Law Commission's report on the assessment of damages (Law Com No 56, HC 373) which bear on this topic. As regards Scotland, we were glad to learn, towards the end of our deliberations, that the Lord President had asked the Procedure Committee of the Court of Session, under the chairmanship of Lord Kincraig, to examine procedure in personal injuries litigation.

Jury trials

729 The Court of Appeal decided in *Hodges* v. *Harland and Wolff* [1965] 1 W.L.R. 523 and *Ward* v. *James* [1966] 1 Q.B. 273 that a court should not exercise its discretion to allow a jury trial in actions for personal injuries, other than in exceptional circumstances. Since these decisions, the use of juries has virtually disappeared from personal injuries litigation in England and Wales. In Scotland and Northern Ireland, jury trial has been retained and is still quite common.

730 The main argument in favour of jury trial in an action for personal injuries is that damages are assessed by reference to the current standards of the ordinary man, and that this is a fairer basis than the views of a specialist judge. This was the main ground on which a majority of the Committee on the Supreme Court of Judicature of Northern Ireland (Cmnd 4292) recommended that jury trial should be kept for personal injury actions (among others) in the province. It also found favour with some of our witnesses, including a majority of the General Council of the Bar of Northern Ireland, and the Faculty of Advocates.

731 On the other hand, jury trials may be said to militate against consistency and predictability in the award of damages, and hence to inhibit settlements. They are also more expensive than trial by a judge alone, and they tend to take longer to arrange and complete. A working group of Scottish judges told us

159

that in their view the uncertainties of assessment would be reduced if jury trials were abolished; and that time would be saved if the question whether a particular case was appropriate for jury trial did not arise. Other Scottish witnesses in favour of the abolition of jury trial included the Faculty of Law of the University of Glasgow, and the Scottish Transport Group.

732 There is a further consideration which has weighed heavily with us. The assessment of damages has become a much more sophisticated exercise in recent years, and our proposals for a modified basis for assessing damages for future loss of income, and for the full offset of social security benefits, would reinforce this trend. This seems to us—as it seemed to the Law Commission—to militate against the use of lay juries.

733 Accordingly we agree with the Law Commission that jury trial should not be reintroduced to personal injuries litigation in England and Wales. We think that there is a good case for the abolition of jury trial in personal injuries litigation in Scotland, but we recognise that this question overlaps with the current remit of the Procedure Committee of the Court of Session.

734 **We recommend** that jury trial should not be reintroduced to personal injuries litigation in England and Wales; and that consideration should be given to the abolition of jury trial in personal injuries litigation in Scotland.

735 Although the considerations we have outlined apply equally to jury trial in Northern Ireland, it was urged upon us by some witnesses that there were special reasons why it should be retained there. A Northern Ireland judge pointed out in his comments on the Law Commission's Working Paper No 41 (which were made available to us) that the small area of the province meant that a judge might know or know of a party to the litigation, or might be able to deduce which insurance company was involved; and that this did not make it any easier to try a case without the assistance of a jury. The same witness also suggested that jury awards in Northern Ireland were surprisingly uniform and predictable, and kept reasonably in step with changes in the value of money. Some members of the General Council of the Bar of Northern Ireland attached importance to consistency with practice in the Republic, where jury trial has been retained. In the light of these views, and in the absence of strong evidence in favour of abolishing jury trial in Northern Ireland, we make no recommendation on this topic.

Adjudication by tribunals and by a judge with assessors

736 We agree with both the Winn Committee and the Law Commission that the assessment of damages should continue to be carried out by the courts, and not by a damages tribunal or other special tribunal. The Council on Tribunals told us that they took the same view. Like the Winn Committee and the Law Commission, we also come down against a system of trial by a judge sitting with expert assessors.

Experts

737   We have considered the separate question whether the courts should be able to appoint an expert whose report would be binding on both parties as to issues within his field of expertise. Such a system operates in France in relation to medical evidence. We think that this is an interesting precedent, which offers some prospect of expediting those cases in which the parties cannot agree on the medical evidence, and deserves further study. We suggest that, if successful, the idea might be extended to other experts, such as actuaries.

738   **We recommend** that consideration should be given to a system whereby, in the absence of agreed expert evidence, the court could, on the application of either party, appoint an expert whose report would have the effect of agreed expert evidence.

Interest on damages

739   In England and Wales by virtue of section 22 of the Administration of Justice Act 1969, and in Scotland by virtue of section 1 of the Interest on Damages (Scotland) Act 1971, a court must award interest on damages for personal injuries, or on such part of them as it considers appropriate, unless there are special reasons to the contrary. In Northern Ireland, the award of interest is discretionary.

740   Guidelines for the award of interest in England and Wales were first laid down by the Court of Appeal in *Jefford* v. *Gee* [1970] 2 Q.B. 130. Lord Denning, Master of the Rolls, giving the judgment of the court, said, 'Interest should not be awarded as compensation for the damage done. It should only be awarded to a plaintiff *for being kept out of money* which ought to have been paid to him.' Like the Law Commission, we agree with this approach.

Past pecuniary loss

741   Also in *Jefford* v. *Gee*, the Court of Appeal held that interest on damages for past pecuniary loss (special damages) should be awarded from the date of injury to the date of trial, at half the rate payable on money in court which was placed on short term investment. (The interest is taxable as income in the hands of the recipient.) The fraction of one-half was an average. Some losses would be incurred at or near the date of injury, and so should theoretically bear interest at the full rate. But others would be incurred shortly before the trial, and so should bear little or no interest.

742   We agree with the Law Commission that the half rate rule is a fair compromise, although we recognise that it sometimes represents only rough justice – for example, where most of the plaintiff's losses are incurred shortly after his injury. Considerations of inflation are not relevant, since the interest rate used is a market rate. **We recommend** that the rule in *Jefford* v. *Gee* that interest on damages for past pecuniary loss should be awarded at half the rate payable on money in court which is placed on short term investment should stand; and that it should be applied in Scotland and Northern Ireland.

Future pecuniary loss

743   We think it follows from the principle that interest should be awarded to a plaintiff only for being kept out of his money that no interest should be awarded on damages for future pecuniary loss. This was the approach adopted in *Jefford* v. *Gee*. **We recommend** that, as at present, no interest should be awarded on damages for future pecuniary loss.

Non-pecuniary loss

744   In *Jefford* v. *Gee*, it was held that interest on damages for non-pecuniary loss should be awarded at the full rate from the date of service of the writ to the date of trial. It was on the date of service of the writ, at the latest, that the defendant's obligation to pay damages arose; and it was from that date that the plaintiff could be said to have been kept out of his money.

745   In the more recent case of *Cookson* v. *Knowles* [1977] 3 W.L.R. 279, however, the Court of Appeal altered this rule in accordance with the recommendation of the Law Commission that no interest should be awarded on non-pecuniary damages. The Law Commission argued, in their report on the assessment of damages, and again in their Working Paper No 66 on Interest, that the plaintiff benefited from any increase in the scale of damages between the date of injury and the date of trial, since the court always assessed damages on the scale prevailing at the time of trial. They felt that the plaintiff should not gain still further from an award of interest.

746   We are not entirely in agreement with this reasoning. It is only in a qualified sense that the plaintiff may be said to gain from any increase in the scale of damages. He receives more pounds, but each pound is worth less because the scale of damages is increased only in line with inflation. He gains nothing in real value for being kept out of his money.

747   Nevertheless, we agree with the Law Commission's conclusion, and with the rule in *Cookson* v. *Knowles*, that no interest should be awarded on non-pecuniary damages. As we have pointed out elsewhere, in present economic conditions an investor may well be unable to do more than maintain the real value of his investment, once tax and inflation are taken into account, if indeed he can manage to do this. To award no interest on non-pecuniary damages may therefore be at least as favourable as the award of interest at a market rate on damages for past pecuniary loss. A more important justification, however, lies in the conventional nature of non-pecuniary damages. We do not think that it would be appropriate to subject essentially arbitrary figures to detailed financial calculations. If an attempt were to be made, allowance would have to be made for inflation in selecting the appropriate interest rate. It would also, strictly speaking, be necessary to apply interest at the half rate only to that part of the damages relating to non-pecuniary loss before trial, assessed on the scale current at the date of injury. This would all be highly artificial.

748   **We recommend** that the rule in *Cookson* v. *Knowles* that no interest should be awarded on damages for non-pecuniary loss should stand; and that it should be applied in Scotland and Northern Ireland.

Damages following death

749   It was held in *Jefford* v. *Gee* that damages for lost dependency should bear interest at the full rate from the date of service of the writ to the date of trial.

750   The Law Commission criticised this rule on the grounds that interest should be awarded only on that part of the damages relating to losses before the trial. They thought that the interest should run from the date of death to the date of trial, and that it should normally be at the half rate. In *Cookson* v. *Knowles*, the Court of Appeal altered the rule in line with the Law Commission's recommendation (although it was not explicitly clear whether interest was to be awarded from the date of death or from the date of service of the writ).

751   We agree with the Law Commission. The old rule in *Jefford* v. *Gee*, that interest should be awarded on the whole sum of damages for lost dependency, seemed to us inconsistent with the principle that damages should be awarded to a plaintiff only for being kept out of money due to him. The analogy with claims for pecuniary loss suffered by a living plaintiff is exact, except that it has not hitherto been the practice to distinguish between past and future pecuniary loss in fatal cases. We think it follows that the same rules should be applied to claims for pecuniary loss caused by death and injury; and that, in particular, interest in fatal cases should run from the date of death and not from the date of service of the writ.

752   **We recommend** that the rule in *Cookson* v. *Knowles* that interest should be awarded only on that part of the damages for lost dependency which relates to losses before trial, at a half-rate, should stand; that it should be applied in Scotland and Northern Ireland; and that such interest should run from the date of death to the date of trial.

753   We are aware that the change in practice brought about by the decision in *Cookson* v. *Knowles* has been criticised on the grounds that it has led to a reduction in total awards to dependants. The fact remains, however, that the previous rule in *Jefford* v. *Gee* resulted in over compensation for which there was no justification in principle. We see no reason why interest should be awarded on damages paid in advance for losses yet to be incurred. Given that the tort system aims to compensate actual losses, we think the rule in *Cookson* v. *Knowles* produces the right result.

754   The Law Commission proposed that damages of £1,000 should be recoverable for non-pecuniary loss suffered by a parent on the death of a minor child, or by a spouse on the death of the other spouse. They considered that such awards should bear interest at the full rate from the date of death to the date of trial.

755   We ourselves have proposed that damages for loss of society, equal in value to one half of average annual industrial earnings, should be recoverable by a spouse, parent or child of the deceased. We do not think that such awards should bear interest. The amount of the loss of society award which we propose for England, Wales and Northern Ireland would keep pace with inflation insofar as earnings did generally. We consider that loss of society awards should be

treated for interest purposes in the same way as other non-pecuniary damages (which, as we have already noted, are also increased approximately in line with inflation).

756 **We recommend** that no interest should be awarded on damages for loss of society.

Itemisation of damages

757 The rules laid down in *Jefford* v. *Gee* in effect required the courts in England and Wales to divide an award of damages for personal injury into three elements – damages for past pecuniary loss (special damages), damages for future pecuniary loss, and damages for non-pecuniary loss. In Scotland it is usual for the court also to sub-divide damages for non-pecuniary loss (*solatium*) into past and future elements. Theoretically the decision in *Cookson* v. *Knowles* means that it is no longer necessary for the purpose of awarding interest to distinguish between damages for non-pecuniary loss and damages for future pecuniary loss.

758 The Law Commission proposed that awards of damages for personal injury (but not for death) should be itemised under twelve heads, falling within the three main divisions required by *Jefford* v. *Gee*. Their proposals were designed to solve the problem of 'overlap', whereby the courts had reduced non-pecuniary damages to take account of the effect on the plaintiff's wellbeing of a large award of pecuniary damages; and to ensure that any amounts awarded under novel heads of damages (such as expenses incurred by others on the plaintiff's behalf) were stated separately.

759 We are at one with the Law Commission on the question of overlap. Damages for pecuniary and non-pecuniary loss are assessed on different principles and serve different purposes. We consider that damages for pecuniary and non-pecuniary loss should always be assessed separately, and that neither should be increased or reduced because of the size of the other.

760 Our proposals in relation to interest on damages would require the courts, as at present, to divide damages for pecuniary loss into past and future elements. Moreover, our majority proposals for handling the deduction of social security benefits from tort damages would require a further division of damages for future pecuniary loss in personal injury cases into damages for future loss of income and damages for future expenses (unless there were no damages or no social security benefits under one of these heads).

761 Accordingly, our majority proposals would normally require the division of awards in respect of personal injury into four parts for the purposes of assessment – damages for past pecuniary loss, future loss of income, future expenses, and non-pecuniary loss. In fatal cases, only three divisions would be necessary since there would be no award for future expenses. In the ordinary case, we would have thought that this degree of itemisation was sufficient. But we would not wish to rule out the possibility of more detailed itemisation, along the lines proposed by the Law Commission, in more complex cases.

762 **We recommend** that damages for pecuniary and non-pecuniary loss should be separately assessed; and that the court should have a discretion, in any particular case, to decide whether the damages should be itemised in more detail than would be required by our recommendations on offsetting social security benefits and our recommendations on interest.

763 We think it important that the itemisation of awards should not encourage unmeritorious appeals. We have no reason to think that the limited itemisation required by the rules in *Jefford* v. *Gee* has had this effect, but for the avoidance of doubt **we recommend** that an award of damages, however itemised, should not be interfered with on appeal unless it is inordinately high or inordinately low as a whole.

Limits of jurisdiction

764 We have already noted that county courts in England and Wales cannot handle a claim for damages for personal injury or death which is worth more than £2,000. Such claims must be made in the High Court. In Northern Ireland, the limit of jurisdiction of county courts is currently £1,000. In Scotland, either sheriff courts or the Court of Session can handle claims of any value.

765 As a result of the existing limits of jurisdiction, and of our proposal that only the Court of Session should have power to award and review periodic payments, claims involving future pecuniary loss caused by death or serious and lasting injury would be confined to the High Court in England and Wales, the High Court in Northern Ireland, and the Court of Session in Scotland. Claims involving less substantial losses, but worth more than £2,000 in England and Wales and £1,000 in Northern Ireland, would also be handled only by the High Courts. But in Scotland, such claims could be handled either by sheriff courts or by the Court of Session. It has been suggested to us that the jurisdiction of sheriff courts in Scotland might be limited in accordance with the limit of jurisdiction of county courts in England and Wales.

766 While we make no recommendation on this matter, we suggest that consideration might in the future be given to the possibility of similarly limiting the jurisdiction of sheriff courts in claims for damages for personal injury and death. If this were done, we think it would be sensible also to align the limit of jurisdiction of county courts in Northern Ireland.

PART V

Combining no-fault and tort

CHAPTER 17

Work

767 Category a of our terms of reference requires us to consider injuries suffered by any person 'in the course of employment'. We have interpreted this requirement so as to include all work related injuries, whether arising from employment or self employment, and also occupational diseases. Although illness as such is outside our terms of reference, we regard occupational diseases as impliedly covered because in the social security legislation they are treated as if they were industrial injuries.

THE PRESENT POSITION

The scale of work injuries

768 Each year in the United Kingdom some 720,000 people are injured at work and 1,300 are killed. This means that there are about twice as many injuries at work as there are on the roads, but less than one fifth as many deaths. Over 80 per cent of work injuries occur to males over the age of 15. Ninety five per cent are suffered by employees as distinct from the self employed. We estimate that there are about 150,000 other injuries indirectly related to work, predominantly those sustained whilst travelling to and from work.

769 The average time for which an employee is away from work as a result of a work accident is about four weeks. Seven out of eight of those injured are able to resume work within eight weeks. About 15 million working days a year are lost as a result of work accidents. The cumulative effect of work accidents on national production is therefore considerable, although even this total is a small proportion of the 330 million days lost annually through all injury or illness.

770 The average accident rate for all industries in the period June 1972–May 1975 was 40 accidents a year for each 1,000 employees. This conceals a wide variation in the rates of different industries or occupations, ranging from 4 accidents for each 1,000 employees in insurance, banking, finance and business services to 198 accidents for each 1,000 employees in mining and quarrying. In deep sea fishing and offshore oil installations the rate of accidental deaths is some 70 times that for all manufacturing industries.

771 It is difficult to be precise about the extent of illness or disease attributable to work. Each year there are some 16,000 new cases of incapacity due to industrial diseases prescribed under the state industrial injuries scheme. On

169

average, these result in longer periods off work than do accidents. Our own survey indicated that, in addition, many employees who had suffered other illnesses felt there was a connection between the illness and conditions at work.

772   Compensation is paid each year through the industrial injuries scheme in over 600,000 new cases of work injury or disease. The total annual cost is about £250 million. In addition about £70 million is paid each year in respect of work injuries to some 90,000 people through the tort system.

Social security benefits

773   In chapter 5 we outlined the history of the industrial injuries scheme. It covers persons in the United Kingdom who are working for an employer whether full time or part time. Benefits are not dependent on contributions, and are paid to those unable to work, or disabled, as a result of an accident 'arising out of and in the course of' employment or because of a prescribed disease related to the nature of such employment. Benefits are also paid to the widow and other dependants of a person who dies as a result of such an accident or disease.

774   Injury benefit is a weekly benefit paid for not more than 26 weeks to a person incapable of work. When this stops, if the person is still incapable of work, invalidity benefit may be payable under the national insurance scheme. Disablement benefit may also become payable when injury benefit ceases. This is not intended to compensate for loss of earnings but for loss of physical or mental faculty as a result of the injury.

775   The payment of industrial death benefits is related to the age and family circumstances of any dependants of the deceased. Benefits include an initial pension for a widow, with increases for children, followed by a long term pension which is flat rate. Small pensions or gratuities may be paid to other relatives.

776   Annex 4 contains a description of all social security benefits.

777   Decisions on title to benefit are given by independent adjudicating authorities – insurance officers, local tribunals and the National Insurance Commissioners. Insurance officers' decisions are given on the basis of documentary evidence including medical certificates and reports from employers and witnesses. An appeal against an insurance officer's decision may be made to a local tribunal which normally consists of an employers' representative, an employees' representative and a legally qualified chairman. There is a further right of appeal to one of the National Insurance Commissioners, who holds oral hearings where necessary. Leading decisions of the Commissioners are published, and form case law.

778   Each year over 600,000 decisions on industrial injuries claims are given by insurance officers. There are about 1,500 appeals to local tribunals and about 400 appeals to the Commissioners.

779 Medical questions arising on claims to disablement benefit are determined by independent medical authorities. These questions include whether
or not an accident has resulted in a loss of faculty, and if so to what degree, and
for what period the extent of resulting disablement is to be assessed. The authorities are medical boards, normally consisting of two general practitioners, and
medical appeal tribunals, consisting of two consultants under a legal chairman.
In prescribed disease cases, decisions relating to diagnosis as well as disablement
may have to be given and the authorities then comprise medical members with
specialised knowledge of pneumoconiosis, byssinosis and other diseases.

780 Nearly 250,000 medical board examinations and over 11,000 medical
appeal tribunal hearings take place each year.

Supplementary schemes
781 Special schemes for supplementing industrial injuries benefit may be
made in any industry under section 158 of the Social Security Act 1975. If
approved by the Secretary of State for Social Services, the schemes may be
administered by DHSS, but must not make use of public funds and must meet
both benefit and administration costs from their own resources. Only one such
scheme has been made – the Colliery Workers Supplementation Scheme – and
we understand that the scheme is being phased out.

Tort
782 To succeed in a civil action for compensation for an injury at work, the
plaintiff must satisfy the court that the injury or disease was caused by the
negligence of the employer or someone acting for or on behalf of the employer,
or that it arose from a breach of a statutory duty imposed on the employer.
It is the practice, in appropriate circumstances, for claims to be based both on
negligence and on breach of statutory duty. Damages in either case may be
reduced if there was contributory negligence by the employee.

783 Actions for negligence are founded on the employer's common law duty
to take reasonable care for the safety of his employees. This duty is a wide
one. It applies whether the employer is an individual or a company, and whether
or not the employer takes any actual part in the conduct of the operations. The
duty is not limited to such matters as the safety of the plant, the place of work,
and the method of work. The employer's duty is to provide for the safety of
the employee in the course of his employment. The courts have taken a fairly
broad view of this duty. It applies when the employee is working at the premises
of other persons; it covers activities normally and reasonably incidental to work
(for example where an employee slipped while going to wash a tea cup); and it
may even include actions in disobedience of orders, provided that they were
undertaken for the purposes of the employer's business.

784 The rule that an employer cannot by delegation divest himself of his duty
of care means that he is usually liable for the negligence of his employees
towards one another. It may also mean that he is liable for the negligence of
independent contractors. The Employer's Liability (Defective Equipment) Act

1969 makes an employer liable for personal injury to employees caused by defects in equipment provided by him, even if the defect is attributable wholly or partly to the fault of a third party, for example a manufacturer or repairer. (The employer retains the right to claim indemnity or contribution from the third party.)

785   Health and safety legislation places on employers stringent requirements for the protection of employees, particularly in dangerous industries. Until the Nuclear Installations Act 1965 and, more recently, the Health and Safety at Work etc. Act 1974, the legislation had not expressly provided for compensation or been concerned with rights of civil action. It has, however, long been established that, where a statute has been passed for the benefit of employees, the common law gives them a right of action against the employer if he is in breach of his statutory duty. As with actions in negligence, the employer cannot avoid liability by delegating responsibility to an employee, agent, or independent contractor, although exceptionally he may escape if he can show that the conduct of the injured employee was the sole cause of the breach.

786   Under the Health and Safety at Work etc. Act 1974, which brings together, under a single authority, matters relating to health, safety and welfare in connection with employment, it is intended ultimately to replace existing legislation with regulations and codes of practice. The Act provides that an action for damages lies for breach of health and safety regulations made under the Act unless the regulations exclude it; liability for breach of the existing codes is not affected, nor is common law liability for negligence.

787   Section 503 of the Merchant Shipping Act 1894, as amended, permits a shipowner to limit his liability for death or personal injury to members of the crew of the ship, with certain exceptions. We understand that it is intended to amend this provision so that the section does not apply in respect of loss of life or personal injury caused to a person on board or employed in connection with a ship under a contract of service governed by United Kingdom law.

Pneumoconiosis Compensation Scheme

788   A provision of particular interest is the National Coal Board Pneumoconiosis Compensation Scheme which provides benefits as a substitute for tort damages.

789   In 1968, a miner who was not receiving compensation under the industrial injuries scheme and had not worked in the mining industry for many years was awarded tort damages for pneumoconiosis with accompanying lung damage (*Pickles* v. *National Coal Board* [1968] 1 W.L.R. 997). This decision opened the way for a large number of similar actions, some of them involving plaintiffs who had developed the disease many years earlier. The National Coal Board and the unions involved agreed that it would be contrary to the best interests of the industry and those employed in it for pneumoconiosis to be the subject of protracted and costly litigation; and in 1974 the National Coal Board Scheme was introduced.

790   The scheme provides lump sum benefits for pain, suffering and loss of amenity (assessed according to age and degree of disablement), together with a loss of earnings allowance of up to 90 per cent of the gross weekly national average earnings in the pre-disease occupation (less national insurance invalidity benefit and special hardship allowance). In fatal cases, dependants receive 60 per cent of the gross pre-disease earnings (less state industrial death benefits). Benefits are reviewed annually to take account of movement in earnings levels and in the rates of state benefits. Acceptance of benefits under the scheme is in lieu of the right to seek compensation under tort; furthermore, the unions agreed not to support a member who decides to claim tort compensation instead of relying on the scheme's benefits.

791   Although the National Coal Board scheme makes use of DHSS medical assessments in determining the level of compensation for pain and suffering and loss of amenity, it is in all other respects independent of the industrial injuries scheme.

FUTURE NO-FAULT COMPENSATION

The basic scheme

792   The industrial injuries scheme, and the national insurance benefits commonly paid to those injured at work, provide a substantial no-fault compensation scheme for work accidents. There are few countries that can in all respects match provision in the United Kingdom. Few of our witnesses advocated total revision of the industrial injuries scheme. Most, including the TUC, whilst criticising specific features of the scheme, felt it provided a sound basis. We agree.   We were impressed by both the range and the level of benefits available or in prospect although we are in no doubt that the scheme can be improved.

793   We have already referred to our hope that the Government will look closely at means of simplifying overall social security provision. We should not wish our approval of existing industrial injuries provision to be taken as an indication that such a review is unnecessary.

794   In considering improvements we looked at a number of detailed criticisms and suggestions on the administration and adjudication of the industrial injuries scheme put forward in evidence. Given the broad base of our enquiry, it was not possible for us to deal with all of these specific issues. We are therefore referring these points to DHSS with a suggestion that they should consider them and, where appropriate, seek the advice of the Industrial Injuries Advisory Council.

795   Two themes strongly influenced our consideration of the existing provision – simplification and harmonisation.

796   The need for harmonisation with existing schemes led us to reject a suggestion that no-fault industrial injuries compensation (together with rehabilitation) should be administered by a body with responsibility for industrial safety,

such as the Health and Safety Executive. Although there might be advantages in such a system, particularly if the scheme were able to give financial support to improving accident prevention, we feel the administrative link with the social security scheme is of much greater importance.

797 **We recommend** that no-fault compensation for work injuries and diseases should continue to be provided by the industrial injuries scheme, augmented as necessary by national insurance provision, and administered as part of the social security system by the Department of Health and Social Security in Great Britain and the Department of Health and Social Services in Northern Ireland.

798 We spent some time in acquainting ourselves with the details of the industrial injuries scheme and other social security provision for the injured. We then concentrated on aspects which we think could be improved. In the discussion that follows we do not touch on those parts of the scheme which should remain as they are. It should be assumed, therefore, that where nothing is said we think no change is called for.

799 The changes we consider and comment on relate first to the amount of benefit payable, secondly to the scope of the scheme and lastly to the method of finance. As to the benefits payable, we looked at ways of compensating for loss of earnings more fully than at present – both for those injured who are unable to do any work and for those who are able to do some work but cannot earn as much as before because of the injury. We then looked at benefits for non-pecuniary loss – loss of faculty benefits – and then at the provision made for widows and other dependants following death. As to the scope of the scheme, we considered whether more earners should be covered – in particular the self employed – and whether more injuries should be included, such as those on the way to and from work and occupational diseases not at present prescribed. Lastly we considered how all these improvements should be financed.

Benefits for total incapacity for work

800 In evidence to us, trades unions, the Confederation of British Industry (CBI), nationalised industries, representative legal associations, and many others advocated that loss of earnings due to injury should be compensated by an earnings related benefit in both the short term and the long term. At present long term benefit is not normally related to the earnings lost. All the oveseas workmen's compensation schemes we studied based their compensation on individual earnings, and there has been a marked trend in this country towards earnings relation, both of benefits and of contributions. We concluded that we should aim to provide earnings related benefits for the full duration of an injured man's incapacity for work.

801 We were faced with a daunting number of possible formulae for relating benefit to earnings. Should we aim for 100 per cent replacement of earnings or some lower figure? Should the benefit be based on gross earnings or post-tax earnings? What would be the effect of making the benefit itself taxable? Should there be an upper limit on the earnings taken into account?

802   When we looked at the effect of various possible schemes we were struck by two facts. First, one of the consequences of relating benefits more closely to earnings was a marked increase, over current benefits, for the single man with high earnings compared with the family man with low earnings. Secondly, in some cases the proposed schemes produced benefits at lower levels than those currently available. The main reason for these results is the current provision of allowances for dependants.

803   If the new child benefit, which is paid for all children whether the parent is working or not, could be increased to the level of the allowance for children paid with incapacity benefit, that would provide a solution to the problem. But we recognise that on cost grounds such a move will not be possible in the foreseeable future, and this must be regarded as a long term solution. It seemed to us that allowances for dependants would have to remain, and would result in a less fully earnings related scheme than we would wish.

804   The new state pensions scheme introduced by the Social Security Pensions Act 1975 will provide an earnings related addition to the flat rate retirement, widows' and invalidity pensions (and will continue to provide allowances for dependants). We think that this scheme will provide an appropriate level of benefit related both to earnings and to family circumstances. But, for our present purpose, it is a major drawback that maximum benefits do not become payable until 1998, when the scheme has been in operation for 20 years. We think that maximum benefits should become payable immediately for those injured at work. This could be effected by accelerating the provisions of the scheme so that all claimants who suffered work injuries would be treated as having been in the scheme for 20 years. This would mean that, until 1998, all people injured at work would receive improved benefits; after that date, those who had worked for less than 20 years would benefit from this acceleration.

805   **We recommend** that, for those injured at work, long term invalidity pensions payable under the Social Security Pensions Act 1975 should be calculated, in all cases, as if contributions under the new pensions scheme had been paid for 20 years. The extra cost would be about £3 million a year after 5 years, falling back to about £1 million a year after 40 years.

806   The proposed new benefit levels represent a substantial improvement on the long term benefits currently payable. But in some cases they are not as high as the current short term benefits payable for the first six months. This is because the existing method of calculation of the short term earnings related supplement to the flat rate benefit provides $33\frac{1}{3}$ per cent of gross earnings between a lower limit of earnings and £30, plus 15 per cent of earnings between £30 and an upper limit. The new pensions scheme for long term benefits provides an earnings related addition of 25 per cent of earnings between (different) upper and lower limits.

807   For the time being, we see no alternative to different systems of earnings related additions to long and short term benefits. But we think that these methods of calculation should be gradually brought into line. As a first step

we suggest that, in industrial injury cases, the proportion of earnings to be paid between £30 and the upper limit should be increased from 15 per cent to 25 per cent for short term benefits.

808 **We recommend** therefore that, for those injured at work, short term injury benefit should comprise the existing flat rate benefit and an earnings related supplement based on 33⅓ per cent of earnings between the short term lower earnings limit and £30, and 25 per cent of earnings between £30 and the upper earnings limit.

809 The short term earnings related supplement is at present not payable to all persons who receive injury benefit. It is payable only where the injured person would also be entitled to sickness or maternity benefit under the national insurance scheme. We think that this restriction should be abolished and that the supplement should be paid to everyone in receipt of injury benefit, regardless of whether or not national insurance contributions have been paid. **We recommend** that an earnings related supplement to injury benefit should be payable without contribution conditions.

810 It is estimated that the cost of making these changes to the short term earnings related supplement would be about £7 million a year after 5 years, reducing to about £5 million a year after 40 years.

811 We considered what would happen when a man receiving the long term invalidity pension reached the age of 65. There would be a danger that, on reaching retirement pension age, an individual's benefit would be reduced. This is because during a period of incapacity for work, contributions credited for retirement pension are at a flat rate and not related to earnings.

812 A proposal that the accelerated invalidity pension rate should continue in payment beyond retirement pension age could lead to anomalies. An injured man with long periods of incapacity for work who returned to work for a short period before his retirement would still receive a comparatively low retirement pension. Nor did we think it right that an injured man with perhaps a short period of incapacity immediately before his retirement should receive an accelerated pension for the rest of his life. To resolve these anomalies, **we recommend** that, during receipt of any incapacity benefits, a man injured at work should be treated, for retirement pension qualification purposes, as having had earnings at his pre-accident level.

813 For those injured at work, the cost of this proposal would be about £1 million a year after 5 years, rising to £8 million a year after 20 years, and falling to £2½ million a year after 40 years.

Benefits for partial incapacity for work

814 One of the more difficult aspects which we considered was compensation for loss of earnings during periods of partial incapacity. By partial incapacity we mean the circumstances in which a man, because of his injuries, is able to return to work only part time or to a different occupation at a lower wage.

176

815   At present, the only attempt to compensate for partial loss of earnings is by way of special hardship allowance payable with industrial disablement pension. The allowance can be paid as an addition to disablement benefit only where the disablement has been assessed at less than 100 per cent. The addition is subject to a specific maximum and the restriction that disablement benefit and the allowance together must not exceed the rate appropriate to 100 per cent disablement.

816   Many who gave evidence to us regarded the present arrangements as inadequate. The TUC, the Post Office Engineering Union, the Industrial Law Society and the Society of Labour Lawyers all suggested that workers should receive either the difference between their earnings before and after the accident or a total income representing some proportion of their pre-accident earnings. We agree that the existing arrangements are inadequate. For those injured at work, there is a relatively low limit on the benefit payable; for those who are sick there is no benefit at all. Additional provision is needed.

817   We have considered ways of improving the provision and examined the administration of special hardship allowance. An appraisal by DHSS, prepared at our request, is at Annex 6. This describes the conditions for the award of the allowance and discusses some of the problems involved. Particular attention is drawn to the difficulties of ascertaining the amount to be paid. Extensive enquiries are necessary, involving the claimant, his employer and a medical board. Prospects of advancement may need to be considered, as may the claimant's capacity to follow suitable employment of an equivalent standard. Then the statutory authorities have to be satisfied that the claimant's inability to follow his pre-accident employment (or that of an equivalent standard) is caused by his injury. It appears that these problems are kept within reasonable bounds only by the effects of low financial limits on the rate of allowance. A further unsatisfactory feature of the allowance is that it combines a benefit for loss of earnings with a benefit for loss of faculty; and, in so doing, blurs the distinction between these fundamentally different forms of compensation. We decided that special hardship allowance could not appropriately be extended to provide satisfactory compensation for partial loss of earnings. We agree with Sir Robert Micklethwait, the former Chief National Insurance Commissioner, who in evidence to us said that the statutory provisions relating to this allowance 'require radical re-thinking'.

818   In a number of continental European countries, incapacity benefits are provided on a sliding scale according to loss of earning capacity or a medical assessment of disability. The Netherlands has seven rates of benefit related to earnings and calculated according to the assessment of incapacity. In Denmark there are three rates. In France and the Federal Republic of Germany there are two rates according to the percentage of earning capacity lost.

819   It seems to us that the time has come to consider extending the invalidity benefit provisions in the United Kingdom so as to end the disparity of treatment between the person who is totally incapacitated and the person who is capable of some work. Some of the problems encountered in administering special

177

hardship allowance will no doubt apply to any scheme for partial incapacity. But in other countries these seem to have been lessened by dealing with loss of earnings in broad bands. This issue is not confined to those incapacitated by work injury or, for that matter, any other type of injury. The question of what no-fault benefits should be paid to those unable to maintain their former standard of living goes well beyond our terms of reference and applies across the whole field of injury, sickness and even, arguably, unemployment.

820 **We recommend** that European provisions for compensating for partial incapacity should be studied with a view to the early introduction in this country of a scheme of compensation for partial incapacity for work.

821 Although the existing special hardship allowance is unsatisfactory, as we have not been able to make specific alternative proposals we are forced to conclude that the allowance should remain in payment for the time being. The existing cost of the allowance has therefore been included in the calculations of the total cost of our proposed industrial injury scheme.

Loss of faculty benefits and allowances

Disablement benefit
822 An injured man, particularly if he suffers some permanent or long term disablement, may have lost not only his ability to work. His ability to pursue leisure or other activities may have been impaired. Although there are obvious difficulties in determining the appropriate level of compensation, we think that some payment should be made in addition to that for loss of earnings.

823 Some of our witnesses felt that this compensation should extend to pain and suffering or to loss of expectation of life, but we do not agree. Payment of a benefit related to the degree of disablement (as is done at present) is in our view the right approach. By comparing the faculties of an injured person with the faculties of someone of the same age and sex who is not injured, it is possible to go some way towards an objective assessment of the loss suffered. We are aware that the list or schedule of disablements used in this assessment does not cover all possibilities (which would, in any event, hardly be feasible), but we think that it provides a useful guide to medical boards. We also think that the current system of paying benefit in the form of a gratuity for less serious disablement and in the form of periodic payments for the remainder is sensible and should continue.

824 **We recommend** that basic industrial disablement benefit should continue in its present form.

825 Despite that recommendation, however, we recognise that the total benefit levels payable may cause problems. Our proposals on long term incapacity benefits mean that families with two children would receive up to £63·60 a week at January 1977 prices. Larger families would receive more. Taking the same set of benefit levels as an example, payment of disablement benefit could add a further £25 a week. Although each element in the total is

in our view justified, there can be little doubt that there would be problems over incentives to return to work. Such high benefit levels might also be socially unacceptable.

826   Our proposals for long term incapacity benefits do no more than accelerate the provisions in existing legislation. The Government will therefore be faced with this issue in due course. The issue of total levels of social security benefits and the related issue of whether or not benefits should be taxable apply across a much wider field than compensation for injury. We do not think it would be helpful to add to the debate on these topics in the comparatively narrow area of compensation for injury, but we think that the Government should consider total benefit levels in the light of their long term plans for social security.

Attendance allowances
827   In the industrial injuries scheme, disablement benefit may be increased where the beneficiary requires constant attendance. There are four different rates of constant attendance allowance according to the extent to which the beneficiary is 'dependent on such attendance for the necessities of life'. Additionally, where either of the two highest rates is in payment, and the need for attendance is likely to be permanent, an exceptionally severe disablement allowance may also be paid.

828   Under the general social security provisions, an attendance allowance which took no account of the cause of disability was introduced in 1971. Nor was it restricted to people who had paid national insurance contributions. Under section 35 of the Social Security Act 1975 the allowance is payable to a person who is so severely disabled physically or mentally as to require 'frequent attention . . . in connection with his bodily functions' or 'continual supervision . . . in order to avoid substantial danger to himself or others'. (It is not payable in addition to the constant attendance allowance at a higher rate.)

829   Originally, the section 35 allowance was paid where attention was required by day and by night; in 1973 a lower rate was introduced for those requiring attention either by day or by night. Because of the different sets of conditions, it is not possible to compare exactly the rates payable under each scheme. But the maximum payable under the industrial injuries scheme is substantially in excess of the higher rate general allowance, and the industrial injuries scheme usually provides a higher allowance for any given degree of disablement.

830   Less than 3,000 persons are receiving constant attendance allowance or exceptionally severe disablement allowance under the industrial injuries scheme. Some 280,000 persons receive the section 35 attendance allowance.

831   These two allowances are clearly intended to cover the same kinds of cir- cumstances. As the need for attendance in each case is identical, we considered whether or not the cause of disablement should lead to different rates of payment or different conditions for payment. This question is not restricted to attendance allowances but is relevant to all benefits. We felt that, at these extremes of

179

disablement, cause is less important than effect and that on grounds of both principle and administrative expediency the two types of attendance allowance should be rationalised, so as to rely in future on a single scheme.

832   We considered a number of possibilities, and concluded that the most sensible course would be to adopt the conditions governing the award of the section 35 allowance. These were formulated comparatively recently, and it would in any event be going beyond our terms of reference to recommend any major change in an allowance which is payable for both illness and injury. For costing purposes we have assumed that the existing rates of the industrial allowances would be frozen until the nearest equivalent general allowance rates equalled or exceeded them.

833   **We recommend** that the constant attendance allowance and the exceptionally severe disablement allowance should eventually be abolished for those injured at work, who should thereafter rely on the attendance allowance payable under section 35 of the Social Security Act 1975. We suggest, however, that constant attendance allowance and exceptionally severe disablement allowance should not be withdrawn immediately. They should continue in payment, but frozen at present rates both to existing beneficiaries and to new work injury cases.

834   It is estimated that the saving from this recommendation would be about £$\frac{1}{2}$ million a year, but that this saving would be offset by the extra cost of new awards of constant attendance allowance and exceptionally severe disablement allowance to people who, under proposals made later in this chapter, would be brought into the industrial injuries scheme for the first time.

Death benefits
Widows
835   The industrial death benefit payable to the widow of a man who dies as a result of industrial injury is at a flat rate with additional allowances for children. Under the national insurance scheme, many widows are also entitled to an earnings related supplement to the flat rate pension for the first six months; this can be paid with industrial death benefit. As with invalidity benefits, widows' long term benefits will gradually be improved under the new pensions scheme by the addition to the flat rate pension of an earnings related element of up to 25 per cent of the husband's relevant earnings. The conditions for the payment of widow's benefit which relate to the age of the widow when her husband dies, or when her children cease to be dependent, differ between the industrial injuries scheme and the national insurance scheme.

836   We were in no doubt that a pension should be paid to the widow of a man killed in an industrial accident. We also felt, particularly in the light of our decisions on incapacity benefit, that in appropriate cases a widow should receive, in both the short and long term, a benefit related to the earnings of her husband. Again, the evidence we received and a study of various overseas schemes suggested a wide range of possible benefits. However for two reasons we discarded all of these and decided to build on the existing system. First,

we had already decided to make use of both the existing short term benefit arrangements and the new pensions scheme to provide improved incapacity benefits for people injured at work; we would have needed powerful reasons to depart from this basis for widows in the industrial injuries scheme. Secondly, we wished to frame our proposals in such a way as to make it relatively simple for all widows eventually to be treated alike. We have already said that, at extremes of disablement, cause is less important than effect; we think that this principle applies equally to fatal cases.

837   Although we were concerned to ensure that widows in the industrial injuries scheme received appropriate compensation, and although our proposals would significantly increase the benefits payable to many of them, we could see no justification for the different sets of conditions relating to the widow's age and family circumstances. We think that these conditions should be harmonised and that in future provisions for widows in the industrial injuries scheme should be brought into line with provision for all other widows.

838   We agree with the principle that, after the initial stage of widowhood, payment of further benefit should depend on the widow's age and whether or not she has any children. It is not in our view unreasonable, particularly in the light of the recent trend towards equal employment opportunities for women, to expect a young childless widow to support herself. We do not, however, feel that this applies to an older widow nor to a mother bringing up young children.

839   Under the national insurance scheme, long term widows' benefit is payable only to widows with dependent children or those over the age of 40. Scaled benefit rates are payable to those becoming widows between the ages of 40 and 50. We think that this scaling is a sensible way of determining an appropriate rate of benefit. We preferred it to the more rigid approach of the industrial injuries scheme whereby full benefit is payable if the widow is over 50 when her husband dies or over 40 when her children cease to be dependent, but otherwise a much smaller pension is payable. We think that the national insurance conditions should be applied in future to widows covered by the industrial injuries scheme.

840   As to benefit levels, we think that after six months widows in the industrial scheme should receive the existing flat rate benefit, allowances for children and an earnings related addition calculated as in the new pensions scheme. Again, however, we feel that the provisions of the new pensions scheme should be accelerated for widows in the industrial injuries scheme so as to provide maximum pensions immediately (that is pensions containing an earnings related addition of 25 per cent of the late husband's relevant earnings). Long term pensions for widows in the industrial injuries scheme have a preference of 55 pence a week over pensions in the national insurance scheme. As we think all widows should be treated alike we consider that this marginal preference should be phased out. For the same reason we think that the small pension (£4·59 a week at January 1977 levels) payable to all widows in the industrial injuries scheme who, because of age or family circumstances, do not qualify for a full rate pension should also be phased out. We do not think that pensions currently in payment should be withdrawn or reduced.

841 **We recommend** that long term benefits should be payable to widows covered by the industrial injuries scheme at the same rates and under the same conditions relating to age and family circumstances as will apply to widows under the provisions of the new state pensions scheme, except that the earnings related addition to a widow's pension under the industrial injuries scheme should be calculated in all cases as if the late husband had been contributing to the scheme for 20 years. The extra cost of this proposal would be about £2 million a year after 5 years falling to less than £1 million a year after 40 years.

842 We think that, for the first six months of widowhood, a widow under pensionable age should, as usually happens now, be paid a benefit made up of a flat rate element, allowances for any dependent children, and a supplement related to the earnings of her late husband. **We recommend** that the method of calculating the earnings related supplement to short term widows' benefit under the industrial injuries scheme should be improved in line with our proposals for short term injury benefit; and that the supplement should be payable in all cases. It is estimated that the cost of these changes is less than £½ million a year.

843 Industrial death benefit for widows ceases on remarriage, as it does in most overseas schemes, but a lump sum payment of a year's benefit is made. It was suggested to us that payment of industrial death benefit for a widow should continue after remarriage. We do not agree. Such a measure would lead to over compensation. **We recommend** that widows' benefit under the industrial injuries scheme should, as now, cease on remarriage; and that the provision of a lump sum payment of a year's benefit to the widow should continue.

844 As a further step towards equal treatment for all widows, we suggest that the Government should consider removing the contribution conditions for flat rate widows' benefit under the national insurance scheme. This step would be in line with the trend towards non-contributory benefits for the more severely disabled. The Government Actuary has advised us that the cost of this suggestion would be about £20 million a year. As this suggestion goes well beyond our terms of reference the estimate of cost is not included in the Government Actuary's report, nor are we including it in the combined cost of all our proposals.

Widowers
845 Under the existing industrial injuries scheme, widowers' benefit can be paid only where the widower is incapable of self support. The new state pensions scheme provides, in effect, a widowers' benefit based on the late wife's earnings where either the widower is incapable of self support or is over retirement age (and is not entitled, on his own earnings, to a retirement pension of an equivalent standard).

846 We think that industrial injuries compensation should go further than this. Changing employment opportunities and attitudes to family structure have altered the work patterns of many families. Increasingly, families are relying on the combined income of both the husband and the wife; and some-

times there is an almost total reversal of the traditional roles of mother and father. It is our view that this change should be reflected in a change in the provision of widowers' benefit so that payment is no longer conditional on the widower being incapable of self support.

847 Widowers should receive a benefit based on the earnings of the late wife and calculated in the same way as widows' benefit, although we recognise that it may not be possible or desirable to transfer all the features of widows' compensation to widowers. **We recommend** that, as far as possible, all widowers covered by the industrial injuries scheme should be treated, for benefit purposes, in the same way as widows. It is estimated that the cost of this recommendation would be about £½ million a year after 5 years, rising to about £1 million a year after 40 years.

Other dependants
848 No-fault compensation for common law wives raises a range of social issues with which we were reluctant to become involved. We note that, under the existing industrial injuries scheme, a small flat rate benefit is payable to a woman who was residing with the deceased and has care of his children; we think that this provision should continue and that any improvement should be in the context of any changes in social security provision for common law wives.

849 We also note that the existing industrial injuries scheme provides compensation, sometimes in the form of a lump sum, to a wide range of relatives who were wholly or partly supported by the deceased. These include parents, grandparents, grandchildren, and brothers and sisters. There are few beneficiaries under these arrangements – some 300 pensions are currently in payment. In 1975 there were only ten new awards. Rates of benefit are low – £1·50 a week for two dependent parents living together and a gratuity of £52 for relatives who were only partly supported by the deceased. These rates of benefit have not been changed since they were introduced in 1948.

850 There is now, particularly with the introduction of non-contributory benefits, much wider social security provision. It is likely that many, if not all, of those dependants would be entitled to benefits in their own right. **We recommend** that industrial death benefits for relatives other than widows and children should be abolished. This would help to simplify the industrial injuries scheme and would be one more step towards harmonisation of industrial death benefits with the new pensions scheme.

The self employed
851 In general, self employed people are not covered by the industrial injuries scheme, notwithstanding that some of them are exposed to considerable risk of injury at work. Those who have paid sufficient contributions are, however, entitled to flat rate sickness and invalidity benefits under the national insurance scheme. Of about 25 million contributors, some 1¾ million are classed as self employed.

852   Overseas practices vary. The self employed have cover for industrial injury in a number of European countries, although in some instances insurance is on a voluntary basis or is restricted to agricultural workers. In Canada and Australia the self employed are excluded. In New Zealand they are included.

853   Our view is that, in principle, a self employed man is just as deserving of compensation for a work accident as is an employed earner. Among those who gave evidence to us supporting the inclusion of the self employed in the industrial injuries scheme were the National Farmers Union, Professor Atiyah and the Post Office Engineering Union. We are also aware of the view, expressed to us by the National Federation of Self Employed, that contributions by the self employed to the social security scheme are not matched by the benefits available to them.

854   DHSS drew our attention to the difficulties in determining whether or not a self employed person was injured while 'in the course of his employment'. In particular, the extent and continuity of employment for a self employed person may not be closely defined and there is no employer who can be required to provide evidence on the circumstances of an accident. We acknowledge these difficulties but do not consider them to be overwhelming. They appear to have been solved in other countries.

855   But there is a further practical issue which presents difficulties. In neither the existing social security scheme nor the new pensions scheme is there provision for earnings related benefits for the self employed. Any fundamental change would have significant repercussions for both sickness benefit and retirement pensions. We were, therefore, forced to conclude that benefits for the self employed, and their widows, should be on a flat rate basis until earnings related supplements become payable to them under the social security scheme. The self employed would, however, for the first time, become eligible for disablement benefit.

856   **We recommend** that self employed persons should be covered by the provisions of the industrial injuries scheme; but that, for the time being, benefits should be at a flat rate.

857   It is estimated that the inclusion of the self employed in the industrial injuries scheme would cost about £6 million a year after 5 years, rising to £13 million a year after 40 years. This cost would then represent some 4 per cent of the total cost of the industrial injuries scheme.

Commuting accidents

858   Broadly speaking, a person travelling to or from work is not 'in the course of' his employment and is not, therefore, covered by the industrial injuries scheme. Where the employee is travelling in transport (other than public transport) provided by his employer he is brought within the scheme by section 53 of the Social Security Act 1975.

859   A number of other state industrial injuries schemes, particularly in Europe, cover commuting accidents. In France employees are included if they do not

deviate from their normal route; in the Federal Republic of Germany minor deviations, such as taking children to school, are allowed. Cover is also provided in Sweden, Australia and New Zealand, but not in most parts of Canada or the USA. And even if there is a scheme providing cover for employees, it may not extend to the self employed.

860   In considering the inclusion of commuting accidents in the industrial injuries scheme in the United Kingdom, we took into account the effect of our proposed no-fault scheme for motor injuries (see chapter 18). We estimate that about 60 per cent of people injured in commuting accidents would be entitled to compensation under the no-fault road scheme. Accidents involving motor vehicles tend to be more serious than other commuting accidents, and the Government Actuary has estimated that about 80 per cent of the value of no-fault benefits for commuting accidents would become payable under the road scheme.

861   The Post Office Engineering Union argued to us that the exclusion of commuting accidents was 'a serious limitation in the coverage of the present scheme and one which ought to be rectified'. The Union contended that 'the process of travelling to and from work is just as much a part of industrial and commercial activity as the work itself, and the individual ought to be safe-guarded in the same way'. The TUC suggested that coverage of the scheme should 'include all injuries occurring while travelling to and from home and the normal place of employment'.

862   Some of us attached considerable weight to these arguments and points of view, supported as they are by the International Labour Organisation's Recommendation 121 adopted on 8 July 1964. This Recommendation said that 'accidents sustained while on the direct way between the place of work and the employee's principal or secondary residence' should be treated as industrial accidents.

863   Commuting is not, however, normally regarded as a part of employment in this country. It is not so regarded for income tax purposes in that a man is not deemed to be engaged in the performance of his duties until he has reached his place of work.   Nor does the employer usually have control over the manner in which his employees travel to work or how far away they choose to live. The risks involved in a particular individual travelling to work may be totally different from those associated with his particular type of employment. Indeed, they are risks commonly shared by many other people engaged in multifarious activities. That being so, a number of us felt that there was no justification what-ever for imposing compensation costs of commuting accidents on employers.

864   We noted the practical difficulties in determining whether or not an accident may properly be described as a commuting accident. One is that many employees break their journey to or from work and it is not easy to devise simple rules to cover all such cases, for example to differentiate between the man who slips on the ice outside his house just before he enters it on his way home from work and the one who slips just after calling at his house. But this problem has had to be faced overseas and the majority of us felt that case law would soon

develop on this point, much as it has done on other borderline issues within the industrial injuries scheme. Another practical difficulty is that we are recommending that self employed people be covered in the industrial injuries scheme in future and it is likely to be even harder in such cases to determine whether they are commuting when an accident occurs. As noted earlier, not all overseas schemes do cover self employed people.

865   We were all concerned about the anomalies that would arise whether or not commuting accidents were included in the industrial injuries scheme. Some of us felt unable to justify paying our proposed no-fault benefits for work injuries to a person who was injured on the way to work but not to a person injured, perhaps in identical circumstances, whilst out shopping. Others felt that a far greater anomaly would arise through compensating a commuter injured in a road accident but denying our proposed benefits to commuters injured in other accidents, even though the latter type of anomaly would be reduced in the case of rail accidents by virtue of our recommendations in chapter 21.

866   The arguments for and against the inclusion of commuting accidents are very finely balanced. Eight of us (our Chairman, Lord Allen, Mr Anderson, Mr Marsh, Professor Schilling, Mr Skerman, Mrs Brooke and Mr MacCrindle) thought that commuting accidents should be included in the industrial injuries scheme. Seven of us (Lord Cameron, Professor Duthie, Mr Marshall, Professor Prest, Professor Stevenson, Mr Stewart and Mr Ure) were against specific compensation for commuting accidents.

867   **We recommend,** by a majority of one, that injuries occurring on the way to and from work should be included in the industrial injuries scheme.

868   The total cost of including commuting accidents (including those involving motor vehicles) in an industrial injuries scheme embodying all our other recommendations would be about £11 million a year after 5 years rising to £23 million after 40 years. By that time, commuting accidents would account for some 7 per cent of the total cost of the industrial injuries scheme. The net cost of including commuting accidents (after taking into account notional savings in the proposed road scheme) is £2 million a year after 5 years and £5 million a year after 40 years. Our main estimates of the cost of our proposals both in this chapter and in chapter 32 reflect the inclusion of commuting accidents in the industrial injuries schemes. As we were so evenly divided on this issue we also include an indication in chapters 18 and 32 of the effect on the cost of our proposals if commuting accidents were not included.

Occupational diseases

869   In most cases it is relatively easy to establish whether or not a particular injury resulted from an accident. The onset of the injury is usually sudden, and frequently immediately follows a particular incident. Although it is more difficult to establish a causal connection between a particular disease and a person's environment or activity, there is no doubt that some occupations inevitably expose those in them to an abnormal risk of particular diseases.

It has long been a matter of general agreement that where an occupational disease is contracted, the employee should be entitled to no-fault compensation as if he had suffered an injury by accident.

Prescription

870   Many countries, including the United Kingdom, simplify the issue of causation by prescribing a list or schedule of diseases (and related occupations) for which benefits will be paid. Such a schedule has been in use in the United Kingdom since 1906. Six diseases were originally specified under the workmen's compensation acts, namely anthrax, ankylostomiasis, and poisoning by lead, mercury, phosphorus or arsenic. Over the years, various diseases were added. By 1948, 41 diseases were included. Pneumoconiosis and byssinosis were also covered by means of special schemes.

871   The diseases prescribed on the introduction in 1948 of the industrial injuries scheme were broadly the same as those which had been covered previously but there were some substantial extensions in the occupations covered. There are currently 50 prescribed diseases together with pneumoconiosis and byssinosis. The most recent additions are occupational deafness, viral hepatitis and certain diseases associated with poisoning by vinyl chloride monomer. There are significant differences in the incidence of the diseases. Of the 16,000 or so new cases each year over 60 per cent are in respect of dermatitis. Inflammation of the hand or forearm accounts for over 20 per cent of cases, pneumoconiosis and byssinosis for over 6 per cent.

872   The conditions to be satisfied before a disease is prescribed are set out in section 76(2) of the Social Security Act 1975 which provides that the Secretary of State must be satisfied that the disease:

'... ought to be treated, having regard to its causes and incidence and any other relevant considerations, as a risk of their [the employed earners'] occupations and not as a risk common to all persons; and

(b) it is such that, in the absence of special circumstances, the attribution of particular cases to the nature of the employment can be established or presumed with reasonable certainty'.

The effect of prescription is that, in most cases, once a claimant has established that he has the disease and that he is in one of the specified occupations, the disease is presumed to be due to the nature of his employment. The schedule of prescribed diseases and related occupations is at Annex 7.

873   In practice, the question whether a disease meets the prescription requirements is referred to the Industrial Injuries Advisory Council for consideration and report. This independent body, which has a membership of 17 including representatives of the medical profession and both sides of industry, invites evidence on the disease under consideration before reaching its conclusion. The Council may request that a particular disease be referred to it for consideration.

874   We are aware that there is a widely held view that the procedures for scheduling diseases take too long, and a number of our witnesses told us that they

thought that the procedures should be simplified and speeded up. We understand that the last four cases have taken some 18 months to 2 years to prescribe after reference to the Council. Others have taken much longer and there have been examples of diseases being identified by medical experts as occupational in origin many years before they were scheduled.

875 We appreciate, however, that in view of the presumption which normally follows prescription, and its consequent effect on benefit payments, adding a disease to the list is a major step requiring careful and expert evaluation of medical and other evidence.

876 Whilst recognising the problems involved, **we recommend** that the appropriate procedures should be examined to see whether there is any means of reducing the time taken to prescribe occupational diseases.

Restrictive conditions
877 The EEC, in its Recommendation of 20 July 1966, referring to lists and schedules of prescribed diseases, advocated the abolition of systematic restrictive conditions relating to the description of the symptoms of the disease, the type of activity stated to be capable of causing the disease, and the periods of exposure to the risk. In the United Kingdom scheme, restrictive conditions have been applied to occupational deafness, where the number of occupations covered for benefit is limited, and to byssinosis, where it is a requirement that the claimant has been in the prescribed occupation for at least five years.

878 We understand that cover for occupational deafness is restricted by a shortage of diagnostic experts. We think it unfortunate that this should be a reason for denying industrial injuries compensation and hope that whatever action is necessary to expand cover for this disease will be taken as soon as possible. Although we are aware that byssinosis is a difficult disease to diagnose because of its similarity to other, non-occupational, respiratory diseases common to the public at large, we note that there has recently been a reduction (from 10 to 5 years) in the period of exposure prescribed. We hope that ways might be found to remove the restriction altogether.

879 **We recommend** that, in accordance with the EEC Recommendation of 20 July 1966, the restrictive conditions relating to the prescription of occupational diseases should be removed.

An individual proof system
880 But if the prescription of diseases were expedited and freed from restrictive conditions, would the arrangements for compensating occupational diseases be adequate? Many of our witnesses think not, and we agree with them. A common theme in the evidence submitted to us on occupational diseases was that an employee should be entitled to industrial benefits if he could show that his disease was occupational in origin. This was not only the view of the trades unions. Among others, Sir Robert Micklethwait advocated such a provision.

881 We also noted that, in a Recommendation dated 23 July 1962, the EEC proposed the introduction of a mixed system of compensating occupational

diseases. The International Labour Organisation made a similar recommendation (No 121) in July 1964. The system would consist both of a list of prescribed
diseases and an opportunity for individual proof. Individual proof would mean
establishing that a disease not on the list was occupational in origin and was a
particular risk of that occupation. Such a mixed system has been operating in
the Federal Republic of Germany since 1963.

882   The system of individual proof impresses us for two reasons. It provides
scope for compensation for an individual suffering from an unlisted occupational disease. It also serves to give a positive indication of occupational diseases
which should be considered for scheduling.

883   Special arrangements might need to be devised for adjudicating on cases
in which an individual claims that an unlisted disease was occupational in origin.
These cases might well require the resolution of difficult and contentious issues,
often involving conflicting medical evidence. It might also be that some way
should be found to deal quickly with claims of a trivial nature. We think these
difficulties can be solved. Any remaining difficulties would provide an added
incentive to speed up the prescription process so that claims could be dealt
with under that simpler system.

884   There is, however, a danger in an individual proof system. Unless the
claimant were required to prove that the disease was a particular risk of his
occupation, the way would be open for a large number of claims in respect of
illnesses which were common to the employed and also the non-employed
population. Bronchitis is an obvious example.

885   We do not think that industrial injuries compensation should be extended
to people who happen, by chance, to contract an illness at work, unless that
chance was substantially greater for those in that occupation than for the public.

886   The results of our personal injury survey suggest that a substantial
number of people consider that they are ill because of their work but are
not suffering from one of the prescribed diseases (details are in Volume Two,
chapter 19). We treated the result of this survey with caution. The view on
whether there was a connection between work and the illness was subjective
and not tested against any specific criteria; furthermore the survey included
illnesses where work was thought to be only a contributory factor, not the sole
cause.

887   We think that the mixed system of compensating occupational diseases
should be adopted in the United Kingdom. Therefore **we recommend** that in
addition to compensating the occupational diseases listed on the schedule of
prescribed diseases, benefit should become payable where the claimant could
prove that his disease was caused by his occupation and that it was a particular
risk of his occupation.

Slate quarrymen
888   We have received a considerable volume of evidence from, among others,
Gwynedd County Council, Mr Dafydd Wigley MP and Plaid Cymru about
compensation for workers in the slate and other quarrying industries suffering

from such lung diseases as pneumoconiosis. The subject has also been raised in Parliamentary debates.

889 These quarrymen, who are eligible for the same benefits under the industrial injuries scheme as are, for example, coal miners, experience difficulty in obtaining tort compensation because of the number of employers who have gone out of business. It has been suggested that a special scheme, similar to the National Coal Board Pneumoconiosis Compensation Scheme which we described earlier, should be set up to provide additional compensation.

890 While we sympathise with these quarrymen, they are not unique, even among those disabled at work, in being denied tort compensation if there is no defendant. The essential difference between the circumstances of coal miners and quarrymen is that in the former case compensation can be provided by a single, existing employer (the National Coal Board), whereas in the latter case it cannot. Any scheme which provided additional compensation for slate quarrymen would inevitably have to be financed by the Exchequer.

891 There is clearly a distinction between a scheme financed by the Exchequer and one set up by an individual employer, albeit a nationalised industry. Any state scheme would, in our view, have to compensate all employees who had failed, through no fault of their own, to obtain tort compensation. We are forced to the conclusion that it would not be possible to justify providing what would in effect be enhanced state benefits for particular groups of workers.

892 We therefore feel unable to recommend that a special compensation scheme should be set up for workers in the slate and other quarrying industries.

'Arising out of and in the course of' employment

893 An industrial accident was defined as an accident 'arising out of and in the course of' employment in the Workmen's Compensation Act 1897. The definition has remained unchanged since then. It is now in section 50 of the Social Security Act 1975.

894 Over the years the interpretation of the phrase has become less restrictive. An accident can now normally be held to have arisen out of employment if it arose from something the employee was authorised by his employer to do, either expressly or by implication, or arose from something so closely incidental to the employment that it was reasonable for the person to do it. The provisions may be satisfied even if the employee was acting in contravention of any regulations or orders, provided that the act was for the purposes of the employer's trade or business. An accident occurring away from the employer's place of business may be held to arise out of and in the course of the employment if the employee was travelling to or from work in his employer's transport or under the direction of his employer.

895 The TUC, referring to the phrase 'out of and in the course of employment' observed that it 'is capable of different interpretations and some injuries have

been excluded by the authorities'. The TUC urged that we should suggest amending the statutory definition of an industrial accident so that it was even less restrictive.

896   We noted, in our visit to the International Labour Organisation, that the phrase 'attributable to employment' was used to define an industrial accident in the rules governing the Organisation's own staff. We were not, however, convinced that the use of any such phrase would necessarily reduce or eliminate difficulties in interpretation. A considerable body of case law has developed around the existing definition and we should be reluctant to change the definition after such a long period of use.

897   The inclusion of commuting accidents in the industrial injuries scheme would necessitate an exception to the definition (since such accidents are not 'in the course of' employment). We do not, however, think that the scope of the industrial injuries scheme should be extended beyond the additional categories of injury or disease specifically referred to in this report. **We recommend** that the basic definition of an industrial accident should continue to be an accident 'arising out of and in the course of' employment.

Financing the no-fault scheme

898   There is not now a separately financed industrial injuries scheme. Benefits are paid from the national insurance fund which is financed by earnings related contributions payable by employers and employees, together with an Exchequer supplement of 18 per cent of these contributions. On earnings over £15 a week in the 1977/78 tax year, employees paid a national insurance contribution of 5·75 per cent of all earnings up to £105 a week. Employers paid a contribution of 8·75 per cent of the same earnings. Employers also paid a surcharge of 2 per cent of earnings, but this surcharge was a form of taxation, and not a contribution to the national insurance fund.

899   We first considered whether the additional cost of the improvements we were recommending for the industrial injuries scheme should be financed independently of the existing scheme. But we rejected this approach. Although on the initial implementation of our proposals there might seem to be some logic in financing the additional cost from a separate source, in the future it would appear increasingly odd for an arbitrary proportion of a single scheme to be financed in this way.

900   We looked at the possibility of introducing some form of differential contribution or premium. This might reflect the degree of risk of a work accident either in a particular company or on the wider basis of an industry as a whole. Such systems were urged on us by, among others, the TUC and the Royal Society for the Prevention of Accidents. The latter organisation, commenting on industrial safety, observed:

'. . . it is considered essential that premiums should be so assessed as to provide a strong incentive on management to establish and maintain safe working conditions, i.e. speedy and substantial changes in premiums, upwards or downwards, as appropriate'.

We also noted that, in most overseas schemes, work accident compensation is financed by differential contributions based either on the specific accident record of individual firms or on the overall accident record of the particular industry. In addition to the accident prevention aspect there are many who believe that, as far as possible, responsibility for financing compensation should be related to the risk created. We were attracted to the concept of financing the industrial injuries scheme by differential contributions and looked at possible ways of introducing such a system.

901 We considered financing the state no-fault scheme through a levy on employer's liability insurance premiums. But there were a number of practical objections to such a scheme. We doubted if private insurers would be prepared to raise large sums of money to finance a state scheme over which they had no control or influence. Conversely the Government might not, for a state scheme, wish to rely on an apportionment of contributions determined by the private sector. Additionally, many of us felt it would be inappropriate to finance no-fault compensation through a component of tort compensation when the latter may well decline in scale and significance. A levy on employer's liability insurance premiums would be wholly out of proportion to the premiums themselves. Total premium income is about £170 million a year. The cost of the industrial injuries scheme under our proposals would ultimately be about £370 million a year. In the light of all this, we do not think it is feasible to finance the state no-fault scheme through a levy on private insurance premiums.

902 We next considered the possibility of differential state scheme contributions. To be most effective in accident prevention, such differentiation would have to be related not just to industries but to individual employers. But we doubt whether differentiation at employer level would be administratively practicable. Assessing the accident risk of every employer would require a large organisation together with some mechanism for appeals. Bearing in mind the relatively small effect on an employer's total labour costs of an increase in industrial injuries contributions, we think that, from the point of view of its contribution to improved safety, the benefits of such a scheme would be far outweighed by the administrative costs and disadvantages.

903 There remained the possibility of differentiation at industry level. Although differentiating by industry would provide some incentive for individual employers to improve standards within the industry as a whole, the results of their own efforts would be likely to be marginal when combined with the accident experience of employers in the same industry who were less conscious of the need for safety. The main advantage of this form of differentiation is that it relates the cost of the industrial injuries scheme more closely to the risk potential of the industry concerned. While we were attracted to this proposition as a theory, most of us felt that, given its very limited effect on accident prevention, it was not appropriate to introduce it. It would require a major change in the existing system of financing national insurance and involve the reintroduction of a separate industrial injuries contribution. We do not think that the economic and social benefits justify such a change.

904 **We recommend**, with one dissentient, that the industrial injuries scheme should continue to be financed through the existing system of national insurance contributions and Exchequer supplement; and, subject to the following recommendation, that the additional cost of the changes proposed should be met by an increase in the employers' contribution only. Professor Prest dissents from this recommendation. His note of reservation appears at the end of this chapter.

905 We see no alternative to continuing to finance benefits for the self employed in the same way as at present. **We recommend** that the benefits which we propose for the self employed should be wholly financed by an increase in their national insurance contributions.

TORT

Should tort be retained?

906 The existence of a substantial no-fault scheme for industrial accidents, and the significant body of opinion which has drawn attention to the adverse effects of the tort system in the field of accident prevention, prompt serious consideration of the abolition of the tort action as a means of providing compensation for work accidents.

907 In 1972 the Robens Committee, in their report 'Safety and Health at Work' (Cmnd 5034), expressed concern over the effect on industrial safety of litigation between employer and employee on compensation for personal injury. The Committee drew attention to the criticism that the prospect of such litigation made the task of framing, maintaining and enforcing effective regulations for the prevention of accidents more difficult than it need be. Employers, trades unions and others who were involved in preparing and interpreting those regulations were likely to be concerned with the implications not only for accident prevention but also for compensation. The Committee also referred to the effect of possible compensation litigation on accident investigation. The need for each side to present its own case in the best possible light might well hinder an objective investigation of the circumstances of any particular accident, and might result in a deterioration in industrial relations.

908 This concern was echoed by many of our witnesses. The CBI observed that potential defendants often feared that the introduction of new safety measures after an accident might be interpreted as an admission that previous practices were deficient in some way.

909 But there is an opposite point of view. Some of our witnesses felt strongly that retention of the tort system, far from being a hindrance to safety at work, was necessary to maintain standards of accident prevention. They pointed to stringent surveys by insurance companies, and the effect on employers of the risk that unsafe practices would be exposed in court.

910 We recognise that tort creates difficulties in the field of accident prevention, but it seems to us likely that their impact, in such areas as accident investigations and co-operation in drafting safety regulations, will be reduced by the provisions of the Health and Safety at Work etc. Act 1974.

911 It was also put to us that an injured workman should not be denied a right which was available to others, even where that remedy had a number of disadvantages. Many witnesses, in particular the TUC, took the view that tort should be abolished only if the no-fault scheme could be significantly improved.

912 We noted that where tort actions for work accidents have been abolished or severely restricted in other countries, this has usually been accomplished at the time when a no-fault scheme was introduced. That is not the position here, and it does not seem to us that the scale of the improvements which we are recommending for the industrial injuries scheme is such as to justify abolishing tort actions for work injuries, and for work injuries alone.

913 **We recommend**, with one dissentient, that an injured workman's right of action for damages against his employer should be retained. Professor Schilling dissents from this recommendation. His note of reservation appears at the end of this chapter.

The basis of liability

914 Having decided, by a majority, that the tort action for work injuries should remain, we considered the basis of liability for such actions. We have already explained that tort actions for work injuries can be based either on negligence or on breach of statutory duty. We noted that in July 1946 the Final Report of the Departmental Committee on Alternative Remedies (Cmd 6860) – the Monckton Report – recommended no change in the basis of liability for tort actions for work injuries. Most actions allege a breach of statutory duty and, in view of the wide powers to make new safety regulations under the Health and Safety at Work etc. Act 1974, this is likely to remain so.

915 Our strategy has been to look at each category of tort action for personal injury to see whether or not the basis of liability should be made more strict. For work injuries, we have concluded that the widely used action for breach of statutory duty goes far enough in this direction.

916 **We recommend** that there should be no change in the basis of liability in tort for work injury.

917 In making this recommendation, however, we are conscious of the difficulties that can arise in basing a tort action on legislation primarily intended to be part of the criminal law. We think that care should be taken to differentiate in legislation between civil liability and criminal offences and note, with approval, that section 47 of the Health and Safety at Work etc. Act 1974 makes specific reference to such matters as the defences available for civil proceedings. Such a distinction should, in our view, be made in any future legislation of this type.

The burden of proof

918 At present, the injured plaintiff has to prove that his injury was caused by negligence or breach of statutory duty on the part of the employer or somebody acting on the employer's behalf. A number of our witnesses urged that

the burden of proof should be reversed, so that the onus was on the employer to prove that he was not at fault.

919 Difficult cases will arise whether the burden of proof is on the employer or whether it is on the plaintiff. There will be occasions on which the employee could not be expected to be aware of, and hence prove, the chain of events leading up to the accident; and in the case of a fatal accident a plaintiff may have particular difficulty in proving the circumstances. It was argued to us that in current industrial conditions, and particularly bearing in mind industrial safety legislation, an employer should be required to demonstrate that an industrial accident was not his fault.

920 But there is also the not uncommon case in which the events leading up to the accident are known only to the injured plaintiff. The employer may have no first hand knowledge and may be unable to obtain any information about the accident. If the burden of proof were reversed, employers might find themselves unable to defend actions even if on the true, but unascertainable, facts the accident was due solely to some reckless act of the plaintiff. In such a case, whilst it is right that the injured employee should receive suitable no-fault compensation through the social security system, it may be thought unjust for the employer to be deemed to have been personally or vicariously at fault.

921 We took into account the fact that persons injured at work are already in a favoured position in relation both to other injured persons and to the much greater number of persons incapacitated by illness. The persons injured at work already have the industrial preference in the social security system. They also have the action for breach of statutory duty as well as the action for negligence, and the statutory duties are many and far reaching. We were not persuaded that it was right to add a further advantage which might result in a magnification of the tort action by encouraging employees to make a claim, however weak their case, in the hope that the employer would have no means of resisting the claim and so would have to make a payment in settlement.

922 **We recommend** that there should be no formal reversal of the burden of proof in actions for damages for work injury.

THE EFFECT OF OUR PROPOSALS

Details of the new benefit levels

923 In tables 14 and 15 we compare our proposed benefits for loss of earnings with the existing benefits and with gross and net earnings before injury or death. Benefits for loss of faculty (which would remain unchanged) are not included. The tables give January 1977 benefit levels and assume the rates of tax and allowances applicable at that date. For the purposes of illustration and simplification, however, it has been assumed that the child benefit scheme, which is being introduced in stages up to April 1979, is fully implemented. No child tax allowances have been included, and the increases of benefit for children have been reduced by £2·50 a week. Total family income would, therefore, be net earnings or benefits plus child benefit payable at the same rate before or after the accident.

195

Table 14 Comparison of existing and proposed benefits for loss of earnings
(disablement benefit may be payable in addition)

i Injured man, aged 35 with a dependent wife and two dependent children

£ a week at January 1977 levels

Gross earnings	Net earnings[1]	Benefits for the first 6 months		Benefits after 6 months	
		Existing[2]	Proposed[3]	Existing[4]	Proposed[5]
60	42·80	36·23	38·33	36·40	47·65
80	54·70	38·75	42·55	36·40	52·65
105	69·50	38·93	42·83	36·40	58·90

ii Injured man, age 35, with no dependants

£ a week at January 1977 levels

Gross earnings	Net earnings[1]	Benefits for the first 6 months		Benefits after 6 months	
		Existing[6]	Proposed[6]	Existing[6]	Proposed[6]
60	40·50	25·13	27·23	17·30	28·55
80	52·30	27·65	31·45	17·30	33·55
105	67·20	27·83	31·73	17·30	39·80

1 Gross earnings less (i) tax at 1976/77 rates, assuming no other income, and no tax allowances apart from personal allowances (in particular no tax allowance for children), and (ii) social security contributions at April 1977 rates, i.e. 5·75% of earnings up to £105 a week.

2 Includes flat rate benefit (£15·65), increase for wife (£8·00), increase for children (£1·55 each, i.e. assuming child benefit rate of £2·50) and an earnings-related supplement of $33\frac{1}{3}$% of gross earnings from £11–£30 and 15% of earnings £30–£69 (earnings in 1975/76 fiscal year, assumed to be 15% lower than January 1977 earnings levels). Supplements are £9·48, £12·00 and £12·18.

3 Benefits as in note 2 above except for earnings related supplement which is $33\frac{1}{3}$% of earnings from £11–£30 and 25% of earnings £30–£69. Supplements are £11·58, £15·80 and £16·08.

4 Includes flat rate benefit (£15·30), increase for wife (£9·20), increase for children (£4·95 each, i.e. assuming child benefit rate of £2·50) and an invalidity allowance (£2·00). On implementation of the new pensions scheme benefits will, over 20 years, rise to those shown under proposed benefits.

5 Benefits as in note 4 plus an earnings related addition of 25% of current gross earnings in the range £15–£105.

6 Benefits as for table 14 i except that no increases for wife or children are payable.

Table 15 Comparison of existing and proposed benefits for widows

(Benefits are shown gross – they are subject to tax)

i Widow with two dependent children

£ a week at January 1977 levels

Husband's		Benefits for the first 6 months		Benefits after 6 months	
Gross earnings	Net earnings[1]	Existing[2]	Proposed[3]	Existing[4]	Proposed[5]
60	42·80	40·78	42·88	25·75	36·45
80	54·70	43·30	47·10	25·75	41·45
105	69·50	43·48	47·38	25·75	47·70

ii Widow aged 50 or over with no dependants

£ a week at January 1977 levels

Husband's		Benefits for the first 6 months		Benefits after 6 months	
Gross earnings	Net earnings[1]	Existing[6]	Proposed[6]	Existing[6]	Proposed[6]
60	40·50	30·88	32·98	15·85	26·55
80	52·30	33·40	37·20	15·85	31·55
105	67·20	33·58	37·48	15·85	37·80

1 Husband's gross earnings less (i) tax at 1976/77 rates assuming no other income, and no tax allowances apart from personal allowances (in particular no tax allowance for children), and (ii) social security contributions at April 1977 rates, i.e. 5·75% of earnings up to £105 a week.

2 Includes flat rate benefit (£21·40), increase for children (£4·95 each, i.e. assuming child benefit rate of £2·50) and an earnings related supplement of $33\frac{1}{3}$% of husband's gross earnings from £11–£30 and 15% of earnings £30–£69 (earnings in 1975/76 fiscal year, assumed to be 15% lower than January 1977 earnings levels). Supplements are £9·48, £12·00 and £12·18.

3 Benefits as in note 2 above except for earnings related supplement which is $33\frac{1}{3}$% of earnings from £11–£30 and 25% of earnings £30–£69. Supplements are £11·58, £15·80 and £16·08.

4 Includes flat rate benefit (£15·85) and increases for children as in note 2 above. On implementation of the new pensions scheme benefits will, over 20 years, rise to those shown under proposed benefits (plus 55p additional flat rate benefit).

5 Includes flat rate benefit (£15·30), increases for children as in note 2 and an earnings-related addition of 25% of husband's current gross earnings in the range £15–£105.

6 Benefits as for table 15 i except that no increases for children are payable.

A further important qualification to the tables is that benefit rates are expressed in gross terms. At present, benefits for injured people are not taxed; widows' benefits are taxed.

924   It will be seen that the effect of our proposals would be to provide slightly higher short term benefits for injured people and much improved long term benefits. The maximum rate of short term injury benefit for a single man would rise by 14 per cent to £31·73 a week. For a married man with two children our proposals would result in a maximum short term benefit of £42·83 a week and in a payment of £42·55 to the man on average earnings (about £80 a week, gross).

925   Long term benefits for injured people would be improved by the provision of an earnings related addition to the existing flat rate benefit. This improvement is based on, and would eventually be matched by, the new pensions scheme, but maximum benefits under that scheme will not become payable until after 20 years. Under our proposals, maximum long term benefits for a single man aged 35 would more than double from £17·30 a week to £39·80 a week. A married man of the same age, with two children, would receive up to £58·90 a week; those on average earnings would receive £52·65, so that existing provision would be increased by 45 per cent.

926   In addition to the benefits for loss of earnings, disablement benefit of up to £25 a week might be payable, as might attendance allowance and mobility allowance.

927   In the first six months of widowhood, benefits under our proposals would be improved by £3·90 a week to a maximum of £47·38 a week for a widow with two children. Widows without children would receive up to £37·48 a week (an improvement of 12 per cent over existing provision). As with cases of injury, long term widows' benefits would be improved by the provision of an earnings related addition. Maximum long term benefit for a widow with two children would be improved from £25·75 a week to £47·70 a week (an increase of 85 per cent); if her husband had average earnings, the widow's pension would be £41·45 a week. For a widow aged 50 or over with no children, maximum long term benefits would more than double from £15·85 a week to £37·80 a week.

The cost of the changes

928   At January 1977 price levels, the cost of our recommendations for improving the industrial injuries scheme (with compensation for commuting accidents included) would, after 5 years, be about £33 million a year, including additional administration costs of £4 million. After 40 years, the cost of the improvements would be about £58 million a year, of which about £7 million represents additional administration costs. This ultimate annual cost represents an increase of about 18 per cent on the projected cost of the existing scheme.

929   We have recommended that the cost of improvements for employees should be financed by increased employers' national insurance contributions. We estimate that this increase would be unlikely to exceed 0·1 per cent of employers' total wage costs.

930   Our recommendations on the assessment of tort compensation would have a significant effect on work injuries compensation as a whole. It is difficult to allocate precisely to specific categories the costs or savings of these recommendations, but it seems that the level of tort compensation for work injuries would decline by about £34 million a year and that the amount spent on administration would fall by about £13 million a year. We also expect that, as a result of our recommendations, the annual amount spent on occupational sick pay schemes would be some £2 million lower than it otherwise would have been. Most of these savings would accrue soon after our recommendations were implemented.

931   We estimate that these reductions would mean that employer's liability insurance premiums would fall, in real terms, by about 25 per cent.

932   If commuting accidents were not included in the industrial injuries scheme the cost of the improvements to that scheme would, after 5 years, be about £21 million a year and, after 40 years, about £33 million a year. The combined effect of a reduction in the level of tort compensation and an improved industrial scheme which did not include commuting accidents would be to reduce the overall cost of compensation for work injuries, diseases and deaths by about £28 million a year (including administration) after 5 years and by about £16 million after 40 years.

933   If commuting accidents were included in the industrial injuries scheme, in accordance with our majority recommendation, the combined effect of all our proposals in respect of work injuries, diseases and deaths would, after 5 years, be a reduction of £7 million a year in level of compensation accompanied by a fall of £9 million a year in administration costs. After 40 years, however, the level of compensation would be increased by £15 million a year, although there would be a fall of £6 million a year in administration costs. The ultimate net cost of our proposals for work accidents and diseases is, therefore, £9 million a year.

Summary

934   In this chapter, having decided that the basic structure of compensation for work injuries was sound, we have looked at ways of improving the industrial injuries scheme. This we have done on two fronts, improving the benefits and extending the scope of the scheme.

935   We have recommended that there should be better earnings related short and long term benefits for injured people and their dependants; that disablement benefit should continue; that widowers should be treated in the same way as widows; and that entitlement to retirement pension should be more adequately protected during periods of injury. We have also recommended that the Government should consider ways of introducing a benefit for partial incapacity for work and that as a first step towards simplification of the industrial injuries scheme, constant attendance allowance and industrial death benefits for certain relatives should be phased out. We have recommended that the scope of the scheme be extended to include commuting accidents, benefits for the self employed and additional cases of occupational disease.

936   We think that all of these improvements should be financed by an increase in the national insurance contributions paid by employers and the self employed.

937   Tort should be retained for work injuries as a means of supplementing the no-fault industrial injuries benefits.

938   Annex 8 contains an outline of our proposed changes in the industrial injuries scheme, and a more detailed description is in the Government Actuary's report in Volume Two. Our proposals on compensation for work injuries are brought together in the List of Recommendations in Part VII of this Volume.

939   We believe that our proposals on compensation for work injuries will lead to a significant improvement in provision. But if, taken as a whole, our recommendations in this area seem less than revolutionary, it is not because we underestimate the importance of compensation for work accidents. It is rather that, precisely because of this importance, successive governments have developed a system, which, in the view of most of us, is fundamentally sound. The TUC told us that their approach had been to see what might be done to improve the industrial injuries scheme and the tort system, rather than abolish them. That has been our approach too.

NOTE OF RESERVATION ON THE FINANCE OF COMPENSATION FOR WORK INJURIES

by Professor Prest

940   As a general principle, it must make sense to relate the charges necessary to finance injury compensation to the risk potential of different activities. No one would dream of arguing that the price per pound of very decayed cod should be the same as that of very fresh salmon; or at least no one who argued for such an arrangement would volunteer to clear up its consequences. Similarly, the consequences of not relating charges to the probabilities of generating industrial injuries can easily be seen in terms of what amounts to cross-subsidisation between safer and riskier industries, the lack of incentives to install safety devices and the like. This argument has been abundantly explored in recent years by G Calabresi[10] and by P S Atiyah[6] but it was also endorsed earlier, at least in part, by Beveridge (Social Insurance and Allied Services, Cmd 6404, HMSO, 1942, paragraph 89). So there is no lack of highly respectable authority for the application of the general economic principle of relating prices to costs in this particular context.

941   At an empirical level, it is quite clear that risks of injury and the like do differ very considerably between industries in this country. Some details are given in paragraph 770 above and the Health and Safety Executive's publication Health and Safety Statistics 1975 (HMSO, 1977) makes very clear that there is, for instance, a far higher risk of injury in mining and quarrying than in manufacturing industry. Nor can it be argued with the slightest degree of conviction that it is impracticable to relate charges to risks when countries as different as

the United States, Canada, France and New Zealand (to take a few examples only) do precisely that. If the further proposition is advanced that the additional administrative costs outweigh the economic benefits, one has to ask the general question: what is the evidence, given that differentiation is common practice in other countries? If one is marching out of step with nearly everyone else, the first thing to ask is whether there is not something wrong with oneself rather than with everyone else. And if more detailed evidence is required it is easy enough to quote instances of the benefits likely to be obtained from loading extra charges on to firms with bad records (for example, Canada; see Volume Two, chapter 26, and Volume Three, chapter 2, paragraph 71).

942 In fact, there is at present some degree of risk relation in the United Kingdom system by virtue of employer's liability premiums. No doubt their application is not perfect. Nor do they cover everyone liable to suffer injury at work (for example, the self employed) but a very substantial proportion of those at risk is covered all the same. On the other hand, contributions to the national insurance fund were never risk related; and, of course, the separate injuries contribution has of late disappeared entirely. But the Commission's proposals broadly amount to a reduction in the role of employer's liability premiums and an increase in that of (undifferentiated) employer contributions. Therefore, if one takes the work area as a *whole* the degree of risk relation is *reduced*. This can only be described as making a bad situation worse and cannot possibly be supported if there is any reasonable alternative.

943 It is submitted that there is an immediate alternative, i.e. to levy a surcharge on employer's liability premiums. There is also a longer run possibility to be kept in mind with employer national insurance contributions. We shall now consider the possible objections.

944 The first objection might be that a surcharge source of finance could not be all inclusive in that, for instance, self employed people could not be charged in this way. This is perfectly true and one would have to accept that additional national insurance contributions be raised in such cases. But it seems perverse to argue that because a particular charging device cannot be applied to everyone, then it should not be applied to anyone. Nor is it at all persuasive that the 'purity' of the national insurance fund would be better maintained by clinging like a limpet to the present system of employer contributions; after all, part of the system is already financed out of general government revenue and so there would be nothing at all inconsistent in adding another source. The omission of the self employed from a risk related surcharge would also mean that the correlation between charges and risk creation would be reduced compared to the situation if everyone could be brought within the surcharge – but not compared to the situation prevailing if one simply collects the funds from a uniform percentage addition to employer national insurance contributions.

945 A second objection is that employer's liability premiums amount to some £170 million a year compared to the projected outlay of over £350 million from the state work injuries scheme. So a surcharge on the former can be pilloried as an example of a tail of a small dog wagging the body of a large one. If at a

future date the role of the state scheme were to be further enlarged and that of tort compensation further diminished, it could be argued that this objection would hold *a fortiori*.

946   The answer to this kind of objection is twofold. In the short run, if one only has to raise the additional £20 million a year needed to finance the state work scheme five years after inauguration (excluding all commuting injuries), there is no real difficulty in that this sum is very substantially less than the £170 million a year present total of employer's liability premiums. It would in fact partially offset the savings in tort compensation which would result from the change of system. This leads to an important further argument about 'spare funds' of insurance companies but as this will be developed at length in the note of reservation on road finance one can simply note it at this stage without going into it in detail.

947   The second part of the answer relates to the longer run. We can clear one point out of the way at once: even if the work scheme figures are taken at maturity the additional state scheme cost (excluding commuting injuries) is less than one fifth of the employer's liability premium total, in 1977 terms. So once again, the surcharge needed to maintain the present overall balance between those charges which are risk related and those which are not is perfectly feasible. The more important question is what would one do if tort compensation is this area were whittled further away or even reduced to zero? The answer is surely perfectly plain: there would then be an overwhelming argument for introducing a risk related element (whether on an industry or a firm basis) into employer contributions to the state scheme – in fact for bringing it into line with what happens in the great majority of other countries, and as is envisaged by Professor Schilling in his note of reservation. So the answer to those who propagate the tail wagging the dog objection to a surcharge on employer's liability premiums is quite simply: are they prepared to visualise a situation with absolutely no element of work injuries charges related to risk generation? Let it be emphasised that there is no recommendation here that employer contributions to the state scheme be changed immediately in this way – but simply that it may have to be borne in mind as a longer run possibility.

948   The final objection to the surcharge proposal is the extra administrative costs entailed. But it must be emphasised that the relevant comparison is with additional administrative costs of raising more revenue from national insurance contributions *relatively* to the extra benefits from preserving a greater degree of risk relation in one case than the other. Both limbs of the argument must be taken into account and not just one on its own if a true assessment is to be made of comparative advantages.

NOTE OF RESERVATION ON RETAINING THE TORT ACTION FOR WORK INJURIES
by Professor Schilling

949   The arguments for and against retention of tort as a means of providing compensation for personal injury are discussed fully elsewhere in this report.

I am one of those who believe that the arguments against substantially outweigh those for its retention, but would still prefer not to abolish tort completely but rather to see it become superfluous and wither away as no-fault compensation and social security provisions become more extensive. There are, however, special reasons for recommending that tort be abolished for work injuries. These reasons do not apply with anything like the same force to other types of personal injury.

950   Many people concerned with health and safety at work strongly hold the views expressed by the Robens Committee, namely, that the present tort law which allows an employee to take an action against his employer for damages for a work injury is counter-productive to accident prevention. The reasons given by the Robens Committee are set out in paragraph 907 and need not be repeated. Tort may also delay remedial measures before the claim is settled for fear that this may be taken as an admission of negligence or breach of statutory duty. Tort may also have an adverse effect on relations between employer and employee, causing harm to both parties.

951   One of the advantages of the tort system claimed by some witnesses is that its retention is necessary to maintain standards of accident prevention because it encourages stringent surveys by insurance companies and discourages unsafe practices by employers through fear of exposure in court. This is not the view generally held by those directly concerned with occupational safety and health. Surveys by HM Inspectors, the threat of prosecution, the serving of improvement or prohibition notices under the Health and Safety at Work etc. Act 1974 are much stronger measures for encouraging employers to improve and maintain standards of health and safety.

952   There would be one serious disadvantage in abolishing tort action for work injuries. It would penalise the injured workman by depriving him of additional compensation available to other injured persons. Improvements in no-fault compensation for work injuries such as the inclusion of commuting injuries, which most of us favoured, would go some of the way to redress the balance. Something more tangible, however, would be necessary to make the abolition of tort for work injuries acceptable to employed persons.

953   One method would be to reduce, or even to eliminate in the case of dangerous industries, the contributions of the employee to the national insurance fund and correspondingly to increase the employer's contribution. New rates as from April 1978 will be $6\frac{1}{2}$ per cent of weekly earnings for non-contracted-out employees and 10 per cent for employers, excluding the 2 per cent surcharge. Thus an employee with weekly earnings of £80 would contribute £5·20 a week, which is substantial, and at least a proportion of it could be paid by the employer. With the abolition of tort, employer's liability insurance premiums, which amount to £170 million a year, would cease and could be diverted to the national insurance fund. The amounts paid respectively by employee and employer to the fund could be related to the class of industry (employers in dangerous industries would pay more than those in safe ones). These employers' contributions could also be related to their own accident and occupational disease

experience. This is called 'experience rating', which Atiyah[6] suggests could only be used with any degree of reliability for the larger firms, i.e. those employing 500 or more.

954 It has not been shown with any conviction that experience rating for employer's liability has a significant effect in reducing accident costs. A stronger argument for its use is that of making the compensation scheme more just by relating employers' costs to their injury risks. Thus whatever the merits or demerits of such a system in preventing accidents, it would to some extent meet Professor Prest's criticism that the Commission's present recommendations do not relate employers' compensation costs to their injury risks.

955 Another method of giving the injured workman something in return for the loss of tort action would be to retain the industrial preference whereby short and long term benefits for work injuries and widows' pensions are higher than those provided by national insurance, and not to extend this preference to those injured on the road who would not be deprived of the right of taking tort action. The real value of the difference in payments for sickness and work injury benefits and for widows' pensions has been eroded. The most important aspect of the preference is that disablement benefit for a work injury is payable whether or not earnings are affected. In this way it compensates for loss of faculty.

CHAPTER 18

Road

956   Category b of our terms of reference relates to injuries suffered 'through the use of a motor vehicle or other means of transport'. In this chapter we deal with road transport injuries, including the relatively small number which do not involve a motor vehicle.

957   As elsewhere in our report, we have included in our estimates only those injuries which lead to at least four days' incapacity for work or are of an equivalent degree of severity. The statistics published by the Department of Transport and by the Department of the Environment for Northern Ireland are of road accidents reported to the police, and include minor injuries such as cuts and bruises. On the other hand, many injuries, particularly those involving pedestrians and pedal cyclists, go unreported. We think it is likely that these unreported injuries outnumber minor ones. This is why our estimates are somewhat higher than the departmental statistics. Further details of differences between other published figures and our own are in Volume Two.

THE PRESENT POSITION

The pattern of injury

958   Each year about 7,600 people are killed and some 400,000 are injured in road accidents in the United Kingdom. Almost all the deaths and 85 per cent of the injuries occur in accidents involving a motor vehicle. Eighteen per cent occur on the way to or from work, and a further 13 per cent in the course of work.

959   The risk of road injury cannot be avoided by anyone who enjoys normal mobility; indeed, we doubt whether any other type of accidental injury has a greater impact on everyday life. Department of Transport statistics show that about a quarter of those injured are car drivers, just under a quarter are car passengers, and about a quarter are pedestrians. Most of the others are riders of two-wheeled motor vehicles or passengers on them. About a third of those killed are pedestrians. Men are more likely to be injured than women. Young drivers and motor cyclists, and child and elderly pedestrians, are particularly vulnerable.

960   Road injuries are more likely than most other accidental injuries to be severe or fatal. They account for one in eight of all injuries, but for one in three of all accidental deaths. Our personal injury survey showed that road injury tends to result in a longer than average period of incapacity for work.

Road safety

961 Since 1930, the annual number of road injuries in Great Britain has practically doubled, but the number of deaths has fallen slightly. Over the same period, the population has increased by 25 per cent, and the number of vehicles on the roads by 700 per cent. The total distance travelled in motor vehicles each year has increased by over 400 per cent since 1949. In terms of casualties per vehicle mile, therefore, there has been a substantial improvement in road safety.

962 In Northern Ireland, the casualty rate per vehicle mile has also declined, but recent improvements in road safety have been less marked. Casualty rates per 10,000 vehicles are higher than in Great Britain. For deaths, the Northern Ireland rate is double. It was suggested to us that one reason might be that adequate resources cannot be spared for the enforcement of road traffic law during the present disturbances.

963 The United Kingdom as a whole has a good road safety record by international standards.

964 The possible interaction between the compensation system and road safety has been a major theme in evidence to us. Numerous witnesses suggested ways in which safe driving might be promoted; and, among those coming within our terms of reference, there was support for differential premiums whereby individual contributions to compensation funds are related to an assessment of the risk created.

Liability in tort

965 The tort system plays an important role in the present system of compensation for road traffic injury. But many road accident victims receive compensation from other sources, such as national insurance benefits, industrial injuries benefits, occupational sick pay and first party insurance. Such compensation is often substantial.

966 The common law principle that there is no liability in the absence of fault governed compensation for road traffic injury in the days of the horse and carriage. It has continued to do so during the phenomenal increase in the scale and seriousness of road injury which followed the advent of the motor car.

967 It is well settled that a duty of care is owed by a road user to any other road user near enough to be affected by his actions. The standard of care is always that of a reasonable man in the circumstances. To establish liability, the plaintiff must show that the defendant's conduct fell below that standard.

Contributory negligence

968 Contributory negligence in relation to road injuries has been held to include failure by drivers and front seat passengers to wear seat belts. In *Froom* v. *Butcher* [1976] Q.B. 286, it was held (on appeal) that, in cases where liability was not in dispute, a driver or front seat passenger would normally have his

damages reduced by 25 per cent if injuries could have been entirely avoided by wearing a seat belt, and by 15 per cent if injuries would have been less severe. There has been no similarly authoritative decision in Scotland; but in certain cases damages there have been reduced by 20 per cent.

Assumption of risk

969   If the plaintiff has knowingly and voluntarily incurred the risk of injury, the defendant may plead the defence of assumption of risk (*volenti non fit injuria*). But this defence is rarely successful in road accident cases. The plea failed in the leading case of *Dann* v. *Hamilton* [1939] 1 K.B. 509 where the plaintiff had chosen to ride with a man knowing that he was under the influence of drink. It also failed in the Scottish case of *Fowler* v. *Tierney* (1974) S.L.T. (M) 23, where the injured party had chosen to ride as a pillion passenger even though she had been warned that the motor cyclist had only a provisional licence. Section 148(3) of the Road Traffic Act 1972 provides that willing acceptance by a passenger of the risk of a vehicle user's negligence shall not be treated as negativing the user's liability towards him. The application of the section is, for historical reasons, limited to cases covered by compulsory third party motor insurance. The Unfair Contract Terms Act 1977 will prohibit the exclusion of liability for death or personal injury in a business context.

Compulsory insurance

970   Compulsory insurance or security against third party liabilities was introduced in Great Britain for drivers of motor vehicles by the Road Traffic Act 1930. The Road Traffic Act 1934 restricted the grounds on which insurers could repudiate liability for third party injury claims; and in 1971 cover was extended to liabilities towards voluntary passengers.

971   Compulsory insurance provisions in Great Britain are consolidated in Part VI of the Road Traffic Act 1972, and in Northern Ireland in Part V of the Road Traffic Act (Northern Ireland) 1970. It is an offence for a person to use a motor vehicle on a road, or cause or permit any other person to do so, unless such use is covered by insurance against the risk of injury to third parties (including passengers). There are certain exceptions, of which the most important are vehicles owned by and driven under the control of local authorities, London Transport and Passenger Transport Executives, and police authorities. The requirement also does not apply to the Crown. As an alternative to taking out an insurance policy, vehicle users may deposit as a security the sum of £15,000 with the Accountant General of the Supreme Court.

972   The insurance cover required by law is limited to the risk of third party claims for death or bodily injury (including injury to passengers), and any liability under section 155 of the Road Traffic Act 1972 to pay for emergency medical treatment. In practice, almost all private motor policies also cover third party claims for property damage, injury or damage on private property, and injury or damage caused by passengers. Some 70 per cent of private motorists

hold comprehensive policies which, in addition, provide cover for damage to their own vehicles and sometimes a limited amount of first party cover for personal injury to themselves.

973   Insurance is not required in respect of non-motor road vehicles, such as pedal cycles or donkey carts. One curiosity of the present law, however, is that insurance against third party injury is required in Great Britain (but not in Northern Ireland) in respect of horses hired from riding establishments. The insurance must be taken out by the establishment, and must cover any third party liability for personal injury incurred by a person riding a horse hired from the establishment, whether or not the injury occurs on a road.

Victims of uninsured or untraced motorists
974   In 1946, the compulsory motor insurance provisions were supplemented by the first Motor Insurers Bureau Agreement between insurers and the Government. The Bureau is a company limited by guarantee and financed by a levy on member companies in proportion to their motor premium income. Under this agreement, it undertook to meet judgments against uninsured motorists. It was also agreed that the Bureau would consider sympathetically the making of *ex gratia* payments to the victims of untraced motorists, in circumstances where in its view a claim would lie against the motorist if he could be traced. Compensation for the victims of untraced motorists was put on a more formal basis by a subsequent agreement, entered into in 1969. Both agreements were revised in 1972, to extend the arrangements to cover voluntary passengers; and again in December 1977, to modify the procedure for certain small claims. Similar agreements are in force in Northern Ireland. Section 20 of the Road Traffic Act 1974 requires all authorised motor insurers in the United Kingdom to be members of the Bureau.

International arrangements
975   Three international agreements currently affect insurance against loss or damage caused by motor vehicles: the 'green card' system, EEC Directive 72/166, and the 1973 European Convention on the Contract for the International Carriage of Passengers and Luggage by Road.

976   The 'green card' system, to which the United Kingdom and 29 other countries are party, was designed to facilitate international motor traffic by providing a motorist driving abroad in a participating country with an international insurance document '(green card') covering insurance requirements in that country. Claims are handled under agreements between motor insurers bureaux in participating countries.

977   The object of EEC Directive 72/166, which became effective in the United Kingdom on 1 January 1974, was to remove the need for 'green cards' and insurance checks on traffic between EEC member states. It requires each member state to ensure that contracts covering the use of vehicles normally kept in its territory also cover damage on the territory of other member states in accordance with their compulsory insurance legislation. The directive depends for its effective working on a modification of the existing 'green card'

system by means of supplementary agreements between motor insurers bureaux, which provide for settlement of claims against visiting drivers – whether or not they are insured.

978   The Carriage of Passengers by Road Act 1974 makes provision for applying the 1973 European Convention in the United Kingdom, although the Convention itself is not yet in force and the United Kingdom has not formally acceded to it. Under the terms of the Convention, liability is imposed on an international carrier for death or injury suffered by a passenger carried under a contract. The liability is subject to limited defences. Damages may be reduced for contributory negligence. Where a third party has contributed to the injury, the carrier is nevertheless liable, but without prejudice to any right of recourse he may have against the third party.

The criminal law

979   In a civil action for road traffic injury, breach of the criminal law by a defendant does not of itself provide the basis for a tort claim. It will do so only if the provision in question could be taken to have been introduced primarily to prevent the sort of injury suffered by the plaintiff. A motorist who infringed the Pedestrian Crossings Regulations, and in doing so injured a pedestrian, was held liable for his breach of statutory duty, even though he was not found negligent (*London Passenger Transport Board* v. *Upson* [1949] A.C. 155). But liability does not necessarily follow from a breach of the 'clearway' regulations (*Coote* v. *Stone* [1971] 1 W.L.R. 279), or from infringement of regulations relating to the construction and use of motor vehicles (*Phillips* v. *Britannia Hygienic Laundry Co Ltd* [1923] 2 K.B. 832).

980   Under section 11 of the Civil Evidence Act 1968, section 10 of the Law Reform (Miscellaneous Provisions) (Scotland) Act 1968, and section 7 of the Civil Evidence Act (Northern Ireland) 1971, a conviction for a criminal offence is admissible as evidence in civil proceedings. Under section 37 of the Road Traffic Act 1972 (which applies to Great Britain), and section 115 of the Road Traffic Act (Northern Ireland) 1970, a failure to observe the provisions of the Highway Code may be relied upon as tending to establish civil liability; or, if the defence of contributory negligence is being pleaded, as tending to negative or reduce liability.

Criticisms of the present law

981   Criticism of the present law has come from academic lawyers, legal practitioners, politicians and the public. It is noteworthy that as far back as 1965, the late Lord Parker, Lord Chief Justice, called for the setting up of a strong committee or a Royal Commission to consider the introduction of a no-fault scheme. We have had discussions with a number of critics, including Professors P S Atiyah, Jeffrey O'Connell, T G Ison, Harry Street and André Tunc. We have taken oral evidence on road injury from 40 organisations and individuals, and we have received 268 items of written evidence. A substantial body of evidence, including information about many personal cases, reached us following a BBC 'Nationwide' television programme in December 1975.

The fault principle

982 Under the present law, a person injured by a motor vehicle will recover tort compensation only if the defendant was at fault.

983 Even good drivers make mistakes. A study by the World Health Organisation in 1962 found that a good driver makes a mistake every two miles; and an American study in 1964 suggested that on average a good driver makes nine mistakes every five minutes. A detailed investigation of over 2,000 road accidents in the Thames Valley, carried out over a four-year period by the Transport and Road Research Laboratory, concluded that human mistakes were the sole cause of 65 per cent of accidents, and a contributory factor in a further 30 per cent. Further details are in chapter 7 of Volume Two.

984 Not all driving mistakes constitute legal fault. They may vary in nature from patently reckless conduct in which no reasonable man would indulge, such as drunken driving or racing on the highway, to a minor slip of the sort often made by good drivers. But almost any driving mistake may in certain circumstances cause injury. Whether it does so may depend on factors, such as the condition of the road surface or the presence of other road users, which are outside the driver's control.

985 Those who are injured as a result of driving mishap in which legal fault plays no part recover no tort compensation. The case of *Snelling* v. *Whitehead* (*The Times*, 31 July 1975) provides a tragic illustration. A seven-year old boy went out on his bicycle one evening without his parents' knowledge. On coming out from a minor road he was struck by a car. He suffered severe brain damage. An initial award of over £40,000 was set aside by the Court of Appeal on the grounds that no negligence on the part of the driver had been proved. The boy's father appealed unsuccessfully to the House of Lords. Lord Wilberforce said in his speech that the case was one which in his opinion should attract automatic compensation regardless of fault.

986 A small proportion of road accidents are not caused by anyone's mistake. An example was drawn to our attention by Mr Cecil Parkinson MP. A young man was injured in a road accident when a car swerved into his motor scooter. His leg was badly broken in two places, and he suffered stomach injuries. He underwent three operations and was unable to work for nearly a year. But a *post mortem* showed that the driver of the car had died of a heart attack seconds before the crash. There had been no question of fault, therefore, and the victim was unable to recover tort compensation.

987 Even if injuries have been primarily caused by the defendant's legal fault, the plaintiff's compensation may be reduced by a finding of contributory negligence.

988 We can summarise the objections urged against the fault principle in the field of road injury by quoting from Justice's memorandum of evidence to us:

'Some . . . accidents will happen because the victim has not been quite careful enough for his own safety. Others will happen because someone else has not been quite careful enough for the safety of other people. Yet others will happen because someone has deliberately chosen to take an unwarranted risk. But many will happen despite the fact that everyone concerned has taken as much care as any reasonable person would, in the circumstances, have expected him to take. Not every accident is directly "caused" by anyone's "fault".'

989 The main advantage claimed for the present system is that it encourages individual responsibility and deters unsafe conduct; drivers, it is argued, are influenced in their behaviour on the road by the prospect of incurring a financial penalty if they are careless. We find this a doubtful proposition. It is unrealistic to suggest that the cost of tort compensation is borne wholly, or even largely, by the driver responsible for an injury. Third party claims are met by insurance funds, to which all drivers are required to contribute, and the element of loss incurred by the negligent driver is in practice limited to the possible loss of his no claim bonus or an increase of premium on renewal of his policy. We doubt if the prospect of such a penalty weighs heavily with a driver in the heat of the moment. We agree with many of our witnesses that the criminal law and the fear of personal injury together provide a more effective deterrent.

Fault in practice
990 A plaintiff is also likely to be faced with a number of practical difficulties in establishing a claim for tort compensation, particularly the difficulty of obtaining reliable witnesses. Road accidents, by their nature, are almost instantaneous and usually unexpected; and the lapse of time between the accident and the trial tends to increase the unreliability of the witness' memory, even if witnesses were present and are prepared to come forward.

991 A retired county court judge told us that his 'main difficulty in trying running down cases was the lack of certainty of the evidence. This uncertainty is largely attributable to the very nature of the accidents, the split second timing and the fallibility of the human brain in grasping accurate detail in a moment.' Often the victim is in no position to look for witnesses himself. As one road accident victim, interviewed in a BBC television 'Man Alive' report broadcast in May 1976, put it, 'It's rather awkward if you're lying on the road with your leg sticking through your trousers.'

992 Tort claims for road injury, as for other types of injury, take time to settle. According to figures supplied to us by the BIA, about 9 per cent by number of tort claims for fatal motor injury and about 17 per cent for non-fatal injury are disposed of within six months of the accident. About a half are disposed of within a year, and about 85 per cent within two years. The remaining 15 per cent include a high proportion which are eventually settled for a large sum.

993 Administration costs amount to about 45 per cent of the total cost of tort compensation, for road injuries as for other injuries. Supporters of the present system take the view that the investigation of fault is essential if fairness is to be achieved. There are others, however, who believe that fault investigation is a largely meaningless exercise, since it is subject to much uncertainty

and since the cost of compensation is in reality borne by the whole motoring community through insurance. It would be better, they argue, to spend the money now devoted to fault investigation on extending the scope of compensation.

Proportion of victims obtaining compensation

994   A substantial number of road accident victims receive no tort compensation. Only about a quarter of those covered by our personal injury survey who were injured by motor vehicles succeeded in recovering tort compensation (although this proportion was higher than for other types of injury). Most of the remainder did not make claims in tort at all. Among the reasons this group gave were that they regarded the accident as their own fault or nobody's fault, that their injuries were not serious, that they did not know how to claim, and simply that they did not want to make a fuss. In one respect, claimants injured in a motor vehicle accident have an advantage not enjoyed by people injured in other ways. If their claim is accepted, they seldom experience difficulty in securing payment. Those injured by vehicles of other kinds may be less fortunate, since insurance is not compulsory and there is no counterpart to the Motor Insurers Bureau agreements.

A NO-FAULT SCHEME

995   The criticisms which may be levelled at the present system of tort compensation for road injuries – that too few victims are compensated; that the entitlement to compensation depends too much on chance; and that the system is unduly slow, and expensive to administer – may also be levelled, to a varying degree, at tort compensation for other types of injury. But there are in our view a number of considerations which justify singling out this system for reform.

996   First, motor vehicle injuries occur on a scale not matched by any other category of accidental injury within our terms of reference, except work injuries (which are already covered by a no-fault scheme). Secondly – and here they are to be distinguished from work injuries – they are not confined to any particular group of victims. Thirdly, they are particularly likely to be serious, so that they highlight the difficulties of compensating for prolonged incapacity. Fourthly, road transport itself is an essential part of everyday life, of fundamental importance to the economy as a whole and to the mobility of individuals.

997   The unique features of motor vehicle injury have long been recognised by Parliament. Insurance against third party injury risks has been compulsory for motor vehicle users for nearly half a century. In suggesting special compensation arrangements for motor vehicle injuries, we feel that we are to a large extent reflecting accepted priorities.

998   Changes in the tort system alone would not be enough, since they could not ensure compensation for everyone injured by a motor vehicle. Provided

that some means of financing a scheme without increasing direct public expenditure can be found, we think that the primary element of compensation for injuries caused by motor vehicles should be based on the no-fault principle.

The form of the scheme

999   None of the overseas schemes we examined can be taken as an exact model for a no-fault scheme in the United Kingdom.

1000   There are dangers in applying American experience too closely. In the USA there is no equivalent to the National Health Service, so that meeting medical expenses is an important function of compensation there. Much greater use is made of motor vehicles (although there is a widespread problem of failure to insure) and the social security system is less extensive.

1001   The New Zealand Scheme is intended to replace tort as the sole provider of compensation for road injury. But as we explained in chapter 11, we have decided that tort should be retained as part of a mixed system.

1002   In Australia, the Victoria Scheme provides earnings related benefits for pecuniary loss, but for a limited period (104 weeks) and subject to a maximum amount. It no doubt eliminates many minor tort claims and provides adequate compensation for earners in most cases. It does not cover non-earners, nor does it provide any benefits for non-pecuniary loss. From our point of view, however, its major shortcoming is that it provides compensation for only two years. Thereafter, victims are dependent on a successful tort action. Although such prolonged cases are relatively few in number, they are the ones which require adequate compensation above all others.

1003   We formed the view that the right course was to introduce a no-fault scheme in this country which extended the benefits paid under the improved industrial injuries scheme to the victims of motor vehicle injuries. This would have the advantage of uniformity of treatment with work injuries, in accordance with our aim of reducing the anomalies between compensation for different types of injury; it would utilise a familiar benefit structure, which has stood the test of time; and it would provide more adequate benefits for the seriously injured than a scheme on the lines of the one in Victoria. For reasons on which we enlarge below, we consider that a scheme administered by the state would have important practical advantages over a scheme administered by insurance companies.

1004   **We recommend** that a no-fault compensation scheme should be introduced for motor vehicle injuries; and that it should be based on the improved industrial injuries scheme.

The scope of the scheme

1005   In our view, the cost of no-fault compensation should so far as possible be borne by those who create the risk of injury; and we cannot suggest any means of achieving this result at present in relation to road injuries caused otherwise than by motor vehicles, since there is no system of compulsory insurance or licensing. Although we recognise that the lack of an appropriate source of risk related finance need not be an insuperable obstacle to the extension of the scheme if this seemed desirable for other reasons, we have concluded that our no-fault scheme should be limited to injuries caused by motor vehicles.

1006 We consider that the no-fault scheme should extend to all motor vehicle injuries incurred on land to which the public has access. Nearly all motor vehicle injuries take place on public roads, but we think that the limitation of no-fault coverage to these injuries could occasionally result in harsh anomalies. A pedestrian injured by a motor vehicle while he was walking along a bridlepath or other right of way should in our view be entitled to compensation, whether or not the vehicle user had a right to drive there. Thus the cover of the no-fault scheme would be somewhat wider than the cover of the compulsory insurance provisions of the Road Traffic Acts in respect of tort liability (which are restricted to the use of motor vehicles on roads). But we do not think this would be a serious anomaly, and it seems to us more important to provide a measure of compensation for those injured off roads than to ensure consistency with the tort provisions.

1007 We consider that injuries incurred on private land to which the public has no right of access should be excluded, since our main concern is to cover the risk to the public caused by the use of motor vehicles.

1008 It should not in our view be necessary to establish that the motor vehicle was in motion. It would be wrong to exclude an injury sustained by a cyclist who crashed into the back of a stationary vehicle in an intermittently moving queue of traffic. The test should be whether a motor vehicle was involved.

1009 We recognise that in defining the scope of no-fault compensation we are creating anomalies. A pedal cyclist who collided with a parked vehicle on a dark night would receive compensation. One who collided with a builder's skip would not. A farmer whose tractor overturned in the road would benefit, but if it overturned in a field to which the public had no right of access he would not (although he might qualify for national insurance benefit). Anomalies are inevitable wherever the boundary of no-fault is drawn. If all road injuries were included, there would still be an anomaly between road accident victims and other injured people. We have drawn the boundary at a line which we believe would be relatively easy to determine in practice.

1010 **We recommend** that the scheme should cover injuries involving motor vehicles on roads and other land to which the public has access.

Northern Ireland

1011 Existing British social security legislation, and to a lesser extent British road traffic legislation, are closely paralleled in Northern Ireland. We see no reason to propose an exception in the case of a no-fault scheme for motor vehicle injuries, although we recognise that in applying such a scheme to Northern Ireland the Government would need to take into account any special difficulties posed by the volume of traffic across the United Kingdom's only land border. These difficulties would need to be considered in the light of any proposals for reforming motor vehicle injury compensation in the Republic of Ireland.

Benefits

Rates of benefit

1012 At present, the industrial injuries scheme provides better no-fault benefits than those available from national insurance. Our proposals for an improved industrial injuries scheme would maintain this preference, which arises largely from the payment of benefit for loss of faculty. Our recommendation that the same structure of benefits should apply to work and road injuries means that benefit for loss of faculty would also become payable to road accident victims. In this sense we are moving the boundary of the preference. We have also considered, however, whether road injury benefits should be payable at the same rates as work injury benefits, or follow the same structure but at lower rates. The first of these options would leave road and work accident victims with the same 'lead' over all other accident victims. The second would mean that road injury benefits would be lower than work injury benefits, but better than national insurance benefits because of payments for loss of faculty.

1013 A differential between work and road injury benefits could perhaps be justified in principle on the grounds that people at work are entitled to expect greater safety, and hence more compensation in the event of injury, because (unlike road users) they are in an environment largely or completely controlled by their employer. On a more practical level, it might be argued that, if identical benefit rates were set, there would inevitably be pressure to restore the industrial preference by raising the level of industrial injury benefits.

1014 On the other hand, there are powerful arguments in favour of identical rates of benefit. The social security system in this country is already of formidable complexity. Identical rates of benefit would conform with our aim of reducing the anomalies between different groups of accident victims, and there would be one level less to administer. The need to decide whether a particular road injury should be treated as occurring in the course of employment (and hence compensated under the industrial injuries scheme at a higher level) would be avoided; and, unless the differential were substantial, the savings in the cost of the road scheme would be relatively small.

1015 We are not convinced by the argument that work benefits should be higher because employees are subject to an environment controlled by their employer. The risks to which road users are exposed are often equally beyond their own control. We accept that there is likely to be pressure to restore the industrial preference. But we consider that, so far as is practicable, the level of no-fault compensation should depend on the degree of loss sustained, rather than on the particular circumstances in which an injury took place.

We recommend that, subject to the following transitional and other arrangements, rates of benefit under the road scheme should be the same as under the improved industrial injuries scheme.

Attendance allowance

1016 A constant attendance allowance is currently payable under the industrial injuries scheme at a higher level than the attendance allowance which is payable, regardless of the cause of disability, under section 35 of the Social Security Act 1975. We have proposed that this differential should be phased out, by freezing constant attendance allowance at the current rate until it is equalled by the section 35 allowance. **We recommend** that constant attendance allowance and exceptionally severe disablement allowance should not be payable under the road scheme; and that those injured by motor vehicles should continue to rely on the attendance allowance payable under section 35 of the Social Security Act 1975.

Benefits for widows and widowers

1017 We have proposed in chapter 17 a number of changes in the benefits payable to widows and widowers under the industrial injuries scheme. We consider that the benefits payable under the road scheme should be the same as those which would be payable under the improved industrial injuries scheme. This would mean that no pension would be payable under the road scheme to childless widows under 40, and pensions for childless widows aged between 40 and 50 would be subject to the reduction currently imposed on national insurance widows' pensions. We proposed that the grant equal to one year's benefit on remarriage should continue to be payable under the industrial injuries scheme. It should also be payable under the road scheme.

1018 **We recommend** that the benefits payable to widows and widowers under the road scheme should be the same as those which would be payable under the improved industrial injuries scheme.

Non-earners

Entitlement to benefit

1019 The industrial injuries scheme applies only to earners. Exposure to the risk of road injury, however, is almost universal in our society, and children and old people are particularly vulnerable.

1020 Some, but by no means all, overseas no-fault schemes for road injury limit benefits to compensation for pecuniary loss, leaving compensation for non-pecuniary loss to the tort action. No-fault road injury benefits are therefore effectively confined to earners. We do not think that such a limitation is justifiable. Non-pecuniary loss may be suffered by all those injured by motor vehicles, whether or not they are earning; and if no-fault compensation for loss of faculty is to be available to one group of road accident victims, it should be available to all. **We recommend** that, subject to special arrangements for children and retirement pensioners, non-earners should be entitled under the road scheme to the basic flat rate benefits and disablement benefit for loss of faculty.

216

Children and young persons
1021   Under the industrial injuries scheme, those under the age of 18 receive a basic benefit at about three quarters of the adult rate and disablement benefit at about three fifths of the adult rate. Children under the age of 16 and not in full time employment who are injured at work receive the same reduced rate of disablement benefit, but basic benefit at only about a quarter of the adult rate. Naturally, these benefits are seldom paid to those under the age of about 12. Road accidents, however, often involve younger children. We think that to extend the benefits available under the current industrial injuries scheme to all children injured in road accidents would result in over compensation. On the other hand, we have accepted as inevitable that, for the time being at least, road and work injuries should generally be better compensated than most others. We put forward a compromise proposal.

1022   **We recommend** that children under the age of 12 who have been injured in motor vehicle accidents should receive, for as long as they are incapable of normal activity, a basic benefit equal to the allowance we are proposing for severely handicapped children; that children over the age of 12 but under the age of 16 should in addition receive disablement benefit at the reduced rate applicable under the industrial injuries scheme to those under 16 and not in full time employment; and that children over the age of 16 should receive a basic benefit at the level of non-contributory invalidity pension, and disablement benefit at the full adult rate. The full basic benefit under the road scheme should become payable at the age of 18.

Retirement pensioners
1023   For a person injured after reaching retirement age, the flat rate element of the road scheme benefits would normally be provided by a state retirement pension. To avoid double compensation, the two benefits should not be paid together. But we think that the earnings related addition to the flat rate benefit should be paid to a retirement pensioner who was working at the time of the accident. Disablement benefit should also be payable.

1024   **We recommend** that those receiving a retirement pension should not receive the flat rate benefit under the road scheme; but that a retirement pensioner who was working at the time of the injury should receive the earnings related addition to the flat rate benefit and that the addition should be related to his immediate pre-accident earnings.

Administration
1025   Should the no-fault scheme which we propose be administered by private insurers or by DHSS? The issues are essentially practical. Whichever solution is adopted for personal injury claims, private insurers would continue to handle property damage claims. It could therefore be said that administration of injury benefits by some other agency would lead to wasteful duplication in the investigation and handling of claims. It might also be easier to incorporate effective risk assessment in the calculation of contributions to a privately run scheme, in view of the relevant expertise of insurance companies. At a time when the Government is committed to restraining the growth of the public sector, a scheme administered wholly or largely by private companies would have its attractions.

217

1026 Despite these arguments, we think that the scheme should be administered by DHSS in Great Britain, and by the Department of Health and Social Services in Northern Ireland if the scheme is extended there. Private insurers do not have the machinery for administering weekly payments of the scale and complexity required, whereas DHSS already operate the industrial injuries scheme on which our road scheme is based. They have achieved a low ratio of administrative cost to benefits paid out, which, because of the nature of insurance, we doubt whether insurers could match.

1027 **We recommend** that the road scheme should be administered by the Department of Health and Social Security.

Exclusions

1028 We have given a great deal of thought to the possibility of excluding from benefit those whose injuries result from their own misconduct. On the one hand the no-fault principle, when taken to its logical conclusion, requires that an injured person's entitlement to compensation should depend only on the nature of the injury – it should be sufficient for determining entitlement that the injury fell within the scope of the no-fault scheme. On the other hand, we recognise that many people feel strongly that those who injure themselves through their own misconduct should not be cushioned from the economic consequences by a compensation scheme financed by others.

1029 It is important not to confuse the roles of compensation and punishment. The need for compensation arises from the fact of injury; the punishment of wrongdoing is a matter for the criminal law. Society has accepted this separation of roles in the field of medical care, where free treatment is available to the most dangerous criminal, whatever the severity of his subsequent sentence. To a lesser extent it has also come to be accepted in the field of cash benefits. Both sickness benefit and industrial injuries benefits may be withdrawn for misconduct, but in practice they rarely are. The refusal of compensation to those guilty of criminal behaviour could be regarded as a form of double punishment. Nevertheless, we cannot ignore the strength of the evidence given to us, and we accept that in rare cases the result of following the no-fault principle to its logical conclusion might well be repugnant to public opinion.

1030 This problem has been recognised (although not satisfactorily solved, in our view) in the overseas no-fault schemes we have studied. For example, in Saskatchewan no-fault cover is withdrawn if the claimant was injured while under the influence of alcohol or when driving without a licence or riding outside the vehicle, although an exception is made where an offending driver was killed or totally and permanently disabled. The British Columbia scheme excludes suicides, and those driving under the influence of drugs. The Ontario Law Reform Commission have recommended that no-fault benefits should not be paid there for injuries which are deliberately self inflicted, or suffered while committing a crime (other than a driving offence), or in the course of escaping or avoiding arrest.

1031 We do not think that sweeping exceptions are warranted. But most of us consider that there should be some provision for excluding from benefit those who suffer injury through their own serious misconduct. Because of doubts about using such a clause as a form of punishment, those concerned think that its application should be carefully confined. They consider that a power to exclude an injured person from benefit should be available only where there has been a conviction on indictment; and that such a power should be exercised only in exceptional circumstances where the payment of benefit would clearly be repugnant to public opinion. It should also be a necessary criterion that the claimant was injured on his way to or from committing the offence, or in the course of committing it. It would be wrong to exclude injuries which were merely coincidental.

1032 Those in favour of an exclusion clause do not think that it would be reasonable to expect local insurance officers, who are normally responsible in the first instance for decisions on eligibility for benefit, to exercise a discretionary power along the lines proposed. It would not be possible to provide them with guidance which would be adequate to ensure that the exclusion clause was applied consistently over the whole country. Any list of offences entailing the withdrawal of benefit, for example, would be far too arbitrary in its application.

1033 It would be right, they think, for these cases to be decided at one central point; and they take the view that the only possibility would be to entrust the power to the Secretary of State for Social Services. They recognise that this would be an unusual function of central government, but the Secretary of State would be answerable to Parliament for the way in which he operated an exclusion clause, and his decisions would be subject to the limited judicial review provided by the prerogative orders. This proposal bears some slight resemblance – distant but nevertheless relevant – to the powers given to Ministers to order the forfeiture of the pensions of persons in the public service in certain circumstances.

1034 By a majority, **we recommend** that the Secretary of State for Social Services should have a discretionary power to discontinue the payment of road scheme benefits to those injured by motor vehicles on their way to or from committing an offence for which they are subsequently convicted on indictment; or in the course of committing such an offence; but that such a power should be exercised only in exceptional circumstances, where the payment of benefits would clearly be repugnant to public opinion. Mr Marsh and Professor Stevenson do not agree. Their views are set out in a minority opinion at the end of this chapter.

1035 We all agree that a disqualification power should not be used to withhold benefit from the widows and dependants of a criminal who died in a motor vehicle accident. It would in our view be wrong to punish his family in this way. A similar approach has been adopted in Manitoba, Victoria and New

Zealand. **We recommend** that the Secretary of State's discretion to discontinue the payment of road scheme benefits should not extend to benefits paid to the widows and dependants of those who die as a result of injuries incurred in the course of criminal activity.

Legal aid

1036 The introduction of a road no-fault scheme would bring a new type of beneficiary into contact with social security administration and adjudication. Those who claim industrial injury benefit are often advised by their trade unions when preparing their claim or contesting a decision. Equivalent help would not necessarily be available to the victims of road injury. We think that a good case could be made out for extending the legal aid scheme to provide such assistance.

1037 We recognise, however, that the possible extension of legal aid to claimants before tribunals would be a major step, with implications for many aspects of administration outside our terms of reference. It might also be regarded as contrary to the nature of tribunals, which seek so far as possible to avoid the adversarial mode. Accordingly we have decided not to recommend the extension of legal aid to road injury benefit claimants, although we think they should be accorded priority if there is any change in the present position as regards tribunals.

International aspects

1038 A no-fault scheme for motor vehicle injuries would pose difficulties in relation both to those habitually resident in the United Kingdom who are injured abroad, and to those resident elsewhere who are injured in this country. These difficulties would not be new in the field of social security, but because of the increasing amount of international travel they could arise on a considerable scale. This is a complex area, in which a great deal depends on international negotiation; and we can do no more than suggest the broad principles which we think should be followed for the time being.

1039 By analogy with emergency medical treatment under the National Health Service, **we recommend** that road scheme benefits should be available to all those who suffer motor vehicle injury in the United Kingdom, whether or not they are habitually resident here.

1040 **We also recommend** that road scheme benefits should continue in payment to those who were injured in the United Kingdom while habitually resident here, if they subsequently reside abroad. We recognise that this could raise problems in relation to inflation proofing. Benefit rates would normally be adjusted in line with inflation in the United Kingdom; but the recipient who lived abroad might experience inflation at a much lower or higher rate. **We recommend** that consideration should be given to the question of inflation proofing road scheme benefits payable to those residing abroad who were injured in the United Kingdom while habitually resident here.

1041 With one dissentient, **we recommend** that road scheme benefits payable to those injured in the United Kingdom while not habitually resident here should, subject to the terms of any international arrangements, cease when they leave the country and not resume when they return.

1042 Professor Stevenson dissents from this recommendation. She considers that those not habitually resident in the United Kingdom who are eligible for benefits following injury in this country should be entitled to claim when they leave the country, subject to proof of their condition.

1043 We found it difficult to decide what should be done about those habitually resident in the United Kingdom who are injured while temporarily abroad. This group is not confined to those who take their own car abroad. It includes those who are injured by motor vehicles as pedestrians and as passengers. Most of us concluded, not without reluctance, that until suitable international arrangements could be devised it would not be practicable to pay no-fault benefits in respect of motor vehicle injuries incurred abroad. The problems of verifying claims and the scope for abuse would in our view be too great. By a majority, **we recommend** that road scheme benefits should not be payable in respect of injuries suffered abroad.

1044 Professor Schilling, Professor Prest and Professor Stevenson dissent from this recommendation. They consider that road scheme benefits should be payable to those habitually resident in the United Kingdom who are injured abroad, provided that the claimant can establish that his injury was caused by a motor vehicle.

1045 There would be a possibility of double compensation where a person eligible for United Kingdom benefits also recovered tort compensation abroad, if the benefits were not offset by the overseas jurisdiction. We do not think that this problem can be avoided by measures taken in the United Kingdom. The only possibility we can see would be to require a beneficiary who recovered tort damages abroad to declare the fact; the benefit paying authority might then have a discretion to reduce or withhold benefits. We reject this solution. We do not think that it would be right for a person's entitlement to no-fault benefits to depend on whether or not he recovered tort compensation abroad. Nor do we think that a discretion to withhold or reduce benefits should be entrusted to the benefit paying authority.

Financing

1046 In considering financing, as with administration, we were faced with a choice between private insurers and the state. We considered whether it would be desirable to devise a scheme in which benefits were administered by DHSS, but private insurers were responsible for meeting the cost from motor premiums. Our conclusion is that it would not. The BIA and Lloyd's argued convincingly that it was not possible for private insurance to guarantee to provide, for more than a limited period, benefits which kept pace with the cost of living. The state would therefore have to enter into some financial commitment if the benefit structure which we propose were to be implemented. We think that the only logical course would be for the state to assume financial responsibility for the scheme. Support for this view is lent by Australian experience, particularly in Victoria where private insurers have completely withdrawn from the provision of no-fault compensation for motor vehicle injury.

1047   This is not to say that the state should meet the cost of the scheme out of general revenue. Indeed we reject this possibility, since it would mean that the cost of compensation would not be borne by those who created the risk of injury. Among the alternatives suggested by our witnesses were levies on driving licence fees, road fund licence fees, motor insurance premiums, and petrol.

Driving licence fee levy
1048   We did not regard a levy on driving licence fees as a realistic possibility, since driving licences are now normally valid without renewal until the holder's seventieth birthday, and it would be unreasonable to expect motorists to pay a lifetime's contributions to the no-fault scheme in the form of a capital sum.

Road fund licence levy
1049   A levy on road fund licence fees has been adopted in New Zealand. It would be relatively easy to collect here. But it could differentiate only between broad categories of vehicle according to the amount of excise duty payable. Within these categories, contributions would have to be at a flat rate. All car drivers, for instance, would have to make the same contribution to no-fault funds regardless of their accident record or the amount of use which they made of their vehicle.

Motor insurance premium levy
1050   A percentage levy on compulsory motor insurance premiums would use the expertise of private insurers in fixing premiums to achieve the result that contributions to the no-fault scheme were risk related. But the element of risk relation would be only approximate. Motor insurance premiums take account of the risks of property damage as well as personal injury; and the compulsory third party element relates to the risk that the insured person will negligently injure others, but not to the risk that he may (with or without negligence) injure himself. This would be of particular practical importance in relation to motor cyclists, who are less likely than other vehicle users to injure others, but more likely to injure themselves. Despite these difficulties, however, a levy on compulsory motor insurance premiums could no doubt be devised so as to take into account both driver and vehicle characteristics. Some overseas schemes (for example, those in British Columbia and Saskatchewan) provide in addition for a premium surcharge on drivers with a bad accident record.

Petrol levy
1051   Finally, we considered a levy on petrol. The main advantage of financing the scheme in this way would be that contributions could be easily and cheaply collected. Motorists' contributions would relate closely to the amount they used their cars, as well as to other risk related factors such as engine size. It would not however be possible to make any allowance for the accident record of the

driver or the type of vehicle being driven. Financing through a petrol levy has been adopted in Manitoba, and there is a reserve power to do so in British Columbia.

Our conclusions on financing

1052   We rejected on practical grounds a levy on road fund licence fees, since the element of risk relation it could provide would be too tenuous. It is possible, too, that in the long term the revenue now raised from vehicle excise duty would be raised in other ways, and the road fund licence could disappear.

1053   We were attracted to the possibility of a percentage levy on motor insurance premiums. This method of financing could in our view provide more sophisticated risk relation than any other. But most of us concluded that it would not be practicable. The cost of our no-fault scheme represents only a small proportion of annual motor premium income. The expense of collecting a levy would therefore be high in relation to the amount raised. We have been mindful, too, of the fact that (as explained in paragraph 1084 below) the Government has recently abandoned its plan for a levy on premiums to meet the cost of National Health Service treatment of road casualties.

1054   It seems to most of us that, for the reasons given in paragraph 1051, the most practical way of financing a no-fault scheme for motor vehicle injury would be a levy on petrol. We recognise that this would be an example of hypothecation of revenue, and would be a departure from the usual (but not universal) approach to raising revenue. Nevertheless, with one dissentient, **we recommend** that the road scheme should be financed by a levy on petrol. We envisage that the levy would be collected as an insurance charge alongside petrol duty and value added tax; and that the proceeds would be paid into the national insurance fund, out of which the benefits would be paid.

1055   Professor Prest dissents from this recommendation. His views are recorded in a note of reservation at the end of this chapter.

1056   An element of cash no-fault compensation is already provided for motor vehicle injury, for example in the form of sickness benefit. This compensation costs about £36 million a year in respect of injuries not covered by the industrial injuries scheme. It comes from the national insurance fund, which is financed partly by employers' and employees' contributions and partly by general taxation. Under our proposals, cash no-fault compensation for motor vehicle injuries outside the sphere of employment would be provided through a single scheme with a unified benefit structure. We do not think that it would be sensible to meet a part of the cost, corresponding to the existing level of no-fault benefits, from national insurance contributions and general taxation, and only the additional cost of the improvements which we have proposed from a petrol levy. Although there may in principle be a case for contributions from general taxation on the grounds of community responsibility, we can see no logical justification for imposing on one special group (employers and employees) the cost of injuries caused by another special group (motorists). **We recommend** that the amount raised by a petrol levy should be enough to cover the whole cost of cash no-fault compensation for motor vehicle injuries outside the sphere of employment, including the present cost of social security benefits and the cost of administration.

Cost

1057 The estimates prepared for us by the Government Actuary show that the extra cost of the scheme we propose, excluding administration costs, would be about £25 million a year after 5 years, rising to about £48 million a year after 40 years, at January 1977 prices. The additional cost of administration would be about £3 million a year after 5 years and about £6 million a year after 40 years. The total cost of cash no-fault compensation, including compensation payable under present arrangements and including administration costs, would be about £64 million after 5 years and about £90 million after 40 years. At January 1977 prices, the cost initially could be met by a levy on petrol of about one penny a gallon.

1058 The inclusion of motor vehicle injuries caused by commuting accidents in the road scheme rather than the work scheme would add a further £9 million a year after 5 years, and a further £18 million a year after 40 years (excluding administration costs), to the cost of the road scheme. The total cost of cash no-fault compensation, including compensation payable under present arrangements and including administration costs, would be about £90 million a year after 5 years, and about £125 million a year after 40 years.

TORT

1059 In chapter 11, we explained why we recommend keeping the tort action for motor vehicle injury. Our recommendations as a whole nevertheless imply a considerable diminution in the importance of tort as a provider of compensation for road injury. Our proposal that in assessing tort damages the no-fault compensation should be fully deducted, together with our proposed changes in assessing damages for non-pecuniary loss, would we believe have the effect of restricting the tort action to cases of serious injury and substantial pecuniary loss.

The basis of liability

1060 In the context of the more limited role which we envisage for tort compensation for motor vehicle injury, we have considered whether any change in the present basis of liability is desirable. In practice, this would mean imposing strict liability.

1061 Under a regime of strict liability, the owner or driver of a motor vehicle (in continental systems, the 'keeper') would be liable for any injury caused by his vehicle whether or not he was to blame, subject to such defences as were permitted. In most continental systems of strict liability, these include the defences that the injury resulted from a sudden and unexpected event beyond the defendant's control (the defence of act of God, or *force majeure*), or from the act of a third party. Sometimes it is also a complete defence to prove that the victim suffered injury through his own gross negligence. Damages are usually reduced for contributory negligence.

1062   Arguments in favour of strict liability tend to be based on the principle of liability for risk created. It is contended that the motor vehicle is a 'dangerous thing', capable of causing grievous injury to third parties, and that those who expose the public to this risk should be liable for any damage caused. This principle would be imposed in respect of both personal injury and property damage by the 1973 Council of Europe Convention on Civil Liability for Damage Caused by Motor Vehicles. The terms of the Convention are reproduced as Annex 9. It has been signed, but not yet ratified, by the Federal Republic of Germany, Norway and Switzerland. It is not yet in force. The United Kingdom Government took part in its development, but has remained non-committal, pointing out that application of the risk principle in relation to motor vehicles in the United Kingdom might result in considerable uncertainty and a good deal of litigation.

1063   The concept of a keeper would not be new in English law. The Road Traffic Act 1974 (which does not extend to Northern Ireland) introduced a regime of owner liability for certain road traffic offences (mainly parking offences) which carry a fixed penalty. In proceedings for such an offence there is a conclusive presumption that the owner is responsible for the acts or omissions of the driver of the vehicle. Similarly under a regime of strict liability, the keeper of the vehicle would be liable for any injury caused by it whether or not he was the driver at the time when the injury was incurred.

1064   In December 1975 the Rt Hon Graham Page MP introduced a Bill (the Road Accident (Compensation) Bill) to impose a form of strict liability, backed by compulsory insurance, on users of motor vehicles. This Bill was debated in the House of Commons on 12 March 1976, but fell for lack of Parliamentary time. In the course of the debate, the Parliamentary Secretary to the Law Officers' Department argued that implementation of the proposal would pre-empt our recommendations. (Official Report (HC) 12.3.76, Vol 907 col 882).

1065   Many of our witnesses were in favour of strict liability for motor vehicle injury as an alternative to no-fault. It was argued by a majority of the Bar Council, for example, that 'the action of bringing a motor car on the road should impose a special responsibility for any injury caused by its presence'. Other witnesses considered that the scope of strict liability should be more limited. It might be confined to injuries suffered by pedestrians, pedal cyclists and passengers, with compensation for injury suffered by drivers continuing to depend on proof of fault.

1066   Some witnesses were opposed to strict liability, on the grounds that it departed from the principle that it was for the plaintiff to prove his case. Some, including the Royal Automobile Club, argued that strict liability would impose heavy financial burdens and penalise the innocent driver.

1067   We state in chapter 31 our belief that those in charge of 'dangerous things' which are likely to cause serious injury if they go wrong should in principle be subject to a more stringent liability in tort than the present law of negligence provides. But even though a motor vehicle might be regarded as a 'dangerous thing' in the sense in which we use the term, we are agreed that strict liability should not be imposed for motor vehicle injury. Strict liability improves the victim's chances of obtaining compensation. For motor vehicle injury, we have argued that this need should be met by the introduction of a no-fault scheme. The imposition of strict liability in addition would in our view place an unfair financial burden on the motorist.

1068 **We recommend** that there should be no change in the basis of liability in tort for motor vehicle injury. **We also recommend** that there should be no change in the basis of liability in tort for injury resulting from road accidents involving vehicles other than motor vehicles.

The burden of proof

1069 We have considered the separate question whether the burden of proof should be reversed in tort actions for motor vehicle injury. Over 40 years ago, in 1932, Lord Danesfort introduced a Bill (the Road Traffic (Compensation for Accidents) Bill) to reverse the burden of proof in cases where pedestrians or cyclists were injured or killed in accidents with motor vehicles. He argued that the motorist should bear the risk inherent in bringing a 'dangerous thing' on to the public highway. Despite Government support, the Bill did not become law.

1070 Some of us were impressed by the arguments in favour of reversing the burden of proof. As we have pointed out, the plaintiff injured by a motor vehicle is often handicapped by lack of witnesses or the reluctance of witnesses to come forward; and by the infirmity of human observation and recollection of fast moving events, over what may be a long period between the events and the trial. It has been put to us that the defendant (usually the driver) is in a better position to say what happened, and that he should have the burden of disproving the plaintiff's allegations.

1071 We have also pointed out that the exercise of reasonable care is not always sufficient to avoid the risk of personal injury. It was suggested that the capacity of the motor vehicle for causing injury is such that it would be fitting to introduce a statutory inference that a motorist should be liable unless he can show that an injury caused by his vehicle was not due to a failure on his part to exercise due care. Part of the justification for such an inference would be that the motorist would be insured or else his liability would be covered by the Motor Insurers Bureau, whereas the plaintiff might well be uninsured against the risk of personal injury to himself. In effect, a reversal of the burden of proof would shift the loss from the individual plaintiff to the motoring community, where the facts were in serious doubt.

1072 It has also been suggested that such a change in the law would tend to increase the proportion of tort claims for motor vehicle injury which were settled without trial; and it has been pointed out that a reversal of the burden of proof appears to operate satisfactorily in more than one European jurisdiction.

1073   There are, however, arguments the other way if our proposed no-fault scheme for motor vehicle injury is implemented. Some of the arguments are similar to those which arose when we discussed (and rejected) a reversal of the burden of proof for work injuries. Those injured by motor vehicles, like those injured at work, would be in a favoured position, as compared with other injured people, because of the availability of no-fault compensation; and we were not persuaded that it would be justifiable to increase this preference still further by giving those injured by motor vehicles an advantage in the field of tort. If the burden of proof were reversed for motor vehicle injuries but not for work injuries, there would be the further problem that those injured at work would be less favoured than those injured by motor vehicles.

1074   A reversal of the burden of proof would add an uncertain, but quite possibly large, amount to the cost of tort compensation for motor vehicle injury. It might be thought unreasonable to impose this cost, as well as the cost of a no-fault scheme, on motorists. But more importantly for some of us, such an outcome would go against the sense of our recommendations as a whole, which is to shift the balance of the provision of compensation away from the tort system towards no-fault schemes.

1075   On balance, we think that the arguments against reversing the burden of proof should prevail. **We recommend** that there should be no formal reversal of the burden of proof in actions for damages for motor vehicle injury.

1076   **We also recommend** that there should be no formal reversal of the burden of proof in actions for damages for injury resulting from road accidents involving vehicles other than motor vehicles.

Children

1077   The courts have been increasingly reluctant to reduce damages awarded to young children for motor vehicle injury on the grounds of the child's contributory negligence. We believe that this development should now be given statutory force. It is in our view unreasonable to expect adult standards of behaviour from young children. The definition of 'young' is necessarily arbitrary, but we consider that the age of 12 would be a sensible dividing line. It would be the age at which, under our proposals, road accident victims would become eligible for a no-fault disablement benefit; and the choice of any lower age might make the law more stringent than the present practice of the courts. **We recommend** that the defence of contributory negligence should not be available in cases of motor vehicle injury where the plaintiff was, at the time of the injury, under the age of 12.

1078   This would not mean that a child under 12 would always succeed in recovering tort compensation for road injury (though he would receive no-fault benefits under the proposals we have already described). Where the defendant was not at fault at all, the child would have no grounds for a tort claim and the question of contributory negligence would not arise.

Compulsory insurance

1079   **We recommend** that, subject to the following minor change, the present compulsory third party insurance provisions for motor vehicles should be retained.

1080 At present, a vehicle user may deposit the sum of £15,000 as a security with the Accountant General of the Supreme Court or the Accountant General of the Supreme Court of Northern Ireland instead of taking out third party insurance. This sum is now far too low to ensure the payment of compensation for serious road traffic injury. We are aware that the Government intends to propose a substantial increase at a suitable opportunity; but we do not think there is a strong case for any exemption from the requirement to insure, apart from the public bodies who are presently exempted by statute. **We recommend** that the deposit alternative to compulsory third party insurance for motor vehicles, under section 144(1) of the Road Traffic Act 1972 and section 75(2)(b) of the Road Traffic Act (Northern Ireland) 1970, should be abolished.

International traffic

1081 We consider that the Motor Insurers Bureau agreements, embodying the United Kingdom's obligations under the 'green card' system and EEC Directive 72/166, ensure adequate insurance cover for meeting successful tort claims against foreign motorists driving in the United Kingdom.

Road accident treatment costs

1082 In Great Britain, under section 154 of the Road Traffic Act 1972, any hospital providing treatment to the victim of a road traffic accident can recover the cost, up to a limit of £20 for an out-patient and £200 for an in-patient, from a motor liability insurer or depositor paying damages to the victim. Under section 155, hospitals and doctors can also recover £1·25 in respect of each person, plus travelling costs, as part of the cost of emergency treatment given immediately after a motor vehicle accident. In contrast to the section 154 provision, this sum may be demanded from the person using the vehicle which caused the injury, whether or not he was negligent. If it is subsequently established that someone else was at fault, the person who paid the treatment costs has a claim against the wrongdoer.

1083 In Northern Ireland, section 84 of the Road Traffic Act (Northern Ireland) 1970 provides similarly to section 154 of the British Act, except that it does not permit recovery of the cost of treating out-patients. There is no provision analogous to section 155.

1084 The amount currently recovered by the National Health Service by means of these provisions is probably less than 5 per cent of the costs incurred, which amounted to nearly £50 million in 1976. The administrative cost of recovery is not precisely known, but it is likely to be high in relation to the amount obtainable. In October 1976, the Government proposed that the existing provisions should be replaced by a flat rate levy on motor insurance premiums, at a level sufficient to recoup from vehicle users the whole cost of National Health Service treatment of road casualties. The scheme was withdrawn after discussions between the Government, insurers and the motoring organisations, on the grounds that it had inherent practical difficulties and would be administratively expensive.

1085   We are in no doubt that the present provisions for recovering the cost of treating road accident victims are ineffective, and that any new proposal should not require investigation of the circumstances of individual injuries. But the question of recouping National Health Service costs from particular groups of patients raises issues of equity and broad social policy which fall outside our terms of reference.

THE EFFECT OF OUR PROPOSALS

1086   The proposed no-fault scheme for motor vehicle injuries would provide compensation for a substantially higher proportion of road accident victims than at present. Annex 8 contains an outline of the scheme. The Government Actuary has estimated that the number of new injuries which would come within the scheme each year would be 185,000, of which 130,000 would be injuries to people of working age. He has assumed that people injured in circumstances which would qualify them both for industrial injury benefit and for benefit under the road scheme would draw industrial injury benefit.

1087   Many minor tort claims would be eliminated; but the action for damages would continue to have a role as a provider of supplementary compensation in cases of serious and prolonged injury, and where the victim suffered heavy pecuniary loss. Tort would remain the principal provider of compensation for road injuries not involving motor vehicles, and for property damage.

1088   Our proposals envisage the administration of no-fault benefits within the social security system; but they would not require an increase in direct public expenditure. Indeed they would reduce the burden on the Exchequer, since we recommend that the whole cost of our no-fault scheme, including the cost of administration and the cost of the compensation now provided through national insurance contributions and general taxation, should be recovered from motorists in the form of a petrol levy. The cost initially could be met by a levy on petrol of about one penny a gallon.

1089   Against this, as a result of the changes in the assessment of damages which we recommend elsewhere, the level of tort compensation for motor vehicle injury would fall by about £28 million a year. About £17 million a year of this reduction would be due to offsetting the additional no-fault benefits which we have proposed. Tort administration costs would fall by about a further £12 million a year, so that the total reduction in the cost of tort compensation would be about £40 million a year.

1090   We have no reason to doubt that this saving would be passed on to motorists in view of the keen competition in the motor insurance market. But if it became apparent that real savings were not being passed on, we expect that the Government would intervene. On average, we think that the element of motor insurance premiums covering liability for injury to third parties should fall by about 14 per cent, and motor premiums as a whole should fall by about 4 per cent, in real terms. In money terms, premiums are likely to continue to increase because of continuing inflation. But our proposals should mean that the increase would be less than it would otherwise have been.

MINORITY OPINION ON EXCLUSIONS FROM THE ROAD SCHEME
by Mr Marsh and Professor Stevenson

1091   We are unable to agree with the recommendation in paragraph 1034. We note that our colleagues themselves emphasise the differing roles of compensation and punishment. In the light of that difference our own view is that if a person is killed or injured in circumstances otherwise covered by the proposed motor vehicle no-fault scheme, neither he nor his dependants should be deprived of the right to compensation under the scheme because his death or injury had a certain connection with an offence of which he has been convicted.

1092   However, if it is thought desirable in deference to the feared impact of public opinion to exclude from the motor vehicle no-fault scheme persons who in certain exceptional circumstances have been convicted of offences, we consider that those circumstances should be defined in advance – as, for example, they are under the Saskatchewan scheme – and susceptible of interpretation by the ordinary legal processes. We would regard it as most undesirable to allow those circumstances to be defined by the executive from case to case under the pressure of what may appear to be public opinion at the time, even if it is anticipated that compensation would only rarely be refused and that the decision would be made at a high executive level. Such a system appears to us to constitute a dangerous inroad on the basic principles of the rule of law.

NOTE OF RESERVATION ON THE FINANCE OF COMPENSATION FOR ROAD INJURIES
by Professor Prest

1093   In deciding whether to raise the necessary finance by means of a surcharge on insurance premiums or a supplementary levy on petrol there are three main issues: risk involvement, administrative costs and 'spare funds' of insurance companies. It will be appropriate to discuss each in turn.

Risk involvement

1094   We have already discussed the general case for relating charges to risks in the note of reservation on work injuries and so we can proceed straight to the application of the principle in the roads context.

1095   We must distinguish between two main cases: the same type of vehicle travelling different distances and different vehicles travelling the same distance. In the first case, a tax on petrol would clearly bear some relation to the risk of accident involvement, on the assumption that there is a relationship between such risks and the distance travelled. A surcharge on third party premiums will also roughly suffice in so far as such premiums are greater for a policy holder travelling long distances with his vehicle (as with a commercial traveller) than if only short distances are involved.

1096   In the second case of equal distances but different vehicles, a petrol tax would score very badly. A motor cycle would use much less petrol than a heavy truck travelling the same distance and hence would pay much less in supplementary petrol tax. But the possibility of injury is clearly much greater for the motor cyclist than for the truck driver. So the petrol tax would fail to be risk related for both reasons. It might seem at first sight that a surcharge on third party premiums would also be unsatisfactory in that one would expect it to be less for the motor cyclist than for the truck owner. But this conclusion does not necessarily hold. If the surcharge were not simply a proportionate addition to third party insurance premiums but also differentiated between vehicle groups (for example, higher percentage addition for motor cyclists than for truck owners) one could get at least part of the way to a true risk related charge. It would not be perfect. But it would be demonstrably better than what is possible in the petrol tax case: there could, after all, be no possibility whatever of levying a higher supplementary charge per gallon of petrol sold to a motor cyclist than that on petrol sold to a truck driver.

1097   One further point should be noted. The surcharge principle is clearly not applicable in those cases where road vehicle insurance is not compulsory (for example, many public sector vehicles). The petrol tax is, on the other hand, paid in the great majority of such cases. As a substitute for insurance surcharges one might have to resort to flat rate contributions differentiated according to the type of vehicle – somewhat analogously to payments in lieu of local rates in respect of Crown property. Whether much is lost by such a system relatively to the petrol tax must be a matter of some doubt given that the costs of such payments are not reflected in relative prices in the same way as in the private sector of the economy.

1098   So, overall, the possibilities of relating charges to risks are likely to be greater in the insurance premium surcharge case than with the petrol tax levy. The relevant concept of risk relation is much more that of a first party than a third party principle, in that the former is applicable to drivers/passengers injured in accidents not involving anything other than vehicles and the latter only to policy holders of vehicles injuring pedestrians, cyclists and the like.

Administration

1099   It is perfectly fair to say that it is not completely straightforward from an administrative viewpoint to levy an insurance premium surcharge and to point to the breakdown of the 1976 proposals for a hospital contribution to be raised in that way. But there are two points to be made on the other side. The first is that if one is using this method for both financing compensation and for financing hospitals, the necessary administrative costs are being spread over two objectives, and not just one. It is not appropriate to argue the hospital financing case here in detail, but there is surely a case in principle for such an arrangement – on the basis set out by the Government in 1976.

1100   The second point is that it seems to be assumed that there are no administrative problems in levying a supplementary petrol tax. In fact, the details of any such operation are far from clear cut. Paragraph 1054 speaks of 'an insurance charge alongside petrol duty and value added tax', but such a statement conceals more points than it explains. Presumably such a charge would be collected by HM Customs and Excise. In that case, exactly how is it to be related to the existing excise duty and to value added tax? Is it to be a charge on the price of petrol, including excise duty? If so, how does this fit into EEC proposals for the harmonisation of excise duties? And, if value added tax is levied on the price of petrol including excise duty and insurance surcharge is one going to say that not just the surcharge but also an element of value added tax is really earmarked for compensation purposes? And if so, how does one calculate such a figure? Parenthetically, the hypothecation issue can be overdone in this context: the national insurance system is, after all, a giant example of the hypothecation which is so abhorred and deprecated by all loyal servants of Her Majesty's Treasury.

'Spare funds'

1101 The costings data show that tort outgoings for roads will fall by £28 million a year (plus administrative savings of about £12 million a year) shortly after the introduction of a new road scheme on the lines suggested. This immediately raises the question of how such benefits are to be channelled back to payers of premiums rather than mysteriously swallowed up in insurance company accounts (except for public sector vehicles for which road insurance policies are not taken out). It so happens that the additional social security expenditure on roads compensation would amount to £34 million (plus administrative costs) some five years after the scheme was implemented, if motor vehicle commuting injuries were included in the road scheme. This means that a surcharge levied on premiums to pay for this compensation would fairly closely match the excess of insurance company receipts over expenditures which would otherwise obtain at that time. Naturally, this would not be so for individual companies and still less, individual motorists. But it would at any rate be a very neat and convenient way of ensuring that the additional cost of the state schemes was met without any overt initial increase in taxes or charges and without the danger of the improvement in the financial position of the insurance companies inuring, in the short run at any rate, to the benefit of the companies rather than that of the motoring community.

1102 It is submitted that taking all three of the reasons set out above, the levy on insurance premiums is a superior method of finance to that of the special petrol charge.

CHAPTER 19

Air

1103   In the last 25 years, more than 30,000 people – passengers, crew and bystanders – have been killed in aircraft accidents throughout the world. About two thirds of the victims were travelling on regular passenger services operated by recognised airlines. When compared with, say, road transport, air transport has a good record of safety, but a distinguishing feature of air accidents is their high rate of fatality. The problem of air accidents is not a purely domestic one, and comparison with other causes of injury within our remit has had to be made with this in mind.

1104   Commercial aviation is less than 60 years old. In that time, the rate of travel has increased from 100 miles an hour to supersonic speeds, and aircraft have become much larger. When accidents occur, there may be casualties on a considerable scale. The great increase in air traffic has caused safety problems. particularly in the airspace around airports, and levels of safety vary from one airport to another.

1105   There are some 164 private flying clubs in the United Kingdom. Over the past ten years, an average of 19 crew and 11 passengers have been killed each year in non-commercial flying. Figures for serious injury are 6 and 4 a year respectively.

The present law
1106   Until 1929, the rights of air passengers on recognised airlines had not been defined on an international basis. Rights and liabilities depended on the laws of the country in which a suit happened to be brought following an accident, and on the terms of the contract made with the particular carrier. In the United Kingdom the basis of liability was the ordinary common law rule of negligence.

The Warsaw Convention
1107   The Warsaw Convention of 1929, which has been accepted by most countries, provided international regulation for the first time. It was given effect in the United Kingdom by the Carriage by Air Act 1932, which came into force in May 1933. The Act provides that the carrier's liability under the Convention is to be substituted for any liability of the carrier towards his passengers or their dependants under common law. The Convention applies to all international carriage. This is defined as carriage in which the point of departure and the point of destination are situated within two states both of which are parties to

the Convention, or carriage within the territory of a single state which is a party to the Convention, provided that there is an agreed stopping place in a second state, whether or not the second state is a party to the Convention. The Convention reverses the burden of proof in negligence in favour of the plaintiff. Under Article 20, however, if the carrier proves that he and his agents took 'all necessary measures to avoid the damage or that it was impossible for him or them to take such measures', he will not be liable for passenger injury. The defence of contributory negligence of the victim is also open to the carrier.

1108 Liability in respect of any one passenger is limited under the Convention to the sum of 125,000 Poincaré gold francs (the then standard unit of account, of which the January 1977 sterling equivalent of 125,000, specified by Order, was £5,350). But, under Article 22 of the Convention, it is permissible for the carrier and passenger to increase the limit by means of a special contract. In addition, the carrier's liability will be unlimited if the damage was caused by his own wilful misconduct, by that of his servants or agents, or by such default on his part or on the part of his servants or agents as is considered to be the equivalent of wilful misconduct. Liability will also be unlimited if a ticket was not delivered to the passenger as required by the Convention.

The Hague Protocol
1109 Most countries, including the United Kingdom but not the USA, have ratified the 1955 Hague Protocol to the Warsaw Convention. This Protocol doubled the limit of liability to 250,000 gold francs (£10,700). The provision for unlimited liability in the case of 'wilful misconduct' was slightly altered under the Hague Protocol; the plaintiff can recover unlimited damages against a carrier if he is able to prove intentional or reckless misconduct. The amendments to the Warsaw Convention were implemented in the United Kingdom by the Carriage by Air Act 1961. This came into effect in June 1967 when the necessary number of ratifications had been made.

The Guadalajara Convention
1110 The Guadalajara Convention of 1961 provides that the rules of the Warsaw Convention, as amended at The Hague, shall apply to international carriage by air performed by a carrier other than the one with whom the passenger has contracted to fly. The Guadalajara Convention is given effect in the United Kingdom by the Carriage by Air (Supplementary Provisions) Act 1962, which came into force in May 1964.

The Montreal Agreement
1111 In respect of journeys to and from the USA, or with an agreed stopping place there, special rules apply. The USA is a party to the Warsaw Convention and a signatory to the Hague Protocol, but has not ratified the Protocol because the limits which it provides are significantly less than the level of awards for personal injury in the United States courts. In the past, the Warsaw Convention limits were often vastly exceeded, in suits brought in the USA, by the plaintiff's attorney invoking or threatening to invoke the 'wilful misconduct' clause of the Warsaw Convention. Carriers have been prepared to settle for compensation

in the USA well in excess of Convention limits. In order to avoid the USA denouncing the Warsaw Convention, international airlines agreed through the International Air Transport Association, in Montreal in 1966, that on all journeys to or from or with a stopping place in the USA they would apply a special limit of liability in respect of death or bodily injury; and that for the same journeys they would waive their defence under Article 20 of the Warsaw Convention, which in other circumstances continued to permit them to escape liability if they could show that all necessary measures to avoid the damage had been taken or that it had been impossible to take such measures. The limit under the Montreal Agreement is $58,000 (£34,000) exclusive of legal fees and costs. This agreement is in effect a 'special contract', permitted under Article 22 of the Warsaw Convention, which is imposed unilaterally on all carriers operating into and from the USA. The United States Civil Aeronautics Board will not issue a permit to land in the USA to an airline not a party to this Agreement.

Special contracts
1112 Many airlines, including all British and most European airlines, also operate special contract limits under Article 22 of the Warsaw Convention. In respect of journeys to, from or touching the United States, all airlines are obliged to apply at least the Montreal Agreement limits. For other flights abroad, the limit applied by British airlines is £25,000. We understand that this limit will shortly be raised to $58,000 (£34,000); and that some other European airlines already apply a limit up to or beyond that figure or its equivalent.

The Guatemala Protocol
1113 A further amendment to the Warsaw Convention was signed in Guatemala in 1971. This Protocol would raise the limit of liability to 1·5 million gold francs (£64,200), but this limit may not be exceeded even if the damage was caused by wilful misconduct, and even if the required passenger ticket was not delivered. Moreover, there is no provision for the making of special contracts between carrier and passenger by which the amount of liability can be increased. On the other hand, the Protocol abrogates entirely the defence of 'unavoidable damage', so that liability would in effect become strict. The defence of contributory negligence would remain. Ratification by at least 30 states is required before the Protocol becomes effective.

The Montreal Protocol No 3
1114 It is, however, unlikely that the Guatemala Protocol will ever be ratified, as it has now been superseded by the additional Montreal Protocol No 3 of 1975. This reproduces the provisions of the Guatemala Protocol relating to liability in respect of passengers, and substitutes for 1·5 million gold francs the broadly equivalent liability limit of 100,000 special drawing rights of the International Monetary Fund. We understand that the USA is considering whether to ratify the Montreal Protocol No 3. If it does so, other countries, including the United Kingdom, are expected to follow suit.

Non-international carriage
1115 The Warsaw Convention, its subsequent Protocols and the special contracts made under it are all intended to regulate international carriage.

None of these provisions applies to non-international travel of which the obvious example is a flight wholly within the territory of a single state. There is, however, no simple classification into 'international' travel on the one hand and 'non-international' travel on the other. For the purposes of the Convention, international travel is not merely travel between two states. As has been explained, it can include carriage within the territory of a single state which is party to the Convention if there is an agreed stopping place in a second state, whether or not this state is party to the Convention. It can also include carriage on a round trip ticket from one state which is a party to the Convention to another state which is not, and back. Yet it excludes carriage on a single ticket between a state which is a party to the Convention and another state which is not (*Philippson* v. *Imperial Airways Ltd* [1939] A.C. 332).

1116   The United Kingdom has made special provision for its own non-international carriage through the Carriage by Air Acts (Application of Provisions) Order 1967. To all such carriage the Order in effect applies the Hague Protocol, but with two important differences. The first is that the complicated ticketing provisions of the Protocol do not apply. The second is that the Protocol liability limit is raised to the sum of 875,000 gold francs (£37,450).

Variations in liability regime
1117   The present law in the United Kingdom is therefore complex. The complications which result from the differing liability regimes applied to individual contracts of carriage may be illustrated by a few examples. Liability in respect of a passenger on a British Airways flight from Paris to London might be up to £25,000 under that airline's special contract if the aircraft crashed on landing at Heathrow. Liability to another passenger in respect of a similar journey by an airline operating without a special contract and therefore governed by the Hague Protocol might be limited to £10,700. On another similar journey, liability to a further passenger who was booked through to New York could be up to £34,000 under the Montreal Agreement. If the aircraft had been flying from Ankara to London, passengers ticketed only for that journey would not be covered by the Warsaw Convention and therefore liability might be up to £37,450 under the Carriage by Air Acts (Application of Provisions) Order 1967.

1118   Table 16 summarises the various limits which may apply to flights to, from or within the United Kingdom.

1119   Article 28 of the Warsaw Convention puts some limitation on the freedom of potential litigants to select the arena of trial against the air carrier. It provides that an action can be brought, at the plaintiff's option, only in the court having jurisdiction where the carrier is ordinarily resident or has his principal place of business; or where the carrier has an establishment by which the contract for carriage has been made; or at the final place of destination. (Where a ticket is for a round trip, the place of destination will be the same as the point of departure.) This still leaves scope for 'forum shopping'. A plaintiff having a choice as to the jurisdiction in which he brings his claim will tend to choose the one which is likely to produce the highest award of damages; the calculation of damages is not identical in all countries; and attitudes to what constitutes intentional or reckless misconduct can differ widely, particularly if findings in this regard are decided by juries.

Other liabilities
1120 The liabilities which the carrier may incur under international conventions are not the only basis on which an action for damages may be brought. The international rules govern the relationship between the carrier and his own

Table 16 Liability limits applying to air carriers
i   Liability limits affecting flights to, from and within the United Kingdom

	Point of departure or arrival		
	United Kingdom domestic	USA	Rest of the world
All British airlines	£37,450	£34,000	£25,000
European airlines with special contracts		£34,000	£25,000–£40,850
Non-European airlines with special contracts		£34,000	£25,000–£34,000
Carriers without special contracts		£34,000	See ii below

ii   Carriers without special contracts – liability limits applicable to flights into and from United Kingdom

	Warsaw Convention	Hague Protocol	Carriage by Air Acts (Application of Provisions) Order 1967
Liability limit	£5,350[1]	£11,700	£37,450[1]
Point of departure or destination	e.g. Guyana Indonesia Jamaica Lebanon Malta Sri Lanka	e.g. Greece Italy Spain	e.g. Chile Turkey

1 Unless on a round trip ticket from the United Kingdom, when the Hague Protocol applies.

passengers. But where the cause of injury is attributable to someone other than the carrier, an action will lie according to the ordinary principles of liability of the relevant jurisdiction against anyone who has caused the loss. In the United Kingdom this means that an action will have to be based on the general principles of negligence. These actions might involve air traffic controllers or ground controllers or the operators of aircraft whose alleged negligence has caused death or injury to passengers in another aircraft. Since none of these actions is covered by the international conventions, the passengers are entitled to bring claims for damages which are not limited by the conventions.

1121   Aircraft are 'premises' within the meaning of the Occupiers' Liability Act 1957 and the Occupiers' Liability (Scotland) Act 1960. The occupiers of an aircraft would normally be the operators, whether owners or not, and they are bound to make it as reasonably safe as any other premises. Occupiers' liability is described more fully in chapter 28.

1122   In the United Kingdom, there is a special rule of strict liability for damage caused to things or people on the ground. Section 40(2) of the Civil Aviation Act 1949 imposes strict liability on the owner of an aircraft, subject to a defence of contributory negligence, for damage caused 'to any person . . . on land or water by, or by a person in, or an article or person falling from, an aircraft while in flight, taking off or landing'. If someone other than the owner of the aircraft may be held liable for the damage, for example the operator, the owner may have a right of indemnity against him.

1123   An aircraft is a manufactured article, and an accident leading to death or bodily injury of passengers and others may be caused as easily by a defect in the aircraft as by some act of negligence of the carrier. An example of a suit brought against a manufacturer is that of the Turkish Airlines DC10 which crashed near Paris in March 1974 with the loss of 346 lives. Numerous actions have been brought in California based on the allegation that the crash was attributable to a design defect in the cargo compartment door of the aircraft. These actions have been brought not only against the manufacturers, McDonnell-Douglas, but also against their sub-contractors, General Dynamics Corporation, who manufactured part of the aircraft involved in the dispute, and against the Federal Aviation Authority, which licensed the DC10 for public transport. Products liability is discussed more fully in chapter 22.

Private flying
1124   Private flying within the United Kingdom is not at present subject to any of the international rules. Liability is governed by the common law principle of negligence. Carriage for reward or gratuitous carriage by an air transport undertaking (for example an air taxi service) is, however, subject to the rules under the Carriage by Air Acts (Application of Provisions) Order 1967. A discretion vested in the Secretary of State by Article 8 of that Order to permit the exclusion of liability in respect of such carriage has been removed by the Unfair Contract Terms Act 1977.

Commercial flying – possible changes in the law

1125   The rapid growth of the volume of air traffic since the last war is likely to continue, boosted by low cost flights by charter or shuttle. As we have seen, the law is far from consistent in the level of tort compensation provided in respect of commercial flights. The liability limits governing a minority of flights into and from the United Kingdom are far below the level of court awards for death or personal injuries in other cases; and a random element may exist, depending on the availability of a claim based on products liability against the aircraft manufacturer and on the national jurisdiction in which a claim may be brought. Any recommendations we may make must necessarily be limited to claims for compensation in the United Kingdom, but in so far as such claims are, or should be, based on international conventions, we can properly express views as to what would be suitable provisions in such conventions.

No-fault

1126   We considered but rejected the possibility of a no-fault scheme for air accidents. Such a scheme would represent a major departure from the international conventions to which the United Kingdom is party. Without further international agreement, there would be difficulty in raising contributions from foreign airlines flying into the United Kingdom.

Strict liability

1127   We looked instead at the basis of the carriers' liability. There is the commercial aspect of this to be borne in mind. Air transport is a highly competitive industry, and, if a particular airline seeks to give a lead by paying generous compensation for injury to passengers, that airline will have to pay higher insurance premiums and be less competitive in consequence. In principle, the right course (although we appreciate the practical difficulties of bringing this about) would be to settle by international convention (as was in effect achieved in the Warsaw Convention) what should be the basis of liability to passengers of the world's principal airlines – ideally all the airlines – and how, if at all, this liability should be limited.

1128   We consider that there are good reasons for imposing on the airlines at least a high standard of care, and preferably strict liability. As we have explained (paragraph 1122), strict liability already applies to the owner of an aircraft in respect of persons other than passengers in the circumstances specified by the Civil Aviation Act 1949; and we think this is right. It seems to us that similar considerations apply to the remedy which should be available to passengers against operators. Perhaps only in the relationship between doctor and patient does a potential victim resign his fate so completely into the hands of another. Modern aircraft are of a great complexity and the average passenger is likely to be ignorant of the skills and techniques which control the machine on which, for a few hours, his life will depend. Furthermore, in the event of an accident, multiple fatalities are almost certain to follow.

Ratification of the Montreal Protocol No 3
1129   Passengers pay a price for the relative ease with which the law already permits recovery against the airlines. In the absence of intentional or reckless misconduct, the passengers' rights to damages are limited to the sums stipulated under the provisions we have described. Where the limit is high enough, this may be regarded as a fair price to pay, although even the limit of £37,450 under the Carriage by Air Acts (Application of Provisions) Order 1967 could be regarded as inadequate if compared with sums of well over £100,000 awarded by the courts to motor accident victims. It is clear that the level of limits requires revision in order to keep abreast with awards for other types of accident. Under the Montreal Protocol No 3 to the Warsaw Convention the limit, depending on the current conversion rate for sterling, would be in the region of £70,000. We think that this would offer an acceptable level of compensation for the time being. **We therefore recommend** that the United Kingdom should ratify the Montreal Protocol No 3 as soon as the USA has done so.

1130   We expect that implementation would have the further advantage of making the settlement of claims speedier. Under this Protocol, the carrier could not invoke the defence under Article 20 of the Warsaw Convention that he and his agents took all necessary measures to prevent the accident or that such measures were impossible, whereas at present there may be delay while the parties contest the availability of this defence. Moreover, liability would be strict and clearly defined, and the victims' right to compensation more immediately apparent. In making this comment, however, we are aware that the Article 20 defence may be of more significance in theory than it is in practice.

Interim measures
1131   The limits of £5,350 and £10,700 which apply to a small number of flights into and from the United Kingdom are manifestly too low. Such flights are not an insignificant proportion of our international travel routes. For example, passengers flying to Greece, Italy and Spain on the national carriers of any of those countries are subject to the £10,700 limit under the Hague Protocol, and passengers flying to Jamaica are subject to the limit of £5,350 under the unamended Warsaw Convention. In view of the difficulties of securing reform by international agreement, we consider that the United Kingdom would be justified in taking steps unilaterally to end these anomalies. Whether or not the Montreal Protocol No 3 is implemented, therefore, **we recommend** that, in relation to all flights entering or leaving the United Kingdom, there should be a limit of liability equivalent to the special contract limit applied by British airlines. There is a precedent for unilateral action in the Montreal Agreement.

Possibility of limiting other liabilities
1132   We considered but rejected the possibility of imposing limits on the liability of persons other than the carrier. We recognise that there is anxiety among insurers and manufacturers about the level of damages which may arise out of products liability claims, although to some extent the high figures of the kind being discussed in, for example, the cases arising from the Tenerife disaster

of March 1977, are attributable to the coincidence of the location in the USA of major manufacturing plants and the high level of damages awarded there. But we are not suggesting such a limit for other forms of products liability, and we see no reason why, if a person is unfortunate enough to suffer injury or death in an aircraft, he or his dependants should be placed at a disadvantage compared with other victims of defective products, or, more widely, with other victims of negligence. Insofar as the present situation encourages plaintiffs to sue the aircraft manufacturer rather than the carrier, we think that the problem arises from the existence of limits on the liability of carriers, not from the absence of limits on the liability of manufacturers.

Channelling

1133   Some of those submitting evidence to us suggested that, instead of the possibility of pursuing separate claims against airlines, manufacturers and air traffic controllers, liability should be channelled to a single party. This system would have the apparent merit of simplicity. But we consider that its broader implications would be inconsistent with our other recommendations, and, as those advocating it recognised, there would have to be international agreement, which we think would not be susceptible of achievement.

1134   We propose elsewhere that a producer should be strictly liable for death or injury caused by his defective products. To recommend that some other party should assume this liability, whether with some arrangement for the sharing of insurance costs or not, would be inconsistent with the principle that a producer should bear the risk of the injury his products may cause. Furthermore, we doubt whether agreement would be reached internationally so as to permit the unlimited recovery we propose for product losses. Both the Society of British Aerospace Companies and the Civil Aviation Authority suggested to us that liability should be unified and borne by the operator; but it is not difficult to imagine a situation where some unfairness would arise. Liability associated with product defects would remain unlimited, whereas operators could still claim the protection of the international conventions where no product liability was at issue. **We recommend** that there should be no channelling of liability to a single party in respect of air transport injuries.

Compulsory insurance

Commercial aircraft

1135   An aircraft registered in the United Kingdom must not carry passengers for reward except in accordance with an air transport licence granted by the Civil Aviation Authority. By virtue of section 22(2) of the Civil Aviation Act 1971, the authority are required to refuse a licence unless satisfied that, 'the resources of the applicant and the financial arrangements made by him are adequate for discharging his actual and potential obligations in respect of the business activities in which he is engaged (if any) and in which he may be expected to engage if he is granted the licence'. The practice of the Authority is to ensure that each operator has in force a certificate of insurance of an adequate amount with a reputable insurer, or an acceptable reserve fund, to meet third party liability. There is therefore, in effect, a system of compulsory insurance for British commercial aircraft.

1136   Foreign carriers are not under the scrutiny of the Civil Aviation Authority in this respect. The Authority told us that, in their view, a system of compulsory insurance extending to foreign carriers would be complicated to administer and difficult to enforce. They also expressed the view that no system of insurance would be effective unless supported by a system similar to that of the Motor Insurers Bureau to compensate victims of an uninsured defendant. It would clearly be unreasonable to expect British aircraft operators to subscribe to a fund to compensate the victims of uninsured foreign operators; and the extent of compulsory insurance arrangements abroad is not sufficient to provide a basis for reciprocal arrangements. Despite the difficulties with respect to foreign carriers, we think that the present arrangements regarding the insurance of aircraft in commercial operation are adequate. The Civil Aviation Authority told us that in practice all major airlines insure up to 'a very high figure'. In all the circumstances, we propose no change in the requirement for liability insurance of commercial aircraft.

Private aircraft
1137   In considering the scope for extending compulsory insurance, we concentrated on the position of private aircraft, including those few commercial operators who are exempt from the requirement of an air transport licence and so do not need to satisfy the Civil Aviation Authority that they are adequately insured. The problem is not a large one. The great majority of owners of private aircraft now have insurance cover for third party liability up to £100,000. The Civil Aviation Authority have recently recommended that owners should take out cover for liability up to £500,000, and it can be expected that a number of owners will increase their policies accordingly. The Department of Trade informed us that, despite the absence of compulsory insurance, no third party in the United Kingdom has gone uncompensated for lack of insurance cover.

1138   All compulsory insurance systems require both supervision of insurers and a means of making sure that individuals take out policies. Since the latter cannot be guaranteed, there could still be unsatisfied judgments unless something along the lines of the Motor Insurers Bureau were set up – and this, in turn, would probably not be acceptable to insurers unless there were an adequate degree of supervision. In addition, the insurance money would not be available if the owner, although insured, were in breach of a condition of his policy by flying in contravention of the Air Navigation Order or Regulations. It would, therefore, be necessary to restrict by statute the defences available to insurers. If a compulsory scheme were introduced for aircraft registered in the United Kingdom, it would be possible to provide that a copy of the policy or cover note must be produced when renewing an aircraft's certificate of airworthiness. Even this requirement, however, would not be a certain check as the policy might have lapsed due to non-payment of premiums, or might have been cancelled.

242

1139   If a compulsory third party insurance scheme were introduced for all aircraft flying in United Kingdom airspace, one of the biggest problems would be how to ensure that foreign registered aircraft were covered. Third party damage might well be caused by an aircraft overflying the United Kingdom, and it is difficult to envisage how the insurance arrangements for such aircraft could be checked. Checks on policies could also cause problems in relation to foreign aircraft landing in the United Kingdom. How does the verifying official know a policy is valid, or even that the document produced is a policy if written in, say, Japanese or Arabic? How could he be certain of the adequate financial standing of the foreign insurers? Something along the lines of the 'green card' system used for motor cars might be possible; but this would need some consensus on what level of insurance should be carried and on what terms and conditions it should be.

1140   In broad terms, there are two possible points of view on this issue. On the one hand, it could be argued that there is no evidence that compulsory insurance is necessary, and that to set up the necessary administrative machinery could not be justified. On the other hand, it could also be argued that, in this relatively small and tightly controlled field, it would not be difficult to administer a scheme of compulsory insurance; and that it is better to have such protection as compulsory insurance would give.

1141   Our overall approach to the imposition of compulsory insurance, which we have set out in chapter 11, did not lead us to a firm conclusion in respect of private aircraft. Nevertheless, the issues deserve further study. **We recommend** that further consideration should be given to the possibility of imposing compulsory third party insurance in respect of private aircraft.

CHAPTER 20

Sea and inland waterways

1142 There are few accidental deaths of passengers in United Kingdom merchant ships. There were seven in 1975 and five in 1976. Deaths of passengers at sea are more commonly from individual personal accidents than from catastrophes. (Fatal accidents to crew members are more frequent; they are relevant to our chapter on work injuries.) Comparable figures for non-fatal injuries are not available.

Sea transport – the present law

The basis of liability

1143 The Maritime Conventions Act 1911 laid down rules of contributory negligence and joint liability as part of maritime law long before they were extended to the law of tort generally. Under that Act, after a collision claimants can sue the owners of either vessel for the full amount of the damages or can proceed against the owners of both vessels jointly. If damages are recovered against the owners of one vessel in excess of their proportion of fault, those owners can claim contribution from the owners of another vessel to the extent of the other vessel's proportion of fault. Negligence remains the basis of a claim for damages for personal injury at sea. In addition, a passenger injured on the voyage may be able to sue the carrier for breach of the contract of carriage.

1144 Normally, an injured passenger will bring his action against the shipowner, who can be an individual or a partnership, but is more often a large company. In accordance with the general law, the shipowner is vicariously liable in tort for injuries caused by negligence or other fault of his shipmaster or crew members or other employees.

The Brussels Convention

1145 Claims against a shipowner, including personal injury claims by passengers and persons not carried in the ship, are subject to a statutory overall limit when they arise from a single maritime incident, provided that the shipowner proves that he was not personally to blame for the accident – that the wrongful act or omission occurred 'without his fault or privity'. (The courts have to give to the expression 'without his fault or privity' a special application when the shipowner is a company. The expression is then taken to mean without the fault or privity of the senior management or directing mind of the company.) If the shipowner does not prove this requirement, his liability is unlimited. If he does prove it, he still has vicarious liability, but only for a limited amount.

1146   This limit was originally fixed by section 503 of the Merchant Shipping Act 1894 at £15 a ton of the ship's net registered tonnage, but it was increased by the Merchant Shipping (Liability of Shipowners and Others) Act 1958, which gave effect to an international Convention made at Brussels in the previous year. Under this Act, the limit is 3,100 Poincaré gold francs (the then standard unit of account) for each ton of the ship's net registered tonnage; and a proportion of the total amount available may be appropriated to satisfy property claims. The January 1977 sterling equivalent of 3,100 gold francs, as specified by Order, is about £133. For the purpose of this limitation, and in respect of personal injury claims, any ship of less than 300 tons is deemed to be a ship of 300 tons. This provides a 'floor' of approximately £40,000. The limit is 'for each incident' and not 'for each claim', so that in respect of any one incident the shipowner is not bound to pay more than the limited amount, however many people may have been injured.

1147   The right to limit liability for each incident is also extended to 'any charterer and any person interested in or in possession of the ship, and, in particular, any manager or operator of the ship'. This provision covers circumstances in which the charterer, instead of leaving the navigation and management of the ship to the owner, takes over the ship, operates it with his own master and crew, and himself becomes liable. The same provision also covers others, such as shipbuilders or repairers, who may be in sole possession of a ship.

1148   The 1958 Act limits the liability of the master, crewmen and other servants of the shipowner in respect of personal injury, notwithstanding their actual fault or privity in the matters which are the subject of complaint. The main objective of this provision is to ensure that the limit on liability for each incident cannot be circumvented by bringing an action directly against an employee rather than against the shipowner or other carrier who is vicariously liable and entitled to invoke the limit.

1149   The provisions of the 1958 Act apply equally in respect of claims by persons not carried in the ship who are injured through the fault of those in charge of that ship. This covers, for example, the passengers of another ship with which the first ship is in collision.

The Athens Convention and the Unfair Contract Terms Act
1150   Until now, the shipowner has also been able to exclude or limit his liability towards passengers by a term in the contract of carriage, and in practice has invariably done so. The position has changed following the Athens Convention of 1974. This Convention prohibits the carrier from contracting out of his liability, but limits his liability for death or personal injury to 700,000 gold francs (about £30,000) for each passenger. (A subsequent protocol to the Convention substitutes special drawing rights of the International Monetary Fund as the units of account.) If a claimant can prove that the incident giving rise to the injury arose from an act or omission of the carrier done with the intent to cause such damage, or recklessly and with knowledge that such damage would probably result, the carrier is then subject to unlimited liability.

The same provisions apply to actions brought directly against the carrier's servants or agents. The Convention has received only one of the ten ratifications needed to bring it into force, although it has been signed by a number of states, including the United Kingdom.

1151   In the meantime, the liability provisions of the Athens Convention have in effect been enacted by the Unfair Contract Terms Act 1977. The Act provides, as a temporary measure, that liability to passengers may not be excluded or restricted except insofar as the exclusion or restriction would have been effective if the provisions of the Athens Convention of 1974 had the force of law in relation to the contract. In other words, the restriction imposed by the 1977 Act on the right of shipowners to contract out of liability may be avoided if the provisions of the Convention, insofar as these bear on the restriction or exclusion of liability in contracts for the sea carriage of passengers, are incorporated into the contract. We understand that substantive legislation implementing the rules of the Athens Convention, in respect of both domestic and international carriage, is expected soon. When this legislation is brought into force, it will supersede the temporary provisions of the 1977 Act.

1152   The combined effect of current legislation, therefore, is that a shipowner is in practice able to limit his liability in negligence for personal injury to £30,000 for each passenger, and is further able to apply a total limit to each incident, which may give rise to claims other than passenger claims. Where both limits apply, the total limit for the incident may effectively reduce the limit for each passenger to a figure below £30,000.

Sea transport – the London Convention 1976

1153   A new convention – the London Convention – was adopted in 1976 by a conference on liability for maritime claims, with the intention of replacing the 1957 Brussels Convention. It will enter into force one year after 12 states have become party to it, but so far only the United Kingdom has signed it, the signature being subject to ratification.

1154   Insofar as it relates to personal injury claims, the London Convention is complementary to the Athens Convention. It deals with a shipowner's total liability for each incident in such a way that the Athens Convention's limit for each passenger cannot normally be reduced. It is the intention of the London Convention that the overall limit for each incident should be the number of passengers which the ship is authorised to carry multiplied by an amount equivalent to the Athens Convention's limit of about £30,000 for each passenger, subject to a ceiling of 25 million special drawing rights (about £17 million).

1155   For a claim made against a party other than the owner, charterer, manager or operator of the passenger's own ship or his servants, limitation would remain on a global basis, but the limit would be based on the gross registered tonnage of the vessel against which the claim was made, rather than its net registered tonnage as at present, and the level of limits would be substantially raised. For a ship of 500 tons, the total limit of liability would be about £340,000 at January 1977 values, about £230,000 being available for the satisfaction of personal injury claims (not all of which need be claims by passengers), and the remainder for the settlement of property claims and unsatisfied personal injury claims. The corresponding figures under the present law are about £66,400 and £45,000 respectively.

1156 Article 4 of the London Convention provides that a person liable is not entitled to limit liability if it is proved that the loss resulted from his personal act or omission committed with the intent to cause the loss, or recklessly and with knowledge that the loss would probably result.

Sea transport – possible changes in the law

1157 Perhaps because of the relative safety of sea travel, the law governing compensation has not attracted as much comment as that relating to other forms of transport. Leaving aside the point now covered by the Athens Convention through the Unfair Contract Terms Act 1977, the main criticism made in our evidence was that the rules regarding the limitation of liability could provide limits which were unrealistically low. In addition, some witnesses addressed themselves to the wider questions of whether a no-fault scheme would be desirable or whether strict liability should replace negligence as the basis of liability so as to bring sea transport into line with international rail and air transport.

No-fault

1158 It did not appear to us that a no-fault scheme would be appropriate. It could be extended only to carriers and shipowners subject to United Kingdom law and its cost would have to be borne by the suppliers and users of the service. The cost of a no-fault scheme could put British shipping at a competitive disadvantage if similar schemes did not apply to foreign vessels. We thought that the better course would be to improve the existing law so as to provide reasonably adequate compensation.

Strict liability

1159 The liability of a shipowner or charterer is at present based on the negligence of himself or his servants in operating the ship. At first sight, it seemed an attractive course to recommend that sea transport should be brought into line with the strict liability rules for international rail and air transport. This recommendation was urged upon us, for example, by the Council of Her Majesty's Circuit Judges. The British Railways Board told us that they already accepted liability without proof of fault in disasters involving their ships.

1160 There is, however, an economic argument against a unilateral imposition of strict liability on carriers subject to United Kingdom law. Where there had been a collision, it would be easier to recover against such a carrier than against a foreign carrier subject only to the existing law. We were impressed by the BIA's reasoning that the additional cost of strict liability would put the British shipping industry at a competitive disadvantage. In an area governed traditionally by international agreement, we considered it inappropriate to recommend a new system of liability for the United Kingdom alone.

Limits on liability

1161   We welcome the provisions of the London Convention of 1976 whereby the limits on the carrier's liability for each incident would be brought into line with the limit for each passenger under the Athens Convention. The new 'floor' of liability of about £30,000 a passenger would not be far out of line with the limit applicable under the special contracts for air travellers.

1162   The limits applying in claims against another vessel would also be raised by the London Convention. One of the criticisms of the present law is that, if a small ship causes extensive injury or death to passengers of a large ship, the small amount payable has to be shared among many victims. The new limit could still be inadequate, but it would be better than the existing one.

1163   **We recommend** that the United Kingdom should ratify the London Convention; and we hope that the Convention will soon be brought into force.

Other possibilities for change

Inland waterways

1164   All vessels, unless propelled by oars, are subject to the same rules regarding liability and limitation as sea going ships. We are aware of a Convention produced in 1973 by the Economic Commission for Europe of the United Nations, relating to the limitation of the liability of the owners of inland vessels. This Convention substantially repeats the terms of the present United Kingdom law.

1165   An accident to a vessel inland may not necessarily give rise to personal injury claims on such a scale that the limitation provisions of the Merchant Shipping (Liability of Shipowners and Others) Act 1958 would come to be invoked. Nevertheless, **we recommend** that the provisions of the London Convention should be applied to inland craft.

Hovercraft

1166   Hovercraft are hybrid vehicles treated for some purposes as aircraft, for others as ships, and for insurance purposes as ships, aircraft or motor vehicles (Insurance Companies Act 1974, section 83). The legislation relevant to our remit – the Hovercraft Act 1968 and the Hovercraft (Civil Liability) Order 1971 – for the most part considers hovercraft to be ships. The Admiralty jurisdiction of the High Court and county courts is applied to them. Since the greatest use for hovercraft at present appears to be for speedy travel over water, this is probably appropriate.

1167   Liability for bodily injury to passengers is governed by the provisions of the Carriage by Air Act 1961 and the Carriage by Air (Supplementary Provisions) Act 1962, together with certain modifications made by the 1971 Order. In this respect, therefore, British hovercraft are subject to the provisions of the Warsaw Convention relating to carriage by air, as amended in 1955 at the Hague. The carrier is liable without proof of fault, but may escape liability if he proves that he took all necessary steps to avoid the damage. In place of the Convention limit on liability of 250,000 gold francs (£10,700), the Order provides for a limit of £12,000. As with aircraft, the limit does not apply if the owner is guilty of intentional or reckless misconduct. The limit may be increased by special contract between the carrier and the passenger, but the limit cannot be reduced and liability cannot be excluded altogether.

1168   Whereas hovercraft are treated in relation to injury caused to passengers as though they were aircraft, in relation to persons other than passengers they are treated as ships. The Merchant Shipping Acts apply, but only if at the time of the incident the hovercraft is travelling over navigable waters, which may be inland waters. There is a different limit, namely £3·50 a kilogram of the maximum authorised weight. Where a hovercraft is of less than 8,000 kg maximum authorised weight, it is deemed for this purpose to have a relevant weight of 8,000 kg. There is therefore a global minimum of £28,000 where a hovercraft causes death or personal injury to persons outside the hovercraft.

1169   Until such time as there is an international convention, we propose no change in this differentiation between liability to passengers and liability to others, and we envisage that our recommendations in respect of aircraft and ships would be followed as appropriate. We are, however, concerned about the current limit on liability to passengers. **We recommend** that, pending implementation of the Montreal Protocol No 3, the limit in respect of liability for death or personal injury to passengers on international hovercraft journeys should be raised to the equivalent of the special contract limit applied by British airlines; and that the limit for journeys within the United Kingdom should be increased to the equivalent of 875,000 gold francs. We recognise that this proposal would introduce an anomaly as between international and internal journeys, but it is consistent with the present law in respect of aircraft as it would be modified by our recommendations.

Ships as premises
1170   Ships and hovercraft are 'premises' for the purpose of the Occupiers' Liability Act 1957. We consider the liabilities of occupiers of premises in chapter 28.

Ships as products
1171   Ships and hovercraft are also manufactured articles. As with aircraft, we considered whether shipbuilders should be exempted from our recommendation elsewhere that producers should be strictly liable for death or injury caused by their defective products. We recognise, again as with aircraft, that if an injured person were able to mount a successful action based on products liability, such an action would effectively circumvent the liability limits enjoyed by the carrier. But we do not see this as a conclusive objection to making United Kingdom manufacturers and importers strictly liable for injuries caused by defects in their products.

CHAPTER 21

Rail

1172   The world's first passenger carrying railway, the Swansea and Mumbles, was opened on 25 March 1807. The first railway to carry goods and passengers entirely by steam traction was the Liverpool and Manchester Railway. The first fatality in railway history coincided with the opening ceremony of that railway in 1830 when William Huskisson MP, former President of the Board of Trade, was accidentally killed.

1173   Today, rail is the safest form of land passenger transport in the United Kingdom. Over the years 1962 to 1971, deaths for each 100 million passenger miles averaged 0·06. The next lowest figure for the same period was 0·2 for bus and coach travel. In 1975 there were 424 deaths on the railways; 46 were railmen, 69 were passengers, 90 were trespassers, 12 were other persons on railway property, and 207 were suicides. During 1975, some 163 passengers suffered serious injury. Accidents involving a large number of passengers are rare.

The present law

Negligence
1174   The liability of British Rail (apart from international journeys), London Transport and other railway undertakings toward passengers and others injured or killed, whether by trains or on railway premises, is, and has always been, governed by the common law principle of negligence. In major disasters there usually arises an inference of negligence on the part of the railway undertaking. The inference may sometimes be rebutted by proof that the accident was attributable to a third party, that it was unforeseeable, or that no exercise of due care on the part of the railway could have prevented it. But it is quite likely that the railway will admit liability. Following the Moorgate disaster on the London Underground in 1975, the cause of which was unknown, the London Transport Executive agreed to pay compensation.

1175   The railways were held liable in negligence to a volunteer who, in consequence of assisting in rescue work at the scene of the Lewisham railway disaster in 1957, suffered emotional shock which hastened his death (*Chadwick v. British Transport Commission* [1967] 1 W.L.R. 912).

Limitation of liability
1176   It used to be possible in certain circumstances for a railway undertaking to limit its liability for bodily injury to passengers. British Rail and London Transport were able to do so in respect of passengers travelling on a free pass.

Other railway undertakings were able to do so in respect of any passengers. Under the Unfair Contract Terms Act 1977, however, no railway undertaking will now be able to limit its liability in these ways.

International journeys

1177   The United Kingdom is party to the International Convention Concerning the Carriage of Passengers and Luggage by Rail 1961 (known as the CIV (*Convention Internationale des Voyageurs*) Convention), which was reviewed in 1970, and to the Additional Convention of 1966. The CIV Convention provided a basis for the contract of carriage between passengers and the railway undertaking, but left liability for death or injury to passengers to be determined by national law. The Additional Convention, which was given effect in the United Kingdom by the Carriage by Railway Act 1972, lays down rules of strict liability. Any part of an international journey undertaken in the United Kingdom is subject to the Additional Convention. Article 2 provides that, 'The railway shall be liable for damage resulting from the death of, or personal injury or any other bodily or mental harm to, a passenger, caused by an accident arising out of the operation of the railway and happening while the passenger is in, entering or alighting from a train'. Certain defences are permitted to the railway; that the accident was 'due to a third party's behaviour which the railway, in spite of taking the care required in the particular circumstances of the case, could not avoid and the consequences of which it was unable to prevent'; or was 'due to the passenger's wrongful act or neglect or to behaviour on his part not in conformity with the normal conduct of passengers'. The railway undertaking is also relieved of liability if the accident was caused by circumstances not connected with the operation of the railway which the undertaking, in spite of having taken the care required, could not have avoided.

1178   There are no limits of liability under the Additional Convention, which prohibits the railway undertaking from introducing such limits by contract. This is in contrast with the position of air and sea carriers.

1179   Because the Additional Convention applies only to international travel, different liability rules can exist in relation to passengers travelling on the same train. Someone travelling from Paris to Edinburgh by way of London can recover damages without proof of fault if he is injured when getting out of the train at Edinburgh. But his companion travelling only from London would have to show that a similar accident sustained by him was due to the fault of British Rail. The terms of the Additional Convention accord with the general practice for domestic journeys in other European countries, where passengers can successfully sue the railways without proof of fault. In Belgium and France, a passenger who is injured may claim for breach of the contract of carriage and the strict liability provisions of the Civil Code may be invoked by others injured by moving trains. In Austria, Denmark and the Federal Republic of Germany there are statutory rules of strict liability in tort.

1180   The various underground systems are not covered by the Carriage by Railway Act 1972. Accordingly, that part of any international journey undertaken on the underground is not subject to the rule of strict liability which the Act lays down.

Possible changes in the law

No-fault

1181 In the evidence submitted to us, most of those favouring change advocated the inclusion of rail accidents in a comprehensive no-fault scheme. But we do not recommend such a scheme. We have not found that the arguments which have led us to propose a no-fault scheme for road accidents would justify establishing a similar scheme for rail accidents.

1182 We accept that a no-fault scheme for rail transport would be financially feasible. As the number of railway undertakings is limited, there would be little administrative difficulty either in placing the cost on those undertakings or in collecting the levy. Nor would the cost be large. On the other hand, the number of persons killed and injured on the railways is much smaller than on the roads, and the shortcomings of the tort system are less likely to result in large numbers of people failing to obtain compensation. One of the major criticisms of the tort action for road accidents is that the plaintiff is often hampered in establishing his claim by uncertainties as to the facts surrounding the accident. This problem is less likely to face someone claiming against the railway. Experience has shown that British Rail and London Transport display a readiness to compensate in major accident cases regardless of arguments about liability, although the amount paid may not always be regarded as adequate by the plaintiff. A further consideration is that a no-fault scheme would be open to abuse by those who were thrown about on a train as a result of their own carelessness, such as badly behaved football supporters. For all these reasons, we have decided not to recommend a no-fault scheme for rail transport.

Reversed burden of proof

1183 We considered whether there would be merit in reversing the burden of proof in negligence, although no such suggestion was made in the evidence and we are not aware of any foreign system where such a provision operates in this context. It seems to us that, in most serious railway accident cases where a number of passengers are involved, a reversal of the burden of proof already takes place in practice, since the plaintiffs are able successfully to invoke the maxim *res ipsa loquitur* (the facts speak for themselves); and that to recommend a formal change would have little effect in the very cases where injury was likely to be most serious.

Strict liability

1184 We received a good deal of evidence supporting the idea of imposing strict liability on railway undertakings. We were impressed by the arguments. Certain aspects of the operation of railways can be characterised as inherently hazardous. Although railway trains are normally safe, the consequences of an accident involving a moving train can be grave.

1185 At the same time, there are many accidents on the railways which are in no way associated with the potentially disastrous risks inherent in the movement of hundreds of tons of metal, often at great speeds, about the country. British Rail owns narrow strips of land 12,000 miles long, and there is considerable scope for accidents on their premises. There is no reason why the type of accident which could happen to a passenger or bystander as easily on other premises, for example, an accidental fall on the station platform, should give rise to any higher duty of care on the part of the railway than is owed by anyone else.

1186 **We recommend** that railway undertakings should be strictly liable in tort for death or personal injury which is wholly or partly caused by the movement of rolling stock.

A regime of strict liability

Defences to strict liability
1187 We considered what defences should be open to the railway undertaking where strict liability applies.

1188 There could be circumstances in which the facts would enable the railway to invoke the defences of contributory negligence or *volenti non fit injuria* (voluntary assumption of risk), if those defences were allowed. A passenger injured when leaning out of a carriage window might be held to have been contributorily negligent; another who had deliberately jumped from the moving train might be held voluntarily to have assumed the risk of injury, in the restricted sense required by the law before this defence can be accepted. Where such circumstances arise, we think it reasonable that the damages for which the railway undertaking is liable should be reduced or eliminated. **We recommend** that the defences of contributory negligence and voluntary assumption of risk should be permitted to a railway undertaking where strict liability applies.

1189 Particular difficulties arise from derailments caused by an obstruction accidentally or unlawfully placed on the railway track. Under the present law, the railway undertaking would not normally be held negligent in such circumstances, and we considered whether the railway should be able to invoke the defence of 'act of a third party' where strict liability applied. The defence is available in respect of international journeys. It could be argued that railways are particularly vulnerable to interference by third parties, and that it would be unreasonable for the operator to be held liable for accidents which he would usually be unable to prevent. On the other hand, the passenger himself has no control over the moving railway carriage in which he is travelling; and, where a derailment leading to death or injury has occurred because of an obstruction on the line, we think that the payment of tort compensation should not be thwarted by this defence. The risk of obstruction or other malicious or accidental interference with trains in motion is one of the risks inherent in the operation of a railway. **We recommend** that the defence of act of a third party should not be available to a railway undertaking where strict liability applies. Under our proposals, a cause of action would not arise in the first place if the accident was wholly caused by the third party's action, as opposed to being wholly or partly caused by the movement of rolling stock.

Rail   *Chapter 21*

1190   **We also recommend** that the defence of act of God, or *force majeure*, should not be available to a railway undertaking where strict liability applies. In practice, the opportunity for deploying such a defence would rarely arise.

Trespassers
1191   We considered whether strict liability should apply in respect of injury or death to trespassers. Although it is impossible for railways to be fully securely fenced, or for there always to be a warning notice, we think it reasonable to assume that someone trespassing on a railway line knows the risk of doing so. **We recommend** that railway undertakings should not be strictly liable for injury or death to trespassers; and the questions whether they owe any duty of care to a particular trespasser, and if so how it could be performed, should be determined as in the case of other occupiers of property.

The effect of our proposals
1192   Our proposal for extending the rule of strict liability could be expected to affect only a minority of claims against the railway. It is unlikely therefore that the additional burden of cost thrown on to railway undertakings would be large. Since the operators of public railways are self insurers, we do not expect this dual standard of liability, whereby strict liability would apply in some cases but not in others, to give rise to insurance difficulties.

254

CHAPTER 22

Products

1193 Category c of our terms of reference covers 'the manufacture, supply or use of goods or services'. This chapter is concerned with compensation for death or personal injury suffered by any person through the manufacture, supply or use of goods. We use the word 'products' rather than the word 'goods' because 'products liability' has become an accepted term of art in this field.

1194 As a working definition, we have taken 'products' to include all goods, whether natural or manufactured, but not 'immovables' such as buildings and bridges. We have also adopted a working definition of the word 'injury' broad enough to include diseases caused by the use of a particular product, so as to cover, for example, certain side effects of drugs.

Products liability and the consumer

Consumer protection
1195 Products liability must be considered in the context of public concern to protect the interests of the consumer. The recent growth of pressure groups and other organisations representing those interests is a world wide phenomenon. Much of this activity is concerned with the need to minimise the risk of death or personal injury caused by defective products.

1196 Recent years have seen a parallel growth of interest in products liability itself. Again this is international; and indeed the subject has international dimensions. The manufacture of components, the assembly of the finished product, the purchase of the product and the injury itself – these could all take place in different countries with different legal provisions. The Standing Conference on Private International Law at the Hague produced in 1973 a Convention designed to establish greater uniformity in deciding which country's laws should be applicable in such circumstances. As to what those laws should be, international deliberations have included discussions by the United Nations Commission on International Trade Law, and a spate of conferences.

1197 Two international documents bear directly on our remit. The first is the Council of Europe's 'Convention on Products Liability in regard to Personal Injury and Death', known as the 'Strasbourg Convention'. This Convention was opened for signature by member states in January 1977. It has been signed by Austria, Belgium, France and Luxembourg. The terms of the Convention are at Annex 10. The second of these documents is a draft EEC Directive,

255

on which we understand that the Economic and Social Committee and the European Assembly are expected to report shortly to the EEC Commission. The latest version is at Annex 11.

1198   The Strasbourg Convention is confined to personal injury and death. The draft EEC Directive covers damage to personal property. Both envisage the imposition of strict liability on the producer. Either accession to the one or the issue of the other would mean substantial changes in the negligence based system of tort liability which applies to producers in the United Kingdom at present. We are not alone in this respect. For example, neither the Nether-lands nor the Federal Republic of Germany have a regime of strict liability in tort for products.

The Law Commissions' report
1199   In November 1971, the Lord Chancellor asked the Law Commission, and the Lord Advocate asked the Scottish Law Commission, 'to consider whether the existing law governing compensation for personal injury, damage to property or any other loss caused by defective products is adequate, and to recommend what improvements, if any, in the law are needed to ensure that additional remedies are provided and against whom such remedies should be available'. Our own subsequent terms of reference with respect to products liability overlapped with theirs. There were nevertheless important differences. The Law Commissions were asked to consider 'damage to property or any other loss', as well as personal injury, whereas our own terms of reference excluded property damage. On the other hand, the Law Commissions saw themselves as limited to considering change within the framework of tort and contract law, whereas we were not thus confined.

1200   We have benefited from these concurrent deliberations in three respects. First, our own consideration of the issues was assisted by the publication in 1975 of the Law Commissions' joint working paper (Law Commission Working Paper No 64; Scottish Law Commission Memorandum No 20). Secondly, the Commissions were good enough to send us copies of the comments they received on that working paper, provided that the contributor concerned had no objection. Thirdly, we have been able to take account of the Com-missions' final report (Law Com No 82; Scot Law Com No 45; Cmnd 6831) in the course of drafting our own. We have thought it right to explain our own views and emphasise those considerations which carried the greatest weight with us; but the working paper and the report have made our job easier.

The importance of products liability
1201   The number of injuries caused by products is relatively small, and the risk of death is lower than for other categories of injury. There are no published statistics, but our personal injury survey suggests that between 30,000 and 40,000 injuries a year (about 1 per cent of all injuries) may be caused by defective products other than drugs. Of these, something over 10,000 occur during the course of work, and a further 10,000 involve services as well as defective products.

1202 We estimate that around 5 per cent of these 30,000 to 40,000 injuries attract compensation either through tort or through contract. The average amount paid is less than £500, half the average for tort compensation as a whole. Claims in respect of liability for products and services represent about 1 per cent of all claims on insurers, but account for only 0·3 per cent of business in the courts. These estimates, and other evidence from the insurance survey, suggest that claims involving products liability tend to be disposed of at an earlier stage than other claims.

1203 These estimates do not give a complete picture, since they give no indication of the growing nature of the problem. Until a fairly late stage in the industrial revolution most goods were manufactured by small businesses, often selling direct to the user. Now the situation is transformed by the scale of production, the complexity of technology, the number of processes, producers and distributors involved with any one item, and the sheer quantity of goods produced and consumed. The consumer is dependent on producers he does not know and processes he does not understand.

1204 Potentially dangerous defects in manufactured goods are commonly divided into two categories. First, there is the 'manufacturing defect' – the defective manufacture of a single item in an otherwise normal production run. This may be due to a material weakness, for example, a flaw in the steel used to make a particular bicycle. An EEC Commission working document pointed out that it may be possible to discover such weaknesses only at disproportionately high cost, such as by an X-ray examination of all the steel used to make all the bicycles. Secondly, there is the 'design defect' – a basic flaw common to a whole product type. For an illustration, one need look no further than the thalidomide disaster. Products liability claims may be comparatively few in number, but the range of risk extends from minor harm to major catastrophe.

The present law
1205 United Kingdom law provides two ways in which a victim injured by a product may be able to obtain redress. One is in contract and the other is in tort.

Liability in contract
1206 Purchases of a product by one person from another are purchases under a contract. Under the Sale of Goods Act 1893, as amended by the Supply of Goods (Implied Terms) Act 1973, a contract of sale in the course of a business normally implies that the goods are of 'merchantable quality', that is to say that they are reasonably fit for the purpose for which goods of that kind are usually bought. If a buyer asks the seller for a ladder, the seller is bound to provide him with a ladder fit for the purpose for which ladders are used. In addition, if the buyer makes it clear that he requires the goods for a special purpose other than that for which the goods are usually bought, and the goods are sold to him as being suitable for that special purpose, then the contract will normally imply that the goods are reasonably fit for that purpose.

1207 If an article is defective, and as a result of the defect an injury results from using it in the way in which it was intended to be used, it is manifestly unfit for its purpose. Irrespective of whether or not the seller has been negligent, the buyer can then sue him for damages in respect of the injury sustained. The effect of contract law is therefore to impose strict liability.

1208 Action in contract, however, has two limitations. First, it is available only against the seller. The article concerned might well have been sold by a retailer in a package sealed by the manufacturer, but it is the retailer who is liable, irrespective of whether or not he is in turn able to bring a successful action in contract or in tort against the manufacturer. Secondly – and subject to the reservation that in Scotland a third party may sue under a contract if, and insofar as, it is made for his benefit – the action is available only in favour of the purchaser. If the ladder has been bought by a man but is used by his wife, the wife will have no remedy in contract if she is injured because a rung breaks.

Liability in tort
1209 The action available in tort is at once wider and more restricted. It is wider in that it may be brought against whoever is responsible for the defect and in favour of whoever suffers injury by it. It is more restricted in that the plaintiff must prove negligence. As a general rule, he must prove not only that the product was defective and that the defect caused the injury, but also that the defendant had failed in his duty of care because the injury was a foreseeable consequence of the defect.

1210 That a duty of care is owed by a manufacturer to the consumer was established by the celebrated case of *Donoghue* v. *Stevenson* [1932] A.C. 562, 1932 S.C. (H.L.) 31. The relevance of the finding to modern manufacturing and marketing conditions was made clear in Lord Atkin's judgment:

'A manufacturer of products, which he sells in such a form as to show that he intends them to reach the ultimate consumer in the form in which they left him with no reasonable possibility of intermediate examination, and with the knowledge that the absence of reasonable care in the preparation or putting up of the products will result in an injury to the consumer's life or property, owes a duty to the consumer to take that reasonable care.'

It is a question of fact rather than of law whether in all the circumstances of a particular case the nature of the defect raises a *prima facie* inference that there must have been some negligence in the design or manufacture of the article. The existence of a dangerous defect will often raise such an inference, and the manufacturer will then have the burden of proving the absence of negligence.

1211 In addition to disputing the facts alleged against him, a producer may raise other defences. Contributory negligence may apply if the plaintiff had used a product for a purpose for which it was not intended, or if he had departed from the instructions for use. Or it may be alleged that the plaintiff had used the product knowing that it was defective and had taken the risk on himself. Where there has been a 'design defect', the producer may raise a defence based on 'the state of the art', contending that he exercised all reasonable care in designing the product, given the level of knowledge and stage of technological development at the time that he did so.

Exclusion of liability

1212   Under the Unfair Contract Terms Act 1977, it will no longer be possible for anyone acting in the course of business to exclude or limit liability for negligence resulting in death or personal injury. (Exclusions and limitations of liability for negligence resulting in other loss or damage will be subject to a test of reasonableness.) Similarly, in contracts where one party is a consumer or is dealing on the other's standard terms of business, any purported exclusion or limitation of liability for breach of contract will be upheld only insofar as it is shown to be reasonable.

Breach of statutory duty

1213   An element of strict liability has been introduced in Great Britain by the Consumer Protection Act 1961, and in Northern Ireland by the Consumer Protection Act (Northern Ireland) 1965. These Acts enable regulations to be made imposing safety requirements for any class of goods. Breach of these regulations is an offence in itself, and is also actionable as breach of statutory duty owed to any other person who may be affected by the contravention of, or non-compliance with, the requirement in question. In effect, the seller is strictly liable if he sells goods in breach of the regulations. Although the retailer is the natural point of redress for the consumer, it is open to the consumer to take action against any seller in the chain of supply, and the right of action is not confined to the buyer, as it would be in an action in contract. Some 16 sets of regulations have been made under the Consumer Protection Act 1961, covering a wide range of goods, including electrical equipment, heating appliances, children's clothing, toys, cooking utensils, pencils and graphic instruments, and glazed ceramic ware. The recently published Consumer Safety Bill, which enables the Secretary of State to make regulations relating to the safety of goods, would further extend the range of actions for breach of statutory duty.

The evidence

1214   Less evidence than we should have liked came to us from producers in response to our circulars. We received none from the CBI, and little from agricultural interests. There was some tendency among producers who did submit their views to represent that a change in the existing law would be undesirable or impracticable. These views, however, were by no means unanimous. A desire for change in favour of consumers was expressed by consumer interests, but there were a number of different views on what was needed.

1215   The evidence which came to us by way of the Law Commissions covered a rather wider range of producer interests, but a narrower range of consumer interests. The tendency among industrial and trade interests was to favour little or no change. Many of the comments, reflecting the emphasis of the Commissions' questions in their working paper, concerned the detailed operation of a system of strict liability if one were to be introduced.

The case for change

Shortcomings of the present system
1216   The term 'products liability' is an American invention. It does not desig-
nate a distinct category of law in the United Kingdom. As we have explained,
the law which applies to liability for injury caused by defective products lacks
coherence.

1217   It has been argued to us that the importance of the discrepancies between
tort and contract law is less than might appear, since a producer's liability
in tort is in practice more strict than theory suggests. The arguments are that
the great majority of products claims are of a relatively minor nature; that they
are normally dealt with quickly and to the satisfaction of both parties; and that
the producer may well settle a claim, in the interests of keeping good relations
with his customers, even where there is no liability at law. It has also been put
to us that the difficulties faced by the plaintiff in proving negligence are often
exaggerated.

1218   On the other hand, there is some evidence from the survey of insurance
claims to suggest that a lower proportion of products claims result in payment
than happens with some other types of claim. The survey also showed little
evidence of settlements being reached where no liability is admitted. One view
is that, in a normal products claim, there are a number of potential defendants,
from the retailer to the original manufacturer; and that, since actions involving
a number of defendants are costly and likely to be time consuming, many
complaints are not pursued to legal action. It is also maintained that it is difficult
to define 'negligence' in relation to modern mass production methods which
include a reasonable level of checks to ensure that there are no dangerous
defects.

1219   Above all, it is suggested, the present position is uncertain. It was put
to us that if liability is stricter than it appears, it can only be of assistance to
customers and insurers to make the position clear. If it is not, then the consumer
does not have a remedy which is consistent with modern manufacturing and
marketing conditions or with the current climate of opinion.

International developments
1220   The Explanatory Report on the Council of Europe Convention notes
'an almost general trend towards stricter liability of producers'. There is
clearly a case for harmonising with these developments.

What changes should be made?
1221   We came to the view that the present law should not be left as it is. We
considered four main options – a no-fault scheme for injuries caused by defective
products; an alteration to the law of contract, allowing rights of action to
third parties; a statutory reversal of the burden of proof in the tort action;
and a new tort of strict liability for defective products.

A no-fault scheme

1222 Various forms of no-fault scheme were advocated by witnesses, particularly, although not exclusively, by organisations representing consumer
interests. We noted that Article 11 of the Strasbourg Convention allows for the
possibility of such a scheme 'provided that the victim shall receive protection
at least equivalent to the protection he would have had under the liability
scheme provided for by this Convention'.

1223 It would be difficult to finance a no-fault scheme on an acceptable basis.
There is no system of compulsory insurance in the products field, and, as we
explain later in this chapter, we think that the imposition of compulsory
insurance would result in a disproportionate expenditure of money and manpower. It would therefore not be practicable to proceed by way of a levy on
insurance premiums.

Altering contract law

1224 A change in favour of the consumer through the medium of contract
law would involve modifying, or dispensing with, the rule of 'privity of contract',
the rule that only the parties to a contract may sue on it. There have been
modifications of this kind in other countries, particularly in the direction of
enabling the buyer to sue the manufacturer (in France and the USA), and to a
lesser extent in the direction of enabling an injured party other than the buyer
of the product to sue (also in the USA). In the USA, such developments were
based on the concept of an 'implied warranty', a general warranty of safety and
fitness for purpose.

1225 We do not think the solution lies in this direction. The effect of abandoning the privity rule would be essentially the same as introducing strict
liability in tort, except that it would necessitate a somewhat fictional extension
of 'implied warranty' to third parties. As we understand it, even in the USA
such extensions of contract law have in practice been superseded by the strong
trend towards strict liability in tort.

Reversed burden of proof

1226 Among our own witnesses, there was little support for a statutory
reversal of the burden of proof as a complete solution, although a number of
those commenting to the Law Commissions were in favour of it. We agree
with the Law Commissions that this expedient would not make much difference.
Even under present circumstances, the existence of a dangerous defect in a
product will in most cases, it seems to us, raise a *prima facie* inference that there
must have been some negligence in its design or manufacture, and the manufacturer will then have the burden of proving the absence of negligence. If so,
a statutory reversal of the burden of proof would usually make no difference.
An injured person could still be left with considerable problems – for example,
challenging the defendant's evidence where this necessitated a knowledge of
the latter's manufacturing processes. Nor would a retention of liability in
negligence remove the anomaly that strict liability is currently placed only on
the seller of the goods and in favour only of the buyer.

The rationale of strict liability

1227   Of all possible changes, the introduction of strict liability in tort was the one most widely discussed both in our evidence and in the comments made to the Law Commissions. In the light of developments elsewhere in Europe and in the USA, and in view of the fact that the Law Commissions had particularly canvassed such a change, this reaction is hardly surprising.

1228   A number of objections to strict liability were put to us. In particular, it was suggested that, in some industries at least, insurance premiums would have to be increased substantially; that such increases would act as a restraint on technical innovation; and that, especially in industries where there is a risk of the kind of catastrophe exemplified by thalidomide, it might prove impossible to obtain insurance cover adequate to meet the potential liability. These problems are undoubtedly a cause of widespread concern among both producers and insurers. It is likely, too, that insurers would find it difficult to assess the appropriate levels of premium until the effects of strict liability on the number and success of claims could be assessed from experience. We appreciate that the problem of catastrophe risks is a real one, not only in the case of drugs, but also, for example, in respect of aircraft design and construction (a problem highlighted by the Turkish Airlines DC10 crash near Paris in March 1974).

1229   On the other hand, for most industries, the cost of products liability insurance would be small in relation to other costs, and would be affected by our recommendations elsewhere for full offsetting of social security benefits and for a threshold on damages for non-pecuniary loss. Strict liability would also apply to domestic competitors, and overseas trends towards strict liability suggest that it would apply increasingly to foreign competitors too.

1230   We concluded in favour of strict liability. Our conclusion rests on practical and policy grounds which, taken as a whole, are peculiar to defective products.

1231   First, we are influenced by the existence of the Strasbourg Convention and draft EEC Directive. We do not regard these documents as pre-empting our recommendations – the United Kingdom Government is not committed to either the Convention or the Directive; and harmonisation of the legal basis of liability might have only a limited effect on relative production costs so long as such factors as the attitudes of courts and levels of damages continue to vary between different countries. Nevertheless, the Convention and the draft Directive indicate a strong European trend towards strict liability in this field.

1232   Secondly, it seems right to extend to all consumers the benefits of strict liability which are currently enjoyed by the purchaser under the law of contract.

1233   Thirdly, there is the practical point which underlies the concept of 'implied warranty' in the USA. When a producer markets his product, he should be expected to do so on the basis that it satisfies a certain standard of safety for the consumer. If his product range is a success, the producer will no doubt claim public credit; if a product within that range is dangerously defective, he should be prepared to accept a claim for compensation.

1234 Fourthly, we hope that strict liability might encourage producers to ensure the highest possible standards of safety (even though we recognise that in some circumstances the additional cost of insurance cover might still be less than the cost of changing production methods).

1235 Finally, the producer is in the best position to arrange the necessary insurance cover, and can be expected to pass on through his prices the bulk at least of the cost of doing so. We think it justifiable and sensible that consumers as a whole should pay for the cost of insuring against injuries caused by a product from which they benefit, just as they pay for its other costs.

1236 **We recommend** that producers should be strictly liable in tort for death or personal injury caused by defective products. It remains to consider the detailed application of this recommendation.

The definition of 'defect'

1237 We propose that strict liability should be confined to 'defective' products. **We recommend** that 'defect' should be defined in accordance with Article 2 of the Strasbourg Convention, which states that 'a product has a "defect" when it does not provide the safety which a person is entitled to expect, having regard to all the circumstances including the presentation of the product'. These words couple the producer's responsibility to produce safe goods with a responsibility on the consumer to use them with care. The definition would allow the producer to show that the victim should have taken heed of warning notices, such as those on cigarette packets; or instructions, such as an indication that a fire extinguisher is not suitable for use on electric fires. A victim would be able to point to the absence of such instructions or warnings as a relevant circumstance, for example in the case of a known allergic reaction to a particular product.

The respective liabilities of producers and distributors

The channelling of liability

1238 The chain of production and marketing is often a long one. An everyday manufactured product may involve a number of component manufacturers, working either in sequence or in parallel or both; the manufacturer of the finished product, whose work may consist in little more than assembling the component parts; and then the wholesaler and retailer. A similar chain will often apply to natural products.

1239 For the purpose of considering on whom strict liability should be placed, these various links in the chain can be grouped into three categories: component producers, producers of the finished product, and distributors. The broad options we considered were the placing of liability on all three categories ('enterprise liability' as it is known in the USA); on both component producers and producers of the finished product, but not on distributors; or exclusively on the producer of the finished product. We have assumed that existing remedies, in negligence and in contract, would be retained. Strict liability would in any event be restricted to production or distribution in the course of a business.

1240   There would be much to be said for confining strict liability to the producer of the finished product. This would provide a fairly straightforward line of redress for the consumer to a single, identifiable person or company. It would also be the cheapest option. If all the producers and distributors in a chain needed to insure against strict liability, the costs of insurance, administration and litigation would undoubtedly be greater – by how much it is impossible to estimate. It would also be easier to identify the defectiveness of a finished product as against a component (including the equivalent of the 'component' in the case of food, such as the meat in the pork pie), because it is this which needs to be safe when it reaches the consumer, and because a given component may be used in a wide range of finished products. This last consideration also has a bearing on cost. As the Law Commissions said in their working paper, 'The more basic the component (such as the nut and bolt) the greater the range of dangers and the higher the insurance premium, both in absolute terms and in relation to the value of the product'. The guiding principle would be to place strict liability on whoever first puts a product into circulation in the form in which it is intended to be used or consumed.

1241   A solution along these lines is nevertheless open to a number of objections. The main one is that there would be a greater risk that the injured person would be deprived of a remedy, for example if the producer of the finished product proved to be either bankrupt or uninsured. There might even be a deliberate evasion of liability by setting up an expendable company as a front for the real producer; and, even where that was not done, component producers would often be more substantial companies than the producer of the finished product, and to that extent better able to bear the burden of insurance. Such considerations do not apply exclusively to the producers of finished products, but the more widely liability is spread, the more certain the remedy is likely to be. If strict liability were to be confined to the producer of the finished product, there might sometimes be difficulty in distinguishing the finished product from the component, perhaps especially with respect to natural products.

1242   At the same time, we have no wish to see imported into the United Kingdom the blunderbuss of enterprise liability, with all that that would mean in terms of proliferating legal actions and escalating costs. Bearing in mind that the bulk of the cost would ultimately be borne by the consumer, we have tried to identify the point at which greater sureness of remedy could no longer justify the resultant increase in cost. On this basis, **we recommend** that both producers of finished products and component producers should be strictly liable in tort for defective products; but that, subject to our recommendation in paragraph 1244 below, distributors should not. This compromise would be consistent with the terms of the Strasbourg Convention and the draft EEC Directive.

1243   We have it in mind that the nature of the component producer's liability would be consistent with that envisaged in the Explanatory Report to the Strasbourg Convention. In particular, the component part would not be 'defective' if a defect in the finished product arose solely because the design of that finished product made the component part unsuitable for incorporation in it; nor would the component part be 'defective' if made according to erroneous technical specifications provided by the producer of the finished product.

The liability of distributors

1244 It would usually be easy to identify the producer of a finished article, but not always. **We recommend** that a distributor who has sold a defective product in the course of a business should be under an obligation to disclose to a person injured by the product either the name of the producer of the goods or the name of his own supplier; and that failure to do so within a reasonable time should render the seller himself strictly liable in tort. This recommendation is consistent with provisions included in the Strasbourg Convention and the draft EEC Directive. We note the suggestion in the Government's consultative document 'Consumer Safety' (Cmd 6398), that the Secretary of State for Prices and Consumer Protection might be enabled to require products to be marked with the name and address or trademark of the manufacturer or distributor. Such powers are now contained in the Consumer Safety Bill.

1245 The Annex to the Strasbourg Convention includes a provision which enables a contracting state to treat specially the retailer of primary agricultural products, including fish and animal products. Under this provision, he would be exempted from the responsibility to disclose the name of the producer or his own supplier, provided that he disclosed to the claimant all the information in his possession. The Convention's Explanatory Report explains that such products are often mixed with similar products from different suppliers, so that it may be difficult for the retailer to determine the source of a given item.

1246 We do not think that there should be such an exemption. It is important that a remedy should be available for injury or illness caused by primary products – shell fish, for example, are known carriers of disease. An obligation on the retailer to disclose his supplier's name would encourage him to be sure that he knew where such produce had come from; and he would in any event be in a better position than the injured person to bear the risk.

1247 Particular problems are posed by 'own brand' goods, that is to say goods which a distributor has had produced to order and is selling under his own brand name to the exclusion of the producer's. It was put to us by some witnesses that such a practice should not be allowed to affect the producer's liability. In particular, the Retail Consortium suggested that retailers were no more able to exercise detailed control of quality for these goods than for others, and implied that the problem would be met by an obligation to disclose the producer's identity such as we are recommending. We were nevertheless impressed by the argument that 'own branding' implies a greater acceptance by the retailer of responsibility for the goods, and that sellers of such goods, in particular large supermarkets chains, will often be bigger concerns than the producers. **We recommend** that, in respect of 'own brand' products, strict liability in tort should apply to those who brand them, as well as to their producers.

Products made to a specification
1248 Some witnesses opposed the imposition of strict liability on producers whose business consisted in making products to special order and usually to the design or specification of their customers. We think it important to distinguish between component parts and finished products. A component part should not be regarded as 'defective' if it has been made to the specification of the producer of the finished product. Among finished products, it is important to make a further distinction between 'own brand' goods and other products made to a specification, sometimes on a one-off basis such as a piece of furniture or a boat made to the specification of an individual customer. With respect to finished products other than 'own brand' goods, the producer would normally be in the better position to insure against the risk of injury, and it is particularly important to ensure that a remedy is available in the event of an injury to a third party. If a producer were not satisfied with the safety of the specification, it should be incumbent upon him either to obtain an indemnity from the specifier or to refuse to do the work. **We recommend** that producers should not be exempt from strict liability in respect of defective finished products which have been made to a specification. Where it is the specifier himself who has been injured, the defence of contributory negligence, which we discuss below, might be relevant.

Liability of others in the chain
1249 It would be possible under strict liability for an action to succeed against one producer even though another producer, earlier in the chain, had actually been negligent. We see no reason to remove the component producer's present liabilities to the final producer, either in negligence or in contract.

Imported goods
1250 Much of the discussion in the preceding paragraphs assumes that the defective products concerned are produced as well as sold in this country. We think it essential also to ensure that the injured person has a remedy in strict liability in respect of imported goods. It could be difficult and costly for him to trace and pursue the producer of such goods, and, even if he were able to do so, the law of the exporting country might not provide an adequate remedy. **We recommend** that importers should be treated as producers for the purpose of products liability. We note that the draft EEC Directive would treat the Community as a single trading area for this purpose.

Defences

The plaintiff's burden of proof
1251 It is implicit in what we have already said that anyone injured by a defective product, or that person's dependants if he has been killed, should be entitled to sue. We would include any bystander who is injured, as well as any user of the product. But the introduction of strict liability would still leave the injured person with the burden of proving three initial contentions – that the product was defective; that his injury had been caused by the defect; and that the defendant was the producer of the product. It would be open to the defendant to try to disprove any of these contentions. We have considered what defences he should be allowed in addition.

The producer's liability for defects

1252   We think it a reasonable corollary of strict liability that the producer should not only have produced the product but also have put it into circulation in the course of his business, whether by selling it to someone later in the chain of production or distribution, or by releasing it for public consumption. It might not have been put into circulation by him. It might have been stolen from him. Or the defect might have been caused after he had put it into circulation, perhaps through inadequate servicing or through excessive delay in selling perishable food. **We recommend** that it should be a defence for the producer to prove either that he did not put the product into circulation; or that the product was not defective when he did so; or that he did not put it into circulation in the course of a business.

1253   It sometimes happens that, after a product has been put into circulation, its producer tries to withdraw it. He may not succeed. For example, the drug eraldin (practolol) continued to be prescribed and dispensed after it had been withdrawn by its manufacturer because of serious side effects. It might appear hard on the producer to hold him strictly liable in such circumstances. But those who had failed to respond to his attempts to withdraw the product might not in the event have either the resources or the insurance cover to indemnify the producer even if they could be held liable to do so; and it is essential that any new system of tort compensation should cover the kind of risks exemplified by eraldin. Subject to any element of contributory negligence – we discuss this defence below – **we recommend** that it should not be a defence for the producer merely to prove that he had withdrawn, or attempted to withdraw, his product.

1254   Mr Marshall dissents from this recommendation in so far as it applies to aircraft, and considers that the range of defences open to producers should be supplemented in respect of aircraft manufacturers. In his view, the manufacture and operation of aircraft, particularly commercial airliners, present problems which are unique in the products liability field. As a result of experience, aircraft manufacturers, with Civil Aviation Authority approval, from time to time in the interests of safety lay down modifications required to be carried out, alterations in the stipulated useful life of component parts, alterations in operating conditions or changed requirements of inspection and maintenance prior to flight. These are invariably supplied by the manufacturer immediately to all operators of aircraft of the type affected, records of owner-ship and operation being kept up to date by the manufacturer. In such conditions, where the manufacturer has conveyed in due time to the owner/operator any amendments of this kind, and then with full knowledge of them the operator deliberately or carelessly fails to comply with the requirements or recommendations, it seems to Mr Marshall wrong that the manufacturer should remain saddled with strict liability for death or injury caused by the defect during operation of the aircraft concerned. No aircraft operator on such facts would be likely to escape full legal liability to the victims on the basis of wilful misconduct, and the normal defences under the Warsaw Convention as amended would be unavailable. This situation is quite different from that of manufacturers of other products such as motor cars, where no record of the operator of each vehicle is held and where it seems right that so far as the victim is concerned strict liability for injury by defect should attach to the manufacturer. In the case of accidents to aircraft due to the operator's failure to comply with requirements or recommendations, Mr Marshall argues that the aircraft itself should not be regarded as one which was defective when it left the manufacturer's hands and thus attract strict liability.

1255   Most of us, however, whilst acknowledging that aircraft manufacturers are in a special position in terms of their relationships with commercial airlines, do not accept that this should be allowed to affect the manufacturer's liability. If the plaintiff had to discover what instructions had been given by the manufacturer to the operator before a cause of action could be established, this would add further to his burden of proof. More fundamentally, if a defect arises in a product after the producer has put it into circulation, the producer should not be held liable for any death or injury caused; this is a principle on which, as we have indicated, we are all agreed. This would apply in respect of an aircraft which is rendered defective by, say, faulty maintenance. But if the aircraft manufacturer had put his product into circulation in a defective state, most of us think that, whatever steps he subsequently took to have the defect rectified, strict liability should apply. In this respect, the aircraft manufacturer's position would differ from that of other producers only in that he would be in a better position to take remedial action. Nevertheless, in view of the specially close relationship between aircraft manufacturers and commercial operators, **we recommend** that the manufacturer of an aircraft should be given a right to be indemnified by a user or operator who has wilfully or negligently ignored his instructions to rectify defects or modify service schedules.

Contributory negligence
1256   It is at present a partial or complete defence to liability in negligence that the plaintiff was partly or wholly responsible for his own injury. There remains some potential scope for such a defence to strict liability. Where the plaintiff had ignored instructions or warnings marked on the product concerned, it might be easy enough to prove that there was no 'defect'; but there might be cases where the plaintiff could demonstrate both that there was a defect and that the defect caused the injury, but still be open to the charge that he was at least partly at fault. This could occur perhaps through misusing the product, or through persistence in using it even after he had been made aware that it was defective. He might have injured his hand as a result of a screwdriver shaft breaking away from its handle and the break might not have occurred but for a defect in the join of shaft to handle; nevertheless, if he had been aware of the defect but continued to use the screwdriver, or if he had been using it as a lever, it might be claimed that he was at least partly at fault himself.

1257   In considering whether or not the defence of contributory negligence should be open to the producer, it is relevant to ask whether it is reasonable for the price of his product to reflect the cost of the insurance cover needed to provide for full tort compensation even where an individual consumer has failed to exercise a reasonable level of responsibility for his own safety. We believe that it is not reasonable, and **we recommend** that the defence of contributory negligence should be available to a producer.

Development risks
1258   There is a further possibility of providing for a special defence for 'development risks'. A dangerous 'design defect' has a greater potential than a 'manufacturing defect' for widespread injuries caused by a single product range. The risks involved particularly affect industries which produce potentially dangerous products, such as chemicals, drugs, aircraft and motor cars, and the more so where these are subject to continuous technological improvements. It is important to such industries to consider whether there should be carried over into a system of strict liability something parallel to the 'state of the art' defence available under the present system of liability in negligence. The production of a new drug is a striking example of the kind of development risk which might be covered by such a defence.

1259   It can be argued that to hold the producer liable in such cases would be to impose on him – and, through him, on the product's consumers as a whole – a responsibility for compensating injuries even when it might have been impossible to prevent the defect occurring. It is further argued that this responsibility, and the cost of insuring against the risks involved, might severely deter the development of new products, particularly those small developments which might lead cumulatively to a major advance; and that this is sufficiently contrary to the interests of consumers themselves to outweigh the case for tort compensation, at least through the medium of strict liability. On the other hand, to exclude development risks from a regime of strict liability would be to leave a gap in the compensation cover, through which, for example, the victims of another thalidomide disaster might easily slip. **We recommend** that the producer should not be allowed a defence of development risk. We consider below whether, in part as a corollary of this conclusion, some limits should be placed on the producer's liability.

Official certification
1260   A related possibility, again of particular though not exclusive relevance to the pharmaceutical industry, is that it might be a defence for the producer to show that his product's safety had been certified by an official scrutinising body such as the Committee on Safety of Medicines. **We recommend** that the producer should not be allowed a defence of official certification. Such a defence would be inconsistent with our approach to strict liability. And, as regards medicines in particular, we were told by the Association of the British Pharmaceutical Industry that that industry does not regard approval of a new product by the Committee on Safety of Medicines as diminishing their own responsibility for it. We think this is right.

Contracting out
1261   Under the Unfair Contract Terms Act 1977, a producer will not be able to exclude or limit liability for negligence resulting in death or personal injury. We think that the same provision should apply in respect of strict

liability. If a product is known or feared to be unsafe in particular respects, the producer should make this clear and rely on the definition of 'defect' as a defence against any claims for compensation. **We recommend** that producers should not be enabled to contract out of strict liability.

Limitation on liability and problems of insurance

1262 Strict liability for defective products, coupled with the restrictions we propose on the defences available to the producer, raises the question whether any upper limits should be placed on such liability, either in amount, or in time, or both. There are two main issues. The first is whether the absence of such a limitation imposes an unreasonable burden on the producer and, through his prices, on the consumers of his products. The second is whether, in the absence of such a limitation, the producer would be able to secure adequate insurance cover to the full potential extent of his liability. The particular problems of the products field in this latter respect were put to us as follows by Lloyd's:

> 'Products' liability differs from other forms of liability insurance in that it is extremely difficult to estimate the number of potential victims involved in the case of any given producer. In Employers' liability, on the other hand, the number of employees at risk is known within reasonable limits, while in motor vehicle third party liability the number of individuals likely to be injured by any one vehicle is not large. The result is that, while policies with no limit of liability are available for motor and Employers' liability insurance, they are not available for products' liability.'

It would be possible to have insurance limits without limits on liability, but the consequent gap in insurance cover, especially in cases of catastrophe, could either bankrupt the producer, or leave victims uncompensated, or both. It would also thereby aggravate the danger that the development of new products might be inhibited.

Limitation in amount

1263 We understand that the typical insurance policy in this field at present contains a limit on the total liability which may be incurred by the insured during the period of the policy, which in the products liability field is normally only a year. A large producer may be able to secure one or more excess policies in order to increase the total indemnity, but there will still be a limit. In this context, there are attractions to producers in the idea of some form of global limitation on their liabilities. The draft EEC Directive would impose such a limit; the Strasbourg Convention makes one optional.

1264 **We nevertheless recommend** that there should be no financial limits on the producer's liability. Any universal limit would inevitably be unnecessarily high in relation to some products and potentially too low in relation to others; and, if it were pitched high enough to ensure that only exceptional catastrophes would find it too low, substantial gaps in insurance cover would be likely to remain. There would be many practical difficulties, and the cost of insurance might be inflated by a tendency for producers to seek insurance up to the limit even where this was unnecessary. Most important, perhaps, as a Select Committee of the House of Lords[11] and the Law Commissions in their recent report, have already pointed out, a global limit could produce appalling problems in cases where the effects of a given product, such as a drug, together with the number of people injured by it, emerged only slowly over a period. An equitable division of the total sum would be impossible without unacceptable delay, and the outcome could be to leave those last in the queue uncompensated.

1265 There can be no doubt that insurance companies will continue to provide cover for defective products only within limits, and indeed that the greater the catastrophe risks the more wary they will be. We recognise that a continuing discrepancy between limited insurance and unlimited liability would make the introduction of strict liability more burdensome on producers, and less watertight for consumers, than we should ideally like, but we believe that this must be accepted. As we suggest in chapter 31, we envisage that the Government would be under strong pressure to intervene with financial assistance in the event of an under insured catastrophe such as one caused by a defective drug.

Compulsory insurance
1266 The extent of voluntary insurance in respect of products is not known, but we believe that only a small minority of producers would be unable to meet claims against them, whether by insurance or from their own resources, even under a regime of strict liability. There are formidable difficulties in the way of imposing compulsory liability insurance. There would be great problems in the way of enforcing any requirement at a reasonable cost in money and manpower; and it would be necessary in each case to provide for some limitation of the amount of cover required. This latter requirement would present difficulties similar to those we have just described in the case of financial limitations on liability. **We recommend** that compulsory liability insurance should not be introduced for products.

Limitation in time
1267 We have also considered the possibility of imposing a limitation in time, that is a number of years after which the producer's liability would expire completely. Here the difficulties are not so severe. Both the Strasbourg Convention and the draft EEC Directive, in slightly different terms, provide for a limit of ten years from the circulation of the product. (The Convention makes is clear that it is referring to the 'individual product which caused the damage', not merely a class of product such as a type of drug.)

1268 Any such universal limitation would of necessity be arbitrary, the more so given the wide variations between classes of product in what would be appropriate in the case of each, for example, as between fresh food and domestic hardware. In some cases the limit would be of little or no value to the producer. Nor would it necessarily bear any relationship to the length of time over which an insurance company is prepared to continue renewing its insurance cover for any given range of products. It could also preclude a tort action in some hard cases, notably if the adverse effects of a drug on a particular individual were not manifest until later in his life.

1269 **We nevertheless recommend** that the producer's strict liability in tort should be subject to a cut-off period of ten years from the circulation of the product. Without such a term to his liabilities, the producer would be faced with increasing difficulties. The relevant records would be more and more difficult to trace, especially where a company had changed hands; it would be more and more difficult to distinguish defect from wear and tear; and the producer would have to insure in perpetuity. Across the broad range of products, we do not think that our recommendation would detract unreasonably from the consumer's remedies.

Lapse of time

1270 We also considered the period within which the injured person must start proceedings. The Strasbourg Convention provides for a formula of 'three years from the day the claimant became aware or should reasonably have been aware of the damage, the defect and the identity of the producer'. The draft EEC Directive has a similar formula, and it is broadly in line with current law in the United Kingdom. **We recommend** that the Government should adopt the provisions of the Strasbourg Convention on the limitation period within which the person injured by a defective product must start proceedings.

Non-pecuniary losses

1271 It has been suggested that strict liability should not apply to non-pecuniary as well as to pecuniary losses. Either course would be consistent with the Strasbourg Convention, which leaves heads of damage to national laws. But, although the draft EEC Directive is itself silent on this issue, its Explanatory Memorandum makes it clear that non-pecuniary loss is not included as damage, and that strict liability would not apply to such loss. This would be a new distinction in the United Kingdom. The main argument in its favour is that there might be many spurious claims for damages for pain and suffering if such a distinction were not adopted. Since we recommend elsewhere a means of limiting minor claims for non-pecuniary loss, however, **we recommend** that damages for non-pecuniary loss should not be excluded from products liability actions.

Possible exclusions

1272 It remains to consider whether any particular classes of product should be excluded from a regime of strict liability of the kind we propose, or subjected to some form of special treatment.

Drugs

1273 Drugs represent the class of product in respect of which there has been the greatest public pressure for surer compensation in cases of injury. The application of strict liability to drugs, however, is subject to a number of particular problems. We are concerned here not so much with proprietary medicines which are sold direct to the public as with medicines which are available only on prescription. It is these which carry a real, if small, risk of catastrophe. In the light of our decision not to recommend either a special defence for development risks or a financial limit on liability, the case for special treatment may be thought the stronger.

1274   There are other, related, considerations. The injured person would still have to prove causation, and there could be particular difficulties in tracing the cause of the injury to the drug. We have been informed by the Medicines Commission that, because of the many formidable difficulties involved, 'it is improbable that any practicable programme of testing could offer an absolute safeguard'. The responsibility for safety rests not only on manufacturers and the Committee on Safety of Medicines, but also on the doctors who prescribe. It has been made clear to us that the pharmaceutical industry is opposed to strict liability.

1275   We acknowledge the force of these arguments, and we recognise that the difficulties faced by drug manufacturers would if anything be aggravated by the imposition of strict liability. We have nevertheless concluded that no special treatment could be justified. The demand for fuller and surer compensation for injuries caused by drugs is now an international phenomenon. The context is one in which the industry finds itself under pressure, whatever its legal liabilities in any one country. These difficulties, and the more fundamental problem of trying to produce safe drugs, would not be solved by avoiding a change to strict liability in the United Kingdom.

Human blood and organs
1276   **We recommend** that human blood and organs should be regarded as 'products', and the authorities responsible for distributing them as their 'producers', for the purpose of products liability.

Movables incorporated into immovables
1277   **We also recommend** that movable products incorporated into immovables should be regarded as 'products' for the purpose of products liability. This would cover building materials incorporated into a house, and would be consistent with our view that strict liability should extend to component producers. We have also been impressed by the risk of indefensible anomalies arising from the exclusion of such goods. A bag of defective cement purchased by a private consumer and used by him in building work on his house should obviously attract strict liability where the defect causes a personal injury. We think the same bag of cement should also attract strict liability if it were used by a contractor.

The cost of our proposals
1278   It is not possible to estimate accurately the cost of our proposals. On the basis of data supplied to us by the BIA, the number and current value of

tort payments stand at about 1,700 and £1·6 million a year, respectively. Much would depend on the extent to which victims and their legal advisers would be encouraged by strict liability to pursue more claims. The experience of other countries, for example France and the USA, does not provide us with a consistent model. A further unknown is whether there might be future disasters of the dimensions of the thalidomide tragedy. The cost of insurance cover is the more difficult to assess because insurance companies would themselves need to make such predictions, on little evidence at first, producer by producer. Nevertheless, we have no reason to believe that the total effect of introducing strict liability would be more than a small proportion of product costs as a whole. We think this a justifiable price for consumers and producers to pay for the benefits which the victims stand to gain by it.

CHAPTER 23
Services

1279 As with products, there is no distinct category of legal liability for injury arising out of the rendering of services either in English or Scots law; and liability is governed by the law of negligence and contract.

1280 There is an overlap between the supply of services and the supply of products as, in many cases where services are rendered, products may also be supplied. Services related to products may include the fitting of products, advising about them, maintaining or modifying them or designing them (although under our proposals faulty design could be a defect in a product, for which the maker who puts it into circulation in the faulty state could be liable).

1281 In this chapter, we include personal services such as hairdressing, the supply of professional, managerial or labour services in person or otherwise, and information and advisory services, as well as those services which are related to products. We do not touch on transport services and medical services. These raise distinct issues and are dealt with separately (chapters 18–21 and 24).

1282 Actions arising out of the injurious performance of services can be found in the law reports of the fifteenth century, long before the distinctions between contract and tort evolved in their present form.

The present law
Liability in contract
1283 One peculiarity of service related injuries is that the person injured is often in a contractual relationship with the person causing injury. It is important to distinguish, however, between contracts *of service* and contracts *for services*. A contract of service is a contract between an employer and his employee, and injuries arising in this context are work injuries. It is the latter category – contracts for services – which concerns us here.

1284 The law normally implies into a contract for services a condition that the contract shall be performed in a proper and workmanlike manner. If something goes wrong because of the carelessness or lack of skill of the performer, and injury is caused, this will amount to a breach of the condition and thus of the contract. If the injury is the result of careless or unskilful performance of the task, liability will follow, but not if the injury results from some unforeseeable event or consequence of the performance. There will then have been no breach of the implied provision for proper and workmanlike performance.

1285   Sometimes an express warranty of safety may be given. For example, a cosmetic operation may be stated to be 'harmless' in terms intended to reassure anyone who might doubt it. Any injury which then results to a person undergoing the operation will amount to a breach of the warranty of 'harmlessness', and thus of the contract. Liability for breach of warranty is strict.

1286   Liability in contract may therefore be strict or be based on lack of care, according to the contract terms. It is unusual for the contract (which frequently is not made in writing) to lay down expressly the extent to which the performer shall be liable. The possibility of injury is usually not something which either party to a contract wishes to think about. In the event of a dispute, the legal effect of the contract has to be determined by a court. The court will consider the matter as a whole. It will take into account the object of the contract, the words used, the manner in which the contract was made, and the nature of the injury. It will reach its conclusions on the basis of what it deems would have been the expectations of each party, at the time of making the contract, as to the way in which injury should be dealt with.

1287   A person who is injured as a result of a contract made between other persons cannot normally sue in contract.

Liability in tort
1288   Tortious obligations are imposed by the law independently of the wishes of those affected by them. They do not depend on the existence of a contract. It is only necessary to repeat here that the law imposes on all persons a duty to take reasonable care not to cause injury to those near enough to be within the range of foreseeable injury if care is not taken.

Special skills
1289   The requirements of workmanlike performance in contract, or the exercise of proper care in tort, frequently receive special formulation in connection with professional services, or wherever a person holds himself out as possessing a particular skill. The law will then demand of the performer not only that he takes all reasonable precautions to prevent injury, but also that in the exercise of his professional skills he displays a reasonable standard. This standard is usually described as 'ordinary skill and competence'. It is recognised that, in any field of skill, some practitioners will be more skilful than others. The standard required is not that of the most accomplished.

Exclusion of liability
1290   Under the Unfair Contract Terms Act 1977, it will no longer be possible for anyone acting in the course of a business to exclude or limit liability for negligence resulting in death or personal injury. In addition, in contracts where one party is a consumer or is dealing on the other's standard terms of business, any purported exclusion or limitation of liability for breach of contract will be upheld only insofar as it is shown to be reasonable.

Services involving the supply of products
1291   The result of our proposals on products liability would be that, where a service involved the supply of a product, the consumer (and anyone else injured

by the product) would have recourse to the manufacturer if injury resulted from a defect in the product. He might then have two causes of action. The hairdresser who had made his own shampoo would be strictly liable for defects in the shampoo which he had put into circulation by using it on his customer's head. At the same time, and under the present law, he would be liable in respect of the service he had rendered insofar as it is negligence to shampoo customers with a mixture which one knows, or ought to know, is defective.

Possible changes in the law

The evidence

1292 Some witnesses favoured the inclusion of services in a comprehensive no-fault scheme. A few witnesses suggested that strict liability was appropriate. But most of our evidence was against change in the existing law.

1293 The Bar Council considered that the existing law was satisfactory, that the present test of liability was a reasonable one, and that any higher standards of care required would be counter productive. People would be deterred from offering their services at all if too onerous a duty were imposed on them. The same view was taken by the Faculty of Law at the University of Glasgow. They thought it would be difficult to conceive a viable alternative test. There was evidence too from the construction industry in favour of the present system

No-fault

1294 Because of the enormous number and variety of services which could give rise to a claim for compensation, there would be problems in organising and financing a no-fault scheme. One main difficulty would be that of determining which services should be covered. The rendering of services embraces an infinite variety of relationships between individuals. For example, if a no-fault scheme were not limited to services rendered in the course of a business, a housewife escorting a neighbour's child to school would be regarded as rendering a service, and injury *en route* could give rise to a claim. We see no reason why these kinds of injury should be singled out for no-fault compensation, even if the practical difficulties could be overcome.

1295 The 'open endedness' of service relationships is also at the root of the second objection to a no-fault scheme – the difficulty of finance. It might be possible to collect contributions from large firms providing services repetitively, but it would be impracticable to put a levy on those operating casually or without fixed business premises.

1296 In sum, it would be difficult to devise an economic and enforceable scheme.

Strict liability

1297 The BIA proposed a variation of the existing tort law which seemed to us in effect to amount to strict liability. They suggested that those who offered services should be under a duty to render these services in a manner which ensured such a degree of safety as the user of them was reasonably entitled to expect. The National Federation of Consumer Groups favoured strict liability. So did Judge Rowland.

1298 There are clearly areas of overlap between liability for services and liability for defective products. As we recommend that producers should be strictly liable for defective products, we naturally considered whether the same reasons applied in the case of services. We concluded that there were sufficient differences between products and services to require a different recommendation.

1299 There would be a formidable array of difficulties in applying strict liability to services. There would be problems in defining the range of services to be covered, even if strict liability were confined to services provided in the course of a business. For example, we considered the position of those, such as architects and designers, who provide technical information services. We feel that they might be discouraged from supplying advice and information if they were to be strictly liable for any injury caused as a result. Their advice might represent only the best available knowledge in an uncertain field.

1300 Furthermore, many of those who provide services in the course of a business have small businesses and few fixed assets. This may be contrasted with the position of many producers of goods, who are more able to bear or insure against the cost of their liabilities.

1301 The evidence submitted to us did not indicate that it was excessively difficult to recover compensation from those who provided services. The difficulties posed by modern methods of mass production do not apply in the same degree to services. Nor do we have to take into account the prospect of an EEC Directive imposing strict liability in the near future.

Reversed burden of proof
1302 We also doubt whether reversing the burden of proof in negligence would be a desirable course in respect of services. In the case of products, under the present law, the defendant already has the burden of exculpating himself once the plaintiff has established the *prima facie* defectiveness of the product. This would also be the position where the facts raised an inference that injury would not have occurred but for the negligent rendering of a service. But we do not think that a formal reversal of the burden of proof should be applied to every service. If it were, those rendering services would find themselves subject to claims for injury the cause of which was susceptible of a number of explanations. For example, if a builder did certain repairs on a house and later some collapse occurred causing injury, he would be under the onus of proving that the collapse was not due to his negligent workmanship, even though there were a number of possible explanations not involving his negligence. We believe that the present law works reasonably well, giving rise in practice to a reversal of the burden of proof where the facts warrant it. We also feel that to recommend a reversal of the burden of proof in all cases could give rise to a proliferation of unwarranted claims.

Conclusion

1303 **We recommend** that there should be no change in the basis of liability for injury arising out of the rendering of services; and that there should be no formal reversal of the burden of proof. We are well aware that to adopt different regimes for products and for services would lead to anomalies. There are small organisations making products and large ones providing services repetitively; and there would be occasions when the 'state of the art' defence would be used successfully by a person providing services and yet, under our proposals, would be denied to a producer. But we think that it is better to accept these anomalies than to adopt any other form of tort compensation in respect of services.

CHAPTER 24
Medical injury

1304 For injuries arising from services generally we have suggested no changes in the basis of liability, but medical services have unique and long standing features which call for separate consideration. Medical skill is exercised by one person on another, creating a special relationship between patient and doctor. The sick person is seeking help which the doctor tries to give, but this help is limited by the boundaries of medical science, and within those boundaries by the doctor's own knowledge and experience. In the words of Savatier, 'Disease, infirmity and death are . . . part of the human condition. In the end, they will always have the last word against the doctor'[12].

1305 Medical decisions involve risks, and if things go wrong, the patient may die or be permanently disabled.

1306 By 'medical injury', we mean an impairment of a person by a physical or mental condition arising in the course of his or her medical care. This impairment may be a foreseeable and acceptable outcome of the approved treatment necessary for the patient's condition. On the other hand it may be the result of a medical accident, whether or not due to negligence; or it may be due to a medical omission.

1307 It would be unreasonable to compensate for injury which is a foreseeable and acceptable outcome of treatment, for example, baldness as a side effect of drug therapy for cancer, or an amputation for gangrene. In this chapter, therefore, we are concerned only with medical injury which can be said to be caused by accident. Injury by accident includes within its scope injury caused by professional negligence.

The position at present
Negligence
1308 Negligence occurs when practice by any member of the team caring for a patient falls below the accepted standards of professional competence and training. For hundreds of years there has been liability for negligent medical treatment causing injury.

1309 The patient's remedy at law is to sue his doctor for damages. He must prove that, on the balance of probabilities, the defendant was negligent. A doctor can clear himself if he can show that he acted within approved practice at the time when the alleged negligence occurred. As Lord Clyde said, 'To establish liability . . . where deviation from normal practice is alleged, three facts require to be established. First of all it must be proved that there is a usual and normal practice; secondly . . . that the defender has not adopted that practice; and thirdly (and this is of crucial importance) . . . that the course the doctor adopted is one which no professional man of ordinary skill would have taken if he had been acting with ordinary care'. (*Hunter* v. *Hanley* 1955 S.C. 200 at p 206). It has also been established that the doctor must take care to recognise a case which is beyond his skill, and refer it to another practitioner having the requisite skill.

1310 Health authorities are liable for any negligence in the treatment by those whom they have employed or engaged to provide it. If a hospital has undertaken to carry out an operation which involves surgical, anaesthetising and nursing services, the health authority is liable for any negligence in the performance of those services by the professional persons which it employs or engages for that purpose. If the patient himself engages a surgeon to come into the hospital and operate on him, then the health authority is not liable for the negligence of the surgeon.

1311 A complication is that the plaintiff may not know whose act or omission injured him. It may, for example, have been the negligence of an ambulance man, a nurse, an anaesthetist or a surgeon. In 1951 a plaintiff succeeded in an action in negligence against the Ministry of Health after post-operational treatment by hospital staff left his hand useless (*Cassidy* v. *Ministry of Health* [1951] 2 K.B. 343). It was held that there had been no rebuttal of the evidence showing a *prima facie* case of negligence on the part of the persons caring for the plaintiff. As the doctors involved were employed under contracts of service to the hospital authorities the defendants were liable to the plaintiff whether the negligence was that of the doctor or of a member or members of the nursing staff. It is now required by statute that in cases arising in the National Health Service the health authority be sued in the first instance.

1312 General medical and dental practitioners, together with others who provide services by arrangement with National Health Service Family Practitioner Committees (in Scotland, with Health Boards), are not employees of health authorities. They must therefore be made the defendants in any action in negligence.

Breach of contract
1313 Private patients may sue their doctors for a breach of contract if inadequate or faulty services have been provided, for example, if a swab has been left in the abdomen after an operation or if blood of the wrong blood group has been used in a transfusion. Under the National Health Service, however, there is no contract between patient and doctor and a plaintiff must rely on an action in tort. But the National Health Service patient is in no worse position than the private patient, because the same considerations determine if there has been a breach of duty whether the case is brought in contract or in tort.

Consent to treatment
1314   It is generally accepted that consent is essential for medical treatment because of the human right to self determination. This principle applies even when the patient is under age, and whether or not he or she is capable of appreciating the reason for, and the importance of, the treatment. If a doctor carries out an operation for which consent has not been given he may be prosecuted for assault under the criminal law. He may also be sued for damages in tort as such an operation constitutes a trespass to the person. There are, however, many exceptions for giving treatment without consent in emergencies; and consent is frequently sought from the next of kin.

1315   How much detail is given to the patient of the nature and significance of the therapy and the possible side effects, and whether he is told that in the opinion of the practitioner it will cause damage to the patient's health, will depend on the patient's own understanding and whether such information is likely to cause further harm to his health. A balance has to be maintained between the possible consequences of treatment and the possible outcome if the treatment is not carried out. It may not be necessary to inform the patient in any great detail about risks which occur rarely, or about unlikely side effects which a reasonable patient would not consider to be significant.

Insurance
1316   In order to cover a possible liability for damages, most doctors in the United Kingdom subscribe to one of three medical defence organisations, the Medical Defence Union, the Medical Protection Society and the Medical and Dental Defence Union of Scotland. Hospital doctors in the National Health Service must either be members of a defence society or subscribe to an insurance arrangement approved by the Government. Subscribing to a defence society is usually also made a condition of employment for doctors and dentists who join private services.

1317   The societies defend members who are accused of negligence and provide compensation for patients who have suffered by negligence. The annual subscriptions are in the region of £40 for doctors and £20 for dentists. Proposals for an insurance backed professional indemnity scheme considered by the British Medical Association in 1977 would have introduced differential rates of premiums for different specialities, as is done in France, the Netherlands and Switzerland, but the proposals were not adopted.

Increase in claims
1318   Fifty or sixty years ago, claims against doctors were rare. The position has changed somewhat, particularly since the inception of the National Health Service in 1948. It is estimated that malpractice claims against doctors and dentists have recently been about 500 a year. The Medical Defence Union, whose membership includes some 50,000 of the 85,000 doctors and dentists in the United Kingdom, calculates that the percentage of its members involved in malpractice claims in 1971 was about double the average for the previous

25 years. The experience in continental European countries has been similar. In France the number of malpractice claims involving surgery or the administration of anaesthetics more than doubled between 1973 and 1976.

1319   In the USA, according to the American Medical Association, the number of medical negligence claims rose by 1,000 per cent between 1969 and 1975. This increase has been combined with high awards of damages – in some cases amounting to more than $1 million. These developments have led to an enormous rise in insurance premiums and in some states it has been necessary to introduce legislation to guarantee the provision of insurance cover. Another effect has been that, in an attempt to avoid litigation, some doctors include in their treatment costly tests and X-rays which are not necessary for treating the patient. This practice is known as 'defensive medicine'.

1320   Because of the concern over this situation, a Commission on Medical Malpractice was appointed by the Secretary to the United States Department of Health, Education and Welfare. The Commission, in its report in 1973, pointed to a change in public attitudes as one reason for the increase in claims. Patients who previously took illness and its consequences for granted now had unrealistic expectations about medicine's capabilities and aired their disappointments in court; more people could afford medical care, necessarily increasing the possibility of malpractice; and a shift away from a personal relationship between doctor and patient to treatment by groups or teams had made the patient less reluctant to sue. The contingent fee system, under which the legal fee is a proportion of the damages obtained, was regarded by the Commission as particularly relevant. It had not only allowed many claimants with injuries entitling them to compensation to obtain legal counsel which they could not otherwise afford, but it had also encouraged lawyers to accept claims with little merit if the potential rewards were high.

1321   Fears have been expressed of a similar problem here, since some ingredients of the American situation are present in this country.

1322   The public attitude towards litigation is changing; people are more likely to sue an impersonal body; and there may have been of late some weakening in the relationship between doctors and patients due to the growth of group practices and the increasing use of weekend and night emergency services. In evidence to us DHSS referred to defensive medicine, pointing to 'the rapid growth of requests for diagnostic work in both pathology and radiology, not all of which is equally productive . . . a great deal . . . is directed towards eliminating the risk of litigation in case a diagnosis is missed'.

1323   But there are considerations pointing the other way. There is no such thing as a contingent fee system in this country. Another element of the American problem which does not exist in England and Wales is the practice of jury trial in civil cases; the use of juries in assessing damages in the USA is said to lead to higher awards. Further, although there has been an increase in the number of claims here, the practice of resorting to the courts is still not widespread and the total of claims is as yet insignificant compared with the number of people who receive treatment. Each year some six million in-patients are treated in National Health Service hospitals and some 19 million people attend out-patient or accident and emergency departments. Yet in a year probably no more than 1,000 claims are made against doctors, dentists, pharmacists or health authorities in respect of negligence.

1324   We do not think that we need fear in this country a problem of American proportions, but we should not be complacent. The possibility of some escalation of claims cannot be ignored.

Criticisms of the present compensation provisions

1325   Criticisms of the present compensation provisions fall into two parts. First, there are those which relate to the difficulty of making claims following negligent treatment. Secondly, there are those concerning the lack of provision for medical accidents.

Proving negligence

1326   The proportion of successful claims for damages in tort is much lower for medical negligence than for all negligence cases. Some payment is made in 30–40 per cent of claims compared with 86 per cent of all personal injury claims.

1327   We received a good deal of evidence about the difficulty of proving negligence. It was said that it was not always possible to obtain the necessary information on which to base a claim. The patient might not know what had happened and he might have difficulty in obtaining the services of a medical expert to assist him. When a doctor was accused of negligence, his colleagues might naturally be reluctant to give evidence. The medical records might not contain all the details of the case, leaving ample scope for different interpretations by witnesses for and against.

1328   One of our number, who attended a Council of Europe colloquy on the civil liability of physicians, held in Lyons in June 1975, reported that most of the doctors and lawyers there agreed that information should be more readily available to the patients' advisers.

1329   In England and Wales, on an order for discovery, the court may direct disclosure to the applicant or his solicitors. The courts have taken the line that, normally, disclosure would be only to a nominated medical adviser of the applicant. In Northern Ireland, the courts have decided that disclosure may be made to the applicant. This is also the position in Scotland.

1330   Any patient may approach the Health Service Commissioners for investigation of his complaint, but the Commissioners are expressly prevented from investigating a claim in respect of which the person aggrieved has or had a remedy in law (unless it would not be reasonable to expect him to resort to it) or in respect of any action taken solely in consequence of the exercise of clinical judgment.

Medical accidents

1331   We have so far discussed the evidence we received about negligence. But there are many more cases where individuals suffer injury which was not due to negligence. We received a good deal of evidence that the position here was unsatisfactory.

1332   The Royal College of Physicians instanced, 'the possible sequelae of coronary arteriograms, kidney biopsies or amniocenteses'. Injury or death might be associated with, 'the development of hypersensitivity to a drug or anti-bacterial substance that was properly prescribed'. Dr White Franklin pointed out that a patient who stopped breathing under properly administered and controlled anaesthesia might die or recover with faculties grossly impaired.

1333   Some of these patients (or their dependants) would receive social security benefit, but many would receive no cash benefit of any kind.

What should be done?

1334   Our evidence showed that there was considerable dissatisfaction with the present position and some unease about the future.

1335   We considered various ways of compensating medical accidents with or without negligence. We look first at tort, where liability at present is based on negligence, and consider the possibility either of reversing the burden of proof or of imposing strict liability. Then we go on to examine the possibility of a no-fault scheme which would cover medical accidents irrespective of negligence.

Tort compensation
Reversed burden of proof
1336   Some witnesses suggested that, if the burden of proof were reversed, the patient's difficulties in obtaining and presenting his evidence would be largely overcome. It was said that doctors were in a better position to prove absence of negligence than patients were to establish liability. At the Council of Europe colloquy, however, although it was agreed that the patient was at a disadvantage when he sought to establish a claim, serious doubts were expressed on the desirability of making a radical change in the burden of proof. We share these doubts. We think that there might well be a large increase in claims, and although many would be groundless, each one would have to be investigated and answered. The result would almost certainly be an increase in defensive medicine.

Strict liability
1337   We also considered whether strict liability should be introduced. Whilst this would avoid the difficulties of proving or disproving negligence, there would remain the difficulty of proving that the injury was a medical accident, that is to say that it would not have occurred in any event. It would be necessary to define the area to be covered. For example, the foreseeable result of medical treatment such as amputation of a limb in a case of gangrene would not be included. The problems in defining the scope of medical injuries to be included would be the same as those we consider later in connection with the possibility of introducing a no-fault scheme.

1338   Even if it were possible to limit the scope satisfactorily, the imposition of strict liability, as with reversing the burden of proof, might well lead to an increase in defensive medicine. It would tend to imply rigid standards of professional skill beyond those which the present law requires to be exhibited, and beyond those which (in our view) can fairly be expected. We decided not to recommend that strict liability should be introduced, except for one special category of people – those who volunteer for research or clinical trials.

Volunteers for medical research
1339   People may volunteer to take part in research or clinical trails of new forms of treatment or new drugs. Strict precautions are imposed, including the screening of experiments by medical ethical committees. Nevertheless the Medical Research Council stated in their evidence to us:

'despite the exercise of the highest degree of care and skill by the medical investigator concerned, death or a personal injury which was quite unforeseen and indeed quite unforseeable might be suffered by a person who volunteers to participate in such an investigation. For example, a volunteer taking part in a recent trial of live attenuated influenza vaccine developed a neurological lesion shortly after the administration of the vaccine – the first known neurological sequela to any attenuated influenza virus despite the fact that many hundreds of thousands of such inoculations had been given during the preceding ten years; a causal connection between the administration of the vaccine and the neurological lesion could neither be proved nor disproved. In such a situation, the Medical Research Council would seek authority to make an *ex gratia* payment from public funds to the volunteer or his dependants and such a payment has been approved for the volunteer who developed the lesion in question.'

Patients undergoing clinical trials
1340   Patients as well as healthy volunteers may be asked if they will agree to accept a new form of treatment in the interests of research. If a patient is given such treatment, and through it suffers injury, or a worsening of his condition which would not have been expected with conventional treatment, he is in the same position as a healthy person volunteering to take part in research.

1341   We think that it is wrong that a person who exposes himself to some medical risk in the interests of the community should have to rely on *ex gratia* compensation in the event of injury. **We recommend** that any volunteer for medical research or clinical trials who suffers severe damage as a result should have a cause of action, on the basis of strict liability, against the authority to whom he has consented to make himself available.

The negligence action
1342   In most of the evidence from the medical profession it was urged that tort should be retained. It was argued that, even if some other system were introduced, the tort action based on negligence should continue alongside. Liability was one of the means whereby doctors could show their sense of

responsibility and, therefore, justly claim professional freedom. If tortious liability were abolished, there could be some attempt to control doctors' clinical practice to prevent mistakes for which compensation would have to be paid by some central agency. It was said that this could lead to a bureaucratic restriction of medicine and a brake on progress. It was further argued that the traditions of the profession were not sufficient in themselves to prevent all lapses which, though small in number, might have disastrous effects. Some penalty helped to preserve the patient's opportunity to express disapproval and obtain redress.

1343   We record these views as put to us, although some of us feel that they are unsound and at the least overstated. We also feel bound to ask whether the growth of insurance cover does not mitigate the effect claimed for the value of the tort action. On this point, the Medical Defence Union said that, although they paid the compensation, their investigation into the circumstances brought home to the doctor the part he had played and encouraged a sense of personal responsibility. We add the comment that the cases that come to court must often be those in which the Union advises the doctor to contest the claim because he has a good defence, whereas the much smaller number of cases of gross negligence must usually be settled out of court. The system, therefore, would appear to expose to publicity those doctors whose behaviour is on the face of it the least reprehensible.

1344   Nevertheless, in spite of the doubts we express about the particular arguments put to us by the medical profession for the retention of the tort action, it is clear that there would have to be a good case for exempting any profession from legal liabilities which apply to others, and we do not regard the special circumstances of medical injury as constituting such a case.

1345   We were impressed by the difficulties facing a patient who wishes to establish a case, but we doubt if the confidentiality of medical records adds significantly to the plaintiff's difficulties in view of the powers of the courts to order disclosure.

1346   Although the powers of the Health Service Commissioners are restricted to some extent, we note with interest the possibility of change following a report published in November 1977 by the Select Committee on the Parliamentary Commissioner for Administration (HC45) about an independent review of hospital complaints in the National Health Service. The Committee considers that there should be a simple straightforward system for handling complaints in every hospital with emphasis on listening carefully to the patient's or relative's concern and dealing with it promptly. When the complainant is not satisfied he should be able to pursue the matter with the District Administrator. For the most serious cases the Secretaries of State should continue to set up inquiries under the relevant Acts. All other cases not resolved by this procedure should be referable to the Health Service Commissioner, including complaints concerning clinical judgment.

1347 **We recommend** that, subject to our recommendation on volunteers for medical research or clinical trials, the basis of liability in tort for medical injuries should continue to be negligence.

No-fault compensation

1348 Changes made to improve the prospects of getting compensation in the cases of negligence could have no effect on the very much greater number of medical accidents where nobody is at fault.

1349 The employment of new techniques and the development of medical science have increased the ability of the doctor to attempt the treatment of severe diseases and to effect a cure, but at the same time have widened the area in which medical accidents may occur. This trend of greater risks for greater gain is likely to continue.

1350 An operation may have unexpected consequences. Blood products may be used which contain viruses the presence of which could not be foreseen. There are now 3,000 drugs in common use and 10,000 listed drug interactions, both detrimental and beneficial. More will doubtless be discovered.

1351 Many of our witnesses urged us to recommend the introduction of a scheme of no-fault compensation for medical accidents. Dr White Franklin said that negligence should not be the key to any form of monetary compensation. A circuit judge suggested that subsistence level compensation would be appropriate for a medical injury which did not involve negligence. The Royal College of Psychiatrists suggested that over the whole field of personal injury, compensation should not be tied to fault or negligence and should be based on the need of the individual and his family.

1352 Most of our witnesses saw a no-fault scheme as an addition to tort. It was put to us that such a scheme would often overcome the difficulties of proving negligence; and that a special scheme for medical injuries would be justified because of the reliance of the patient on the doctor to preserve his health and perhaps his life.

Overseas experience

1353 No-fault schemes which cover medical accidents have recently been introduced in New Zealand and Sweden. In Volume Three we give a detailed description of the provisions; in this chapter we touch only on some relevant features.

1354 New Zealand's accident compensation scheme covers medical, surgical, dental and first aid misadventure. In an appraisal of the first two years' operation of the scheme, Professor Geoffrey Palmer refers to the Accident Compensation Commission's 'restrictive interpretation' of 'medical misadventure' which 'seems concerned to avoid sliding down the slippery slope and compensating illness or death every time medical treatment fails'. This means that in many cases the claimant is left only with recourse to the common law. The view that the Accident Compensation Commission is treading carefully in this difficult area is supported by reported decisions of the Commission.

1355   The Patient Insurance Scheme in Sweden provides no-fault compensation which is based on the rules for the assessment of tort damages. This includes provision for loss of earnings, necessary medical expenses not covered by social insurance, and non-pecuniary loss. The scheme is financed by the Government and by the county councils who are responsible for the hospitals and for public health facilities. Liability is limited to 20 million kronor (about £3 million) for each incident involving injury and there is an overall limitation of 60 million kronor (about £8½ million) for such injuries in the whole country in one year. This is about £1 a head of the population.

1356   Payments under the scheme are relatively modest because they supplement existing social insurance payments which cover virtually all the adult population, including housewives. Social insurance sickness benefit is 90 per cent of earnings with an earnings ceiling of over £10,000 a year. The Patient Insurance Scheme makes up the payments to 100 per cent. Under industrial agreements, benefit for work accidents is made up to 100 per cent and this further reduces the scope for the payments under the Patient Insurance Scheme. Of the compensation paid during the first year only 12½ per cent was for loss of income.

1357   The scheme covers injury or illness which has occurred as a direct consequence of examination, medication, treatment or any other similar procedure, and does not constitute a natural or probable consequence of an act justified from a medical point of view. Mental illness is not covered unless it results from bodily injury. Injuries resulting from risks which are justified in order to avoid a threat to life or of permanent disability or would have occurred regardless of the treatment are also excluded.

1358   The Swedish scheme is administered by the main insurance companies. The amount of compensation is settled in the same way as tort awards. Disputed claims and questions of principle are referred to a panel consisting of a chairman and one member appointed by the government, two members appointed by county councils and two by insurance companies. Specialist medical advice is available. Only 50 cases have been referred to the panel in the first 23 months of the scheme. The advice of the panel has been accepted in every case. There has been no need to use the arbitration machinery under the Swedish Arbitration Act.

1359   The Swedish and New Zealand schemes cater for relatively small populations, so that it is possible to ensure consistency in decisions by dealing with all difficult or borderline cases centrally. Both schemes have been in operation for a short time and claims will take some time to build up. It will be a few years yet before a useful appraisal can be made.

A no-fault scheme for the United Kingdom?
1360   In considering the possibility of a no-fault scheme for this country we looked first at the question of cost. There are two aspects: the overall cost of any scheme; and the machinery for financing it.

1361   It is difficult to be precise about cost. Minor injuries and complications of treatment could reasonably be excluded as in Sweden, where there has to be some incapacity for work for more than 14 days. If there were as many as 10,000 cases a year, and benefits were provided on the same lines as in our suggested work and road schemes, the total additional cost of compensation over the existing form of compensation would be about £6 million a year. Some addition would have to be made for the cost of administration. This could well be substantial. Judging by the Swedish experience there would be at least two claims for every one that was successful.

1362   We think that it would be appropriate to finance any such scheme through the National Health Service. But the question of what to do about medical accidents in private practice would raise difficulties. Although it might be argued that many doctors have both National Health Service and private patients, that private doctors use National Health Service facilities and that all taxpayers contribute to the National Health Service, nevertheless we think that it is out of the question that a no-fault scheme provided by public funds should cover injuries received in the course of private treatment. There might be other ways of solving the problem. For example, such injuries could be covered by private no-fault insurance, or it might be possible to provide no-fault compensation through a levy on the subscription to medical defence societies. But in view of the decision we come to, as explained below, not to recommend a no-fault scheme because of other even more compelling considerations, we have not worked out in any detail possible ways of meeting this particular difficulty over finance.

1363   Any attempt to devise a no-fault scheme would also run into the problem of whether, and if so, how, treatment given by the 'paramedical' professions should be covered. Most of those in such professions, for example, nurses and physiotherapists, work with or mainly under the direction of doctors or dentists; but there would remain the problem of treatment not given by a medical team, for example chiropody. Outside the National Health Service, there would by the further problem whether other practices, such as osteopathy, should be covered.

Establishing causation
1364   The main difficulty in the way of a no-fault scheme is how to establish causation, since the cause of many injuries cannot be identified. The Medical Research Council said that while future research was likely to establish more causal relationships it would also reveal increasingly complex interactions which would heighten the problems of proving causation in the individual case.

1365   Even with our definition of medical injury we were forced to conclude that in practice there would be difficulty in distinguishing medical accident from the natural progression of a disease or injury, and from a foreseeable side effect of treatment. It is quite normal for a patient not to recover completely for several weeks or months after a major operation; for complications to ensue after operation; and for a patient to find that the drugs prescribed cause serious side effects.

1366   How should words like 'expected' or 'foreseeable' be interpreted? Even rare side effects such as vaccine damage not caused by negligence are often foreseeable in the sense that they are well known to medical science. If such injuries were to be included in a no-fault scheme, where would the line be drawn between them and the accepted risks of treatment? If they were to be excluded, the scheme would do little more than convert the negligence test of tort into a statutory formula, thereby making it easier for the victims of negligence to obtain compensation, but doing nothing for those suffering medical injury from other causes.

1367 In establishing causation, who should take the decision? We envisage that a no-fault scheme would be the responsibility of DHSS. The use of its adjudication procedure, however, would either place more burdens on the medical manpower available, or would put the onus of making the initial decision on the shoulders of junior officials who have neither the experience nor the training to determine these issues.

1368 To establish causation would involve deciding whether the condition was the result of the treatment and, if so, whether it was a result that might have been expected. This would have to be disentangled from the conditions resulting from the progress of the disease or advancing age or from some other purely fortuitous circumstances.

1369 It is easy to distinguish the completely unexpected result from that which was expected. The grey areas in between pose serious difficulties in knowing where to draw the line.

Conclusions on no-fault compensation
1370 We concluded that we could not recommend the introduction of a no-fault scheme for medical accidents in the United Kingdom. Some of us found this was a difficult decision and thought the arguments were finely balanced. All of us appreciate that circumstances may change, and that our conclusions may have to be reviewed in the future.

1371 **We recommend** that a no-fault scheme for medical accidents should not be introduced at present; but that the progress of no-fault compensation for medical accidents in New Zealand and Sweden should be studied and assessed, so that the experience can be drawn upon, if, because of changing circumstances, a decision is taken to introduce a no-fault scheme for medical accidents in this country.

CHAPTER 25

Vaccine damage

1372 Vaccination (or immunisation) increases the body's resistance to diseases caused by harmful bacteria and viruses. It involves inoculation, a process of putting into the body a substance (the vaccine) which raises an anti-body to neutralise a particular species of bacterium or virus which can cause infectious disease.

1373 Vaccination was introduced by Jenner in 1796 by inoculation with cowpox. The virus of cowpox resembles smallpox closely enough to provoke immunity to both diseases. The term 'vaccination' was later applied to the principle of using modified organisms to confer immunity to more dangerous ones. For example, Pasteur in 1885 attenuated (weakened) the virus of rabies by infecting a series of rabbits; virus taken from the twenty-fifth rabbit was dried and was a safe vaccine against the disease.

1374 Vaccines are now prepared either by attenuating the organism or by killing it. Preparations of killed organisms are used for immunisation against cholera, typhoid and pertussis (whooping cough); and as vaccines against the virus infections such as influenza and poliomyelitis (Salk vaccine). Examples of live vaccines prepared from attenuated organisms in general use are those against rubella, measles, yellow fever and poliomyelitis.

1375 Vaccination of children against smallpox was compulsory from 1853 to 1948 although exemption could be claimed on grounds of conscience. Since 1971, it has no longer been offered as a routine procedure in early childhood; the risk of contracting the disease is considered to be less than the risk of adverse reaction to the vaccine. Smallpox vaccination is still recommended for certain health service staff who may come in contact with smallpox victims, and for travellers to and from areas where smallpox is endemic.

The immunisation programme

1376 The prime object of vaccination in the United Kingdom is to reduce the risk of children catching serious diseases. In addition, adults may be advised to have specific vaccinations if their occupation exposes them to a special risk of disease in times of epidemic or otherwise. Vaccination against influenza may be of particular value to the elderly, the chronically ill or other special groups.

1377 Vaccinations may be advised before visits to certain foreign countries, but we are here concerned with vaccinations in the interests of the community in this country. Our recommendations do not apply to vaccinations for visits abroad.

1378   There is now no compulsory vaccination in the United Kingdom. But DHSS, and the Health Departments of Scotland, Wales and Northern Ireland, recommend for children a programme of vaccinations against diphtheria, tetanus, whooping cough, poliomyelitis, measles, and tuberculosis, and rubella for girls only. Apart from the benefits to the individual, the vaccination of a high proportion of the population makes these diseases less likely to spread.

1379   In making these recommendations, the Health Departments offer detailed advice to general practitioners and health authorities on the precautions to be observed and, in particular, on contra-indications, that is to say medical conditions or histories which may be associated with serious reactions to vaccination. There are contra-indications relevant to all vaccination, for example, certain immunodeficient conditions; and contra-indications which are specific to a certain vaccine, for example, a family history of epilepsy, or a severe reaction to a preceding dose, in respect of whooping cough vaccine. It is the individual's doctor who decides whether or not to vaccinate in any particular case.

1380   Recently, there has been controversy about whooping cough vaccine, following allegations that its administration has caused serious brain damage in a number of children. The recommended programme includes the administration of a triple vaccine, which protects against diphtheria, tetanus and whooping cough. The Joint Committee on Vaccination and Immunization, set up in 1963 to advise the Health Ministers on medical aspects of vaccination and immunization, has reaffirmed that whooping cough vaccine should be offered in infancy, the first dose preferably being given at the age of three months. Where there are parental objections or medical contra-indications to the whooping cough component, the Committee has recommended that vaccination against diphtheria and tetanus only should be offered instead. This is to try to ensure that the wider immunisation programme is not adversely affected by parental objections to whooping cough vaccination.

1381   In England, by the end of 1972, 81 per cent of children born in 1970 had been vaccinated against diphtheria and tetanus, 79 per cent against whooping cough, and 80 per cent against poliomyelitis. By the end of 1976, in respect of children born in 1974, these figures had fallen, respectively, to 75 per cent, 38 per cent, and 74 per cent. This decline was probably caused to some extent by the adverse publicity given to cases of vaccine damage, especially following vaccination against whooping cough. It may also have been partly due to complacency about the dangers of diseases which were once common but are now comparatively rare.

1382   Some reduction in the number of deaths from the diseases referred to in the previous paragraph had been apparent before vaccination was introduced, due perhaps in part to improvements in living standards and to better management of illness. But the number suffering from these diseases, and in particular the number of deaths, has decreased much more sharply since vaccination was introduced. Whooping cough notifications in England and Wales declined from about 85,000 in 1957, when routine immunisation was introduced, to less than 2,500 in 1973. Deaths dropped from 88 to 2. There were over 6,000 notifications of poliomyelitis and 270 deaths in 1955, before immunisation was introduced nationally. In 1973, there were 5 notifications and no deaths.

1383   In addition to the main immunisation programme for children, there is a further circumstance in which vaccination may be recommended. Where a case occurs of one of certain specified communicable diseases, the appropriate medical officer of the local authority concerned is empowered to vaccinate, without charge, anyone who has been in contact with the infection or is at risk of such contact. The officer must be satisfied that this is in the public interest, and the person at risk must be willing to be vaccinated.

1384   It remains open to individual patients to seek vaccination, and to general practitioners to recommend it, in circumstances other than those for which it is recommended by the Government or by local authorities. We regard this as a medical matter outside the concern of this chapter.

1385   Vaccines are produced in the United Kingdom and bought from the manufacturers either centrally or by health authorities. Before vaccines are released, samples have to pass tests of purity and potency under standards laid down by the National Institute for Biological Standards and Control, at present administered jointly by DHSS and the Medical Research Council.

Risk of injury

1386   There is an element of risk in any vaccination, as in any medical procedure. In the overwhelming majority of cases, there is no serious or lasting damage; there may be a minor adverse reaction, such as a swollen arm or a few days' feverish illness. Quite exceptionally, a child may suffer severe and permanent brain damage following vaccination, and particularly following vaccination against whooping cough. In such circumstances, it may be difficult to establish whether the vaccination causes the damage or whether it is coincidental.

1387   This brain damage may lead to forms of physical and mental handicap and, sometimes, death. We were told in evidence of loss of sensation in the lower part of the body, confinement to a wheelchair, fits and hyperactivity, epileptic fits with partial paralysis, and the need to be fed and dressed.

1388   Most of the evidence we received concerned children. The Association of Parents of Vaccine Damaged Children, which was formed in August 1973, represented to us that, because there was no hope of recovery from injury due to vaccine damage, normal family life was impossible; holidays were limited; great expense was incurred, for example on special education, special shoes, clothing and food; and families sometimes broke up under the strain. The Association has since told us that, of the 356 cases of serious damage from vaccination registered by them, 240 are in respect of whooping cough vaccination.

1389   The Association's figures have not been officially confirmed. DHSS accepts that severe damage can occur, albeit rarely, but considers that problems over establishing causation make it difficult to produce reliable figures. The Joint Committee on Vaccination and Immunization says in its recent Review of the Evidence on Whooping Cough Vaccination (London, HMSO, 1977) that, 'infants frequently develop convulsions for the first time in the first two years of life. By chance some of these will occur shortly after a child has been vaccinated and will be wrongly attributed to the vaccine.' It is hoped that the essential data to establish how far childhood convulsions and brain damage can be related to immunisation will ultimately be provided by the National Childhood Encephalopathy Study which began in July 1976. It is not possible to say in advance what the reaction will be in any individual case, save possibly if there are contra-indications.

1390   The Joint Committee considers that the present balance of evidence continues to favour the benefits of immunisation for the individual child and for the community at large, although, in respect of whooping cough vaccine, medical opinion as a whole is not unanimous on this point. The Committee's view is not based simply on comparing the numbers of complications resulting from the disease and those resulting from immunisation; it takes account also of the burden of illness in the community.

1391   We have so far considered mainly children, but older people cannot be left out. It is unusual for individuals over 16 to suffer more than temporary ill effects from vaccination, but the risk of more serious damage exists. For example, in the USA a number of people have suffered serious effects from vaccination against swine fever.

Compensation
The present position
1392   In the United Kingdom there is compensation provision for members of HM Forces through the armed forces pension scheme and, where appropriate, the war pensions scheme. Smallpox vaccination is usual. If a serviceman refuses the vaccination, he must sign a declaration that he has done so. Section 10 of the Crown Proceedings Act 1947 precludes the bringing of a case against a member of the services – in this case the service doctor – if the injured serviceman has been compensated under the war pensions scheme.

1393   Civilians who are damaged by vaccination arising out of their work may be eligible for benefits under the industrial injuries scheme and, in some cases, under their own pension scheme. It is open to anyone to pursue an action for negligence if he considers that the circumstances justify this course.

Should more be done?
1394   Several Members of Parliament have urged that compensation should be paid to all vaccine damaged children. Mr Jack Ashley MP asked the Parliamentary Commissioner for Administration to investigate the cases of four children who were said to have suffered brain damage after whooping cough vaccinations. In February 1977 the Commissioner agreed to investigate a complaint that the Health Departments had failed to make available to parents all the information that they should have taken into account before they agreed to have their children vaccinated. The Commissioner's report (Whooping Cough Vaccination, HC 571) had no general criticism to make of the action taken by the Health Departments to make information available to doctors; but he considered that they should have recognised earlier the desirability of alerting parents to the risks and contra-indications.

1395   The Association of Parents of Vaccine Damaged Children considers that, since vaccination is recommended by the state, the state ought to compensate where vaccination causes injury. It claims that in the past the state made no mention of risks attendant on whooping cough vaccination. It argues that all handicapped children are deserving of assistance, but that vaccine damaged children have a prior claim to compensation because they have been placed at risk and injured in the national interest. In 1975, the Association appealed to the European Commission of Human Rights for aid in securing compensation, which, it contends, should be retrospective.

1396   Other witnesses also advanced arguments for compensating all vaccine damaged children. These witnesses included the British Medical Association; the Royal College of Physicians and Surgeons of Glasgow; the Royal College of Surgeons, Edinburgh; the Association of the British Pharmaceutical Industry; and the British Insurance Association. The Standing Medical Advisory Committee of DHSS told us that in its view there was a reasonable case for paying compensation where vaccination was proved as the cause of the damage.

1397   Nobody argued in the contrary sense.

1398   We concluded that there is a special case for paying compensation for vaccine damage where vaccination is recommended by a public authority and is undertaken to protect the community. We had reached this conclusion when we were asked by the Government for our views. Our Chairman explained that we had concluded that some kind of financial assistance should be made available for very serious injury resulting from vaccination recommended by a public health authority, but that we were unable to produce an interim report as we thought it essential to look at the problem of vaccine damage in the light of our remit as a whole.

1399   On 14 June 1977 the Secretary of State for Social Services (Mr Ennals) said that, in the light of the conclusion which the Royal Commission had reached, the Government had decided to accept in principle that there should be a scheme of payments for the benefit of those who were seriously damaged as a result of vaccination, and that it should apply to existing, as well as to new, cases.

Overseas systems

1400   Before deciding what form of compensation to recommend, we looked at practice overseas. Specific compensation for vaccine damage is still the exception, but four European countries have provided for such compensation.

1401   In France, vaccination is compulsory for smallpox, diphtheria, tetanus, poliomyelitis and tuberculosis. The vaccines most frequently involved are those for smallpox and, to a lesser degree, tuberculosis. The main sufferers from vaccine damage are children. State compensation, which is available both to the victim and to the parents, is assessed by a tribunal and covers established pecuniary and non-pecuniary loss and provision for future support, taking into account payments under social security schemes. The tribunal has a discretion whether to award a lump sum or periodic payments, although a preliminary award for periodic payments is made until the victim's condition has stabilised.

1402 In the Federal Republic of Germany, smallpox vaccination is compulsory. Other vaccines are officially recommended. Compensation is provided for damage caused by any officially recommended vaccination. It includes a pension, where earning capacity has been impaired, based on federal invalidity pension regulations. It also covers medical and other costs. The probability of a causal relationship is sufficient to establish a claim.

1403 In Switzerland, a federal law on epidemics obliges all cantons to provide free vaccination against smallpox and other dangerous epidemic diseases. The cantons have the discretion to make the vaccination compulsory or voluntary. The law also requires cantons to compensate damage caused by compulsory or officially recommended vaccination, in so far as the damage is not covered otherwise, for example by social security payments or private personal insurance.

1404 In Denmark, there is a statutory vaccine damage compensation scheme covering vaccination against smallpox, diphtheria, whooping cough, polio and tuberculosis, and anti-tetanus where this is combined with one of these. The main compensation is for loss of earning capacity, and a vaccine damaged child does not receive this until he has reached the age of 15. No compensation is payable where the disability is less than 5 per cent; for disability between 5 and 50 per cent a lump sum is paid, and for 50 per cent or more, an annuity.

1405 In the USA, strict liability applies to vaccine manufacturers. There have been some substantial awards of damages against the manufacturer of the Salk vaccine which was used in a polio immunisation programme. There was also a substantial award against the Federal Government which had certified and released an allegedly defective polio vaccine.

Our proposals

1406 The problem of establishing causation with certainty in any individual case may well be difficult. The overriding need is that, where there is serious damage, there should be prompt recognition that some form of compensation should be payable. We do not think it is right to try to distinguish one severely disabled child from another, and to produce a situation where two children have the same needs, but one is compensated and the other is not. We decided, therefore, that vaccine damaged children should be considered with other severely disabled children, irrespective of the cause of disablement. We explain our conclusions in chapter 27.

1407 For those children who can be shown to have been victims of vaccine damage, we consider that there is a case for an additional remedy in the field of tort.

1408 Under the present law, an action in tort against a doctor who performs a vaccination in the recognised circumstances and using the recognised methods would be unlikely to succeed since he could not be said to be acting outside the bounds of proper practice, and would not be negligent. We are not aware of any successful actions. We think an alternative remedy should be made available. Where vaccine damage can be proved to have followed from medical procedures recommended by the Government or a local authority, those who suffer serious and lasting damage should be entitled to bring an action in tort for damages against the Government or the authority concerned. This would normally apply only to children, but we think that adults should also be included, in order to cover those exceptional circumstances in which the Government or a local authority might recommend adults to be vaccinated in the public interest.

1409   We think that the basis of liability should not be fault but should be strict, that is to say that, where a plaintiff can show on the balance of probabilities that the injury suffered was attributable to the administration of a vaccine on the recommendation of the Government or a local authority, he should be entitled to compensation. Subject to these matters of causation and fact, there should be no defences. We reach these conclusions because vaccination is recommended by the state for the benefit of the community; and where it causes injury the state ought to provide compensation, as part of the cost of providing protection for the community as a whole.

1410   We are conscious of the view that special compensation provision for vaccine damage might act as a deterrent to vaccination, on the grounds that it would imply that there must a be real danger. But there is also the opposite view, which we share, that the Government must be confident about vaccination before it would make such provision. We naturally hope that any increase in litigation resulting from our recommendations, and any attendant publicity, will not have an adverse impact on the future vaccination programme.

1411   We are aware that proof of causation could pose problems for the courts. The convulsions which may be symptomatic of damage by whooping cough vaccine, for example, can also occur naturally, and we are aware of no clinical tests which could distinguish the one from the other. Nevertheless, we see no need to suggest that the courts should adopt a different approach to the proof of causation than that of assessing the balance of probabilities as in the case of other tort actions. No doubt case law would develop on this difficult matter.

1412   We are also aware that the courts would need to assess what is severe damage if, as we propose, a remedy in strict liability is to be confined to such cases.

1413   **We recommend** that the Government, or the local authority concerned, should be strictly liable in tort for severe damage suffered by anyone (adult or child) as a result of vaccination which has been recommended in the interests of the community.

CHAPTER 26
Ante-natal injury

1414   Ante-natal injury was specifically included in our terms of reference because of the thalidomide tragedy. It is thought that there are 8–10,000 children in the world who were born with deformities because their mothers took thalidomide when they were pregnant. Some 400 of these children are in this country.

1415   Thalidomide was developed by a West German firm, Chemie Grünenthal, and came on the international market in 1958. In this country it was manufactured under licence by the Distillers Company Ltd. It was prescribed for coughs and colds and for insomnia and was used as a sedative especially in cases of *hyperemesis gravidarum* (severe vomiting in pregnancy).

1416   In November 1961 the drug was withdrawn from the market because it was suspected that it was causing polyneuritis in adults and gross deformities in the children of women who took it during pregnancy. It was later established that thalidomide ingested during the fourth to sixth weeks of pregnancy affected the unborn child, resulting in limblessness, absence of eyes or ears, or deformities of internal organs. A number of the deformed children did not survive.

1417   Sixty two actions for damages for negligence were brought against the Distillers Company starting in November 1962, but it was not until 1967 that they approached trial. Distillers always denied negligence. They held that Chemie Grünenthal were at fault in not making sufficient tests before marketing the drug. Nevertheless, Distillers said that if all allegations of negligence were withdrawn, they would pay the children 40 per cent of what a court would have awarded for a successful negligence claim. This was accepted on behalf of the claimants and approved by the court. When legal advisers were unable to agree the amount of such an award, two cases were considered as test cases to determine this. As a result in 1968 Distillers paid £1 million to the children concerned, payments being made according to disability.

1418   More families were then given leave to bring actions out of time and a further 341 claims were made. In negotiations in 1971 Distillers suggested that a charitable trust be set up into which they would pay £3·25 million over ten years. Some families objected as there would be no enforceable claims. A new offer was made, with the alternative of a cash payment of £2·9 million.

1419   Following considerable public discussion and adverse criticism of Distillers, a greatly increased offer of compensation was made. This was accepted in 1973 and provided in the first place £6 million for lump sum compensation to the 341 children. In addition, Distillers agreed to pay into the trust fund, over seven years, £2 million a year plus annual payments of up to 10 per cent of this amount to offset inflation. In sum, Distillers were to make payments totalling over £20 million.

1420   The Government recognised that when the parents accepted the Distillers' offer, they were not aware that payments made by the trust fund would count as taxable income and that, had they known that, they might not have accepted the offer. To offset the tax payable, the Government in October 1974 made a single payment of £5 million to the trust.

1421   The public interest aroused in the thalidomide tragedy brought to the forefront the question of compensation. One of the difficulties was whether there was a right to recover in respect of ante-natal injury. There have been decisions in the courts of other countries, but the question had never been decided in the English or Scottish courts. The nearest approach was a case at Liverpool Assizes in 1939 when a ladder fell on a pregnant woman, and as a result her child was born the next day and lived only one day. The parents brought a claim for damages for the child's loss of expectation of life and accepted a payment of £100 in settlement of their claim.

1422   In view of the uncertainty, at the end of 1972 the Lord Chancellor referred the matter to the Law Commission, and the Lord Advocate referred it to the Scottish Law Commission. The Law Commission were asked to advise what the nature and extent of civil liability for ante-natal injury should be. The Scottish Law Commission were asked what the present law of Scotland was, and whether there should be liability if there were none under the present law.

The Law Commissions' Reports

1423   The Scottish Law Commission reported in August 1973 (Scot Law Com No 30, Liability for Ante-natal Injury, Cmnd 5371). They said that established principles were sufficient to afford a remedy to a child in respect of ante-natal injury, 'although there is no express Scottish decision on the point, a right to reparation would, on existing principles, be accorded by Scots law to a child for harm wrongfully occasioned to it while in its mother's womb, provided that it was born alive'. Legislation should be considered only if it were thought that, because there had been no Scottish decisions directly in point, it were desirable to put the matter beyond argument.

1424   The Law Commission, reporting in August 1974 (Law Com No 60, Report on Injuries to Unborn Children, Cmnd 5709) thought that it was highly probable that the English common law would in appropriate circumstances provide a remedy for a plaintiff suffering from an ante-natal injury caused by another's fault. As there was some doubt on this question, and as regulation of the right was desirable, there should be legislation. The legislation should deal with the rights of a living person and no rights should be given to the foetus. A draft Bill, the Congenital Disabilities (Civil Liability) Bill, was annexed to the Law Commission report.

The Congenital Disabilities (Civil Liability) Bill

1425 The Bill provided that a person was answerable to the child if he was liable in tort to the parent or would if sued in due time have been so. If the defendant had committed a breach of duty in common law, or a breach of statutory duty, to the parent so that he was liable to the parent for resulting injury, or would have been so liable if injury to the parent had resulted, then the child when born alive with a congenital defect caused by the defendant's breach of duty to the parent should be entitled to recover damages from the defendant. No damages should be available for loss of expectation of life unless the child lived for at least 48 hours.

1426 The child should have the right to sue his father, but should not have the right to sue his mother except where the injury was caused by the mother's negligent driving of a motor vehicle. In an action against the father, doctor or drug manufacturer or any other defendant, however, the mother's contributory negligence should be available as a partial defence.

1427 A defendant in an action by the child should be able to rely on a contractual term binding on the mother excluding or limiting the defendant's liability either towards her or towards her unborn child, and on the mother's voluntary assumption of risk.

1428 For injuries caused by events before conception there should be a cause of action only if at the time of conception the parent(s) neither knew, nor ought to have known, of the risk of the child being born disabled as a result of the relevant injury. This limitation would not apply if a father was being sued for injury caused before or at conception.

1429 A claim for ante-natal injury should be limited to the first generation, that is to the person who suffered the ante-natal injury, but descendants would not have a claim.

1430 The Law Commission considered that under the existing law a person acting in a professional capacity was not liable for negligence if he acted in accordance with the then received professional opinion. But in the light of their consultation with the medical profession they took the view that it would be useful to formulate a professional man's liability as arising only if he failed to take reasonable care having due regard to the existing received professional opinion.

Legislation on ante-natal injury

1431 We were concerned at the prospect of legislation on ante-natal injury before we had submitted our report. When the Law Commission report was published we had not completed our consideration of ante-natal injury, but such preliminary attention as we had given to the subject, coupled with an examination of the evidence that was coming in, prompted misgivings about steps being taken to confirm the tort action in this field.

1432 We expressed our misgivings to the Government but our views were not accepted. Later, when it was clear that the Law Commission's Bill was to be presented by a private member with Government support, we thought it right to make our views more widely known. Accordingly our Chairman wrote on our behalf to the Editor of *The Times*. The letter was published on 28 January 1976 and includes the following:

'Parliament should . . . be made aware of the special objections which can be and have been urged against relying on the operation of the tort action in the field of ante-natal injuries:—

   i According to the expert evidence which we have received it is only in the rarest of cases that even the physical cause of a congenital deformity can be ascertained, and even if that is ascertainable the plaintiff in an action of tort would still have to prove that the deformity was caused by fault, usually negligence, on the part of the defendant.

   ii Thus the Bill, so far from dealing comprehensively with a widespread and highly distressing social problem, could result in compensation for no more than a minute proportion of the children concerned. The Bill therefore would raise many false hopes, not least by its very title.

   iii There would still be delay and expense, especially in difficult and complicated actions.

   iv The accusations and counter-accusations in such cases could have an adverse effect on family relations and on relations between doctors and patients. For example, in an action against a drug company or a doctor, the defence might allege that the damage to the unborn child was caused by the mother's own action such as smoking or drug addiction.'

1433   The Bill received wide support in both Houses of Parliament although some doubts were expressed as to the suitability of the tort action in this area. Our Chairman explained the attitude of the Royal Commission to the Bill when he spoke in the Second Reading debate in the House of Lords on 27 May 1976 (Official Report (HL) 27.5.76, Vol 371, cols 374–377).

1434   The Bill was passed and came into effect on 22 July 1976. Any child born disabled in England, Wales or Northern Ireland on or after that date as a result of ante-natal injury has the right to sue for damages in accordance with the provisions of the Act. We are not aware of any actions brought under the Act.

1435   An ante-natal injury claim was settled out of court in 1976 for £78,692 but as the occurrence giving rise to the claim took place in 1971, the 1976 Act did not apply.

1436   It may be asked why any further consideration of the subject of ante-natal injury is necessary when two experienced law reform bodies have already pronounced on the subject and when Parliament has legislated in accordance with the views expressed by one of them. There are several reasons.

1437   First, the Law Commissions were asked for advice within the context of the present law of tort. Our remit is wider and we have to concern ourselves with the question whether the basis of the law of tort should be changed.

Indeed the Congenital Disabilities (Civil Liability) Act 1976 has been described as a temporary clarification of the current law. In introducing the Bill, Mr Ray Carter, MP said, 'it may prove to be no more than an interim measure'. The Solicitor General in referring to the Royal Commission stated, 'anything we do today and in the course of our deliberations on the Bill will not prejudge or prejudice our consideration of whatever recommendations the Commission may make' (Official Report (HC) 6.2.76, Vol 904, cols 1591 and 1645).

1438 Secondly, the Bill could be said to have raised false hopes. Some of the publicity it attracted suggested that all children born with some malformation would automatically receive large amounts of compensation; the need to prove causation and negligence was not always sufficiently appreciated or explained.

1439 Thirdly, our remit is not restricted to ante-natal injury, but embraces all injuries for which compensation is recoverable. We think that the provision of compensation for ante-natal injury needs to be fitted into the future pattern of compensation for injuries generally. The Law Commission referred to the different background to their consideration when they said in their report, 'We are asked to consider one class of injury only . . . and we are asked to consider what the nature and extent of civil liability for such injury should be. It seems to us to be inevitable that such an inquiry should be conducted within the context of . . . the present law of tort' and also, 'it is our view that any legislation based on our proposals neither can nor should prejudice the much wider issues which the Royal Commission is considering'.

1440 On the legal issues, we were greatly helped by the reports of the Law Commissions. We accept their exposition of the law and would refer our readers to their reports for a clear and helpful survey of the various authorities, including a description of the regimes in other countries.

Causes of ante-natal injury

1441 Before we came to conclusions we thought it essential to know more about ante-natal injury and its causes. So we commissioned reports from Professor J P M Tizard, Professor of Paediatrics, University of Oxford, on 'Birth Injury' and from Dr J H Renwick of the London School of Hygiene and Tropical Medicine on 'The Biology of Human Pre-natally Determined Injury'. These reports are at Annex 12 and Annex 13. In addition, we had the benefit of evidence from many expert witnesses, as well as access to the evidence given to the Law Commission in response to their Working Paper No 47.

1442 The basis of most congenital defects is still uncertain, but it is now considered doubtful whether external physical injury to the mother causes a congenital defect. It is unthinkable that in the present state of knowledge a decision could be given such as that in the Canadian case of *Montreal Tramways Co* v. *Léveillé* ([1933] 4 D.L.R. 337). Damages were awarded to the child born with club feet two months after the mother was injured descending from a tram when she was seven months pregnant.

1443 We understand that most abnormalities from faulty development originate within the first eight weeks, during which period the unborn child is generally described as an embryo. After the eighth week the unborn infant is described as a foetus. By this time it has acquired its essential form and its organs and become recognisably human.

1444 Most congenital abnormalities have more than one cause and some are not injuries. For example, there may be genetic or inborn error at the time of conception such as microcephaly (abnormally small or imperfectly developed brain) or spontaneous genetic mutations or chromosomal anomalies which arise during the division of cells. Environmental influences occur within the womb or as an occurrence during the process of birth itself. These include injury to the mother during invasive investigation; diseases, such as rubella; irradiation; food, drink and tobacco; pre-conceptional agents; and previous abortion and drugs. There are also unknown and possibly chemical influences from the mother which affect the foetus.

1445 Foetuses with severe malformations rarely survive the embryonic period. All but a few with chromosomal defects are eliminated as early abortions. Twenty per cent of perinatal deaths, that is, deaths immediately before or after birth (6 in each 1,000 births), are due to serious malformations.

1446 The Law Commission said that their consultation with the medical profession left them, '. . . in little doubt that we are in an era of rapidly expanding knowledge as to the aetiology of congenital defects'. Although the proof of causation of ante-natal injury presented great difficulties, rapid progress was being made and they concluded that, '. . . we must be prepared for much greater certainty both in the identification of teratogenic agents and the proof of causation of specific disabilities in the future'.

1447 In the light of our evidence, we think that these statements are over optimistic. In a paper submitted by Professor R J Berry and Dr A G Searle it is stated:

'Since almost all mutagenic chemicals known so far have a quantitative effect on mutation (increasing the rate of a naturally occurring process) rather than a qualitative one (producing a distinct class of mutations) it may hardly ever be possible to *prove* that heritable genetic damage is caused by a particular environmental agent.'

And again:

'As a rule, harmful effects of dominant mutations will be expressed in the first generation after exposure to the mutagenic agent; so will most chromosome aberrations, though some will show up in the second generation. The adverse effects of recessive mutations, however, are likely to emerge over 5–10 generations at least, by which time any link between cause and effect will have vanished.'

1448 Dr Renwick states in his paper:

'. . . experiments using embryo cultures and transplants will advance our understanding but, because of the difference in environment between a cultured and a natural embryo, deductions about the effects of added chemicals on human concepti will be of dubious reliability'.

1449   Our consultations have led us to the conclusion that, as the boundary of knowledge increases, so does the area of uncertainty. The British Medical Association asserted that, 'the vast majority of congenital defects and diseases are of unknown causation and the number of instances which can be unequivocally ascribed to any particular act of omission or commission are few'. This view was supported by, among others, the Royal College of Obstetricians and Gynaecologists, the Medical Defence Union and the Medical Research Council.

1450   We received no evidence that causation is becoming easier to establish. On the contrary, we understand that birth defects do not all have the same basis. The effect of a drug may be to cause a pre-existing and latent genetic defect to become manifest rather than to act directly on the unborn child. Goya, who lived 200 years ago, portrayed a child with the same malformations as those of some of the thalidomide children.

1451   It is possible for apparently identical effects in different individuals to be due to different causes. Radiation is an example. According to Lord Platt, 'The chance of a certain mutation occurring in a chromosome may be X in 100,000 births. If radiation is being used, or something of that kind, it may be X + 10 in 100,000 births, but no one can possibly tell whether this particular case is one of the naturally occurring ones or one of the extra ones which occur when radiation is used in certain circumstances' (Official Report (HL) 27.5.76, Vol 371, col 380).

1452   We are forced to conclude that only a minute proportion of those who are born with congenital defects may be able to establish causation and prove that it was due to negligence, and that there is little prospect that this proportion will increase.

A definition of ante-natal injury

1453   We tried to arrive at a working definition of ante-natal injury, and to establish the number of children affected. We think that ante-natal injury may be defined as 'an acquired change or event, before or after conception, which leads to any derangement in the developing tissues or 'organs of the embryo or foetus, or any other event which may harm the fully developed foetus before birth'. We would extend this to include perinatal injury.

Numbers

1454   Significant malformations are usually detectable in the first two weeks of life in just under 20 in each thousand total births. By the age of five years, another 5 or 6 in each thousand will have been recognised. If to these one adds serious metabolic defects, such as fibrocystic disease of the pancreas, and those undetected or appearing later, a figure of 30 in each thousand is reached, which is probably a conservative estimate for significant birth defects.

1455   According to an estimate made by Mr Jonathan Bradshaw of the University of York,[13] the number of children under 16 living at home with congenital disability of a severe kind is about 6 in each thousand, or about 90,000.

1456   Of these 90,000 severely handicapped children, probably no more than one half per cent have grounds for claiming tort compensation. These include the thalidomide children; and it is not known whether Distillers would have been held to be negligent and legally liable to pay compensation if the issue of liability had come before the courts.

The present law of the United Kingdom

1457   The present law of England, Wales and Northern Ireland is governed by the Congenital Disabilities (Civil Liability) Act 1976. Its provisions are for the most part the same as those in the draft Bill summarised in paragraphs 1425 to 1429.

1458   The present law in Northern Ireland has one aspect peculiar to that province. The Criminal Injuries (Compensation) (Northern Ireland) Order 1977 includes unborn children among the possible beneficiaries. No claims have been determined under this Order or under the Criminal Injuries to Persons Act (Northern Ireland) 1968. One claim under the Act is pending.

1459   In Scotland, there has been no legislation on ante-natal injury. The Scottish Law Commission considered that:

' . . possible objections to the child's right to sue would be met by the application of either or both the following principles, namely, (1) the principle . . . that the fault or breach of duty persists until the damage is suffered, or at any rate emerges as a wrong at that stage, and (2) the equitable principle, derived originally from Roman law, that if subsequently born alive, a child *in utero* should be regarded in law as having already been born whenever so to regard it is to its advantage'.

The role of tort

1460   We now turn to the question whether tort should play a part in the case of civil liability and compensation for ante-natal injury. It seems to us that there are three objections to retaining the tort action in this area – first, that only rarely will tort be able to provide compensation; secondly, that in those rare cases there is risk of grave damage to family relations; and thirdly, that there is some risk of damage to relations between doctors and patients.

1461   The fact that the tort action can provide for only an insignificant number of cases is not a conclusive reason for its abolition; and it would no doubt be argued that, even if tort cannot provide for all, there is no reason why it should not provide for a few.

1462   The second objection is more formidable. Damage to family relations could arise from actions in respect of ante-natal injuries in several ways. First, there could be an action by the child against a parent. Secondly, another person, being the defendant to an action by the child, might seek to prove that the child's ante-natal injury was solely due to the fault of a parent and therefore not due to any fault of the defendant. A defendant could not reasonably be deprived of his right to resist a claim in this way. Thirdly, the Act of 1976 has provided in effect that a parent's contributory negligence can diminish the extent of a defendant's liability to the child. This is an innovation, because otherwise the rule is that only the plaintiff's own contributory negligence (or that of the deceased in a fatal accident case) can diminish the extent of a defendant's liability, if he is liable at all. In any of these ways, one or both of the parents could become involved in the litigation and be accused of having by negligence or other fault caused the child's injury and consequent deformity. If such an accusation appeared to be even possibly justified, it could gravely damage family relations and therefore the interests of the whole family, including especially the injured child.

1463 As regards the third objection – the possible adverse effect on relations between doctors and patients – a doctor sometimes has to take a difficult decision between conflicting interests of the mother and the unborn child. If he prefers the interests of the mother, he may afterwards have to face an accusation of negligence and an action for damages on behalf of the child. We think that this possibility would be unlikely to affect the doctor's decision, but we do not think that it can be completely ignored. There is a danger that, in an action against a doctor, the allegation that the mother's own action caused the damage to the unborn child might be used in defence.

1464 In spite of the difficulty of proving the cause of action, and in spite of the risk of grave damage to family relations, we consider that it would be unfair to discriminate against the child whose injuries were suffered before birth. When a child who has suffered post-natal injuries has a right of action against anyone who has wrongfully caused them, a similar right of action should not be withheld from a child whose injuries are ante-natal. If another disaster similar to the thalidomide disaster should occur and it could be proved to have been caused by the fault of some person sued as a defendant, there should be no doubt that the victims have a legally valid cause of action against him. By a majority, **we recommend** that, subject to the recommendations in paragraphs 1471 and 1472, a child born alive suffering from the effects of ante-natal injury caused by the fault of another person should continue to have a right of action for damages against that person. But we also think that, in order to diminish the risk of grave damage to family relations, there should be special provisions to protect the parents, so far as possible, from becoming involved in the litigation.

1465 Many of our witnesses felt that parental liability should be wholly excluded. Mrs Justice Lane felt that, 'potential disruption of family life and bitterness would be occasioned between parent and child, which disadvantages would far outweigh any financial benefit to the child, even assuming the parents' ability to pay damages'. Judge Rowland spoke of 'horrific possibilities', and asked, ' . . . can it be seriously suggested that a defective child should have a right of action against its mother because she smoked during pregnancy? In my opinion it would be against public policy for a child to have a right of action against its parents for pre-natal injury.'

1466 We were impressed also with the evidence in the same sense given to the Law Commission by the Bar Council and by Sir George Baker, President of the Family Division. Extracts from Sir George's evidence are quoted in the Law Commission Report. He felt that a child should not be able to sue the mother or the father. He said:

'My reasons are really very simple. Logic and love are not always congenial bedfellows. I would go so far as to say that it would be cruel to allow such an action against a mother, and even against a father. But the real danger is that it would give a new weapon to the unscrupulous spouse – and there are many . . . . The vindictive father might be dissuaded in all but a few cases from seeking to take action on behalf of the child against the mother whom he is seeking to divorce and whom he now hates. But what of the father who is seeking custody of the child or children? An action against the wife for her supposed negligence while carrying the child would be a splendid additional weapon in his armoury, and I have no doubt it would be used.'

1467   The National Council of Women of Great Britain said to us:

'The intimate relationship between parent and child would . . . be jeopardised by the existence of such a right, especially if any action were taken to enforce the right . . . The fact that a child is born with some deformity or incapacity may well result in great grief to parents and produce an even higher degree of devotion and care than is normally bestowed on a child. This devotion ought not to be poisoned, nor care endangered by the prospect or possibility of a financial claim by the child or on behalf of the child.'

The Christian Economic and Social Research Foundation gave us as their view that it was more important to preserve the wellbeing of the family than to afford economic revenge or compensation to a child suing its parents.

1468   Dr Thomas Weihs, a psychiatric and medical consultant to the Camphill-Rudolf Steiner-Schools for children in need of special care, said in written evidence that it was not helpful to suggest a cause of action where there was injury to the foetus. He continued:

'There can be no doubt that for a child to sue his mother or father would prove detrimental to the child's own moral development and would seriously impair not only his relationship to his parents, but theirs to him. Parents would begin to regard their handicapped children as potential enemies, and parental love and support, vital to all children but still more to the handicapped, would be exposed to more untenable strain than is already the case today . . . It seems to me that true and effective advancement lies in helping people to achieve fortitude and responsibility in the face of any harm they may have inadvertently done to their children and that the intrusion of monetary compensation into the most intimate and complex of human relationships is in principle an avoidance of primary issues.'

1469   The Scottish Law Commission have commented:

' . . . there has been a marked trend in recent years in favour of permitting actions between parties who are closely related to each other . . . The question whether the trend is sound or whether it ought to be reversed in certain limited fields, or even more generally, is one which in our opinion would involve an investigation going well beyond the present reference and which, because of the possible effects on well-settled principles of law in a number of different fields, as well as the important social implications involved, would make wide consultation essential.'

1470 It can be argued that, as a child retains full right of action against its parents in respect of any injury inflicted after birth, he should be able to sue either or both parents in respect of ante-natal injury.

1471 We believe, however, that the social argument which has impressed so many of our witnesses should prevail. The argument is particularly strong in the case of the mother, but the danger of disrupting family life applies also to the father. We turn in the next paragraph to possible exceptions; but by a majority, **we recommend** that, subject to the recommendation in the next paragraph, a child should not have a right of action for damages against either parent for ante-natal injury.

1472 The Act of 1976, although generally providing immunity for the mother from liability in respect of the child's ante-natal injuries, creates an exception in the case of the injuries having been caused by the mother's negligence in driving a motor vehicle. If this exception is to continue, we think it should be widened to apply to the father as well as the mother and to any activity for which insurance is compulsory. The advantage of the exception is that it enables the family to obtain compensation from the insurers. There is a question whether this advantage outweighs the disadvantage of a parent being held responsible for the child's injury and resulting deformity. We believe that the exception does not have much practical importance, because the foetus in the womb is so well protected that any impact injury is rare. We are divided in opinion whether the exception should be continued or not. By a narrow majority we have decided in favour of continuance and its extension to other compulsory insurance situations. By a majority, **we recommend** that a child should have a right of action for damages against either parent for ante-natal injury arising from any activity for which insurance is compulsory.

Contributory negligence
1473 Under section 1(7) of the Act of 1976 contributory negligence of a parent could be used as a partial defence diminishing the extent of the defendant's liability. The accusation would be damaging if made against either parent, but especially if made against the mother. It would bring into open court matters with which the mother could be reproached by the child when he grew up. It produces a weapon for a vindictive husband or other member of the family. A mother's conduct during pregnancy would have to be investigated. Smoking and drug taking by the mother could affect her unborn child. Many pregnant women take medicines which are not prescribed, or which they have been warned to stop taking.

1474 Intimate details concerning the birth of the child could be made public, for example, that the father (who might not be the mother's husband) was syphilitic, or that the parents were advised by a genetic counsellor that any child conceived might be born defective.

1475 In view of the social objections we see to an action taken against the mother, it would seem strange to allow the same sort of situation to come in by a side door through contributory negligence.

1476 We note the Law Commission's view that if the defence were not available it would be unfair to tortfeasors and their insurers. But this is only one element in the situation and against this has to be weighed the objections to involving either parent in the court action. We do not think it logical to accept the arguments in the one case and not in the other.

1477 We think, therefore, that the new concept of a parent's contributory negligence diminishing the extent of the defendant's liability to the child is undesirable and **we recommend** that section 1(7) of the Congenital Disabilities (Civil Liability) Act 1976 should be repealed. We recognise that this deals with only part of the problem. If a defendant wishes to contend in his defence that the ante-natal injury was caused solely by the fault of a parent and therefore not at all by any fault of the defendant, he must be free to do so. Such a contention would increase the costs of the action and a defendant would be unlikely to rely on it unless he was advised that it had a good chance of success.

Pre-conception injury

1478 The 1976 Act provides that:

'In the case of an occurrence preceding the time of conception, the defendant is not answerable to the child if at the time either or both of the parents knew the risk of their child being born disabled (that is to say, the particular risk created by the occurrence), but should it be the child's father who is the defendant, this subsection does not apply if he knew of the risk and the mother did not.'

1479 This follows the recommendation of the Law Commission, who thought that the child should have a remedy, if born disabled as a result of some tortious injury suffered by its mother or father before conception. Examples they quoted were a physical injury to a woman's pelvis causing injury to the child subsequently conceived and born, and radiation which might cause gene mutations. The limitation which they suggested on the range of actions which might be possible followed a suggestion by the Bar Council. This was that if the parents knew or ought to have known at the time of conception that 'because of something which has happened to one of them previously there is a risk that a child born of the intercourse will be disabled' this knowledge could properly be held to break the chain of causation between the act or omission and the injury.

1480 In Scotland, liability would be incurred whether the wrongful act occurred before or after conception.

1481 Any pre-conception injury caused by a parent (for example, through one of them being infected with syphilis) would be excluded under our proposal that neither parent should be capable of being sued. As far as other persons are concerned, the inclusion of pre-conception injury, without qualification, was recommended by a few of our witnesses, but a majority, including most medical witnesses, were against it.

1482 On balance, we accept the Law Commission's reasoning and **we recommend** that there should be no change in the provisions of the Congenital Disabilities (Civil Liability) Act 1976 relating to pre-conception injury, beyond the removal of the father as a potential defendant.

1483 We think it desirable to achieve uniformity on this matter in the United Kingdom. **We recommend** that liability for pre-conception injury should be limited in Scotland to the same extent as in the rest of the United Kingdom.

Damages for loss of expectation of life

1484 Under the 1976 Act, no damages for loss of expectation of life are available unless the child lived at least 48 hours. This provision has been criticised because, in many cases which are hopeless, life may often be maintained by artificial means beyond 48 hours. If, however, the recommendations we make elsewhere about damages under this head are accepted, there would be no claim, since we are suggesting that damages for loss of expectation of life should be abolished. This would mean a consequential amendment to the 1976 Act.

Wrongful life

1485 The Law Commission considered that there should be no liability for 'wrongful life', that is, where the child has suffered harm from being born and it would have been better for it not to have been born at all. The weight of the evidence we have received supports the Law Commission's recommendation. The Mothers' Union said that, if actions were allowed, a doctor would be obliged to urge a woman to have an abortion if there was the slightest chance that her child would be born defective.

1486 We agree with the Law Commission and **we recommend** that there should be no cause of action for damages for 'wrongful life'.

Ante-natal injury and compensation

1487 The question of tort damages is a minor part of compensation for ante-natal injury and some of us feel that the tort action for ante-natal injury should disappear altogether. We found the legal problems intriguing but in tracing these intricate pathways, which sometimes verged on the metaphysical, we think it is possible to lose sight of the real problem. There are children deprived of normal limbs, of their mental faculties, of the ability to behave like other children and to grow up and work and play like others. We think that it is right to consider their position as part of the problem of all children who are injured whether before or after birth. This we do in our next chapter.

CHAPTER 27

Children

1488　In considering ante-natal injury, we found that the cause of such injury could rarely be established with certainty. There are some 90,000 severely handicapped children whose condition is due to congenital disability, but only those whose condition is caused by injury before or at birth are within our terms of reference. These children cannot be distinguished from those whose condition is caused by genetic abnormality or disease, and it is simply not feasible to devise a separate scheme of compensation for the children who are within our terms of reference. The question is whether provision should be made for none or for all.

1489　Recent legislation and practice relating to the compensation and care of severely handicapped children suggest that Government policy is based on the principle that they are to be treated alike, without regard to the cause of their condition. We decided to follow suit. It would not be sensible to allow the constraints of our terms of reference to prevent us from seeking the right solution. We are fortified in this belief by Mr Peter Archer MP, the Solicitor General, who wound up the Second Reading debate on the Congenital Disabilities (Civil Liability) Bill for the Government with these words:

> 'We all hope that the Royal Commission may be able to propose some means by which all disabled children can be given the support that they need.' (Official Report (HC) 6.2.76, Vol 904, col 1643.)

1490　We have regarded as 'children' all those aged under 16 (the school leaving age) and those under 19 who are undergoing full time education. This follows the definition adopted for social security purposes. On this basis, the number of children in the United Kingdom is about 14 million.

The special position of the child

1491　Originally, the common law recognised the natural right of the parent to have custody of the child and his duty to maintain and protect him; but, during the last century, these rights and duties have been considerably modified on the principle that the welfare of the child is 'the first and paramount consideration' (Guardianship of Infants Act 1925). It is now accepted that it is sometimes necessary in the interests of the child's welfare to remove him from parental custody.

1492　This change of attitude is reflected in the United Nations Declaration of the Rights of the Child which was adopted in 1959. It states, '. . . the child by

312

reason of his physical and mental immaturity, needs special safeguards and care, including appropriate legal protection, before as well as after birth . . . the best interests of the child shall be the paramount consideration'.

1493   In looking at the problems affecting children, the first question we considered was whether the provision for compensating a child who had suffered injury should differ from the provision for an adult who had suffered a similar injury.

1494   In theory, a child has the same opportunities of seeking tort compensation as does an adult, although he must do so through an adult. In England, Wales and Northern Ireland this adult is called his 'next friend' and in Scotland his tutor or, at a later age, curator. If the child's father is alive, he will fulfil the function. In practice, few children seek tort compensation. According to our survey about one per cent of children injured after birth, as compared with about seven per cent of injured adults, obtain any reparation or payment through tort. Recent awards of damages to children suffering permanent severe mental or physical handicap as a result of accidental injury have been between £60,000 and £125,000.

1495   We received evidence from a number of witnesses about children injured in road accidents. The National Society for the Prevention of Cruelty to Children said that children often failed to recover damages following street accidents where the cause could not be established. There was often no competent or unbiased adult witness, and the child might be incapable of giving an account of the accident himself.

1496   In chapter 18 on road injuries we have made two recommendations relating particularly to children. We have made proposals for compensation for child road accident victims under our suggested no-fault scheme; and we have suggested that the defence of contributory negligence should not be available in an action where the plaintiff is a child who was under the age of 12 at the time of the injury.

1497   Two witnesses suggested that children injured at school should be entitled to compensation under a scheme similar to the industrial injuries scheme. In the Federal Republic of Germany, injuries suffered at kindergarten or school, or on the way to or from kindergarten or school, have been brought within the work injuries scheme. But we do not consider that children injured at school are in a disadvantageous position when compared with children injured elsewhere, and we see no reason to make special provision.

1498   We have studied the Report of the Court Committee – 'Fit for the Future' – which was published in December 1976 (Report of the Committee on Child Health Services, Cmd 6684). The Committee in recommending improvements in the health services for children state:

'. . . we want to see a child and family centred service; in which skilled help is readily available and accessible; which is integrated in as much as it sees the child as a whole, and as a continuously developing person. We want to

313

see a service which ensures that this paediatric skill and knowledge are applied in the care of every child whatever his age or disability, and wherever he lives, and we want a service which is increasingly orientated to prevention.'

1499 Implementation of the recommendations of the Committee should reduce the number of children injured and therefore the need for compensation; but this would require many more paediatricians, child health nurses and child health visitors, and the programme would take a long time to implement. The Committee made an estimate of 15 to 20 years. Even if the programme were implemented and its aims achieved, the problem of what to do with those children who were injured or disabled, would still remain.

What should be done ?

1500 We are naturally sympathetic to the problems of any physically injured child. But we do not believe it to be practicable for compensation to be provided for all the hundreds of thousands of injuries to children which occur every year. It seems to us that the important problem is that of helping severely handicapped children. Their needs are much the greatest, and our recommendations are directed towards their problems.

Severely handicapped children

1501 We define the term 'severely handicapped child' as a child suffering from a long term mental or physical handicap (but not necessarily a permanent one) which causes the child's performance or development to fall far below those of other children of the same age. We recognise that a severely handicapped child is a member of a severely handicapped family, and this family is bound to be in need of additional support.

1502 In oral evidence to us, the Royal College of Physicians said that support should be provided for the family as a whole, including possibly the provision or adaptation of a house; this should be done regardless of fault. The British Paediatric Association said that the need was for a system of comprehensive and universal assistance, including the provision of services on both a community and an individual basis, and also financial assistance. The Association said that services were probably best provided by local authorities, but that the need for financial help would still exist even if local authority services for the handicapped child were as good as the Association would like them to be. The National Society for the Prevention of Cruelty to Children supported the view that there should be comprehensive services provided for all children irrespective of the cause of injury.

1503 The forms of support required cover a wide range. They can include special needs such as wheelchairs, adaptations to houses, extra clothing and bedding, and also needs such as holidays and portable television and radio sets.

Support available now

1504 The support available for severely handicapped children takes various forms. Central government provides periodic payments in the form of attendance allowance and mobility allowance; local authorities provide services and lump sums for home conversions; and the Family Fund provides additional assistance. Other voluntary organisations provide a significant level of support for handi-capped children. The activities of many such organisations are co-ordinated through the work of the Voluntary Council for Handicapped Children.

Attendance allowance
1505   Attendance allowance is a tax free allowance for adults and children aged two or over who are severely disabled and require the presence of an adult to a far greater extent than is normal for their age.   There are two rates of payment according to the amount of attendance required. Payments are currently being made in respect of 42,000 children, at a total cost of £22 million a year.

Mobility allowance
1506   Mobility allowance is a taxable allowance which is being progressively introduced for people who are physically unable or virtually unable to walk, and likely to remain so for at least a year. For a child, the claim is made by a parent (normally the mother). Children from age five became eligible to claim from 1 January 1977.   It is estimated that up to 20,000 children are eligible, at a gross cost of £7¼ million a year.

Local authority provision
1507   Local authority provision under the relevant legislation covers a wide range of services. In practice the amount of help given varies considerably amongst the different authorities. It includes services provided by social workers, residential care, special fostering and boarding out arrangements, adaptations to houses, aids and telephones.

1508   No reliable estimate can be given of the value of local authority services currently provided to severely handicapped children, but it is probably less than £1 million a year. We have the impression that local authorities, in distributing their limited resources, tend not to give high priority to provision for severely handicapped children. We appreciate that, at a time of severe financial restraint, the ordering of priorities poses complex and sometimes painful choices. Handi-capped children are often being cared for by their parents, whereas many disabled adults have no such care. It has been suggested to us by local authority representatives themselves that the children perhaps suffer from the lack of a powerful lobby to support them and from the lack of a definition by central government of what their normal needs are.

Family Fund
1509   The Family Fund was set up by the Government at the beginning of 1973 following an undertaking given in Parliament in November 1972 during a debate on the thalidomide compensation issue. Initially, £3 million was made available to complement the provision of services and cash benefits from both statutory and voluntary sources and so to help in relieving stress on families having the care of a child with a severe congenital disability. The Joseph Rowntree Memorial Trust, an independent charitable body, agreed to assume responsi-bility for the Fund.

1510   At the end of 1974, the requirement that the disability should be congenital was removed. Any family with a severely handicapped child under the age of 16 became eligible for help. The Fund was allotted a further £3 million for 1974, £2·5 million for 1976 and £1·8 million a year for 1977 and 1978. The help given includes assistance with transport problems, equipment for dealing with laundry, help with family holidays and unusual adaptations to houses of a kind not normally financed by local authorities.

1511   It was originally intended that the Fund should operate centrally and provide services complementing those of the local authorities. In practice, the Fund was obliged to employ its own social workers in some areas, and we were told that some local authorities tended to regard the Fund as a substitute for their own activities.

The value of the services
1512   There is no doubt that much help can be given to the families of handicapped children, in cash or in services, by central government, local authorities, the Family Fund and voluntary organisations. We were able to see extracts from some of the letters received by the Family Fund. The following examples illustrate the value of such help to the families concerned. A mother of three children wrote to express thanks for a holiday saying:

'. . . how much [she] enjoyed her holiday. Perhaps you will also be interested to know that [she] had no epileptic fits during our holiday, and has maintained this improvement, so that her drugs have been drastically reduced. The holiday proved of great value for all of us, because we all relaxed together, and [her] joy was infectious.'

Another family, with two sons suffering from muscular dystrophy, were given a grant to buy a van in which the whole family could travel with the wheelchairs. Their letter said:

'Since we have had the van, we have been able to visit many places which are of interest to the boys. These places include the seaside, zoos and many other places. My wife and I have also gained much pleasure just from seeing the happiness on the boys' faces when we go out.'

Ignorance of the services available
1513   There is a wide variety of help available. In spite of the efforts made to distribute information through, for example, citizens advice bureaux and local radio, we are told that many parents are unaware of the services available and do not know how to claim or to whom to apply. This is an aspect of the wider problem of the 'take up' of benefits and services, a problem well recognised by those who administer such provision and probably in part attributable to the complexity of the present arrangements.

Number of severely handicapped children
1514   An estimate made at York University of the number of children living at home who are qualified to receive help from the Family Fund, and whose

condition is believed to approximate to our definition of a severely handicapped child, is some 100,000.[13] We have no way of knowing whether this number is likely to increase or diminish, and we have assumed that it will remain at about the same level for the foreseeable future.

1515   The figure of 100,000 may be divided into three main groups.

1516   The first, and by far the largest, is a group of some 90,000 children suffering from congenital disability. This disability may be due to ante-natal injury, inheritance of genetic abnormality or to birth injury or disease; but the medical evidence we have received is to the effect that the cause of the handicap can seldom be ascertained.

1517   Medical developments can serve to increase or reduce the numbers of children surviving with handicaps. On the one hand it has become increasingly possible to prolong the lives of children born with defects. On the other hand many defects can be corrected, or the sufferer enabled to lead a substantially normal life; where this cannot be done, doctors are increasingly having misgivings about prolonging life at any cost. An example which appears to demonstrate the effect of medical practice on the numbers of survivors is given in a study of spina bifida.[14] It shows that the percentage of children born with spina bifida who were alive at 12 months rose from 16 per cent in 1954 to 70 per cent in 1969, as the use of techniques for prolonging their lives became more common. Thereafter, the proportion declined to 59 per cent in 1972, following a change in medical and public opinion.

1518   In recent years, there has been a fall in the birth rate among women over 40, who are at particular risk of bearing handicapped children. At the same time facilities have become more generally available for genetic counselling and ante-natal diagnosis followed by termination of pregnancy where foetal abnormality is detected. The Court Committee have recommended an expansion of these facilities. Nevertheless we must plan on the basis that considerable numbers of children will continue to be born with severe defects.

1519   The second group within the 100,000 severely handicapped children consists of some 1,000–2,000 children who are disabled through post-natal injury and suffer from prolonged or permanent handicap. This group includes children injured on the road or in accidents in the playground or at home; vaccine damaged children; and those handicapped as a result of assault.

1520   The third group consists of some 8,000 children who have suffered from disabling diseases acquired after birth, such as meningitis, leukaemia and epilepsy. These children can be as severely handicapped as those in the other groups. We think that their needs should be covered in the same way.

Future action

1521   Even when account is taken of all the existing forms of support, a gap remains. Obviously the degree of need varies from family to family, but it is possible to express it as an average. The need arises at about the child's second birthday when the extent of the handicap generally becomes fully apparent.

1522   Research at York University suggests that, after allowing for all available support, the extra cost to a family of looking after a severely handicapped child was on average about £3 a week at 1975 levels.[15] We understand that later research has identified some items previously omitted. Allowing also for the fall in the value of money, we think that there is justification for an average extra provision of £4 a week (at January 1977 levels) from age two for a severely handicapped child. This is the measure of the need. We discuss below three possible ways in which it might be met.

1523   First, a permanent and strengthened organisation on the lines of the Family Fund could be established. We do not think that this would be appropriate. Such an organisation would have to be bigger than that now existing, and would be likely to duplicate much of the work of the social services departments of local authorities.

1524   Secondly, the money available to local authorities might be increased through the rate support grant. We do not think that this would be the right answer, in view of the difficulties under this system of earmarking a sum specifically for the needs of severely handicapped children. There is a related point which we think should be pursued. We are aware of the difficulties which local authorities are experiencing in implementing the present statutory objectives. We hope that, despite restraint on public expenditure, they will be enabled within the next few years to develop much more fully their services to the handicapped and will be encouraged to accord handicapped children a higher priority than heretofore.

A new allowance
1525   The third possibility, which is the one we favour, is the provision of a disability income, in the form of a new non-taxable allowance of £4 a week from age two. For preference, this allowance should be paid to the mother as an addition to child benefit. The allowance would not be a substitute for local authority services; but, as against the first two possibilities we have described, it would have the advantage of putting more money into the hands of the parent or guardian of the severely handicapped child. The allowance should cease when the child became eligible for non-contributory invalidity pension at age 16, or at age 19 if receiving full time education.

1526   We envisage that the assessment of what constituted severe handicap in order to qualify for the new allowance would not depend solely on medical certification by doctors, but should include assessment by other members of the health care professions. We think that DHSS should administer the benefit, and lay down the detailed procedures. It is important that there should be no avoidable delay in determining entitlement to this benefit.

1527   As with attendance allowance and mobility allowance, parents should be given, and should be made aware of, an appeal procedure if they are refused the allowance, whether it be appeal to a local tribunal or appeal to a medical board. The allowance should be reviewed as the child grows as there may be some improvement in his condition, and this review should also be subject to appeal. Again it would be for DHSS to consider the arrangements in detail.

1528   If DHSS administers the allowance we would hope that the Department would inform the parents that the local authority social services departments could be approached concerning the provision of services.

1529   As to the children who should qualify for the new allowance, we have already indicated that there should be no distinction between the different causes of handicap. We think also that it would be invidious to have an artificial distinction between children who become handicapped after a certain date and those who are already handicapped. We hope therefore that the Government will consider all severely handicapped children as eligible. On this basis the cost of the allowance would be some £15 million a year, plus administration costs of £2 million a year.

1530   We can find no practicable alternative to putting the cost directly on the Exchequer. The causes of injury to children are diverse, and many of them unknown. There is no obvious source of finance comparable with those we are suggesting for work and road accidents.

1531   Accordingly **we recommend** that there should be a new non-taxable disability income of £4 a week for all severely handicapped children, payable from age two as an addition to child benefit, financed by the Exchequer and administered by the Department of Health and Social Security.

Extending mobility allowance
1532   The new allowance is the main new form of support we recommend, but we have some additional proposals.

1533   Mobility allowance is now payable from age five. We are aware of the argument, referred to by the Working Party on Mobility Allowance set up by the Central Council for the Disabled, that the need for mobility assistance for the disabled child does not assume major proportions until the child reaches school age. But it seems to us that there are many severely handicapped children whose parents need help from the time their child, had it been normal, could have been expected to walk. The demands of such a child on its mother can be very great. **We recommend** that mobility allowance should be payable from age two. This would cost about £1 million a year.

1534   We note that the conditions of eligibility for the allowance exclude substantial numbers of children with serious mobility problems, for example, those with physical handicaps such as uncontrolled epilepsy, severe asthma or cystic fibrosis; those who are blind and deaf; and overactive mentally handicapped children, who require constant supervision. But we understand too that recent decisions on the award of mobility allowance are in effect extending entitlement to it. **We recommend** that the conditions of eligibility for mobility allowance should be reviewed so as to help those children who may be technically mobile, but whose mobility is subject to special difficulties.

Future of tort
1535   We consider that, even if compensation is available to all severely handicapped children on the lines proposed, it should still be possible to bring

tort actions for post-natal injury (subject to the changes we are recommending for offsetting social security benefits). It would probably be only infrequently that it could be established that the child's condition was due to negligence, but we see no reason to withhold from children the right to seek tort damages which we are recommending for adults.

CHAPTER 28

Occupiers

1536 Category d of our terms of reference refers to personal injury suffered by any person 'on premises belonging to or occupied by another'. These words, if understood literally, would cover nearly all injuries at work and also most injuries by motor vehicles, since these occur on highways and the surface of a highway is usually vested in a highway authority. But to avoid duplication with other categories, we have interpreted Category d as referring to injuries which not only happen to occur on somebody else's premises but also have, or might be alleged to have, resulted from the state of the premises or from the use of the premises. The first part of this chapter is mainly concerned with occupiers' liability, and the second part with liability in respect of highways.

1537 We estimate that in 1973 there were about 190,000 injuries coming within Category d as we have interpreted it. About 100,000 of these were on public highways.

Occupiers' liability – England, Wales and Northern Ireland
The law before 1957
1538 The basic pattern of the law relating to occupiers' liability was laid down in a number of judicial decisions at a time when the wide general principle of liability for negligence had not been fully developed. Persons entering other persons' premises were divided into classes, and the extent of the occupier's duty to a particular entrant depended on the class to which the entrant belonged. One class was of persons entering in pursuance of a contract. The duty of the occupier was governed by the express or implied terms of the contract. In its most stringent form, it could amount to a warranty that the premises were as safe for the purposes contemplated by the contract as reasonable care and skill could make them. Entrants of another class were known as 'invitees'. This word was used in a special sense covering persons entering the premises for a purpose in which the occupier had a material interest, whether or not an actual invitation had been given. The occupier's duty to an invitee was to use reasonable care to prevent damage from unusual danger of which the occupier knew or ought to have known. There was a third class of entrants known as 'licensees'. They were persons entering with express or implied permission from the occupier but for purposes beneficial to them and not of material interest to him. A licensee had to take the premises as he found them, except that if the occupier knew of a concealed danger it was his duty to give warning of it to the licensee.

1539   In addition, there were the unlawful entrants, the trespassers, forming a fourth class. The civil law took a severe view of trespassing. The occupier did not owe to the trespasser any general duty of care, and would not be liable to him except for 'some act done with deliberate intention of doing harm to the trespasser or at least some act done with reckless disregard of the presence of the trespasser' (*Robert Addie & Sons (Collieries) Ltd* v. *Dumbreck* [1929] A.C. 358, 1929 S.C. (H.L.) 51).

The Occupiers' Liability Act 1957
1540   The rigidity of the different degrees of duty owed by an occupier towards different classes of visitor caused uneasiness. In 1952, the Lord Chancellor invited the Law Reform Committee to consider whether the law in England and Wales needed to be improved, simplified or amended. The Committee's report in 1954 (Cmd 9305) recommended that the distinction between invitees and licensees should be abolished, but did not recommend any change as regards trespassers. The proposals in this report led to the Occupiers' Liability Act 1957, which applies to England and Wales. Legislation modelled substantially on this Act applies in Northern Ireland – the Occupiers' Liability Act (Northern Ireland) 1957.

1541   The Occupiers' Liability Act 1957 regulates the duty which an occupier of premises owes to his 'visitors' in respect of dangers due to the state of the premises or to things done or omitted to be done on them. 'Visitors' are the persons who would at common law have been treated as invitees or licensees. The duty owed by the occupier to any of his visitors is the 'common duty of care', and that is defined as 'a duty to take such care as in all the circumstances of the case is reasonable to see that the visitor will be reasonably safe in using the premises for the purposes for which he is invited or permitted by the occupier to be there'. A person occupying or having control over any fixed or movable structure, including any vessel, vehicle or aircraft, owes in effect the same common duty of care to those who enter the structure as to visitors to other premises. The distinction between invitees and licensees has become obsolete.

1542   Under the Act there are two other classes of persons to whom the occupier owes the common duty of care in addition to the class of 'visitors'. The first is 'persons who enter premises for any purpose in the exercise of a right conferred by law'. There is doubt as to the ambit of this class, but at any rate it includes persons exercising statutory rights to entry, for instance public utility officials acting under the Rights of Entry (Gas and Electricity Boards) Act 1954. This class is considered to exclude persons exercising public or private rights of way. Secondly, the occupier owes the common duty of care to a person entering in pursuance of a contract, unless the contract provides otherwise; and, under the Unfair Contract Terms Act 1977, the occupier will not be able to exclude or restrict his liability in respect of business premises.

1543   The 1957 Act excludes from the class of 'visitors' those who may be called 'authorised ramblers' (that is to say persons entering on land in exercise of rights conferred by virtue of an access agreement or order under the National

Parks and Access to the Countryside Act 1949). The Act did not deal with the occupier's duty to trespassers, nor with his duty to persons entering in exercise of a public or private right of way.

Trespassers
1544   For trespassers, the common law rule as formulated in *Addie* v. *Dumbreck* continued to limit the occupier's duty to one of abstaining from 'some act done with deliberate intention of doing harm to the trespasser or at least some act done with reckless disregard of the presence of the trespasser'. The rule operated unfairly in the case of child trespassers, who might stray on to premises dangerous for them either in all innocence, or at any rate without adequate appreciation of the dangers; and was modified by judicial action of the House of Lords in *British Railways Board* v. *Herrington* [1972] A.C. 877.

1545   That was a case of a child trespasser, who, from a place open to the public and used as a playground, made his way over a broken down railway fence on to the electrified line and suffered severe injury. The fence had been in a dilapidated condition for a considerable time, and there was an unofficial short cut over the fence, over the line, and through a hole in the fence on the other side of the line. Children had been seen on the relevant sector of the line two months before, but no action had been taken to repair the fence. It was held that the claim of the injured child against the British Railways Board for damages for negligence must succeed and that the rule laid down in *Addie* v. *Dumbreck* must be modified. Separate opinions were however given by the five judicial members of the House of Lords who heard the case, and doubts were afterwards expressed as to the precise nature of the modified duty now falling on the occupier. One suggestion was that it was a duty of common humanity rather than reasonable care. If so, what did common humanity require? Consequently, in April 1972, the Lord Chancellor asked the Law Commission 'to consider in the light of the decision of the House of Lords in *British Railways Board* v. *Herrington* the law relating to liability for damage or injury suffered by trespassers'.

The Law Commission report
1546   The Law Commission made their report in 1976 (Law Com No 75, Cmnd 6428). They annexed a draft Bill which would supplement the Occupiers Liability Act 1957, but not repeal it. The report and the draft Bill were primarily concerned with trespassers, but the opportunity was taken to deal with 'uninvited entrants', that is the three classes of persons who were not dealt with in the Act of 1957. These classes were trespassers; those whom we have called 'authorised ramblers'; and persons exercising a private right of way.

1547   Clause 2 of the draft Bill provides that:
'(1) An occupier of premises owes a duty to an uninvited entrant upon the premises in respect of a danger if, but only if, the danger is one against which, in all the circumstances of the case, the occupier can reasonably be expected to offer him some protection.

'(2) The duty owed by an occupier in accordance with subsection (1) above is a duty to take such care as is reasonable in all the circumstances of the case to see that the entrant does not suffer personal injury or death by reason of the danger.'

1548   In our view, that is a satisfactory provision. Under it, the particular occupier would not necessarily owe to the particular trespasser any duty at all. The court would have to consider whether there was some danger against which the occupier could reasonably be expected to offer some protection to the trespasser; and, if so, whether the occupier had failed to take such care as was reasonable. If the injured trespasser had come to steal the farmer's turkeys, he would have difficulty in satisfying the court on these issues. Nuisance and loss are caused to farmers by urban trespassers who come in their cars and leave gates open, or allow their dogs to chase the farm animals, or leave litter which is dangerous to the farm animals. Much of the evidence we received expressed anxiety about increasing the standard of care towards trespassers, although some witnesses favoured an increase in the standard of care towards small children. The flexible formula proposed by the Law Commission in their draft Bill would enable the courts to do justice according to the facts of the particular case. The discretion given to the courts would be wide, just as it is under the Act of 1957, but a wide discretion is needed because of the variety of situations which can arise.

1549   The Bill would cover authorised ramblers. As they come to walk about in open country, they cannot complain of the natural hazards and usual activities which may be encountered in open country, but there may be unexpected or concealed dangers against which the occupier might reasonably be expected to afford them some protection. Similarly, the person exercising a private right of way is not entitled to have the way kept in good repair by the owner or occupier of the 'servient tenement' (the land over which the way runs), but, if there is some special danger, some protection against it may be reasonably required.

1550   **We recommend** that, for England and Wales, the law laid down in the Occupiers' Liability Act 1957 should be supplemented by enactment of the Law Commission's proposals for 'uninvited entrants'; and that similar steps should be taken in Northern Ireland.

1551   As to contract terms and notices excluding or restricting occupiers' liability, the Law Commission proposed that a test of reasonableness should be applied. Clause 3(2) of their Bill provides that 'any such contract term or notice is ineffective to the extent that it is shown that, in all the circumstances of the case, it would not be fair or reasonable to allow reliance on it'. This proposal has now been superseded, however, insofar as under the Unfair Contract Terms Act 1977 liability for death or personal injury on business premises cannot be excluded or restricted.

Other provisions
1552   In some special situations, the owner of premises may have a liability in tort for injuries caused by the defective condition of the premises. If he is

the owner of a block of flats, and retains control of the entrance and staircase and other parts used in common by the tenants and their families and guests or callers, he is the occupier and they are his 'visitors', and he owes to them the common duty of care in respect of the parts which he controls. An owner letting or selling premises may incur liability under the Defective Premises Act 1972. If an owner 'lets a nuisance', he may at common law be liable to a person injured soon afterwards by the nuisance. We see no need for any change.

Occupiers' liability – Scotland
The law before 1960
1553   Until 1929, the law in Scotland relating to occupiers' liability was based on the general principle of *culpa* (fault). No rigid legal categorisation of persons entering premises was known to Scots law. Reasonable care was required to be taken for the safety of a person entering on premises, and what was reasonable in any given case might be affected by the circumstances in which the person had entered (including his right, or absence of it, to be there). Under English law, no duty of care was owed to a person classified as a trespasser; but under Scots law, trespass, which in Scotland is regarded more as a popular than as a legal term, was not by itself considered to constitute a bar to an action in delict.

1554   With the House of Lords decision in the case of *Addie* v. *Dumbreck*, the rigidity of the English categories and restrictions relating to persons entering on premises was held to overlay the system which had hitherto prevailed in Scotland. The categories of invitee, licensee and trespasser had to be recognised and the standard of care appropriate to each, as laid down by the English courts, had to be applied by the Scottish courts to the class or category in question. In practice, the Scottish courts attempted to restrict the application of these rules as far as possible, but, where they were applicable, the primary task of the courts became that of ascertaining the category to which the injured person belonged. Then the nature and extent of the duty of care (if any) owed to him flowed from his status as 'invitee', 'licensee' or 'trespasser'.

The Occupiers' Liability (Scotland) Act 1960
1555   The growing resistance to the inconvenience presented by the introduction of the English rules of occupiers' liability into the law of reparation in Scotland was given recognition by the first report of the Law Reform Committee for Scotland in 1957 (Cmnd 88). It recommended that fault should be restored as the basis of liability in Scotland, irrespective of the lawful or unlawful nature of the entry on to the premises in question. This recommendation was implemented by the Occupiers' Liability (Scotland) Act 1960, which has broadly reinstated the former common law rule of *culpa* as the basis of occupiers' liability under Scots law. The rule provides for the duty of care to be shown by occupiers of premises, including such property as the common stairs of tenement buildings. The Act also extends the rule to persons having control of fixed or movable structures such as vessels, vehicles or aircraft, and to property damage as well as personal injury.

1556 The 1960 Act requires the occupier to show any person entering the premises such care as in all the circumstances of the case is reasonable: no distinction is made between trespassers and lawful visitors. What is required in order to discharge a duty towards others varies according to the circumstances. An occupier may not be expected to be as diligent in pursuit of the welfare of trespassers as he would of those whom he had invited or permitted to come on to his land. Under section 16(1) of the Unfair Contract Terms Act 1977, an occupier of business premises in Scotland will, as in England, be prevented from relying on an exemption clause in a contract so as to avoid liability which would attach to him as occupier of those premises where death or injury was caused to any person.

1557 **We recommend** that there should be no change in the law governing occupiers' liability in Scotland. Enactment of the Bill proposed by the Law Commission would in effect bring English law into line with Scots law as it stands under the Act of 1960.

Public rights of way – England, Wales and Northern Ireland
The liability of highway authorities
1558 In England and Wales, public highways (that is, streets or roads or paths over which the public have a right of passage) are maintainable at the public expense under section 38 of the Highways Act 1959. Formerly, the highway authority was liable only for injuries caused by 'misfeasance' (positively doing something which made the highway unsafe) and not for 'non-feasance' (merely leaving the highway unrepaired even if it becomes dangerous). But now, under the Highways (Miscellaneous Provisions) Act 1961, there can be liability for injury caused by non-feasance. The position is similar in Northern Ireland – under the Roads (Liability of Road Authorities for Neglect) Act (Northern Ireland) 1966.

1559 Section 1(2) of the 1961 Act provides that, 'In an action against a highway authority in respect of damage resulting from their failure to maintain a highway maintainable at the public expense, it shall be a defence . . . to prove that the authority had taken such care as in all the circumstances was reasonably required to secure that the part of the highway to which the action relates was not dangerous for traffic'. In effect, if the injured plaintiff in an action against a highway authority proves that his injury was due to non-repair of a highway, the highway authority then has the burden of proving that they took such care as was reasonably required. In doing that, they are assisted by subsection (3) which specifies (rather favourably for the authority) certain matters to which the court should have regard in deciding whether the authority took such care as was reasonably required.

Unadopted highways
1560 The other kind of public highway is the 'unadopted' path or road or street which the owner of the subjacent soil or his predecessor has impliedly dedicated as a public highway by prolonged acquiescence in the use of it by the public. There is no statutory provision imposing on anyone a duty to keep

such a highway in good repair or in a safe condition, and it is not plain that there is any such duty at common law. The owner of the subjacent soil cannot reasonably be treated as the occupier of the surface used as a public highway because he has no power to exclude others from it and no more right to use it than anyone else has. The Law Commission said in their report that it appeared that there was a gap in English law, in that nobody was liable to a person injured by the defective condition of an unadopted public highway.

1561   We agree that there is a gap in the law. In *Greenhalgh* v. *British Railways Board* [1969] 2 Q.B. 286, it was held that a person exercising a public right of way was not a 'visitor' for the purpose of the 1957 Act, as he would not have been an invitee or licensee at common law, and that he therefore had no claim for damages. As the Law Commission pointed out, this gap results in the anomaly that, whereas there is a duty of care towards trespassers, there is no such duty towards certain lawful entrants.

1562   We could find no just and effective way of meeting this problem. It is the more difficult in that it extends beyond unadopted roads to public footpaths, sometimes over necessarily hazardous country. It would be a hardship if the person who has allowed the public to walk or ride or drive over his land were rewarded for his generosity by having the burden of repair imposed on him. He might well have insufficient resources for meeting the liability unless he was insured, and compulsory insurance would be an excessive requirement owing to the expense and the difficulty of enforcement. On the other hand, if a liability were imposed on the highway authority or the local authority, they would need to inspect all the unadopted public highways in their areas and to remove any danger disclosed by the inspection, and for that purpose they would need power to interfere with the subjacent soil. These public highways would virtually become repairable at public expense. That would be a major step. We should not feel justified in recommending it.

Public rights of way – Scotland

1563   In Scotland, there is no statutory provision governing the liability of highway authorities in respect of persons injured as a result of using public highways, and the law of delict therefore applies. Liability is dependent on possession and control, which are not necessarily coincidental with ownership. Statutory responsibility for the maintenance of certain roads is given to the appropriate highway authorities, but Scots law has no distinction between 'misfeasance' and 'non-feasance', and the onus of proof is on the claimant to show that the road authority has been negligent in any particular case.

1564   As regards roads which have not been taken over by the appropriate roads authority, liability will again depend on possession and control, but the title deeds to the subjacent soil will be highly influential in allocating responsibility. The problem illustrated by the *Greenhalgh* case would not arise in Scotland. Under the Occupiers' Liability (Scotland) Act 1960, the occupier owes such duty of care as is reasonable in the circumstances to anyone entering on the premises; and accordingly the starting point of the court's enquiry would be, not whether the entrant could be classified as a 'visitor', but whether the occupier had shown such care as was reasonable to see that the entrant should not suffer injury. The result in another *Greenhalgh* case might turn out to be the same in Scotland as in England. But the underlying principles on which it was based would be different.

Alternative compensation provisions

1565   We have considered whether no-fault compensation or strict liability should be introduced into this branch of the law.

No-fault

1566   We concluded that a no-fault scheme would not be appropriate. No-fault compensation could be financed by a surcharge on the rates, but we think there would be complications affecting enforcement. A no-fault scheme financed by the state is another possibility, but we see no reason why the state should, at the expense of the taxpayer, provide compensation for this class of injured persons in preference to others. Injuries on other persons' premises which are attributable to the defective condition of the premises are happily not so frequent as to constitute a social problem serious enough to require special action.

Strict liability

1567   We also came to the conclusion that strict liability would not be suitable in respect of most premises. The occupation of premises is not normally an activity creating significant danger of injury to others. Special cases which do involve significant dangers and so might suitably be made the subject of strict liability are considered in chapter 31.

CHAPTER 29

Criminal

1568 Compensation for criminal injuries is now provided by criminal injuries compensation schemes set up in Great Britain in 1964 and in Northern Ireland in 1969.

The present schemes

Great Britain

1569 The scheme in Great Britain resulted from public discussion of a proposal that compensation of the victim of personal violence should be paid by society, which had failed to protect him. The late Miss Margery Fry was active in initiating this idea. In 1964, the Government, while rejecting the concept of state liability, accepted that compensation should be paid at public expense as an expression of public sympathy to the victims of violent crime. They announced a scheme which provided that compensation could be paid even where the criminal had not been found and prosecuted, and including cases where an individual had been hurt when helping the police to make an arrest. Compensation would be *ex gratia* and in the form of lump sums. The scheme, which was to be administered by a compensation board, would be experimental and non-statutory. The victim would remain free to sue the offender, but would have to repay the board any compensation received from it out of any damages he obtained from the offender.

1570 The Criminal Injuries Compensation Board, at present comprising a chairman and 13 members (all legally qualified), operates throughout Great Britain. It is financed by a grant-in-aid from public funds.

1571 To qualify for compensation under the scheme, the circumstances of the injury must either have been the subject of criminal proceedings or have been immediately notified to the police, unless the Board waives these requirements. Injuries caused by traffic offences are excluded unless there is a deliberate attempt to run the victim down.

1572 The scheme excludes offences committed against a member of the offender's family living with him at the time of the offence. The Board must be satisfied that the victim's character, way of life and conduct generally justify an award being made.

1573 Compensation for injury or death is based on common law damages, but the rate of loss of gross earnings (and, where appropriate, of earning capacity) to be taken into account is not to exceed twice the average of gross industrial earnings at the time the injury was sustained. Compensation may also be paid for non-pecuniary loss. The injury must be one for which not less than a minimum figure would be awarded. This minimum, which was originally set at £50, was increased to £150 in March 1977.

1574 There is a requirement that compensation should be reduced by the value of any entitlement to social security benefits (and analogous payments from Government funds) which accrue as a result of the injury or death to the person to whom the award is made. But no indication is given as to how the value of social security benefits is to be calculated. Compensation is also reduced by the amount of any damages awarded in civil proceedings, or compensation paid under an order made by a criminal court. No account is taken of occupational pensions where the victim is alive, but, where the victim has died, the Board is required to offset 80 per cent of any part of a pension which is payable because the injuries were sustained while the victim was on duty or performing a duty connected with his employment.

1575 The number of awards made, and the total paid out in compensation, have been increasing year by year. In the first full year, 1965/66, there were 1,164 awards, with payments amounting to about £400,000; in 1976/77 there were 13,951 awards, with payments amounting to about £9·7 million.

1576 The average level of award is now about £700. About 68 per cent of awards are below £400, and 1·5 per cent greater than £5,000. The highest award in 1976/77 was £55,250, made to a woman who had been blinded by a shotgun.

1577 The Queen's Bench Division of the High Court in England and Wales has on occasion exercised its jurisdiction by prerogative order to supervise the discharge of the Board's functions and to review awards or refusals of awards.

1578 In March 1973 the Home Secretary set up an interdepartmental working party of officials, on which there was Scottish representation, to review the working of the scheme. It has not yet published its report, but we were informed of its provisional views.

Northern Ireland
1579 Northern Ireland has a separate scheme, under the Criminal Injuries to Persons (Compensation) Act (Northern Ireland) 1968, which came into operation in 1969. The scheme was reviewed by a Northern Ireland Office working party which reported in June 1976. As a result, the scheme was amended by the Criminal Injuries (Compensation) (Northern Ireland) Order 1977, which came into effect in August 1977.

1580 The basis of the Northern Ireland scheme is much the same as in Great Britain, but the method of administration is different. Under the original scheme compensation was awarded by a county court, and the Northern Ireland Office or the applicant could appeal to a higher court. Under the 1977

Order the Secretary of State now determines the claims, but there is provision for appeal to the courts on matters of both law and fact. It is thought that this change should reduce the load on the courts.

1581   Under the original scheme, although the character of the injured person was not normally taken into account when awarding compensation, the court could have regard to any provocative or negligent behaviour by the victim and to other relevant circumstances. Under the 1977 Order, compensation is not payable to anyone who is or has been a member of an unlawful association or has been involved in an act of terrorism, unless the Secretary of State exercises a discretion to make payments where he considers it in the public interest to do so.

1582   Originally, there was a lower limit of £50 on the amount of an award, but under the 1977 Order this was increased to £150, the same as for Great Britain. Many claims have been made for 'nervous shock' – mental reaction to a crime of violence. No such claim now attracts compensation unless at least £1,000 is payable for pain, suffering and loss of amenity. Pensions and gratuities paid by the Crown or an employer are deducted in full. There is also a requirement to deduct social security benefits in full (but no guidance as to how this calculation is to be made).

1583   Over the period 1 March 1969 to 31 May 1977, 21,769 claims were resolved and about £28·3 million paid out. In the first complete year, 1969/70, the total compensation was about £132,000; in 1975/76 it was about £7·9 million and in 1976/77 about £6·3 million.

1584   The average level of award is now about £1,700. About 42 per cent of awards are below £400, and about 8 per cent greater than £5,000. Awards have been made in respect of injuries caused by terrorists which have resulted in brain damage and severe injury to, or loss of, limbs and eyes. The highest award in 1976/77 was £85,000, made to a 12-year old boy who had been injured by a booby trapped transistor radio.

Possibilities for change

The principle of the schemes
1585   We have received a considerable volume of evidence about criminal injuries. But we do not think it necessary, or indeed appropriate, to duplicate the thorough reviews of the compensation schemes recently completed in respect of Northern Ireland, and in an advanced stage in respect of Great Britain. We confine ourselves to comment on the principle of the schemes and on the possible application of our general proposals for changes in the assessment of tort damages.

1586   One criticism of the principle of the scheme for Great Britain which has come to our notice is that made by Professor P S Atiyah. In his book 'Accidents, Compensation and the Law'[6], he refers to the ability of victims to obtain compensation from social security or other sources, and says that 'the idea of selecting yet another group of unfortunates for special treatment is not easily defensible'. He argues that there is no social principle on which state compensation for criminal injuries alone could be justified, and that the decision appears to have been taken on 'practical' grounds, including perhaps the relatively low total cost.

1587 He also says that injuries similar to those compensated under the scheme can arise by pure accident, and that indeed some of the injuries which have been compensated were really accidental. He points out that a high proportion of awards go to policemen and others whose occupations make them particularly vulnerable to the risk of criminal assault, thus duplicating the industrial injuries scheme. He says also that the administrative costs of the scheme are higher than those of social security.

1588 On the other hand, there is widespread support for the argument advanced by the Government when introducing the scheme in Great Britain, that compensation for criminal injury is morally justified as in some measure salving the nation's conscience at its inability to preserve law and order. The scheme has now been in operation for 13 years, and the basis on which it was introduced appears to have been generally accepted by the communit. They scheme in Northern Ireland has been working for 8 years, and there was no suggestion when the revision of this scheme was debated in Parliament that the principle was wrong.

1589 It is relevant that similar schemes (usually statutory) have been set up in New Zealand, the Federal Republic of Germany, the Netherlands, Sweden, Australia, most of the provinces of Canada and several states of the USA. The New Zealand scheme has now been absorbed in the general accident compensation scheme. The Council of Europe has recently adopted a Resolution inviting its members to make special provision for criminal injuries compensation where compensation cannot be ensured by other means.

1590 If there were a comprehensive scheme of no-fault compensation for personal injury there would be strong grounds for embracing the criminal injuries schemes within it. But we are not recommending a comprehensive scheme.

1591 We think that criminal injuries form a special category; criminals may not be found or convicted, they often have no funds of their own and there is, obviously, no compulsory insurance. We think that it is right that there should be reasonable provision for the victims of crime, and we accept that these compensation schemes have come to stay. Indeed **we recommend** that the criminal injuries compensation scheme for Great Britain should be put on to a statutory basis.

The assessment of compensation
1592 **We recommend** that compensation under the criminal injuries schemes in Great Britain and Northern Ireland should continue to be based on tort damages.

1593   Our report contains a number of recommendations for changes in the assessment of such damages. We draw attention to two which are particularly relevant in the present context.

1594   First, those of us who consider that compensation for future pecuniary loss should normally take the form of periodic payments in cases of death or serious and lasting injury think that the Government should consider how this proposal might be applied to compensation for criminal injuries. Secondly, experience suggests that, not surprisingly, those concerned have found some practical difficulties in applying the provision for compensation to be reduced to take account of social security benefits; and we hope that the Government will review the practice of the schemes in the light of what we propose about offsetting social security and other payments against tort awards.

1595   **We recommend** that consideration should be given to applying to the criminal injuries compensation schemes our recommendations for changes in the assessment of tort damages.

Administration
1596   We take the view that, whether statutory or not, the scheme in Great Britain should continue to be administered by a separate board rather than by the courts. We have received few complaints on this score. Administration by a single statutory board would considerably reduce the practical difficulties which would be involved in a review of periodic payments and to which we refer in chapter 14; and seems to us appropriate to a scheme which is in effect making payments from a fund rather than adjudicating between adversaries. We would not suggest that the scheme should be administered through the social security system. The questions which have to be decided are of a different kind from those dealt with under that system.

CHAPTER 30
Animals

1597 The number of injuries and deaths caused by animals is not known exactly. On a broad estimate, there may be 50,000 injuries each year, together with a small number of deaths. Most injuries involve either dogs, of which there are some 6 million, or horses, of which there are about half a million.

1598 Some occupations give rise to particular risk. For example, in 1974 3 people were killed and 574 injured as a result of farm accidents involving animals in England and Wales; and each year about 170 postmen have four or more days off work as a result of dog bites. Few injuries are caused by wild animals.

The present law

Civil liability – England, Wales and Northern Ireland
1599 The law of civil liability for animals in England and Wales is largely defined by the Animals Act 1971, which implemented the recommendations in the Law Commission report 'Civil Liability for Animals' (Law Com No 13). Since 1 January 1977 the law in Northern Ireland has broadly corresponded to the Animals Act in accordance with the Animals (Northern Ireland) Order 1976.

1600 The 1971 Act codified the common law, which since medieval times has distinguished between animals *ferae naturae* (wild) and animals *mansuetae naturae* (domestic). As early as the fourteenth century it was recognised that an action would lie for redress for damage caused by a wild animal. The keeper was assumed to know the animal's character, and kept the animal at his peril.

1601 Under the common law, whether an animal fell into one class or the other was decided by the court by reference only to the species. For example, a docile circus elephant was 'wild'. The court was bound by judicial precedent to ignore the difference which existed between the wild elephant in the jungle and the trained elephant in the circus. (*Behrens* v. *Bertram Mills Circus Ltd* [1957] 2 Q.B. 1). On the other hand, camels were held to be 'domestic'. (*McQuaker* v. *Goddard* [1940] 1 K.B. 687 C.A).

1602 In the case of an injury by a domestic animal, the plaintiff had to prove that the defendant kept the animal knowing that it was dangerous and had departed from the peaceful habits of its species. An action of this kind, based on the defendant's knowledge, was called a *'scienter'* action. In *Fitzgerald* v. *Cooke Bourne* (*Farms*) *Ltd* [1964] 1 Q.B. 249, there was no liability in *scienter* for personal injuries inflicted by a young horse following its natural propensities in galloping up to and prancing round lawful visitors to a field. But if the defendant knew of a tendency to do harm, *scienter* must be found. The rule was clearly established in *May* v. *Burdett* (1846) 9 Q.B. 101, where the plaintiff recovered damages without proof of negligence after a bite by the defendant's monkey. The defendant was held to have been aware of the monkey's vicious disposition.

1603   In addition to the imposition of strict liability for certain animals, there might be ordinary liability in tort, for example, in negligence. This liability has not been disturbed by the Animals Act.

1604   Under the Animals Act 1971, animals which belong to a species not commonly domesticated in the British Isles, and, when fully grown, have such characteristics that they are likely, unless restrained, to cause severe damage, are considered as belonging to a 'dangerous' species for the purpose of the Act. The person in control of such an animal, referred to in the Act as the 'keeper', is strictly liable for damage caused by it.

1605   If an animal which does not belong to a dangerous species causes damage, the keeper will be strictly liable if the damage is of a kind which the animal, unless restrained, was likely to cause or which, if caused by the animal, was likely to be severe; and if the likelihood of the damage or of its being severe was due to characteristics of the animal which are not normally found except at particular times or in particular circumstances, and the keeper (or his representative) was aware of these characteristics.

1606   The defence of contributory negligence is available; and the keeper is not liable where the damage was due wholly to the fault of the person suffering it, or where that person was trespassing on property and the animal which injured him was not kept there to protect persons or property or, where it was so kept, it was not unreasonable to do so. Voluntary assumption of risk on the victim's part is also a complete defence. Where a person employed as a servant by a keeper incurs a risk incidental to his employment, he is not treated as accepting it voluntarily.

1607   The Animals Act requires that fences be properly maintained and steps taken to prevent animals straying on the highway. But it imposes no duty to fence where the land is common land or a village green, or is situated in an area where fencing is not customary; and, where animals stray from such land, the owner is not to be regarded as in breach of a duty of care merely because he placed his animals on the land in pursuance of a right to do so.

1608   The first, and so far only, case under the 1971 Act to be reported was heard in 1976 by the Court of Appeal (*Cummings* v. *Granger* [1977] Q.B. 397). The defendant occupied a breaker's yard behind a public house where he kept an untrained Alsatian guard dog which he knew was liable to attack people. The dog was allowed to roam the yard loose at nights. The plaintiff entered the yard one night, although she had no permission to do so. The dog attacked her and caused injuries to her face. She brought an action under section 2(2) of the Act, but the court held that she had voluntarily accepted the risk. Her action failed.

Civil liability – Scotland

1609 In the older law in Scotland, it was accepted that it was unnecessary to prove fault in respect of damage caused by animals *ferae naturae,* and even by those characterised as *mansuetae naturae* which had known vicious propensities. To that extent, liability was regarded as being strict. This view of the law was accepted as recently as 1963 by the Law Reform Committee for Scotland in their report on civil liability for loss, injury and damage caused by animals (Cmnd 2185). The Committee found that there had been some doubt whether the principles of the modern law of negligence could be applied to questions of liability for damage caused by animals, and asked whether there was, apart from the absolute duty to confine dangerous animals, a duty on the owner of the animal to take reasonable care to prevent it injuring others. The uncertainty of the law, as it was then, was criticised in the report. The Committee proposed, among other things, that the distinction between animals *mansuetae naturae* and *ferae naturae* should be abolished; and that liability for animals should in every case depend on whether there had been a failure to exercise reasonable care to prevent the animal causing injury.

1610 The trend in more recent cases points to *culpa* (fault), as evidenced by negligence or foreknowledge, being the basis for liability for damage caused by animals. Although the view was expressed in one case that 'this is a chapter of the law in which there is still a certain degree of uncertainty as to the true legal principle which in Scots law has to be applied' (*Sneddon* v. *Baxter* 1967 S.L.T. 67 (Notes)), on balance it was considered that liability was probably founded on *culpa.* Other recent cases have supported such a view. Unlike the position as it was in English law before the Animals Act 1971, Scots law recognises that the owner of an animal may be liable for injury caused by it while straying on the highway (*Gardiner* v. *Miller* 1967 S.L.T. 29).

1611 The doctrine of *culpa* in relation to animals has in recent times been re-examined by the courts and defined as consisting not merely of the ordinary duty to take reasonable care, but also of a duty to confine effectually. 'If a man were to keep a tiger and failed to confine it effectually with the result that it devoured a passing pedestrian, the inference of *culpa,* would, in most circumstance, be irrebuttable' (*Henderson* v. *John Stuart (Farms) Ltd* 1963 S.C. 245).

1612 Although the practical results of actions relating to liability for animals in English and Scots law have often been similar, the underlying principles differ. The principle underlying the English *scienter* action is the principle of strict liability that a man acts at his peril; the principle of *culpa* as applied in Scotland in effect consists of increasing the duty of care imposed to correspond to the dangerous nature of the animal concerned. In Scotland, unlike the English common law position, it is a defence to an action against the owner or custodian of an animal that the release of the animal was due to the act of a third party.

Safety legislation in Great Britain

1613   There are three other relevant Acts which apply to Scotland as well as
to England and Wales, although not to Northern Ireland. These are the Rabies
Act 1974, the Guard Dogs Act 1975 and the Dangerous Wild Animals
Act 1976.

1614   Rabies is caused by a virus which is generally transmitted to man by
saliva in a bite by a rabid animal. Although over the past 50 years there has
been virtually no rabies in this country, the safeguard of quarantine can be
seriously threatened by the smuggling of animals. Since the passing of the
Rabies Act 1974 there has been a marked reduction in the number of cases of
attempted smuggling, probably due to the anti-rabies publicity campaign as
well as to the greatly increased penalties imposed by the Act. There is no case
law on the question whether, if a person is bitten by a dog with rabies, the
owner is strictly liable. But there can be little doubt that if the owner knew
that the dog had the disease, then in England and Wales he would be strictly
liable, and in Scotland he would have to overcome a virtually irrebuttable
inference of *culpa*.

1615   The Guard Dogs Act 1975 prohibits the use of guard dogs unaccompanied
by handlers except on agricultural land and in private houses and gardens.
It also provides for the licensing of guard dog kennels.

1616   The Dangerous Wild Animals Act 1976 regulates the keeping of certain
wild animals. There had been growing concern, especially within the veterinary
profession, that too many private individuals were keeping exotic animals without
being aware of the dangers involved. Under the Act, a licence issued by a
local authority is now required for keeping a dangerous animal, except in
zoos (including safari parks), pet shops, circuses and research laboratories.

Possible changes in the law

1617   Under the existing law in England, Wales and Northern Ireland, there
is strict liability for keeping an animal of a dangerous species or a domestic
animal which is known to be dangerous. Does this afford sufficient redress
for those who suffer personal injury caused by animals?

Our evidence

1618   In New Zealand, persons injured by animals receive no-fault compensation under the Accident Compensation Act 1972. This is the only instance
known to us of no-fault compensation in other countries. None of our witnesses
positively advocated a no-fault scheme for the United Kingdom (although two
witnesses thought it might be considered). The Women's National Commission
were in favour of strict liability for the owners of all animals (as in France,
the Federal Republic of Germany, the Netherlands and Switzerland); and the
Royal College of Surgeons, Edinburgh, thought that liability without fault
should be seriously considered.

1619   The British Veterinary Association thought that the Animals Act of
1971 had to a large extent rationalised a previously unsatisfactory branch of

the common law. 'It does, however, place an additional burden upon the veterinarian in that responsibility for the control of a dangerous animal is placed by the Act upon its "keeper". If such an animal escapes and causes damage, it is the keeper (who is not necessarily the owner) who is liable therefor. This must cause a veterinary surgeon to hesitate before agreeing to hospitalise such an animal, if there is any possibility of it escaping, even though it may be essential for the animal that it should receive treatment.' The Association suggested that full compensation should be paid for any injury for which the injured person had no personal responsibility. They said that they would like to see a central fund established, based on universal compulsory insurance, to compensate victims injured by animals through no fault of their own.

1620 Evidence was given of several personal cases where no compensation had been obtained for injury and death caused by animals.

1621 Witnesses with major interests in this context, including the National Farmers' Union and the Country Landowners' Association, considered that the existing law was satisfactory. One witness, Master Ball, considered that the Animals Act tilted the scale against the landowner. It was almost impossible to keep some kinds of animals in if they were determined to stray. 'The user of the countryside should take it as he finds it and nobody should expect to be safeguarded against all the possible perils of existence.'

1622 We have received some special representations about dogs. In Sweden, some Canadian provinces and several Australian states, the dog owner is strictly liable for damage done by the dog to human beings. The Law Society pointed out that there was a strict liability under the Animals Act when a dog killed or injured livestock, and suggested that it was anomalous that a similar principle did not apply when people were injured.

No-fault
1623 Our conclusion is that a case has not been made out for a scheme of no-fault compensation for injuries caused by animals. There is no ready and cheap method by which all of the large number of keepers of animals could be made to contribute and there is a relatively small number of serious injuries caused by animals (other than those covered by the industrial injuries scheme and the proposed motor vehicle injuries scheme). We think that any attempt to provide no-fault compensation for all people injured by animals would involve administrative effort quite out of proportion to the benefits.

1624 We considered whether there was sufficient justification for a special no-fault scheme covering injuries caused by dogs; the dog licence fee, suitably increased, could provide a means of financing such a scheme. Our attention was drawn in particular to the problem of unidentified dogs. An interdepartmental working party on dogs, under the chairmanship of Mr W J S Batho of the Department of the Environment, published a report in 1976 which included an invitation to us to consider whether a compensation fund might be set up from licence revenue to meet claims for injury by people who had been attacked by unidentified dogs.[16] On balance, we feel that the hardships caused by the lack of a special scheme, whether for all dogs or just for unidentified dogs, are not sufficient to justify the administrative machinery which would be required.

Tort liability

1625   An alternative to a no-fault scheme for injuries caused by dogs would be to impose strict liability on the keepers of dogs (or perhaps only on the keepers of pet dogs, and not on the keepers of farm dogs, guard dogs or other dogs kept for business purposes). We concluded against this, too, largely on the grounds that ordinary domestic animals do not readily fall into the category of dangerous things to which we recommend elsewhere that strict liability would be particularly appropriate.

1626   **We recommend** that there should be no change in the law relating to liability for injuries caused by animals in England, Wales or Northern Ireland. At the same time, we think it reasonable that Scots law should be brought into line with English law in this respect. **We therefore recommend** that provisions parallel to those of the Animals Act 1971 should be enacted for Scotland.

Insurance limits

1627   Our attention was drawn to two similar problems arising, respectively, out of the Dangerous Wild Animals Act 1976, to which we have already referred, and the Riding Establishments Acts 1964 and 1970 (which, like the 1976 Act, do not apply to Northern Ireland). One of the conditions for the issue of a licence for a dangerous wild animal or a riding establishment is that the applicant should hold a suitable third party insurance policy as specified by the appropriate Act. We understand that, in each instance, this provision is interpreted as requiring unlimited cover; but that, in practice, insurers normally refuse to issue policies which give cover beyond certain financial limits. For riding establishments, the Home Office have sent a circular to licensing authorities in England and Wales recommending that they ensure that such establishments have the maximum cover obtainable.

1628   We think that the present law is unsatisfactory, and we doubt whether unlimited insurance cover can realistically be expected in either instance. **We recommend** that the Dangerous Wild Animals Act 1976 and the Riding Establishments Acts 1964 and 1970 should be amended, either to specify practical limits to the third party insurance cover required, or to give the licensing authorities discretion to determine what is a satisfactory amount.

CHAPTER 31
Exceptional risks

1629 As we have explained in chapter 11, we concluded that, leaving aside defective products, negligence should normally remain the basis of liability in tort except where there were exceptional risks. In this chapter, we consider what risks should be regarded as exceptional for the purposes of tort liability, and how tort should deal with them.

1630 Perhaps we should repeat that, in referring to strict liability, we mean liability which does not require the plaintiff to prove that the defendant was negligent and which (in contrast to a liability in negligence with a reversed burden of proof) does not exempt the defendant from liability if he proves simply that he was not negligent. Strict liability may provide for special defences, of varying number and width; these determine whether the strict liability in question comes near, at the one extreme, to an absolute liability or, at the other, to a liability for negligence with a reversed burden of proof.

Strict liability under statute
The present law
1631 In a number of instances, strict liability has already been imposed by statute. In conformity with international conventions to which the United Kingdom is a party, there is strict liability for death, personal injury or damage to property arising from nuclear installations – under the Nuclear Installations Act 1965. There is strict liability for loss or damage to persons or property on land or water caused by a civil aircraft while in flight (or by an article or person falling from such an aircraft) or while taking off or landing – under the Civil Aviation Act 1949. Strict liability applies to the underground storage of gas in Great Britain – under the Gas Act 1965. In the previous chapter we discussed the imposition of strict liability by the Animals Act 1971 in England and Wales.

Recommendations elsewhere in our report
1632 Under recommendations made in earlier chapters, the statutory scope of strict liability would be further extended to cover rail transport, defective products, vaccine damage and volunteers for medical research.

The common law
England, Wales and Northern Ireland
1633 Except in Scotland, strict liability has been applied to certain other situations by decisions of the courts as part of the common law. These have

been analysed by the Law Commission in their report on Civil Liability for Dangerous Things and Activities (Law Com No 32; HC 142). We need not repeat their detailed description of a highly technical branch of the law. It will suffice to say that, under English law, strict liability applies under the so-called rule of *Rylands* v. *Fletcher* (1866) L.R. 1 Ex. 265, affirmed (1868) L.R. 3 H.L. 330, to the occupier of land in respect of dangerous things which escape from that land and do damage; to some extent in cases of fire; to some aspects of nuisance; and, so far as liability for the negligence of an independent contractor is concerned, to a number of situations, notably where damage has resulted from 'ultra-hazardous activities'.

Scotland

1634   In Scotland, the tendency of the law has been to resist the introduction of strict liability, and to rely instead on the general basis of *culpa* (fault) adapted where appropriate to meet particular circumstances. Both *Rylands* v. *Fletcher* and the similar but earlier Scottish case of *Kerr* v. *Earl of Orkney* (1857) 20 D. 298 are regarded in Scotland as cases of liability for negligence. The activities which resulted in the damage in each case demanded a high standard of care. Failure to meet the standard of care required, coupled with *res ipsa loquitur* (the facts speak for themselves), was held to be sufficient to establish liability on the part of the defender.

1635   Nor has Scots law found it necessary to single out the particular categories listed in paragraph 1633 as heads of strict liability under English law. Fault may to some extent at least be presumed from the circumstances of the case, especially where dangerous things and activities are involved, and has usually been regarded as a sufficient basis on which to found liability.

The case for change

Defects in the common law

1636   The Law Commission concluded that the application of strict liability under English common law was 'complex, uncertain and inconsistent in principle'. Our own studies would confirm that conclusion. For example, the scope of the rule in *Rylands* v. *Fletcher* is so uncertain, and the permissible defences so wide, that its practical importance is rather slight.

1637   An example of a potential anomaly is as follows. A person who is injured inside a building by an explosion not attributable to the occupier's negligence will not recover damages, although he might have been successful if he had been injured by the same explosion when in a street outside the building, provided that what exploded had the necessary quality of 'dangerousness' and that its employment by the occupier amounted to a 'non-natural use' of the building (which is one of the requirements of the occupier's liability).

1638   Strict liability under the rule in *Rylands* v. *Fletcher* does not apply to activities carried out under mandatory statutory powers. Nor does it apply under permissive powers unless there is a specific reservation of liability for nuisance. This is apparently on the doubtful justification that, in giving such powers, Parliament must be taken to have intended that there should be liability only for negligence. In this connection, the provisions of the Reservoirs (Safety Provisions) Act 1930 are of interest. This Act was passed after the Dolgarrog Dam disaster of 1925, when a reservoir 1,400 feet above sea level and holding 200 million tons of water burst, causing widespread damage and loss of life. Section 7 of the Act provides that the fact that a reservoir was built under statutory powers shall not exonerate the undertakers from liability. This means that the rule in *Rylands* v. *Fletcher* applies. But for section 7, the undertakers would not be liable in the absence of negligence.

1639 We think it unsatisfactory that a person's ability to recover damages for personal injuries should depend on such fine distinctions.

A new principle
1640 The Law Commission's terms of reference did not entitle them to reconsider the principles of liability governing accidents involving personal injury as distinct from other accidents; and they took the view that it would be necessary to consider making such a distinction if they were to investigate the role of strict liability. We think that, in cases of death or personal injury, it is particularly important that the plaintiff is not faced with undue uncertainty as to the availability of a remedy. Compensation for loss of property need not necessarily be provided with the same degree of certainty as compensation for injury to life and limb.

1641 Most personal injury accidents relate to risks which are capable of being covered by insurance; and it is generally more practicable and less expensive for the controller of a specific thing or activity to insure against its miscarriage (whether or not by reason of his negligence) than for every potential victim to take out first party insurance against that risk. We think that the case for strict liability is stronger where a person is in control of a thing or operation in the course of a business (under which we include the supplying of non-commercial services by public bodies). The incidental cost of personal injuries can then normally be charged to the cost of the business, and so ultimately spread over all the consumers of the goods or services in question (or over the body of ratepayers or taxpayers who enjoy the public services in question).

1642 Behind the relatively few cases where strict liability has been imposed by statute (most clearly, perhaps, in relation to nuclear damage) and, in a more uncertain way, behind the cases of strict liability in English common law, we believe that there is a valuable principle to be extracted and more widely and consistently applied. This principle can be broadly stated as one of strict liability for personal injury caused by dangerous things or activities.

Categories of dangerous things
1643 We recognise that there is no sharp line between things or activities which are inherently dangerous and those which are not. The most innocent object can be a source of danger if wrongly used. **We recommend** that strict liability should be imposed on the controllers of things or operations in each

of two categories – first, those which by their unusually hazardous nature require close, careful and skilled supervision, the failure of which may cause death or personal injury; and, secondly, those which, although normally by their nature perfectly safe, are likely, if they do go wrong, to cause serious and extensive casualties. In the first category would fall such things as explosives and flammable gases or liquids. In the second category would fall such things as large public bridges, dams, major stores and stadiums and other buildings where large numbers of people may congregate.

1644   It is true that the courts, as cases have come before them, have to some extent shown themselves capable of providing a remedy for victims in the first category of accidents, even within the framework of negligence liability, by adjusting the standard of care required to the degree of dangerousness of the thing or operation in question. But this is an uncertain process and one involving a somewhat artificial conception of 'negligence'. We think it better that the controller of a thing or operation which, unless properly controlled, has a high risk of causing death or personal injury should be responsible in law for those consequences, so that both he and the potential victim know in advance where they stand.

1645   The second category of things for which we envisage strict liability covers those which would be generally regarded as a potential cause of public disasters. It seems to us only right – and indeed what in the event the public would be likely to demand – that someone who is responsible for a thing or activity which, even without negligence on his part, is capable of causing widespread death or personal injury should bear the resulting loss. This should be so whether or not the accident is on a disastrous scale. The alternative (as we saw in the thalidomide tragedy) is likely to be extra-legal pressure exerted to secure compensation for the victims.

Our options
1646   We looked at three main possible ways of imposing strict liability on the controllers of dangerous things and activities. The first was to follow the example set by the American Law Institute's Restatement of the Law of Torts (1938), and formulate a general principle to apply to instances involving dangerous activities on the lines of section 519, which provides that:

'. . . one who carries on an ultra-hazardous activity is liable to another whose person, land or chattels the actor should recognise as likely to be harmed by the unpreventable miscarriage of the activity for harm resulting thereto from that which makes the activity ultra-hazardous . . .'

By section 520, an activity is defined as ultra-hazardous, if it:

'(a) necessarily involves a risk of serious harm to the person, land or chattels of others which cannot be eliminated by the exercise of the utmost care, and,

(b) is not a matter of common usage.'

1647   We do not, however, think that such provisions, if introduced into our law and left to be applied by the courts, would prove a satisfactory way of giving effect to the principle we have in mind. Apart from the consideration that liability for ultra-hazardous activities under the Restatement would appear to be somewhat narrower in scope than the principle we have recommended, we would foresee practical disadvantages in effecting an important change in the substance of liability by what would in effect be a long drawn out process of judicial legislation. It would be difficult to effect insurance, or at least to determine the appropriate level of the premiums involved, until in a substantial number of cases the full significance of the new pattern of liability had been worked out; and meanwhile the basis for settlements would be uncertain, to the detriment of plaintiffs and defendants.

1648 Somewhat similar objections may be raised against the second possibility we considered. This was to implement the proposal made by Professor Jolowicz some ten years ago in his article 'Liability for Accidents'.[17] The proposal was that the courts should be left with the task of deciding from case to case on whom the loss arising from any particular incident should fall, taking full account of the availability and feasibility of insurance and also of the ways in which loss would be distributed.

1649 We prefer the third course, a statutory scheme. We think that there should be a statute setting out the nature of liability to be applied in respect of dangerous things and activities as we have defined them, and providing for a list of those things and activities to be specified by statutory instrument and added to by subsequent statutory instruments. This view is supported by evidence we received from Master Elton of the Queen's Bench Division who urged that statutory provision should be made for strict liability to attach to persons controlling 'dangerous things' or carrying on 'dangerous activities' as listed in regulations and that specified defences such as contributory negligence should be available in actions founded on such strict liability.

1650 We would hope that, by means of such an approach, potential defendants and their insurers would receive fair notice of the risks for which they would be responsible, while at the same time there would be available reasonably expeditious machinery for adding new, or newly discovered, risks to the list of those giving rise to strict liability.

1651 **We recommend** that there should be a statutory scheme making the controller of any listed dangerous thing or activity strictly liable for death or personal injury resulting from its malfunctioning; that this scheme should involve a parent statute and statutory instruments made under it; that the parent statute should contain general provisions and authorise the making of statutory instruments; and that each statutory instrument should apply the general provisions of the parent statute to particular dangerous things and activities set out in a list, and should also contain any special provisions relating to one or more of the listed things or activities.

Defences

1652 We considered to what extent the parent statute should define the extent of strict liability, by specifying the defences to be permitted; and to what extent it should be left for the statutory instruments to specify the defences applicable to each particular thing or operation. We differ in one aspect of our conclusions on these issues, but we begin our discussion of them with three recommendations on which we are all agreed.

The defence of statutory authority

1653   First, **we recommend** that statutory authority (which is a defence where liability under the rule in *Rylands* v. *Fletcher* is in question) should not be a defence in respect of any listed thing or activity. By this, we mean that the fact that activities are being carried out under statutory powers should not of itself give rise to any implication that the activities in question are exempt from any strict liability to which they would otherwise be subject. It would be open to a body acting under statutory powers to represent that its activities should not be listed as dangerous, and Parliament could, if it saw fit, confer an express immunity in relation to a particular thing or operation which might otherwise involve strict liability.

Contributory negligence and voluntary assumption of risk

1654   Secondly, **we recommend** that two defences should be specified by the parent statute as applicable in respect of all listed things and activities, namely contributory negligence and voluntary assumption of risk. In the case of voluntary assumption of risk, we think that the defence should be qualified. If an employed person is injured by reason of the malfunctioning of a thing or operation, and that malfunctioning is a risk incidental to his employment, we do not think that by reason of his employment alone he should be treated as having voluntarily accepted the risk. In this we follow section 6 (5) of the Animals Act 1971.

Trespass

1655   Thirdly, we are also agreed on our approach to the defence of trespass. We gave much thought to the question whether it should be a defence laid down in the parent statute that the plaintiff at the time he was injured was trespassing on the defendant's property. In seeking an answer to this question we have looked at such modern statutory models as are available. The strict liability imposed by section 40 (2) of the Civil Aviation Act 1949 is not subject to any defence that the plaintiff was a trespasser. Nor is there such a defence to the gas authority's liability in respect of underground storage of gas under section 14 of the Gas Act 1965, or to the licensee's liability in respect of nuclear occurrences under sections 7, 12 and 13 of the Nuclear Installations Act 1965. On the other hand, strict liability for certain animals under section 2 of the Animals Act 1971 is subject to the defence provided by section 5 (3) of that Act. This is that the animal was kept on the premises on which the plaintiff was trespassing other than for the protection of persons or property; or (if the animal was kept there for one of those purposes) the keeping of it for that purpose was not unreasonable. We have expressed our agreement with the Law Commission's recommendations under which a trespasser would be able to recover for the negligence of an occupier of land only in respect of dangers against which it was reasonable to offer him protection.

1656 These models, however, were rather inconclusive for our present purpose. Damage arising in respect of the operation of aircraft, with regard to underground storage of gas or as a result of a nuclear incident may well have been regarded only as particular risks where tort compensation should be available even to a trespasser. If, under our recommendations, a stand at a football stadium was by statutory instrument made the subject of strict liability, we ourselves would not wish to exclude an injured person from a claim, in the event of the collapse of the stand, solely because he had wrongfully avoided payment for entry. Bearing in mind the somewhat different approach taken by Parliament in 1971 to the trespassing plaintiff where strict liability for an animal is in question, we have reached the conclusion that the propriety of a defence that the plaintiff was a trespasser must be decided in the light of the particular risk involving strict liability. **We recommend** that the maker of a statutory instrument imposing strict liability should be authorised by the parent statute, if he thinks fit, to provide for a defence that the plaintiff was a trespasser, and to state the conditions on which such a defence would operate. If there is no such provision, there should be no such defence.

Other possible defences

1657 Our difference of view arises in our approach to other possible defences – in particular, act of a third party, but also *force majeure* or act of God (for instance an earthquake).

1658 As we have already emphasised, strict liability is a somewhat indeterminate concept as far as the strictness of the liability is concerned. Most of us think it important to make clear the extent of the strict liability which we intend to apply if a thing or operation is specified in a statutory instrument. This means that the parent statute should itself lay down the defences which would be available in any case where strict liability applied. If this were not done, there might be a tendency to extend the list of things and activities which were subject to strict liability, at the expense of weakening the liability itself.

1659 By a majority, **we recommend** that, with the exception of trespass, any defences which might be thought necessary in addition to contributory negligence and voluntary assumption of risk should be laid down in the parent statute as applicable in respect of all listed things and activities.

1660 Those of us who subscribe to this recommendation also consider that it should never be a defence under the scheme we are proposing that the accident was caused by a negligent, malicious or criminal act of a third party. The risk of malfunction of the thing or activity in question should be regarded as one of the risks for which strict liability is intended to provide. It may certainly be difficult for the controller to prevent the third party intervention, but where strict liability is concerned that is not the decisive consideration. The question is, rather, whether it is right to put the risk of death or personal injury on the victim himself, bearing in mind that he is likely to have even less possibility than the controller of preventing the third party intervention. By a majority,

we recommend that act of a third party should not be a defence in respect of any listed thing or activity. We make no recommendation on the defence of act of God, which is likely to be invoked only rarely.

1661 Our Chairman, Mrs Brooke, Mr MacCrindle and Mr Marshall think that, while the defences of contributory negligence and voluntary assumption of risk should be allowed in all cases by general provisions in the parent statute, the Minister making the statutory instruments should have a discretion to include or exclude certain other defences in relation to particular things or activities which were being listed. He should have this discretion because it might be right to list certain things or activities only if certain defences were allowed, and also because it might be necessary to define the circumstances in which a certain defence was to operate in relation to a particular thing or activity. In addition to trespass, such discretion would apply to the defences of act of a third party and act of God. The discretion could be restricted by general provisions in the parent statute to the effect that certain defences should be included or excluded unless there are special reasons to the contrary.

Other provisions

Heads of damage

1662 We considered whether it would be right to limit the categories of damage covered by our proposed scheme, for example to exclude recovery for non-pecuniary loss. Two considerations persuaded us not to recommend this course. The first was that there is no exclusion of recovery for non-pecuniary loss in any of the cases where, by statute or at common law, strict liability now exists. The second, and more decisive, consideration was that the main argument in favour of excluding non-pecuniary loss – that it might serve to discourage undeserving or frivolous claims – would be met by our overall proposals on the assessment of damages. **We recommend** that the parent statute should lay down that, wherever strict liability applies to any listed thing or activity, the damages recoverable for death or personal injury should be under the same categories of loss as would apply to tort generally.

Inclusion of things and activities in the scheme

1663 **We recommend** that the parent statute should set out the principles on which any subsequent statutory instruments imposing strict liability would have to be made. The principles involved are those recommended in paragraph 1643 above.

1664 To decide whether a particular thing or activity should be subject to strict liability could involve considering a variety of factors, including accident statistics, economic considerations and insurance factors. **We recommend** that the parent statute should provide for setting up an advisory committee; authorising it to consult the Health and Safety Commission; and requiring that a statutory instrument laid before Parliament should be accompanied by a report on the proposal from the advisory committee.

1665 We are aware that the Health and Safety Commission is to propose regulations requiring the notification of all potentially hazardous installations, so that closer scrutiny can be exercised and the opportunity provided for tighter controls to be imposed where appropriate. It hopes that, for the first time, there will be a complete picture of all hazardous installations. In the meantime, it expects that many firms will notify their activities voluntarily.

1666 Statutory instruments imposing strict liability would always deal with three matters. First, they would define the thing or activity giving rise to strict liability. Secondly, they would specify the particular risks connected with the thing or activity in respect of which strict liability was to apply. For example, if the activity was the transport by road vehicle of certain types of chemicals, the instrument would have to make it clear that the strict liability did not apply to every accident in which the vehicle was involved when carrying such chemicals, but only to those in which the carrying of chemicals would be a relevant factor, for example where the chemicals had caught fire. Similarly, if those in control of a public bridge were to be made strictly liable on the grounds that its malfunctioning might cause death or personal injury on a large scale, it would have to be made clear that strict liability would not apply to the pedestrian who tripped on a broken paving stone on the bridge and broke his leg, but that it would apply if the bridge collapsed and the pedestrian were drowned, even if he were the only victim. Thirdly, the instrument would specify the person to be regarded as the 'controller' of the thing or operation subject to strict liability. Often this would be self evident, but sometimes it would be desirable to treat someone as the controller who did not have an obvious immediate physical connection with the thing or operation in question, as for example when one person was in physical control of a structure but another was responsible for its repair and maintenance.

1667 **We recommend** that the statutory instruments imposing strict liability should require affirmative resolutions of both Houses before coming into effect.

Compulsory insurance
1668 We considered whether the listed things and activities should be subject to compulsory third party insurance. Although we would not go so far as to say that compulsory insurance should be automatic in every case where strict liability was imposed, we would expect it to be found appropriate in most cases. One of the difficulties involved in imposing compulsory insurance is the practical one of supervising and enforcing it. Where, however, strict liability had been imposed in specific cases by statutory instrument, this difficulty should be less acute. **We recommend** that the maker of a statutory instrument imposing strict liability should have the power, although not the duty, to lay down a requirement of third party insurance (and the minimum permissible cover in any particular case) in respect of the risk to which strict liability is to apply.

1669 We recognise that, even where compulsory insurance has been imposed, there might be a disaster on such a scale that the insurance cover was inadequate to meet all claims for tort compensation. In these circumstances, however, we envisage that the Government would in any event be under strong pressure to intervene with financial assistance.

Relationship with the existing law on strict liability

1670   We considered the relationship between the strict liability for the new categories we envisage and that for the existing categories covered by statute and at English common law. We think it would be more satisfactory for potential defendants, as well as for potential plaintiffs, to know with certainty when strict liability would apply, and what its significance would be. It would also be more satisfactory and more just if the cases to which strict liability applied were based on coherent principles. As we have said, this is not the present position. Nevertheless, we do not think that it is for us to attempt to rationalise the existing categories of strict liability. The same applies to the relevant applications of *culpa* under Scots common law. We are concerned only with accidents giving rise to death or personal injury, whereas the cases to which strict liability and *culpa* at present apply are not so limited. Tackling this problem would take us well outside our terms of reference.

PART VI
Costs and some concluding reflections

CHAPTER 32

The cost of our proposals

1671 Our terms of reference required us to consider various categories of injury, '. . . having regard to the cost and other implications of the arrangements for the recovery of compensation . . .' This chapter gives a broad summary of the changes in cost and the distribution of costs arising from our proposals taken as a whole. We also put these changes in the context of the existing cost of compensation for injury.

1672 Further information is given in the chapters relating to individual categories of injury, in particular chapters 17 and 18 on work and road injuries and chapters 12, 13 and 15 on the assessment of tort damages. In Volume Two more detailed information is given on costs together with a description of the methods of estimation.

Changes in social security and tort

1673 The estimates fall into two main categories – social security and tort. The Government Actuary's report on the cost of our proposals for improving social security benefits for work and road injuries is published as an Annex to Volume Two. We have made our own estimates of the cost of improving social security benefits for children and of the saving in cost resulting from changes in the tort system.

1674 In this chapter and elsewhere in our report the costs quoted are at January 1977 price levels. References to an increase or decrease in costs are in real terms, assuming no other changes.

Taxation
1675 We were faced with the difficulty of combining the annual cost of social security benefits with the annual cost of tort compensation. Some social security benefits are taxable and some are not. Lump sum tort compensation is not taxable, but we have recommended that periodic payments of tort compensation should be taxed as earned income. Lack of information about the level of taxation on injured people means that we have been unable to assess the aggregate amount of taxation on compensation and benefits. But it was clearly necessary to give the combined cost of our proposals. We have, therefore, followed established practice in combining the total cost of both taxable and non-taxable compensation and benefits. The effect of taxation would result in the net cost of our proposed social security benefits being slightly lower than the estimates we have made

353

Injuries on the way to and from work

1676   We have recommended, by a narrow majority, that injuries on the way to and from work should be included in the work injuries scheme and the compensation financed through that scheme. Except where otherwise stated, the costs presented in this chapter reflect that recommendation. An indication is also given of the effect on these costs if compensation for commuting accidents had not been recommended as part of the work injuries scheme. Broadly, the result would be a smaller cost for the work injuries scheme and, because a significant proportion of commuting accidents occur on the road, a larger cost for the road injuries scheme.

The initial and ultimate changes

1677   The two main elements in our estimates are an increase in social security expenditure, particularly on work and road injuries, and a net decrease in the cost of tort. The full effect of our proposals would not be felt immediately. The increase in social security costs could be expected to build up over a number of years, whereas the reduction in tort compensation would be accomplished after a much shorter time. We therefore give two summaries of the changes.

1678   Table 17 summarises the changes after 5 years (the initial change in cost). Table 18 shows the position after 40 years (the ultimate change in cost). The changes would not necessarily be limited to the range between these estimates. Social security costs in the first two or three years would be even lower than those expected after 5 years, although the full tort reductions might not all have been made. But we think that a period of 5 years gives a realistic indication of the initial change in cost, as by that time claim patterns would have settled down. Although the picture might change after 40 years we might expect to approach a plateau of ultimate change in cost by this time.

Table 17   Estimates of changes in costs after 5 years

£ million a year at Jan 1977 prices

	Total	Work	Road	Other
Social security benefits[1]	69	29	25	15
Social security administration	9	4	3	2
Social security total	78	33	28	17
Tort compensation[2]	−61	−34	−28	1
Tort administration	−25	−13	−12	–
Tort total	−86	−47	−40	1
Occupational sick pay	− 3	− 2	− 1	–
Total compensation	5	− 7	− 4	16
Total administration	−16	− 9	− 9	2
Overall change	−11	−16	−13	18

1, 2 See footnotes to table 18.

Table 18   Estimates of changes in costs after 40 years

£ million a year at Jan 1977 prices

	Total	Work	Road	Other
Social security benefits[1]	115	51	48	16
Social security administration	15	7	6	2
Social security total	130	58	54	18
Tort compensation[2]	−61	−34	−28	1
Tort administration	−25	−13	−12	−
Tort total	−86	−47	−40	1
Occupational sick pay	− 3	− 2	− 1	−
Total compensation	51	15	19	17
Total administration	−10	− 6	− 6	2
Overall change	41	9	13	19

1 Commuting injuries and deaths are included under work injuries. 'Other' costs relate to the additional benefits for children.

2 Most tort compensation for commuting injuries and deaths is paid in respect of road injuries, and therefore the cost of such compensation is included under road.

1679   Table 19 compares the proposed levels of provision of social security and tort after 40 years with the expected levels if the present arrangements continue unchanged.

Table 19   Present and proposed levels of compensation after 40 years (excluding administration)

£ million a year at Jan 1977 prices

	Total	Work	Road	Other[1]
Social security benefits at proposed levels[2]	455	333	80	42
Social security levels at present benefits[3]	340	282	32	26
Change in social security benefits	115	51	48	16
Tort compensation at proposed levels[4]	141	35	90	16
Tort compensation at present levels[5]	202	69	118	15
Change in tort compensation	−61	−34	−28	1

1 For social security, benefit for children; for tort, compensation other than that paid under employer's liability or motor policies.

2 Commuting injuries and deaths are included under work injuries.

3 Cost of present schemes are estimated costs in 2023/24 of benefits under the industrial injuries and national insurance schemes at January 1977 rates and corresponding earnings levels. 'Other' costs are estimates of mobility allowance and attendance allowance paid to children.

4 Most commuting injuries and deaths are included under road injuries.

5 Equivalent at January 1977 prices, of payments in 1975.

The change in social security costs

1680   Initially, the amount paid out in social security benefits would increase by £69 million a year, and administration costs by about £9 million. Ultimately, social security provision would increase by £115 million a year and administration costs by about £15 million. Total provision for those injured at work or on the road would then be about one third higher than it would otherwise have been.

Work injuries

1681   Improvements in benefits for work injuries would cost about £29 million a year initially (excluding administration), rising to £51 million a year after 40 years. By then, provision would be improved by 18 per cent. If commuting injuries were not included, improvements to the work scheme would cost about £18 million a year initially (excluding administration), rising to £28 million a year.

Road injuries

1682   Improvements in benefits for road injuries (outside the sphere of employment) would cost about £25 million a year initially (excluding administration), rising after 40 years to £48 million a year. The provision of state benefits for this category of injury would by then be improved by 150 per cent. If injuries to commuters were not included in the work scheme (leaving many such injuries to be compensated by the road scheme), the improvements to the road scheme would cost £34 million a year (excluding administration) initially, rising to £66 million a year.

Children

1683   The provision of an allowance for severely handicapped children and the wider entitlement to mobility allowance for children would cost £15 million a year initially (excluding administration), rising by £1 million over 40 years. By then, total provision for handicapped children (which currently consists of mobility allowance and attendance allowance) would be improved by 62 per cent.

The change in tort costs

1684   As the full effect of our proposed changes in tort compensation would be felt after the first few years, the estimates of the initial and ultimate changes in costs in tables 17 and 18 are identical. These estimates allow for full offsetting of the improved social security benefits and take account of the majority proposals for a threshold for non-pecuniary loss under tort and for the use of modified multipliers as described in chapter 15.

1685   We estimate that, as a result of our proposals, the level of tort compensation would decline by about £61 million a year, a decline of 30 per cent in total tort compensation for personal injury. There would be a further reduction of about £25 million in administration costs.

Work injuries
1686   Tort payments in respect of work injuries would be reduced by £34 million a year, that is to about half their level under present arrangements. There would also be a reduction of £13 million in administration costs.

Road injuries
1687   Tort payments in respect of road injuries would fall by £28 million a year, representing a decline in such compensation of 24 per cent. The reduction in administration costs would be about £12 million a year.

Other injuries
1688   Our proposals would have a small effect on tort compensation for injuries incurred otherwise than at work or on the road. We estimate that these proposals, which include the extension of strict liability to new categories and the limitation of damages for non-pecuniary loss, would result in a net increase of about £1 million a year in such compensation.

Occupational sick pay
1689   Our proposals are not directly concerned with occupational sick pay, but as many employers deduct social security benefits from sick pay, we expect that the increase in such benefits would lead to a reduction of about £3 million a year in the total level of occupational sick pay.

The combined effect of our proposals
1690   Initially, we expect total compensation payments to increase by £5 million a year. Compensation in respect of work and road injuries would fall, but payments to severely handicapped children would increase. Savings in administration costs would total £16 million a year. There would, therefore, be an initial reduction of £11 million a year in the cost of compensation for personal injury.

1691   Ultimately, the combined effect of all our proposals would be to increase compensation payments by £51 million a year. This increase represents over 9 per cent of the £542 million a year payable in injury compensation at present levels through both tort and social security. At the same time, we expect overall administration costs to decline by about £10 million a year, leaving a net increase in cost of £41 million a year. If commuting injuries were not included in the work scheme, there would ultimately be an overall increase of £46 million a year in compensation payments, at a net cost (after taking into account savings in administration costs) of £36 million a year.

Work injuries
1692   Aggregate compensation in respect of work injuries and diseases would initially be reduced by about £7 million a year. A further reduction of £9 million in administration costs would lead to a total initial decrease of about £16 million a year in the cost of such compensation.

1693   Ultimately, total work injuries compensation would be increased by £15 million a year (an increase of about 4 per cent). There would be a saving in administration costs of about £6 million a year, resulting in an increase of £9 million a year in the eventual cost of compensation for work injuries.

1694   If commuting injuries were not included in the work scheme, the initial reduction in overall compensation for work injuries would be £18 million a year. Ultimately, such compensation would be reduced by £8 million a year.

Road injuries
1695   Initially, compensation payments in respect of road injuries (outside the sphere of employment) would be reduced by about £4 million a year. A further reduction of £9 million in administration costs would result in a fall in total costs initially of £13 million a year.

1696   Ultimately, there would be an increase of £19 million a year (13 per cent) in compensation payments in respect of road injuries.   A saving of £6 million a year in administration costs would lead to an overall increase of £13 million a year in the ultimate cost of compensation for road injuries.

1697   If commuting injuries were not compensated through the work scheme, aggregate compensation for road injuries would be increased initially by £5 million a year and ultimately by £37 million a year.

The distribution of compensation costs
1698   Our proposals would result in some redistribution of the cost of compensation for personal injury.   Costs in the state social security scheme (including administration) would ultimately increase by £130 million a year (£125 million a year if commuting injuries were not included in the work scheme). Tort compensation costs, which are met in the first instance mainly by insurers in the private sector, would decrease by £86 million a year and occupational sick pay by £3 million.   We have tried to ensure that, despite this transfer from the private to the public sector, broadly speaking the costs of the proposed compensation arrangements would ultimately fall on the same groups as at present and would not involve a large increase in general taxation.

Work injuries
1699   We have recommended that the increase in state provision for the industrially injured should be financed by increasing national insurance contributions from employers and the self employed.   The cost of this increased provision would ultimately be £58 million a year, of which £14 million would be attributable to the self employed.

1700   The total of employers' contributions to the national insurance fund in 1977/78 was expected to be about £5,000 million.   Our proposals would add less than one per cent to the aggregate value of employers' national insurance contributions.   As the employers' contribution in the 1977/78 tax year was 8·75 per cent of the employees' relevant earnings, the increase in total employers' wage costs on this account would be unlikely to exceed 0·1 per cent.

1701 Contributions by the self employed to the national insurance fund in 1977/78 were expected to be about £300 million. Our proposals would add about 5 per cent to the aggregate value of national insurance contributions from the self employed.

1702 We have not allowed in our calculations for any Exchequer contribution to the national insurance fund. If the Exchequer contributed 18 per cent towards the extra cost, as it does already to the national insurance fund, additional costs for employers and the self employed would be lower.

1703 Our recommendations would ultimately result in a reduction of £47 million a year in tort compensation in respect of work injuries. We estimate that over 90 per cent of such compensation is met by employer's liability insurance policies. The total value of employer's liability insurance premiums is currently some £170 million a year. Assuming that competition ensures that the savings in compensation costs are passed on to the employer, a reduction in insurance premiums of about 25 per cent could be expected. As we have explained, however, this reduction is in real terms (and ignores any movement in price levels), and assumes no other changes.

Road injuries
1704 Our recommendations for the provision of improved and new state benefits in respect of those injured in road accidents (outside the sphere of employment) would ultimately result in an increase in cost of some £54 million a year. We have proposed that this cost and the cost of existing benefits, currently about £36 million a year (including administration), should be met by an additional levy collected with petrol tax.

1705 The increase in motoring costs should be partially offset by a reduction in motor insurance premiums. We expect that the cost of tort compensation for road accidents would decline by about £40 million a year. The total value of motor insurance premiums is currently about £1,000 million a year, of which some £280 million is for personal injury insurance. Motor insurance premiums might therefore be expected to fall in real terms by about 4 per cent (subject again to the reservations about any other changes that might affect the level of motor insurance premiums).

Children
1706 We have recommended that improved provision for severely handicapped children should be financed solely by the Exchequer. This would mean an increase in general taxation of £18 million a year.

The cost in perspective
1707 Ultimately, the net cost of our proposals is £41 million a year. The increase in public expenditure through the social security system is £130 million a year. This figure must be compared with a total social security budget, including retirement pensions, of almost £12,000 million a year. In respect

of the road scheme, motorists would pay £90 million a year extra (while employers, employees and the Exchequer would pay £36 million less in national insurance contributions). In respect of the work scheme, employers would pay £58 million a year more. Motorists and employers could expect a reduction, in real terms, in existing private insurance premiums. Only £18 million a year, the cost of the proposed benefits for severely handicapped children, would be a new burden on the Exchequer to be financed from general taxation.

1708   The changes proposed would result in improved compensation for many injured people and their dependants. Some would become entitled to compensation for the first time. Whatever other views may be expressed on our report, we do not believe that it can be argued that the small extra cost of our proposals is too high a price to pay for the provision of more appropriate compensation for personal injury.

CHAPTER 33
Concluding reflections

1709   Our enquiry has proved to be a long and complicated one. We learned much from our study of overseas schemes, but we never expected that these could have been copied in the United Kingdom without regard to our national circumstances.

1710   Differing opinions can legitimately be held on many of the interlocking issues within our remit, and our own report is not free from reservations and minority recommendations. But we have reached a substantial measure of agreement on what should be done – albeit within the confines of our terms of reference, and within the circumstances which now prevail.

1711   We are conscious that our terms of reference have precluded us from looking at the whole range of compensation for personal injury. Of the three million or so injuries which are sustained each year, over a third (mainly those occurring in the home) are not our concern. Nor have we been able to consider all aspects of compensation for sickness. We estimated that in addition to the cost of our proposals, the cost of extending to all injuries the kind of scheme we are recommending for road injuries would be some £250 million a year in 40 years' time (at January 1977 prices). This would be 25 per cent more than the total cost of social security and tort compensation for injuries, after our proposals had come fully into effect. Extension to all illness as well as all injuries would cost perhaps an extra £2,000 million a year, an 80 per cent addition to the total cost of social security and tort compensation for illness and injury.

1712   We were also clearly not intended to consider accident prevention or rehabilitation. Both are invaluable, not only for reducing pain, suffering and disability, but also for cutting the cost of compensation. The question which we have not answered – and we were not the body to answer it – is whether more needs to be done by extending and co-ordinating rehabilitation services and by promoting more research and educational programmes on safety. We are well aware that in some other countries the extra costs are met by a levy on insurance contributions or from other sources of finance for compensation.

1713   After our extensive enquiries and discussions, we naturally have views on ultimate objectives for the development of compensation. There are among us broadly three schools of thought, which we will indicate only briefly as they go in part beyond the scope of our terms of reference, and wholly beyond our conclusions and recommendations.

361

1714   Some of us would welcome an eventual extension of no-fault compensation beyond the spheres of employment and road traffic to cover the other categories of accident within our terms of reference (such as accidents arising from the use of services), and those accidents which are outside our terms of reference (such as accidents in the home). In the long run, too, they would see little justification for distinguishing between the injured and the sick. The cost of introducing a comparable no-fault scheme covering both sickness and injury would be substantial, there are those of us who believe that it is a socially desirable objective.

1715   Some of us who look forward to considerable extensions of no-fault provision are also doubtful about the permanent value of the tort system of compensation as a means of supplementing what can be obtained from social security. In their view the tort system is too costly, too cumbersome, too prone to delay and too capricious in its operation to be defensible; and they do not accept, having regard to the availability of liability insurance, that the tort action is an effective deterrent to accidents in general. They regard our present, limited recommendations as providing, if implemented, a time for testing the capacity of the social security system to cope with the new demands which those recommendations would put upon it. In the light of that experience they think it would be possible to find acceptable ways of providing an overall no-fault scheme of compensation without reliance on tort. Compensation would be related to lost income and special needs which have arisen as a result of injury. They do not think, however, that compensation should necessarily be restricted to state benefits. Greater facilities, for example, by way of tax concessions or otherwise, might be offered for additional cover by first party insurance.

1716   Others among us hope, and believe, that there would always be a role for the tort system, whatever happened to no-fault provision. They would argue that tort would remain uniquely well equipped to compensate the widest possible range of the particular losses suffered by a given individual; that, despite the role of liability insurance, tort would continue to embody the socially valuable principle that, where a person negligently or intentionally caused injuries to another, amends should be made for the consequences of his fault; and that the continued existence of tort would, of itself, be some safeguard against a system of total dependence on the state.

1717   In addition it is felt that no-fault compensation, with no recourse to tort, might involve or lead to abandoning the common law principle of *restitutio in integrum* (making up to the injured party, so far as money can serve, the loss and injury which he has sustained) and the replacement of this principle by a statutory tariff determined, not by practice and accepted custom, but by governmental regulation. There would then be no court awards independent of the tariff to give guidance as to its sufficiency; and there could be changes in the tariff for reasons other than the interests of injured persons. Adjudication by statutory tribunals, however careful and impartial, might not be accepted as an adequate substitute for the existing right of the subject to seek reparation for personal injury from the independent courts of the realm. Those who hold this view would also maintain that there is another factor which goes deeply into the structure of society. A sense of responsibility for the effect of one's actions on others, and a sense that one does have a duty of care towards one's fellow citizens, is an essential element in a civilised community, and a lapse in the discharge of that responsibility is a matter of blame – in other words fault or *culpa*. They would regard the continued existence of the law of tort or delict as a measure of deterrence against general irresponsibility and a positive encouragement to a sense of individual responsibility towards one's fellows.

1718   Then there are yet others of us who take the view that, in the light of all the uncertainties, it would be best to wait until it is possible to assess the social and practical consequences of our proposals, in particular our road scheme, before trying to judge, even in principle, in which direction it would be appropriate to move next.

1719   But speculation about the future takes us well beyond our terms of reference. We have tried to deal with some of the most urgent problems which relate to compensation for death and personal injuries; and to provide a vantage point from which a number of possible routes into the future could be mapped out.

1720   We should like to end with a few thoughts on what we have sought to achieve.

1721   Although we have been concerned with many issues, at the heart of our enquiry has been the relationship between tort and social security. They are derived from different philosophies. In the past they have been allowed to develop side by side as though they had little to do with each other, so that they even use different words to describe what are basically the same things. The Monckton Committee surveyed some aspects of their interrelationship thirty years ago. But, since then, social security provision for the injured and bereaved has greatly expanded and has become much more complicated, and the common law of tort has further evolved and been supplemented by a number of statutory provisions. It was high time for a further review.

1722   In the event, we have not recommended that tort should be abolished. But the changes which we have proposed represent a considerable shift of emphasis from the tort to the social security system of compensation.

1723   Some of our recommendations are based on majority decisions, in one or two cases narrow majorities. They nevertheless add up to a considerable programme.

1724   We have proposed a new no-fault scheme for road accidents.

1725   We have proposed changes in the industrial injuries scheme, among them benefits based on the new pensions scheme; the inclusion of the self employed; and cover for commuters.

1726   We have suggested a new benefit for severely handicapped children.

1727 We have recommended changes in the tort system, notably provision for inflation proofed periodic payments, and a more realistic method of calculating lump sum payments. We have suggested a threshold for damages for non-pecuniary loss. We have recommended introducing strict liability in tort in respect of rail transport, defective products, vaccine damage, and things and activities involving exceptional risks.

1728 We have suggested ways of avoiding duplication of compensation, mainly by the full offsetting of social security benefits against tort awards.

1729 We have devised means of financing the suggested changes which would involve only a modest additional charge on general taxation, needed to meet the cost of our proposals for severely handicapped children.

1730 More people than at present would benefit; delays, with all the anxieties that they involve, would be cut down; costs of administration would be reduced; and the better distribution of what funds were available should ensure that more of them went to the seriously injured and the bereaved who were in the greatest need.

1731 We have not removed anomalies (and could not have done so under our terms of reference); we have merely moved the boundary lines. We think that the new boundary lines are more sensible, but those who fall on the wrong side may not agree. Some people who at present can look for modest tort awards would in future get nothing but their social security payments. Our decision that the calculation of tort awards should take account of our taxation system, and fully offset social security benefits which are based on different principles from those of tort awards, will result in some redistribution of new benefits from tort towards higher earners and single people. This may be regarded by some as regrettable but we have had to accept it as an inevitable and logical consequence of our policy in relation to offsetting, which we believe to be right. Our proposals for fully offsetting social security payments against tort awards, taken with our other suggestions and the consequent saving in administrative costs, would have the result that, in real terms, there would be a temporary drop in the overall cost of compensation.

1732 Nevertheless, we feel in no doubt that, looking at the whole picture, our proposals would result in a better balance in the distribution of the funds devoted to compensation for personal injuries and would give greater help to those who most need it. We hope too that, after this report, it should no longer be possible to think that there is no relation between compensation for the injured and bereaved provided by the social security system on the one hand and that provided by the common law of tort on the other. The two systems work in different ways and operate from different philosophies, and tort will become the junior partner. But we have shown how, by fitting them together more effectively, compensation for injured people and their dependants can be appreciably improved and extended.

PART VII

Conclusions and recommendations

Summary of conclusions

General

Our compensation systems should be looked at as a whole. Tort should be retained and, while the two systems of tort and social security should continue side by side, the relationship between them should be significantly altered. Social security should be recognised as the principal means of compensation. Double compensation should be avoided by offsetting social security benefits in the assessment of tort damages. Money available should be spent on the more serious injuries rather than minor injuries. The range of those receiving compensation should be extended.

No-fault compensation should be introduced for motor vehicle injuries. The no-fault provision for work injuries should be improved. A new benefit for all severely handicapped children should be introduced.

The range of tort should be extended by introducing strict liability in some areas. Under tort, provision should be made for periodic payments for pecuniary loss.

In administering compensation existing systems and institutions should be used, but considerable simplification of the highly complicated social security system is desirable.

Our terms of reference do not cover all injuries, and at least one million injuries every year, mostly those occurring in the home, would remain outside the scope of our proposals.

A list of recommendations follows this section. It includes references to minority views.

Summary of conclusions

TORT AND THE ASSESSMENT OF DAMAGES

We concluded that the action of tort, of which there are many criticisms, should nevertheless be retained. Liability in tort should remain a liability in negligence except where there are special reasons for imposing strict liability. We found special reasons for strict liability in respect of products, rail transport, volunteers for medical research, vaccine damage and things and operations involving exceptional risks.

So far as possible, the principle of making full reparation for the loss suffered should be continued. Damages should continue to be awarded for pecuniary loss and non-pecuniary loss, but changes should be made in the method of assessment and in the method of payment. In particular tort damages should be reduced by taking into account the full amount of the social security benefits payable as a result of the injury, thus avoiding double compensation. The number of small claims should be reduced by imposing a threshold for damages for non-pecuniary loss. A system of periodic payments should be introduced for pecuniary loss caused by death or serious and lasting injury, although the parties should still be at liberty to settle a claim for an agreed lump sum. The method of calculating the loss when expressed as a lump sum should take fuller account of the effects of the plaintiff's tax position and of inflation.

Recommendations 1–71

WORK INJURIES

We concluded that the industrial injuries scheme administered by DHSS should provide the basis for improved provision for those injured at work. Higher benefits should be paid for the first six months of incapacity or widowhood, followed by pensions calculated in the same way as in the new state pensions scheme, but in all cases at the improved levels that would accrue if contributions to the scheme had been paid for 20 years. Widowers should be treated in the same way as widows. The scheme should be extended to cover the self employed and to include commuting accidents. The conditions for compensation for occupational diseases should be less restrictive. The increased compensation costs should be met by employers.

Recommendations 72–95

ROAD INJURIES

We concluded that a no-fault compensation scheme should be introduced for injuries caused by motor vehicles, modelled on the scheme we recommend for work injuries with benefits at broadly the same level. Special provision should be made for children and non-earners, including housewives and retirement pensioners. The scheme should be administered by DHSS and should be financed by a levy on petrol.

Recommendations 96–120

368

AIR TRANSPORT

We **concluded** that because liability is largely governed by international conventions the scope for change is limited. Nevertheless we draw attention to existing anomalies and to those areas where change is desirable. In particular, we would welcome action to increase the minimum limit of carriers' liability on all flights to, from and touching the United Kingdom.

Recommendations 121–124

SEA AND INLAND WATERWAYS

We **concluded** that, in an area traditionally governed by international agreement, it would be inappropriate to recommend a new system of liability for the United Kingdom alone. We therefore reject the idea of imposing strict liability, but we think that the limits of liability for negligence or other fault should be increased as proposed in the London Convention. Our proposals in respect of aircraft and ships should be applied to hovercraft where appropriate.

Recommendations 125–127

RAIL TRANSPORT

We **concluded** that a no-fault scheme would not be appropriate for railway accidents but that strict liability should be introduced for injuries caused by the movement of rolling stock.

Recommendations 128–132

PRODUCTS LIABILITY

We **concluded** that there is no justification at present for introducing a no-fault scheme for injuries caused by defective products. Strict liability would meet most of the objections to the present law. A scheme based broadly on the Council of Europe Convention and the draft EEC Directive should be introduced.

Recommendations 133–153

SERVICES OTHER THAN MEDICAL AND CARRIAGE

We **concluded** that, for these services, liability in negligence should be retained. While recognising that different treatment of services and products would result in some anomalies, we thought that this would be preferable to the problems which could arise if strict liability for services were imposed.

Recommendation 154

MEDICAL INJURY

We **concluded** that a no-fault scheme for medical accidents should not be introduced at present; but that the progress of no-fault compensation for medical accidents in New Zealand and Sweden should be studied and assessed, so that

369

the experience could be drawn upon, if it was decided to introduce a no-fault scheme for medical accidents in this country. The negligence action should remain. Volunteers for medical research should have a right of action for tort damages based on strict liability.

Recommendations 155–157

VACCINE DAMAGE

We concluded that vaccine damaged children should, if severely handicapped, be entitled to the benefit which we propose for severely handicapped children generally. In addition, there is a special case for paying tort compensation for vaccine damage where vaccination is recommended by the state and is undertaken to protect the community: the authority concerned should be strictly liable in tort for severe damage suffered by anyone, adult or child, as a result of such vaccination.

Recommendation 158

ANTE-NATAL INJURY

We concluded that as the cause of congenital malformation can rarely be established, it is not practicable to identify those cases within our terms of reference and to devise a separate scheme for them. Children who are injured before birth should be considered as part of the problem of compensation for all children who are injured. The tort action provided under the Congenital Disabilities (Civil Liability) Act 1976 should be retained, but its operation should be restricted because there are grave objections to the tort action within the family in the sphere of ante-natal injury. The introduction of strict liability for products would provide a remedy for ante-natal injury caused by 'defective' drugs.

Recommendations 159–165

CHILDREN

We concluded that all children who are severely handicapped should be treated in the same way no matter what the cause of their handicap. A special benefit for severely handicapped children should be introduced. As there is no obvious source of finance related to the causes of handicap, the cost should be borne by the Exchequer.

Recommendations 166–168

OCCUPIERS' LIABILITY

We concluded that no change is needed regarding injuries on other persons' premises, beyond that required to implement the Law Commission's recommendations on uninvited entrants.

Recommendations 169–170

370

CRIMINAL INJURIES

We concluded that a state scheme for criminal injuries is desirable in principle. The existing criminal injuries schemes should be reviewed in the light of our proposals on tort and the assessment of damages.

Recommendations 171–173

ANIMALS

We concluded that no major change is needed in the law of England, Wales and Northern Ireland relating to injuries caused by animals, but that Scottish legislation might be aligned with that for the rest of the United Kingdom.

Recommendations 174–176

EXCEPTIONAL RISKS

We concluded that some provision should be made for exceptional risks that could not be adequately covered under any of the categories we have considered. Strict liability should be imposed on controllers of things or operations which by their unusually hazardous nature require supervision because of their potential for causing death or personal injury; and on controllers of things or operations which, although normally safe, might cause serious and extensive casualties if they go wrong.

Recommendations 177–188

THE COST OF OUR PROPOSALS

As far as possible the cost of compensation should be borne by those creating the risks. Compensation should be redistributed in favour of the seriously injured. By removing double compensation, eliminating tort compensation for trivial injuries and reducing the amount spent on administration the overall cost of compensation for personal injury would be reduced in the early years, although ultimately there would be an overall increase of £41 million a year (at January 1977 prices). This change reflects an increase in the cost of social security compensation of £130 million a year and a reduction in the cost of tort compensation and other payments of £89 million a year.

Details of costs are in chapter 32.

371

List of recommendations

THE ASSESSMENT OF TORT DAMAGES

The heads of claim (Chapter 12)

1 In England, Wales and Northern Ireland, as under the present law in Scotland, damages for loss of income by a living plaintiff should be recoverable on the basis of his pre-accident life expectancy, subject to a deduction for the amount which he would have spent on his own living expenses (paragraph 335).

2 Loss of earning capacity should be regarded as a factor to be taken into account when assessing damages for future loss of earnings (paragraph 338).

3 Section 2(4) of the Law Reform (Personal Injuries) Act 1948 and section 3(4) of the Law Reform (Miscellaneous Provisions) Act (Northern Ireland) 1948 should be repealed; and in their place it should be provided that private medical expenses should be recoverable in damages if and only if it was reasonable on medical grounds that the plaintiff should incur them (paragraph 342).

4 Damages should continue to be recoverable for an injured person's need to have services rendered and expenses incurred by others for his benefit; such damages should be recoverable by the injured person in his own right; the injured person should not have a legal obligation to account to, or hold the damages in trust for, those rendering the services or incurring the expenses; and such damages should continue to be assessed on the basis of what is reasonable (paragraph 351).

5 Damages should be recoverable by an injured person for the loss of his capacity gratuitously to render services to others, where those to whom the services were rendered are within the class of relatives entitled to bring an action for loss of support under the Damages (Scotland) Act 1976; and such damages should be assessed on the basis of what is reasonable (paragraph 358).

6 Damages for loss of expectation of life as a separate head of damage should be abolished (paragraph 372).

7 Damages should continue to be recoverable for loss of amenity; such damages should continue to be awarded as a single sum; and a scale of damages should not be introduced (paragraph 380).

8 (By a majority) Damages should continue to be recoverable for pain and suffering; and such damages should continue to be awarded, together with damages for loss of amenity, as a single sum (paragraph 381). (Note of reservation, paragraphs 448 to 464.)

9 (By a majority) No damages should be recoverable for non-pecuniary loss suffered during the first three months after the date of injury (paragraph 388).

10 We are equally divided on the question whether a ceiling (of five times average annual industrial earnings) should be imposed on damages for non-pecuniary loss (paragraphs 390 to 392).

11 Non-pecuniary damages should no longer be recoverable for permanent unconsciousness (paragraph 398).

12 The relatives entitled to claim damages for lost dependency in England, Wales and Northern Ireland should be the same as those entitled to claim damages for loss of support under the Damages (Scotland) Act 1976 (paragraph 404).

13 In assessing damages for lost dependency, changes in a dependant's earnings which have taken place before the trial as a direct result of the death should be taken into account; but the possibility of changes in a dependant's earnings after the trial should normally be left out of account (paragraph 408).

14 In assessing damages for lost dependency, the court should be able to take into account the remarriage of a widow before trial; and the court should continue to be able to take into account the remarriage of a widower before trial (paragraph 412).

15 In assessing damages for lost dependency, the possibility of divorce between a widow or widower and the deceased if he or she had lived should be disregarded, if taking the possibility into account would be to the detriment of the plaintiff (paragraph 417).

16 (By a majority) Damages for loss of society should be recoverable by a husband or wife for the death of the other, by a parent for the death of an unmarried minor child, and by an unmarried minor child for the death of a parent (paragraph 424). (Dissenting paragraphs 425 and 426.)

17 Damages for loss of society in England, Wales and Northern Ireland should be set at half average annual industrial earnings (paragraph 427).

18 Damages for loss of society in Scotland should continue to be unlimited (paragraph 429).

19 In England, Wales and Northern Ireland, as under the present law in Scotland, a claim for damages for pecuniary loss in the 'lost years' should not survive for the benefit of the claimant's estate (paragraph 437).

20 In England, Wales and Northern Ireland, as under the present law in Scotland, a claim for loss of society should not survive for the benefit of the claimant's estate (paragraph 441).

21 In England, Wales and Northern Ireland, claims for pain and suffering and loss of amenity should continue to survive for the benefit of the claimant's estate; and in Scotland such claims should continue not to survive (paragraph 444).

22 The actions for loss of services and loss of consortium (*per quod servitium amisit* and *per quod consortium amisit*) should be abolished (paragraph 447).

Offsets (Chapter 13)

23   The full value of social security benefits payable to an injured person or his dependants as a result of an injury for which damages are awarded should be deducted in the assessment of the damages (paragraph 482).

24   For the purpose of offsetting, social security benefits should be divided into categories; the benefits in each category should be deducted in assessing the corresponding portion of the tort award; and there should be no carry over between categories (paragraph 487).

25   (By a majority) For the purpose of offsetting, there should be three categories of social security benefits – those compensating for loss of earnings, for expenses, and for non-pecuniary loss (paragraph 488). (Minority opinion, paragraphs 543 to 548.)

26   (By a majority) The proposed allowance for severely handicapped children (recommendation 166) should be set off against damages for expenses, where a child succeeds in a tort claim for the injury which caused his handicap (paragraph 495). (Minority opinion, paragraphs 543 to 548.)

27   (With one dissentient) Where damages are reduced on account of contributory negligence, only the equivalent proportion of the relevant social security benefits should be deducted (paragraph 498).

28   *Ex gratia* payments made to the plaintiff by his employer should continue to be left out of account in the assessment of damages, unless the employer is the defendant (see recommendation 37) (paragraph 501).

29   Occupational sick pay should continue to be taken into account in the assessment of damages, unless either the plaintiff is by his contract of service under a contractual obligation to refund it from damages, or it was advanced by his employer as a loan on the express understanding that it would be repaid if damages were recovered (paragraph 505).

30   The value of maintenance provided by a public authority should be taken into account in the assessment of damages (paragraph 512).

31   Payments received under a first party contract of insurance should continue to be left out of account in the assessment of damages (paragraph 516).

32   Occupational disability pensions should continue to be left out of account in the assessment of damages for loss of earnings (paragraph 520).

33   Occupational disability pensions should continue to be taken into account in the assessment of damages for loss of retirement pension (paragraph 523).

34   Widows' benefits provided by occupational pension schemes which are not contracted out of the state scheme should be left out of account in the assessment of damages; and, in the case of contracted out schemes, only the full equivalent state benefit should be deducted (paragraph 528).

35   Benefits provided under a policy of permanent health insurance taken out by an employer for his employees should be left out of account in the assessment of damages (paragraph 529).

36   Subject to recommendation 37, charitable gifts and other donations to the plaintiff should continue to be left out of account in the assessment of damages (paragraph 532).

37   Payments made by the defendant should be taken into account in the assessment of damages unless

either   i   the payments were made subject to an express contractual provision that they would be repaid from any damages recovered;

or   ii   the payments were in the form of contributions to a general fund from which people other than the plaintiff also benefited (paragraph 536).

38   In England, Wales and Northern Ireland, as under the present law in Scotland, benefits derived from the deceased's estate should be disregarded in the assessment of damages for lost dependency (paragraph 539).

The form of damages (Chapter 14)

39   Damages for past pecuniary loss should continue to be awarded as a lump sum (paragraph 551).

40   (By a majority) Provision should be made, in accordance with recommendations 41 to 54, for damages in the form of periodic payments for future pecuniary loss caused by death or serious and lasting injury (paragraph 573). (Minority opinion, paragraphs 615 to 630.)

41   The court should be obliged to award damages for future pecuniary loss caused by death or serious and lasting injury in the form of periodic payments, unless it is satisfied, on the application of the plaintiff, that a lump sum award would be more appropriate (paragraph 576).

42   The parties in a claim for future pecuniary loss caused by death or serious and lasting injury should remain free to negotiate a settlement for damages in the form either of a lump sum or of periodic payments; but the plaintiff's professional adviser should be under a duty to point out the advantages of periodic payments and the normal court practice in such cases (paragraph 578).

43   The court should have a discretion to award damages in the form of periodic payments for future pecuniary loss caused by injuries which are not serious and lasting (paragraph 580).

44   The recipient of an award of damages in the form of periodic payments should be entitled to apply to the court for its commutation at any stage during the currency of the award, based on his total future expectation of periodic payments in the light of his circumstances when the application is considered; the court should have a discretionary power to grant or refuse the application; and, in exercising this discretion, the court should apply the same criteria as for applications for lump sums at the time of the award (paragraph 582).

List of recommendations

45   Where the plaintiff is suffering from a serious and lasting injury which is not, at the time of the trial, causing him pecuniary loss, the court should, subject to recommendation 46, be able to give a declaratory judgment (paragraph 584).

46   Declaratory judgments should be given only if the defendant is a public authority, or is insured in respect of the plaintiff's claim (paragraph 585).

47   Awards in the form of periodic payments should be subject to review by the courts (paragraph 589).

48   The review of an award in the form of periodic payments should be confined to changes in the plaintiff's pecuniary loss brought about by changes in his medical condition, and to cases which are the subject of a declaratory judgment (paragraph 591).

49   If both the parties to a settlement for damages in the form of periodic payments wish its terms to be subject to the review procedure, they should be able either to register the settlement with the court or to ask the court to make an order by consent (paragraph 592).

50   Where the recipient of an award in the form of periodic payments dies prematurely as a result of his injury, his dependants should be able to bring an action for lost dependency in respect of the years when but for his injury he would still have been alive (paragraph 594).

51   Periodic payments provided by insurance should be administered by insurers; and payments should be made no less often than monthly (paragraph 597).

52   Periodic payments should be revalued annually in line with the movement of average earnings (paragraph 600).

53   Periodic payments provided by insurance should be financed by a fixed escalation scheme based on the contracting out provisions of the Social Security Pensions Act 1975 (paragraph 608).

54   The court should have power to require an uninsured defendant to deposit a lump sum with an insurance company, in order to provide an income to meet an award for periodic payments; and the income derived from this lump sum should be inflation proofed by the fixed escalation scheme (recommendation 53) (paragraph 611).

55   Damages for non-pecuniary loss should continue to be awarded as a lump sum (paragraph 614).

The calculation of damages (Chapter 15)

56   There should be no change in the present method of calculating damages for past pecuniary loss, except that relevant social security benefits (see recommendations 23 to 27) should be deducted in full (paragraph 634).

57   The starting point for the assessment of damages for future pecuniary loss should be the plaintiff's net annual loss, that is his net pecuniary loss at the date of the award, adjusted as necessary and expressed as an annual figure (paragraph 641).

58   (By a majority) The net annual loss should be calculated according to the procedure set out in paragraphs 662 to 674 (paragraph 642). (Minority opinion, paragraphs 709 to 726.)

59   The initial annual amount of damages for future pecuniary loss in the form of periodic payments should be the gross equivalent of the net annual loss; and the payments should be taxed as earned income in the hands of the recipient (paragraph 644).

60   Damages for future pecuniary loss in the form of a lump sum should continue to be calculated by multiplying the net annual loss by the appropriate multiplier (paragraph 650).

61   (By a majority) The appropriate multiplier for calculating lump sum damages for future pecuniary loss should be determined by the modified multiplier method (paragraph 658). (Minority opinion, paragraphs 709 to 726).

62   There should be no fixed rule for calculating the offset of social security benefits from damages for non-pecuniary loss; but multipliers based on a 2 per cent discount rate for all plaintiffs may be helpful as a guide to the value of the benefits (paragraph 691).

Adjudication (Chapter 16)

63   Jury trial should not be reintroduced to personal injuries litigation in England and Wales; and consideration should be given to the abolition of jury trial in personal injuries litigation in Scotland (paragraph 734).

64   Consideration should be given to a system whereby, in the absence of agreed expert evidence, the court could, on the application of either party, appoint an expert whose report would have the effect of agreed expert evidence (paragraph 738).

65   The rule in *Jefford* v. *Gee* that interest on damages for past pecuniary loss should be awarded at half the rate payable on money in court which is placed on short term investment should stand; and it should be applied in Scotland and Northern Ireland (paragraph 742).

66   As at present, no interest should be awarded on damages for future pecuniary loss (paragraph 743).

67   The rule in *Cookson* v. *Knowles* that no interest should be awarded on damages for non-pecuniary loss should stand; and it should be applied in Scotland and Northern Ireland (paragraph 748).

68   The rule in *Cookson* v. *Knowles* that interest should be awarded only on that part of the damages for lost dependency which relates to losses before trial, at a half rate, should stand; it should be applied in Scotland and Northern Ireland; and such interest should run from the date of death to the date of trial (paragraph 752).

69   No interest should be awarded on damages for loss of society (paragraph 756).

70   Damages for pecuniary and non-pecuniary loss should be separately assessed; and the court should have a discretion, in any particular case, to decide whether the damages should be itemised in more detail than would be required by our recommendations on offsetting social security benefits and our recommendations on interest (recommendations 23 to 27 and 65 to 69) (paragraph 762).

71   An award of damages, however itemised, should not be interfered with on appeal unless it is inordinately high or inordinately low as a whole (paragraph 763).

COMBINING NO-FAULT AND TORT

Work injuries (Chapter 17)

72   No-fault compensation for work injuries and diseases should continue to be provided by the industrial injuries scheme, augmented as necessary by national insurance provision, and administered as part of the social security system by the Department of Health and Social Security in Great Britain and the Department of Health and Social Services in Northern Ireland (paragraph 797).

73   For those injured at work, long term invalidity pensions payable under the Social Security Pensions Act 1975 should be calculated, in all cases, as if contributions under the new pensions scheme had been paid for 20 years (paragraph 805).

74   For those injured at work, short term injury benefit should comprise the existing flat rate benefit and an earnings related supplement based on $33\frac{1}{3}$ per cent of earnings between the short term lower earnings limit and £30, and 25 per cent of earnings between £30 and the upper earnings limit (paragraph 808).

75   An earnings related supplement to injury benefit should be payable without contribution conditions (paragraph 809).

76   During receipt of any incapacity benefits, a man injured at work should be treated, for retirement pension qualification purposes, as having had earnings at his pre-accident level (paragraph 812).

77   European provisions for compensating for partial incapacity should be studied with a view to the early introduction in this country of a scheme of compensation for partial incapacity for work (paragraph 820).

78   Basic industrial disablement benefit should continue in its present form (paragraph 824).

79   The constant attendance allowance and the exceptionally severe disablement allowance should eventually be abolished for those injured at work, who should thereafter rely on the attendance allowance payable under section 35 of the Social Security Act 1975 (paragraph 833).

80   Long term benefits should be payable to widows covered by the industrial injuries scheme at the same rates and under the same conditions relating to age and family circumstances as will apply to widows under the provisions of the

new state pensions scheme, except that the earnings related addition to a widow's pension under the industrial injuries scheme should be calculated in all cases as if the late husband had been contributing to the scheme for 20 years (paragraph 841).

81   The method of calculating the earnings related supplement to short term widows' benefit under the industrial injuries scheme should be improved in line with our proposals for short term injury benefit (recommendation 74); and the supplement should be payable in all cases (paragraph 842).

82   Widows' benefit under the industrial injuries scheme should, as now, cease on remarriage; and the provision of a lump sum payment of a year's benefit to the widow should continue (paragraph 843).

83   As far as possible, all widowers covered by the industrial injuries scheme should be treated, for benefit purposes, in the same way as widows (paragraph 847).

84   Industrial death benefits for relatives other than widows and children should be abolished (paragraph 850).

85   Self employed persons should be covered by the provisions of the industrial injuries scheme; but, for the time being, benefits should be at a flat rate (paragraph 856).

86   (By a majority of one) Injuries occurring on the way to and from work should be included in the industrial injuries scheme (paragraph 867).

87   The appropriate procedures should be examined to see whether there is any means of reducing the time taken to prescribe occupational diseases (paragraph 876).

88   In accordance with the EEC Recommendation of 20 July 1966, the restrictive conditions relating to the prescription of occupational diseases should be removed (paragraph 879).

89   In addition to compensating the occupational diseases listed on the schedule of prescribed diseases, benefit should become payable where the claimant could prove that his disease was caused by his occupation and that it was a particular risk of his occupation (paragraph 887).

90   The basic definition of an industrial accident should continue to be an accident 'arising out of and in the course of' employment (paragraph 897).

91   (With one dissentient) The industrial injuries scheme should continue to be financed through the existing system of national insurance contributions and Exchequer supplement; and, subject to recommendation 92, the additional cost of the changes proposed should be met by an increase in the employers' contribution only (paragraph 904). (Note of reservation, paragraphs 940 to 948.)

92   The benefits proposed for the self employed should be wholly financed by an increase in their national insurance contributions (paragraph 905).

379

93   (With one dissentient) An injured workman's right of action for damages against his employer should be retained (paragraph 913). (Note of reservation, paragraphs 949 to 955.)

94   There should be no change in the basis of liability in tort for work injury (paragraph 916).

95   There should be no formal reversal of the burden of proof in actions for damages for work injury (paragraph 922).

Road injuries (Chapter 18)

96   A no-fault compensation scheme should be introduced for motor vehicle injuries; and it should be based on the improved industrial injuries scheme (paragraph 1004).

97   The scheme should cover injuries involving motor vehicles on roads and other land to which the public has access (paragraph 1010).

98   Subject to recommendations 99 and 100, rates of benefit under the road scheme should be the same as under the improved industrial injuries scheme (paragraph 1015).

99   Constant attendance allowance and exceptionally severe disablement allowance should not be payable under the road scheme; and those injured by motor vehicles should continue to rely on the attendance allowance payable under section 35 of the Social Security Act 1975 (paragraph 1016).

100   The benefits payable to widows and widowers under the road scheme should be the same as those which would be payable under the improved industrial injuries scheme (paragraph 1018).

101   Subject to recommendations 102 and 103, non-earners should be entitled under the road scheme to the basic flat rate benefits and disablement benefit for loss of faculty (paragraph 1020).

102   Children under the age of 12 who have been injured in motor vehicle accidents should receive, for as long as they are incapable of normal activity, a basic benefit equal to the allowance proposed for severely handicapped children (recommendation 166); children over the age of 12 but under the age of 16 should in addition receive disablement benefit at the reduced rate applicable under the industrial injuries scheme to those under 16 and not in full time employment; and children over the age of 16 should receive a basic benefit at the level of non-contributory invalidity pension, and disablement benefit at the full adult rate (paragraph 1022).

103   Those receiving a retirement pension should not receive the flat rate benefit under the road scheme; but a retirement pensioner who was working at the time of the injury should receive the earnings related addition to the flat rate benefit and the addition should be related to his immediate pre-accident earnings (paragraph 1024).

104   The road scheme should be administered by the Department of Health and Social Security (paragraph 1027).

105 (By a majority) The Secretary of State for Social Services should have a discretionary power to discontinue the payment of road scheme benefits to those injured by motor vehicles on their way to or from committing an offence for which they are subsequently convicted on indictment, or in the course of committing such an offence; but such a power should be exercised only in exceptional circumstances, where the payment of benefits would clearly be repugnant to public opinion (paragraph 1034). (Minority opinion, paragraphs 1091 to 1092.)

106 The Secretary of State's discretion to discontinue the payment of road scheme benefits (recommendation 105) should not extend to benefits paid to the widows and dependants of those who die as a result of injuries incurred in the course of criminal activity (paragraph 1035).

107 Road scheme benefits should be available to all those who suffer motor vehicle injury in the United Kingdom, whether or not they are habitually resident here (paragraph 1039).

108 Road scheme benefits should continue in payment to those who were injured in the United Kingdom while habitually resident here, if they subsequently reside abroad (paragraph 1040).

109 Consideration should be given to the question of inflation proofing road scheme benefits payable to those residing abroad who were injured in the United Kingdom while habitually resident here (paragraph 1040).

110 (With one dissentient) Road scheme benefits payable to those injured in the United Kingdom while not habitually resident here should, subject to the terms of any international arrangements, cease when they leave the country and not resume when they return (paragraph 1041). (Dissenting paragraph 1042.)

111 (By a majority) Road scheme benefits should not be payable in respect of injuries suffered abroad (paragraph 1043). (Dissenting paragraph 1044.)

112 (With one dissentient) The road scheme should be financed by a levy on petrol (paragraph 1054). (Note of reservation, paragraphs 1093 to 1102.)

113 The amount raised by a petrol levy should be enough to cover the whole cost of cash no-fault compensation for motor vehicle injuries outside the sphere of employment, including the present cost of social security benefits and the cost of administration (paragraph 1056).

114 There should be no change in the basis of liability in tort for motor vehicle injury (paragraph 1068).

115 There should be no change in the basis of liability in tort for injury resulting from road accidents involving vehicles other than motor vehicles (paragraph 1068).

116 There should be no formal reversal of the burden of proof in actions for damages for motor vehicle injury (paragraph 1075).

381

List of recommendations

117   There should be no formal reversal of the burden of proof in actions for damages for injury resulting from road accidents involving vehicles other than motor vehicles (paragraph 1076).

118   The defence of contributory negligence should not be available in cases of motor vehicle injury where the plaintiff was, at the time of the injury, under the age of 12 (paragraph 1077).

119   Subject to recommendation 120, the present compulsory third party insurance provisions for motor vehicles should be retained (paragraph 1079).

120   The deposit alternative to compulsory third party insurance for motor vehicles, under section 144(1) of the Road Traffic Act 1972 and section 75(2)(b) of the Road Traffic Act (Northern Ireland) 1970, should be abolished (paragraph 1080).

Air transport (Chapter 19)

121   The United Kingdom should ratify the Montreal Protocol No 3 as soon as the USA has done so (paragraph 1129).

122   In relation to all flights entering or leaving the United Kingdom, there should be a limit of liability equivalent to the special contract limit applied by British airlines (paragraph 1131).

123   There should be no channelling of liability to a single party in respect of air transport injuries (paragraph 1134).

124   Further consideration should be given to the possibility of imposing compulsory third party insurance in respect of private aircraft (paragraph 1141).

Sea and inland waterways (Chapter 20)

125   The United Kingdom should ratify the London Convention (paragraph 1163).

126   The provisions of the London Convention should be applied to inland craft (paragraph 1165).

127   Pending implementation of the Montreal Protocol No 3, the limit in respect of liability for death or personal injury to passengers on international hovercraft journeys should be raised to the equivalent of the special contract limit applied by British airlines; and the limit for journeys within the United Kingdom should be increased to the equivalent of 875,000 gold francs (paragraph 1169).

Rail transport (Chapter 21)

128   Railway undertakings should be strictly liable in tort for death or personal injury which is wholly or partly caused by the movement of rolling stock (paragraph 1186).

129   The defences of contributory negligence and voluntary assumption of risk should be permitted to a railway undertaking where strict liability applies (paragraph 1188).

130   The defence of act of a third party should not be available to a railway undertaking where strict liability applies (paragraph 1189).

131   The defence of act of God, or *force majeure*, should not be available to a railway undertaking where strict liability applies (paragraph 1190).

132   Railway undertakings should not be strictly liable for injury or death to trespassers; and the questions whether they owe any duty of care to a particular trespasser, and if so how it could be performed, should be determined as in the case of other occupiers of property (paragraph 1191).

Products liability (Chapter 22)

133   Producers should be strictly liable in tort for death or personal injury caused by defective products (paragraph 1236).

134   'Defect' should be defined in accordance with Article 2 of the Strasbourg Convention, which states that 'a product has a "defect" when it does not provide the safety which a person is entitled to expect, having regard to all the circumstances including the presentation of the product' (paragraph 1237).

135   Both producers of finished products and component producers should be strictly liable in tort for defective products; but, subject to recommendation 136, distributors should not (paragraph 1242).

136   A distributor who has sold a defective product in the course of a business should be under an obligation to disclose to a person injured by the product either the name of the producer of the goods or the name of his own supplier; and failure to do so within a reasonable time should render the seller himself strictly liable in tort (paragraph 1244).

137   In respect of 'own brand' products, strict liability in tort should apply to those who brand them, as well as to their producers (paragraph 1247).

138   Producers should not be exempt from strict liability in respect of defective finished products which have been made to a specification (paragraph 1248).

139   Importers should be treated as producers for the purpose of products liability (paragraph 1250).

140   It should be a defence for the producer to prove either that he did not put the product into circulation; or that the product was not defective when he did so; or that he did not put it into circulation in the course of a business (paragraph 1252).

141   It should not be a defence for the producer merely to prove that he had withdrawn, or attempted to withdraw, his product (paragraph 1253).

142   The manufacturer of an aircraft should be given a right to be indemnified by a user or operator who has wilfully or negligently ignored his instructions to rectify defects or modify service schedules (paragraph 1255).

143   The defence of contributory negligence should be available to a producer (paragraph 1257).

383

144 The producer should not be allowed a defence of development risk (paragraph 1259).

145 The producer should not be allowed a defence of official certification (paragraph 1260).

146 Producers should not be enabled to contract out of strict liability (paragraph 1261).

147 There should be no financial limits on the producer's liability (paragraph 1264).

148 Compulsory liability insurance should not be introduced for products (paragraph 1266).

149 The producer's strict liability in tort should be subject to a cut-off period of ten years from the circulation of the product (paragraph 1269).

150 The provisions of the Strasbourg Convention on the limitation period within which the person injured by a defective product must start proceedings should be adopted (paragraph 1270).

151 Damages for non-pecuniary loss should not be excluded from products liability actions (paragraph 1271).

152 Human blood and organs should be regarded as 'products', and the authorities responsible for distributing them as their 'producers', for the purpose of products liability (paragraph 1276).

153 Movable products incorporated into immovables should be regarded as 'products' for the purpose of products liability (paragraph 1277).

Services (Chapter 23)

154 There should be no change in the basis of liability for injury arising out of the rendering of services; and there should be no formal reversal of the burden of proof (paragraph 1303).

Medical injury (Chapter 24)

155 Any volunteer for medical research or clinical trials who suffers severe damage as a result should have a cause of action, on the basis of strict liability, against the authority to whom he has consented to make himself available (paragraph 1341).

156 Subject to recommendation 155, the basis of liability in tort for medical injuries should continue to be negligence (paragraph 1347).

157 A no-fault scheme for medical accidents should not be introduced at present; but the progress of no-fault compensation for medical accidents in New Zealand and Sweden should be studied and assessed, so that the experience can be drawn upon, if, because of changing circumstances, a decision is taken to introduce a no-fault scheme for medical accidents in this country (paragraph 1371).

Vaccine damage (Chapter 25)

158   The Government, or the local authority concerned, should be strictly liable in tort for severe damage suffered by anyone (adult or child) as a result of vaccination which has been recommended in the interests of the community (paragraph 1413).

Ante-natal injury (Chapter 26)

159   (By a majority) Subject to recommendations 160 and 161, a child born alive suffering from the effects of ante-natal injury caused by the fault of another person should continue to have a right of action for damages against that person (paragraph 1464).

160   (By a majority) Subject to recommendation 161, a child should not have a right of action for damages against either parent for ante-natal injury (paragraph 1471).

161   (By a majority) A child should have a right of action for damages against either parent for ante-natal injury arising from any activity for which insurance is compulsory (paragraph 1472).

162   Section 1(7) of the Congenital Disabilities (Civil Liability) Act 1976 should be repealed (paragraph 1477).

163   There should be no change in the provisions of the Congenital Disabilities (Civil Liability) Act 1976 relating to pre-conception injury, beyond the removal of the father as a potential defendant (paragraph 1482).

164   Liability for pre-conception injury should be limited in Scotland to the same extent as in the rest of the United Kingdom (paragraph 1483).

165   There should be no cause of action for damages for 'wrongful life' (paragraph 1486).

Children (Chapter 27)

166   There should be a new non-taxable disability income of £4 a week for all severely handicapped children, payable from age two as an addition to child benefit, financed by the Exchequer and administered by the Department of Health and Social Security (paragraph 1531).

167   Mobility allowance should be payable from age two (paragraph 1533).

168   The conditions of eligibility for mobility allowance should be reviewed so as to help those children who may be technically mobile, but whose mobility is subject to special difficulties (paragraph 1534).

Occupiers' liability (Chapter 28)

169   For England and Wales, the law laid down in the Occupiers' Liability Act 1957 should be supplemented by enactment of the Law Commission's

proposals for 'uninvited entrants'; and similar steps should be taken in Northern Ireland (paragraph 1550).

170　There should be no change in the law governing occupiers' liability in Scotland (paragraph 1557).

Criminal injuries (Chapter 29)

171　The criminal injuries compensation scheme for Great Britain should be put on to a statutory basis (paragraph 1591).

172　Compensation under the criminal injuries schemes in Great Britain and Northern Ireland should continue to be based on tort damages (paragraph 1592).

173　Consideration should be given to applying to the criminal injuries compensation schemes our recommendations for changes in the assessment of tort damages (paragraph 1595).

Animals (Chapter 30)

174　There should be no change in the law relating to liability for injuries caused by animals in England, Wales or Northern Ireland (paragraph 1626).

175　Provisions parallel to those of the Animals Act 1971 should be enacted for Scotland (paragraph 1626).

176　The Dangerous Wild Animals Act 1976 and the Riding Establishments Acts 1964 and 1970 should be amended, either to specify practical limits to the third party insurance cover required, or to give the licensing authorities discretion to determine what is a satisfactory amount (paragraph 1628).

Exceptional risks (Chapter 31)

177　Strict liability should be imposed on the controllers of things or operations in each of two categories—first, those which by their unusually hazardous nature require close, careful and skilled supervision, the failure of which may cause death or personal injury; and, secondly, those which, although normally by their nature perfectly safe, are likely, if they do go wrong, to cause serious and extensive casualties (paragraph 1643).

178　There should be a statutory scheme making the controller of any listed dangerous thing or activity strictly liable for death or personal injury resulting from its malfunctioning; this scheme should involve a parent statute and statutory instruments made under it; the parent statute should contain general provisions and authorise the making of statutory instruments; and each statutory instrument should apply the general provisions of the parent statute to particular dangerous things and activities set out in a list, and should also contain any special provisions relating to one or more of the listed things or activities (paragraph 1651).

179   Statutory authority should not be a defence in respect of any listed thing or activity (paragraph 1653).

180   Two defences should be specified by the parent statute as applicable in respect of all listed things and activities, namely contributory negligence and voluntary assumption of risk (paragraph 1654).

181   The maker of a statutory instrument imposing strict liability should be authorised by the parent statute, if he thinks fit, to provide for a defence that the plaintiff was a trespasser, and to state the conditions on which such a defence would operate (paragraph 1656).

182   (By a majority) With the exception of trespass, any defences which might be thought necessary in addition to contributory negligence and voluntary assumption of risk should be laid down in the parent statute as applicable in respect of all listed things and activities (paragraph 1659). (Dissenting paragraph 1661.)

183   (By a majority) Act of a third party should not be a defence in respect of any listed thing or activity (paragraph 1660). (Dissenting paragraph 1661.)

184   The parent statute should lay down that, wherever strict liability applies to any listed thing or activity, the damages recoverable for death or personal injury should be under the same categories of loss as would apply to tort generally (paragraph 1662).

185   The parent statute should set out the principles on which any subsequent statutory instruments imposing strict liability would have to be made (paragraph 1663).

186   The parent statute should provide for setting up an advisory committee; authorising it to consult the Health and Safety Commission; and requiring that a statutory instrument laid before Parliament should be accompanied by a report on the proposal from the advisory committee (paragraph 1664).

187   The statutory instruments imposing strict liability should require affirmative resolutions of both Houses before coming into effect (paragraph 1667).

188   The maker of a statutory instrument imposing strict liability should have the power, although not the duty, to lay down a requirement of third party insurance (and the minimum permissible cover in any particular case) in respect of the risk to which strict liability is to apply (paragraph 1668).

ALL OF WHICH WE HUMBLY SUBMIT FOR YOUR MAJESTY'S GRACIOUS CONSIDERATION

Pearson (Chairman)
Allen of Abbeydale
John Cameron
W C Anderson
Norman S Marsh
Richard S F Schilling
R S Skerman
M Brooke
Robert B Duthie
R A MacCrindle
D A Marshall
A R Prest
Olive Stevenson
James Stewart
Alan W Ure

Elizabeth Parsons (Secretary)
David Pilkington (Assistant Secretary)

January 1978

388

Annexes

Annexes

Annex 1
(referred to in paragraph 2)

Extracts from Hansard 19 December 1972 when the appointment of the Royal Commission was announced

The Prime Minister (Mr Edward Heath): 'The House will have noticed that the terms of reference require the Royal Commission to consider in what circumstances and by what means compensation should be payable in respect of death or personal injury caused in a number of different ways. Injury suffered in the course of employment is included – as the Robens Committee recommended – and so is injury suffered through the use of a motor vehicle or other means of transport.

The Royal Commission will also have to consider the question of liability for injury suffered through the manufacture, supply or use of goods or services. Hon. Members will observe that this will enable the Commission to consider the principles governing the award of compensation for injury caused by the administration of a drug such as thalidomide, though I must make it plain that no recommendation the Commission may make could have any retrospective effect.

One of the difficulties which arose in the thalidomide cases was whether there is a right to recover compensation in respect of ante-natal injuries. My noble and learned Friend, the Lord Chancellor, has asked the Law Commission to consider the matter and I understand that the Commission expects to be able to report in the course of next year. A similar request has been made to the Scottish Law Commission by my right hon. and learned Friend, the Lord Advocate. The Royal Commission should thus be able to take into account the report of the Law Commissions on this aspect of the matter and any action which Parliament may have taken on it in the meanwhile.'

(Official Report (HC) 19.12.72, Vol 848, col 1120.)

The Lord Chancellor: 'Of course I am familiar with the New Zealand work. As the noble and learned Lord is aware, there they have hit upon a particular scheme. So, in America has the State of Massachusetts and certain other States. They are quite different schemes, based on different principles, although I think both up to a point rely upon no-fault liability as the basis of compensation. That being so, obviously the Royal Commission will want to examine both these and other types of possible model, and indeed the *status quo* as a possible model. I should not like to comment upon these various possible models, but it will be precisely that sort of thing which will engage part of the attention of the noble and learned Lord, Lord Pearson . . .'

(Official Report (HL) 19.12.72, Vol 337, cols 974–5.)

'. . . as to whether it is within the terms of reference of the Royal Commission to consider a State scheme, the answer is clearly that it is within the terms of reference to do so but I should have thought that the Government's thinking at the moment is that *prima facie* compensation should derive from the person or persons promoting the activity which gives rise to the injury. Clearly, the New Zealand scheme, for example, includes an important element of State involvement . . . and it will be within the terms of reference of the Royal Commission to consider that kind of thing . . .'

(Official Report (HL) 19.12.72, Vol 337, col 976.)

Royal Commission on Civil Liability and Compensation for Personal Injury

---

1.   The Commission are about to begin their inquiries and have decided to direct their attention initially to the first two categories of personal injuries mentioned in their terms of reference, namely,

   a   injuries in the course of employment, and

   b   injuries through the use of a motor-vehicle or other means of transport,

and under b to consider at this initial stage only road transport injuries (deferring to a later stage consideration of air, rail and water transport injuries).

2.   The Commission will initially consider especially the basis or bases on which compensation should be recoverable, and what arrangements would be suitable if some new basis were introduced or some existing basis were given a more extended application, and also whether, if and in so far as the existing basis or bases be retained, any major changes should be made. Memoranda on matters within the scope of this initial inquiry will be particularly welcome. Memoranda on other matters falling within the terms of reference will also be welcome, but consideration of them may be deferred to a later stage of the Commission's operations. The Commission intend at a later stage to invite memoranda on other matters which fall within the scope of the initial inquiry. It is contemplated that in some cases the Commission will ask for oral evidence to supplement memoranda.

3.   In the course of the statement made by the Prime Minister in the House of Commons on the 19th December, 1972, when he announced that the Commission was being established, he said:

> "The Government have been considering proposals made from time to time in the past, which are now particularly relevant in the light of the Report of the Robens Committee on Safety and Health at Work and in connection with the recent concern over the thalidomide cases, that there should be an inquiry into the basis of civil liability in the United Kingdom for causing death or personal injury. It is the Government's view that a wide-ranging inquiry is required into the basis on which compensation should be recoverable."

4.   The Commission's terms of reference are as follows:–

"To consider to what extent, in what circumstances and by what means compensation should be payable in respect of death or personal injury (including ante-natal injury) suffered by any person –

a   in the course of employment;

b   through the use of a motor-vehicle or other means of transport;

c   through the manufacture, supply or use of goods or services;

d   on premises belonging to or occupied by another; or

e   otherwise through the act or omission of another where compensation under the present law is recoverable only on proof of fault or under the rules of strict liability,

having regard to the cost and other implications of the arrangements for the recovery of compensation, whether by way of compulsory insurance or otherwise."

5.   It is not intended to make any opening forecast of the eventual scope of the whole inquiry. But the initial stages indicated in paragraph 1 above will involve consideration of the basis or bases on which compensation for injuries resulting from accidents should be recoverable. As those interested in the inquiry are invited to send memoranda, it may be helpful to point out what seems to be at least an important issue and perhaps the fundamental issue in the whole inquiry.

6.   At present the predominant basis of entitlement to compensation for personal injuries is that of tortious liability, which is *liability for fault*. An injured person is entitled to judgement for damages as plaintiff in a civil action if he is able to prove that his injuries were caused by some fault (negligence or breach of statutory duty) of the defendant or a servant or agent of the defendant. In the case of a road transport accident, that is the only basis on which an injured person can be entitled to compensation, and therefore claims are settled on that basis. In the case of an accident in the course of employment, the injured person has, if he is able to prove his case, the same right to recover damages on the basis of another person's liability for fault, but he also has rights to receive benefits, without proof of any person's fault, under the National Insurance (Industrial Injuries) Acts.

7.   It has been suggested in books and addresses that there should be a system of *"liability without fault."* This would be a new system in the case of road transport accidents, but could be an extension of the existing system in the case of accidents in the course of employment. The phrase "liability without fault" is a convenient short phrase, but it must be understood in a wide sense so as to include (among other possible arrangements) the liability of a statutory authority to pay compensation out of a fund to persons entitled to such compensation under statutory provisions. One can achieve greater accuracy, but with loss of brevity, by describing the entitlement instead of the liability: under a system of "liability without fault" an injured person could be entitled to compensation on proof that he had received injuries of a particular category (e.g. road transport injuries) without having to prove that the injuries were caused by the fault of another person. The broad issue is whether it is (a) feasible and (b) desirable to introduce a system of "liability without fault" (or to extend such a system where it already exists). The other side of the issue is whether the existing system of tortious liability is satisfactory and sufficient.

8.   In the case of road transport injuries it will be necessary to compare the list of advantages and disadvantages of the existing systems of tortious liability (liability for fault) with the list of advantages and disadvantages of some possible new system of "liability without fault". Assistance in drawing up the lists would be welcome and so would views as to the relative weight of any item in the list and what system or combination of systems might be preferred.

9.   Many questions can be raised as to the nature and incidence of a possible new system of liability without fault for road transport injuries. For instance —

a   should it apply only in respect of motor vehicles or also to other forms of road transport?

b   should there be (as there is now) compulsory insurance? If so —

    i   who should have to take out or contribute to the insurance, e.g. in the case of motor-vehicles the owners and/or drivers and/or some other class of persons?

    ii   should the insurers be commercial (insurance companies or underwriters) or governmental (a statutory authority)?

    iii   how should the premiums or contributions be collected?

    iv   should the State make some contribution out of general revenue?

    v   how should the rates of premiums or contributions be determined?

    vi   should endeavours be made, by means of differential rates of premiums or contributions or otherwise, to encourage safe driving?

    vii   what could be done for prevention of accidents?

    viii who should be entitled to benefit from the insurance - owners, drivers, their families, passengers, or anyone suffering a transport injury?

    ix   should a claim for compensation or insurance money be subject to adjudication both in respect of entitlement and in respect of amount by a Court of Law or by an administrative officer subject to appeal to a special tribunal, or how otherwise?

    x   what should constitute total incapacity and partial incapacity, and what benefits should be paid in respect of each, and how should the amounts of such benefits be assessed?

    xi   in the case of a fatal accident, what benefits or payments should be payable to whom?

    xii   should the benefits or insurance money be in the form of lump sums paid once for for all or in the form of periodical payments or partly in the one form and partly in the other?

    xiii should periodical payments be at flat rates or related to earnings? Should there be maxima and minima?

    xiv   to what extent, if at all, should compensation be payable for non-economic loss (disability, loss of function, loss of amenities, pain and suffering)?

    If you have already sent to the Law Commission a memorandum on any of the aspects covered by questions x-xiv above would you authorise us to obtain it from them?

(c) If a system of "liability without fault" is introduced, should it be in substitution for or in addition to the existing system of tortious liability? In other words, should the system   of tortious liability be abolished or should it be retained and operate alongside the new system and if so should it be restricted in any way? And if it is to be retained, should the benefits received or receivable under the new system be taken into account fully or partially or not at all in the assessment of damages for tortious liability?

10.   In the case of injuries in the course of employment, a similar comparison of advantages and disadvantages of the two systems will be needed, and similar questions will arise. The difference is that there is already a partial system of "liability without fault" under the National Insurance (Industrial Injuries) Acts which have taken the place of the former Workmen's Compensation Acts. Should the premiums or contributions be payable by the employers or the employees or both? Should the State make contributions out of general revenue?

11. If no new system on the basis of "liability without fault" is introduced should the burden of proof be imposed on the owner (or driver) of the motor vehicle or on the employer, so that he would have to prove that the accident was not caused by any fault of himself or his servant or agent? In the case of a motor vehicle accident should the owners (or driver) also have to prove that the accident was not caused by any defect in the vehicle?
We are not, for the time being at any rate, asking for evidence or suggestions as to possible changes in the methods of assessing damages, because this subject has very recently been considered by the Law Commission.

12. Costing will be an important element in the comparison of the two systems, and any help in the search for statistics will be welcome. If compensation is in the form of periodical payments, there will be mounting liabilities for many years, both because there will be more injured persons receiving compensation and because if inflation continues the amounts will need to be increased. Is there any evidence as to what happens to large lump sums awarded as damages — to what extent, for example, are they invested?

13. Written evidence should be sent to:

> The Secretary,
> Royal Commission on Civil Liability and
>   Compensation for Personal Injury,
> 22, Kingsway,
> London WC2B 6LE

from whom further copies of this circular may be obtained.

April 1973 (reprinted February 1974)

Royal Commission on Civil Liability
and Compensation for Personal Injury

Royal Commission on Civil Liability and Compensation for Personal Injury

Notes on Categories b ii, c, d and e of Terms of Reference

The Commission's first circular referred to categories a and b i — injuries at work and road transport injuries. This circular deals with the remaining categories.

CATEGORY b ii ("THROUGH THE USE OF TRANSPORT BY AIR, RAIL OR WATER")

Carriage by air

1.   The Carriage by Air Act 1961, S.1, gives the force of law to the provisions of the Warsaw Convention, the most material provisions of which are Articles 17, 20, 21, 22, and 25 with effect that :—

   (1)   an injured passenger can recover damages from the carrier, unless the carrier proves the accident was not caused by negligence of the carrier, his servants or agents;

   (2)   damages cannot exceed 250,000 gold francs[1] (currently about £8,000) per passenger, unless the plaintiff proves intent to cause damage or recklessness on the part of the carrier or his servant or agent acting within the scope of his employment;

   (3)   damages are extinguished or reduced if the carrier proves contributory negligence by the passenger.

On the assumption that a change could be made is any change desirable?

Carriage by sea

2.   In the absence of any contractual exclusion of liability the shipowner is liable to passengers and others for personal injuries caused by negligence or other fault of the ship-

---

[1]   For internal flights, 875,000 gold francs (currently about £27,000)

owner, his servants or agents. The Merchant Shipping Act, S.503, as amended by the Merchant Shipping (Liability of Shipowners and Others) Act 1958, S.1, limits to 3100 gold francs (currently somewhat under £100) for each ton of the ship's tonnage the liability of a shipowner for loss of life or personal injury without the actual fault or privity of the shipowner. Apart from an alteration in the amount, S.503 has been in force since 1899. As in the case of carriage by air there are also international Conventions in the area. Is any change desirable?

Carriage by rail

3.   Generally the railway authority is liable to passengers and others for personal injuries caused by the negligence or other fault of the authority, its servants or agents. The authority is carrying on a public enterprise for the benefit of the public. Is any major change desirable? In particular should the authority have an absolute liability (liability without proof of fault) or some form of strict liability (liability unless fault is disproved) for injuries caused to:—

    (a)   passengers;

    (b)   other persons lawfully on railway property, eg., persons coming to buy tickets or meet passengers or buy things at railway book-stalls or kiosks;

    (c)   persons trespassing on railway property?

The Carriage by Railway Act 1972, relating to international rail travel, does already provide for strict liability on the carrier.

CATEGORY c ("THROUGH THE MANUFACTURE, SUPPLY OR USE OF GOODS OR SERVICES")

4.   The development of products liability has been extensive in the United States of America and has been prompted by changes in marketing methods. Nowadays the retailer often merely displays the manufacturer's products in sealed packages, and the customer chooses in reliance on the manufacturer's advertisements. It can be suggested that in such aa situation the customer should have a direct right of action against the manufacturer if the goods are defective. Where, as in most cases, the defects cause only commercial loss to the customer, the subject is outside the Royal Commission's terms of reference, though it is within the scope of an investigation of the whole subject of products liability being carried out by the Law Commission and the Scottish Law Commission jointly. Sometimes, however, the defect may cause personal injury to the customer, or to a member of his family or a friend or bystander who is a reasonably foreseeable victim of the defect. That is within the Royal Commission's terms of reference.

5.   Under existing law the injured person would in many cases have a cause of action in tort [1] against the manufacturer under the principle of *Donoghue v. Stevenson* [1932] A.C. 562, as applied in subsequent cases, on the ground that the manufacturer negligently, or otherwise culpably, manufactured and supplied and thus put into circulation goods of unreasonably dangerous character which caused the plaintiff's injury. One has to use some such phrase as "unreasonably dangerous" (which is taken from the American Restatement of the Law of Torts Section 402A) because there are some goods which, though correctly made and supplied and safe when properly and carefully used by a normal person, are dangerous when misused or negligently used or used by a person with a special allergy. Under existing law the plaintiff has to prove not only that the goods as supplied by the manufacturer were unreasonably dangerous and this caused the plaintiff's injury, but also

---

(1)   Broadly speaking, "tort" means a civil as opposed to a criminal wrong, and "tortious liability" means responsibility for compensating the person wronged. Tortious liability is also to be distinguished from contractual liability. The contractual liability of a seller of goods to the buyer under the Sale of Goods Act 1893 has been extended by the Supply of Goods (Implied Terms) Act 1973.

that their dangerous character was due to some negligence by or other fault of the manufacturer, his servants or agents. The plaintiff may have considerable difficulty in proving these two matters if there were several intermediate transactions before the goods reached the plaintiff.

6. Is any change in the law necessary or desirable? If so, one possible change would be to shift the burden of proof, so that if the plaintiff proved that he suffered injury by reason of the dangerous character of the product it would be for the manufacturer to exculpate himself by showing either (a) that the product was not unreasonably dangerous when he supplied it and must have become so afterwards or (b) that the dangerous character was not due to any negligence by or other fault of the manufacturer, his servants or agents but to some unavoidable extraneous cause.

7. Another possible change would be to impose some "no-fault" liability on the manufacturer, so that he would be required to stand by his product and his advertisements of it and would be liable, without proof of fault, if the dangerous character of the product which caused injury was present when the manufacturer supplied it. It would seem unfair to hold the manufacturer liable for defects caused afterwards. If there were a no-fault liability of this kind, should there be compulsory insurance?

8. One has to consider also the liabilities of retailers and of intermediaries such as distributors, factors and wholesalers. Retailers selling direct may have contractual as well as tortious liability [2] under the existing law or some proposed extension of it. If a retailer was sued he might bring in an intermediary as third party in the action. An intermediary may also have a tortious liability to the injured person if the dangerous character of the goods, which caused the injury, was due to the intermediary's fault. It can be suggested that there might be a no-fault system rendering any person supplying unreasonably dangerous goods liable for any personal injury caused by them, and that, if so, there should be compulsory insurance.

9. A complication is that a large selling organisation may put its own brand name on goods manufactured to its order by another person, and it may advertise them. In such a case would it be appropriate to impose any no-fault liability on the large selling organisation rather than on the manufacturer? There are other special problems. For instance, what should be the respective liabilities of (i) makers and suppliers of artificial joints and other medical implants (ii) importers (iii) makers of component parts (iv) assemblers? To what extent should disclaimers of responsibility be allowed to have effect?

10. Also to be considered are injuries caused in the rendering of services, eg., hairdressing; faulty repair work causing accidents in the home — by electrocution for example. At present there is no civil liability without proof of fault. Should there be any change in the law in this respect?

CATEGORY d ("ON PREMISES BELONGING TO OR OCCUPIED BY ANOTHER) [3]

11. The occupier, being in control of the premises, has the main duty of taking care of the safety of entrants on the premises. He has different duties in relation to different classes of entrants, as follows.

    i. *Employees.* The occupier's duty to his own employees falls to be dealt with under category a of the Terms of Reference.

---

(2)   See footnote to paragraph 5.

(3)   If you have already submitted views on this head to the Law Commission your permission to obtain them would save you repetition. But you may wish to add further comment in the light of a possible change in the basis of compensation.

ii.   *Visitors*, as defined in the Occupiers' Liability Act 1957, are persons invited or permitted by the occupier to enter or use the premises, (S.1(2)), and the occupier owes them "the common duty of care", which is to take such care as in all the circumstances is reasonable to see that they will be reasonably safe in using the premises for the purposes for which they are invited or permitted by the occupier to be there (S.2(2)).

iii.   *Lawful Entrants.* S.2(6) of the same Act provides that "persons who enter premises for any purpose in the exercise of a right conferred by law are to be treated as permitted by the occupier to be there for that purpose, whether they in fact have his permission or not". The effect is to apply the "common duty of care" mutatis mutandis, and the occupier's duty to them is much as in ii. There may, however, be doubts as to who such persons are. Presumably a rating surveyor making his survey and the electricity or gas meter-reader are included. It has been held that a person who uses a bridge in pursuance of a public right of way is not included. (*Greenhalgh v. British Railways Board* [1969] 2 QB 286 CA).

iv.   *Entrants under Access Agreement or Order.* S.1(4) of the same Act provides that "A person entering any premises in exercise of rights conferred by virtue of an access agreement or order under the National Parks and Access to the Countryside Act 1949 is not, for the purposes of this Act, a visitor of the occupier of these premises". The object of an access agreement or order is to enable the public to have access for open-air recreation to open country (S.59(1) of the 1949 Act). Those taking advantage of it are, so to speak, "authorised ramblers", and S.60(1) provides that they are not to be treated as trespassers. S.66(2) provides that "The operation of subsection (1) of S.60 in relation to any land shall not increase the liability under any enactment not contained in this Act or under any rule of law, of a person interested in that land or adjoining land in respect of the state thereof or of things done or omitted thereon". But what is the liability which is not increased? The occupier cannot treat them as trespassers, and therefore cannot keep them off the land or remove them from it. Presumably he must treat them with common humanity and not expose them to serious risks. Is some clarification required?

v.   *Entrants under Right of Way.* The occupier is not obliged to keep the premises in good repair for the benefit of persons exercising a right of way. But what care should he take to avoid exposing them to risks of injury? Again is some clarification required?

vi.   *Trespassers.* As these range from a child to a burglar, some flexible definition of the duty of care is needed. Until recently the English common law took the hard line that for a right of action for damages against the occupier to exist there had to be "some act done with the deliberate intention of doing harm to the trespasser, or at least some act done with reckless disregard of the presence of the trespasser" (per Lord Hailsham L.C. in *Robert Addie & Sons (Collieries) Limited v. Dumbreck* [1929] AC 358. 365). That statement was consistent with earlier authorities, but not with the development of the law of negligence in recent times, and it was eventually overruled by the House of Lords in *British Railways Board v. Herrington* [1972] AC 877, when five separate opinions were pronounced, all broadly to the same effect but with differences in the reasoning.

12.   On 21st April 1972 the Lord Chancellor asked the Law Commission to consider in the light of that decision the law relating to liability for damage or injury suffered by trespassers. On 6th July 1973 the Law Commission issued Working Paper No. 52 on "Liability for Damage or Injury to Trespassers and related Questions of Occupier's Liability", making tentative proposals and inviting comments, and it remains to be seen how in their Report the occupier's duty to trespassers will be formulated and the "related questions" dealt with. These include the duties of occupiers to the "authorised ramblers" referred to above and to persons exercising a right of way. They also include questions as to contractual provisions restricting liability and whether it should be permissible for an occupier to allow persons to use his premises for certain purposes at their own risk.

13. In Scotland the duty of occupiers to trespassers and other entrants is regulated by the Occupiers' Liability (Scotland) Act 1960, S.2(1). But the content of the duty towards trespassers, who come unasked and unwanted, may differ from that towards visitors invited or permitted or authorised by law to come. The occupier can take steps to save the trespasser from harm by keeping him out of the premises or removing him and this action may be sufficient discharge of the occupier's duty, but such steps are not available in the case of lawful visitors or entrants.

14. There can also be a landlord's liability. The Occupier's Liability Act 1957, S.4(1), has now been replaced by the Defective Premises Act 1972, S.4(1), which provides that "Where premises are let under a tenancy which puts on the landlord an obligation to the tenant for the maintenance or repair of the premises, the landlord owes to all persons who might reasonably be expected to be affected by defects in the state of the premises a duty to take such care as is reasonable in all the circumstances to see that they are reasonably safe from personal injury or from damage to their property caused by a relevant defect". Also a landlord may in some cases have a liability under the law of nuisance.

15. The Royal Commission will thus be considering some of the questions considered by the Law Commission, but in a different context. The Law Commission are considering what the duties of the occupier should be within the existing system of tortious liability whereas the Royal Commission are required to consider what the basis of liability should be. Should there be introduced some system of strict liability (imposing on the occupier the burden of proving that the injury to an entrant was not caused by any fault of the occupier, his servants or agents) or some system of absolute liability or no-fault compensation? Could there be any system of compulsory insurance against liability to persons injured on the premises for (i) all occupiers of premises or (ii) occupiers of premises used for business purposes or (iii) occupiers of some other class of premises? Should there be some special regime – e.g. a regime of liability without proof of fault – for public authorities carrying on their undertakings (e.g. railways, gas, water or electricity) for the benefit of the general public? To what extent should disclaimers of responsibility be allowed to have effect?

CATEGORY e ("OTHERWISE THROUGH THE ACT OR OMISSION OF ANOTHER WHERE COMPENSATION UNDER THE PRESENT LAW IS RECOVERABLE ONLY ON PROOF OF FAULT OR UNDER THE RULES OF STRICT LIABILITY") – THE RESIDUAL CATEGORY.

i. *Injuries by "accidents" in the course of medical treatment*

16. "Medical treatment" can be widely defined as including medical, surgical, psychiatric, dental, ophthalmic, osteopathic, physiotherapeutic, nursing and other treatment.

17. At present there is tort liability for negligent medical treatment causing injury to the patient. Should there be added to, or substituted for, the present tort system some new no-fault scheme under which a patient would be entitled to compensation in respect of "accidents" in the course of medical treatment?

13. "Accidents" would be difficult to define. The general idea is of unexpected or unwonted injuries. A surgical operation frequently involves making a wound, and the prescription of a medicine or regime frequently involves interference with the normal chemistry or action of the human body. Such things are not "accidents". But the treatment may have side-effects, of which some are likely, some unlikely but possible, and some so unlikely as to be virtually unpredictable. Could a line be drawn between mere mishaps which should not be compensated and errors or disasters which should? If some unmistakable error were made, that would be an "accident" for the purposes of a no-fault scheme, but it would also be negligence under a fault system so that it would be compensatable without any no-fault scheme. There is also the individual having a peculiar allergy. There is the kill-or-cure operation or the operation which will make the patient either much better or much worse; the risk is recognised and accepted: if the patient dies or is made worse, should there be compensation?

19. If there were a no-fault scheme, should the compensation be payable out of a fund, and if so, from what source should the fund be provided? Or should some authority (e.g. the National Health Service) or the individuals giving medical treatment be held liable? If individuals might be liable, should there be compulsory insurance?

ii. Compensation for Criminal Injuries

20. Since 1964 compensation has been payable under the Criminal Injuries Compensation Scheme on an ex gratia basis to victims of crimes of violence and those hurt as a result of attempts to arrest offenders or to prevent offences. Compensation is assessed on the basis of common law damages and in the form of a lump sum payment. There is a limit on the loss of earnings to be taken into account and no sum is payable in the form of exemplary or punitive damages. There are provisions for avoiding double payments from public funds. The Scheme is at present under review by a Working Party and they are seeking views on certain points on the scope of the scheme e.g. whether compensation should be paid for injuries received at the hands of a suspected offender, and what should be the degree of nexus between the criminal act and the injury of which the act is alleged to be the cause; is it right to have a minimum limit in the amount payable – at present £50, and if so, should this amount be revised in view of the fall in the value of money; should compensation be assessed on loss of faculty rather than loss of earnings; should compensation continue to be in the form of a lump sum or by way of periodical payment? If you have sent comments on this scheme to the Working Party would you like us to get these and take them into account? Are there any other ways in which you think the Commission might take account of this scheme, e.g. as a model for any other part of their studies?

iii Other contingencies

21. Provisions in the Animals Act 1971 replaced the rules of the common law in England and Wales on civil liability for damage done by animals. Damage is defined in section 11 as including "the death of or injury to, any person (including any disease and any impairment of physical or mental condition)". In some cases there is strict liability subject to exceptions (S.2 and 5), in other cases a duty to take reasonable care (S.8). No accurate short summary is possible, but the Act itself contains only thirteen sections. Is any change in the basis of liability or other major change required?

22. Category e covers only injuries "through the act or omission of another", so not all accidental injuries are included. But other possibilities include injuries resulting from organising dangerous sports and admitting spectators to watch them; providing or managing circuses, fairgrounds or adventure playgrounds; selling or using fireworks; carrying on school activities at or away from the school; and allowing children to use airguns or bows and arrows. There is the fire risk in hotels and places of public entertainment etc. No doubt there are many others, e.g. injury by falling branch of a tree; accidents to pedestrians using faulty roads or footpaths; injury sustained during an attempt to rescue a child or other person.

23. Generally the primary question is whether any change in the basis of liability or other major change is desirable. If the change would involve increased expenditure, it has to be considered where the money would come from, and, if the answer is "from compulsory insurance", then who should be required to insure, and how could they be compelled to do so?

Royal Commission on Civil Liability
and Compensation for Personal Injury

February 1974

Royal Commission on Civil Liability and Compensation for Personal Injury

Some General Issues

1.   The Commission's first circular dated April 1973 dealt with categories a and b i — injuries at work and road transport injuries. The Second Circular refers to the remaining categories. This Third Circular invites comment on certain issues, often common to the whole field.

2.   These are —

i   the difficulties of overlapping compensation, which arise especially under categories a and b i;

ii   the merits of recurrent payments as opposed to lump sums (or maybe some discretion for a choice or even a mixture of the two);

iii ante-natal injury, which can have many causes;

iv   whether, if some other remedy such as a no-fault scheme is introduced or extended, tort should exist alongside it or be abolished;

v   whether any alteration ought to be made in the present system of adjudication;

vi   whether differential contributions or premiums have merit.

i   OVERLAPPING COMPENSATION

3.   There is at present a dual system of compensation for accidents at work. The injured employee is entitled (i) to benefits under the National Insurance (Industrial Injuries) Acts without proving that the injury was caused by anyone's fault (ii) to recover damages from his employer, if he can prove "fault" (negligence or breach of statutory duty) on the part of the employer, his servant or agent. There is thus some overlapping.

4.   In the days of Workmen's Compensation the injured workman had to elect: he could not have both, though if he failed in a claim for damages he could still have the Workmen's Compensation payments. In at least some overseas schemes of Workmen's Compensation the benefits are the only compensation provided, actions of tort [1] being excluded.

---

(1)   Broadly speaking a "tort" is a civil as opposed to a criminal wrong, and "tortious liability" means responsibility for compensating the injured party.

5.   The Beveridge Report[2] and the Monckton majority Report on Alternative Remedies in 1946 recommended that there should be no overlapping. However, a minority report recommended that as the injured person contributed to the Industrial Injuries fund, benefits should, no less than payments under private accident insurance policies, be wholly disregarded in assessing damages. In the end there was a compromise whereby only half the scheme benefits for five years are taken into account when assessing damages in tort. (S.2(1) of the Law Reform (Personal Injuries) Act 1948[3].

6.   Clearly there can be a large overlap. A young man injured at work may draw permanent disablement benefit in full for, say, 35 years. But in calculating the damages in the tort action only half of the benefit for 5 years will be deducted.

7.   Again, a person injured in a road accident (not being a working driver), or otherwise having a claim for personal injury, can receive (i) social security benefits if he has qualified by contributions to national insurance, (ii) damages in addition if he can prove causation of the injury by the negligence of another. Under the Law Reform (Personal Injuries) Act, 1948, S.2, as amended by the National Insurance Act, 1971, there is, as with accidents at work, no deduction for benefits payable after five years. The overlapping of benefits and damages in road accidents is similar in principle to the overlapping in accidents at work but less in amount because disablement benefit is payable only in the case of accidents at work.

8.   Is the present position satisfactory? If not what changes should be made? The following possibilities have been suggested:—

   (1)   The action for damages for such injuries could be preserved (a) with full damages or (b) with the existing overlapping of damages and benefits or (c) with a proportion of the benefits for a different period taken into account.

   (2)   The action could be only for nett damages arrived at by deducting the estimated value of past and future social security benefits from the gross damages. The plaintiff would get as damages his actual nett loss – the income lost less the benefits gained. There are precedents in Canada and the USA in relation to motoring cases. Or the action for damages could be limited to certain heads of damage not covered by benefits.

   (3)   Damages could be subject to a minimum limit – a "floor" or "threshold".No damages would be recoverable unless the injuries were serious, and it would be necessary to define "serious" injuries. There are precedents in the USA in relation to motoring cases.

   (4)   The damages could be subject to a maximum limit – a "ceiling". This would bear hardly on persons very severely injured.

   (5)   Full damages would be recovered in the action of tort, but the benefit-paying authority would be entitled to receive out of the damages a sum in principle equal to the benefits paid or payable.

   (6)   The action for damages could be abolished.

The position of dependants in regard to overlapping benefits

9.   Under the existing statutory provisions in the Fatal Accidents Act 1959, there is overlapping compensation for dependants. For example, a widow whose husband has been killed

---

(2)   Paragraph 260 of the Report on Social Insurance and Allied Services (Cmd. 6404) 1942: "An injured person should not have the same need met twice over. He should get benefit at once without prejudice to any alternative remedy, but if the alternative remedy proves in fact to be available he should not in the end get more from the two sources together than he would have got from one alone"

(3)   This provides that "... there shall in assessing these damages be taken into account, against any loss of earnings or profits which has accrued or probably will accrue to the injured person from the injuries, one half of the value of any rights which have accrued or probably will accrue to him therefrom in respect of industrial injury benefit, industrial disablement benefit or sickness benefit for the 5 years beginning with the time when the cause of action accrued". A reference to invalidity benefit was added by the National Insurance Act 1971.

at work through the fault of the employer or another employee may receive a pension from the employer in full, plus social security benefits in full, plus damages under the Fatal Accidents Acts in full. It has been suggested that under these arrangements the economic loss is more than fully compensated.

10. On the other hand there is no compensation for non-economic loss. Soon after the original Fatal Accidents Act of 1846, the English Courts decided that nothing but the bare pecuniary loss should be taken into account in damages for dependants. This can be reconsidered in to-day's very different circumstances when under the Employers' Liability (Compulsory Insurance) Act 1969 employers must insure against such liability and the damages are not paid by the individual employer but by the insurance company out of the general fund of premiums. Should, for example, the loss of the husband and father just be treated as the loss of a mere breadwinner; should not the dependants be compensated for the loss of his general contribution to the well-being of the family? Do similar considerations apply to the loss of a wife and mother, or the loss of a son or daughter? In Scotland there is a solatium to assuage the grief of the relatives. In England there has been no solatium, but now the Law Commission in paragraphs 172-180 of their "Report on Personal Injury Litigation - Assessment of Damages" have proposed that there should be damages in respect of personal bereavement. The Scottish Law Commission in paragraphs 102-113 of their "Report on the Law relating to damages for injuries causing death" have proposed that an award of damages for loss of society and guidance should be substituted for solatium.

11. Also, under Section 4 of the Law Reform (Miscellaneous Provisions) Act 1971, a widow who has in fact remarried is deemed for the purposes of assessing compensation to be still unmarried.

12. Are the present arrangements satisfactory? If they include undesirable elements of overlapping and fiction, could removal of such elements be suitably balanced by provision of compensation for non-economic loss, something like a dowry on re-marriage, or better provision for children?

ii   PERIODICAL PAYMENTS VERSUS LUMP SUMS

13. This subject has been examined by the Law Commission, who in a published Working Paper[4] expressed the opinion that at least an optional alternative to the customary lump sum ought to be available. But in their Report[5] they concluded after hearing evidence from the many interests involved, that in a fault-based system periodical payments would not be useful and indeed would not be used. But, while bowing to the weight of opinion, they saw merit in at least providing for "provisional awards" in suitable cases leaving the final assessment of damages over until the long-term situation had resolved itself or at least become clearer.

14. The Law Commission (and those whom they consulted) were of course considering the subject within the current framework of the law of tort. It will be necessary for the Royal Commission to reconsider the subject in relation to possible changes in the system or basis of compensation. It has been suggested that periodical payments have certain advantages over lump sum payments. For instance:—

   (1)   Assuming the system is sufficiently flexible, such payments can be adapted to allow for changes in the condition and other relevant circumstances of the injured person, and for the effects of inflation.

   (2)   They ease (by making less important) the problems of prognosis, an uncertain matter on which a view has nevertheless to be taken when lump sums are awarded.

---

(4)   Law Commission Published Working Paper No. 41, paras. 226-252.
(5)   Law Commission No. 56, 24 July 1973.

The scope for error either way is very great — awarding too much against a possible deterioration which may not eventuate or too little for the opposite reason.

(3) They provide for the future maintenance of the injured person or his dependants, whereas a lump sum may be lost through inexperience or bad investment advice or spent rapidly, with the result that future maintenance has to be provided by social security.

On the other hand, lump sums have the advantages of simplicity and finality.

15. Opinions on this subject would be welcome.

iii   ANTE-NATAL INJURIES

16. There is, first, the legal problems. If there is injury to the foetus by the negligence or other fault of some person, can the child when born defective as a result have a cause of action for damages against that person? There are technical difficulties, but Courts in the USA,[6] Canada[7] and Australia,[8] the Scottish Law Commission in their Report on Liability for Ante-natal Injury and the Law Commission in their Working Paper on Injuries to Unborn Children have decided or proposed that there is or should be a cause of action in such a case. There are subsidiary but important questions whether a child should be allowed to sue (a) his mother (b) his father for causing ante-natal injury, and whether it should be permissible to trace the chain of causation backwards beyond the time of conception, and whether there should be a cause of action for "wrongful life" (ie. for being allowed or even caused to be born defective instead of being aborted).

17. Both the main question and the subsidiary questions are under consideration by the Law Commission in the light of comments and discussions and after extensive consultation with the medical profession. The Law Commission is considering them in the context of the existing system of tortious liability. The Royal Commission may have to reconsider them in the context of possible changes in the basis of liability, taking into account a wide range of matters in the sphere of social policy. How many babies are born with serious defects, and in what proportion of the cases can the cause of the defect be sufficiently identified and attributed to some person's negligence? Would there be too much discrepancy between the position of some children recovering large sums of damages as successful plaintiffs and that of many other children with similar handicaps but unable to establish any claim for damages? Would such litigation tend to impair the doctor/patient relationship, if there is conflict between the interests of the mother and her unborn child? Could a serious strain be imposed on the parent/child relationship? Would some employers be placed in difficulty? Is the real need for some immediate practical help rather than simply monetary compensation?

18. On the other hand, if, according to the law as it now is (or, so far as legal considerations are concerned, reasonably could be), a child born defective has a right of action against any person who can be proved to have caused the defect by negligently injuring the foetus, would it be right to deprive any child born defective in the future of such a right of action which he might otherwise have?

19. Opinions would be welcome. If memoranda bearing on these aspects of social policy have already been sent to the Law Commission would you wish them to be available to the Royal Commission? You may well prefer to await the Law Commission's Report before expressing your views.

---

(6)   *see White v Yup* [1969] 458P. 2d. 617

(7)   *Tramways v Leveille* [1933] 4 DLR 337

(8)   *Watt v Rama* [1972] VR 356

iv   SHOULD THE LAW OF TORT CO-EXIST WITH SOME OTHER BASIS OF
     COMPENSATION?

20.   The following list of possibilities, though not claimed to be exhaustive, has been derived
from material studied. They are not necessarily unique solutions, but one or more choices
might be made for the different fields:—

   (1)   The present system of tortious liability without any major modification;

   (2)   A system of "strict liability" whereby in an action of tort an onerous burden of
        proof is imposed on the defendant, so that when the plaintiff has proved the
        happening of the accident, the defendant is liable unless he proves that it was not
        due to any fault of himself or any servant or agent of his (nor to any defect in his
        equipment), or that it was due to some fault of the plaintiff or a third party; this
        system already applies in certain cases under common law or governed by statute,
        eg. the Nuclear Installations Act, 1965;

   (3)   A system of no-fault insurance * operated by insurance companies and under-
        writers and supplemented by tortious liability with suitable modifications;

   (4)   A system of no-fault insurance * operated by insurance companies and under-
        writers, tortious liability for the particular category or categories of injury being
        abolished;

   (5)   A system of no-fault insurance * operated by a governmental agency and supple-
        mented by tortious liability with suitable modifications;

   (6)   A system of no-fault insurance * operated by a governmental agency, tortious
        liability for the particular category or categories of injuries being abolished.

Questions of co-ordination and compatibility of compensation for different categories of
injuries will also have to be considered.

v   SHOULD ANY CHANGE BE MADE IN THE SYSTEM OF ADJUDICATION?

21.   Again, a number of different methods of adjudication have been suggested. The
alternatives might be simply stated as follows:—

   (1)   Whatever changes may be made in the basis of compensation, the function of the
        Courts should continue as at present.

   (2)   Some simplified "small claims" procedure might be introduced for claims below a
        a certain figure, the larger cases still being handled by the Courts.

   (3)   Lay tribunals should hear cases in the first instance, with appeals

        (a)   to Commissioners (with perhaps appeal to courts only on points of law)

   or   (b)   to the Courts

   (4)   Officials like those who at present administer the Industrial Injuries scheme
        should first deal with the case, with provision for appeal. Then there are more
        general matters. For example, should provision be made for actuarial or economic
        evidence or assessments? And there are problems where compensation is governed
        by international convention and practice, eg. in air transport and shipping.

22.   Again, opinions would be welcome.

---

*   i.e. a system of no-fault liability covered by compulsory insurance

vi　IS THERE MERIT IN DIFFERENTIAL RATES OF CONTRIBUTION?

23.　Then there is the matter of differential rates of contribution and premiums. Differentiation exists to some extent already in private car insurance (loss of 'no-claim' bonus, penal rates of premium for drivers with a bad record), in fire insurance (depending on assessed risk and extent of safeguards and precautions) and in insurance of plant and machinery, but not, apparently, to any great extent for employer's liability insurance, in private insurance as well as in the state scheme. Should there be more differentiation in the interests of safety or for any other reason?

Royal Commission on Civil Liability and
Compensation for Personal Injury

February 1974

Annex 3

(referred to in paragraph 12)

Organisations and individuals who gave evidence in the United Kingdom

* denotes both written and oral evidence ; ** oral only

Mr Howard Abbott
The Honourable Mr Justice Ackner
Action on Smoking and Health (ASH)
Mr J E Adams
Adamsdown Community and Advice
    Centre
Agricultural Engineers Association
Airline Users Committee
Mr A Alexander
David Alexander (Public Loss
    Assessors) Ltd
Mr J Allen
Mr and Mrs J A Armitage (through
    Mr Marcus Kimball, MP and direct)
Mr G Armstrong
Mrs K Arnold
Mr W Ashelby
Mrs N Ashton
Association of Anaesthetists of Great
    Britain and Ireland
Association of Assistant Mistresses
*Association of the British
    Pharmaceutical Industry
*Association of Chief Police Officers of
    England, Wales and Northern Ireland
Association of Chief Police Officers
    (Scotland)
*Association of Directors of Social
    Services
Association of Education Committees
Association of Independent Cinemas
Association of Law Teachers
*Association of Parents of Vaccine
    Damaged Children
Association of Public Health Inspectors
*Association of Public Passenger
    Transport Incorporated
Mr E A S Astill
*Professor P S Atiyah
Professor C R Austin
Mr D Austin
Automobile Association
Mr C Aves

Mr F Bagnall
Miss B G Bailey
Mrs P Baird

Master R E Ball, Chief Chancery
    Master
Mrs V E Banford
Mr S W D Banks
Baptist Union of Great Britain and
    Ireland
*Bar Association for Commerce,
    Finance and Industry
Mr E M Barendt
Mr D Barkshire
**Dame Josephine Barnes (with the
    Honourable Mrs Justice Lane)
Mr R N Barnes
Mrs E Barraclough
Mr J E Barrie
Mrs C Bartlett
Mrs L M Batty
Mrs J Baxter
Mr J Bays
Mr H Bean
Mr J M Beard
Mr G H Beeby
Mr H Beesley
Mrs W Beesley
Mrs M Bellamy
Mrs M Bentley
Mr R Berry (through Mr Lewis
    Carter-Jones, MP and the
    Lord Chancellor)
Professor R J Berry
Dr F Ray Bettley
Mrs M Bews
Mrs V Bibby
Mr G A Bilby
Mrs M Billige
Mrs C J Bird
Mrs M Birrell
Mr D H Blades
Blair Bell Research Society
Mr R Blaza
*Board of Inland Revenue
*Boots Company Ltd
Professor G J Borrie
The Hon Robert Boscawen, MP
Bournemouth College of Technology –
    Students at
Mr S H Bowden
Dean W F Bowker (Canada)

Mr Jonathan Bradshaw
Mr S L Bragg
Dr Jeremy Bray, MP (for
  Mr G Gordon)
Miss M Bremner
Bremner, Sons and Corlett (Solicitors)
Brick Development Association
Bristol Polytechnic
British Agrochemicals Association
British Air Line Pilots Association
*British Airways
British American Tobacco Co Ltd
British Association of Grain, Seed,
  Feed and Agricultural Merchants
British Association of Sewing
  Machine Manufacturers
British Brush Manufacturers
  Association
British Chemicals and Dyestuffs
  Traders Association
British Dental Association
British Electrical and Allied
  Manufacturers Association
British Federation of Hotel and
  Guest House Associations
British Fire Services Association
British Helicopter Advisory Board
British Horse Society – Riding
  Establishments Act Committee
British Industrial Truck Association
*British Institute of Radiology
*British Insurance Association
British Insurance Law Association
British Legal Association
British Mechanical Engineering
  Confederation
*British Medical Association
British Metal Castings Council
*British Motorcyclists Federation
British Non-Ferrous Metals
  Federation
*British Paediatric Association
British Paper Machine Wire
  Manufacturers Association
British Photographic Manufacturers
  Association
British Printing Industries Federation
*British Railways Board
British Society of Dental Radiology
*British Steel Corporation
British Sugar Refiners Association
British Textile Machinery Association
British Toy Manufacturers Association

*British Veterinary Association
British Waterways Board
Mrs I Brooker
Mrs E Brown (through
  Mr D E Thomas, MP)
Mr G A Brown
Mr L Brown
Mrs R Bryan
Mr H V Bucknall
Dr D Burrows
Miss D M Burrows
Burt, Brill and Edwards (Solicitors)
Mr M Burton
Business Equipment Trade Association

Mr J S Cameron
Mrs E Campbell
Mr H Caplan
Mr A R Carmichael (through
  Mr Robin Corbett, MP)
*His Honour Sir Walker Carter, QC
Catholic Union of Great Britain
Central Council for the Disabled
*Central Statistical Office
Dr D R Chambers
Chemical Industries Association
Cherry Willingham Liberal Association
*Christian Economic and Social
  Research Foundation, and also
  on behalf of Mr J D Carmichael
Citizens Advice Bureau, Walthamstow
*Civil Aviation Authority
Civil Service Department
Civil Service Motoring Association
Mr C Clark
Mr B Clarkson
Clinical Genetics Society
Mr R L Cobb
Dr R R A Coles
College of Justice in Scotland
Mrs J Collier
Mr and Mrs H Collins
Mr H C Collins
Committee of Associations of
  Specialist Engineering Contractors
Committee of Professors of Clinical
  Pharmacology and Therapeutics
Compound Animal Feeding Stuffs
  Manufacturers National
  Association
*Confederation of British Industry
*Consumers' Association
Consumers' Medical Charter

Continental Freight Drivers Club
Mrs E Cooper
Professor B Coote
Council of British Fire Protection
  Equipment Manufacturers
Council of Her Majesty's Circuit
  Judges
Council of Her Majesty's Circuit
  Judges – Wales and Chester Circuit
Council on Tribunals
*Country Landowners Association
Countryside Commission for Scotland
*Courtaulds Ltd
Covent Garden Market Authority
Mrs M E A Cox
Mrs W Coyle
Creda Electric Ltd
Miss J Cresswell
Mr C Cullinan
Mr G Cunningham, MP
Mr J Cunningham
Mr R J Cunningham
Cycling Council of Great Britain
Cyclists Touring Club

Dr T J David
Mr A Davies
Mr D J Davies
Mrs E Davies
Mr G Davies
Mr J Davies
Mr M Davies (through
  Mr D E Thomas, MP)
Dawley Urban District Council
Mr G W D'Costa
The Right Honourable Lord Denning
Mr W H Dennison
Mr C Denny
Mr I G Dennys
Department of Commerce, Northern
  Ireland
*Department of Employment
Department of Energy
Department of the Environment
**Department of the Environment,
  Northern Ireland
*Department of Health and Social
  Security
Department of Industry ⎫ formerly Depart-
Department of Trade ⎬ ment of Trade
                     ⎭ and Industry
Developmental Pathology Society

Mr J Devlin
Mr J Dick
Disability Alliance (direct and through
  Professor P Townsend)
Disablement Income Group
  (Llanberis and District Branch)
Mr N Doherty
Mr L Dolamore
The Honourable Mr Justice Donaldson
Mrs I Dover
Mr K B Dubash
Miss M J Duffy
Mrs M Duncan
Mr E G Dunn

Mr E Eder
*Edinburgh Corporation
Educational Institute of Scotland
Mr J H Edwards
Dr R G Edwards
Electricity Council
Electronic Components Board
Electronic Components Industry
  Federation (the Board's successors)
Electronic Engineering Association
Mr J A Elliott
Mrs F M Ellis
Miss I W Ellis
*Professor P C Elmes
*Master J B Elton
Professor A E H Emery
*Engineering Employers' Federation
Engineering Industries Association
Eugenics Society
European Dialysis and Transplant
  Association
Mr I Evans
Mrs M Evans
Mr W Evans (through
  Mr D E Thomas, MP)
His Honour Judge Everett, QC

*Faculty of Advocates
Mr J Fane
Mr J D Fearn
Federation of Associations of
  Materials Handling Manufacturers
Federation of Associations of
  Specialists and Sub-Contractors
Federation of British Port Wholesale
  Fish Merchants Association
Federation of Manufacturers of
  Construction Equipment and
  Cranes

Federation of Wire Rope
  Manufacturers of Great Britain
Mrs A Felshin
Fencing Contractors Association
Mrs P J Ferguson
Finance Houses Association
Fire Research Station
Firework Makers' Guild
Professor A A Fitzpatrick
Mr E Flaherty
Mrs K M Foley
Foreign and Commonwealth Office
Mrs V Forshaw
Sir John Foster, QC
Miss M E Foulkes
Mrs N Fowler (through Mr Cecil
  Parkinson, MP)
His Honour Judge Francis
Mr P R Francis
Dr A White Franklin
Mr Michael Freeman
Mrs U M Freer (through Lord
  Chancellor's Office)
Mr K Furniss

Mr T Gardner
Professor D J Gee
*General Council of the Bar of
  England and Wales
*General Council of the Bar of
  Northern Ireland
*General Council of British Shipping
  Ltd (formerly British Shipping
  Federation and Chamber of Shipping
  of the United Kingdom)
General Federation of Trade Unions
General Nursing Council
General and Municipal Workers Union
Mr D Ghosh
Mr R Gibson
*Professor R H Girdwood
Glasgow Chamber of Commerce
Mrs M Glasson
Mr John Golding, MP
Mr H Golsong, Council of Europe
*Government Actuary's Department
Mrs D Graham
**Mr L M Graham (New Zealand)
Grain and Feed Trade Association
Mr John Grant, MP (for
  Mr and Mrs Cook)
Professor R H Graveson

Greater London Council Staff
  Association
Mr D A R Green
*Professor D S Greer
Mr J Gregory
Mr A Griffith
Mr E Griffith
Mr W G Griffith
Mr A H Griffiths
Mr J Grindley
Mr W Grove
Gun Trade Association
Mr Duncan Guthrie
Gwynedd County Council

Mr A Haddon (through Mr David
  Steel, MP)
Mr C E Hadfield
Hairdressing Council
Mr W J Halcro
Mr F D Hanley
Mr R N Harding
Mrs M Hardy
Mrs A Hargrave
Harlow Industrial Health Service
Dr J B Harman
**Mr D R Harris
Mrs M Hart (through Mr Michael
  Fidler, MP)
Mr R Hart
Hawker Siddeley Group Ltd
Mr T J Hazeldine
Mrs M A Hazelton
Mrs A Hedley
Mr Eric S Heffer, MP (for Mr E Lynch)
Mr D Herbert
Mr C Heskin
Mr P J Hewitt
Mrs J Higgs (through Mr Barry
  Jones, MP)
Mr J W Hill (John Williams
  Insurance Consultants)
Mr L F Hill
Mr A Hoffman
Mr A Hollis
*Home Office
Mrs D Hook
Hoover Ltd
Mr E Horobin (through Mr Leslie
  Huckfield, MP)
Horstmann Gear Co Ltd
Horwood and James (Solicitors)
  (for Mr G C Sachar)

Hotel, Catering and Institutional
  Management Association
Mr A A M Hotter
Howard League for Penal Reform
Mrs M W Howarth
Mrs L E Hudson
Mrs A Hughes
Mr G Hughes
Mr H D Hughes
Mr H R Hughes
Mrs K L Hughes
Humphries, Kirk and Miller
  (Solicitors)
Mr J R Humphrey
Mrs D Hutchinson
Mr P G Hyde

Imperial Tobacco Co Ltd
Incorporated Law Society of
  Northern Ireland
Incorporated Society of Valuers and
  Auctioneers
Industrial Fire Protection Association
  of Great Britain
*Industrial Law Society
Mr A Inglese
Inland Waterways Association
Institute of Actuaries
Institute of Advanced Motorists
Institute of Biology
Institute of Trading Standards
  Administration
International Chamber of Commerce
  (British National Committee)
International Computers Ltd
Invalid Children's Aid Association
Iron and Steel Trades Confederation,
  Temple 5 (through Miss Joan
  Maynard, MP)
Mr G W Isgar

Mrs D Jackson
Mrs D James
Mr D Jardine
Mr W H Jaycock
Mr R J Jennings
Mr I M Johnson
Joint Committee of Ophthalmic
  Opticians
The Right Honourable Lord Justice
  Jones (Northern Ireland)
Mr A Jones
Mr A M Jones
Mrs B Jones

Miss D Jones
Mr E B Jones
Mr E C Jones
Mrs Ellen Jones
Mrs Ellen Jones (for Mr Ifor Jones)
Mr H Jones
Mr I Jones
Mrs P M Jones
Mr R D Jones
Mr R E Jones
Mr R H Jones
Mr R J Jones
Mr W Jones
Mr W B Jones
Mr W R Jones
Mr Michael Jopling, MP
*Justice
Justice (Scottish Branch)

Mrs J Kates
Mr J C Kaye
Mr J Kayes
Mrs B C Kebby
Mr Richard Kidner
Kingsley-Smith and Associates Ltd
Mrs M Kinread
Mr D Kirk
Mrs Jill Knight, MP (for Miss M E
  O'Brien)

Mrs Lalliment
Mr J L Lancett
*The Honourable Mrs Justice Lane
Mr G Latta (with Mr R Lewis)
*The Law Society
*The Law Society of Scotland
Lay Observer, Royal Courts of Justice
  (about Mr Redmond)
League of Safe Drivers
Dr G L Leathart
Mr J J Leeming
*Professor D S Lees
Legal and Civil Rights for Children
  Society
Leicester Polytechnic
*His Honour Judge H C Leon
Mr J Lewis (through Mr D E
  Thomas, MP)
Mr M Lewis
Mr R Lewis (with Mr G Latta)
*Professor A M Linden, QC (Canada)
Liverpool Polytechnic
Llanberis Council of Churches

*Lloyd's
Mrs L Loach
Mr and Mrs E Lodwig
*London Solicitors Litigation
  Association
*London Transport Executive
Dr J Lorber
Mr R R Lord
*Lord Chancellor's Office
Mr John Loveridge, MP (for
  Mr Malcolm Cousins)
Mr A W Low
Mrs G P Lowe
Mr W A Lyster
Mr J McCluskey
Professor D N MacCormick
The Right Honourable Lord
  MacDermott (Northern Ireland)
Mrs M McDonald (through
  Mr Kenneth Lomas, MP)
**Mr R H M Macdonald
The Honourable Mr Justice MacKenna
Magnesium Industry Council
Mail Order Traders' Association of
  Great Britain
Manpower Services Commission
Mr G B Marks (through Sir
  Geoffrey Howe, MP)
Married Women's Association
Mr J E Marsh
*Mr Peter Martin
Lady Masham
Miss I Mason
*Miss Joan M Matheson
Mr I Mathias
Mr Michael Meacher, MP
**Mr Justice Meares (Australia)
Mr J Mechaniow
Medical Commission on Accident
  Prevention – Occupational
  Safety Committee
*Medical Defence Union
Medical Protection Society,
  covering also Medical and Dental
  Defence Union of Scotland
*Medical Research Council
Medicines Commission
Merchant Navy and Airline Officers'
  Association
Mr W T Merritt
Methodist Church – Division of
  Social Responsibility
Mr G A Meynell and others

*Sir Robert Micklethwait, QC
Mr C J Miller
*Dr Henry Miller
Professor I P Miller
Mrs S Millyard
Ministry of Agriculture, Northern
  Ireland
Ministry of Defence
Mirror Group Newspapers Ltd
Mr E J Mishan
Mr T Mitchell
Professor P Mittler
The Honourable Mr Justice Mocatta
Dr R H Mole
Mr C Monk
Mrs K Moore
Mr M Morad (through Mr Cecil
  Parkinson, MP)
Mrs C Morgan
Mrs C Morris,
Mr Charles Morris, MP (for
  Miss A M Williams)
Mr H Morris
Mr J Morrison
Mrs J Morton
Mrs S Moseley
Mr D Moss
*Mothers' Union
Motor Agents' Association
*Motor Insurers Bureau
Mr R W Mowat
Multiple Shops Federation
Mr A K Murray (through Alex
  Lauriston and Son, Solicitors)
Mrs E Myles
Mr A T Mynard
National Association for Deaf/Blind
  and Rubella Children
National Automobile Safety Belt
  Association
National Chamber of Trade
*National Coal Board
National Council of Building
  Material Producers
*National Council of Women of
  Great Britain
*National Farmers' Union
National Federation of Building
  Trades Employers
National Federation of Consumer
  Groups
National Federation of Old Age
  Pensions Associations

National Federation of Professional
  Workers
National Federation of Self Employed
National Federation of Wholesale
  Grocers and Provision Merchants
National Federation of Women's
  Institutes
National Freight Corporation
National Pharmaceutical Union Group
National Society for Mentally
  Handicapped Children
*National Society for the Prevention
  of Cruelty to Children
National Television Rental Association
National Union of Public Employees
National Union of Teachers
Mr S A Naylor
Mr C H Nellist (through
  Mr A G F Hall-Davis, MP)
Mrs E E Newton
North Eastern Circuit Bar
*Northern Ireland Office
Northern Ireland Seed Trade
  Association
Mrs Q M Nunn

Mr F W Oakes
**Professor Jeffrey O'Connell (USA)
The Honourable Mr Justice O'Donnell
  (Northern Ireland)
*Herr Carl Oldertz (Sweden)
Office of Fair Trading
*Office of Law Reform, Northern
  Ireland
*Office of Legislative Draftsmen,
  Northern Ireland
*Mr Michael Ogden, QC
Professor R Oliver
The Right Honourable Lord Justice
  Ormrod
Mrs S Y Osborn (through Simpson
  Millar (Solicitors), Mr Airey
  Neave, MP and the Lord
  Chancellor)
Mr G Owen
Mr G E Owen
Mrs M A Owen
Mr W Owen and others
Oxford Polytechnic

Panel of Four – representing the
  British Association of the Hard of
  Hearing; British Deaf Association;

National Deaf Children's Society;
  Royal National Institute for the
  Deaf
Mr E Parker (through Mr Barry
  Jones, MP)
**Mr Michael Parkington
Mr W H Parry
Mr G Parsons
Mr M L S Passey
Patent Judges (with the Honourable
  Mr Justice Ackner)
Patients Association
Mr C T Peach
*Pedestrians Association for Road
  Safety
Mr C E Perkins
Mr N Perry
Mr M Peters
Pharmaceutical Society of Great
  Britain
Mr G Piper
Plaid Cymru
Plaid Cymru, Llanberis and
  Dyffryn Ogwen Branches
Police Superintendents' Association
  of England and Wales
Mr A J B Porch
Mr J C Porritt
*Post Office Engineering Union
  (direct and through Mr John
  Golding, MP)
Post Office Management Staff's
  Association
Mrs C Powley
Mr B W Powys
Mrs P Pratt
Mr G S Prevost
Councillor Emrys Pride
Mr C Pritchard
Process Plant Association
*Proprietary Association of Great
  Britain
*Public Road Transport Association
Public Trustee Office
Mrs E Purnell

Radio and Electronic Components
  Manufacturers Federation
Mr and Mrs J Ratcliffe
Mr T Reeks
Mrs A J Regan
Mr R Reid
Retail Consortium

Mr K Richards
Richardson and Sweeney
Mr L G Ridyard
Mrs D Robe
Mr G Robelon
**Lord Robens
Mr Alun Roberts
Mr B Roberts
Mrs E Roberts (for Mr A G Roberts)
Mrs Elizabeth Roberts
Mr R M Roberts
Mr T A Roberts (through
  Miss Joan Maynard, MP)
Mr W Roberts
Robinson, Jarvis and Rolfe
  (Solicitors)
Mrs W Rogers
Mr W H Rogers
Her Honour Judge Rowland
Joseph Rowntree Memorial Trust
*Royal Automobile Club
Royal British Legion Scotland
*Royal College of Obstetricians and
  Gynaecologists
Royal College of Pathologists
*Royal College of Physicians
Royal College of Physicians,
  Edinburgh
*Royal College of Physicians and
  Surgeons of Glasgow
*Royal College of Psychiatrists
Royal College of Radiologists
*Royal College of Surgeons, Edinburgh
Royal College of Surgeons of England
*Royal Faculty of Procurators in
  Glasgow
Royal National Life-boat Institution
Royal Scottish Automobile Club
Royal Society for the Prevention
  of Accidents
Mr E B Roycroft
Mrs J Rudge

The Right Honourable Sir Eric Sachs
**Mr K L Sandford (New Zealand)
Mr A A Sapey
Scottish Development Department
Scottish Fishermen's Federation
Scottish Landowners' Federation
Scottish Law Agents Society
Scottish Office
Scottish Police Federation
*Scottish Transport Group

Mr W Seal
Dr A G Searle
Mr N Seymour
Shaen, Roscoe & Bracewell (Solicitors)
Shaftesbury Project
*Professor Marshall S Shapo (USA)
Mr Marcelli Shaw
Mr J D Sheerin
  (for Mrs J M Hancock)
Ship and Boat Builders' National
  Federation
Mr Charles Simeons
The Right Honourable Lord Simon
  of Glaisdale
Mr T B W Simon
Mr A Simpson
*Smaller Businesses Association
Mr B Smith
Dr H Smith
Miss H Smith
Mr H Smith
Mr J D Smith
Smith, Kline and French Laboratories
  Ltd
Mr P C Snelling
*Society of British Aerospace Companies
Society of Community Medicine
*Society of Conservative Lawyers
Society for Drug Research
*Society of Labour Lawyers
Society of Motor Manufacturers
  and Traders
Society of Occupational Medicine
*Society for the Protection of
  Unborn Children
Society for Radiological Protection
Society of Solicitors in the Supreme
  Courts of Scotland
Solicitors' Law Stationery Society
*Soroptimist International of Great
  Britain & Ireland
Spastics Society
Mrs E Speak
Mr Austen Spearing
Standing Medical Advisory Committee
Mr W Stapleton
Mrs M State
Steel Castings Research and Trade
  Association
Mrs P A Steele
Mr R Stokes
Mr S Stokes
Mr R Stone

**Professor H Street
Sutton and District Consumer Group
Mr G N C Swift
Mrs E M Szmyrko

Mrs N Tait
Tavistock Institute of Human
  Relations
Mr J C Taylor
Mr N Leigh Taylor
Dr H Teff
Mr N G Tether
Thalidomide Children's Trust
Mr D E Thomas, MP
Mr E O Thomas
Mr H Thomas
Mr J E Thomas
Mr R Thomas
Mr W H Thomas
*Mr B Thompson
Mrs L Thompson (through the
  Lay Observer, Royal Courts of
  Justice)
Mrs K S Thomson
Mrs N Thorley
Mrs D Thornton
Mr J E Timmins
Mr and Mrs D A Toulson
Mrs E Towells
*Trades Union Congress
Transport and General Workers Union
**Chief Justice Traynor (USA)
*HM Treasury
**Professor André Tunc (France)
Mrs E J Turton

University of Birmingham
University of Bristol – Faculty of Law
*University of Glasgow – Faculty of
  Law

Mr T B Veitch (through Mr David
  Steel, MP)

Mr S M Waddams
Mrs G Wakerell
Mr Ivor Walker (through Mr James
  Hamilton, MP and the Lord
  Chancellor)
Sir John Walley
Mr E Walmsley
Mr B E Walsh

Mr Clifford Ward
Mrs P Ward
Mr J G Waters
Mr L W Webb
Mrs H M Webster
Dr T J Weihs, Camphill-Rudolf
  Steiner-Schools
Mr L Wetton
Mr A Wharam
Mr M H Whincup
Mrs V I Whitbread
Mr W J Whitehead
Miss Katherine Whitehorn
Col R A Wiggin
Mr Dafydd Wigley, MP
Mrs M P Wilkins
Mrs J Wilkinson
Mrs A Wilks
Mrs A Williams
Mr D O Williams
*Mr D W Williams
Mr E Williams
Mr Ezra Williams
Mr E R Williams
Mr E W Williams (through
  Mr D E Thomas, MP)
Mr E Wyn Williams
Mr F Williams
Mr H Williams
Mr I Williams
Mr J F Williams
Mr O Williams
Mr R T Williams
Mr T C Williams
*The Right Honourable Sir Gordon
  Willmer
*Women's National Commission
**Professor J C Wood
Mr W Wood
**Mr Justice Woodhouse (New Zealand)
  (now the Right Honourable
  Sir Owen Woodhouse)
Mrs B Woodward
Mr H J Woolford
*Working Group of Scottish Judges
Professor B A Wortley
Drs Arthur and Margaret Wynn
Mrs M Wynne

Miss Priscilla Young
Dame Eileen Younghusband

Another 13 witnesses who submitted written evidence asked that their names should
not be published.

Annex 4

(referred to in paragraph 135)

Social Security Benefits and Allowances as at 1 January 1977

Résumé by the Department of Health and Social Security

Attendance allowance

Attendance allowance is a tax free allowance for adults and children over the age of 2 who are severely disabled, either physically or mentally, and have needed a lot of looking after for at least 6 months.

A higher rate of £12·20 a week can be paid if one of the day requirements and one of the night requirements are satisfied for a period of at least 6 months.

A lower rate of £8·15 a week can be paid if one of the day or night requirements is satisfied for a period of at least 6 months.

Child benefit – commences 4 April 1977

Child benefit replaces family allowances in April 1977 and will be tax free. From April 1977 child tax allowances for children under 11 will be phased out over 3 years and allowances for older children correspondingly reduced. It is not a national insurance benefit and is not means-tested.

Rate of benefit

Child benefit is payable for each child for whom a person is responsible. The weekly rate for a first or only child is £1·00. For each other child the weekly rate is £1·50.

There will be an increase in the rate of child benefit for the first or only child of some lone parents. This increase will be 50p a week and will bring the rate of child benefit for such a child to £1·50. The increase will be payable to those parents who were entitled to child interim benefit – see child interim benefit for one-parent families – and those persons who become lone parents after 3 April 1977.

Child interim benefit for one-parent families – ceases on 3 April 1977 – see Child Benefit. This is a benefit for the first or only child in certain one-parent families. It will be replaced by child benefit and child benefit increase in April 1977.

The conditions

The benefit is payable to a lone parent, e.g. divorced, separated or an unmarried person who is not living with someone as man and wife, and who has at least one of their children living with them. The child must be either under 16, or under 19 and still in full-time education. Lone parents who are already receiving certain social security benefits, for instance, widow's allowance or widowed mother's allowance, are not entitled to child interim benefit since the benefit they receive already includes a higher rate for the first or only child to make up for the absence of family allowances for that child.

Rate of benefit

Benefit is payable at the rate of £1·50 a week. It is taxable and is taken into account as income in assessing supplementary benefit and FIS.

Child's special allowance for children of divorced women

This allowance is available to a woman on the death of her former husband if their marriage had been dissolved or annulled and, at the time of his death she has a child towards whose support he was contributing, or had been liable to contribute, at least 25p a week in cash or its equivalent. The allowance cannot be paid if the woman has remarried.

The rate of the allowance is £7·45 for the first or only child, and £5·95 for each other child.

The allowance is based on the former husband's contribution record.

417

Death grant

A death grant is a sum paid on the death of a contributor, or the wife, husband or child of a contributor. It may also be payable on the contributions of a near relative, in respect of an incapacitated person who has never been able to work and pay contributions. If the deceased person left a will, or letters of administration have been taken out, the grant is normally paid to the executors or administrators; otherwise it is paid to the person meeting the funeral expenses or to the next of kin.

No death grant is payable if the contribution condition is not satisfied by the person on whose contributions the grant is claimed.

Amount of grant

The amount of the grant depends on the age of the person who has died:

Age	Amount
Under 3 years	£9
3–5 years inclusive	£15
6–17 years inclusive	£22·50
Man aged 18 or over born on or after 5 July 1893	£30
Woman aged 18 or over born on or after 5 July 1898	£30
Man born on or after 5 July 1883 but before 5 July 1893	£15
Woman born on or after 5 July 1888 but before 5 July 1898	£15

Earnings related supplement

Earnings related supplement is payable after the first 12 days of a period of interruption of employment to people under minimum pension age (65 for a man, 60 for a woman) who are entitled to sickness benefit, unemployment benefit or maternity allowance. The supplement is payable for a maximum of 6 months and cannot be paid with invalidity benefit.

The rates

The rate of supplement depends on the amount of the claimant's 'earnings factor' for the relevant tax year. The earnings factor is the amount upon which Class 1 (employed earner's) contributions have been paid.

Where the weekly rate of supplement exceeds the amount by which the claimant's benefit (without a supplement but including increases for dependants) falls short of 85 per cent of his earnings factor in the relevant income tax year, the amount of the supplement payable is limited to that amount. Where benefit already exceeds 85 per cent of the reckonable weekly earnings no supplement is payable (though the benefit itself is not subject to any reduction).

Family allowances – Ceases on 3 April 1977 – See Child Benefit

Amount of the allowances

Family allowances are cash payments, for the benefit of the family as a whole, to families with more than one child under the age limits. The rate is £1·50 a week for each child after the first.

Family allowances are not an insurance benefit and there are no contribution conditions. The cost is met entirely from taxation. The allowances are treated as part of income for tax purposes.

The conditions

A child is under the age limits up to the minimum school-leaving age and during any further period before his nineteenth birthday while he is receiving full time instruction at a school, college or university, or can qualify as an apprentice. A parent (usually the mother) may claim for children if they are living with or maintained by her/him. A person may include in his family another person's children who are not eligible for inclusion in their own parent's family for family allowances purposes. But he must be contributing more than anyone else towards their maintenance. The contribution towards maintenance must be at least £1·50 a week.

Family income supplement

Family income supplement is a benefit for people in full-time work who have at least one dependent child and whose normal gross weekly income is less than amounts prescribed by Parliament.

The prescribed amount is £39·00 for a family with one child and this amount goes up by £4·50 for each additional child.

Rate of supplement

The amount of the supplement is one half of the difference between a family's normal gross income and the appropriate prescribed amount. Family allowances (but not child benefit after April 1977) and other sources of income – such as wife's earnings – are included in the total income but the income of children is not. The maximum supplement payable is £8·50 a week for families with one child, increasing by 50p for each additional child in the family; the minimum is 20p a week. Awards are normally made for a period of 52 weeks and are not affected by changes of circumstances.

Guardian's allowance for orphaned children

A guardian's allowance is a payment of £7·45 a week to the person who takes into his family an orphan child. The age limits are the same as for child benefit or family allowances. In the ordinary way both parents of the child must be dead but the allowance can sometimes be paid on the death of only one parent where the parents were divorced; where the child is illegitimate and the mother is dead; where one parent was missing at the time the other died and cannot be traced; or where the surviving parent is serving a long term of imprisonment.

One of the child's parents must have been a British subject who was born in the United Kingdom. If neither parent satisfied this condition, one of them must have satisfied a special residence test.

Industrial injuries benefits

The industrial injuries scheme provides cash benefits for those unable to work, or those disabled, because of an accident at work or one of the prescribed industrial diseases. Where death results, benefits are paid to dependants. Generally the scheme covers anyone working for an employer under a contract of service or apprenticeship, or an office holder (e.g. a company director) with emoluments chargeable to income tax under Schedule E. Some people employed through agencies and wives employed by their husbands (and *vice versa*) may also be covered.

Entitlement to benefit under the scheme does not depend on payment of contributions.

Industrial death benefit

Industrial death benefit is a pension, allowance or a gratuity for a death resulting from an industrial accident or disease.

For a widow who was living with her husband at the date of his death the benefit is £21·40 a week for the first 26 weeks plus any earnings-related supplement that would have been payable had she been entitled to national insurance widow's allowance; thereafter a pension of £15·85 or £4·59 a week is paid according to circumstances. For other dependants the benefit is a pension, allowance or gratuity according to the relationship to, and the extent to which they were being maintained by, the deceased at the time of his death.

419

For children of the deceased's family an allowance of £7·45 for the first or only child and £5·95 for each other child, in addition to family allowances, may be paid to the widow. If the children are in the care of someone other than the widow the allowances for them are £4·05 a week for the first or only child and £2·55 a week for each other child, in addition to family allowances. The rates for the first or only child will change when child benefit is introduced.

Industrial disablement benefit

Disablement benefit is a pension or gratuity for any disablement which remains when injury benefit stops. It can be claimed right away if the disablement has not kept the claimant away from work. The amount of benefit depends on the extent of disablement as assessed by a medical board.

The pension varies from £25·00 a week for 100 per cent disablement to £5·00 a week for 20 per cent disablement. There are lower rates for people under 18. For disablement of 19 per cent or less, benefit is usually paid as a gratuity.

Disablement benefit can be increased for various reasons as below:

Special hardship allowance – up to £10·00 a week, as long as the benefit and allowance together do not come to more than £25·00 a week, if as a result of the injury or disease the claimant is unable to return to his regular job and cannot work at a job of a similar standard.

Unemployability supplement – £15·30 a week, with increases for dependants at the invalidity benefit rates, for anyone who is likely to be permanently unfit for work as a result of the injury or disease. An 'age of onset of incapacity' allowance similar to invalidity allowance is also payable with this supplement. The supplement and special hardship allowance cannot be paid at the same time.

Constant attendance allowance – up to £10·00 a week for anyone who needs constant care and attention as the result of the effects of the injury or disease and whose disablement is 100 per cent (disablement due to certain other causes, e.g. war injuries, may be taken into account for this purpose). This allowance can be increased in cases of exceptionally severe disablement to a maximum of £20·00.

Exceptionally severe disablement allowance – £10·00 a week for anyone who is in receipt of constant attendance allowance at a weekly rate above £10·00 (or would be but for the fact that he is in hospital) and whose need for such attendance is likely to be permanent.

Hospital treatment allowance – raises benefit to the 100 per cent rate, while the claimant is in hospital and receiving treatment for the injury or disease.

For anyone who is incapable of working, sickness benefit or invalidity benefit as appropriate can be paid in addition to disablement benefit unless an unemployability supplement is also being paid.

Industrial injury benefit

Injury benefit is payable for incapacity for work due to the industrial accident or disease during the period of 26 weeks from the date of the accident or development of the disease, but not usually for the first 3 days. Generally flat-rate sickness benefit (or invalidity benefit) cannot be drawn at the same time as injury benefit, but anyone who is still unable to work after the 26 weeks can get sickness benefit (or invalidity benefit as appropriate) on the usual conditions.

The weekly rate of injury benefit for a person aged 18 or over is £15·65 with increases for an adult dependant and children normally at the sickness benefit rate. If, however, sickness benefit would have been replaced by invalidity benefit or retirement pension but for the payment of injury benefit, the more favourable increases payable with invalidity benefit will be paid.

The weekly rate for someone under 18 is £12·90. But anyone who is entitled to an increase for a dependant is paid the adult rate. There are special rates for children under school-leaving age.

A person receiving injury benefit can also qualify for earnings-related supplement if he would have got sickness benefit but for receiving injury benefit.

Injury benefit is paid in the same way as sickness benefit.

Invalid care allowance
Invalid care allowance is payable to people of working age who are unable to work because they have to stay at home to care for a severely disabled relative. The benefit is not means-tested and there are no contribution conditions but it is taxable. Generally married women cannot qualify for the allowance.

The conditions
The claimant must be regularly and substantially engaged, for at least 35 hours a week, in caring for the severely disabled relative.

The severely disabled relative must be in receipt of attendance allowance (or constant attendance allowance at the normal maximum rate or more).

The claimant must satisfy presence and residence conditions.

The claimant must be under pensionable age (65 for a man, 60 for a woman) to qualify for the allowance but once in payment it can continue beyond pensionable age provided the caring conditions are still satisfied and it is not replaced by retirement pension. The allowance can continue in payment beyond retirement age (70 for a man, 65 for a woman) and the caring conditions no longer have to be satisfied.

Rate of allowance
The allowance is payable at the rate of £9·20 a week and increases may be paid for dependants.

Invalidity benefit
Invalidity benefit consists of invalidity pension and invalidity allowance. Invalidity pension is paid for incapacity for work and replaces sickness benefit after 168 days' entitlement to sickness benefit in a period of interruption of employment. (Spells of incapacity and/or unemployment separated by no more than 13 weeks link to form the same period of interruption of employment.) Invalidity allowance is paid in addition to the pension to people who become chronically sick while they still have a large part of their normal working lives ahead of them. Earnings related supplement is not payable with invalidity benefit. See also 'Non-contributory invalidity pension'.

The rates
Invalidity benefit is paid at the following rates:

Invalidity pension
Personal rate £15·30 a week.

Invalidity allowance
Payable at three rates depending on age at which incapacity in the present period of interruption of employment began:

for a person then under the age of 35 (or whose incapacity began before 5 July 1948)	£3·20 a week
for a person then aged at least 35 but under the age of 45	£2·00 a week
for a man then aged at least 45 but under the age of 60 or for a woman then aged at least 45 but under the age of 55	£1·00 a week

The rate of invalidity allowance stays the same as long as the incapacity lasts.

Invalidity pension can be paid up to retirement (on or after pension age) or to the age of deemed retirement whichever is earlier. Over pension age, benefit is payable at the claimant's retirement pension rate.

A person who does not qualify for invalidity benefit because of failure to qualify for sickness benefit in the first place may be able to qualify for the non-contributory invalidity pension.

Dependants
Like sickness benefit, invalidity pension can be increased for dependants. The increase for a wife or other dependant is £9·20. The children's increases are £7·45 for the first child, and £5·95 for each other child in addition to any family allowances. The rate for the first dependent child will change when child benefit is introduced. The wife of a man drawing invalidity pension can earn £35·00 a week before the increase paid for her is affected, so long as she resides with him.

Maternity benefits
Maternity grant
The maternity grant is £25 and is intended as a contribution towards the general expense of a confinement. It may be paid on either the mother's own contribution record or her husband's, but not on both.

Maternity allowance
This allowance is payable only to women who have themselves paid sufficient contributions as employed or self-employed persons. It is usually payable for 18 weeks starting 11 weeks before the week in which the baby is expected (but it cannot be paid for any period during which the woman works). The standard rate is £12·90 a week. Earnings-related supplement may be payable with maternity allowances. The allowance may be increased in some circumstances if the woman has an adult dependant or a dependent child.

Mobility allowance

This allowance is for severely disabled adults under pensionable age (65 for men, 60 for women) and children from age 5 who are unable or virtually unable to walk and is being gradually phased in over the next few years.

As at 1 January 1977 the allowance is payable to children aged 11 or over and adults who were born after 1 April 1925. Children aged 5–10 will be included from 13 April 1977.

As from 24 August 1977 the allowance will be payable to adults who were born after 24 August 1923. Adults born before 25 August 1923 but still under pensionable age will be included at a later date.

Rate of allowance
The allowance is payable at £5 a week and is taxable.

It is payable together with other social security benefits unless, exceptionally, any supplementary benefit in payment includes a special addition for mobility, in which case the supplementary benefit will be adjusted. Mobility allowance cannot be paid in addition to a vehicle or private car allowance provided under the National Health Service. People who have a vehicle or car allowance under the old scheme, will be allowed to switch to mobility allowance without further medical examination and without age limit.

Non-contributory invalidity pension

Non-contributory invalidity pension is for people of working age who are incapable of work because of sickness or disablement and who do not qualify for invalidity benefit. The pension is tax-free and is not subject to a means test. It is not generally payable to married women at present, but it is to be extended in November 1977 to married women who are incapable of their normal household duties and also incapable of work.

The conditions

The pension does not depend on payment of national insurance contributions.

To qualify for non-contributory invalidity pension a person must be at least 16 and under 60 (women) or 65 (men) and have been *continuously* incapable of work for at least 28 weeks and satisfy residence conditions. Once the pension is in payment, and assuming continuing incapacity, it can continue beyond pension age unless it is replaced by retirement pension.

Rate of pension

The pension is payable at £9·20 a week and increases are payable for dependants. The rate may be reduced if certain other benefits or allowances are payable.

Pneumoconiosis, byssinosis and miscellaneous diseases benefit scheme

Allowances may be paid to people who are suffering from pneumoconiosis or byssinosis, or certain other slowly developing diseases, due to employment before 5 July 1948 but who do not qualify for workmen's compensation or industrial injuries benefit.

Retirement pension

At 65 (60 for a woman) a man who retires from regular work and satisfied the contribution conditions can get a retirement pension. When he reaches 70 (65 for a woman) he can get his pension whether he has retired or not. A married woman can get a retirement pension on her husband's contributions when he retires and draws his pension provided she is then over 60 and has herself retired from regular work other than her domestic duties or she has reached age 65. If a woman qualifies for a pension both on her own and her husband's contributions she receives whichever pension is the higher.

How the pension is made up

A pension can be made up of the following parts:

Basic retirement pension. The standard weekly rate is £15·30 but reduced rates are payable where the contribution conditions are only partially satisfied. For a married woman qualifying on her husband's contributions the standard weekly rate is £9·20.

Increase for a wife who is not entitled to a pension herself or, in some circumstances, for another dependant instead. The standard weekly rate is £9·20.

Increases for children if they are within the age limits, of £7·45 a week for the first child and £5·95 for each other child, in addition to family allowances.

Extra pension earned by deferring retirement beyond 65 (60 for a woman). Up to April 1975 an extra 6p a week could be earned for every 9 flat rate contributions actually paid for weeks of employment or self employment between 65 and 70 (60 and 65 for a woman). From 6 April 1975 the pension is increased by ⅛ per cent of its rate for every 6 days (excluding Sundays) for which a person has given up his pension between these ages, but there must be at least 48 such days unless one 6p increase was earned before 6 April 1975. Days of deferred retirement for which another benefit, such as unemployment benefit, was received do not count. A married man can also earn extra pension for his wife.

423

Graduated pension which depends on the amount paid in graduated contributions between 6 April 1961 when the graduated pensions scheme began and 5 April 1975 when graduated contributions ceased. A man gets 2½p a week for each 'unit' of £7·50 of graduated contributions paid by him, and a woman 2½p a week for each 'unit' of £9 paid. An odd half unit or more in the final total of contributions counts as a whole unit.

Extra graduated pension can also be earned by a person who defers his retirement beyond age 65 (60 for a woman). Half the graduated pension which a person would have been paid if he had retired at age 65 (60) will count as an extra graduated contribution towards further graduated pension when he does retire or reach 70 (65 for a woman).

Age addition of 25p a week payable to all pensioners aged 80 or over.

Persons who defer retirement and who satisfy the contribution conditions will be entitled to unemployment or sickness benefit or invalidity pension during periods of unemployment or incapacity for work up to age 70 (65 for women). The rate of benefit payable is the basic rate of retirement pension which would be payable if the claimant had retired.

How earnings affect the pension

Because the retirement pension is for people who have retired, it is reduced if a pensioner under 70 (65 for women) earns more than a certain amount. The pension is reduced by 5p for every 10p of earnings (after deduction of reasonable expenses incurred in connection with the employment) between £35 and £39 and by 5p for each 5p earned over £39.

A dependency increase for a pensioner's wife (or woman having the care of his child) who resides with him is reduced in the same way as the earnings of a pensioner. If, however, she does not reside with him the increase is not payable at all if her earnings (after deducting admissible expenses) are more than £9·20 unless she is employed by the pensioner to care for his child, when her earnings may not affect the increase. For widow retirement pensioners there are special provisions.

Non-contributory retirement pension for people over 80

Anyone who is 80 or over and is not getting a national insurance retirement pension or who is getting one at less than the current rate of non-contributory retirement pension may qualify for the latter if certain residence conditions are satisfied. The current rates are £9·45 (£5·85 for a married woman). These amounts include the 25p age addition referred to above.

Pensions for women who are or were married to men aged 65 or over on 5 July 1948

Payable to women who are or were married to men born before 6 July 1883. A woman may qualify even if, after her husband died or the marriage was dissolved or annulled, she remarried when over 60. Age and residence conditions have to be satisfied according to the woman's status at the time of claim, and she should not be receiving a national insurance pension at a rate higher than £9·20 (widow, excluding any increase for a child, or divorced woman) or £5·60 (married woman).

Sickness benefit

Sickness benefit is payable for incapacity for work because of illness or disablement. Only employed and self employed contributions count towards this benefit.

The rates

The standard weekly flat rate benefit for a man or woman (except a married woman) is £12·90 with increases of £8·00 for an adult dependant, £4·05 for the first dependent child and £2·55 for each other child in addition to any family allowances. The rate for the first dependent child will change when child benefit is introduced. No increase is payable for a wife (or other adult female dependant) whose net earnings are more than £8·00 a week unless she is employed to care for the beneficiary's child, when her earnings may not affect the increase.

The weekly flat rate benefit for a married woman is £9·20. But she may be paid the £12·90 rate in the following cases:

if she is living with her husband and he is receiving invalidity or retirement pension or unemployability supplement;

if she is entitled to an increase of benefit for her husband;

if she is living apart from her husband and receiving less than £3·70 a week from him towards her support.

Under the new pensions scheme the lower rate of benefit for married women is being abolished with effect from April 1978.

Earnings related supplement may also be payable.

After pension age, benefit is paid at the claimant's retirement pension rate. It can be paid until retirement (on or after pension age) or to the age of deemed retirement, whichever is the earlier.

To qualify for the benefit two contribution conditions have to be satisfied. There are special rules to help widows and divorced women.

Benefit is not paid for the first 3 days of a period of interruption of employment (see section on 'invalidity benefit' for definition of a period of interruption of employment) or for isolated days of incapacity unless 2 or more of these occur within 6 consecutive days.

Supplementary benefit

Supplementary benefit is a non-contributory benefit. It is payable to anyone aged 16 or over who has left school and is not in full time work to the extent that their resources (if any) fall short of their requirements. It can supplement other state benefits or private resources.

Supplementary pension is payable to people over state pension age (65 for a man, 60 for a woman).

Supplementary allowance is payable to people below state pension age.

Conditions
Claimants who are under state pension age and fit for work may have to register for work at an employment office as a condition for getting benefit.

How benefit is worked out
The amount of supplementary benefit payable is worked out by taking a claimant's 'requirements' (i.e. what he needs) and deducting from these his 'resources' (i.e. what he is already receiving).

The 'requirements' and 'resources' of a married couple in the same household and those of any dependent children living with them are counted together. Only the husband can claim in these circumstances.

A couple who, although not married, are living together as husband and wife are normally treated as if they were married.

Requirements

A person's 'requirements' are made up of the appropriate scale rate(s) from the table below *plus* an addition for rent *plus* any special additions to which the claimant has entitlement. Where a claimant is entitled to attendance allowance the 'requirement' is increased by the amount of attendance allowance payable.

Calculation of requirements

Weekly scales		Ordinary scale	Long term scales* Claimant (and wife) under 80	Claimant or wife 80 or over
Married couple		£20·65	£24·85	£25·10
Single householder		£12·70	£15·70	£15·95
Any other person				
18 or over		£10·15	£12·60	£12·85
16 to 17		£7·80	—	—
Dependent child	13 to 15	£6·50	—	—
	11 to 12	£5·35	—	—
	5 to 10	£4·35	—	—
	under 5	£3·60	—	—
Blind people				
married couple	one blind	£21·90	£26·10	£26·35
	both blind	£22·70	£26·90	£27·15
single person	18 or over	£13·95	£16·95	£17·20
	16 to 17	£8·70	—	—

*The long term scale rates apply to (a) supplementary pensions and (b) people under pension age, except the unemployed, who have received supplementary benefit for a continuous period of two years or more. These higher scale rates include a margin of 50p (75p for the over 80 rate) towards special expenses.

Rent: an amount for rent is added to the basic requirements.

A householder will generally have the full amount of rent and rates added (but see below). If the claimant owns the house in which he lives, outgoings including payments of mortgage *interest*—but not of capital – and rates, etc will be treated as rent.

The rent addition will be less than the full rent if this includes such items as heating or lighting, if it is unreasonably high, or if there are any payments from sub-tenants. Part of the rent may be attributed to other members of the household who are not dependent on the householder.

Rent rebates or allowances and rate rebates are not normally made available by local authorities to people who receive supplementary benefit for continuous periods of more than eight weeks. When someone claiming supplementary benefit already has a rent rebate or allowance or rate rebate, the relevant amount is deducted from the amount to be added for rent in the supplementary assessment.

A claimant living as a member of someone else's household has £1·20 added for rent.

A boarder who pays an inclusive charge for board and lodging does not have an amount added for rent. Requirements in this case are assessed as the amount of the board and lodging charge (up to a reasonable level) *plus* £4·10 (£4·60 for long term beneficiaries) for personal expenses.

Special additions are added to requirements where there are exceptional circumstances, for example where a special diet or domestic help is needed or extra expenditure is necessarily incurred in centrally-heated accommodation. Help with heating costs can also be given where a claimant or a dependant has difficulty in moving about, or is seriously ill or suffering from a chronic illness (such as chronic bronchitis) or where the living accommodation is difficult to keep warm.

The long term rate of benefit already includes a margin of 50p (75p for the over 80 rate) towards special expenses and this will be deducted from any additional requirements other than for heating or for special expenses of children.

Resources

In calculating 'resources' different kinds of income are treated as follows:

Earnings: generally the first £4 a week of any part time earnings plus the first £4 of a wife's earnings are not counted. In the case of the parent of a one-parent family, £6 is ignored. But someone who is unemployed and required to register for work at the unemployment benefit office has only £2 ignored. The earnings of children under 16 or over 16 and in full time secondary education are disregarded entirely. Earnings, for this purpose, means the net amount received after deducting tax, national insurance and pension contributions, trade union subscriptions, fares to work and other expenses connected with work.

Child benefit and most national insurance benefits: fully taken into account.

Maintenance payments (voluntary or under court order): fully taken into account.

Occupational pensions or weekly payments under a redundancy scheme: first £1 a week is disregarded.

Disablement and war widow's pensions: up to £4 is disregarded.

Other income: up to £4 a week of the total of most other forms of income is disregarded. *The total of income other than earnings which can be disregarded is limited to £4.*

Savings and capital: if a man or his wife owns the house they live in, its value will be ignored. Other savings, such as money in the National Savings Bank or building societies, are treated as capital. If a man and his wife and dependants have between them capital of less than £1,250, it will be ignored and so will any income it produces. If capital amounts to £1,250 or more, the actual income from it will not be counted; a weekly income, which is fully taken into account, will be calculated at the rate of 25p for each complete £50 on the basis that a person can reasonably be expected to draw something from capital over this amount for normal living expenses.

Exceptional needs

If a person has exceptional needs, lump sum payments of benefit may be made in certain circumstances. Such payments may be made, for example, where a person has inadequate stocks of bedding, or is without essential furniture or other household equipment. They may also be made where there is an exceptional need for clothing or footwear.

Emergencies

In an emergency such as flood or fire the local social security office will usually help in the task of relief. They can also help in less serious emergencies: for example, some payment may be made when a person has lost wages by being unavoidably prevented from going to work, or when he is in some other temporary emergency, and has insufficient resources for his immediate requirements. If the person is in full time work the money may be recovered.

Automatic entitlement to other benefits

People receiving supplementary benefit and their dependants are also entitled to exemption from or refund of National Health Service charges for prescriptions, wigs and fabric supports, dental treatment and dentures and certain glasses; children under school age and expectant mothers are also entitled to free milk and vitamins;

children at school do not have to pay for school meals; members of the family attending hospital for treatment under the National Health Service may claim a refund of fares.

Unemployment benefit

Unemployment benefit is paid to persons who are unemployed, capable of work and available for work as an employee. Availability for work is normally shown by registering for a job at an office of the Employment Service Agency. Contribution conditions have to be satisfied, and normally only Class 1 (employed earners) contributions count. There are special rules to help widows and divorced women.

The rates of unemployment benefit, including increases for dependants, are the same as for sickness benefit.

Flat rate unemployment benefit is payable for up to 312 days in any period of interruption of employment. (Spells of unemployment and sickness not separated by more than 13 weeks count as one period of interruption of employment.)

Once benefit has run out it cannot be paid again until the claimant has been back at work for an employer for 13 weeks or more.

Benefit is not paid for the first three days of any period of interruption of employment, nor for isolated days of unemployment.

War pensions

Pensions and allowances for those disabled as a result of service in the 1914–18 and 1939–45 wars (including civilian casualties of the 1939–45 war) or of service in the Armed Forces since the end of the 1939–45 war, and for the widows, parents and certain other dependants of those who have died as a result of such service.

The pensions are payable at the same rates and under the same basic principles which apply to industrial injuries disablement benefit (see above). They also attract similar increases by way of constant attendance allowance, exceptionally severe disablement allowance, unemployability supplement and an allowance for a lowered standard of occupation which is the parallel benefit to special hardship allowance under the industrial injuries scheme (see above).

There are however some additional allowances paid with war disablement pensions which include rank additions, allowances for a wife and children, educational allowances for children, a severe disablement occupational allowance, comforts allowance, an age allowance for those aged 65 or over whose assessment is 40 per cent or more and a clothing allowance where the disablement causes exceptional wear and tear on clothing.

Treatment allowances may also be paid in certain circumstances, raising the pensioned disablement to the 100 per cent rate.

War widows' pensions are payable at a standard rate (plus rank additions) for widows aged 40 or over or under 40 with child(ren) or under 40 incapable of self-support. The standard rate is £19·80 a week. Allowances for children are also payable. These include a rent allowance of up to £4·59 a week and a maximum education allowance of £120 a year where appropriate. Childless widows under 40 capable of self-support receive a lower rate of £4·59 a week. An age allowance of £1·95 a week is payable to all widows on attaining age 65, increasing to £3·90 a week at age 70.

Widow's benefits

General

For the first 26 weeks of widowhood, widow's allowance is generally payable. After that, payment of widow's benefit depends on individual circumstances such as family responsibilities and age.

Only the husband's contributions count for widow's benefit.

Widow's allowance
The rate of the allowance is £21·40 a week payable for the first 26 weeks of widowhood, with increases for dependent children of £7·45 for the first child and £5·95 for each other child.

If a woman is widowed when 60 or over she can get the allowance only if her husband was not a retirement pensioner.

A widow may qualify for earnings related addition for the same period as her widow's allowance where her husband had an earnings factor of more than 50 times the lower earnings limit for the income tax year relevant to her claim. The addition is calculated in the same way as earnings related supplement described above but is based on the late husband's earnings factor, not that of the widow. The limitation to 85 per cent of reckonable weekly earnings does not apply to the addition.

Widowed mother's allowance
A widow left with a dependent child will usually get a widowed mother's allowance when she has finished drawing her widow's allowance. The standard rate of widowed mother's allowance is £15·30 a week, and reduced rates are payable where the contribution conditions are only partially satisfied. There are increases for each qualifying child at the same rates as those paid with widow's allowance.

A widow can get widowed mother's allowance, without increases for children, if she has residing with her a son or daughter under 19 who does not count as a child because he or she has left school and is not an apprentice.

Widow's pension
A widow's pension may be paid to a widow:
after her widow's allowance ends, if she does not qualify for widowed mother's allowance and was 40 or over when her husband died; or
after she ceases to be entitled to a widowed mother's allowance if she is then 40 or over.

The standard rate of widow's pension is £15·30 a week if the widow was over 50 when her husband died or when her entitlement to widowed mother's allowance ended. If she was between 40 and 50 at that time, however, the standard rates range from £14·23 a week for the widow who was 49 to £4·59 a week for the widow who was then 40. Where the contribution conditions are only partially satisfied, however, widow's pension may be payable at less than the standard rate.

A widow whose husband was over 65 on 5 July 1948, when the National Insurance scheme began, and who was herself 40 or over when her husband died may, subject to certain residence conditions, qualify for a non-contributory widow's pension. The standard rate of the pension payable where the widow was 50 or over when widowed is £9·20 a week. If she was between 40 and 50 at that time, the rate of the pension is scaled down from the full age 50 rate of £9·20 a week in the same way as the contributory widow's pension.

Remarriage or living with a man as his wife
Widow's benefit stops if the widow remarries or lives with a man as his wife but is not married to him.

Widows who are 60 or over
Since 5 April 1971 all widows over 60 who are getting widow's pensions can get a retirement pension of at least as much as the widow's pension they were receiving previously.

429

Workmen's Compensation (Supplementation) Scheme
In certain cases supplementation allowances are payable to people with rights to compensation under the Workmen's Compensation Acts for accidents occurring or diseases contracted in employment before the National Insurance (Industrial Injuries) Act came into force on 5 July 1948.

Contributory benefits
The benefits listed below are paid out of the National Insurance Fund. Entitlement will depend, among other things, on the amount and class of contributions paid or credited.

Class 1	Class 2	Class 3
Unemployment benefit	Sickness and	Maternity grant
Sickness and	invalidity benefits	Widow's benefits
invalidity benefits	Maternity benefits	Retirement pension
Maternity benefits	Widow's benefits	Child's special
Widow's benefits	Retirement pension	allowance
Retirement pension	Child's special	Death grant
Child's special	allowance	
allowance	Death grant	
Death grant		

Duplication of benefits
Certain of the main benefits listed above cannot be paid at the same time. The general principle is that if there is title to more than one benefit only the higher will be paid if the benefits are for the same contingency. For example, unemployment benefit cannot be paid at the same time as sickness or invalidity benefit or retirement pension as these benefits are for replacement of earnings.

The new state pensions scheme
A new pensions scheme starts in April 1978. Under the new scheme, retirement, widows' and invalidity pensions will, from April 1979, be in two parts—

a basic pension equivalent to the present flat-rate pension, and
an additional pension related to earnings.

Employees who are members of an occupational pension scheme which meets the necessary requirements may be contracted out of the additional pension for retirement and half the additional pension for widowhood. A contracted out occupational pension scheme assumes responsibility for providing that part of the additional pension. The state scheme will then provide the whole of any invalidity pension, basic, and any balance of additional, widows' benefits, and any basic retirement pension. It will also continue its present cover for sickness, unemployment, maternity and industrial injuries benefits.

The additional pension will be related to earnings between lower and upper earnings limits for contribution liability. These limits are reviewed annually and, from April 1978, are expected to be £17·50 (which is the basic pension rate) and about seven times that amount. Additional pension will be calculated as 1/80th of these earnings for each year of contributions to the scheme up to a maximum of ¼ (20/80ths) of these earnings after 20 years of contributions.

It will thus take 20 years for the full amounts of additional pension to build up but people who retire, are widowed or become entitled to invalidity benefit before then will benefit proportionately (even when, for retirement pension, widowed mother's allowance or widow's pension, they do not satisfy the contribution conditions for the flat rate benefit).

430

Those who contribute for more than 20 years will have their additional pension calculated by reference to their best 20 years of earnings.

Women will get the same personal benefit as men with the same earnings.

A widow will get any additional pension earned by her husband with her widowed mother's allowance or widow's pension. A widow retirement pensioner will be able to add together the entitlements on her own and her husband's contributions up to the maximum that one person could have earned.

A man whose wife dies when they are both over state pension age will also be able to inherit his wife's pension rights, in the same way as a widow.

Certain people who have recently been widowed may be able to use their late spouse's earnings record for invalidity pension if this gives a more favourable result than their own.

Basic pension rights will be protected without the need to pay contributions for tax years during which a person cannot work because of home responsibilities, such as bringing up children (to age 16) or caring for a person receiving an attendance allowance. Women will not benefit from this provision, however, for years in which they keep the right to pay reduced contributions.

Contributions for employees will continue to depend on the amount earned, but naturally, better pensions must mean higher contributions. The exact contribution rates and upper and lower earnings limits from 6 April 1978 are not yet known but the employee's rate will not be more than 6½ per cent of pay.

Women aged 60 or over and men 65 or over will cease to be liable for contributions.

Newly married women can no longer choose to pay reduced rate contributions. However, some married women and widows may retain their right to pay at the reduced rate.

Inflation proofing

Basic pension will keep up with the average increase in earnings or prices – whichever is the higher.

Additional pension will be protected in two ways:

The earnings on which additional pension will be based will be revalued in line with the general movement of earnings from the year in which they were received up to the last tax year before entitlement to pension arises.

The pension awarded will keep up with the average increase in prices.

Annex 5
(referred to in paragraph 135)

Principal rates of social security benefits and allowances

£ per week

	15 November 1976 to 13 November 1977	From 14 November 1977
Injury benefit		
Personal benefit	15·65	17·45
Adult dependant	8·00	9·10
First child	3·05²	3·50³
Other child	2·55²	3·00³
Industrial disablement benefit		
100 per cent disability pension	25·00	28·60
Special hardship allowance		
Maximum rate	10·00	11·44
Constant attendance allowance		
Normal maximum	10·00	11·40
Exceptionally severe disablement		
allowance	10·00	11·40
Unemployability supplement	15·30	17·50
Industrial death benefit[1]		
Widow's pension for first 26 weeks	21·40	24·50
Higher permanent widow's pension	15·85	18·05
Lower permanent widow's pension	4·59	5·25
First child	6·45²	7·40⁴
Other child	5·95²	6·90⁴
Sickness benefit		
Men and single women: 18 and over	12·90	14·70
Adult dependant	8·00	9·10
First child	3·05²	3·50³
Other child	2·55²	3·00³
Invalidity pension		
Personal benefit	15·30	17·50
Adult dependant	9·20	10·50
First child	6·45²	7·40⁴
Other child	5·95²	6·90⁴
Invalidity allowance		
Up to 34	3·20	3·70
35–44	2·00	2·30
45–59 (men)	1·00	1·15
45–54 (women)	1·00	1·15

£ per week

	15 November 1976 to 13 November 1977	From 14 November 1977
Widow's national insurance benefits[1]		
Widow's allowance for first 26 weeks	21·40	24·50
Widow's pension, standard rate	15·30	17·50
First child	6·45[2]	7·40[4]
Other child	5·95[2]	6·90[4]
Attendance allowance		
Lower rate	8·15	9·30
Higher rate	12·20	14·00
Mobility allowance[1]	5·00	7·00
Non-contributory invalidity pension		
Personal benefit	9·20	10·50
Adult dependant	5·60	6·30
First child	6·45[2]	7·40[4]
Other child	5·95[2]	6·90[4]
Invalid care allowance	9·20	10·50
Increase for adult dependant	5·60	6·30
Child benefit		
First child	1·00[2]	1·00
Each other child	1·50[2]	1·50
One-parent families: each child	1·50[2]	1·50
Retirement pension	15·30	17·50
Adult dependant	9·20	10·50

1 Taxable.

2 From April 1977.

3 From April 1978 rates will be £2·20 a week for each child, assuming child benefit is increased to £2·30 a week for each child.

4 From April 1978 rates will be £6·10 a week for each child, assuming child benefit is increased to £2·30 a week for each child.

Annex 6

(referred to in paragraph 817)

Special hardship allowance

Note by the Department of Health and Social Security

Introduction

1 The main benefit of the industrial injuries scheme (disablement benefit) is based on the principle of giving compensation for the injury itself (i.e. 'loss of faculty') instead of for loss of earning capacity which was the basis of compensation under the Workmen's Compensation Acts which the scheme replaced. When the scheme was introduced it was, however, accepted that compensation based solely on loss of faculty without regard to the effect of the injury on earning capacity would not be entirely equitable as a comparatively slight injury could in some cases have a quite disproportionate effect on earnings; the classic instance is the compositor who loses an index finger. This led to the provision of a supplementary benefit for such exceptional cases – known as 'special hardship allowance'.

2 Assessments of disablement are related to a period. Disablement pension will be paid if the loss of faculty is assessed at 20 per cent or more; for an assessment of less than 20 per cent a gratuity will in general be the form of award. Special hardship allowance is payable as an increase of disablement benefit and therefore can be awarded only for a period during which the claimant is suffering from a loss of faculty.

3 Although, as the name suggests, special hardship allowance was originally envisaged as a minor feature of the scheme, it has developed so that almost any claimant who can show that he has lost his 'regular' occupation as a result of an industrial accident – even though this may involve only a slight change of duties – and has suffered an earnings loss of a very small amount can qualify for the allowance. In 1973 80,000 of the 202,000 disablement pensioners were drawing special hardship allowance and a further 61,000 allowances were being paid to persons who had been awarded disablement gratuities. It has therefore come to play a very significant role in the scheme.

The conditions

4 A person entitled to disablement pension or gratuity can qualify for special hardship allowance if, as a result of the relevant loss of faculty, he is incapable of following his regular occupation *and* is incapable of following employment of an equivalent standard which is suitable in his case *and* either:

(a) is likely to remain permanently incapable of following his regular occupation; or

(b) has, at all times since the end of the injury benefit period, been incapable of following his regular occupation or employment of an equivalent standard.

The 'continuous' condition ((b) above) was designed to overcome the difficulty which might arise from the reluctance of doctors to certify an injured person as permanently incapable of his regular work until they were quite certain that there was not going to be complete recovery. It also means that title to special hardship allowance is virtually automatic if the claimant continues to be incapable of work at the end of the injury benefit period. There are provisions allowing certain periods of work in the regular occupation, after the end of the injury benefit period, to be disregarded for the purpose of the continuous condition in certain circumstances, e.g. where the claimant has returned to his regular occupation to ascertain whether he has recovered from the effects of the injury or where he is awaiting surgical treatment for those effects.

5   It will be apparent that the effect of the conditions is such that a claimant will not be able to qualify for an allowance for odd weeks of incapacity for his regular occupation.

How the rate of allowance is determined

6   If a claimant satisfies the conditions for an allowance, the rate payable is determined by comparing the standard of remuneration in his regular occupation with the probable standard in the employments, if any, which are suitable in his case and which he is likely to be capable of following. The rate payable will be the difference between the two sets of earnings, subject to

(*a*)   the maximum rate (£10 a week at January 1977 levels). This rate is traditionally equivalent to the rate of disablement pension payable for a 40 per cent assessment. Over four fifths of the allowances are being paid to persons whose disablement assessment is 30 per cent or less. For the majority of the beneficiaries therefore the allowance represents the major part of their benefit from the scheme. This restriction does not prevent the acquisition of more than one special hardship allowance. A man may, because of a series of accidents or diseases, suffer a series of earnings losses. He can be entitled to an allowance for each of them. The limit of £10 applies only to each individual loss, though the limit described in (*b*) below will prevent an aggregate of allowances and disablement benefit worth more than 100 per cent;

(*b*)   the disablement pension and the special hardship allowance must not together exceed the rate of disablement pension appropriate to 100 per cent disablement. It follows that if the claimant is already receiving disablement pension of 70 per cent or more his allowance will be restricted. A man with a 100 per cent disablement pension cannot receive a special hardship allowance whatever his earnings loss may be.

7   The effect of the maxima is to remove the need for the earnings loss to be precisely calculated in the many cases where it is immediately apparent that the loss is well in excess. It is only of academic interest that on one interpretation a man's loss may be £12 and on another £13 when either will secure the maximum allowance. Account has to be taken however of the fact that the maxima are regularly uprated in line with the movement in disablement benefit itself.

8   The allowance is awarded for specified periods, usually of up to 12 months; a longer period may be given where the claimant has passed retirement age. The rate awarded may be reviewed if there are any relevant changes of circumstances.

9   Special hardship allowances cannot be awarded where the claimant is already in receipt of unemployability supplement, the latter being the benefit under the industrial injuries scheme which caters for the circumstances in which the claimant is incapable of work, and likely to remain permanently so, because of the effects of the accident; the law provides that the two benefits may not be paid together. The allowances may however be paid together with benefits under the main scheme, such as sickness, invalidity and unemployment benefits and with retirement pension.

How the conditions work in practice

10   Unless it is clear that there is no title to an allowance, e.g. where the claimant is already receiving disablement pension at the 100 per cent rate, enquiries will normally need to be made

(*a*)   of the claimant, by correspondence and then, perhaps, by interview, to establish the nature of his regular pre-accident occupation;

(*b*)   of the medical board, for advice as to whether the claimant is capable of that regular occupation and, if not, whether the relevant loss of faculty contributes materially to that incapacity and whether the incapacity is likely to be permanent or temporary. Advice is also required as to the claimant's capacity for alternative work and as to the nature of any limitations imposed by the relevant loss of faculty;

(c) of the employers at the time of the accident, as to the normal current earnings in the regular occupation, including overtime and bonuses, and as to whether over-time is a regular feature of the occupation. The employers are also asked whether there were any special circumstances which were applicable to the claimant which would make his earnings more or less than those of other employees in the same grade and occupation;

(d) of any employers in any post-accident employment for similar information as to earnings.

It may also be necessary to seek information from Departmental records and to obtain further general or particular information as to the level of earnings in occupations followed in the locality, for example from the Employment Services Agency, from local employers and from press advertisements.

Regular occupation
11 It will usually be the case that the occupation being followed at the time the accident happened was the claimant's regular occupation but this will not necessarily be so. He might have been following a temporary occupation at the time, so that his regular occupation would be different from the job in which he suffered the accident, or indeed the claimant might not have had a regular occupation at the time of the accident. Adequate details of the description and nature of the regular occupation need to be obtained so that the statutory authorities may obtain the necessary medical advice and then consider whether the claimant is incapable of following the occupation and, if so, whether the relevant loss of faculty has materially contributed to that incapacity. Difficulties may arise on subsequent claims if adequate details are not obtained on the initial claim. This may happen where, for example, the man is totally incapable of work due to the accident when the initial claim is determined and it is clear that the maximum rate of allowance is payable. In these, and in other cases where the maximum is payable, there will be little or no incentive for the claimant to challenge the basis of the award. Years later, however, if the rate then falls to be reduced on the basis of the original information, the claimant may challenge the validity of that information and at that time it may be difficult or impossible to obtain the necessary confirmation.

12 Even though a claimant may appear to have resumed his regular occupation after the accident further detailed enquiries may be necessary before the claim can be determined. The enquiries will need to cover matters such as whether the claimant's tasks and duties have been changed because of his disablement, whether he is unable to use particular tools or operate particular machines or, perhaps, whether he is not now able to accept the grade to grade advancement which was an essential part of his regular occupation. The enquiries may show that there have been no such changes but that the claimant just works more slowly or less productively.

13 Where the claimant contends that there is some difference in the conditions under which he has been re-employed in his regular occupation, it will have to be considered whether he is able, despite the relevant loss of faculty, to fulfil all the ordinary duties which employers expect of a person in the relevant occupation; this will entail establishing the requirements of the employer. Even if it is accepted that a man is incapable of following his regular occupation because he has returned to it under easier conditions it will not necessarily follow that he will be entitled to an allowance; it may be that the employment will be regarded as of a standard equivalent to that of his regular occupation.

436

Loss of 'prospects of advancement'

14 If it can be established that at the date of the accident the claimant belonged to a class of employed persons who are normally advanced to better paid work and that his prospects of such advancement were as good as others in his class, then the regular occupation is regarded as extending to include the better paid work to which he would have been advanced. This provision does not cover the circumstances where, although the claimant may have good personal prospects of promotion or advancement, he does not belong to a class of employed persons who are normally so advanced. If the claimant would not have been advanced to the higher paid work during the period of award the loss of prospects would not be taken into account when the standard of remuneration in the regular occupation was being determined. Where a claimant contends that he has lost prospects of advancement enquiries would need to be made of the employer for confirmation.

'Equivalent standard'

15 Where it can be accepted that the claimant is incapable of following his regular occupation because of the effects of the relevant loss of faculty, it will then need to be considered whether he is also incapable of following employment of an equivalent standard. This will entail comparing the standard of remuneration of the regular occupation and that of the alternative occupation which can be regarded as suitable in his case. Where the regular occupation was carried out full time, the standard of remuneration means the normal level of earnings in the employment for the normal number of hours worked by persons employed in that employment. It will be assumed that the norm for the employment represents the claimant's earnings unless the employer indicates otherwise on the earnings enquiry form sent to him or there is other clear evidence to the contrary. The local office will need to make further enquiries where the employer has indicated that the claimant's earnings were different from those of other employees or where the claimant disputes the figures. If the enquiries establish that the claimant earned consistently more than the norm his personal earnings in the regular occupation will be taken for the purpose of the initial comparison to decide whether there is title to an allowance. Where, on the other hand, the claimant consistently and regularly worked fewer hours or shifts than the norm for a full time worker and so had lowei earnings than the norm the lower figure will be used for the comparison purpose.

16 The impersonal standards of the two employments are used when it is being considered whether the alternative employment is of equivalent standard. Once title has been established, however, the amount of allowance is determined by comparing the claimant's personal standards in the regular and alternative employments.

Overtime

17 When it is a regular feature of the employment overtime is taken into account in assessing the standard of remuneration of both regular and post-accident employments. In relation to the regular occupation, the claimant's actual overtime earnings will be taken into account and not the full amount he might have earned had he worked all the voluntary overtime available to him. Where in regard to the post-accident employment it is considered that the claimant has not acted reasonably in relation to the overtime available to him, with the result that his actual earnings are not a fair measure of his capacity, account may need to be taken of the overtime earnings of the claimant's colleagues working under the same conditions.

18 Where the relevant disablement prevents a claimant from working overtime on resuming his regular occupation the incapacity test may be regarded as satisfied where it is established that the employer would not normally engage anyone unable to work overtime in the particular employment. Where however the working of over-

time in the regular occupation is entirely voluntary it will be disregarded in considering the requirements of the employer whether or not there is medical evidence that the claimant is unable to work overtime.

19   If a claimant does regular overtime in his post-accident occupation, this may serve to reduce entitlement to the allowance; for example, a man who earned £60 in a 40 hour week in his regular occupation will get no allowance if he is able to earn £60 for a 48 hour week in his post-accident occupation (if these are the regular hours including any regular overtime). Similarly his allowance will fall to be reduced if regular overtime ceases in the regular occupation.

'Suitable' employment
20   In considering whether an alternative occupation would be 'suitable' for the claimant, it is necessary to examine what fields of employment were open to the claimant before the relevant accident occurred, having regard to his physical and intellectual powers, his education, training, employment history, age and any other then existing physical or mental disabilities. It would then have to be considered to what extent the field had been restricted subsequently by the effects of the industrial accident. In this connection any factors supervening after the date of the accident would need to be ignored. Such an exercise involves not only a detailed interview with the claimant but enquiries of employers and, perhaps, the specialised advice of disablement resettlement officers.

21   An employment may be regarded as 'suitable' for the purpose of the provisions even though there may be family and domestic responsibilities which restrict the claimant's availability for the work. Moreover, the fact that the claimant may not be able to obtain such employment will also be irrelevant.

'As a result of the relevant loss of faculty'
22   In addition to considering whether the claimant is incapable of his regular occupation and of employment of an equivalent standard, the statutory authorities have to be satisfied that such incapacity arises 'as a result of the relevant loss of faculty'. Although advice on the question may be obtained from a medical board and, occasionally further advice from a consultant, there may be other, and perhaps conflicting, medical evidence on the matter and it will be for the statutory authorities to decide on the question of fact; they will however be obliged to accept that the 'relevant loss of faculty' was as determined by the medical authorities. The assessment of the relevant disablement may be increased due to the interaction of the relevant loss of faculty with another condition which was not due to the accident. An incapacity which results only from this other 'connected' condition itself will not be regarded as resulting from the relevant loss of faculty. It is possible however for a condition which was not included in the relevant loss of faculty to be regarded as a sequela of it, in which case incapacity arising from that sequela may be taken as having arisen from the relevant loss of faculty.

Pneumoconiosis cases
23   In the case of someone receiving disablement benefit for pneumoconiosis there is a special provision if they have received a 'letter of advice' from a pneumoconiosis medical board. These letters are issued by boards to all claimants who are diagnosed by a board as suffering from the disease unless, because of age or illness, the claimant is unlikely ever to work again. The letter may advise the claimant to work in a dust free atmosphere, or that he may continue to work in his normal job provided that certain conditions are fulfilled. If, following receipt of this advice he changes his job, regulations provide that for SHA he is deemed to be incapable of his regular occupation or of an occupation of an equivalent standard, although it is possible to rebut this presumption if there is evidence (other than the letter of advice itself) with which to

438

do so. This is of importance particularly in the coalmining industry where many miners with a 10 per cent assessment for minimal pneumoconiosis are advised that they may continue in their normal job provided it does not involve work in the most dusty conditions. (Such letters are issued in about 20 per cent of all newly diagnosed cases.) If, for whatever reason, on receipt of such a letter of advice or later the miner decides to move to less onerous and less well paid work he may claim SHA and it will be presumed that he moved because he was incapable of his normal occupation. The presumption will only be challenged if e.g. the man faces redundancy, or suffers from some other incapacitating condition, or he is within two years of retirement.

The 'permanent' and 'continuous' conditions
24   If it is accepted that, as a result of the relevant loss of faculty, a claimant is incapable of following his regular occupation and suitable employment of an equivalent standard it has then to be considered whether either the permanent or continuous condition is satisfied.

25   'Permanence' in this context is interpreted as meaning for the remainder of the claimant's life. The award of a life assessment for the purpose of the basic disablement benefit does not of course mean that necessarily the claimant is permanently incapable of his regular occupation; the relevant disability may not affect his working capacity. Moreover, even if permanency is accepted on the initial claim it does not follow that it will continue to be accepted at subsequent renewal stages; the claimant's condition may improve so that he is no longer considered likely to be permanently incapable. Conversely, a medical opinion that incapacity is not likely to be permanent may be reversed at a later stage of the claim.

26   As an alternative to the 'permanent' condition, the claimant may be able to satisfy the 'continuous' condition which requires him to show that, as a result of the relevant loss of faculty, he has been continuously incapable of following his regular occupation, and employment of equivalent standard, since the end of the injury benefit period. If the claimant received injury benefit to the end of the 156 days of the injury benefit period and remained incapacitated thereafter because of the relevant injury, the 'continuous' condition will normally be regarded as satisfied. If however the claimant has returned to work it will be necessary to show that he continued to be incapable of both his regular occupation and employment of equivalent standard. It is however possible for periods of work in the regular occupation to be disregarded in certain circumstances when the work was done for rehabilitation or training, or for ascertaining whether he had recovered from the effects of the injury sufficiently for him to work in his regular occupation or in work of equivalent standard, or where the claimant was awaiting surgical treatment for the effects of the relevant injury.

The effect of retirement
27   As has been stated, special hardship allowance is paid on a large scale to recipients of sickness, invalidity, unemployment and retirement benefits. Furthermore, the earnings loss calculated for allowance purposes takes no account of benefit income, so that special hardship allowance and the other benefits can both be in payment to cover the same loss. The main area of duplication, with retirement pension, arises because the industrial injuries scheme does not recognise or deem retirement at any age. If an SHA recipient retires or leaves employment for any reason, other than a worsening of his relevant disability, he is imputed with a suitable employment which he could perform (i.e. which he could perform in the light of his disability, not in the light of his age or other intervening factors) and he continues to be compensated on the gap between this and his regular occupation. In practice this usually means that he is treated as if he had remained in his last post-accident job. If there are shifts in the differential between the man's two hypothetical occupations this can lead to a

reduction of SHA when the man is in his 70s or 80s, which is difficult to explain to the recipient. In other cases changes in differentials can lead to an increase in the allowance or even create title to a first award after retirement, even though the claimant spent his entire post-accident working life in what was throughout an occupation of equivalent standard. Variations in award can also arise from changes in the man's medical condition even though his age alone may render him unfit for employment.

The award

28 If it is established that the claimant is entitled to an allowance, the award is normally made for a period of up to twelve months. As the allowance is an increase of disablement benefit it cannot of course be awarded for any period beyond the terminating date of the current disablement benefit assessment. Title to special hardship allowance is considered afresh when the period of award expires. The allowance is paid weekly, usually by order book together with the basic disablement pension. If the disablement benefit was a gratuity the award of special hardship allowance can allow the claimant to elect to have a pension in lieu. Where a gratuity has been paid as a lump sum the special hardship allowance will need to be paid separately by order book.

Some comments on the system

29 The principle underlying special hardship allowance is that, while the basic disablement benefit takes account of disabilities that may or may not affect earning capacity, there should be an additional provision to compensate those with lower levels of disablement where the disability involved has had a disproportionate effect on earning capacity. Thus the scheme gives recognition to two factors, the disablement and the loss of earnings. As might be expected, much of the difficulty experienced in administering the provisions arises from the problems involved in establishing the essential link between the two factors and in determining the extent of the consequential loss.

30 It does not of course follow that lower post-accident earnings will necessarily be a consequence of the accident nor is it necessarily the case that the lower earnings represent the limit of the person's earning capacity. In some industries it is not unusual for a man to move to a less strenuous and lower paid occupation in the latter part of his working life or there may be other reasons, quite unconnected with the accident, why the person should prefer to work in the lower paid occupation. Furthermore, the existence of the allowance may itself constitute an incentive for the man to prefer such lower paid work.

31 Although, in the process of establishing the link between the two factors, there is access to the independent medical boarding doctors, their essential function as medical authorities is to determine whether the accident has resulted in a loss of faculty and, if so, what is the extent of the disablement. It cannot be expected that doctors will be in a position to exercise the same level of expertise when they come to consider the secondary question regarding the effect the disablement may have had on the individual claimant having regard to the particular nature of his work. Much will depend on the extent to which doctors are seized of the precise nature of all the tasks involved in the occupation concerned.

32 The subsequent stage, the earnings comparison, which entails finding the difference between the gross pre- and post-accident earnings, may look reasonably simple – and particularly so where the operation of the maxima means that the allowance has become virtually a flat rate benefit, with some 90 per cent of beneficiaries receiving the maximum rate. In practice, however, while there are many cases which are reasonably straightforward, given the nature of benefit, the determination of the claim often involves a not inconsiderable administrative effort.

33   Determining notional current earnings can itself give rise to difficulties but they are few compared with the problems which arise in calculating notional earnings in the regular occupation or in a suitable post-accident occupation when the claimant is out of employment for reasons unconnected with his accident. With the passage of time such difficulties multiply and there are more and more claimants whose accidents occurred many years previously and whose current earnings, had they remained in their regular occupations, become increasingly conjectural. One set of problems arises where the former employer has gone out of business and comparisons have to be made with work with other employers or with local or regional rates of pay.

34   In some cases entire industries have vanished and the claimant has to be notionally re-deployed in his regular occupation or, in some cases, the phantom of the regular occupation is preserved with the earnings being determined in relation to national earnings in a comparable employment. In other cases the job structure of an industry may have been completely reorganised so adding to the difficulty of keeping track of jobs which used to be more readily identifiable.

35   These problems may be compounded when a second set of notional earnings has to be determined when the claimant is not in work. In cases of short term sickness or unemployment, previous earnings, or earnings in the occupation for which the claimant has registered, may provide a reasonably acceptable basis but where a person is not in work but is not registering for employment there have to be complex procedures so that the statutory authorities may come to some conclusion as to the suitable employments to be imputed to the claimants concerned. For some married women such an exercise has to be quite arbitrary and with the chronic sick and the retired the problem of vanished employments and reorganised occupations once again emerges.

36   Earnings comparisons may often be distorted by the varying incidence of over-time and bonuses. A man who has been obliged to take a less skilled job because of the effects of an accident may find some years later that his title to the allowance has disappeared because of the reduced availability of overtime in his erstwhile regular occupation.

37   The administrative problems involved, the burdens on the employers and the Department's staff, the complex case law which has developed all make this a comparatively costly benefit to administer, bearing in mind that in many cases the finely sifted results achieved could, even if compensation were in full, only bear a tenuous and sometimes hypothetical relationship to what would have happened but for the industrial disablement. The problems referred to would of course have been much more intractable if there had been no maximum rates which serve to reduce the guesswork to rather more manageable proportions. Moreover, were there no maxima there would be a significant increase in the number of appeals as to the level of benefit to be awarded.

38   The practical difficulties experienced in operating the present provisions do not of course in themselves invalidate the case for the inclusion of a special 'loss of earning capacity' allowance in the industrial injuries scheme. Nevertheless, it is right to take account of these difficulties in considering whether a proper balance has been struck in the industrial injuries scheme between 'loss of faculty' and 'loss of earnings' provision.

441

Annex 7

(referred to in paragraph 872)

**Extracts from Industrial Injuries (Prescribed Diseases) Regulations
made under the Social Security Act 1975**

List of prescribed diseases and injuries and the occupations for which they are prescribed (except pneumoconiosis and byssinosis)

Description of disease or injury	Nature of occupation
Poisoning by:	Any occupation involving:
1 Lead or a compound of lead.	The use or handling of, or exposure to the fumes, dust or vapour of, lead or a compound of lead, or a substance containing lead.
2 Manganese or a compound of manganese.	The use or handling of, or exposure to the fumes, dust or vapour of, manganese or a compound of manganese, or a substance containing manganese.
3 Phosphorus or phosphine or poisoning due to the anti-cholinesterase action of organic phosphorus compounds.	The use or handling of, or exposure to the fumes, dust or vapour of, phosphorus or a compound of phosphorus, or a substance containing phosphorus.
4 Arsenic or a compound of arsenic.	The use or handling of, or exposure to the fumes, dust or vapour of, arsenic or a compound of arsenic, or a substance containing arsenic.
5 Mercury or a compound of mercury.	The use or handling of, or exposure to the fumes, dust or vapour of, mercury or a compound of mercury, or a substance containing mercury.
6 Carbon bisulphide.	The use or handling of, or exposure to the fumes or vapour of, carbon bisulphide or a compound of carbon bisulphide, or a substance containing carbon bisulphide.
7 Benzene or a homologue.	The use or handling of, or exposure to the fumes of, or vapour containing, benzene or any of its homologues.
8 A nitro- or amino- or chloro-derivative of benzene or of a homologue of benzene, or poisoning by nitrochlorben-zene.	The use or handling of, or exposure to the fumes of, or vapour containing, a nitro- or amino- or chloro-derivative of benzene or of a homologue of benzene or nitrochlorbenzene.
9 Dinitrophenol or a homologue or by substituted dinitro-phenols or by the salts of such substances.	The use or handling of, or exposure to the fumes of, or vapour containing, dinitrophenol or a homologue or substituted dinitrophenols or the salts of such substances.
10 Tetrachloroethane.	The use or handling of, or exposure to the fumes of, or vapour containing, tetrachloro-ethane.

Description of disease or injury	Nature of occupation
Poisoning by:	Any occupation involving:
11 Tri-cresyl phosphate.	The use or handling of, or exposure to the fumes of, or vapour containing, tri-cresyl phosphate.
12 Tri-phenyl phosphate.	The use or handling of, or exposure to the fumes of, or vapour containing, tri-phenyl phosphate.
13 Diethylene dioxide (dioxan).	The use or handling of, or exposure to the fumes of, or vapour containing, diethylene dioxide (dioxan).
14 Methyl bromide.	The use or handling of, or exposure to the fumes of, or vapour containing, methyl bromide.
15 Chlorinated naphthalene.	The use or handling of, or exposure to the fumes of, or dust or vapour containing, chlorinated naphthalene.
16 Nickel carbonyl.	Exposure to nickel carbonyl gas.
17 Nitrous fumes.	The use or handling of nitric acid or exposure to nitrous fumes.
18 Gonioma kamassi (**African boxwood**).	The manipulation of gonioma kamassi or any process in or incidental to the manufacture of articles therefrom.
19 Anthrax.	The handling of wool, hair, bristles, hides or skins or other animal products or residues, or contact with animals infected with anthrax.
20 Glanders.	Contact with equine animals or their carcases.
21 (*a*) Infection by leptospira ictero-haemorrhagiae.	Work in places which are, or are liable to be, infested by rats.
(*b*) Infection by leptospira canicola.	Work at dog kennels or the care or handling of dogs.
22 Ankylostomiasis.	Work in or about a mine.
23 (*a*) Dystrophy of the cornea (including ulceration of the corneal surface) of the eye, (*b*) Localised new growth of the skin, papillomatous or keratotic, (*c*) Squamous-celled carcinoma of the skin, due in any case to arsenic, tar, pitch, bitumen, mineral oil (including paraffin), soot or any compound, product (including quinone or hydroquinone), or residue of any of these substances.	The use or handling of, or exposure to, arsenic, tar, pitch, bitumen, mineral oil (including paraffin), soot or any compound, product (including quinone or hydroquinone), or residue of any of these substances.

Description of disease or injury	Nature of occupation
	Any occupation involving:
24	
25 Inflammation, ulceration or malignant disease of the skin or subcutaneous tissues or of the bones, or blood dyscrasia, or cataract, due to electro-magnetic radiations (other than radiant heat), or to ionising particles.	Exposure to electro-magnetic radiations other than radiant heat, or to ionising particles.
26 Heat cataract.	Frequent or prolonged exposure to rays from molten or red-hot material.
27 Decompression sickness.	Subjection to compressed or rarefied air.
28 Cramp of the hand or forearm due to repetitive movements.	Prolonged periods of handwriting, typing or other repetitive movements of the fingers, hand or arm.
29	
30	
31 Subcutaneous cellulitis of the hand (Beat hand).	Manual labour causing severe or prolonged friction or pressure on the hand.
32 Bursitis or subcutaneous cellulitis arising at or about the knee due to severe or prolonged external friction or pressure at or about the knee (Beat knee).	Manual labour causing severe or prolonged external friction or pressure at or about the knee.
33 Bursitis or subcutaneous cellulitis arising at or about the elbow due to severe or prolonged external friction or pressure at or about the elbow (Beat elbow).	Manual labour causing severe or prolonged external friction or pressure at or about the elbow.
34 Traumatic inflammation of the tendons of the hand or forearm, or of the associated tendon sheaths.	Manual labour, or frequent or repeated movements of the hand or wrist.
35 Miner's nystagmus.	Work in or about a mine.
36 Poisoning by beryllium or a compound of beryllium.	The use or handling of, or exposure to the fumes, dust or vapour of, beryllium or a compound of beryllium, or a substance containing beryllium.
37 (a) Carcinoma of the mucous membrane of the nose or associated air sinuses. (b) Primary carcinoma of a bronchus or of a lung.	Work in a factory where nickel is produced by decomposition of a gaseous nickel compound which necessitates working in or about a building or buildings where that process or any other industrial process ancillary or incidental thereto is carried on.

Description of disease or injury	Nature of occupation
	Any occupation involving:
38 Tuberculosis.	Close and frequent contact with a source or sources of tuberculous infection by reason of employment—
	(a) in the medical treatment or nursing of a person or persons suffering from tuberculosis, or in a service ancillary to such treatment or nursing;
	(b) in attendance upon a person or persons suffering from tuberculosis, where the need for such attendance arises by reason of physical or mental infirmity;
	(c) as a research worker engaged in research in connection with tuberculosis;
	(d) as a laboratory worker, pathologist or person taking part in or assisting at post-mortem examinations of human remains where the occupation involves working with material which is a source of tuberculous infection.
39 Primary neoplasm of the epithelial lining of the urinary bladder (Papilloma of the bladder) or of the renal pelvis or of the ureter or of the urethra.	(a) Work in a building in which any of the following substances is produced for commercial purposes:—
	(i) alpha-naphthylamine or beta-naphthylamine;
	(ii) diphenyl substituted by at least one nitro or primary amino group or by at least one nitro and primary amino group;
	(iii) any of the substances mentioned in sub-paragraph (ii) above if further ring substituted by halogeno, methyl or methoxy groups, but not by other groups;
	(iv) the salts of any of the substances mentioned in sub-paragraphs (i) to (iii) above;
	(v) auramine or magenta:
	(b) the use or handling of any of the substances mentioned in sub-paragraphs (i) to (iv) of paragraph (a), or work in a process in which any such substance is used or handled or is liberated;
	(c) the maintenance or cleaning of any plant or machinery used in any such process as is mentioned in paragraph (b), or the cleaning of clothing used in any such building as is mentioned in paragraph (a) if such clothing is cleaned within the works of which the building forms a part or in a laundry maintained and used solely in connection with such works.

Description of disease or injury	Nature of occupation
	Any occupation involving:
40 Poisoning by cadmium.	Exposure to cadmium fumes.
41 Inflammation or ulceration of the mucous membrane of the upper respiratory passages or mouth produced by dust, liquid or vapour.	Exposure to dust, liquid or vapour.
42 Non-infective dermatitis of external origin (including chrome ulceration of the skin but excluding dermatitis due to ionising particles or electro-magnetic radiations other than radiant heat).	Exposure to dust, liquid or vapour or any other external agent capable of irritating the skin (including friction or heat but excluding ionising particles or electro-magnetic radiations other than radiant heat).
43 Pulmonary disease due to the inhalation of the dust of mouldy hay or of other mouldy vegetable produce, and characterised by symptoms and signs attributable to a reaction in the peripheral part of the bronchopulmonary system, and giving rise to a defect in gas exchange (Farmer's lung).	Exposure to the dust of mouldy hay or other mouldy vegetable produce by reason of employment – (*a*) in agriculture, horticulture or forestry; or (*b*) loading or unloading or handling in storage such hay or other vegetable produce; or (*c*) handling bagasse.
44 Primary malignant neoplasm of the mesothelium (diffuse mesothelioma) of the pleura or of the peritoneum.	(*a*) The working or handling of asbestos or any admixture of asbestos; (*b*) the manufacture or repair of asbestos textiles or other articles containing or composed of asbestos; (*c*) the cleaning of any machinery or plant used in any of the foregoing operations and of any chambers, fixtures and appliances for the collection of asbestos dust; (*d*) substantial exposure to the dust arising from any of the foregoing operations.
45 Adeno-carcinoma of the nasal cavity or associated air sinuses.	Attendance for work in or about a building where wooden furniture is manufactured.

Description of disease or injury	Nature of occupation
	Any occupation involving:
46 Infection by brucella abortus.	Contact with bovine animals infected by brucella abortus, their carcases or parts thereof or their untreated products, or with laboratory specimens or vaccines of or containing brucella abortus, by reason of employment – (a) as a farm worker; (b) as a veterinary worker; (c) as a slaughterhouse worker; (d) as a laboratory worker; or (e) in any other work relating to the care, treatment, examination or handling of such animals, carcases or parts thereof, or products.
47 Poisoning by acrylamide monomer.	The use or handling of, or exposure to, acrylamide monomer.
48 Substantial permanent sensorineural hearing loss due to occupational noise amounting to at least 50dB in the better ear, being the average, after exclusion of hearing losses not due to occupational noise, of pure tone losses measured by audiometry over the 1, 2 and 3 kHz frequencies (occupational deafness).	(a) The use of pneumatic percussive tools or high-speed grinding tools in the cleaning, dressing or finishing of cast metal or of ingots, billets or blooms, or (b) the use of pneumatic percussive tools on metal in the shipbuilding or ship repairing industries, or (c) work wholly or mainly in the immediate vicinity of drop-forging plant or forging press plant engaged in the shaping of hot metal.
49 Viral hepatitis.	(a) Close and frequent contact with human blood or human blood products; or (b) close and frequent contact with a source of viral hepatitis infection by reason of employment in the medical treatment or nursing of a person or persons suffering from viral hepatitis, or in a service ancillary to such treatment or nursing.
50 (a) Angiosarcoma of the liver; and (b) Osteolysis of the terminal phalanges of the fingers	Work in or about machinery or apparatus used for the polymerization of vinyl chloride monomer, a process which, for the purposes of this provision, comprises all operations up to and including the drying of the slurry produced by the polymerization and the packaging of the dried product; or work in a building or structure in which any part of the aforementioned process takes place.

Occupations for which pneumoconiosis is prescribed

1 Any occupation involving –

(*a*) the mining, quarrying or working of silica rock or the working of dried quartzose sand or any dry deposit or dry residue of silica or any dry admixture containing such materials (including any occupation in which any of the aforesaid operations are carried out incidentally to the mining or quarrying of other minerals or to the manufacture of articles containing crushed or ground silica rock);

(*b*) the handling of any of the materials specified in the foregoing sub-paragraph in or incidental to any of the operations mentioned therein, or substantial exposure to the dust arising from such operations.

2 Any occupation involving the breaking, crushing or grinding of flint or the working or handling of broken, crushed or ground flint or materials containing such flint, or substantial exposure to the dust arising from any of such operations.

3 Any occupation involving sand blasting by means of compressed air with the use of quartzose sand or crushed silica rock or flint, or substantial exposure to the dust arising from such sand blasting.

4 Any occupation involving work in a foundry or the performance of, or substantial exposure to the dust arising from, any of the following operations:–

(*a*) the freeing of steel castings from adherent siliceous substance;

(*b*) the freeing of metal castings from adherent siliceous substance –

(i) by blasting with an abrasive propelled by compressed air, by steam or by a wheel; or

(ii) by the use of power-driven tools.

5 Any occupation in or incidental to the manufacture of china or earthenware (including sanitary earthenware, electrical earthenware and earthenware tiles), and any occupation involving substantial exposure to the dust arising therefrom.

6 Any occupation involving the grinding of mineral graphite, or substantial exposure to the dust arising from such grinding.

7 Any occupation involving the dressing of granite or any igneous rock by masons or the crushing of such materials, or substantial exposure to the dust arising from such operations.

8 Any occupation involving the use, or preparation for use, of a grindstone, or substantial exposure to the dust arising therefrom.

9 Any occupation involving –

(*a*) the working or handling of asbestos or any admixture of asbestos;

(*b*) the manufacture or repair of asbestos textiles or other articles containing or composed of asbestos;

(*c*) the cleaning of any machinery or plant used in any of the foregoing operations and of any chambers, fixtures and appliances for the collection of asbestos dust;

(*d*) substantial exposure to the dust arising from any of the foregoing operations.

10 Any occupation involving –

(*a*) work underground in any mine in which one of the objects of the mining operations is the getting of any mineral;

(*b*) the working or handling above ground at any coal or tin mine of any minerals extracted therefrom, or any operation incidental thereto;

(*c*) the trimming of coal in any ship, barge, or lighter, or in any dock or harbour
        or at any wharf or quay;

(*d*) the sawing, splitting or dressing of slate, or any operation incidental thereto.

11   Any occupation in or incidental to the manufacture of carbon electrodes by an
industrial undertaking for use in the electrolytic extraction of aluminium from
aluminium oxide, and any occupation involving substantial exposure to the dust
arising therefrom.

12   Any occupation involving boiler scaling or substantial exposure to the dust
arising therefrom.

Occupations for which byssinosis is prescribed

Any occupation in any room where any process up to and including the winding or
beaming process is performed in factories in which the spinning or manipulation of
raw or waste cotton or of flax is carried on.

Annex 8

(referred to in paragraphs 938 and 1086)

An outline of the proposed schemes for work and road injuries

Introduction

The industrial injuries scheme of compensation for those injured at work would be improved, and the scheme would be used as a basis for compensating for motor vehicle accidents.

(*Benefit rates quoted are at January 1977 levels.*)

Work injuries

Scope

All persons at present insured for industrial injuries would be covered, and in addition self employed persons but with title to flat rate benefits only until they are brought within the earnings related state pensions scheme.

All injuries and diseases at present covered by the industrial injuries scheme and in addition cover for accidents on the way to and from work.

Additional cover for industrial diseases, where the claimant could prove that the disease was occupational in origin and was a particular risk of his occupation.

Benefits

Short term incapacity benefit (up to 6 months from date of injury)

Basic flat rate (£15·65 a week) plus earnings related supplement of 33⅓ per cent of gross earnings from £11 to £30 and 25 per cent of gross earnings from £30 to £69. Increases for dependants payable at current levels.

Long term incapacity benefit (after 6 months incapacity)

Benefits calculated in the same way as invalidity benefits under the new state pension scheme. The number of years' earnings recorded for pension purposes should be treated as 20 years in all cases. Basic flat rate (£15·30 a week) plus earnings related addition of 25 per cent of gross earnings from £15 to £105. Increases for dependants and invalidity allowance payable at current levels.

Benefits for non-pecuniary loss

Industrial disablement pensions and gratuities would continue as at present, that is to say, up to £25 a week or a gratuity according to the degree of disablement.

Special hardship allowance would be replaced eventually by a new benefit for partial loss of earnings.

Constant attendance allowance and exceptionally severe disablement allowance would be phased out in favour of the general attendance allowance.

Hospital treatment allowance would continue.

Unemployability supplement would be rendered largely obsolete by the long term incapacity benefit.

Short term widow's benefit (for the first 6 months)

Benefits would comprise a flat rate (£21·40) plus earnings related supplement calculated on the late husband's earnings as for short term incapacity benefit. Increases for dependent children payable at current levels.

450

Long term widow's benefit (after 6 months)
Benefits calculated in the same way as widow's pension under the new state pension scheme (and with the same conditions as to age and family circumstances). The number of years' earnings recorded for pension purposes should be treated as 20 years in all cases. Benefits would comprise a flat rate (£15·30) plus earnings related addition calculated on the late husband's earnings as for long term incapacity benefit. Increases for dependent children payable at current levels.

Widowers
As far as practicable widowers would be treated in the same way as widows.

Retirement pension
For pension purposes, an injured person would be credited with contributions, for the period of his incapacity, at a level equivalent to his pre-accident earnings.

Benefit rates
Benefits would be protected against inflation, as now.

Finance
Scheme to be financed by an increase in the national insurance contributions paid by employers and the self employed.

Administration
Scheme to be administered by DHSS, as now.

Motor vehicle injuries
Scope
Injuries involving motor vehicles on roads and other land to which the public has access would be covered. Motor vehicle injuries in the course of work and whilst travelling to and from work would be classed as work injuries.

Benefits
Incapacity benefits
Incapacity benefits for *earners* would be identical to those payable under the improved industrial injuries scheme. For *non-earners* incapacity benefits would be as follows:
  i   under age 16 – £4 a week
  ii   ages 16 and 17 – £9·20 a week
  iii from age 18 to pensionable age – £15·65 a week
  iv   over pensionable age – no benefit payable.

Benefits for non-pecuniary loss
Disablement benefit including its allowances to be identical to those payable under the improved industrial injuries scheme, except that:
  i   disablement benefit not payable to children under the age of 12
  ii   reduced rate disablement benefit payable from ages 12–15 (inclusive)
  iii constant attendance allowance and exceptionally severe disablement allowance not payable.

Widows and widowers
Benefits identical to those payable under the improved industrial injuries scheme.

Finance
Scheme to be financed through a levy on petrol.

Administration
Scheme to be administered by DHSS.

Annex 9

(referred to in paragraph 1062)

Council of Europe: European Convention on Civil Liability for Damage caused by Motor Vehicles, 14.5.73

Preamble

The member States of the Council of Europe, signatories of this Convention,

Considering that the aim of the Council of Europe is to achieve a greater unity between its Members;

Considering that the steady growth of road traffic has resulted in an increase in the number of accidents, which calls for an improvement of the systems of liability for damage;

Considering that international road traffic is at present subject to legal systems of liability which differ from one State to another;

Considering that it is appropriate to harmonise the law in this matter and to improve the position of victims;

Have agreed as follows:

Article 1: Duties of Contracting States

1 Each Contracting State shall make its national law conform with the provisions of this Convention not later than the date of the entry into force of the Convention in respect of that State.

2 Each Contracting State shall communicate to the Secretary General of the Council of Europe, not later than the date of the entry into force of the Convention in respect of that State, any text adopted or a statement of the contents of the existing law which it relies on to implement the provisions of this Convention, including any option of which the State avails itself.

Article 2: Scope of the Convention

This Convention shall apply to civil liability for damage caused by a vehicle and resulting from an accident connected with traffic. Each Contracting State may, however, limit the application of the Convention to accidents connected with traffic on the public highway and in grounds open to the public.

Article 3: Definitions

1 For the purpose of this Convention:

(a) 'vehicle' means a vehicle which is provided with a motor for its propulsion and intended to travel on the ground, other than a vehicle running on rails or a hovercraft;

(b) 'keeper', in relation to a vehicle, means the person who controls the use of the vehicle. The person under whose name a vehicle is registered or, in the absence of registration, the owner of a vehicle shall be presumed to control the use of the vehicle, unless the contrary is proved. The occasional user of a vehicle shall not be considered to control the use of the vehicle, unless he has taken possession of the vehicle illegally. Each Contracting State may, however, implement the provisions of this sub-paragraph with the modifications it considers necessary.

2 For the purposes of this Convention, damage caused by the vehicle includes damage caused by a trailer or any object hauled by or attached to the vehicle or by anything transported even when detached accidentally.

452

Article 4: Principle of liability

1 The keeper of a vehicle shall be liable for damage caused by the vehicle, subject to the restrictions provided in this Convention.

2 Each Contracting State may provide that the direct liability of an insurer shall be wholly or partly substituted for the liability of the keeper under this Convention, provided that the victim shall be protected to the same extent as if the keeper were liable.

Article 5: Contribution of the victim to the damage

1 If a victim or person suffering damage, other than a keeper of a vehicle involved in the accident, has committed a fault which contributed to the damage, the compensation may be reduced or disallowed having regard to the circumstances of the accident within the meaning of Article 9.

2 The same shall apply when the contribution to the damage is due to circumstances in which the victim or the person suffering damage would be liable irrespective of his fault.

Article 6: Liability of two or more keepers to third parties

1 When, as a result of an accident, damage is caused by two or more vehicles to persons other than the keepers of the vehicles involved, the keepers of the vehicles which caused the damage shall, subject to the provisions of Articles 8 and 10, each be liable for such damage in full (*in solidum*).

2 In this case, in the mutual relations between the keepers liable, the damages shall be apportioned having regard to the contribution of the vehicles to the damage.

Article 7: Damage to keepers

When as a result of an accident, one or more keepers of the vehicles involved in the accident suffer damage, each keeper liable shall be liable only for his share of the damages according to the contribution of the vehicles to the damage. Each Contracting State may, however, derogate from this rule by providing for liability in full (*in solidum*).

Article 8: Exceptions to the keepers' liability in full

1 As regards damage for which the keeper of a vehicle is not liable by virtue of Article 10 or under the terms of a contract permitted by national law, the keepers of other vehicles which have contributed to the damage shall not be liable under this Convention for the share of the damages which would fall on the keeper in question having regard to the contribution of the vehicles to the damage.

2 When the keeper of a vehicle is liable for damage caused to the driver of the vehicle, each Contracting State may nevertheless provide that the keepers of other vehicles which have contributed to the damage shall not be liable for the share of the damages that falls on the keeper in question.

Article 9: Apportionment of liability between keepers

1 For the purposes of this Convention, the contribution of the vehicles to the damage shall be determined having regard to the circumstances of the accident, such as the fault or ill-health of a driver or passenger, the inherent risks of the vehicles or the irregular behaviour of a vehicle, whatever may be its cause, for instance a defect of the vehicle, the intervention of a third party, or a natural event other than a grave natural disaster of an exceptional nature.

2 If the circumstances do not indicate otherwise, the contribution of the vehicles to the damage shall be regarded as equal.

453

3   If and to the extent that the share of the damages for which a keeper is liable cannot be recovered wholly or partially from him, from the insurer, or from a guarantee fund or a similar body, it shall be borne by the other keepers in proportion to the contribution of their vehicles to the damage.

Article 10: Damage excluded

1   The keeper of a vehicle shall not incur liability under this Convention in respect of any damage to that vehicle, a trailer or any object hauled by or attached to the vehicle or any thing transported by the vehicle even when detached accidentally, with the exception of the personal effects, such as clothes and luggage, of a person carried.

2   Each Contracting State may provide that the keeper of a vehicle shall not be liable under this Convention for damage caused to the driver of the vehicle.

Article 11: Exceptions to the application of the Convention

1   This Convention shall not apply to:

(a)   damage caused by a vehicle and resulting from its use exclusively for a non-vehicular purpose;

(b)   nuclear damage;

(c)   damage directly due to an act of armed conflict, hostilities, civil war, insurrection or a grave natural disaster of an exceptional character.

2   Each Contracting State shall have the option not to apply this Convention to damage caused by specified categories of vehicles creating little risk for the traffic, for example pedestrian-controlled vehicles, certain agricultural machines and mopeds of low power and speed.

Article 12: Matters left to national law

1   Amongst the matters left to the law of each Contracting State are the following:

(a)   the nature, form, extent and any limits on the amount of compensation;

(b)   actions for damages against persons other than keepers and recourse actions brought by or against such persons;

(c)   recourse actions brought by keepers in respect of the share of the damages of another keeper for which they are made liable under Article 9, paragraph 3;

(d)   whether a claim may be defeated or the compensation may be reduced because of the assumption of an exceptional risk by the victim or the person suffering damage, or because of his criminal conduct or his acquiescence in such conduct of the driver.

2   Each Contracting State may assimilate wholly or partially to a keeper of a vehicle involved in an accident any other person involved in the accident who, according to national law, is liable irrespective of fault for damage resulting from the accident.

3   Each Contracting State shall have the option to derogate from this Convention so as to avoid conflicts with its law on workmen's compensation or any social security scheme.

Article 13: Extended protection and application

This Convention shall not prevent the Contracting States:

(a)   from adopting rules more favourable to persons suffering damage, except as regards the mutual relations between keepers liable;

(b)   from applying the rules of the Convention to accidents, damage or means of transport other than those covered by this Convention.

454

Article 14: Entry into force of the Convention

1   This Convention shall be open to signature by the member States of the Council of Europe. It shall be subject to ratification or acceptance. Instruments of ratification or acceptance shall be deposited with the Secretary General of the Council of Europe.

2   This Convention shall enter into force six months after the date of deposit of the third instrument of ratification or acceptance.

3   In respect of a signatory State ratifying or accepting subsequently, the Convention shall come into force six months after the date of the deposit of its instrument of ratification or acceptance.

Article 15: Accession of a State not a Member of the Council of Europe

1   After the entry into force of this Convention, the Committee of Ministers of the Council of Europe may invite non-member States to accede.

2   Such accession shall be effected by depositing with the Secretary General of the Council of Europe an instrument of accession which shall take effect six months after the date of its deposit.

Article 16: Territorial scope of the Convention

1   Any Contracting State may, at the time of signature or when depositing its instrument of ratification, acceptance or accession, specify the territory to which this Convention shall apply.

2   Any Contracting State may, when depositing its instrument of ratification, acceptance or accession or at any later date, by declaration addressed to the Secretary General of the Council of Europe, extend this Convention to any other territory or territories specified in the declaration and for whose international relations it is responsible or on whose behalf it is authorised to give undertakings.

3   Any declaration made in pursuance of the preceding paragraph may, in respect of any territory mentioned in such declaration, be withdrawn according to the procedure laid down in Article 19 of this Convention.

Article 17: Reservations

1   No reservation shall be made to the provisions of this Convention except that mentioned in the Annex to this Convention.

2   The Contracting State which has made the reservation mentioned in the Annex to this Convention may withdraw it by means of a declaration addressed to the Secretary General of the Council of Europe which shall become effective as from the date of its receipt.

Article 18: Declarations concerning options

1   Each Contracting State which wants to avail itself of one of the options set forth in Article 2, Article 3, paragraph 1 (*b*), Article 4, paragraph 2, Article 7, Article 8, paragraph 2, Article 10, paragraph 2, Article 11, paragraph 2 and Article 12, paragraphs 2 and 3 shall, when signing this Convention or when depositing the instrument of ratification, acceptance or accession, declare by means of a notification to the Secretary General of the Council of Europe its intention to do so and in what way it intends to exercise the option.

2   If, after the entry into force of the Convention in respect of a Contracting State, that State deems it necessary to avail itself of one of the options mentioned in the preceding paragraph, it shall notify the Secretary General of the Council of Europe of its intention to do so before the entry into force of the relevant provisions under domestic law.

3 Each Contracting State may, at any time, by means of a notification addressed to the Secretary General of the Council of Europe, declare that it no longer avails itself of an option exercised in accordance with the preceding paragraphs. The notification shall indicate the date on which the change takes effect.

Article 19: Duration of the Convention and denunciation

1 This Convention shall remain in force indefinitely.

2 Any Contracting State may, in so far as it is concerned, denounce this Convention by means of a notification addressed to the Secretary General of the Council of Europe.

3 Such denunciation shall take effect six months after the date of receipt by the Secretary General of such notification.

Article 20: Functions of the Secretary General of the Council of Europe

The Secretary General of the Council of Europe shall notify the member States of the Council and any State which has acceded to this Convention of:

(a) any signature;
(b) any deposit of an instrument of ratification, acceptance or accession;
(c) any date of entry into force of this Convention in accordance with Article 14 thereof;
(d) any reservation made in pursuance of the provisions of Article 17, paragraph 1;
(e) withdrawal of any reservation carried out in pursuance of the provisions of Article 17, paragraph 2;
(f) any communication received in pursuance of the provisions of Article 1, paragraph 2, Article 16, paragraphs 2 and 3 and Article 18, paragraphs 1, 2 and 3;
(g) any notification received in pursuance of the provisions of Article 19 and the date on which denunciation takes effect.

In witness whereof, the undersigned being duly authorised thereto, have signed this Convention.

Done at Strasbourg, this 14th day of May 1973, in English and in French, both texts being equally authoritative, in a single copy, which shall remain deposited in the archives of the Council of Europe. The Secretary General shall transmit certified copies to each of the signatory and acceding States.

Annex (to the Convention)

Belgium may, at the time of signature or when depositing its instrument of ratification or acceptance of the Convention, declare that she reserves the right to exclude from the scope of the Convention material damage to vehicles, for a period of three years from the date of the entry into force of the Convention in her respect.

Annex 10

(referred to in paragraph 1197)

Council of Europe: Convention on Products Liability in regard to Personal Injury and Death, 27.1.77

Preamble

The member States of the Council of Europe, signatory hereto,

Considering that the aim of the Council of Europe is to achieve a greater unity between its Members;

Considering the development of case law in the majority of member States extending liability of producers prompted by a desire to protect consumers taking into account the new production techniques and marketing and sales methods;

Desiring to ensure better protection of the public and, at the same time, to take producers' legitimate interests into account;

Considering that priority should be given to compensation for personal injury and death;

Aware of the importance of introducing special rules on the liability of producers at European level,

Have agreed as follows:

Article 1

1   Each Contracting State shall make its national law conform with the provisions of this Convention not later than the date of the entry into force of the Convention in respect of that State.

2   Each Contracting State shall communicate to the Secretary General of the Council of Europe, not later than the date of the entry into force of the Convention in respect of that State, any text adopted or a statement of the contents of the existing law which it relies on to implement the Convention.

Article 2

For the purpose of this Convention:

a   the term 'product' indicates all movables, natural or industrial, whether raw or manufactured, even though incorporated into another movable or into an immovable;

b   the term 'producer' indicates the manufacturers of finished products or of component parts and the producers of natural products;

c   a product has a 'defect' when it does not provide the safety which a person is entitled to expect, having regard to all the circumstances including the presentation of the product;

d   a product has been 'put into circulation' when the producer has delivered it to another person.

Article 3

1   The producer shall be liable to pay compensation for death or personal injuries caused by a defect in his product.

2   Any person who has imported a product for putting it into circulation in the course of a business and any person who has presented a product as his product by causing his name, trademark or other distinguishing feature to appear on the product, shall be deemed to be producers for the purpose of this Convention and shall be liable as such.

3   When the product does not indicate the identity of any of the persons liable under paragraphs 1 and 2 of this Article, each supplier shall be deemed to be a producer

for the purpose of this Convention and liable as such, unless he discloses, within a reasonable time, at the request of the claimant, the identity of the producer or of the person who supplied him with the product. The same shall apply, in the case of an imported product, if this product does not indicate the identity of the importer referred to in paragraph 2, even if the name of the producer is indicated.

4   In the case of damage caused by a defect in a product incorporated into another product, the producer of the incorporated product and the producer incorporating that product shall be liable.

5   Where several persons are liable under this Convention for the same damage, each shall be liable in full (*in solidum*).

Article 4

1   If the injured person or the person entitled to claim compensation has by his own fault contributed to the damage, the compensation may be reduced or disallowed having regard to all the circumstances.

2   The same shall apply if a person, for whom the injured person or the person entitled to claim compensation is responsible under national law, has contributed to the damage by his fault.

Article 5

1   A producer shall not be liable under this Convention if he proves:
a   that the product has not been put into circulation by him; or
b   that, having regard to the circumstances, it is probable that the defect which caused the damage did not exist at the time when the product was put into circulation by him or that this defect came into being afterwards; or
c   that the product was neither manufactured for sale, hire or any other form of distribution for the economic purposes of the producer nor manufactured or distributed in the course of his business.

2   The liability of a producer shall not be reduced when the damage is caused both by a defect in the product and by the act or omission of a third party.

Article 6

Proceedings for the recovery of the damages shall be subject to a limitation period of three years from the day the claimant became aware or should reasonably have been aware of the damage, the defect and the identity of the producer.

Article 7

The right to compensation under this Convention against a producer shall be extinguished if an action is not brought within ten years from the date on which the producer put into circulation the individual product which caused the damage.

Article 8

The liability of the producer under this Convention cannot be excluded or limited by any exemption or exoneration clause.

Article 9

This Convention shall not apply to:
a   the liability of producers *inter se* and their rights of recourse against third parties;
b   nuclear damage.

Article 10

Contracting States shall not adopt rules derogating from this Convention, even if these rules are more favourable to the victim.

Article 11

States may replace the liability of the producer, in a principal or subsidiary way, wholly or in part, in a general way, or for certain risks only, by the liability of a guarantee fund or other form of collective guarantee, provided that the victim shall receive protection at least equivalent to the protection he would have had under the liability scheme provided for by this Convention.

Article 12

This Convention shall not affect any rights which a person suffering damage may have according to the ordinary rules of the law of contractual and extra-contractual liability including any rules concerning the duties of a seller who sells goods in the course of his business.

Article 13

1   This Convention shall be open to signature by the member States of the Council of Europe. It shall be subject to ratification, acceptance or approval. Instruments of ratification, acceptance or approval shall be deposited with the Secretary General of the Council of Europe.

2   This Convention shall enter into force on the first day of the month following the expiration of a period of six months after the date of deposit of the third instrument of ratification, acceptance or approval.

3   In respect of a signatory State ratifying, accepting or approving subsequently, the Convention shall come into force on the first day of the month following the expiration of a period of six months after the date of the deposit of its instrument of ratification, acceptance or approval.

Article 14

1   After the entry into force of this Convention, the Committee of Ministers of the Council of Europe may invite any non-member State to accede thereto.

2   Such accession shall be effected by depositing with the Secretary General of the Council of Europe an instrument of accession which shall take effect on the first day of the month following the expiration of a period of six months after the date of its deposit.

Article 15

1   Any State may, at the time of signature or when depositing its instrument of ratification, acceptance, approval or accession, specify the territory or territories to which this Convention shall apply.

2   Any State may, when depositing its instrument of ratification, acceptance, approval or accession or at any later date, by declaration addressed to the Secretary General of the Council of Europe, extend this Convention to any other territory or territories specified in the declaration and for whose international relations it is responsible or on whose behalf it is authorised to give undertakings.

3   Any declaration made in pursuance of the preceding paragraph may, in respect of any territory mentioned in such declaration, be withdrawn by means of a notification addressed to the Secretary General of the Council of Europe. Such withdrawal shall take effect on the first day of the month following the expiration of a period of six months after the date of receipt by the Secretary General of the Council of Europe of the declaration of withdrawal.

Article 16

1   Any State may, at the time of signature or when depositing its instrument of ratification, acceptance, approval or accession, or at any later date, by notification

addressed to the Secretary General of the Council of Europe, declare that, in pursuance of an international agreement to which it is a Party it will not consider imports from one or more specified States also Parties to that agreement as imports for the purpose of paragraphs 2 and 3 of Article 3; in this case the person importing the product into any of these States from another State shall be deemed to be an importer for all the States Parties to this agreement.

2   Any declaration made in pursuance of the preceding paragraph may be withdrawn by means of a notification addressed to the Secretary General of the Council of Europe. Such withdrawal shall take effect the first day of the month following the expiration of a period of one month after the date of receipt by the Secretary General of the Council of Europe of the declaration of withdrawal.

Article 17

1   No reservation shall be made to the provisions of this Convention except those mentioned in the Annex to this Convention.

2   The Contracting State which has made one of the reservations mentioned in the Annex to this Convention may withdraw it by means of a declaration addressed to the Secretary General of the Council of Europe which shall become effective the first day of the month following the expiration of a period of one month after the date of its receipt by the Secretary General.

Article 18

1   Any Contracting State may, in so far as it is concerned, denounce this Convention by means of a notification addressed to the Secretary General of the Council of Europe.

2   Such denunciation shall take effect on the first day of the month following the expiration of a period of six months after the date of receipt by the Secretary General of such notification.

Article 19

The Secretary General of the Council of Europe shall notify the member States of the Council and any State which has acceded to this Convention of:

a   any signature;

b   any deposit of an instrument of ratification, acceptance, approval or accession;

c   any date of entry into force of this Convention in accordance with Article 13 thereof;

d   any reservation made in pursuance of the provisions of Article 17, paragraph 1;

e   withdrawal of any reservation carried out in pursuance of the provisions of Article 17, paragraph 2;

f   any communication or notification received in pursuance of the provisions of Article 1, paragraph 2, Article 15, paragraphs 2 and 3 and Article 16, paragraphs 1 and 2;

g   any notification received in pursuance of the provisions of Article 18 and the date on which denunciation takes effect.

In witness whereof, the undersigned, being duly authorised thereto, have signed this Convention.

Done at Strasbourg this 27th day of January 1977, in English and in French, both texts being equally authoritative, in a single copy which shall remain deposited in the archives of the Council of Europe. The Secretary General of the Council of Europe shall transmit certified copies to each of the signatory and acceding States.

Annex (to Convention)

Each State may declare, at the moment of signature or at the moment of the deposit of its instrument of ratification, acceptance, approval or accession, that it reserves the right:

1   to apply its ordinary law, in place of the provisions of Article 4, in so far as such
    law provides that compensation may be reduced or disallowed only in case of gross
    negligence or intentional conduct by the injured person or the person entitled to
    claim compensation;

2   to limit, by provisions of its national law, the amount of compensation to be paid
    by a producer under this national law in compliance with the present Convention.
    However, this limit shall not be less than:

    a   the sum in national currency corresponding to 70,000 Special Drawing Rights
         as defined by the International Monetary Fund at the time of the ratification,
         for each deceased person or person suffering personal injury;

    b   the sum in national currency corresponding to 10 million Special Drawing
         Rights as defined by the International Monetary Fund at the time of ratification,
         for all damage caused by identical products having the same defect;

3   to exclude the retailer of primary agricultural products from liability under the
    terms of paragraph 3 of Article 3 providing he discloses to the claimant all infor-
    mation in his possession concerning the identity of the persons mentioned in
    Article 3.

(referred to in paragraph 1197)

Draft EEC Directive on Products Liability: Proposal for a Council Directive relating to the Approximation of the Laws, Regulations and Administrative Provisions of the Member States concerning Liability for Defective Products

(Presented by the Commission to the Council on 9 September 1976)

The Council of the European Communities,

Having regard to the Treaty establishing the European Economic Community, and in particular Article 100 thereof,

Having regard to the proposal from the Commission,

Having regard to the Opinion of the European Parliament,

Having regard to the Opinion of the Economic and Social Committee,

Whereas the approximation of the laws of the Member States concerning the liability of the producer for damage caused by the defectiveness of his products is necessary, because the divergencies may distort competition in the common market; whereas the rules on liability which vary in severity lead to differing costs for industry in the various Member States and in particular for producers in different Member States who are in competition with one another;

Whereas approximation is also necessary because the free movement of goods within the common market may be influenced by divergencies in laws; whereas decisions as to where goods are sold should be based on economic and not legal considerations;

Whereas, lastly, approximation is necessary because the consumer is protected against damage caused to his health and property by a defective product either in differing degrees or in most cases not at all, according to the conditions which govern the liability of the producer under the individual laws of Member States; whereas to this extent therefore a common market for consumers does not as yet exist;

Whereas an equal and adequate protection of the consumer can be achieved only through the introduction of liability irrespective of fault on the part of the producer of the article which was defective and caused the damage; whereas any other type of liability imposes on the injured party almost insurmountable difficulties of proof or does not cover the important causes of damage;

Whereas liability on the part of the producer irrespective of fault ensures an appropriate solution to this problem in an age of increasing technicality, because he can include the expenditure which he incurs to cover this liability in his production costs when calculating the price and therefore divide it among all consumers of products which are of the same type but free from defects;

Whereas liability cannot be excluded for those products which at the time when the producer put them into circulation could not have been regarded as defective according to the state of science and technology ('development risks'), since otherwise the consumer would be subjected without protection to the risk that the defectiveness of a product is discovered only during use;

Whereas liability should extend only to moveables; whereas in the interest of the consumer it nevertheless should cover all types of moveables, including therefore agricultural produce and craft products; whereas it should also apply to moveables which are used in the construction of buildings or are installed in buildings;

Whereas the protection of the consumer requires that all producers involved in the production process should be made liable, in so far as their finished product or component part or any raw material supplied by them was defective; whereas for the same

462

reason liability should extend to persons who market a product bearing their name, trademark or other distinguishing feature, to dealers who do not reveal the identity of producers known only to them, and to importers of products manufactured outside the European Community;

Whereas where several persons are liable, the protection of the consumer requires that the injured person should be able to sue each one for full compensation for the damage, but any right of recourse enjoyed in certain circumstances against other producers by the person paying such compensation shall be governed by the laws of the individual Member States;

Whereas to protect the person and property of the consumer, it is necessary, in determining the defectiveness of a product, to concentrate not on the fact that it is unfit for use but on the fact that it is unsafe; whereas this can only be a question of safety which objectively one is entitled to expect;

Whereas the producer is not liable where the defective product was put into circulation against his will or where it became defective only after he had put it into circulation and accordingly the defect did not originate in the production process; the presumption nevertheless is to the contrary unless he furnishes proof as to the exonerating circumstances;

Whereas in order to protect both the health and the private property of the consumer, damage to property is included as damage for which compensation is payable in addition to compensation for death and personal injury; whereas compensation for damage to property should nevertheless be limited to goods which are not used for commercial purposes;

Whereas compensation for damage caused in the business sector remains to be governed by the laws of the individual States;

Whereas the assessment of whether there exists a causal connection between the defect and the damage in any particular case is left to the law of each Member State;

Whereas since the liability of the producer is made independent of fault, it is necessary to limit the amount of liability; whereas unlimited liability means that the risk of damage cannot be calculated and can be insured against only at high cost;

Whereas since the possible extent of damage usually differs according to whether it is personal injury or damage to property, different limits should be imposed on the amount of liability; whereas in the case of personal injury the need for the damage to be calculable is met where an overall limit to liability is provided for; whereas the stipulated limit of 25 million European units of account covers most of the mass claims and provides in individual cases, which in practice are the most important, for unlimited liability; whereas in the case of the extremely rare mass claims which together exceed this sum and may therefore be classed as major disasters, there might be under certain circumstances assistance from the public;

Whereas in the much more frequent cases of damage to property, however, it is appropriate to provide for a limitation of liability in any particular case, since only through such a limitation can the liability of the producer be calculated; whereas the maximum amount is based on an estimated average of private assets in a typical case; whereas since this private property includes moveable and immoveable property, although the two are usually by the nature of things of different value, different amounts of liability should be provided for;

Whereas the limitation of compensation for damage to property, to damage to or destruction of private assets, avoids the danger that this liability becomes limitless; whereas it is therefore not necessary to provide for an overall limit in addition to the limits to liability in individual cases;

Whereas by Decision 3289/75/ECSC of 18 December 1975[1] the Commission, with the assent of the Council, defined a European unit of account which reflects the average variation in value of the currencies of the Member States of the Community;

Whereas the movement recorded in the economic and monetary situation in the Community justifies a periodical review of the ceilings fixed by the directive;

Whereas a uniform period of limitation for the bringing of action for compensation in respect of the damage caused is in the interest both of consumers and of industry; it appeared appropriate to provide for a three year period;

Whereas since products age in the course of time, higher safety standards are developed and the state of science and technology progresses, it would be unreasonable to make the producer liable for an unlimited period for the defectiveness of his products; whereas therefore the liability should be limited to a reasonable length of time; whereas this period of time cannot be restricted or interrupted under laws of the Member States, whereas this is without prejudice to claims pending at law;

Whereas to achieve balanced and adequate protection of consumers no derogation as regards the liability of the producer should be permitted;

Whereas under the laws of the Member States an injured party may have a claim for damages based on grounds other than those provided for in this directive; whereas since these provisions also serve to attain the objective of an adequate protection of consumers, they remain unaffected;

Whereas since liability for nuclear damage is already subject in all Member States to adequate special rules, it has been possible to exclude damage of this type from the scope of the directive,

Has adopted this Directive:

Article 1

The producer of an article shall be liable for damage caused by a defect in the article, whether or not he knew or could have known of the defect.

The producer shall be liable even if the article could not have been regarded as defective in the light of the scientific and technological development at the time when he put the article into circulation.

Article 2

'Producer' means the producer of the finished article, the producer of any material or component, and any person who, by putting his name, trademark, or other distinguishing feature on the article, represents himself as its producer. Where the producer of the article cannot be identified, each supplier of the article shall be treated as its producer unless he informs the injured person, within a reasonable time, of the identity of the producer or of the person who supplied him with the article.

Any person who imports into the European Community an article for resale or similar purpose shall be treated as its producer.

Article 3

Where two or more persons are liable in respect of the same damage, they shall be liable jointly and severally.

Article 4

A product is defective when it does not provide for persons or property the safety which a person is entitled to expect.

---

1 OJ L 327 of 19.12.1975. Also the Council Decision of 21.4.1975 on the definition and conversion of the European unit of account used for expressing the amounts of aid mentioned in Article 42 of the ACP-EEC Convention of Lomé, OJ L 104 of 24.4.1975.

Article 5

The producer shall not be liable if he proves that he did not put the article into circulation or that it was not defective when he put it into circulation.

Article 6

For the purpose of Article 1 'damage' means:
(*a*) death or personal injuries;
(*b*) damage to or destruction of any item of property other than the defective article itself where the item of property
   (i) is of a type ordinarily acquired for private use or consumption; and
   (ii) was not acquired or used by the claimant for the purpose of his trade, business or profession.

Article 7

The total liability of the producer provided for in this directive for all personal injuries caused by identical articles having the same defect shall be limited to 25 million European units of account (EUA).

The liability of the producer provided for by this directive in respect of damage to property shall be limited *per capita*
—in the case of moveable property to 15,000 EUA, and
—in the case of immoveable property to 50,000 EUA.

The European unit of account (EUA) is as defined by Commission Decision 3289/75/ECSC of 18 December 1975.

The equivalent in national currency shall be determined by applying the conversion rate prevailing on the day preceding the date on which the amount of compensation is finally fixed.

The Council shall, on a proposal from the Commission, examine every three years and, if necessary, revise the amounts specified in EUA in this Article, having regard to economic and monetary movement in the Community.

Article 8

A limitation period of three years shall apply to proceedings for the recovery of damages as provided for in this directive. The limitation period shall begin to run on the day the injured person became aware, or should reasonably have become aware of the damage, the defect and the identity of the producer.

The laws of Member States regulating suspension or interruption of the period shall not be affected by this directive.

Article 9

The liability of a producer shall be extinguished upon the expiry of ten years from the end of the calendar year in which the defective article was put into circulation by the producer, unless the injured person has in the meantime instituted proceedings against the producer.

Article 10

Liability as provided for in this directive may not be excluded or limited.

Article 11

Claims in respect of injury or damage caused by defective articles based on grounds other than that provided for in this directive shall not be affected.

Article 12

This directive does not apply to injury or damage arising from nuclear accidents.

Article 13

Member States shall bring into force the provisions necessary to comply with this directive within eighteen months and shall forthwith inform the Commission thereof.

Article 14

Member States shall communicate to the Commission the text of the main provisions of internal law which they subsequently adopt in the field covered by this directive.

Article 15

This directive is addressed to the Member States.

Annex 12

(referred to in paragraph 1441)

Birth Injury: Paper by J P M Tizard,

Professor of Paediatrics, University of Oxford

Definition

1 In medical usage the term 'birth trauma' is usually employed to indicate damage to the newborn baby caused by an external physical force, whereas 'birth injury', while including 'birth trauma', also means damage caused by agents other than physical force, such as deprivation of blood supply to a part of the baby's body ('ischaemia') or deprivation of oxygen ('anoxia' or 'asphyxia').

2 Nearly all fatal cases of birth trauma and nearly all cases of birth trauma resulting in survival with permanent and serious handicap are those involving head injury (see below).

Incidence

3 The perinatal death rate is defined as the number of stillbirths plus the number of deaths in the first postnatal week per 1,000 total births. While these figures can be obtained from the Registrar General's Reports, their breakdown into causes of death is unsatisfactory due to lack of uniformity in death certification. Thus in the following table use has been made of the national perinatal mortality surveys carried out under the auspices of the National Birthday Trust in 1958 for three months[1] and of the National Birthday Trust and Royal College of Obstetricians and Gynaecologists in 1970[2] for one week, and of the survey by Dr G A Machin[3] of all perinatal deaths in an area of South East London over a four year period from 1970 to 1973.

		Perinatal Death rates			
		A	B	C	A + B + C
Years	Total	Asphyxia during birth plus cranial trauma	Asphyxia during birth alone	Trauma to the baby's head alone	Total – all cases of cranial trauma and asphyxia during birth
1958[1]	33·2	2·1	10·5	1·0	13·6
1970[2]	23·2	———7·8———		0·4	8·2
1970–1973[3]	21·1	0·6	4·4	0·2	5·2

Notes on table
(a) There has been a marked decrease in perinatal deaths over the past 15 years.
(b) Most cases of fatal birth trauma occur in association with fetal asphyxia rather than as an isolated event.
(c) There has been a marked decrease in death due to cranial trauma alone, a less marked decrease in deaths due to intrapartum asphyxia with or without cranial trauma.
(d) Separate figures for stillbirths and first week deaths have not been provided, but perinatal mortality is fairly evenly divided between the two categories.

4 There are no accurate figures available for the incidence of birth injury or trauma causing serious and permanent handicap in survivors: a figure of 2 per 1,000 would not be far off the mark.

5   The incidence of cerebral palsy (the commonest form of brain disorder in survivors of birth injury or trauma – see below) is falling. A recent survey from Sweden ([4],[5]) showed an incidence of 2·24 per 1,000 live births in 1954 – 1958 compared with 1·34 in 1967 – 1970. (N.B. Not all cases of cerebral palsy are a consequence of birth injury or trauma.)

Birth trauma

6   Parts of the body that may be injured include brain, spinal cord (spinal marrow), nerves connecting the spinal cord to muscles, skin etc., bones, skin and internal organs, especially the liver. Serious injury to the liver may cause death from bleeding, but if detected and treated operatively does not lead to residual damage. In general injuries to skin, bones and nerves are only temporary in their effects: bruises fade, lacerations and broken bones heal perfectly and nerves re-grow. Thus in terms of permanent damage there are, for practical purposes, only the brain and, rarely, the spinal cord to consider. The permanent effects of the latter may amount to paralysis of the trunk and legs. The permanent effects of brain trauma in survivors are considered below.

Causes of birth trauma

7   'Natural', unattended deliveries may result in birth trauma, especially to the head and therefore the brain. The head of a newborn baby has a wider diameter than the trunk and it is a question of the relative size of the head and the bony aperture (pelvic brim) through which it has to pass. Normally the baby's head gradually 'moulds' in the course of labour. This means that the bones of the skull, which are not joined together, overlap so that the head becomes narrow and more elongated to allow its passage through the birth canal. If the baby's head is too large or the mother's pelvic opening too small ('disproportion') or if delivery is too rapid ('precipitate') birth trauma to the head may result. Injury to the head is more likely to occur if the baby is born buttocks first ('breech presentation') rather than head first ('vertex'), because moulding of the head does not take place. Trauma to the head may occur when obstetric forceps are applied to hasten delivery, but it must be emphasised that forceps are far more often protective than damaging to the baby's head. Birth trauma may be caused by the obstetrician or midwife pulling too hard on the presenting part, by the use of forceps on the head or manually to the legs and trunk in the case of breech presentation. The necessity to hasten labour occurs when there is evidence that the baby is suffering from oxygen lack and may die if labour is prolonged (see below).

Birth injury

8   Birth injury, aside from birth trauma, principally takes the form of deprivation of an adequate supply of oxygen to the fetus. Again the brain bears the brunt of the damage. About one third of all perinatal deaths are caused by fetal asphyxia during labour.

9   An inadequate supply of oxygen is a particular hazard to babies who are born too small. Small size at birth is due to one of two causes; either the baby is born too soon ('preterm') or he has grown inadequately in the womb ('small for dates'). All babies are subjected to some deprivation of oxygen in the course of normal delivery. But the small for dates baby is particularly prone to asphyxia during delivery. When this is very severe it may cause the death of the child either during or soon after delivery or its survival with permanent brain damage, which is not always distinguishable from that due to birth trauma.

10   In the case of the preterm baby anoxic damage to the brain is most likely to occur after birth, because of difficulties in breathing and in the circulation of blood to which these babies are prone.

11   About one quarter of all perinatal deaths are due to premature delivery and most of these are early neonatal deaths rather than stillbirths. Some preterm babies, but a decreasing proportion[6], survive with brain damage.

Causes of preterm birth and of fetal stunting

12 The causes both of preterm birth and of stunting of the fetus in the womb are only partly understood. (It is known incidentally that heavy cigarette smoking by a mother during pregnancy contributes to the latter.) Thus preventive measures are today largely experimental and unproved. However it is important to make a distinction between the two conditions in the case of a fetus who appears to be too small for the length of gestation. This has become an even more difficult task today since the introduction of the contraceptive pill. When a woman stops taking the pill for the purpose of a planned pregnancy there may be a loss of menstrual periods ('amenorrhoea') for several months before conception takes place, resulting in the normal guide to the length of pregnancy being unavailable. The importance of making the distinction lies in the fact that early induction of labour may be necessary in the case of the stunted baby to prevent death during natural delivery, whereas early induction to the baby who is small because of a short period of gestation may be disastrous. The best method of making this distinction is to draw off some of the fluid surrounding the baby ('amniotic fluid') by inserting a needle through the mother's belly into the womb. Analysis of this fluid will usually give clear cut information concerning the quantity of a chemical substance manufactured in the lungs of the fetus only when he has reached a certain stage of maturity.

Preventive measures and their dangers

13 It will be readily appreciated that the diagnostic measure just described is not without possible hazards to the fetus and the same consideration applies to almost all measures designed to prevent birth trauma or birth injury (see [7] paragraph 25). The following are examples. A diagnosis of 'disproportion' can often be made by X-raying the mother's pelvis, but it is known that this practice significantly increases the risk of leukaemia in childhood. A breech presentation may be converted into a vertex presentation by manual rotation ('version') of the fetus, but this may lead to separation of the placenta from the wall of the womb and thus produce anoxia resulting in death or injury to the fetus. Birth trauma may be prevented by Caesarean section, but this is a process which obviously injures the mother and which carries certain disadvantages, sometimes serious, to the fetus.

Medical responsibility

14 These examples will, perhaps, suffice to show that the prevention of birth injury or trauma is a matter of fine judgments of relative risks by the attendant doctor. In the best maternity hospitals 'perinatal conferences' are held at regular intervals to enable the obstetricians and paediatricians to discuss in retrospect deliveries that went wrong. At these conferences it is often difficult enough to be wise after the event and it is thus not surprising that judgments before birth are often so difficult. Of course certain standards of ante-natal care are regarded as obligatory, but the latest techniques for ensuring the wellbeing of the fetus may only be available in a few selective hospitals. It cannot be too strongly emphasised that any additional legislation implying medical culpability might have undesirable effects on the practice of obstetrics and of neonatal paediatrics (care of the newborn). One example may be given: it is known that if a preterm baby is given too much oxygen he may become blind, due to a condition called retrolental fibroplasia; if he is given too little oxygen he may die or survive with brain damage. Steering between these two disasters has been made more feasible in recent years. In the meantime, however, blindness due to retrolental fibroplasia has been regarded as grounds for legal redress, whereas death or brain damage due to oxygen lack are still regarded as acts of God. Professor K W Cross ([8] and [9]) has produced evidence that many thousands of babies in the

United States and in this country have died unnecessarily in the last 20 years due to restriction of oxygen therapy, the doctors responsible for their care evidently preferring to risk neonatal death rather than survival with blindness.

Handicap in survivors

15   As indicated above permanent and serious handicap in survivors of severe birth injury and/or trauma is nearly always due to brain damage. The effects of this damage are varied in their nature and extent: they include defects of sensation (sight, hearing and touch), defects of intelligence, epilepsy and defects of movement which are generally termed cerebral palsy, or any combinations of these categories.

16   Isolated defects of sensation and mental retardation alone can seldom be attributed convincingly to birth trauma or injury: a very small minority of cases of epilepsy may be; in contrast a high proportion of cases of cerebral palsy (with or without other brain defects) are so attributable.

Attribution of brain damage

17   There remains the question of the extent to which brain damage in a child can retrospectively be attributed to birth injury or trauma. Untoward happenings at birth and subsequent evidence of impairment of brain function are a common enough association, but in the great majority of cases are almost certainly not causally related. For instance it seems that intellectual impairment as sole evidence of brain dysfunction is very seldom attributable to birth injury, but the following figures illustrate the size of the association.

18   Nearly 20 per cent of all newborn babies suffer birth asphyxia in the sense that they do not breathe within one minute following birth; nearly 5 per cent do not breathe until after three minutes[2]. Follow-up examinations of such babies show that the vast majority survive apparently unscathed.

19   Severe mental subnormality (intelligence quotient less than 50) has an incidence of ℇ per 1,000 of the child population. Mental subnormality not amounting to severe subnormality (to use the jargon of the Mental Health Act 1959) affects a further 25 per 1,000. Severe subnormality may be due to factors that are clearly unrelated to birth processes (e.g. Mongolism, metabolic defects, post-natal brain damage etc. etc.) but in nearly 50 per cent of the cases it is not possible to assign a definite cause. The lesser degrees of mental subnormality are for the most part multifactorially determined and a precise diagnosis of the cause is seldom made.

20   Combining these figures shows that about 6 per 1,000 will both have suffered birth asphyxia and subsequently proved to be mentally subnormal. In the great majority there will be no reason to suppose that the former is even partly responsible for the latter, but this will be impossible to disprove!

21   Much the same considerations apply to epilepsy. Estimates of the incidence of fits in childhood vary but in one reliable survey the figure was no less than 7 per cent. Paediatric experience suggests that birth injury is responsible for only a small fraction of these fits, but again it is impossible to disprove a causal relationship in an individual case.

22   Conversely the most dramatic and apparently serious birth injury may be followed by survival with complete normality. A survey has recently been made of all cases of revival from severe birth asphyxia in babies born at the Hammersmith Hospital over the period 1966–1971[10]. In 48 cases the babies either had no detectable heartbeat at birth (i.e. were apparently fresh stillbirths) or, while the heart was beating, did not breathe for 20 minutes or longer. The results are shown in the table.

	Apparent stillbirth	First breath after 20 minutes	Total
Total numbers	15	33	48
Neonatal deaths	8	17	25
Survival with cerebral palsy	1	5	6
Survival unscathed	6	11	17

23   Of the 23 survivors only 3 – all with cerebral palsy – are mentally retarded*.

24   Attribution of brain damage to untoward events at birth is made the more difficult by the fact that signs of such damage may take weeks, months or even years to emerge. A newborn baby does have some powers of expressing his intelligence, but obviously these are limited, and many of the movements of the newborn are 'automatic' and not under 'voluntary' control. For example, a baby who has suffered severe damage to one-half of the brain may nevertheless move his limbs symmetrically at first, signs of partial paralysis of the opposite arm and leg only becoming apparent after weeks or even months. Thus while the emergence of cerebral palsy in a baby who had been revived from apparent stillbirth would highly probably be due to birth asphyxia it would be impossible to prove that the brain damage had not taken place either before labour began or even later in infancy (cp. [7] paragraph 28).

Loss of expectation of life

25   The Law Commission ([7] paragraphs 98–100) proposes that recovery of damages for loss of expectation of life should only apply to the infant plaintiff who survives birth for 48 hours. Of the severely asphyxiated and apparently stillborn babies referred to above who were only temporarily revived some died within 48 hours of birth, others later. In many hopeless cases life may be maintained by artificial means for 48 hours or longer; indeed, since the outcome may not at first be obvious, artificial ventilation is often appropriate treatment. The legal implications of this fact which, incidentally, may also apply to the severely congenitally deformed baby, are obvious and disquieting.

Summary of conclusions

 i   Birth injury is steadily becoming rarer.
 ii   For practical purposes the serious consequences of birth injury consist in still-birth or neonatal death or in survival with cerebral palsy.
 iii   Prediction and prevention of birth injury are complex and difficult matters. Special investigations or treatment may in themselves be harmful.
 iv   It is never possible to prove with certainty, and sometimes impossible to disprove, that brain damage is a consequence of birth injury.
 v   Adding to the obstetricians' or paediatricians' medicolegal hazards may have unfortunate consequences for their patients.
 vi   Restricting the medicolegal consequences of loss of expectation of life to those infants who survive a fixed period after birth is impracticable.
 vii   The concept of 'wrongful life' should no more apply to survivors of birth injury than to survivors with congenital malformations.

December 1975

---

*It is to be hoped that the Law Commission's rejection of 'wrongful life' as actionable in the case of the malformed fetus who is allowed to survive ([7] paras 89–90) would also apply to the case of the apparently stillborn or severely asphyxiated baby who, with medical aid, survives but survives with brain damage.

References

1 Perinatal Mortality. First Report (1958) by N R Butler and D G Bonham, E & S Livingstone 1963.

2 British Births 1970. Volume I. William Heinemann Medical Books Ltd 1975.

3 G A Machin. Journal of Clinical Pathology. Volume 28, p 428, 1975.

4 & 5 B Hagberg, G Hagberg and I Olow. Acta Paediatrica Scandinavica. Volume 64, p 187 and p 193, 1975.

6 P A Davies and J P M Tizard. Developmental Medicine and Child Neurology. Volume 17, p 13, 1975.

7 The Law Commission Report on Injuries to Unborn Children. Her Majesty's Stationery Office 1974.

8 K W Cross. The Lancet, 27 October 1973.

9 D P G Bolton and K W Cross. The Lancet, 16 March 1974.

10 H Scott. 'The outcome of very severe birth asphyxia' personal communication: to be published 1976.

Annex 13

(referred to in paragraph 1441)

The Biology of Human Prenatally Determined Injury

Report to the Royal Commission by Dr James H Renwick

*Reader in Human Genetics and Population Teratology at the
London School of Hygiene & Tropical Medicine*

Disclaimer

The field covered is so wide that, in many aspects, the author has not been able to call on personal experience. Much of the information comes from the literature. Of those articles that have been traced, not all have been studied thoroughly, and of those studied, not all have been listed here.

In these circumstances, this document, designed for an inquiry into the legislative position regarding prenatal injury, should not be taken to be authoritative in any particular, and, above all, not in any legal proceedings upon which the document may, at any time, be considered to bear. Queries and corrections from any quarter will be welcomed.

Apologies are made to those investigators whose findings have been unwittingly mis-represented or not represented at all.

Acknowledgments

Mrs Anne Possamai, BA, and Miss Vanessa Moore, BSc, are thanked for discussions and assistance; Miss Surini Dissanaike for providing invaluable secretarial and bibliographical help with great patience; and the library staffs at this School and at the Royal Society of Medicine for making the surveying of the literature easy and even pleasurable.

September 1974, updated to April 1977

CONTENTS

475

CONTENTS – *cont.*

I Introduction

Aims

1 This paper, necessarily oversimplified and incomplete, presents background material selected to help in that area which concerns prenatal injury. That area is multifaceted and difficult. The process of development of the human embryo (or any embryo) is one of the least understood processes in nature, partly because of its inherent complexity and partly because of the technical difficulties limiting direct observation or experimentation. In addition, there is the wide variability inherent in all biology.

2 One aim has been to clarify the type of interplay that occurs between causative factors in the field of prenatal injury. Knowledge is continually accumulating on the specific details of the mode of action and on final effects of various noxious agents but such details are not emphasised here. Instead, emphasis has been placed on general principles in the belief that many of these will continue to be valid.

3 This report was submitted in 1974. For the present publication, I have added some recent references, but as my substantive views have not changed for the most part, I have decided against a general recasting.

Definitions

4 *Teratology* is the study of malformation (excluding simple genetical malformations – those in which the influence of the environment in determining the presence or absence of malformation appears to be small). Many other types of prenatally determined injury – those not involving disturbances of developmental processes – are in the purview of *embryotoxicology*.

5 A *teratogen* is an agent (chemical or otherwise) that increases the chance of malformation, though not necessarily in man (unless so specified). So far, excluding chemical analogues, only a score or so of the group of 1,500 teratogenic drugs appropriately mentioned by the Law Commission are known to be teratogenic to man (Report No. 60, paragraph 21, 'Injuries to unborn children'. HMSO, 1974).

6 The adjective *congenital* refers only to presence (of a disease or malformation) at the time of birth or shortly thereafter. This presence may be either detectable at birth or deduced retrospectively. The word does not imply anything as regards cause; or size of genetic contribution; or future unpreventability.

The notion of causality

7 In an area as complex as prenatal injury, simplifications (linguistic or otherwise) are essential. It is, for example, helpful to consider here, as causes or causal factors, only those actions, of individuals or groups, that could conceivably be varied by an exercise of the human will, individual or collective. Those causal factors, such as genetic factors, over which man is unlikely, in the next 25 years, to gain influence, will be mentioned only rarely. (This restricted usage of the word 'cause' is not always appropriate in other contexts.) In this usage, the existence of thalidomide is not in itself a cause of limb deformities; but the making available, prescribing or consuming of thalidomide on a particular day of pregnancy, may each be a cause. (There is also a question whether the drafting of regulations and recommendations by the appropriate national committees, for the testing for safety of pharmaceuticals, might not also be a cause if judged to be inadequate.)

Paucity of facts

8 The task of summarising the hard facts concerning prenatal life and prenatal injury in man might be deemed easy because of the paucity of such facts. Unfortunately,

simple interpretations of a small number of facts, no matter how well established those facts may be, can be seriously inappropriate unless notice is taken of a vast and vague mass of ancillary information, scattered in many books and dozens of journals.

9   Unlike many other sciences, those of embryology (the study of normal development) and teratology are currently handicapped by understandable ethical considerations restricting human experimentation. The result is that firm inferences for man are few. Only a few types of strictly scientific teratological experiment in man are now possible, and these are preventive not causal un nature. One of these is the preventive experiment in which the usual course of events in a 'control' group of pregnancies is compared with a hopefully improved course of events in another similar group that has been subjected to some change. This change may be, for example, a vitamin supplement to the mothers or the reduction in the intake of some foodstuff. Such 'intervention experiments', in which allocation to one or other group is random, are rare, so far, but are likely to be commonplace in the future. This is not to claim that all prenatal epidemiology is experimental. Much of it has to be purely observational, aimed at detecting associations between environmental factors and malformations – associations that, at best, might lead to hypotheses that could be tested by intervention experiments.

II   Conception

10   Biologically (but not legally – Law Commission report, paragraphs 32–33), the beginning of a new individual of the species is taken to coincide with fertilisation – the union of egg and sperm. Most of the information that determines that the conceptus will be a human being (and that largely determines what kind of human being) is carried in the DNA (deoxyribosenucleic acid) of the 23 chromosomes in the nucleus of the egg and the 23 corresponding but not quite identical chromosomes in the head of the sperm. One of the sperm chromosomes determines the sex of the conceptus on a roughly 50 : 50 basis, X for a girl and Y for a boy. The egg carries an X chromosome. Thus the predetermination component in our make-up is largely chromosomal, with the remainder of this component being contributed by the non-nuclear (cytoplasmic) parts of the sperm and egg; especially, indeed overwhelmingly, those of the egg.

11   The union of the human egg and sperm takes place in either the left or right tube of the uterus, some hours or even some days after the deposition of the sperm-containing seminal fluid in the vagina. The successful sperm inside its prize, the much larger egg, retraces its steps, re-entering the body of the uterus. Once every few hours during this return, the conceptus doubles the number of its cells by splitting every cell into two smaller ones.

III   The process of development

12   At first, the total mass of the barely-visible conceptus increases only slowly by a process of feeding from the surrounding fluids; but when, after a few days, the conceptus reaches the body of the uterus, it attaches itself to one of the walls of the uterine cavity and obtains more nourishment. The region of attachment develops eventually into a large organ, the placenta, which, by a partly sieve-like mechanism, permits interchange of chemical constituents between the blood of the embryo and the blood of the mother, without the actual free mixing of the two bloods. The interchange – which is free for some chemicals, restricted for others – constitutes the chief feeding and excretory mechanisms of the conceptus. The sieve is not completely impervious even to particles as large as cells. Red blood cells or white blood cells (leucocytes) do cross

in small numbers in either direction. This crossing occurs mainly at times of physical injury to the placenta (particularly at delivery) and its potentially adverse effects are discussed later (paragraphs 61–65).

13 Throughout pregnancy, the number of chromosomes in the majority of cells remains constant at $23+23=46$, despite the sharing out of chromosomes between the two daughter cells at each cell division. This constancy results from (*inter alia*) the chemical synthesis of an exact copy of each chromosome once and only once between cell divisions.

14 At first, each cell of the conceptus is indistinguishable from others, but after a few cell divisions (about 5) the process of detectable differentiation begins, presumably by the sequential activation of chemical switches, that determine which parts of the chromosomes are active. At any point of time, each cell, while possessing chromosomes that are identical from cell to cell except for the state of certain switches, is potentially unique in its pattern of chromosomal material that is activated. At the stage of chromosome-copying in each cell-division cycle, the current state of the switches is also copied; hence a single differentiated cell gives rise to a set of similar cells, sharing at least this particular switching or its consequences. This set constitutes a cell type, say striated muscle cells or cells that secrete cartilage material. Mutual attractions, repulsions, and other interactions between different cell types account for the basic process of development of the embryo, human or otherwise. These processes include cell migrations, some being controlled by a concentration gradient of a specific chemical substance. They also include differential rates of cell growth, division and death; contractile movements, canalisations and fusions of groups of cells; and extra-cellular syntheses of structural materials, such as fibres (collagen, elastin, etc.) or cartilage or bone, largely from components made inside cells and then extruded.

15 The progressive growth, foldings, rotations, canalisations, fusions, and other changes occur in an ordered manner, despite their three-dimensional complexity, and run to a fairly strict time-schedule in the average conceptus.

IV Effects of prenatal injurious agents

16 An injurious agent may act either on the genetical material (DNA, deoxyribosenucleic acid) that is destined to become the DNA of the conceptus when it is formed by union of egg and spermatozoon (see mutagenesis, paragraphs 92–96): or it may act directly on part or all of the conceptus itself, once formed, or on the uterus in which it is housed. If the action is non-trivial, it will eventually initiate one or more of six possible pathological processes or events. For a descriptive purpose only, these are crudely listed, complete with untidy overlappings, as follows:

i. *In conceptus and/or in placenta.*

Infective process (e.g. rubella).

Maldevelopment (e.g. from thalidomide).

Physical disruption, bruising, scarring from trauma (e.g. during delivery).

Toxic or degenerative process including loss of function and cell death (e.g. deafness arising from quinine taken by the mother in pregnancy).

Tumour formation (e.g. delayed cancer of vagina initiated, up to 25 years previously, by the synthetic hormone, stilboestrol, taken by the mother during pregnancy).

ii. *In uterus*

Change in uterine physiology: e.g. either retention of conceptus (the ingestion of the plant, *Salsola tuberculata*, unduly prolongs pregnancy in sheep – Kennedy,

1971; and subcutaneous injections of somatotrophin do so in rats – Croskerry & Smith, 1975) – or lack of retention (e.g. from a previous delivery or abortion having left a laxity of the mouth of the uterus).

17 Each pathological process may be of short or of long duration, with temporary or permanent consequences.

18 Any one of these processes when initiated by an injurious agent may produce physical handicap; or immediate death of the conceptus with termination of pregnancy; or delayed death, perhaps many years after birth. The brain seems particularly susceptible to injury. A process in any of the categories can lead to brain effects and these will be manifest in diminished mental ability or disturbed behaviour of one sort or another (see review by Barlow & Sullivan, 1975).

19 If the conceptus survives, the child that it becomes shows a degree of disability ranging from trivial to total, and this wide range, remarkably enough, is probably almost equally a feature whatever the class of mechanism at play. There is, for example, no known mechanism of prenatal injury to man that confines itself to trivia.

V Origins of variation in the injury

The timing of a prenatal event as an arbitrator of its effect

20 The adherence to a time-schedule of normal development, mentioned in paragraph 15, has consequences for the effect of a prenatal event. On any specific day of pregnancy, notably in the first three lunar months when organs are being formed, only a limited number of processes will be at a critical stage. An occurrence to the conceptus at such a time tends to produce distortions of those processes and not directly of others. Thus the timing confers specificity of defect to some extent. (As discussed later, a further order of specificity is possible if, at the same time, the injuring agent has a predilection for affecting certain regions of the conceptus – paragraphs 23–24.)

21 Careful appraisal of the full range of body-parts involved in the deformity, together with an appraisal of the times of the maximum vulnerability of these parts during their key phases of development, can give valuable leads to the timing of the injuring event, whatever the agent. For instance, man's gullet is canalised usually in the fifth or sixth week. Failure of canalisation of the gullet (which, in principle, can be distinguished, by microscopy at surgical operation, from later obliteration of the lumen) can therefore be attributed to some influence acting in the fifth or sixth week of pregnancy or earlier. More relevantly, a putative noxious agent which was not administered until some time **after** the sixth week could not reasonably be blamed for the lack of patency. (The uncertainty that often pertains to the exact date of conception unfortunately reduces the otherwise considerable value of this type of argument.)

22 Another consequence of the interaction between the nature of an injuring agent and the timing of its application is that the same agent may produce differing effects according to the timing. When thalidomide is given orally to women on day 27–30 of pregnancy, it is mainly the upper limbs of their children that are shortened and deformed. When it is given three days later, it is mainly the lower limbs that are so affected (see Shepard, 1976). In this and other respects, the deformities in either rhesus or marmoset monkeys correspond closely to the human deformities resulting from thalidomide taken orally (Wilson & Gavan, 1967).

Target predilection of an injuring agent as an arbitrator of its effect

23 In many cases, an agent injures some cell types more than others, hence the abnormalities can vary with the nature of the injuring agent. For example, x-radiation

is particularly damaging to certain types of brain cell and, in sufficient dosage, leads even in the human fetus to a small head coupled with mental retardation. It has been suggested that a learning deficit after smaller doses might be detectable if sought.

24 By contrast, at least in marmoset monkeys, thalidomide appears to have a predilection for damaging not the brain cells but the branch-points of certain developing arteries. This is at the sensitive time, and this time may be different for arterial branch-points in different regions of the body (Poswillo, 1973). Subsequent local bleeding from these branch-points is claimed to lead to the disturbed development of the part. But such uniformity of mechanism does not always imply uniformity of effect. Indeed, there is much variation from case to case. For thalidomide, if the mechanism were as claimed, it would be easy to see how the amount of bleeding could be somewhat variable, enough to account for the incompleteness of symmetry of the deformity as observed on the two sides of the body, both in man and in other primates. (McCredie, 1976, argues that the target is in the nervous system, not in the arterial system, but comparable opportunities for variability would pertain.)

Sources of variation particularly relevant for chemical agents

25 Variability in response is a general phenomenon in the prenatal field and leads to a poor level of predictability of the outcome of, for example, any specific chemical insult received by mouth by the mother. This is true for experimental animals as well as for man. Some of the factors involved are given here.

i. *Variation in rate of absorption*
26 The rate of absorption may be markedly influenced by what is taken orally at the same time or by what is already in the stomach of the mother. For a drug, it may be markedly influenced by the particle size (e.g. cortisone, griseofulvin – Griffin, 1974) or accompanying substances (e.g. calcium phosphate with phenytoin in Australia – Tyrer et al., 1970).

ii. *Variation in rate of conversion to a more toxic substance or to a less toxic substance*
27 The extent of either of these types of conversion depends on such factors as
a   the make-up, inherited and acquired, of the mother and of the conceptus;
b   the biochemical properties of the mix of bacterial and other micro-organisms in the intestines of the mother, this mixture varying from time to time even in the same individual;
c   variation from conceptus to conceptus in the quantities, specific activities and times of appearance and disappearance of each enzyme (a protein catalyst that facilitates each its specific type of chemical transformation).

iii. *Ease of transport of substances from mother to conceptus across the placental barrier*
28 Most substances do cross the placental barrier though not all with equal readiness. The larger proteins, for example, pass only at a low rate. Further, not all placentas offer the same degree of resistance to free passage. (Incidentally, a substance can damage the conceptus without ever reaching it – if it damages the placenta or the mother's health.)

iv. *Variation from conceptus to conceptus in susceptibility of certain tissues to the chemical insult*

v. *Variation from conceptus to conceptus in the rate of its development and, hence, in the timing of a susceptible period*
29 This effect may be small but the unpredictability it leads to is often increased by uncertainties in the date of human conception.

481

vi. *Route of access of a chemical agent to the conceptus*

30   Because some chemical conversions take place in the gut lumen, the giving of a substance by a route of access to the conceptus that by-passes the mother's gut may have an effect different from that by the oral route. Among such routes, those that most deserve mention are certain injectional routes (subcutaneous, intramuscular and intravenous). These clearly by-pass the gut in the first instance. But the resulting freedom from changes mediated in the gut may not be absolute. Depending on the substance injected, some of it may reach the gut later, if only after excretion by the liver down the bile duct. Re-absorption after chemical conversion in the gut by the intestinal bacteria, etc., or by the enzymes in the gut lumen or in its epithelial lining is then possible. When a substance by injectional routes is indeed excreted with the bile and re-absorbed after conversion in the gut, the effects are not very different from those by the oral route.

31   An interesting situation arises with cycasin, a component of a human food (the cycad seed) in some countries. When consumed orally, it is converted into a toxic and cancer-producing compound, methyl-azoxy-methanol (MAM), by a known (ß-glucosidase) enzyme of certain bacteria in the human gut. By *injection* experiments in the *adult* non-pregnant rat, cycasin is found to be harmless – but during pregnancy things are different.

32   Unexpectedly, the rat conceptus (and not its mother) has another glucosidase toxifying enzyme (in its kidneys) and therefore is subject (and, with it, its mother) to the toxic and carcinogenic properties of MAM (see Liener, 1969). This is mentioned to illustrate the surprises that still occur in this field; to emphasise that the pharmacology of a substance in the conceptus need bear little resemblance to that in the adult; and, above all, to highlight the potential relevance of chemical interconversions and hence of the route of intake.

33   One route of intake that by-passes the gut, at least in the first instance, is absorption through skin or mucous membrane. This occurs to a greater degree than is often realised. Cleft palates in mouse embryos can result from instillation of hydrocortisone drops into the mothers' eyes (Hearney, Ballard & Smith, 1975). So far, no case of teratogenesis in man has yet been attributed to such a route but cases could potentially occur. Oestrogenic hormones, once present in certain cosmetics, were absorbed via the skin sufficiently to produce general hormonal effects in the user. Such hormones are teratogenic in mice (Nishihara, 1958), so teratogenic effects must be considered when cosmetics are applied by a pregnant woman. To take another example, selenium compounds in certain hair shampoos are absorbed apparently through the human skin sufficiently to produce in certain individuals the mental symptoms, unpleasant body odour and hair changes of selenium poisoning (unpublished and Liener, 1969). And selenium excess could conceivably damage a conceptus also, even a human one.

34   The route by inhalation is also important. Carbon monoxide, whether from tobacco smoke or otherwise, and certain anaesthetics produce oxygen deficiency (anoxaemia) which, in the opinion of many, can have injurious potential for the conceptus (Fedrick et al., 1971, 1973; Ross et al., 1973; Nisbet, 1973; but see Yerushalmy, 1973). Smoking is discussed again in paragraphs 56–60.

vii. *Variation between mammalian species*

35   It is clear that studies of rat embryology and rat teratology do proceed more rapidly than the corresponding studies in man and are often used to predict risks for man.

But variation has been observed repeatedly from one mammalian species to another in their response to prenatal challenge. (This variation is still largely unforeseeable, so extrapolations involving man are also uncertain.)

36   There are known explanations for a few of the species differences observed. For example, cyclopamine, an alkaloid occurring naturally in one plant in the herbiage of certain parts of North America, produces the single-eye cyclops deformity in sheep. But it does not do so in rabbits unless the acid they (unlike sheep) have in their stomachs is simultaneously neutralised (Keeler, 1970). Cyclopamine is chemically changed by acids and rendered harmless by them.

37   Many of the teratological differences between species of mammal arise indirectly from differences in the thousands of enzymes which each species possesses and which are under genetic control. (As discussed below, man is no exception.) Every item taken in the diet, and every substance administered otherwise, is liable to be influenced by several of these enzymes at all stages – before absorption, during absorption, during the phase of distribution in the body, during storage, or during metabolism (utilisation or break-down). If the mammal is pregnant, dietary items may be also changed during transplacental passage to the fetus, or during excretion via the amniotic fluid or, more externally, via the mother. These influences may raise or lower the concentration of the item in the fetus, may prolong or shorten, intensify or diminish the effects of the item, or convert it to a more toxic form or to a less toxic form. Then different enzymes come into play in dealing with *this* form. When it is remembered that few if any of these enzymes are identical in chemical structure or quantity from one species to another, it is not surprising that few predictions can be made for one species on the basis of experience with another species. Indeed, for some mammals, including man, genetically determined differences can often be detected even between two normal individuals of the one species in an appreciable proportion of their enzymes (Harris, 1970). By the same token, the embryos themselves may also differ from each other in their enzymes and differ from their mothers. Thus, even in experimental animals, safe predictions can but rarely be made about the outcome in a particular pregnancy. Results must always be assessed statistically on a reasonable size of sample in order to average out these individual effects. (For repeatability, investigators usually use genetically homogeneous strains of laboratory animals to the extent that this is possible. Unfortunately, this repeatability, though a requirement for scientific understanding, may simultaneously make the findings of these experiments misleading and too reassuring when applied to a genetically heterogeneous population such as the human one.)

VI   Uncertainty from these sources of variation

38   In those animal experiments in which the aim is to elucidate mechanisms, strenuous efforts are made to evade or standardise as many as possible of the genetic and environmental sources of variation. However, these efforts are never fully effective. With few exceptions, variation in outcome from litter to litter and even within litters is found to be considerable. Only in a statistical sense could most of such experiments be strictly described as repeatable.

VII   Nature-nurture interactions

39   Nature-nurture interactions between an inherent constitution and its environment, common to all biology, are of great importance also in teratology. As two constitutions are involved, and in a sense, two environments, the interactions are often complex. Only a few situations have so far been clarified in man and the haemoglobinopathies (in their interactions with anaesthetics) will serve as an example:

Of the Negro minorities in this country, nearly 10 per cent have some of their haemoglobin molecules in a form (Haemoglobin S) detectably different in one-half of the molecule from the haemoglobin (Haemoglobin A) of their fellows of any race. This reflects the presence from antiquity of an unusual form ($Hb_\beta{}^s$) of the Hb_β part of the DNA of one member of the relevant pair of chromosomes. If the other member of the pair possesses the usual form, it produces sufficient Haemoglobin A to carry sufficient oxygen to permit a healthy normal life under most circumstances. But such a person (an S-carrier) is, among other things, unduly sensitive to environmental anoxia, e.g. that associated with certain anaesthetics such as halothane or nitrous oxide. There is a nature-nurture interaction between those anoxia-producing factors that are inborn (unusual haemoglobin molecules) and those that are environmental in origin (the anaesthetics). If this person be a woman and pregnant, the oxygen deficiency can be severe enough to damage the conceptus. Thus the risk that a particular anaesthetic will do damage might be high mainly for the mother who possesses some biochemical quirk – in this example, an unusual haemoglobin. (Even in normal women patients or medical attendants, the risk from inhalation anaesthetics received during pregnancy might not be negligible – Lancet, 1975; Bussard, 1976; Corbett, 1976; Pharoah et al., 1977.)

VIII Are all substances potentially injurious to the fetus ?

40   The generalisation that any substance can cause injury to any animal including man, at least under certain circumstances, is as true for a conceptus as it is for an adult, although no generalisation of this type is capable of formal proof. The fact that even simple substances such as water, oxygen, salt or glucose, when administered to the conceptus in certain circumstances of dosage, timing and route, can cause toxic damage in an experimental system is not proof that *every* substance will cause damage; but it is nevertheless sufficient to warn us against declaring any substance safe for man in an absolute sense. The word 'injurious' is thus seen to be meaningful only under some supposition about the dose levels that are likely to be at issue. Unfortunately it is just these critical dose levels that are the most variable from one species to another even when adjusted for the species' body-weight on a mg/kg basis. At a particular weight-adjusted dosage, a substance may be highly injurious in one species and not detectably so in another (see Tuchmann-Duplessis, 1972).

41   Is it then true that any substance at some dose level and at some stage of develop- ment can *deform* a conceptus? Probably yes, except for the occasional substance of which the dose required kills the mother. As there is a great range in sensitivity of the various tissues of the conceptus on a particular day, there will nearly always be dosages, between the no-effect range and the range lethal to the conceptus which the conceptus as a whole may survive but which is injurious to certain parts. Repair of the damage, while adequate for survival of the conceptus, may leave an anatomical or functional defect. Naturally, the dosage range (the teratogenic range) in which this chain of events occurs may well be narrow for a particular substance, the actual dose only rarely falling within it. There would then be only a small risk of teratogenesis (in the surviving conceptuses) – but it would not be zero.

42   A complication arises in that, despite this risk of a specific deformity, the total risk over all types of deformity among those that survived exposure to a teratogen could conceivably be lower than normal. This would be so if the substance also had a lethal effect evident preferentially among those conceptuses that were already, for other reasons, malformed. By comparison with normals, a smaller proportion of the malformed fetuses would reach delivery. This possibility (which has not been studied) would have compensation implications only in the hypothetical situation where a drug might conceivably be marketed in the future to kill only deformed

embryos but, while doing this effectively, also induced its own specific malformation at a lower frequency and presumably a lower total burden of cost and incapacity. Liability in a particular case would presumably depend *inter alia* on the degree of confidence with which the specific defect could be attributed to the substance.

IX   The relationship between dosages in animals and man

The basis for dose extrapolation

43   The teratogenic range of dosage seems to be very different from one animal species to another but this raises a question – just how do we determine what dose in one animal, say a rat, corresponds to what dose in another? (By convention, all doses are expressed in mg/kg body weight, without correction for the weight of the pregnant uterus.) How do we allow for possible differences between rat and man in the rate of chemical conversions? A therapeutic index might be comparable in animals and man: that is to say that the ratio of minimum teratogenic dose to the minimum-effect dose is more likely to remain constant from species to species than is any absolute level of dose expressed relative to body weight. For example, the therapeutic index for thalidomide is not convincingly greater than unity for the mouse, the rat or the dog; nor for man. This important matter has been succinctly discussed by Wendel (1973). But considerable controversy about extrapolation remains and is fuelled by the unfortunate fact that the therapeutic index as defined here or as defined otherwise, is small for a large proportion of the therapeutic substances that might be administered during pregnancy. The margin of safety is small. Therefore, relatively minor differences between species could lead to markedly different decisions when extrapolations are made from those species to man. For the testing of a new drug, it would be wise to determine such an index in three species of laboratory animal and, except for life-saving drugs, the index should be of a magnitude adequate to ensure that, when the drug is used, the benefit to the mother justifies the (unavoidable) residual risk of malformation to the fetus.

44   Protocols for teratogenic screening of new drugs have been devised (e.g. Tuchmann-Duplessis, 1974) but they are all unsatisfactory. The above dosage extrapolation problem illustrates the difficulties involved. It alerts us to the unsuitability of any potential legislation if based on the assumption that a body such as the UK Committee on Safety of Medicines can devise a protocol that will establish that a specific dose of a substance is teratogenic or is not teratogenic for man. This is probably not within the realm of possibilities from animal experiments alone. (It is not always feasible to define a safe dose even in the perhaps simpler situations that arise in straight toxicology.) Epidemiological data and clinical-trial data on the human species itself are required for this purpose and these bring their own (high) costs and difficulties in interpretation. Studies in man of an ancillary nature, such as those concerning the absorption, conversions, movements and excretion of the substance, will help; but except when a human calamity has already occurred, as with thalidomide (paragraphs 22, 107, 108) or rubella virus (paragraphs 109–110) or stilboestrol (paragraphs 112–115) or methyl mercury (paragraphs 89–90), even the total data will continue to be inadequate for accuracy in the assessment of the risk for the majority of substances.

Other aspects of dosage

45   Animal work and general considerations indicate that there are few if any generally valid relationships between the effects of a substance on the mother and its effects on the conceptus. For instance, there is no strength in the argument that a dose that

leaves the mother symptomless is necessarily safe for the child. Many of the mothers of thalidomide-deformed babies had no symptoms of thalidomide toxicity, and there are many substances in addition to thalidomide to which the conceptus is more susceptible than is the adult (e.g. hydrocortisone – Chaudhry & Shah, 1972; quinine – Covell, 1936).

46   It is sometimes stated that, to be convincing, a teratogenic response must rise continuously with increasing dose. Such, indeed, is the *simplest* dose-effect relationship to explain, but is not the only one possible on theoretical grounds. For example, beyond a certain dose level an increasing lethality to the conceptus could lead to a diminishing teratogenic response in the *surviving* young. Such a situation is analysable if the experimenter can afford to sacrifice the mother and can score implantation sites and early and late resorptions. But if the experimental animal is a larger mammal (e.g. dog, miniature pig or primate), this will often be impracticable and the anomalous dose-effect relationship could then be misleading.

47   The smallest rate of teratogenic effect (above background) that it is normally practical to seek in animals (say one abnormal conceptus in fifty) is many times greater than the smallest rate that has appreciable consequences in man (say ten in a million). For this practical reason, the doses given in animal experiments are usually relatively large (on *any* basis for comparison). The discrepancies between the high levels of these animal doses and the low levels of human therapeutic doses sometimes invite adverse comment. But, when these discrepancies are considered alongside the fact that an effect has to be large to be detectable in a laboratory experiment of a reasonable size, they are seen to be an inevitable feature of almost any experimental design in animal teratogenesis.

X   Assessment of human risk by extrapolation from animals
Rodents and primates
48   A Canadian Working Party has stated in its otherwise excellent report that extrapolation from rodents to man is as relevant as from non-human primate species (Lalonde et al., 1973). For reasons given later, this claim, as a general statement, is probably indefensible. Presumably, the intention was to claim instead and much more reasonably that, given a fixed budget, and given the existence of inbred strains of rats and the non-existence of inbred strains of any non-human primate; and given the currently diminishing supply of primates of any ancestry; and given the great expertise available for rat teratology which has so far no adequate equivalent for any primate, then an experiment on rats can, in practice, be of a suitable standard in scale and skill, whereas an experiment on a primate species is almost inevitably inadequate in scale and possibly in skill. In these circumstances, the satisfactory rat experiment *is* probably preferable to the unsatisfactory primate experiment.

49   However, on a conceptus-to-conceptus basis of comparison, the primate must undoubtedly weigh more heavily than the rodent when the data are in conflict. This is so because the non-human primates and man, having diverged from a common ancestry in evolutionary prehistory much more recently than did the rat and man, have had less time to diverge biochemically. They are less different, for example, in:

i.   the range and characteristics of their enzymes and hence in the response to toxins;

ii.   size of litter (man usually one; marmoset monkey usually two; rat about ten);

iii.   length of gestation (e.g. man 40 weeks, marmoset 13 weeks, rat 3 weeks);

iv.   general anatomy (e.g. of uterus);

v.   placental morphology: the rat's placenta is constituted quite differently from man's and, in addition, there is another placenta for each conceptus – the yolk-sac placenta. This potentially gives extra scope for divergences in storage or breakdown of a substance, or in the efficiency of its transport to the conceptus and of its excretion, as metabolites, from the conceptus.

Variability within a single species

50 The general unreliability of extrapolation of teratogenic response from animal to animal is brought out clearly by the recent work of Keeler et al. (1976 a, b; 1978) on the teratogenic effects of potato sprouts in golden hamsters. These effects are reproducible in hamsters from Simonsen Laboratories but are not observed in hamsters from Engel Laboratories, derived from the others as recently as 1972. This difference might well reflect genetic divergence, but, whatever its explanation, it shows that extrapolation, even within a species, can be unreliable.

51 *Magnitudes* of effects of given dose-levels, are what we want to know and these are not safely extrapolated. For review, see Palmer (1974).

52 *Qualitative* findings from laboratory animals, however, are sometimes more readily extrapolated. For instance, mechanisms, once worked out, can be assessed for their potential similarity to the corresponding mechanisms in man. Thus, the teratogenicity, in rodents, of crude preparations of the herbicide, 2, 4, 5-trichlorophenol, was shown by Sparschu, Dunn & Rowe (1971); Neubert, Zens, Rothenwallner & Merker (1973) and Moore, Gupta, Zinkl & Vos (1973) to be due to a contaminant, TCDD (tetrachloro-dibenzo-dioxin). This allowed attention to be focused on TCDD. (We still do not know, despite the Seveso mishap – Lancet, 1977 – whether any terata are produced in *man* by TCDD and at what dosages. The 60 or so induced abortions performed in London on worried Italian mothers from the Seveso area in Italy were apparently not examined systematically, either pathologically or biochemically.)

Variability within the human species

53 The human population is a complex mixture of literally millions of genetically different types. No two individuals, other than perhaps identical twins derived from a single fertilised egg, are genetically or enzymatically identical – Harris (1970). (Predictions even from man to man are therefore not totally reliable.) In the light of this heterogeneity in man, the heterogeneity that we cannot yet avoid within a primate colony as used in teratological experiments is not for all purposes a serious drawback, as it simulates the human situation. It does, however, produce difficulties enough with reproducibility, unless experiments are performed on a huge scale.

Imperfection of non-human data for man

54 The present low quality of forecasting of human effects will improve when primate models, despite their difficult budgetary and other problems, have been extensively developed, but no species or set of species can be a substitute for man. Several mammalian species, particularly among the primates, can give useful leads to mechanisms of action and can suggest human experiments; but as Saxén (1969, p 208) says, 'it is abundantly clear that the results of animal experiments cannot be directly extrapolated to clinical medicine'. A similar view is expressed by Shirkey (1972) – 'teratologic animal tests are not directly applicable to man. The animal model is *homo sapiens*'. In my personal view, these are not overstatements of the situation *de facto*.

55 For the possibility of direct testing in man see paragraphs 122–124.

XI Special aspects of certain injurious agents

Tobacco smoking

56 It is now widely accepted (Miller et al., 1976; BMJ, 1976) that smoking during pregnancy, at least after the fourth month, is associated with a low birth-weight of the conceptus, not exclusively due to prematurity of delivery (Butler & Alberman, 1969; Andrews & McGarry, 1972; Goldstein, 1973; Nisbet, 1973; BMJ, 1973b; Butler et al., 1972; Fedrick et al., 1973; Murphy & Mulcahy, 1974, but see Nature, 1973; Yerushalmy, 1973; Hickey et al., 1974). The effect is found within each of the Registrar-General's standard occupational classes. There is no feature of the affected babies themselves that distinguishes them clearly from low-weight babies of other aetiologies, such as those that involve racial or other genetic factors, or undernutrition, or high altitude anoxia. No suit has ever been brought to the courts. The slow fetal growth is perhaps due to anoxaemia from carbon monoxide in the tobacco smoke (BMJ, 1976; Nutrition Reviews, 1973) or, much less likely, to depressed caloric intake by the mother (Rush, 1974; but see Mau, 1976; Spira & Servent, 1976). Nicotine itself might contribute.

57 Mainly as a result of the effect on birth-weight, maternal smoking of over four cigarettes daily appears to raise the late-fetal and neonatal death rate by nearly 30 per cent.

58 There is still insufficient evidence for us to be certain how much of the observed lowering of IQ of those infants that survive is mediated by *prenatal* smoke alone and how much by other factors such as passive exposure to tobacco smoke *postnatally* (Butler & Goldstein, 1973; James, 1974; Harlap & Davies, 1974).

59 Fedrick et al. (1971) but not Yerushalmy (1973) found malformations of the heart to be commoner in the offspring of smokers than of non-smokers, by about one third. Again, the type of lesion appears to be not exclusively related to this cause, so liability would be difficult to establish in an individual case, even if Fedrick's findings are confirmed.

60 Mau & Netter (1974) suggest that the father, by smoking, may, even in the absence of maternal smoking, lower the birth-weight and even raise the malformation risk perhaps three-fold (hare-lip particularly). In the absence of contrary evidence, this may be the effect on the fetus of a smoky, carbon monoxide rich environment for its *mother* during pregnancy rather than a direct effect on the semen or its spermatozoa. In any case, it is necessary to consider in principle whether a child should have a remedy at law against its father. The DHSS warns women against smoking during pregnancy; no comparable warning is given to their husbands.

Cell leakage across the placenta causing immunisation

61 Under certain circumstances, leakage of appreciable numbers of fetal cells across the placenta to the mother's blood can have serious detrimental effects on the subsequent offspring of that mother. The size of the leakage can be estimated, as fetal red blood cells are distinguishable in the mother's blood after suitable staining. Leakage of up to 4 ml of fetal blood at the time of delivery is common (50 per cent of full-term deliveries – Finn, 1970) but leakage may also follow trauma to the uterus and may then be of any magnitude. The damaging chain of events occurs when the fetal cells are genetically such that they carry a blood group substance of a particular type (especially the Rhesus D antigen) that is not present in the mother. She then makes antibody to this substance carried on the leaked cells; and the antibody, in subsequent years, specifically combines with that substance wherever it is encountered. Alas, when

this combining takes place in the fetus itself (in a subsequent pregnancy), coating most of the fetal red blood cells with antibody, the antibody-coated cells are removed from the fetal circulation and broken down. There may be widespread and severe effects of the resulting anaemia and bilirubin accumulation. These can include brain damage (spastic paralysis, inco-ordination, deafness) and even death of the fetus *in utero* or after its birth.

62   Prevention of this maternal-fetal incompatibility reaction in any pregnancy depends on minimising any trauma to the placenta in all previous pregnancies and on neutralising any leak that does occur. This neutralising is achieved by an immediate injection of antibody (intramuscularly) to remove the stimulus for the mother to make her own. The injected antibody, or 99 per cent of it, is destroyed within 6 months, hence it is harmless to subsequent offspring. The promptness of the injection following each leak is critical, hence either a delay in detecting the small leak at delivery or otherwise, or a failure to respond quickly to it will increase the risk to subsequent incompatible offspring. Further, failure to ensure that any blood transfusion received by a girl or woman at any time is of suitable blood group will also increase that risk and will do so to a degree dependent on the amount of blood received – often a large amount (see Finn, 1970; Clarke et al., 1971; Clarke, 1972).

63   Leakage of fetal cells occurs without undue trauma, on occasion, and its routine detection would demand frequent blood testing of pregnant women. This is not normally performed, hence the relative importance of one specific injury might well be difficult for a court to assess.

64   Surgical intervention during pregnancy, particularly to induce abortion (Murray & Barron, 1971) or to obtain amniotic fluid for forecasting the normality or otherwise of the fetus, may occasion a leakage of fetal into maternal blood and it is good practice for this to be looked for routinely and particularly in those women who, by virtue of their blood group, are at risk of producing antibody.

65   With current preventive measures applied at delivery (and at times of surgical intervention), severe maternal-fetal incompatibility reactions leading to permanent disability are now rare in many countries (say 1 in 10,000 live births) and are becoming rarer. Even when prevention of the reaction has failed, treatment of the affected fetus, particularly by exchange transfusion (on occasion, prenatally,) is now effective and has contributed a lot to the reduction in disability.

Medication in pregnancy

i. *Scale of problem*

66   Heinonen et al. (1977) have shown that, in the USA, the proportion of pregnant women taking no medical preparations (other than iron) during pregnancy has fallen from 9·4 per cent in 1958 to less than 5 per cent in 1965. By 1965, about 7 per cent of pregnant women were taking as many as ten different preparations. It is, therefore, reassuring to note that in the USA, despite the increase in this one type of prenatal hazard, the general rate of malformation is not rising.

67   In Edinburgh, medication (prescribed and self-prescribed) is less extensive. Only 1·5 per cent of pregnant women were found by Forfar & Nelson (1972) to be taking ten preparations or more; and 18 per cent were taking none, other than iron. But even in Edinburgh, the consumption trend was upward over the preceding decade, despite the severe warning of the thalidomide tragedy, 1958–61. Yet, as in the USA, the malformation rate in Edinburgh is not rising, even with this rise in medication. (Indeed, it is falling slowly for reasons that are only partly related to known factors, such as improvement in contraception which is narrowing the range of maternal age at confinement.) In normal dosages, therefore, the average drug may generate little additional hazard. The quantities taken of drugs thought to be human teratogens

(see Shepard, 1976; Stevenson, 1973; Schardein, 1976; and see Table 2) were apparently sufficiently small for their effects in a modest sample to be lost in the overall totals of malformations in the Edinburgh study.

68   There could be hope of detecting a new hazard early by this or some other type of epidemiological study, only if the effect were specific and of otherwise great rarity. These pre-conditions were met, for example, in the case of the rare vaginal carcinoma that followed DES treatment (paragraphs 72–76) and, also, in the case of the limb defects of thalidomide (paragraphs 22, 24, 107–108). If a new drug were merely to make a particular common malformation commoner, many hundreds of extra cases might have to be born before the proportionate increase was detectable.

ii.   *The overall risk*

69   The taking of a drug (by prescription or otherwise) during pregnancy is authoritatively regarded as a danger point. With the present inadequacy of any practicable testing procedures, the advice that represents the present state of the art is not to take any drug in pregnancy unless absolutely necessary. Advice of this general tenor has been given by the following:

Lenz (1965) – 'Any tablet given to a pregnant woman is an experiment in human teratology'.

Nelson & Forfar (1971) – 'During pregnancy, it would appear wise to avoid the administration of any drug which carries a suspicion of teratogenicity unless that drug is specifically indicated, and self-medication with common household remedies such as aspirin and antacids should be avoided. These recommendations would also apply to any woman of child-bearing age in whom conception is likely'.

Illingworth (1972) – 'the best advice which one can offer to any pregnant woman is that she should take a medicine in pregnancy only when it is absolutely necessary – and that is rare'.

Shenkel & Vorherr (1974) – 'pregnant women should never use drugs without a doctor's advice; whenever drug treatment appears to be necessary the risks of drug-intake have to be weighed against the benefits'. These authors give a long list of some of the preparations available in USA without prescription.

Stevenson (1969) – 'our only advice to women in very early pregnancy is to avoid taking any drug, however harmless'.

Girdwood (1967) – 'giving of drugs unnecessarily in pregnancy or, indeed, at any time cannot be deprecated too strongly'.

WHO (1967) – 'further efforts must be made to inform the medical profession of the teratogenic risks presented by drugs in spite of their clearance through approved screening methods'.

iii.   *Maternal Epilepsy: to treat or not to treat*

70   A maternal condition equally with its treatment might cause an abnormality in the offspring. For example, epilepsy and its treatment by anticonvulsants, particularly diphenylhydantoin, might each carry such a risk. Epilepsy, by producing temporary anoxia in the mother, might conceivably cause malformations itself, and anoxia in rodents certainly does so. The anticonvulsant, diphenylhydantoin, in rodents produces malformations particularly of the cleft lip and palate type; and there are now extensive data for man, again involving particularly this group of malformations. (The whole constellation of effects in man has been named the fetal hydantoin syndrome. It is, however, rare for a single fetus to manifest all the features of the syndrome

as listed with references in Table 2.) Diphenylhydantoin reduces blood levels of folic acid in rodents and in man (see discussion by Norris & Pratt, 1974). In mice, the teratogenic effects can apparently be prevented by supplements of folinic acid, a prime metabolite of folic acid (Evans, 1977); and, in chick embryos, even folic acid itself is effective (Bellairs, 1954). Whatever the mechanisms, the effects are sufficiently clear and serious that special caution has to be exercised in prescribing, in early pregnancy, diphenylhydantoin and certain other anti-epileptic drugs.

71   We must also bear in mind the interest of the mother. For her, the treatment may be less hazardous than the epilepsy. As mentioned by the Law Commission (paragraphs 90, 95 of their Report to the Royal Commission), such apparent conflicts of interest are not rare. Fortunately, the area of conflict is often more apparent than real as it is not even to the mother's benefit to risk a malformation in a liveborn child.

iv.   *Stilboestrol* – also see paragraphs 112–115

72   Stilboestrol, received by the conceptus via the placenta, illustrates how delayed the effects of some pre-natal injuries can be.

73   Stilboestrol (or DES – di-ethyl-stilboestrol – as it is often called abroad) was used as a synthetic hormone for several years after the war. In pregnancy, it was prescribed widely, usually to prevent a threatened aborting of the conceptus. There are over 200 of such saved concepti known, now young women or teenagers, in whom a malignant tumour of the vagina, of an otherwise very rare form, has developed 8–28 years after the stilboestrol was prescribed orally to the mother. Destructive surgery is required except when the tumour is highly sensitive to radiotherapy. But the overall mortality is high (26 per cent within 2 years – Boronow, 1973).

74   The stilboestrol problem gives rise to a general question. To what extent should a company which markets a drug be expected to contribute to the cost of human screening to detect its ill effects – both as part of the testing of safety and also as a step towards minimising any damage?

75   In the stilboestrol example, screening *has* been suggested for catching the tumours early. There are perhaps a further 10 or so instances expected in the UK, but screening of teenage girls in a search for these would be expensive whether it were to be comprehensive or restricted to those somehow identified as having been exposed to DES – perhaps 1 per cent or so.

76   The fact that a carcinogenic substance, namely urethane, could act by placental transfer had previously been discovered accidentally in experimental animals (Larsen, 1947) but this was not widely known at the time that stilboestrol was being used. It was not until 1976 that an experimental model of the human response to DES was described. This was in golden hamsters (Rustia & Shubik, 1976). So what was painfully learned in humans has been eventually repeated, years later, in an experimental animal. The analogy with thalidomide is obvious and close. Unfortunately, it is, in practice, hard to find something in an experimental animal until we know what we are looking for. For both DES and thalidomide, animal screening would have had to be wideranging and extensive to have had a chance of picking up the hazard before these drugs were made available to pregnant women. Incidentally, in the mother there may well be an increased risk of carcinoma of the ovary (see Hoover et al., 1977).

v.   *Thalidomide* – discussed in paragraphs 22, 24, 107–108.

Drugs of addiction

i. *The data*

77 Drugs of addiction include some which are also used therapeutically. Alcohol, cannabis (marijuana, hashish), lysergic acid diethylamide (LSD), amphetamines, barbiturates, and the hard drugs of the morphine, heroin, methadone and cocaine types are some of the most important.

78 Claims of mutational risk and malformation risk have proved extremely difficult to assess, even if only human data are considered. The human data on, for example, LSD are of three types:

a Data from experiments in which human cells, often fibroblasts, are directly exposed to the drug. These data reflect none of the influences of absorption, toxification or detoxification. Elevation of the rate of chromosome breakage is often used as one index of risk of mutagenesis, but is of limited value for assessing teratogenic risks.

b Data from experiments on non-pregnant human volunteers. The same index is used (though often on a different cell type unfortunately).

c Data from observations on the pregnancies of drug users. Rates of spontaneous abortion, still-birth, neonatal and infant mortality, morbidity and malformation are studied, and compared with those of a control group of pregnancies of women otherwise similar but not exposed to the drug in question. Only rarely can a control group be found that fulfils these criteria (by differing in not taking the drug and by differing in no other way). More commonly the best controls available differ greatly from the drug-takers in life-style and in not taking *any* addictive drugs, not merely the one under study. The problems are similar to those of distinguishing the effects of epilepsy from those of its treatment (paragraphs 70, 71).

ii. *Embryolethality and teratogenicity*

a. LSD (short for LysergSauereDiaethylamid)

79 In a study of LSD effects, Jacobson & Berlin (1972) found an undue rate of early spontaneous abortion (12 out of 28 pregnancies) and, probably, of congenital malformation (8 instances being detected at birth among 83 live-borns). Anecdotal reports (for references, see Broome et al., 1976) are more difficult to interpret. Whether the effect, even if real, is truly due to LSD or to impurities in 'street LSD' or to the associated life-style or use of other psychedelic drugs is, as yet, impossible to say. What can be said clearly is that the drug-taker's life-style as a whole (including the drugs) carries considerable risks to the survival and normal development of the offspring. Follow-up studies of these children are difficult and, so far, leave most of the questions unanswered (Sardemann et al., 1976).

b. Alcoholism

80 There have been claims for centuries that the offspring of women who are chronic alcoholics are at high risk too (see Warner & Rosett, 1975). More scientifically, Jones et al. (1974 a, b), following Lemoine et al. (1968), found mortality perinatally in 17 per cent and, among many of the survivors, the characteristic fetal alcohol syndrome (short palpebral fissures, septal cardiac defect, microcephaly and mental retardation). The relevance of non-ethanol constituents has not yet been adequately studied, but ethanol itself seems the principal culprit, to judge from its known ability to produce, in rats and mice, most of the features of the syndrome (Tze & Lee, 1975; Sandor & Amels, 1971; Chernoff, 1977).

492

iii. *Fetotoxicity*

81   In addition to these difficult mutational and malformational issues, the literature contains undeniable evidence of fetotoxic effects of the addictive drugs individually. These effects may be fatal to the conceptus, before or soon after birth. Some of the toxic effects e.g. irritability, sneezing, sweating, yawning are really symptoms of withdrawal of a drug to which the conceptus has become addicted *in utero*, but the long-term durability of the infant's addiction has not been much studied. Infant mortality (from withdrawal of the addictive drug) is almost 100 per cent without treatment but the immediate case-mortality rate has been inconstant, varying from 3 to 34 per cent among treated infants, the figure depending on the severity of the addiction and the type of treatment (Tylden, 1973).

Teratogens for man in food
see Crosby, 1969; Keeler, 1972.

i. *In natural food*

82   The popular belief that a food that is natural is good, has a reasonable foundation in that, in general, the edibility of a natural foodstuff has been subjected to repeated testing over millions of years by man and his ancestors. There is, of course, inefficiency in the testing wherever there are long lags before adverse effects appear. Such lags obtain in the prenatal field and even more strikingly in the carcinogenic and mutagenic fields. But, even if the selection process had been fully efficient and nothing had been forgotten, and even if a community were making the best possible use of its ability to breed an optimal range of plant foodstuffs, and to plant and harvest them, and were to be equally optimal in animal foodstuffs, it would be unwarrantable to hold that what is the best food yet attained is perfect and non-toxic. 'Belief in . . . what is natural is a source of many errors' (Bertrand Russell, 1950). 'Food is only a mixture of chemicals and not all of them are dietarily beneficial' (Crosby, 1969). Every mouthful of a natural food contains several thousand different chemical entities, some of them specifically selected in plant and animal evolution and in controlled breeding as being toxic to parasites, predators or other threatening species. Some extend their toxicity to man also.

83   There is thus the exciting prospect that the average human diet could be further improved by agricultural means and by extension of food-processing to reduce or remove toxins inherent in the foodstuff itself. Reduction is also possible of toxins present adventitiously, such as those in moulds, insects, weeds, etc., inadvertently incorporated in the food. The current decline in the frequencies of several types of malformation could conceivably reflect recent achievement of a higher quality of foodstuff, particularly from better storage conditions, including refrigeration, to suppress endogenous and exogenous deterioration.

84   Poor storage of food has not yet been shown to cause pre-natal injury to man. However, a high degree of toxicity for adults has been shown for some of the compounds in rotting food. Such compounds may be produced sometimes by the organism responsible for the rotting. For instance, several common fungi, notably *Aspergillus flavus*, produce aflatoxins which are teratogenic at least to hamsters (Elis & DiPaolo, 1967).

85   Or, sometimes, toxic compounds may arise from the food plant itself, as part of its anti-fungal defence mechanisms. Here the best example is ipomeanol which, together with related toxic compounds is produced by sweet potatoes (the tubers themselves) when damaged, or when infected by fungi. Ipomeanol produces lung oedema in adult mammals and probably man but its effect prenatally has not been studied (Wilson et al., 1971). Defence materials of this general origin (phytoalexins) are made

493

by every plant species that has been tested adequately. So far, only a few of the compounds in rotting food have been tested and only a few have been shown, even for laboratory animals, to be teratogenic (Hayes et al., 1974), but there is a good chance that the present burden of natural teratogens for man may be reduced in the future by improvements in the condition of food consumed. Ideally, the general framework of proposed legislation on liability should be flexible enough, therefore, to embrace examples of prenatal injury arising from failure to preserve food in good condition.

86 The public tends to regard natural food as safe and to imagine that the only components of food that are potentially hazardous are the synthetic food additives. (A few of these, such as red food dye-2 and cyclamate and monosodium glutamate – Inouye et al., 1973; Holson et al., 1976 – might indeed be teratogenic or embryolethal for some mammals and might conceivably be so for man – Shepard, 1976, Stone et al., 1971.) But 'the myth that natural substances are *ipso facto* safer than synthetic substances is a fallacy which toxicologists and health officials ought not to help perpetuate' (Oser, 1966). After all, some of the most potent poisons known to man are of natural origin.

87 Even food which is in good condition may not always be safe. Modern techniques of breeding can throw up innovations which, just like the innovations of the pharmaceutical industry, have not yet been subjected to the evolutionary trial period of human experience. And this is particularly true when disease-resistance in a food-plant or food animal is being selected for or when non-edible species are used in the development of new strains. The American potato variety, Kennebec, under some conditions, contains a chemical compound which consists of a steroid part which is found in tomatoes and other plants; and a sugar part which is found in the common potato (Kuc, 1973). This substance which belongs to a generally toxic class of steroid alkaloids has never been tested for safety to man, except unwittingly in the American home during the present century.

88 But, for every one novelty of this nature, there are thousands of chemicals that have always been present in our natural foodstuffs and some dozens of these are acknowledged to be toxic to the human adult (Liener, 1969). It seems almost inevitable, bearing in mind the usually greater susceptibility of the conceptus, that at least some of these are teratogenic to man. Already, a few are known to be teratogenic for at least some species – cycasin from cycad seeds, hypoglycin A from ackee nuts, and a toxin from bracken tips at one time available in cans in the USA, as 'fiddleheads').

(ii.) *As pollutants in food*

Methyl mercury

89 A permanent and severe disorder of the nervous system, with mental deficiency and spasticity, can arise prenatally, following a mother's consumption of methyl mercury in fish from polluted water. The mercury levels in the tissues and the fairly specific set of symptoms allow a good legal case to be made for causality in an individual child, but litigation has so far been mainly confined to Japan and perhaps Iraq, in which countries major outbreaks of adult poisoning by methyl mercury have occurred. Koos & Longo (1976) give an excellent review.

90 The mercury, nearly always of industrial origin, usually reaches man via a chain of intermediate organisms, each feeding on the previous member of the chain. At each stage, the mercury is accumulated, by ingestion, in the absence of an effective excretory mechanism.

Chlorobiphenyl

91   Chlorobiphenyl, used as a heat exchanger, on one occasion leaked from a heating coil into edible fat in Japan. Many 'coca-cola babies', so called for their colour, were born (Taki et al., 1969).

Pre-conceptional exposure

i. *Mutagens*

92   Mutagens are agents that permanently change the DNA – for all time, because the change is faithfully copied in subsequent generations of cells and organism. Whether the change be large (e.g. a microscopically visible deletion of part of a chromosome), or small (a chemical change in one part of one gene), the effects on the person who inherits the mutant DNA can be extreme.

93   Hundreds of agents (including probably all chemical carcinogens) are known to increase markedly the rate of mutation of DNA either directly or indirectly, but few are actually proved to do so in man except by inference from the basic similarity of DNA in all species. X-radiation has been the most studied.

94   It is an important principle that no individual mutational event in man (whole man) can be scientifically timed more precisely than within a generation nor can it be easily attributed to a specific agent as there is little difference, in general, between agents as regards the changes they produce. A typist's misprint gives but scant indication of the nature of the conversation that distracted attention.

95   There are mutagens in natural food and these account for a part of the spontaneous mutation rate. In the germ line – the cells that produce the next generation – the rate of detectable change of a specified type in one generation is very approximately 10 per million cells (among those cells that go on to take part in fertilisation and initiate a recognised pregnancy). Each of us, by accumulation, has received about two such changes of a potentially major nature (Cavalli-Sforza & Bodmer, 1971), but most are manifest in our offspring only if partnered by a similar mutant from the other parent (in which event, serious consequences ensue).

96   Men and women are often exposed to mutagenic hazards. Many are avoidable but, because of the non-specificity of the effect and the delay of one or usually many more generations before detection, litigation is rare and will probably continue so. It may therefore not be necessary to discuss mutation more deeply, except to emphasise that it is not involved at all in most teratogenesis. In general, teratogens act *after* conception, mutagens *before* conception. Teratogens affect *only* the conceptus that is exposed: mutagens, through the mutants they produce, potentially affect *any* of the descendants of the individual exposed. (The fact that a mutagen can act on the fetus's own germ cells during fetal life as readily as at any other time does not obscure the validity of the general statements. Further, there may be a few teratogens that are such by virtue of an ability to produce a mutation in a body-cell of the conceptus. This 'somatic mutation' is similarly an unimportant exception, of a technical nature only: it would not be transmitted to the next human generation.)

ii. *Retained teratogens*

97   Some toxic substances – for example iophenoxic acid, which is used diagnostically in man to visualise by x-rays certain ducts such as the bile-duct – are retained for a long period in the body. If pregnancy intervenes in that period, prenatal damage to the conceptus may result. The iodine in iophenoxic acid induces goitre in the human conceptus, in one instance as long as four years after the injection (Wolff, 1969).

495

iii. *Gonadotrophin*

98 This hormone, given (before conception) for infertility, can be too successful. The subsequent birth even of septuplets has been described (Cameron et al., 1969), six of the seven concepti being born alive. Three still survive but might be handicapped physically and mentally by the low birth-weight. Clomiphene, which stimulates secretion of gonadotrophin, like gonadotrophin itself, has been accused of having teratogenic properties but it might be more likely that it is the reason for its being prescribed (the infertility itself) which is associated indirectly with a propensity to bear malformed children (Ahlgren et al., 1976).

Nutritional deficiency as a factor in teratogenesis

99 It is not clear that nutritional deficiency lies within the remit of the Royal Commission as it is debatable whether it constitutes an 'injury'.

100 However, for completeness, it might be mentioned that a low birth-weight and a high rate of fetal loss result, for example, from zinc deficiency, whether it be from inadequacy of zinc intake or inadequacy of absorption, or from a requirement that is unusually high. Zinc deprivation is rare in the UK but occurs in Iran, Egypt and elsewhere (see Jameson, 1976).

101 Iodide deprivation, sufficient to lead to mental deficiency, deafness and ataxia in the offspring, could occur in certain areas in Derbyshire and elsewhere in the UK, wherever the iodide concentration in the water is low. It does not do so currently because of the present policy of iodisation of the bread (or earlier, of the common salt). Before such preventive measures were instituted, the situation in some UK areas possibly approached that originally found in the Jimi valley of Papua New Guinea. Injections of iodised oil have, since then, relieved the problem in New Guinea (Hetzel & Pharoah, 1971).

102 The question of whether or not folate deficiency influences the risk of neural-tube malformation in the human offspring is not yet resolved. Emery (1977) and Hall (1977) found no evidence for this and the latter attributes the apparently contrary findings of Smithells et al. (1977) to an alleged unsuitability of their controls.

Special aspects: conclusion

103 Disasters such as the thalidomide incident have focused attention on pharmaceuticals but the teratogenic disasters of the future could occur in fields other than the pharmaceutical. Therefore, proposed legislation might with reason be designed to cope simultaneously with a wide range of hazards, including those in foods, drinks, additives, medical instruments, inhalants, cosmetics, packagings, pesticides, etc. Alternatively, legislation might be proposed initially for pharmaceutical products in the knowledge that it could provide a model for optional expansion later. The natures of the agents potentially involved are diverse, as indicated in Table 1.

XII Prevalence rates of human malformations

General

104 The prevalence rates of abnormality in live- and still-births have been discussed by the Law Commission (para 19 of its Report). The lower of the figures given (1–2 per cent) was for abnormality detected at birth or soon thereafter; and the higher (over 5 per cent) included also those detected later, in the first decade of life. Most of the additional cases have lesions of the heart, brain (subnormality), or ear.

105 The causal factors remain largely unknown but, contrary to some popular myths, industrialised societies have no higher risk than other societies (though the

pattern of deformities *is* different). Further, the prevalence rates (at birth) have been slowly declining in most of the United Kingdom, except at the time of the thalidomide disaster, 1958–61.

106   Unreliability of recording and many other factors make all figures for incidence rates of rare events inaccurate. And variations from place to place and from year to year make them hard to interpret anyway. The figures given below are only a rough guide to the scale of the prenatal injury problem and may err by a factor of 10 in some cases. No attempt is made to estimate how many cases might give rise to litigation, even among those defects with an assignable cause – some of which are detailed in Table 2.

Thalidomide Syndrome

107   The thalidomide disaster, 1958–1961, is thought to have produced crippling defects in about 28 children in the USA, 249 children in Britain, an unknown number in Japan and 5,000 or so in Germany, where, in 1956, the drug was first marketed (Lenz, 1966). Nearly half of these are still alive. In West Germany, after 283 days of a criminal trial, charges of homicide, criminal negligence and violation of drug laws were dropped on a financial settlement of nearly $29,000,000 plus $1,600,000 costs (see Curran, 1971). Litigation in the USA and Japan is still continuing.

108   A single 100mg tablet of thalidomide (whether it be called Contergan, Distaval, Kevadon or one of the other 50 names listed by Taussig, 1963) may be sufficient to cripple, if taken at the most sensitive stage of pregnancy, i.e. about day 40. About 2·5 million tablets were sold to the world, including the pregnant world, and the world toll was probably about 7,000 babies.

Rubella Syndrome

109   The impact of the german measles virus (rubella) on the newborn has been declining, partly because of active and passive immunisations. In the UK, about 3,000 pregnant women may be exposed to rubella in an average year but, of these, many are already immune, so only some of those so exposed develop apparent or inapparent infection. The damage to the conceptus is proportional to the severity of the disease in the mother.

110   Particularly since 1967, termination of a pregnancy exposed to rubella has been common and has reduced the numbers of newborn afflicted. If not aborted, the child has a 50–50 risk of being infected and, if infected, he has a 50–50 risk of being disabled (Peckham, 1974). Perhaps about 60 children per year are born in the UK with the brain, eye, ear or heart abnormalities characteristic of rubella, but many more in an epidemic year such as 1964. In that year, in the USA, over 30,000 of these babies were born (Cooper, 1968).

Other Infections

111   Other viruses, whose complicity is suggested by their detection in the fetus, probably do an almost comparable amount of prenatal damage in aggregate, particularly cytomegalovirus, other viruses of the herpes simplex group, and chicken-pox virus. Non-viral infections, particularly by the protozoon, toxoplasma, have less impact, perhaps 10 per year.

Stilboestrol Tumours

112   Between 1945 and 1967, and especially in the years 1946–50, stilboestrol was administered to many women (e.g. 19 per cent of pregnancies at the Mayo Clinic,

USA – a selected sample). It was often given to prevent a threatened abortion. Vaginal or, less commonly, uterine cancer (adenocarcinoma) of a characteristic clear-cell type has appeared at ages 8–28 years, so far in over 200 of the many daughters that resulted from these pregnancies all over the world.

113   The number in the UK is unknown. If, on average, 1 per cent of UK pregnancies were exposed to DES in the 22 years, 1946 to 1967 (when DES was withdrawn), just over 100,000 baby girls were so exposed here. The risk of vaginal adenocarcinoma among these is perhaps one (and no higher than ten) per 10,000 (one US sample was 0/803 – Lanier et al., 1973). So, over the years, perhaps 10 (and not more than 100) vaginal cancers are expected to follow in the UK – few were earlier than 1960 and few will be later than 1990. Uncertainties about dosages given in the UK (probably lower than those in the USA) and about many other factors compel caution with these rough estimates of the hazard.

114   As little as $1\frac{1}{2}$mg DES daily for one week has caused this cancer. Despite treatment of the cancer, its mortality is 26 per cent within two years of onset of symptons.

115   A far commoner result of DES is adenosis of the vagina. Up to 90 per cent of those girls exposed *in utero* show this or an even grosser abnormality of development. There is no general agreement about the size of the increased threat of malignancy conveyed by these changes but surveillance seems advisable (Zerner et al., 1976). In boys, stilboestrol prenatally can perhaps malform the urethra.

XIII   The future

116   The following predictions represent nothing more than very personal guesses.

Indirect testing for prenatal safety

117   Techniques for testing substances for safety will continue to improve, but most rapidly in areas far from the human need. For example, experiments using embryo cultures and transplants will advance our understanding but, because of the difference in environment between a cultured and a natural embryo, deductions about the effects of added chemicals on human concepti will be of dubious reliability. Nevertheless, such work will eventually constitute an extra component in the laboratory screening procedures for teratological safety.

118   Will it eventually be possible to extrapolate to man accurately from any laboratory experiments? This is a subject for disagreement. My own view is that progress towards such an ideal will be as slow as progress towards predicting the weather accurately. Those who work in large experimental teratological laboratories such as that at the National Center for Toxicological Research, Pine Bluff, Arkansas, USA, tend to be more optimistic. But their circumstances give them a vested interest in optimism, perhaps, as justifying the expense of their further work. Many of them previously worked in straight toxicology, where (if we exclude the cyclamate and some other dietary controversies) extrapolation is not quite so difficult. They are apt to assume that a similar success in teratology is merely a matter of time. The teratology of a substance, is, however, much more difficult to analyse than its straight toxicology. At least twice as many factors are involved – all interesting to a greater or lesser degree. Unfortunately, the difficulties in inravelling $2x$ interacting factors are inordinately greater than for x factors and not just twice as great.

119   With or without optimism on this issue, there is little doubt that laboratory screening procedures for teratological safety of chemical substances will continue to be refined and, with modern synthesising and separating techniques, will even be

applied to the numerous chemical constituents of food. However, it may be a long time before these screening procedures look different fundamentally (and not just in scale) from those available before the war.

120 There will be a justified shift from rodents towards the primates, but data from both rodents and primates will have some value. To use a weather analogy – for predicting Luxemburg's weather over a few hours, extrapolation is better from France's data alone than from England's alone; but a meteorologist would sensibly use both.

121 Primates are being rapidly depleted in their natural habitats but it will be possible, even if costly, to breed an adequate number in captivity.

Direct testing for prenatal safety

122 Work with women who come requesting early abortion and who consent to the testing of the safety and pharmacology of a substance in their concepti might seem unexceptionable and even necessary. Kobyletzki (1971) and a US National Commission (1976) argue cogently for at least pharmacokinetic studies of this nature. These were effectively inhibited in this country, despite our liberal abortion Act, by Medical Research Council recommendations and guidelines on the ethics of human experimentation. One issue concerns the alleged lack of a right of parents to volunteer their child's participation in research procedures of any sort that could be potentially injurious. Some controversy exists regarding this issue (e.g. Bradford Hill, 1963; Beecher, 1971; Gairdner, 1977; Clothier, 1977; Dodge & Evans, 1977; Pratt, 1977 and see Smithells et al., 1973); but Skegg (1977) argues convincingly that the English Courts 'will accept that, where a minor is incapable of consenting, a parent can give a largely effective consent to any procedure to which "a reasonable parent" would consent'. Presumably, as for the minor, so for the conceptus, *a fortiori*. One effect of any future implementation of the Law Commission's view (para 10,32 of their Report) that a conceptus should have no separate legal personality and therefore no legal rights until born alive, might be to re-establish even more firmly the adequacy of parental consent for research procedures that involve the conceptus. Society's right to have the opportunity of preventing future calamities of the thalidomide type in its members could then be honoured. Further, the actual effect of any injurious agent could potentially be clarified, at least in part, thus simplifying some decisions in the courts.

123 The situation may be less favourable in the USA. In Boston, Mass., a case of alleged manslaughter (of a fetus) concerned *inter alia* the teratological testing of a pharmaceutical product on a fetus – with the mother's consent. An abortion had previously been arranged to follow the test. But the ruling was unfavourable, so experimentation on selected human concepti – those destined for aborting in any case – might be risky in the USA, even in those States that have liberal abortion Acts.

124 Prof R W Beard said 'I can't see how you can improve the prognosis for the fetus without this type of research' (in discussion of Smithells et al., 1973), but whether or not this type is allowed to proceed, the second-best approach, the epidemiological (intervention) type of experiment on man (see paragraph 9) is almost certain to be encouraged. It will give direct leads on prevention. It will rarely elucidate *mechanisms* of causation in detail, but, for preventive purposes and for legal purposes, a full understanding of the causal chain may not be required. In the future, a good experiment of this type ought, for those purposes, to be accorded a standing equal to that of a good experiment on a laboratory mammal, the human basis of the one more than compensating for the advantage of fewer variables of the other.

125 Further, it is a safe prediction that the recording of abnormalities at EEC, national and other levels will improve.

Future scale of litigation

126   We could ask what will be the proportion of handicaps of prenatal origin that will be attributable to some specific agent in say 1984? – Certainly more than now, even if the causes and incidence rates remain the same. By 1984, the number of pharmaceutical agents the effects of which will be 'attributable' will perhaps have risen to, say, 70 and, in addition, it seems likely that the effects of half a dozen constituents of food will be similarly attributable. Interest is already awakening in the roles of plant breeding, of fungal toxins, and of natural antifungal toxins in food.

127   Each new attribution of a disability to a prenatal agent will generate new opportunities for negligence to be claimed, so there will probably be more litigation, particularly if we assume an increased public awareness of the preventability of many deformities.

128   But this increase in litigation may be limited by other factors. For instance, by 1984, the food and drink industries might have achieved a partial immunity from successful litigation, with the tacit approval of the public; just as the tobacco industry already seems to enjoy a partial *de facto* immunity against successful liability proceedings for lung cancer, apparently also with the tacit approval of the public.

129   Let us hope that methods additional to litigation will soon prove feasible and effective in limiting the prenatal damage from all types of hazard.

XIV References

Aaron H (ed) (1970). Med Letter D & T, **12**, 61.
Ahlgren M et al (1976). Acta Obst Gyn Scand, **55**, 371.
Alderman B (1974). Brit Med J, **4**, 44.
Amin-Zaki L et al (1974). Pediatrics, **54**, 587.
Anderson R C (1976). J Pediat, **89**, 318.
Andrews J & McGarry J M (1972). J Obst Gyn Br Cwlth, **79**, 1057.
Ardran G M & Kemp F H (1972). Brit Med J, **4**, 422.
Astrup P et al (1972). Lancet, **ii**, 1220.
Axelrod L R (1970) Pp 217–230 in *Adv Terat*, Vol **4**. Ed D H M Woollam. London:
    Academic Press.

Barlow S M & Sullivan F M (1975). Pp 103–120, in *Teratology: trends and applications*.
    Eds C L Berry & D E Poswillo. Berlin: Springer.
Barry J E & Danks D M (1974). Lancet, **ii**, 48.
Beaudoin A R (1968). Teratology, **1**, 11.
Beecher H K (1971). Lancet, **i**, 1181.
Bellairs R (1954). Pp 336–365 in *Chemistry and Biology of Pteridines*. Eds G E W
    Wolstenholme & M P Cameron. CIBA Symp. London: Churchill.
Beral V (1974). Lancet, **i**, 1280.
BMJ (1973a). Perinatal therapeutics and toxicology. Brit Med J, **1**, 5.
BMJ (1973b). Smoking hazard to the fetus. Brit Med J, **1**, 369.
BMJ (1974a). Cytomegalovirus again. Brit Med J, **3**, 593.
BMJ (1974b). Synthetic sex hormones and infants. Brit Med J, **4**, 485.
BMJ (1975). Risks of amniocentesis. Brit Med J, **4**, 485.
BMJ (1976). Cigarette smoking in pregnancy. Brit Med J, **2**, 492.
Boronow R C (ed) (1973). J Miss St Med Ass, **14**, 301.
Brinsmead M W (1976). Med J Australia, **1**, 379.
Brogan W F (1975). Med J Australia, **1**, 44.
Broome D L et al (1976). In *Cytogenetics, environment and malformation syndromes*.
    Eds D Bergsma & R N Schimke. Birth Defects Orig Art Ser, **12**, 65.
Burch P R J (1972). Brit Med J, **4**, 668.
Bussard D A (1976). J Am Dent Ass, **93**, 606.
Butler N R & Alberman, E D (eds) (1969). *Perinatal problems*. Edinburgh: Living-
    stone.
Butler N R & Goldstein H (1973). Brit Med J, **4**, 573.
Butler N R et al (1972). Brit Med J, **2**, 127.

Cameron A H et al (1969). J Obst Gyn Br Cwlth, **76**, 692.
Cavalli-Sforza L L & Bodmer W F (1971). *The genetics of human populations*. San
    Francisco: Freeman.
Chan Y–F & Sivasamboo R (1972). J Obst Gyn Br Cwlth, **79**, 761.
Chaudhry A P & Shah R M (1972). J Dent Res, **5**, 1516.
Chernoff G F (1977). Teratology, **15**, 223.
Clarke C A (1972). Clin Sci, **43**, 1.
Clarke C A et al (1971). Brit Med J, **2**, 607.
Clothier C M (1977). Lancet, **i**, 642.
Cooper L Z (1968). In *Birth Defects: intra-uterine infections*. Ed D Bergsma. Orig Art
    Ser, **4**, 23–5. New York: Nat Foundation.
Corbett T H (1976). Ann N Y Acad Sci, **271**, 58.
Covell W P (1936). Arch Otolaryng, **23**, 633.
Cowie V (1960). J Ment Defic Res, **4**, 42.

Cree J E et al (1973). Brit Med J, **4**, 251.
Crosby D G (1969). J Agric Food Chem, **17**, 532.
Croskerry P G & Smith G K (1975). Science, **189**, 648.
Curran W J (1971). New Engl J Med, **284**, 481.

David T J (1972). New Engl J Med, **287**, 487.
Derban L K A (1974). Arch Env Health, **28**, 49.
Desmond M M et al (1972). J Pediat, **80**, 190.
Deutsch M E (1976). J Am Med Ass, **236**, 823.
Dieulangard P et al (1966). Bull Féd Gynécol Obstet, **18**, 85.
DiSaia P J (1966). Obst Gyn, **28**, 469.
Dixon M (1974). Brit Med J, **4**, 45.
Dodge J A & Evans J (1977). Lancet, **i**, 852.
Doig R K & Coltman O M (1956). Lancet, **ii**, 730.
Donald I (1974). Dev Med child Neurol, **16**, 90.

Edwards M J (1971). J Pathology, **103**, 49.
Elbling L (1973). Nature, **246**, 37.
Elis J & DiPaolo J A (1967). Arch Path, **83**, 53.
Emery A E H (1977). Lancet, **i**, 703.
Evans M A (1977). Pharmacologist, **19**, 201.
Evening Post (1972). *Chemist 'with compassion' lands in court*. Evening Post Nov 2.

Fedrick J et al (1971). Nature, **231**, 529.
Fedrick J et al (1973). Nature, **242**, 263.
Feldman H A et al (1974). Pp 110–127 in *Symposium on toxoplasmosis*. Bull NY Acad Med, **50**, 110–239.
Field J H & Krag D O (1973). J Bone & Joint Surg, **55A**, 1035.
Finn R (1970). In *New trends in paediatrics*. Ed J Apley. London: Butterworth.
Fischman H (1973). Lancet, **ii**, 920.
Fleet W F et al (1974). J Am Med J Ass, **277**, 621.
Forfar J O & Nelson M M (1972). Clin Pharm & Therap, **14**, 632.
Fraser F C (1962). Brit Med J, **2**, 479.

Gal I (1974). Brit Med J, **2**, 560.
Gal I et al (1967). Nature, **216**, 83.
Gairdner D (1977). Lancet, **i**, 852.
Gemzell C & Roose P (1966). Am J Obst Gyn, **94**, 490.
Girdwood R H (1967). J Pak Med Ass, **17**, 403.
Giroud A (1973). World Rev Nutr & Diet, **18**, 195.
Gold A P & Michael A F (1958). J Pediat, **52**, 279.
Goldstein H (1973). Nature, **245**, 467.
Grant E C G (1974). Brit Med J, **3**, 115.
Greenberg G et al (1975). Brit Med J, **2**, 191.
Greene R M & Kochhar D M (1975). Teratology, **11**, 47.
Griffin J P (1974). Proc roy Soc Med, **67**, 581.
Griffiths H J (1974). Vet Med SAC, **69**, 177.

Hall M H (1977). Lancet, **i**, 648.
Hamerton L J et al (1977). *Diagnosis of genetic disease by amniocentesis during the second trimester of pregnancy*. Report No 5 of Medical Research Council of Canada. Ottawa: Minister of Supply & Services.
Hanshaw J B et al (1976). New Engl J Med, **295**, 468.
Hanson J W et al (1976a). J Am Med Ass, **235**, 1458 & **236**, 1114.
Hanson J W et al (1976b). J Pediat, **89**, 662.

Harlap S & Davies A M (1974). Brit Med J, **2**, 610.
Harris H (1970). *The principles of human biochemical genetics*, esp p 241. London: North-Holland.
Harris J W S & Ross I P (1956). Lancet, **i**, 1045.
Hart C W & Naunton R F (1964). Arch Otolaryng, **80**, 407.
Hartz S C et al (1975). New Engl J Med, **292**, 726.
Hayes A W et al (1974). Toxicol & Appl Pharmacol, **29** (abstr 196), 157.
Hearney E F et al (1975). Teratology, **11**, 21A.
Heinonen O P, Slone D & Shapiro S (eds) (1977). *Birth defects and drugs in pregnancy.* Littleton, Mass: Publishing Sciences Group.
Henderson B E et al (1976). Pediatrics, **58**, 505.
Herbst A L et al (1975). Clin Obst Gyn, **18**, 185.
Hetzel B S & Pharoah P O D (eds) (1971). *Endemic cretinism* Goroka, Papua: Inst Human Biol.
Heywood R & Palmer A K (1973). Lancet, **ii**, 1021.
Hickey R J et al (1973). Brit Med J, **3**, 501.
Hill A Bradford (1963). Brit Med J, **1**, 1043.
Hill R M (1976). Am J Dis Child, **130**, 923.
Hirsch J et al (1972). Am Heart J, **83**, 301.
Hoefnagel D (1976). Lancet, **i**, 152.
Holson J F et al (1976). J Toxicol Envir Hlth, **1**, 875.
Hoover R et al (1977). Lancet, **ii**, 533.

Illingworth R S (1972). Med News-Tribune, Nov 13 p 12.
Infante P E & Newton W A (1975). New Engl J Med, **293**, 308.
Inouye M et al (1973). Teratology, **8**, 94.

Jacobson C B & Berlin C M (1972). J Am Med Ass, **222**, 1367.
James W H (1974). Brit Med J, **2**, 611.
Jameson S (ed) (1976). Acta Med Scand, (Suppl **593**), 4–64 & 80.
Jespersen C S et al (1977). Acta paediatr Scand, **66**, 367.
Jones K L & Smith D W (1974a). Lancet, **ii**, 349.
Jones K L et al (1974b). Lancet, **i**, 1076.

Kajii T et al (1973). Teratology, **8**, 163.
Kaufman R L (1973). Lancet, **i**, 1396.
Kay C R (1974). Lancet, **ii**, 514.
Keeler R F (1970). Teratology, **3**, 175.
Keeler R F (1972). Clin Toxicol, **5**, 529.
Keeler R F et al (1976a). Bull Envir Contam Toxicol, **15**, 522.
Keeler R F et al (1976b). Res Comm Chem Path & Pharmacol, **13**, 723.
Keeler R F et al (1978). Teratology (in press).
Kennedy P C (1971). Fed Proc, **30**, 110.
Kimmel C A et al (1974). Arch Envir Hlth, **28**, 43.
Klauber G T et al (1976). Urology, **8**, 153.
Kobyletzki D V (1971). Proc Europ Soc Study of Drug Toxicity, **12**, 342–6. In *The correlation of adverse effects in man with observations in animals*. Amsterdam: Excerpta Medica.
Koos B J & Longo L D (1976). Am J Obst Gyn, **126**, 390.
Kopelman A E et al (1975). J Am Med Ass, **231**, 62.
Kuc J A (1973). Teratology, **8**, 333.
Kucera J (1968). J Pediat, **72**, 857.
Kuntz W D (1976). Am Industr Hyg Ass, **37**, 423.

Lalonde M, LeClair M & Johnson A E (eds) (1973). *The testing of chemicals for carcinogenicity, mutagenicity and teratogenicity*. Ottawa: Health & Welfare.

Lancet (1962). Thalidomide and congenital malformations. Lancet, i, 307.
Lancet (1971). Drugs and the fetal eye. Lancet, i, 122.
Lancet (1975). Pregnancy and anaesthesia. Lancet, ii, 169.
Lancet (1977). Seveso. Lancet, ii, 297.
Langer A et al (1974). J Med Soc NJ, **71**, 184.
Lanier A P et al (1973). Mayo Clin Proc, **48**, 793.
Larsen C D (1974). J Nat Cancer Inst, **8**, 63.
Larsson Y & Sterky G (1960). Lancet, ii, 1424.
Lemoine P et al (1968). Ouest Méd, **25**, 477.
Lenz W (1965). Ann NY Acad Sci, **123**, 228.
Lenz W (1966). Am J Dis Child, **112**, 99.
Levin J N (1971). J Pediat, **79**, 130.
Liener I E (1969). *Toxic constituents of plant foodstuffs.* London: Academic Press.
Liston W A & Campbell A J (1974). Brit Med J, **3**, 606.
Löser H et al (1976). Klin Pädiat, **188**, 233.
Loughnan P M et al (1973). Lancet, i, 70.

MacCallum F O (1972). Proc Roy Soc Med, **65**, 585.
Manchester D et al (1976). Am J Obst Gyn, **126**, 467.
Matsumoto H et al (1965). J Neuropath & Exp Neurol, **24**, 563.
Mau G (1976). Lancet, i, 972.
Mau G & Netter P (1974). Deut Med Wschr, **99**, 1113.
McCredie J (1976). Medical Hypotheses, **2**, 63.
McFadyen R E (1976). Clio Medica, **11**, 79.
Merz T (1976). Birth Defects Orig Art Ser, **12**, 19–22. In *Cytogenetics, environment and malformation syndromes.* Eds D Bergsma & R N Schimke. New York: Alan R Liss.
Meyer M B et al (1969). Am J Epidem, **89**, 619.
Mickelsen O et al (1964). Fed Proc, **23**, 1363.
Milkovich L & van den Berg B J (1974). New Engl J Med, **291**, 1268.
Miller R W et al (1976). Pediatrics, **57**, 411.
Milner R D G & Chouksey S K (1972). Arch Dis Child, **47**, 537.
Milunsky A et al (1968). J Pediat, **72**, 790.
Moffitt J M et al (1974). J Am Dent Ass, **88**, 547.
Moore J A et al (1973). Environ Hlth Persp (Expl Issue No 5), 81.
Moore M R et al (1977). Lancet, i, 717.
Mosher H P (1938). The Laryngoscope, **48**, 361.
Murakami U (1972). In *Drugs and fetal development*, eds M A Klingberg et al. London: Plenum Press. Adv Exp Med Biol, **27**, 301.
Murphy J F & Mulcahy R (1974). J Ir Med Ass, **67**, 309.
Murray S & Barron S L (1971). Brit Med J, **3**, 90.

Nahmias A J et al (1970). Adv Pediat, **17**, 185.
Nat Cancer Inst (1976). J Am Med Ass, **236**, 1107.
Nature (1973). Smoking, pregnancy and publicity. Nature, **245**, 61.
Nelson M M & Forfar J O (1971). Brit Med J, **1**, 523.
Neubert D et al (1973). Environ Hlth Persp (Expl Issue No 5), 67.
Nisbet I C T (1973). Nature, **245**, 468.
Nishihara G (1958). Proc Soc Exp Biol Med, **97**, 809.
Nishimura H & Tanimura T (1976). *Clinical aspects of the teratogenicity of drugs.* Amsterdam: Excerpta Medica.
Nora J J & Fraser F C (eds) (1974). *Human genetics: principles and practice*, pp 276–285. London: Kimpton.

Nora J J & Nora A H (1973). Lancet, **i**, 941.
Nora J J et al (1974). Lancet, **ii**, 594.
Nora J J et al (1970). Lancet, **i**, 1290.
Norris J W & Pratt R F (1974). Drugs, **8**, 366.
Nutrition Reviews (1973). Smoking, pregnancy and development of the offspring. Nutr Rev, **31**, 143.

Oser B L (1966). Can Med Ass J, **94**, 604.

Palmer A K (1974). Pp 16–33 in *Experimental embryology and teratology*. Vol **1**. Eds D H M Woollam & G M Morriss. London: Elek Sciences.
Peckham C S (1974). Brit Med J, **1**, 259.
Pendergrass T W & Hanson J W (1976). Lancet, **ii**, 150.
Penrose L S (1956). Fol Hered Pathol, **5**, 79.
Persaud T V N (1973). Anat Anz, **133**, 499.
Pharoah P O D et al (1977). Lancet, **i**, 34.
Plummer G (1952). Pediatrics, **10**, 687.
Pochin E E (1976). Brit J Radiol, **49**, 577.
Poswillo D E (1973). Oral Surg, **35**, 302.
Pratt H (1977). Lancet, **i**, 1052.

Roberts I F & West R J (1977). Lancet, **ii**, 982.
Robinson G C et al (1963). Pediatrics, **32**, 116.
Rosenstein G et al (1976). Pediatrics, **57**, 419.
Ross E M et al (1973). Brit Med J, **3**, 51.
Rossiter E J R & Rendle-Short T J (1972). Lancet, **ii**, 705.
Roy Coll Gen Pract (1974). *Oral contraceptives and health*. London: RCGP.
Rush D (1974). J Obst Gyn Br Cwlth, **81**, 746.
Russell Bertrand A W R (1950). *Unpopular essays*. London: Allen & Unwin.
Rustia M & Shubik P (1976). Cancer Letters, **1**, 139.

Safra M J & Oakley G P (1976). Cleft Palate J, **13**, 198.
Sandor S & Amels D (1971). Rev Roum Embryol Cytol Ser Embryol, **8**, 105.
Sardemann H et al (1976). Arch Dis Child, **51**, 131.
Savage M O et al (1973). Lancet, **i**, 353.
Saxén L (1969). Pp 75–91 in *Pigments in pathology*. Ed M Woollman. New York: Academic Press.
Schardein J L (1976). *Drugs as teratogens*. Cleveland: CRC Press.
Schiff D et al (1970). J Pediat, **77**, 457.
Seip M (1976). Acta Paediat Scand, **65**, 617.
Shaul W L & Hall J G (1977). Am J Obst Gyn, **127**, 191.
Shenkel N & Vorherr H (1974). J Reprod Med, **12**, 27.
Shepard T H (1976). *Catalog of teratogenic agents*. 2nd Edn. London: Johns Hopkins Press.
Sherman S & Roizen N (1976). Lancet, **ii**, 517.
Shirkey H C (1972). In *Drugs and fetal development*. Ed M A Klingberg, et al. London: Plenum Press. Adv Exp Med Biol, **27**, 17.
Shuval H I & Gruener, N (1972). Am J Publ Hlth, **62**, 1045.
Skegg P D G (1977). Lancet, **ii**, 754.
Smith C A (1947). J Pediat, **30**, 229.
Smithells R W et al (1973). Brit Med J, **2**, 464.
Smithells R W et al (1977). Arch Dis Child, **51**, 944.
Sparschu G L et al (1971). Fd Cosmet Toxicol, **9**, 405.
Spira A & Servent B (1976). Lancet, **i**, 1416.

Spyker J M & Smithberg M (1971). Teratology, 4, 242 (abstr).
Srabstein J C et al (1974). J Pediat, 84, 239.
Steen J S M & Stainton-Ellis D M (1977). Lancet, ii, 604.
Stevens D et al (1974). Lancet, ii, 595.
Stevenson A C (1969). Pp 195–205 in *Methods for teratological studies in experimental animals and man.* Eds H Nishimura & J R Miller. London: Pitman Med Publ.
Stevenson R E (1973). Pp 96–125 in *The fetus and newly born infant: influences of the prenatal environment.* Saint Louis: C V Mosby.
Stewart A & Kneale G W (1970). Lancet, i, 1185.
Stone D et al (1971). Nature, 231, 53.

Taki I et al (1969). Fukuoka Acta Med, 60, 471.
Taussig H B (1963). New Engl J Med, 269, 992.
Thacker J (1973). Curr Topics Rad Res Qly, 8, 235.
Titus R J (1972). Internat J Addiction, 7, 701.
Tuchmann-Duplessis H (1972). Teratology, 5, 271.
Tuchmann-Duplessis H (1974). Biologie Médicale, 3, 91.
Tylden E (1973). Adverse Drug Reaction Bull, No 38, 120.
Tyrer J H et al (1970). Brit Med J, 4, 271.
Tze W J & Lee M (1975). Nature, 257, 479.

Ulfelder H (1976). Teratology, 13, 101.
US National Commission for the Protection of Human Subjects of Biomedical & Behavioral Research (1976). *Research on the fetus.* Washington: US Dept Hlth, Education & Welfare.

Vessey M P et al (1974). Lancet, i, 495.
Voorhess M L (1967). J Pediat, 71, 128.

Warkany J (1971). *Congenital malformations: notes and comments.* Chicago: Year Book Medical Publishers.
Warkany J (1976). Teratology, 14, 205.
Warkany J et al (1959). AMA J Dis Child, 97, 274.
Warner R H & Rosett H L (1975). J Studies Alcohol, 36, 1395.
Warrell D W & Taylor R (1968). Lancet, i, 117–8.
Weinstein M R & Goldfield M D (1975). Am J Psychiatry, 132, 529.
Wendel H A (1973). Brit Med J, 4, 230.
West R A (1938). Am J Obst Gyn, 36, 241.
WHO (1967). *Principles for the testing of drugs for teratogenicity: report of a WHO Scientific Group.* Eds J G Wilson et al. Pharmaz Indust, 29, 759.
Wilkins L (1960). J Am Med Ass, 172, 1028.
Williamson A P (1975). Clin Pediat, 14, 533.
Wilson B J et al (1971). Nature, 231, 52.
Wilson J G & Gavan J A (1967). Anat Rec, 158, 99.
Winckel C W F (1948). J Trop Med, 51, 2.
Wolff J (1969). Am J Med, 47, 101.
Wyll S A & Herrmann K L (1973). J Am Med Ass, 225, 1472.

Yerushalmy J (1973). Nature, 242, 262.

Zerner J et al (1976). J Maine Med Ass, 67, 163.

Table 1   Classification by nature of agents that are known to be, or that might be (marked *?*), injurious pre-natally.

A   Chemical Agents – Excess (see also Table 2).

1   In *Foods* (eg methyl mercury in fish from polluted waters – Matsumoto et al, 1965; Murakami, 1972; Amin-Zaki et al, 1974: cycasin from Japanese cycads – Mickelsen et al, 1964; see paragraph 21).

2   In *Drinking water* (eg radioactive strontium–90 from atmospheric fallout; nitrate in excess of 45 mg/l – Shuval & Gruener, 1972).

3   In *Inhalants* (eg tobacco smoke – BMJ, 1976; see paragraphs 56–60; carbon monoxide in city air; in ill-ventilated garages and cars; and in domestic quarters from gas appliances – Warkany, 1971 – p 128; or anaesthetic agents – Pharoah et al, 1977).

4   In *Pharmaceutical Preparations* (eg thalidomide; quinine – giving deafness; virilizing androgens; chenodeoxycholic acid – Heywood et al, 1973; aminopterin; ergot derivatives).

5   In *Cosmetics, Detergents, and Anti-Bacterials that may come in contact with the Skin* (eg hexachlorophene – *?* – Kimmel et al, 1974).

6   In *Contraceptives* used intravaginally (eg mercury-containing spermicide – *?*).

7   From *Internal Sources* (eg anti-D protein leading to Rh blood group incompatability response – jaundice, anaemia, etc – in a conception lacking D antigen genetically; thyroid-stimulating hormone in toxic goitre in a pregnant woman – Beaudoin, 1968).

B   Chemical Agents – Deficiency

1   of *Vitamin* (eg vitamin A).

2   of *Element* (eg iodine-deficient mental-deficiency – Hetzel & Pharoah, 1971 & see paragraph 101; oxygen – Astrup et al, 1972; zinc – Jameson, 1976).

3   of *Hormone* (eg thyroid hormone – neonatal goitre – see Shirkey, 1972).

4   of *Nutrient* (see Langer et al, 1974; Smith, 1947; Giroud, 1973).

C   Organisms

1   *Viruses* (eg rubella virus or even rubella vaccine – MacCullum, 1972; Fleet et al, 1974; Wyll & Herrmann, 1973 – blindness from cataracts, deafness, heart malformation; cytomegalovirus – BMJ, 1974a; Hanshaw et al, 1976; herpes simplex virus – Nahmias et al, 1970; chicken-pox virus – Srabstein et al, 1974; Savage et al, 1973; varicella-zoster – Williamson, 1975; Klauber et al, 1976; measles – Jaspersen et al, 1977).

2   *Bacteria* etc (eg syphilis – treponema pallidum: also ascending bacterial infections).

3   *Fungi* (eg fusarium fungi in cattle abortion, but no example yet known in man).

4   *Protozoa* (eg toxoplasma – mental deficiency, microcephaly, blindness – Feldman et al, 1974).

5   *Worms* (eg toxacara in dog fetuses – Griffiths, 1974).

6   *Co-Twin, Co-Triplet* etc (incidence much increased by gonadotrophin therapy; effects – multiple repercussions of small size of conceptus, eg possible effect on IQ).

D   Physical Factors

1   *Trauma* (eg traffic accident with separation, partial or complete, of placenta from uterus; lack of amniotic fluid from rupture of amnion – Field & Krag, 1973; Persaud, 1973; intra-uterune contraceptive device deforming conceptus when contraception fails – Vessey et al, 1974).

2   *Surgical Trauma* (eg induction of abortion; tapping of amniotic fluid for diagnostic purposes – Hamerton et al, 1977; Brinsmead, 1976; BMJ, 1975: also see Law Commission Report, paragraph 24, 25).

3   *Temperature* (eg feverish body-temperatures, 3°– 4°C above normal, induce many types of malformations in guinea-pigs – Edwards, 1971 – in rats and in calves and presumably in humans; lightning has killed a human fetus ante-natally – Chan & Sivasamboo, 1972).

4   *Ultrasonics* (possibly increased frequency of chromosome breaks from *prolonged* ultrasonic diagnostic procedures in pregnancy. Controversial – see Fischman, 1973; Donald, 1974; Thacker, 1973).

5   *Ionising Radiation* (eg x-rays to a pregnant woman's abdomen can induce microcephaly and mental retardation: possibly also leukaemia and other cancers later in the child – see Cowie, 1960; Meyer et al, 1969; Burch, 1972; Ardran & Kemp, 1972; Plummer, 1952; Merz, 1976).

E   Miscellaneous Factors

1   *Consanguinity* including incestuous consanguinity (eg father-daughter mating with high risk of homozygous, ie double-dose, genetic disorder in the child.)

2   *Prenatal Mismanagement or Interference* (eg possible malformation in a future test-tube fertilisation * ?*).

3   *Failure to abort; Failure to warn* (the public or a person); *Failure to ban* (eg a drug).

4   *Other including 'chance'* (eg low position of the placenta potentially lethal to the fetus and mother at delivery – by haemorrhage; also cord knots).

XVI.

Table 2 SOME PRENATAL AGENTS (other than trauma and viruses and nutritional deficiencies) of which the effects in man are probably attributable in some individual cases. Omission from this list by no means implies safety to the fetus: mere non-specificity of a teratogenic effect was sufficient to exclude a compound by making that effect non-attributable. Industrial hazards in pregnancy are underemphasised here: an introduction to them was given recently by Kuntz (1976). Numerous compounds related to one or other of those mentioned are also marketed and many have prenatal effects, eg aminopterin is like its derivative, methotrexate. For broader tabulations, see Schardein (1976); Shepard (1976); Heinonen et al (1977) and Nishimura & Tanimura (1976).

Agent of prenatal injury	Class	Putative effect on conceptus shown in newborn (E) when given early (in first trimester); (L) when given later in pregnancy	References
barbiturate	sedative	temporary respiratory failure, drowsiness, poor feeding, or withdrawal symptoms – extreme restlessness, 2 weeks after birth. (L)	Desmond et al (1972)
caffeine & theophylline	stimulant	apnoea, in premature infant, as withdrawal symptom, sometimes fatal. (L)	Deutsch (1976)
chenodeoxycholic acid chlorobiphenyl	solubilizer of gallstones accidental heat-exchanger contaminant in edible oil anti-malarial, etc.	necrosis of cells of liver and of adrenal cortex. (L) coca-cola skin for months; low weight; skin loss. (L)	Heywood et al (1973) Taki et al (1969)
chloroquin	anti-malarial, etc.	blindness from retinopathy and inner-ear deafness. (L)	Lancet (1971); Hart et al (1964)
chlorpromazine	anti-depressant, anti-allergic	blindness from retinopathy. (L)	Lancet (1971)
cortisone	adrenal hormone; anti-inflammatory agent	placental failure; cleft palate. (E)	Harris & Ross (1956); Doig & Coltman (1956); Warrell & Taylor (1968); Fraser (1962); Green & Kochhar (1975)
dextroamphetamine	appetite reducer; stimulant	biliary atresia; heart defects, especially dextrocardia. (E)	Levin (1971); Nora et al (1970); Nora & Fraser (1974)
diazepam (valium)	for toxaemia of pregnancy; also tranquilliser	loss of tone and heat; inhalation of feeds, respiratory failure, recovery usual (L); cleft lip/palate. (E)	Cree et al (1973) Safra & Oakley (1976)
diazoxide	hypotensive agent, eg for toxaemia of pregnancy; (also hyperglycaemic agent)	hair abnormalities – loss on head, but hair excess everywhere otherwise. (L)	BMJ (1973a); Milner & Chouksey (1972)

509

Agent of prenatal injury	Class	Putative effect on conceptus shown in newborn (E) when given early (in first trimester); (L) when given later in pregnancy	References
dicoumarol	anti-coagulant	bleeding (L); possibly warfarin-like defects. (E)	Hirsch et al (1972); Warkany (1976)
diphenylhydantoin (phenytoin)	anti-convulsant	fetal hydantoin syndrome (mental deficiency, under-growth, hare-lip, malformed ears, hypertelorism, squint, neuroblastoma – an adrenal tumour, defects of finger-tips and nails, cardiac defects, diaphragmatic hernia). (E)	Sherman & Roizen (1976); Pendergrass & Hanson (1976); Loughnan et al (1973); Anderson (1976); Barry & Danks (1974); Hanson, Myrianthopoulos et al (1976b); Hill (1976)
ergometrine	abortifacient*; contracts muscle of uterus, arteries etc	Poland anomaly – unilateral defects of fingers and of chest muscles. (E)	David (1972 & unpublished)
ethanol	anti-depressant drug	fetal alcohol syndrome: ptosis, cardiac defects, microcephaly, mental retardation (E); fetal addiction. (L)	Hanson, Jones & Smith (1976a); Löser et al (1976)
gonadotrophin	placental hormone	multiple pregnancy – physical and mental handicap from low birth weight. (Pre-pregnancy)	Gemzell & Ross (1966); Cameron et al (1969); Elbling (1973)
haloperidol	tranquilliser	limb defects. (E)	Dieulangard et al (1966); Kopelman et al (1975)
heptachlor	impurity (10%) in chlordane insecticide	tumours in infancy, eg neuroblastoma. (E, L)	Infante & Newton (1975)
indomethacin	inhibitor of labour	pulmonary hypertension. (L)	Manchester et al (1976)
iodide	anti-asthma drug, of dubious benefit	large thyroid in newborn, often with too much or too little hormone. (L)	see Shirkey (1972); Aaron (1970)
iophenoxic acid	opaque contrast medium for x-ray of gall-bladder, etc	large thyroid in newborn; some improvement with age. (L, E or before pregnancy – even 4 years before)	Wolff (1969); & see Shirkey (1972)
lead	environmental hazard, particularly in drinking water	mental deficiency. (E, L)	Moore et al (1977)
lithium	tranquilliser anti-psychotic drug	cardiovascular malformation. (E)	Weinstein & Goldfield (1975); Stevens et al (1974); Nora et al (1974)

Drug	Description	Effect	References
meprobamate	tranquilliser	cardiac or other abnormality. (E)	Milkovich & van den Berg (1976); but see Hartz et al (1975)
methotrexate	anti-leukaemia drug	syndrome of cleft palate, spina bifida, hydrocephalus, short stature. (E)	Milunsky et al (1968); Warkany et al (1959)
methyl mercury	pollutant in fish and molluscs; industrial origin	mental and muscular inco-ordination; blindness; cerebral palsy; small head. (E, L)	Murakami (1972); Derban (1974); Spyker & Smithberg (1971); Amin-Zaki et al (1974)
oxytocin	as ergometrine but used to speed labour	fast pulse, weak delayed breathing; oxygen lack; recovery usual. (L)	Liston & Campbell (1974); Dixon (1974); but see Alderman (1974)
phenobarbitone	sedative; anti-convulsant	as for diphenylhydantoin. (E)	Seip (1976)
podophyllum	cathartic; abortifacient	limb and ear defects, as from thalidomide. (E)	Rosenstein et al (1976)
progestogens**	steroid hormones	masculinised genitals in girls. (L)	Voorhess (1967); Gold & Michael (1958); Roberts & West (1977)
quinine	anti-malarial drug; and as ergometrine qv	inner-ear deafness. (L)	Mosher (1938); Covell (1936); West (1938); but see Winckel (1948)
rifampicin	antibiotic	CNS malformation; limb defects. (E)	Steen & Stainton-Ellis (1977)
stilboestrol (=diethyl stilboestrol, DES)	synthetic hormone for maintaining pregnancy, etc	clear-cell adenocarcinoma of vagina (8–28 years' delay) in about 0·1% of those U.S. pregnancies (♀) heavily exposed 1943–67. In boys, abnormality of urethra. (E)	Ulfelder (1975); Herbst et al (1975); Nat Cancer Inst (1976); Henderson et al (1976); Hoefnagel (1976)
streptomycin & gentamicin	antibiotic	inner-ear deafness. (L)	Robinson et al (1963)
tetracycline	antibiotic	yellow teeth subject to decay. (L)	Saxén (1969); Moffitt et al (1974)
thalidomide	tranquilliser, and anti-emetic for morning sickness	absent or deformed limbs; ear defects, etc. (E)	Lenz (1966); Axelrod (1970); Lancet (1962); Kajii et al (1973); McFadyen (1976)

*For an example of unauthorised supply of this (fallible) abortifacient see *Evening Post*, 2 Nov 1972.

**Also corticotropin (Wilkins, 1960) and testosterone but not progesterone. Hormones in contraceptive pills seem relatively safe fetally but, with their wide use, a risk of 10^{-6} would be worrying. This is not excluded (Grant, 1974; Beral, 1974; RCGP, 1974; Kaufman, 1973; Nora & Nora, 1973; Kay, 1974; BMJ (1974b); Gal, 1974). The testing for pregnancy by the oral administration of hormones is no longer recommended in the UK: several studies indicate a teratogenic risk (Gal et al, 1967; Brogan, 1975; Greenberg et al, 1975).

Agent of prenatal injury	Class	Putative effect on conceptus shown in newborn (E) when given early (in first trimester); (L) when given later in pregnancy	References
tolbutamide	anti-diabetic sulphonamide	multiple malformations (uncertain). (E); thrombocytopenia. (L)	Tuchmann-Duplessis (1972); Larsson & Sterky (1960); Schiff et al (1970)
warfarin	anti-coagulant	chondrodysplasia punctata; mental deficiency. (E); bleeding. (L)	Di Saia (1966); Warkany (1976); Shaul & Hall (1977)
x-rays	ionizing radiation	short head; low IQ; ? risk of leukaemia later. (L)	Merz (1976); Pochin (1976); Meyer et al (1969); Penrose (1956); Stewart & Kneale (1976)
xylene	fat solvent	sacral agenesis. (E)	Kucera (1968)

Notes to Table 2

Note 1: Several other drugs are listed as toxic prenatally by Shenkel & Vorherr (1974), notably:—

morphine	– respiratory failure
aspirin	– bleeding
diphenylhydantoin	– bleeding (and see para 74)
thiazide	– bleeding
phenformin	– acidosis
ammonium chloride	– acidosis
lidocaine	– slow heart rate

These toxic effects can be readily attributed to the drug when it is given late in pregnancy. Toxic effects from intake earlier in pregnancy, while less observable, may also leave permanent damage, particularly of the brain.

Note 2: Impure or 'street' LSD is discussed by Titus (1972) but he thinks it unlikely that the actual effects of this hallucinogen will be known for quite some time. See also Jacobson & Berlin (1972).

Note 3: Bromides taken daily as sedatives or otherwise by mothers may produce mental retardation in the child – Rossiter & Rendle-Short (1972).

Glossary

The following descriptions of terms used in this volume are intended to afford brief explanations, not precise definitions:

Absolute liability	See Liability, absolute.
Benefit, contributory	A social security benefit paid out of the national insurance fund. Entitlement usually depends on the payment of national insurance contributions.
Benefit, non-contributory	A social security benefit paid out of general taxation. Entitlement does not depend on the payment of national insurance contributions.
Breach of statutory duty	Breach of a duty imposed by or under a statute which may give a right of action in tort to a person injured by the breach.
Burden of proof	The task of satisfying the court as to the truth of the facts alleged.
Compensation	The provision of money, services, goods or real property to an injured person or to his dependants or relatives, in consequence of the injury and for the purpose of alleviating its ill effects. In most contexts, the compensation referred to is the provision of money.
Compensation neurosis	A genuine neurosis which develops in an injured person while a tort claim is outstanding, and which tends to prolong illness.
Contributory benefit	See Benefit, contributory.
Contributory negligence	See Negligence, contributory.
Culpa	In Scots law, equivalent to fault (*qv*).
Damages	Compensation awarded by a court of law by way of reparation.
Damages, special	In England, Wales and Northern Ireland, damages for past pecuniary loss.
Damages, general	In England, Wales and Northern Ireland, damages for non-pecuniary loss and future pecuniary loss.
Defendant	The person against whom a legal action is brought.
Defender	In Scots law, equivalent to defendant (*qv*).
Delict	In Scots law, equivalent to tort (*qv*).
Dependency	In actions under the Fatal Accidents Acts in England, Wales and Northern Ireland, the annual amount which the deceased would have spent or applied for the benefit of his dependants if he had lived.
Duty of care	The legal duty to take reasonable care to avoid acts or omissions which are likely to injure those to whom the duty is owed. Breach of this duty gives rise to liability for negligence.
Fault	Negligence or a breach of statutory duty.

Forum shopping	Selection of the court in which to bring an action, where more than one court has jurisdiction, usually in order to maximise damages.
General damages	See Damages, general.
Injury	An injury which is sufficiently serious to lead to four or more days off work, or to an equivalent degree of incapacity for those who are not at work. Except where the context otherwise requires, injury includes death resulting from injury.
Liability, absolute	Liability imposed by law irrespective of fault, and subject to no defences.
Liability, strict	Liability, subject to such defences as are in the particular case prescribed, imposed by law irrespective of fault on the part of the person made liable.
Liability, vicarious	Liability imposed by law on one person for the tort of another.
Loss of society award	An award of damages in recognition of the loss of society and counsel suffered by a close relative of a deceased person.
Negligence	Breach of a duty to take reasonable care.
Negligence, contributory	Negligence of the plaintiff contributing to the causation of his injury. An award of damages is reduced according to the degree of any contributory negligence.
No-fault compensation	Compensation which is provided independent of fault, and by payment from a fund rather than through the tort system.
Non-contributory benefit	See Benefit, non-contributory.
Non-patrimonial loss	In Scots law, equivalent to non-pecuniary loss (*qv*).
Non-pecuniary loss	The intangible results of injury, often summarised as 'pain and suffering and loss of amenity'.
Onus of proof	See Burden of proof.
Patrimonial loss	In Scots law, equivalent to pecuniary loss (*qv*).
Pecuniary loss	The extent to which an injured person is, or is expected in the future to be, out of pocket because of his injury. The major components of pecuniary loss are usually loss of income and additional expenses.
Plaintiff	The person bringing a legal action.
Prescribed disease	An occupational disease, prescribed under section 76 of the Social Security Act 1975, in respect of which industrial injuries benefits are payable.
Pursuer	In Scots law, equivalent to plaintiff (*qv*).
Res ipsa loquitur	Literally 'the thing speaks for itself'. A plaintiff invoking this maxim alleges, in effect, that his injury could not have occurred in the absence of negligence by the defendant, even though he has no specific proof.
Reversed burden of proof	The burden of proof (*qv*), which normally rests with the plaintiff, is transferred to the defendant.

Glossary

Settlement	An agreement between the parties to a legal action, whereby the plaintiff drops his action – usually in return for a sum of money paid by the defendant (probably provided by his insurer).
Solatium	In Scots law: i Until recently, compensation paid to a relative of a deceased person in recognition of his grief. This claim was abolished by the Damages (Scotland) Act 1976, and replaced by the entitlement to a loss of society award (*qv*). or ii Compensation paid to an injured person for non-pecuniary loss (*qv*).
Special damages	See Damages, special.
Strict liability	See Liability, strict.
Subrogation	The transfer from one person to another of rights of action against a third party.
Tort	A wrongful act or omission in respect of which damages can be claimed, but not including a breach of contract as such. Derived from the Latin *tortus* (twisted).
Tortfeasor	One who commits a tort (*qv*).
Vicarious liability	See Liability, vicarious.
Volenti non fit injuria	Literally, 'to a willing person no injury is done'. The doctrine, often known as 'voluntary assumption of risk', whereby a plaintiff who voluntarily exposes himself to a risk of injury which is known to him cannot recover compensation if the injury occurs.

Abbreviations

BBC	British Broadcasting Corporation
BIA	British Insurance Association
CBI	Confederation of British Industry
DHSS	Department of Health and Social Security
EEC	European Economic Community
TUC	Trades Union Congress
USA	United States of America

516

List of References

The majority of references, including all Command papers, Law Commission reports and legal cases, are cited in full in the text and do not, therefore, appear in this list.

1 WIDISS, A I, LITTLE, JOSEPH W, CLARK, ROGER S, and JONES, THOMAS C. No-fault automobile insurance in action; the experiences in Massachusetts, Florida, Delaware and Michigan. New York, Oceana Publications, 1977.

2 Rt Hon LORD PARKER of WADDINGTON. Compensation for Accidents on the Road. Address to the Bentham Society, publ. in Current Legal Problems 1965. London, Stevens & Sons.

3 LORD KILBRANDON. Other People's Law. Hamlyn Lecture. London, Stevens & Sons, 1966.

4 ISON, T G. The Forensic Lottery. London, Staples Press, 1967.

5 ELLIOT, D W, and STREET, HARRY. Road Accidents. London, Allen Lane The Penguin Press, 1968.

6 ATIYAH, P S. Accidents, Compensation and the Law. London, Weidenfeld & Nicholson, 2nd ed. 1975.

7 FLEMING, JOHN G. The Law of Torts. Australia, The Law Book Company Ltd, 4th ed. 1971.

8 O'CONNELL, JEFFREY, and SIMON, RITA JAMES. Payment for Pain and Suffering – who wants what, when and why? University of Illinois, 1972, reprinted by Insurers Press Inc.

9 SMITH, P H N and RAZZELL P E. The Pools Winners. London, Caliban Books, 1975.

10 CALABRESI, GUIDO. The Costs of Accidents: A Legal and Economic Analysis. New Haven and London, Yale University Press, 1970.

11 SELECT COMMITTEE OF THE HOUSE OF LORDS ON THE EUROPEAN COMMUNITIES. Liability for Defective Products. Session 1975–6, Sixty third Report, R/2237/76. London, HMSO, 1976.

12 SAVATIER, RENE. Comment repenser la conception française actuelle de la responsabilité civile. Recueil Dalloz Sirey, 1966, p 149 (chronique). Paris, Librairie Dalloz.

13 BRADSHAW, J. Examining benefits for families with handicapped children. DHSS Social Security Research Seminar paper No 7. London, HMSO, 1975.

14 WEATHERALL, J A C, and WHITE, G C. A study of survival of children with spina bifida. Studies on Medical and Population Subjects, No 31: Child Health: a collection of studies. OPCS, London, HMSO, 1976.

15 BALDWIN, SALLY. The financial problems of families with handicapped children and an evaluation of the Attendance Allowance. University of York, Department of Social Administration and Social Work. Family Fund Research Project paper FF 19/11. 74. SB. Unpublished, 1975.

16 DEPARTMENT of the ENVIRONMENT. Report of the Working Party on Dogs. London, HMSO, 1976.

17 JOLOWICZ, J A. Liability for Accidents. Cambridge Law Journal, Vol 26, No 1, April 1968, pp 50–63.

Index

(References are to paragraph numbers)

Index

Index

Health insurance,
  Employers', 142
  Permanent, 150, 153–4, 166, 529–30
Health Service Commissioners, 1330, 1346
Henderson, Professor R, 24
Henderson v. *John Stuart (Farms) Ltd*, 1611
Hepatitis, viral, 871
High Court, 588, 765
  Queen's Bench Division, 79, 1577, 1649
Highway Code, 980
Highways,
  Injuries on, 1536–7, 1558–64
  Unadopted, 1560–2
Highways Act 1959, 1558
Highways (Miscellaneous Provisions) Act 1961, 1558–9
Hodges v. *Harland and Wolff*, 729
Holmes v. *Mather*, 48
Home Office, 92, 1627
Home Secretary, 1578
Horses, 1597, 1602, 1627–8
Hospital treatment allowance, 101, 490
House of Lords, 53, 364, 394, 517, 985, 1264, 1544–5
Household survey, 14
Housewives, 223, 228, 352–8
Hovercraft, 1166–9, 1170–1
Hovercraft Act 1968, 1166
Hovercraft (Civil Liability) Order 1971, 1166
Human blood and organs, 1276
Hunter v. *Hanley*, 1309
Husbands,
  Common law, 405
  Compensation for loss of, 418–29, 754–6

Incapacity for work,
  Benefits for partial, 814–21, 935
  Benefits for total, 800–13
  Duration of, 40, Table 2, 557
Indexed annuities, 218, 602
Industrial death benefit, 490, 775, 835–50, 935
Industrial Injuries Advisory Council, 794, 873–4
Industrial injuries scheme—*see under* Work injuries
Industrial Law Society, 613, 816
Industrial preference, 97–104, 107–8, 118, 289–91, 840–1, 921, 955, 1012–15
Industrial relations, effect of tort action on, 260, 303, 950
Inflation—*see also* Inflation proofing
  Allowance for in calculating damages, 677–87, 701–8, 723–4, 755
  Effect of, 74, 169, 184, 215–18, 244, 259, 557, 616, 648–9, 651, 712–15, 1040
Inflation proofing, 572, 603, 1040—*see also* Inflation
  Bonds, index linked, 603
  Finland, 218, 602
  France, 215–16, 602
  Scheme to protect periodic payments, 598–608, 611, 615, 645
  Social security benefits, 105–6, 182
  Tort damages, 568, 577, 598–608, 611, 615, 755, 1727
Influenza, 1374, 1376
Injuries, numbers, 37–9, Table 1, 1711

Index

Index

Merchant Shipping (Liability of Shipowners and Others) Act 1958, 1146–9, 1164
Merchant ships, oil pollution from, 320
Michigan road injuries no-fault scheme, 196, 203–4
Micklethwait, Sir Robert, 817, 880
Mobility allowance, 115, 266, 459, 471, 486–7, 490–1, 546, 726, 1504, 1506, 1532–4, 1683
Moeliker v. *A Reyrolle and Co Ltd*, 337
Monckton Committee, 167–8, 477–80, 496, 914, 1721
Montreal Agreement, 1111–12, 1114, 1117, 1129–30
Montreal Tramways Co v. *Léveillé*, 1442
Moorgate train disaster, 421, 1174
Morris of Borth-y-Gest, Lord, 375, 394
Mothers' Union, 1485
Motor cyclists, 959, 969, 1050, 1096
Motor Insurers Bureau, 974, 994, 1071, 1081, 1136, 1138
Multiplier, 627, 647–52, 656–87, Tables 10 and 11, 690–1, 698–703, Table 13, 708, 710–25, 1684

National Assistance Act 1948, 94–5, 129
National Childhood Encephalopathy Study, 1389
National Coal Board, 890—*see also* Nationalised industries
    Pneumoconiosis compensation scheme, 788–91, 889–90
National Council of Women of Great Britain, 1467
National Farmers' Union, 853, 1621
National Federation of Consumer Groups, 1297
National Federation of Self Employed, 853
National Health Service, 29, 128, 176–7, 232, 236, 340–1, 511, 1311–13, 1346
    Availability of, 340–1, 1039
    Recovery of treatment costs in road accident cases, 128, 1082–5
National Health Service Acts, 94
National Institute for Biological Standards and Control, 1385
National Insurance Acts, 92, 94
National Insurance Commissioners, 777
National insurance fund, 942, 944, 953, 1054, 1700–2
National Insurance (Industrial Injuries) Act 1946, 94
National Parks and Access to the Countryside Act 1949, 1543
National Society for the Prevention of Cruelty to Children, 1495, 1502
National Union of Farmers, 1621
National Union of Mineworkers, 155
Nationalised industries, 800
Negligence—*see also* Proof
    Contributory, 57, 496–8, 782, 785, 968, 978, 980, 987, 1061, 1077–8, 1107, 1113, 1122, 1143, 1188, 1211, 1256–7, 1426, 1462, 1473, 1496, 1659, 1661
    Employers', 782–4
    Extensions of, 62–70
    Gross, 1061, 1343
    Medical injury, 1308–12
    Statutory duty, breach of, 65–6, 782, 785–6, 921, 950, 1213, 1425
    Test of, 49, 52–8
    Vicarious liability, 63–4, 784–5, 1144–5, 1147–8
Netherlands,
    Animals, 1618
    Criminal injuries compensation, 1589
    Damages, assessment of, 515
    Medical injury, 1317
    Partial loss of earning capacity, 818
    Products liability, 1198
    Recovery rights, 214
    Road traffic laws, 186
    Visit to, 8

Unfair Contract Terms Act 1977, 72, 243, 969, 1124, 1150–2, 1157, 1176, 1212, 1261, 1290, 1551, 1556
Uninsured or untraced defendant, 585, 609–11, 615, 974
United Nations,
    Commission on international trade law, 1196
    Convention on liability of owners of inland vessels, 1164
    Declaration of the Rights of the Child, 1492
United States of America,
    Accidents to and from work, 859
    Air traffic injury liability, 1111–12
    Criminal injuries compensation, 1589
    Loss of expectation of life, compensation for, 371
    Medical malpractice claims, 1319–20, 1323
    No-fault road injuries schemes, 7, 177, 190–204, 212, 232–5
    Products liability, 1224–5, 1233, 1239, 1242
    Risk rating, work injuries, 941
    Vaccination against swine fever, 1391
    Vaccine damage compensation. 1405
    Visit to, 8
    Work injuries,
        No fault, 187
        Tort action, 212, 235

Vaccination,
    Numbers vaccinated, 1381–2
    Purpose, history and practice of, 1372–85
    Recommended, 1378–9, 1383, 1408–9
    Risk of injury, 1386–91
Vaccination and Immunization, Joint Committee on, 1380, 1389–90
Vaccine damage, 1366, 1372–1413
    Cause, 294, 1411
    Compensation,
        Demand for, 241, 1394–7
        Recommended, 1398–9, 1406–13, 1727
        United Kingdom, present position in, 1392–3
    Law, present, 1408
    Overseas practice, 1400–5
Vaccines, testing of, 1385
Value added tax (VAT), 1054, 1100
Vehicles (other than motor), 1068
Veterinary surgeons, 1619
Vicarious liability, 63–4, 784–5, 1144 5, 1147–8
Victoria (Australia) no-fault road injuries scheme, 205–6, 1002–3, 1035, 1046
Vinyl chloride monomer, 871
Viral hepatitis, 871
Visitors (occupiers' liability), 1541, 1552
Visits overseas, 7–10, 14
Volenti non fit injuria, 969, 1188—*see also* Risk, assumption of

War pensions scheme, 1392
Ward v. *James*, 729
Warranty of safety, 1224–5, 1233, 1285, 1538
Warsaw Convention 1929, 1107–13, 1115, 1117, 1119, 1130–1, 1167, 1254
Watkins J, 430
Wealth tax, 569
Weihs, Dr Thomas, 1468
West v. *Shephard*, 375, 394–5
Whooping cough, 1374, 1378–82, 1386–90, 1394–5, 1404, 1411

Printed in England for Her Majesty's Stationery Office by Oyez Press Limited
Dd 291049 K36 3/78